Insurance policies that practically everybody buys and nobody needs.

Page 357

Secrets of the successful test-takers. How to get much better scores.

Page 19

How to deduct all the interest on personal loan without borrowing against home equity.

Page 433

How to double your chances of winning a sweepstakes.

Page 251

How to collect interest from two banks on same money at same time.

Page 309

BOARDROOM® CLASSICS

Library of Congress Cataloging in Publication Data
Main entry under title:

The Big Black Book.

    Includes index.
      1. Family life education—United States.
2. Consumer education—United States.   I. Boardroom Books
(Firm)
HQ10.5.U6C66   1987   640.73   86-30967
ISBN 0-88723-083-0

Boardroom® Classics is a registered trademark of Boardroom® Reports, Inc.
330 W. 42nd Street, New York, NY 10036

Printed in the United States of America

Contents

1. Family And Social Life

HOW TO MAKE BETTER FRIENDS AND BE MORE INFLUENTIAL

Many people complain that it's harder than ever to make friends. And they're right. *Reason:* There are fewer opportunities for people to meet and interact.

Many of us spend our days involved with machines rather than people. We work with computers and come home and sit in front of televisions. *Result:* The time we spend with people is diminished...and so are the opportunities to practice relating to others.

Also, our society has become more fast-paced. This means people have less time to get to know one another.

Example: In Nebraska, where I grew up, people who first met would spend some time "rolling the cob." The term describes the way Nebraska farmers would sit around rolling a corn cob under their feet and just talking about unimportant things. It was a way to slowly get to know the other person and develop a friendship.

People no longer have time for that sort of slow, easy-going process.

Sign of the times: At one time, people handled disagreements by getting together and talking things out. Today, they are more apt to hire lawyers to settle disputes, creating a litigious society that is costing us a fortune. In addition to all the *new* reasons that it's tough to make friends, the *old* reasons still apply.

Many people have trouble making friends because they're shy and think that they shouldn't impose themselves on others. They feel standoffish, reluctant to push themselves forward to meet and get to know people.

Trap: We all have a *comfort zone*—an area in which it's relatively easy for us to relate to other people. This area is made up of people that we already know—our families, colleagues in business, old friends. Anything that demands we move beyond that area causes discomfort and fear.

Example: At a meeting or party, most people immediately look around for someone they know to chat with, rather than walking up to someone new and introducing themselves.

Although making friends and maintaining friendships involve a variety of skills, there are a few basics that anyone can follow...

- **Overcome shyness.** A big part of shyness is a lack of self-confidence. Before you can accept new friends you have to learn to accept yourself. This calls for self-awareness—knowing both your strengths and weaknesses and accepting them all.

Once you realize that you're a whole person—and that other people also feel awkward and unsure of themselves—it will be easier for you to make the first move. Inside of everyone there's a confident, friendly person who wants to get out.

- **Banish fear.** Millions of people are more afraid of speaking to a group than they are of dying. *Reason:* They're sure they are going to embarrass themselves or appear foolish.

But most people discover that once they stand up to address a group—or approach someone new to start a conversation—it isn't horrible or embarrassing at all.

What we really fear is the unknown. The way to overcome that fear is by doing the thing that scares you...and keep doing it.

- **Broaden your thinking.** We all have a tendency toward "pigeon-hole" thinking—applying what we know to just one part of our lives. But most of our skills can be used in different aspects of our lives.

Example: Many people take our courses thinking that they are going to learn public speaking skills. They're surprised that what they learn helps them get along better with people.

The following tips on how to make friends comes from Dale Carnegie's book, *How to Win Friends and Influence People:*

- Don't criticize, condemn or complain.
- Give honest, sincere appreciation.
- Arouse in the other person an eager want.
- Become genuinely interested in other people.
- Smile.
- Remember that a person's name is to that person the sweetest and most important sound in any language.
- Be a good listener. Encourage others to talk about themselves.
- Talk in terms of the other person's interests.
- Make the other person feel important—and do it *sincerely*.

Source: J. Oliver Crom, president, Dale Carnegie & Associates, Inc., 1435 Franklin Ave., Garden City, NY 11530. The company was founded by Dale Carnegie, pioneer of the self-development movement and author of *How to Win Friends & Influence People*, Pocket Books, Simon & Schuster, Inc., 1230 Ave. of the Americas, New York 10020. The book, which has been revised for the eighties, has sold more than 30 million copies. Dale Carnegie courses in self-development are offered in 68 countries.

LIVING TOGETHER VS. MARRIAGE

Living together is not a satisfying alternative to marriage. In fact, it is a caricature of marriage.

Practitioners are usually 18- to 30-year-olds who are separated from their families while going to college or working in a city. The major motivating factors for living together are to assuage loneliness, to avoid the anxiety of finding dates, or to escape the shallowness of fleeting liaisons.

Sexual relations are generally more satisfying to the men than to the women. Sexual dissatisfaction is the main reason for breakups between those who live together.

Problems: Living together is an uneasy alliance with pseudo-intimacy. The good times are shared, but the bad times and the bad self are hidden. Result: There is really no commitment to a shared life. True commitment seldom occurs until after a marriage ceremony.

Hard fact: Living together is not a replica-tion of nor a preparation for marriage. It may, in fact, actually postpone or complicate the mature intimacy needed for a satisfying marriage. Often major changes occur between people who have lived together once they have exchanged marriage vows. Reason: They have not thought out the serious, long-range side of their relationship.

Source: E. Mansell Pattison, MD, department of psychiatry, Medical College of Georgia, in *Medical Aspects of Human Sexuality.*

MARRIAGE AND CAREERS

Working wives tend to have better mental health than homemakers, but the husbands of working wives feel lower self-esteem and depression more often than the spouses of homemakers. Insight: Husbands who support their wives' careers by taking on some of the household and child-care chores are less likely to become anxious than those who seldom share family responsibilities. Men in the study who had working wives and suffered self-esteem problems were in their 30s, 40s and 50s. Men in their 20s did not have this problem.

Source: Ronald Kessler, Institute of Social Research at the University of Michigan, quoted in *Psychology Today.*

JUNE MARRIAGES

June is still the favorite month of 12.3% of brides marrying for the first time. Among women remarrying, 10.2% choose July and another 10.2% choose December. Most popular day: Saturday (53%). Least popular day: Wednesday (4.2%). Religious ceremonies are chosen by 80% of first-time brides but by only 60% of women who are remarrying.

PUT A LITTLE FUN INTO YOUR MARRIAGE

Life is difficult—marriage even more so. To have a successful marriage, make sure you keep some fun in your marriage. Here are some ideas for you. But the possibilities are, of course, endless, and limited only by your loving imaginations.

• Start a scrapbook. It helps you relive the happy moments of your life together.

• Buy a bulletin board. Keep it in the kitchen or other room where each day you can leave funny and/or meaningful messages.

• Serve breakfast in bed to each other. On odd Sundays it's your turn, even Sundays your mate's.

• Buy a treat a day, large or small, but with a light touch. Example: Kiwi fruit, a little American caviar, a red rose, some champagne, a trinket, a funny sign.

• Make your home beautiful. It should be a place that is fun to return to each night and to be in together away from the harsh world.

• Buy something special for your house that you can both enjoy. Example: A piano, a videorecorder.

• Use satin sheets. They are a treat for special occasions.

• Make yourself look as good as possible. Stay slim, trim and well groomed.

• Read aloud to each other.

• Buy subscriptions to your local theater group. Go together or with close friends.

• Enjoy sports together.

• Do things for each other. Examples: Cut each other's hair, give each other massages, take care of each other's needs.

• Start a hobby together, such as collecting stamps or autographs.

• Go to dancing school. Learn special, fun dance steps that you can practice together.

• Throw a big party for your friends for absolutely no reason at all.

• Plan a really special trip in the coming year. Have fun planning it together.

• Enjoy television together. Subscribe to cable TV, and see games and movies together.

• Plan a treat a week for each other. One week it's your treat, the other week your mate's.

• Buy a hot tub.

• Say nice things to each other. See who can give the best and most compliments.

• Make a ritual of dinner. Replace paper napkins with linen napkins. Use sterling silver, fine china and candles. Drink good wine.

• Become involved in community affairs together.

• Join a health club together and work out daily.

• Take a shower together. It has great potential.

• Allow plenty of time for each partner to "do his or her own thing" alone.

CONFLICTS IN A TWO-CAREER FAMILY

The most important requisites for success in a two-career family are careful planning and a willingness to submerge two individual ego needs. The important decisions in such a marriage, such as the question of whose career comes first and at what point, can be made meaningfully only if both partners are able, when necessary, to turn their focus away from their own personal drives and career ambitions.

Consider potential areas of conflict early on, before job decisions must be made. Questions to ask: Do either or both careers demand a high degree of mobility? Is one of the careers dependent on permanence, such as building up a private legal, medical or accounting practice?

If a conflict could arise from accepting a job offer, transfer or promotion, act now to head it off and minimize the traumas visited on the other partner. One way: Develop a list of possible career alternatives for the partner who may have to put immediate career needs aside in the interest of the other. Essential: The decision to give one career priority must be viewed as temporary, to be altered as circumstances change.

Family stresses are likely to be especially severe in the first five years for a two-career family. They can be worked out only if both partners make a conscious commitment to the marriage unit as early as possible. The constant goal for both must be: To continue as a unit, regardless of sacrifices and setbacks along the way.

Essentials to carry out that goal:

• The ability to communicate freely, even at the risk of hurting feelings, shocking the other partner or threatening the relationship. Airing feelings openly provides a sounding board for decisions, possibly the only one either partner has available. Being honest about a spouse's weakness can prevent unwise career moves and other blunders.

• A nonjudgmental attitude. It is possible to disagree without being self-righteous or moralizing. Avoid the *Who's Afraid of Virginia Woolf* syndrome, where partners constantly score off each other's weaknesses. This attitude is particularly devastating to career-oriented couples with more than their share of external threats and pressures.

• Readiness to give more than your share. A solid relationship is never fifty-fifty at any time. It is more like seventy-thirty. Greatest danger: When both need 70% at the same time. Caution: Beware of continual one-sided giving, where one partner always demands and the other always gives.

• Humor. It's crucial for release of tension and frustration. When the situation seems so grim that nothing seems funny, that is the time one partner has to dig deep and come up with something you can both laugh at.

In career-oriented families, children are especially likely to feel pressure from the outside world at a relatively early age. Being integrated into a strong family unit provides a measure of protection for them. They must be included in decision-making discussions that will affect them and be encouraged to question and express their feelings. Otherwise, they become outsiders looking in at the strong, career-dominated couple.

Resentments are bound to occur despite the best of agreements if the growth of one spouse's career is interrupted for the sake of the other's. A close friend, particularly one in the same or a similar profession, can ease some of the tensions by providing reassurance and by serving as a sounding board for career problems. Caution: Choosing a close friendship with a member of the opposite sex outside marriage can get sticky.

Source: Ronya Kozmetsky, coauthor of *Making It Together,* Free Press, New York.

To make dual-career households work best, the spouses should set aside specific portions of their week to be together and discuss each other's activities. This scheduled time must be inviolate.

Source: Dr. Barrie S. Greiff, psychiatrist, Harvard University School of Business Administration.

IF YOUR SPOUSE RETURNS TO SCHOOL

A spouse's return to school tests a marriage. The student develops new friendships or starts to regard the partner as an intellectual inferior. To make the process easier, enlist your mate's support before enrolling. Agree in advance to share household chores. Don't let all conversations center around school. Develop new activities with your partner to establish a fresh common ground. To keep your sex life healthy, set aside unbreakable dates for time alone together.

WORK VS. HOME CONFLICT

The behavior that makes you a success in your career can cause problems within your family. Typical: A lawyer who speaks to family members in an accusing tone. An accountant who nit-picks about the family's budget. Toning down your business skills at home requires an effort, but it often pays off.

Source: Dr. Marilyn Machlowitz, organizational psychologist and consultant, New York.

RECIPE FOR A HAPPY MARRIAGE

Marriage is a jail when both partners believe they can demand anything of each other. Similarly, if one partner becomes totally dependent on the other, resentment is sure to creep into the relationship. Insight: Love cannot exist under coercion. Way out: Two people with healthy self-esteem can speak openly about their relationship. Both can be free while continuing to live harmoniously together. The best marriage: One that is made up of a husband and wife who respect the needs and rights of the partner while maintaining a sense of their own individuality as well.

HOW TO AVOID DIVORCE

If one or both partners have definitely decided on getting a divorce, there's usually no stopping them. If they are ambivalent, then they ought to spend at least as much time considering the question of divorcing as they did of getting married. (If the courtship took a year, they should spend a year trying to stay together.) It's wise to get counseling or therapy if help is needed.

Two households can't be supported on the same amount of money and in the same style as one household.

Children may have problems at the beginning, but if the situation is handled well, the impact of divorce on children can be minimized. Important: Parents should not denigrate each other or use children as a go-between. Both must give them time, attention and emotional support.

Symptoms of troubled marriages:

• Poor communication: Lack of intimacy, of sense of closeness, of being able to talk, of really being heard when you do talk, loss of sexual desire and a sense of not being understood.
• Sexual infidelity: This is no longer a common cause of divorce, but often it is a symptom of something wrong with the relationship. Today, people are more likely to accept some degree of infidelity. But it is always a sign of trouble in a previously monogamous relationship.
• Children: Increasing use of children in struggles between adults.

Some people fail to make the shift from short-term to long-term bonding. Short-term bonding is the initial period of being intensely in love. The partner isn't seen realistically. There is a strong sexual attraction and a desire to be with the loved one as much as possible. In long-term bonding, love is no longer a "sickness" but a more quietly satisfying caring and building together. The other person is seen more realistically and deficiencies are accepted. Some of the passion wears off, but it can be reawakened from time to time.

Motivation: You have to want to move to long-term bonding and to accept the other person despite some shortcomings. It takes a lot of work to solve the problems of communication. For instance, a person must want to communicate.

Example: A couple with an infidelity problem have to realize where they are in the short-term/long-term cycle. People who have to be intensely in love all the time go from one short-term relationship to another to get their "fix." Do they want to change? Although anger is a common cause of outside affairs, there are people who need them. They may say, "I'm not taking anything away from you. This is the way I am." If the spouse can truly accept it, fine. But if the infidelity is sadly tolerated, the prospects for the marriage are poor.

First step in finding a solution: Once you know why things aren't working out, ask yourself whether you are contributing to the problem. It's easy to see what your spouse is doing wrong, but what are you doing that you should consider changing?

Most likely to succeed:
• Maturity: The best candidates for staying together (or for getting divorced) are the most mature. They know their own minds and are realistic in their expectations.
• Good complementariness: The partners meet each other's emotional needs and they dovetail well.
• Mutual respect: The ability to compromise on both practical and emotional levels is necessary. Example: "I don't mind your being dependent on me at times because it's not that onerous. And when we're at a party, you always make sure I'm having a good time and not standing by myself." Some couples berate each other about personality traits they don't like. But not being able to lovingly accept such characteristics spells trouble.

Source: Dr. Clifford Sager, author of *Marriage Contracts and Couple Therapy,* Brunner/Mazel, and (with Bernice Hunt) *Intimate Partners: Hidden Patterns of Love Relationships,* McGraw-Hill, New York.

STAY FRIENDLY WITH IN-LAWS AFTER THE DIVORCE

To remain friendly with in-laws after the divorce, allow a cooling-off period before making contact. Then don't hesitate to make the first move. Get the approval of the family member who carries the most weight. Call a family meeting to bring resentments out into the open. Don't force your in-laws to take sides. Behave with them as you always have. Be patient—time is on your side. Important: Remember that your in-laws are your children's grandparents. Children need to be reassured that they won't lose other family members in the wake of divorce.

DIVORCE AND INSURANCE

A divorce decree ordered both parties to keep up their current life-insurance policies, which named their children as sole beneficiaries. The court ruled that the provision was not a division of property but a type of child-support order, binding on the parties, but susceptible to future amendment if circumstances warrant.

VETERAN'S PENSION IS NOT MARITAL PROPERTY

A veteran's pension and other benefits were not marital property subject to distribution on divorce, an Illinois court ruled. Federal law makes these benefits the sole property of the veteran, not subject to divorce orders. But this source of income to the veteran could be taken into account in deciding on an equitable division of other property.

In re Marriage of Hapaniewski, Ct. App., Ill., 438 N.E. 2d 466.

SINGLE PARENTING

Girls raised by their mothers without a father are stronger and more independent than those brought up in two-parent households. Key: Most children act the way their parents expect them to act. If a mother wants her daughter to be strong and independent, the daughter will develop these traits. Insight: Fathers often encourage their daughters to exhibit so-called feminine behavior. Daughters learn to act that

way to please fathers rather than to emulate feminine mothers. Role in society of a woman raised by a mother: She will have the same sexual, social or professional problems with men as does any other woman.

Source: Results of several research studies reported in *Savvy.*

Single-parenting produces boys just as masculine and girls just as feminine as those in two-parent families. Scholastic levels: In the long run, both sexes do well, after initial difficulties when parents separate.

Source: Dr. Kathryn Black, associate professor of psychology, Purdue University.

HOW TO BE A GOOD STEPPARENT

Both partners in a remarriage usually have unrealistic expectations about their roles in the new marriage. As parents, they are not prepared for the problems they will have to face when they get their collective children together through various custody and visitation arrangements. The children, of course, are not prepared for difficulties either.

Some people sail through the transition period, but for most there are many fantasies that can cause trouble. Examples:

• Children expect the new parent to replace a deceased parent or to provide something their custodial parent doesn't.
• A stepparent who has never had children anticipates becoming an ideal mother or father with an instant family.
• Parents who have failed with their own children think they have a second chance. But they may not really understand what the failure was about in the first place, and they often end up making a similar mistake.

It is not easy to adapt to new roles in the stepfamily. Here are some of the problems that can arise:

• Children vie for seniority. A girl who has been the oldest in one family finds that she is now number two or three. Result: Rivalry, jealousy, hurt feelings. The role of the new stepfather becomes difficult, too. He is sought after by all the children, which causes conflict between his loyalty to his own children and the need to relate to the stepchild.

• Blood ties versus nonblood ties. It is always more difficult to love, or even to get along with, someone else's children. A parent tolerates more inconvenience and conflict from a natural child than from a stepchild, and suffers from feelings of guilt and hostility.

• Differences in parenting style. Watching one's spouse cope with a child in a way that you do not approve of can exacerbate an already tender situation. Example: A man who had longstanding problems with his adolescent son married a woman he thought would take care of these problems. She didn't consider it her role to be the disciplinarian. As she watched her husband tolerate abuse from his son, she began to lose respect for him.

Marriage and parenting are skills one learns from parents. You blunder along, imitating or rejecting their behavior. But most people never had any role models for stepparenting. Useful guidelines:

• New rules. Families have different rules of conduct. Some rules have to be negotiated between the parents. It is helpful to establish times when the family gets together to work on those decisions the children can be included in.

• Love is not instant. While it is important for members of the family to be considerate and to allow each other space for self-expression, the pressure to love a new family can cause guilt and hurt feelings. Some day you may learn to love stepchildren, and they may learn to love you—but not necessarily.

• Respect old ties. A new stepfamily has many complicated connections with relatives. A natural parent and child have a unique relationship that may never be duplicated by stepparent and stepchild. People should not feel that a new family has to do everything as a group. Allow children time to be alone with natural parents, grandparents or other relatives.

• Co-parenting. The basis for any successful remarriage is for ex-spouses to be as considerate of the children as possible. Conflicts between parents should be dealt with by them.

Children should not feel they are included in these problems.

• Divided loyalties. Even the best stepparent can experience hostility from a stepchild for reasons that have nothing to do with the stepparent. It may arise out of the child's feeling that the natural parent won't approve if the child likes the new stepparent.

• Children can love more than two adults as parents. It's an enriching experience for a child to have more than two parents, two sets of grandparents, etc. The natural family should understand that it may be better for the child to develop a close relationship with someone in the stepfamily. Both sides should stand back and let children choose whom they want to love.

• The couple relationship is primary. This is the core of the new family unit, in spite of the fact that each partner comes in with strong loyalties to their family of origin. Children have to know that the new couple is an unshakable combination and cannot be broken up (which they often try to do in order to get their own parents back together again). Seeing that the partners love and respect each other is an important role model.

• Discipline. You cannot discipline even your blood children without a good relationship. It may take a year or two before this happens with stepchildren. In the meantime, the natural parent should be the disciplinarian for natural children. The authority of an absent natural parent should be vested in the stepparent. This must be made clear to the children.

• Ironing out discipline policy. Parents should discuss priorities and compromises. If they can't work out their differences, they should look into getting professional help.

To keep things in proper perspective, observe before acting. Then step in and do what you can. But don't expect too much. The romantic ideal of the nuclear family was never true, despite some ideal moments. It is the same with a stepfamily. There will be some wonderful moments, but you should be prepared for the pain as well.

Source: Barbara C. Freedman, C.S.W., director of the Divorce and Remarriage Counseling Center, New York.

BABIES' BEHAVIOR

Attending babies when they cry helps prevent future problems. Misconception: That an infant can be spoiled if the parents respond every time it cries. Studies show that babies who are looked after by their parents when they cry during the first six months are less likely to cry during the second six months. Crying is *not* a ploy used by a baby to get attention. Research shows that babies under the age of one year are not capable of knowing that crying is a way to control the behavior of parents.

BABIES' FEEDING

Introduce an infant to solid foods one food at a time (the order isn't important) to see whether the baby has trouble tolerating them. Homemade foods chopped in a blender or processor are fine (don't add salt or sugar). More water is needed once a baby starts on solid food, and crying sometimes indicates the child is thirsty.

Source: Dr. Judith Wurtman, research scientist, Massachusetts Institute of Technology.

YOUR BABY'S WEIGHT

Fat babies do not necessarily become fat adults. The fat-cell theory (that fat babies develop more fat cells, thereby causing adult obesity) has been disproved by Dr. Alexander F. Roche of the Fels Research Institute in Yellow Springs, OH. Major danger to fat babies: Respiratory infections. Recommendation: Moderate feeding. Pay attention to your infant's signals indicating when he or she wants more or has had enough.

DENTAL CARE FOR INFANTS

Dental cavities in children can be eliminated with early proper care. Steps: As soon as the baby's teeth come in, clean them daily with a piece of gauze. Put only water in the baby's overnight bottle—juice contains sugar, and milk has fermentable bacteria. Take the child to the dentist before the age of four. Starting at three or four, have children rinse after every meal, floss once a day and brush with fluoride toothpaste after breakfast.

Source: Stephan Moss, Department of Pediatric Dentistry, New York University, reporting in *Harper's Bazaar*.

KEEP TOXIC SUBSTANCES AWAY FROM YOUR INFANT

Changing diapers on a seven-month-old or older child can be dangerous, according to a survey by a Massachusetts poison control center. Starting at this age, tots have the strength and dexterity to grab the objects around them and put them in their mouths. Particularly hazardous: All the toxic substances that surround the changing table—powder, wipes, shampoo, ointment, oil, etc. (Keep a close watch on the open safety pins, too.) Most poison-prone time of day: Between 5 pm and 9 pm, when the family is busiest and parents are most harried.

Source: *Journal of the American Medical Association*.

TEDDY BEARS CAN MAKE CHILDREN SICK

Teddy bears can cause allergic symptoms in children. Like other stuffed toys, bears are favorite dwellings for dust mites and may release clouds of allergenic mite excrement when squeezed. Alternative: Washable toys made of plastic or vinyl.

Source: *Rodale's Allergy Relief*, 33 E. Minor St., Emmaus, PA 18098.

INFANT SAFETY

Children's cribs should be positioned away from windows, curtains or venetian blinds.

Cords and curtains make it easier for a child to climb out and get into trouble.

Baby-walkers, the device meant to help infants prepare for walking, can tip over with the child inside even on flat surfaces, causing injuries. Worse: Children have fallen down stairs while trapped inside the walkers.

Source: *The Lancet.*

SIGNS OF HIGH INTELLIGENCE

Gifted children show early signs of their abilities. Examples: They walk and talk before others and speak in sentences that employ sophisticated vocabulary. They have good memories, are curious about the world and can entertain themselves for long periods. How to treat gifted children: Do not play up to them or be intimidated by their precocity. They may be smarter than other kids, but their emotional needs are the same as others'.

STRICT VS. LENIENT PARENTING

In a follow-up look at a group of adults whose mothers had been interviewed on parenting practices when the children were five, two patterns emerged. The children who had been subjected to the strictest feeding schedules and toilet training have the highest need to achieve as adults. The youngsters whose mothers were most permissive about sex and aggression (allowing masturbation and fighting with siblings, for example) show the highest need for power as adults.

Practices the researchers expected to relate to adult characteristics did not show clear correlation in the study. How warm the mother was with the infant, or how long the child was breast fed, long assumed to be important to a child's well-being, did not match up directly with specific adult traits.

Source: Study by psychologist David McClelland, Harvard University, reported in *Journal of Personality and Social Psychology.*

ENCOURAGE EXPRESSIVENESS IN CHILDREN

Fear of public speaking begins early. Parents may unwittingly make children feel foolish when they speak. Helpful: Ask for children's opinions, even when they are very young. Let them express negative as well as positive opinions. Avoid correcting or enlarging on everything they say. Encourage discussions at dinner. Tape-record children and, as they mature, offer suggestions.

Source: Clarissa Whitney, speech instructor, Santa Ana College, CA, quoted in *The Toastmaster.*

TEMPER TANTRUMS

A child's temper tantrum is best handled by simply walking away. This usually stops the display, as the child grows bored without the attention. Realize that tantrums are part of the process by which toddlers declare their individuality. They usually occur when the child is tired. Don't rush to the child and try to smother it with affection. This may make you feel better in front of onlookers, but it doesn't help. Don't automatically accept the blame for the problem. Don't berate the youngster. Best: Let the storm pass. Allow the child to have a nap, and don't mention the incident later.

Source: Dr. Dennis Allendorf, pediatrician, Columbia Presbyterian Medical Center, New York.

CHOOSING A NURSERY SCHOOL

Enrollment of three- and four-year-olds has doubled in the last decade. Why: Working parents who need child care, few playmates for children with a parent at home.

Choosing a school: The ideal ratio is one adult to every five children. (At least two teachers should be in charge of a group.) Check for: Fire extinguishers, doors that open out, emergency exits, clean bathrooms and an isolated room for sick youngsters.

What nursery school can do: Teach sharing

and taking turns, build confidence and competence, ease the path to kindergarten. What it can't do: Insure academic achievement for middle-class children in their later school life. (Studies show that it does benefit the deprived.)

WHEN A CHILD NEEDS A THERAPIST

Children don't come to parents and say they need a therapist. They don't perceive the locus of the problem as themselves. They'll blame it on parents or school. Treatment revolves around helping children to see what it does have to do with them.

Most children get into therapy because a teacher or school psychologist suggests it to a parent. Parents often do not recognize deviant behavior until the child goes to school. But many problems can be corrected if they are caught early.

Major tip-off: A child is stuck in development and is not doing what one would expect of a child in his or her age group.

Signs of poor emotional development:

• A four-year-old in nursery school cries and misses his or her mother.
• An eight-year-old with no friends comes home after school and watches television.
• Rigid rituals: The child's bedroom has to be a certain way. Particular foods must be served on certain nights.
• Major sleep disturbances: Frequent nightmares, waking in the middle of the night.
• Lack of learning progress: The child is not performing at grade level in school.
• Psychosomatic illnesses: Whatever the root cause, ailments are exacerbated by stress (ulcerative colitis, asthma, etc.).

When in doubt, ask the school psychologist or pediatrician to recommend a therapist. Don't bring the child in for the first visit. Request a consultation. In some cases, there may not be anything wrong with the child. The parents may be the ones who need help.

Parents should use psychologists and psychiatrists more freely to help assess problems with children. One answer: More parenting centers where parents can go to ask questions and get guidelines about developmental progress.
Source: Dr. Pearl-Ellen Gordon, child psychologist, New York.

LEARNING TO WALK AND YOUR CHILD'S I.Q.

Slow walkers are slow learners, says an old folk tale. The trouble is, it may actually be true. Children who are slow to walk (or slow to walk and talk) have lower IQs. And they experience greater difficulties when they start learning to read. Surprise: Slow talking alone is not associated with low intelligence or with later reading problems.
Source: A long-term study of children by Phil Silva, Rob McGee and Sheila Williams of the University of Otago Medical School, New Zealand.

EARLY SIGNS OF ADOLESCENT DRUG ADDICTION

Boys who were both shy and aggressive in first grade are most likely to become abusers of drugs, alcohol and tobacco later in life, a study shows. These children were usually loners who did not participate in classroom activities and were hostile to their classmates and to school regulations. When these boys became adolescents, 45% smoked marijuana, 60% were heavy cigarette smokers, 18% drank hard liquor and 60% beer or wine. Next most likely: Boys who were aggressive without also being shy. The least likely: Those who were merely shy had the lowest percentages. Only 10% smoked marijuana as adolescents, 5% were heavy cigarette smokers, 20% drank wine or beer and none tried hard liquor.
Source: A study of 1,200 youngsters by Dr. Sheppard Kellam, director, Social Psychiatry Research Center, University of Chicago.

THE IDEAL BABYSITTER

The ideal babysitter is warm, patient, outgoing, well-adjusted and interested in your child. Caution: Very domineering people will undermine your relationship with your child. People who are depressed or have other emotional problems will be more concerned with themselves and will not see to the emotional needs of your child.

DAY CARE CENTERS

Day care is not bad for children, despite a recent rash of antifeminist articles claiming just that. Evidence: A recent study found that children in day care matured faster and were more advanced in learning and social skills than chilen who stayed home. Recommended: Day-care centers with a low ratio of children to staff.

More information: *Daycare* by Alison Clarke-Stewart, Harvard University Press, Cambridge, MA.

WHEN YOU DON'T NEED A BABYSITTER

Leaving children alone without a babysitter depends on the age and emotional maturity of the child. Ages when most children can start to cope: Between 10 and 12. Circumstances to consider: Availability of helpful neighbors. The safety and security of your home. The sex of the child (girls tend to mature earlier). The relationship between siblings (will the younger child listen to the older?). How to tell if they are ready: Give them added responsibility and see how they handle it. Start gradually, leaving them alone for short trial runs. Bottom line: Let your kids grow up. Trust your parental training and their own judgment.

STAY IN TOUCH WITH YOUR CHILDREN WHEN YOU TRAVEL

The same principles of child rearing apply to parents who travel on business as to those who do not. These elements contribute to a child's

emotional health and give him/her the skills to cope with life's problems later on.

Fundamentals:

• Options. Children need to feel that they have choices. If other people make all their decisions for them, children lose their motivation, become depressed or angry and feel helpless. Being offered appropriate choices—which book to read at bedtime, for instance—gives children more motivation to learn. It helps them to make responsible decisions later on and to be less vulnerable to peer pressure.

• Acceptance. All children need to feel that they are accepted, regardless of their strengths or weaknesses. Parents who are high achievers frequently put too much pressure on children. Rather than demand perfection, it is far more important for a parent to make sure a child feels successful at a realistic level.

• Approval. Children need someone to say, "That was a nice job." They also need to be aware of disapproval. Communicate when you are unhappy about something, too. Being a responsive parent doesn't mean you mustn't say no. Disapproval is a response, too.

If you're a responsive parent and feel comfortable giving your children choices, you have laid the groundwork for being able to meet your obligations even while you travel. Not being there to respond can be detrimental to your child, but parents can respond wherever they are.

Here are some of the ways to stay in touch with your children:

• Minimize time away. Although you may travel a great deal, make it a rule to try not to be away from home more than one night at a time.

• Call children twice a day. When you are away, bracket the day with one telephone call in the morning and another at night. Your presence is there even if you're not.

• Plan children's time during your absence. Before going on a business trip, try to set up the options your children will have while you're gone—a guest for dinner, an overnight visit at a friend's house. You participate in their lives even though you're not there. While you're away, you're not supervising or controlling, but simply looking in to see what's going on.

• Gifts should be special. Parents shouldn't be expected to bring back gifts. If you find something special, then it's a surprise that says, "I was thinking of you." But bringing gifts every time you make a trip becomes a ritual. Kids who grow to expect a gift because they have always received a gift can become ambivalent about their parents' traveling. The unfortunate lesson: Materialistic values are more important than human values.

• Take children along. When possible, take your children with you. Missing a day or two of school is well worth it for the benefits of family closeness and the educational experience of travel. For longer trips, arrangements can be made with the school to bring lessons along and to do special projects. (In fact, the trip itself may provide the basis for a personalized school report.)

• Communicate your feelings about separation. Let your children know how much you miss them and that staying in hotels is a lonely business. When you telephone, say to your children, "I wish I were home with you."

• When you return, let the children know how happy you are to be home. It's nice if they can look forward to something special, like dinner out, to celebrate.

Source: Lee Salk, professor of psychology in psychiatry and professor of pediatrics, New York Hospital-Cornell Medical Center.

HOW TO TALK WITH YOUR CHILD ABOUT SEX

Parents who want to give their children mastery of the facts about sexuality have to start early in the child's life. That's when to begin, too, to build the attitudes they will need to enjoy themselves as sexual beings and to respect the sexuality of others.

A child is born sexual, just as he or she is born with the capacities of walking and of talking. Parents delightedly help children to develop their ability to walk and talk but rarely treat sexual pleasure the same way. Once you understand and accept your children's sexuality as normal and beautiful—the same as their other human endowments—you will be free to help them in their sexual socialization.

The process of socialization starts in infancy. You socialize your children in other natural functions such as eating. You praise them for using a spoon instead of plunging their hands into the cereal bowl and for other appropriate eating behavior.

A child also needs the guidance and support of parents in developing appropriate sexual behavior that fits in with the parents' own cultural norm and value system. The beginning:

• Establish a sense of intimacy and trust with a newborn by touching and holding. The cuddling, kissing and hugging should continue—do not stop when the child reaches three, when some parents feel awkward with physical demonstrations of affection, especially with boys.

• When you start the game of naming parts of the body, include the sex organs. Avoidance of the area between the waist and the knees causes confusion and lays the groundwork for problems in adult life.

• Don't interfere with a child's natural discovery and enjoyment of self-pleasuring. Genital play is normal. At six or eight months, a child learns to put its hand where it feels good. Don't slap on a diaper, pull the hand away or look upset or disapproving. Leave the child alone. As the child gets older, teach what you consider appropriate behavior. You don't want your child masturbating in the supermarket or living room even at 15–18 months, so you pick up the child and, smiling, carry it to its bedroom. Explain that the place to pleasure yourself is in your own room with the door closed—that sex is good but should be private.

• Parents need privacy, too. Tell children: "When our door is closed, you don't come in without knocking and being invited. When we see your door closed, we'll do the same for you. Everyone likes privacy during sex games." This is when you can introduce the idea that sex games are something people who love and respect each other can play together.

• Sex play between children is usual. If parents banish the play, it will only drive the child underground. It's better to keep the lines of communication open and to reinforce socially appropriate sexual play. Inappropriate: Sex play with someone older. Child molestation is more commonly practiced by someone in the family or known to a child than by a stranger. The message: You don't have to let anyone touch your body against your will. You are in charge, and you can say *No*.

Few parents are aware of how much sex education is transmitted before nursery school by attitudes and body language—how parents react to scenes on TV, the tone of voice or facial expression in sexual conversations or situations, significant silences.

Children delight in affection openly expressed between their parents. Withholding such demonstrations can indicate sexual hang-ups.

Don't avoid opportunities to discuss sex or to answer questions. Always speak only the truth. You may wish to withhold some of the details until later. Explain appropriate behavior outside the home. ''In our family, we are open with each other about sex. But most other families don't talk about it the way we do. So we keep what we do private. It's a good thing to respect what other people believe.''

A child who doesn't ask questions by the age of four or five has gotten the idea that the parent is uncomfortable about sex or that sex is not an open topic, or was not given straight answers. But parents should be the ones to give children sexual information. Initiate a discussion. One idea: Tell your child about your own questions when you were the same age. If there is no response, try again another day to prove you're available.

Choose a time when you (or both parents) are alone with the child and have plenty of time. Be encouraging about behavior that is appropriate or shows maturation. Give recognition to a good line of thought. Respond positively, even if you are criticized.

Common mistakes:

The most damaging mistake is to associate sexual parts of the body with dirt, ugliness or sin. Guilt and shame transmitted about such a wonderful part of our human birthright will never be erased.

Parents should never lie. They may have to tailor the truth to the level of the child. Example: To a three-year-old who asks, ''Do you have to be married to have a baby?'' the correct answer is, ''No, you don't, but....'' Then you go into your own value system about why marriage is important—on a level that a three-year-old can understand.

Talking with children about sex should be a shared responsibility. A harmonious front is important. Both parents should be clear on attitudes toward standards and rules and on what they agree and disagree on. If there are differences of opinion, call them that. Undermining the other parent shakes the confidence of the child in the one who's doing the undermining. Children trust parents who are *for* each other.

If you have laid the groundwork between birth and six or seven, you can take advantage of the major learning years until 12. Before puberty is when to pour in reliable information about sexually transmittable diseases, reproduction, etc. Keep the lines of communication open. Give opinions when they're asked for. Avoid judgments—they tend to close off discussions. Express your own values frankly and give sound reasons. Young people will respect them, even if they don't share them.

Source: Mary Steichen Calderone, MD, former medical director of the Planned Parenthood Federation of America and co-founder and president of SIECUS (Sex Information and Education Council of the US).

HOW TO EXPLAIN DEATH TO A CHILD

Explaining death to a child of three or four is best done with simple, direct sentences. Example: Explain that death is when a person is broken and no one can fix him—not a doctor, nurse or anyone. Young children know that badly broken toys cannot be repaired, so they can relate to this. Save more complex explanations for when the child is older.

Source: *Salk Letter.*

FINDING THE RIGHT BOOKS FOR YOUR CHILDREN

Teach children how to find books at their reading level. Technique: Tell the child to open the book near the middle and to read from the top of any full page. If there are five words the child doesn't know before getting to the end of the page, the book is too hard.

Source: *Is Your Child Gifted?* by Eliza Brownrigg Graue, Oak Tree Publications, San Diego.

VISUAL PROBLEMS IN THE CLASSROOM

Nearsightedness in children may be more a reaction to school pressures than an inherited visual problem. By emphasizing the acquisition of information in the classroom, educators encourage excessive concentration. This makes youngsters constrict their field of vision. Tension tends to restrict perceptual abilities, including sight. In a public school study, myopia was reduced by 50% among elementary school children when the teaching method changed from one dependent on frequent testing of skills to a more relaxed, multisensory approach to learning.

Source: Ray Gottlieb, a Los Angeles optometrist and vision trainer, writing in *Brain/Mind Bulletin.*

Students who sit near the teacher learn more. They take an active role, establish eye contact and get full attention.

SEX EDUCATION AND PROMISCUITY

Sex education in school does not lead to promiscuity among teenagers. And young women who have had sex education are less likely to become pregnant than those who have not. These are the findings of surveys of teenagers. Overwhelming conclusion: There is no connection between sex education and sexual activity.

Source: *Family Planning Perspectives.*

WHEN TELEVISION VIEWING IS A PROBLEM

Children who watch up to one-half hour of TV a day actually score slightly better on standard school achievement tests than youngsters who watch none. In fact, up to an hour of tube time a day seems to have no adverse effect on academic work. Test scores begin to drop when students spend more than an hour a day watching TV. Scores plummet as much as 30 percentage points when children spend four hours or more a day in front of the set. Variable: Neither social nor economic background seems to affect the correlation of TV watching and achievement scores. Even youngsters with high IQs lose their advantage when they watch too much television.

Source: Study conducted by the California Department of Education.

Block out TV programs that you don't want your children to see with a device that plugs into your TV set. *Censorview 1200* can block out up to eight pre-set time periods of any length in a seven-day span. Limitation: It works only on channels 2–13. To block out cable channels A–W, you have to turn off all cable reception.

SCHOOL SPORTS CAUTIONS

Pushing young athletes can result in "overuse" injuries such as stress fractures, tendinitis of the shoulder, bursitis of the hip and tennis elbow. These injuries in children were unheard of before the advent of organized sports programs after World War II. Even now, doctors rarely see these problems in youngsters who play sports among themselves without special coaching. (Children do not push themselves too hard.)

Most frequent cause of injury: Inappropriate or excessive training. Children are particularly susceptible to injury when they are tired or in pain. Remedy: Make sure that the coaches or trainers who work with your children are sensitive to this issue and that they have a proper perspective on what a sports program is really about.

Source: Dr. Lyle Micheli, director of sports medicine, Children's Hospital Medical Center, Boston, quoted in *The Ladies' Home Journal.*

ASPIRIN CAN BE DANGEROUS

Aspirin given to children who have chicken pox or flu increases the risk of Reye's syndrome, a mysterious illness that sometimes follows viral ailments. Symptoms: Vomiting, fever leading to convulsions, coma and even death in about one-quarter of the cases.

Source: Department of Health and Human Services and the Centers for Disease Control.

BEWARE OF SUGAR IN MEDICINE

Sugar in medicine makes it palatable to children. But it is harmful to their teeth if the medicines are taken regularly. Best: After taking sweet medication, children should rinse their mouths and brush their teeth.

IF YOUR CHILD IS HOSPITALIZED

Parents of hospitalized children are now usually permitted (and often encouraged) to stay, even overnight, with the child in the hospital. This is a sharp departure from previous practice, when parents could visit only during visiting hours. Why the change: Parents provide continuity between the home and hospital. It is important that acutely ill children, especially the very young, don't see the hospital as a place of abandonment.

WHY YOU SHOULDN'T FEED HONEY TO A BABY

Hold the honey for babies under one year of age. Reason: Even ''pure'' or ''filtered'' honey contains tiny amounts of bacteria. Although harmless to older children and adults, these can lead to botulism in an infant. Symptoms: Constipation, lethargy, feeding trouble.

Source: *Vegetarian Times.*

CHOKING EMERGENCIES

If a young child is choking on food, first look in the throat. If you can see the chunk of food, try to dislodge it with an index finger. Should that fail, hold the child upside down by one ankle and slap sharply between the shoulder blades. If the child is too heavy to lift, lay him across your knees, stomach down, head and upper torso hanging down. Then slap between the shoulder blades. Last resort: Call your local emergency number. Note: This advice applies to children between one and five. Do not attempt the Heimlich maneuver on children of this age. The thrust beneath the diaphragm forces an exhalation of air in adults, but it is not recommended for youngsters.

DOGS BITE KIDS

About 90% of all attacks on children by dogs occur within the home. Overwhelming percentage of victims: Children under the age of four. Why: Young children often provoke the dog unintentionally.

WHEN YOU ARE INVADING YOUR CHILD'S PRIVACY

How much should parents know about their children's lives? The answer really depends more on how much the children are on their own than on age. Their lives become more and more their own business as they move away from parental supervision. It's part of growing up to have an increasingly greater private life and to feel you don't have to tell your parents everything.

During the years when children are under your roof, the key to keeping track is dialog. If communications are good, then you've developed a relationship in which children would want to share information with you that you should be aware of. If the relationship is sound and there are matters they don't want to share, they may have a good reason. You should respect their privacy.

How to elicit information: When you are concerned about a serious issue, questions can work. Better: It's more of an invitation to open up if parents talk more about their feelings on what's going on in their own lives—being worried about this or embarrassed about that —or about feelings on something that is happening with the child. This helps create an atmosphere in which the child can talk about feelings, too. Particularly inviting: A non-judgmental parent.

Setting the stage: When you have something difficult to discuss with your children, do it in the car. No one can get up and walk out. You don't have to look at each other, if that is a problem. Pick a trip that will last at least half an hour. Try not to ask questions.

Sometimes it is enough to give your opinion on a subject, even if you elicit no information. Example: A divorced father with custody of a 16-year-old daughter had this conversation about her relationship with a boyfriend: "You and David are getting very close, and I think that's fine. I don't know how active a sex life you're having, but I hope you will delay a full sex life. I think you're too young for that. But whether in six weeks or six years you do go all the way, the one experience I don't want you to have is getting pregnant. I want you to feel free to come to me to ask for the name of a doctor."

Her response: "We're not doing anything like that now." A month or two later, she said she was having problems with menstrual bleeding and asked for the name of a gynecologist. The father had expressed what he wanted to say and had opened the door. The child had not invited him in, but she had certainly received the message.

How serious is the issue? Whether invasion of privacy is justified depends on the stakes. For parents to read a child's diary because they're curious about his or her sex life is indefensible. If the problem is something damaging to a child living under your roof, even if the child is 18, 19, or 20, you should intervene. Example: A parent who suspects a child is getting into drugs should search the child's room thoroughly.

Less serious problems: If the communication is good, the child might tell you about them. But a child on drugs may have a change in personality, and this will probably adversely affect a previously healthy relationship.

When and how you intervene depends on the severity of the issue and how it will affect a child's life. It also depends on what you can effectively do. Examples:

• Movies: Some parents might be concerned about sexuality or violence in films. They wouldn't want a 12- or 14-year-old seeing a frightening or perverted horror film. They might, though, be more lenient about sex that isn't x-rated. For this age group: Strongly advise against an unsuitable film. Refuse to pay for it. If necessary, prohibit seeing it.

• Friends: If you're going to press a negative opinion, have a good reason. Check yourself: Do I object because this is not my preference for a friend? Do I think no one's good enough for my child? Am I afraid of competition? If the association is dangerous, you can refuse to allow the friend in your house, but it is impossible to police whom your child sees outside the house.

How much can a parent control a child? You can exercise more control about what goes on in the house than what takes place outside. If you don't know that your child is getting drunk at parties, there's not much you can do. If your 15-year-old comes home drunk, you can say, "You're grounded. This has got to stop." If you pass a prohibition ("You're not to get high any place at any time"), obviously you have no way of enforcing it.

In general, keep the lines of communication open by expressing your own feelings and values. It may not always yield information, but at least it creates a receptive climate for exploring important issues.

Source: Howard M. Halpern, author of *Cutting Loose: An Adult Guide to Coming to Terms with Your Parents,* Bantam Books, New York.

HOW TO DEAL WITH A DEFIANT TEENAGER

The problem of the teenager who defies parental authority is rooted in changes in the outside world as well as in the relationships in the home. In recent years, we have seen a breakdown in discipline and a disruption of family authority. Family structures are not as strong as they were, nor are roles as well defined. Often there is conflict between parents. Increasingly, peer involvement has usurped family involvement.

In this society, with its breakdown of law and order, children are apt to see parents cheating on income taxes and using drugs. They know of illegal acts committed by people in the highest positions in the country. The Vietnam war and the hydrogen bomb encourage children to ask, "What's the sense of it all?" They say to parents, "Who are you to tell us what to do? Look at how you're living your life and how you messed up the world."

Even with these changes, adolescence is a period when children must separate from the family. At the same time, they still need guidance. Parents still need to know how to exercise the right proportions of flexibility and supervision. How parents set limits will influence their success in maintaining them. Some suggestions:

• Parents should have their own standards, but it's a good idea to check with other parents, and perhaps the school, about the prevailing views on curfews, use of alcohol and allowances. You can't always trust children to report accurately about regulations in other families.
• Both parents should agree on a course of action and support each other. Kids will use every opportunity to take advantage of differences between parents.
• Discuss the rules with children. Explain your position calmly, and be prepared to back up your ideas. Remember: Things have changed a great deal since you were the age of your child. Listen carefully to your children, particularly to the oldest one, who usually has the toughest time because he is a trail blazer for those who follow.
• Rules must be geared to the ability of the child to handle responsibility. Development in adolescence is uneven not only physically but also emotionally. One child of 16 may be able to manage a flexible curfew, but another may not be mature enough.

If rules are being flouted, parents must first examine their own roles, expectations and motivations. Are they contributing to the problem? Are their demands arbitrary and unreasonable? Examples:

• Bad language: What kind of language do the parents use?
• Rushing away from the dinner table—not participating in family discussions: What is the dinner-table ambience? Is it one a child would want to get away from?
• School grades: Are parental expectations realistic?

Next, avoid hostile confrontation and open warfare. Create an atmosphere where attitudes are expressed, where there is a positive feeling about learning, the intellectual spirit and the arts. The child should feel home is a comfortable place to be and that his friends are welcome.

When stress periods come, and calls from the outside begin to run counter to family standards, the child has something to fall back on, a basis on which to make choices and parents to turn to.

Praise the child for what he is doing right before you tell him what he is doing wrong.

If a child is told he is bad, he begins to live up to that reputation and is more likely to get into trouble.

Defiant behavior is most often used to get attention or to test limits.

Always deal with your child with understanding. Children react best to fairness. But it's all right to be angry if your anger is motivated by your concern for his safety. It is your job to protect him.

Don't impose restrictions you can't enforce.

Always give a warning.

Important: Don't make any threats for punishment you're not able or willing to carry out.

Effective punishment requires the cooperation of both parents. What kind of punishment? Withholding part of the allowance or a planned trip or other treat is better than corporal punishment.

Let the punishment fit the crime. Lesser matters (untidy rooms) may not call for the same approach as more urgent ones (drugs, alcohol).

Important: Do not discipline your child in front of other people, including siblings—and especially not in front of his friends.

Source: Clifford J. Sager, M.D., director of family psychiatry, Jewish Board of Family and Children's Services, New York.

UGLINESS AND DELINQUENCY

Physical unattractiveness and delinquency are often linked. Insight: We tend to treat ugly people like delinquents, so they act the role. Delinquency seems less common among the handsome. Suggestion: Be nice to unattractive people.

Source: Sociologist Robert Agnew.

TEENAGE SMOKING

Since 1977, the number of high-school-age youngsters who use cigarettes has dropped 9%, but a recent survey of seniors indicates that 20% still do smoke. Young people smoke for different reasons than do addicted adults. Problem: The kinds of self-help groups that support adults trying to stop don't work with kids. Best approach to teenage smokers: Life-skills training that helps youngsters cope with peer pressures and other problems. When a teenager's self-confidence improves, he doesn't need to smoke to prove himself.

Source: *Changing Times.*

LETHARGY CAN BE CAUSED BY ALLERGIES

Slothful teenagers may be allergic to common foods, not to work. In some youngsters, reactions to staples such as sugar, milk, corn, wheat or eggs can interfere directly with brain function, causing an inability to concentrate or to think clearly. Some signs beyond lethargy: Nasal congestion, headaches, abdominal pains, pallor and dark circles under the eyes. Test: A special diet that eliminates the patient's favorite foods. If dramatic improvement in health lasts more than 48 hours, an allergy seems likely. By reintroducing the youngster's regular foods one at a time, the source of the problem can be identified.

Source: William G. Crook, pediatrician, writing in *Medical Tribune.*

HOW TO GET BETTER TEST SCORES

• Keep current. Prepare for tests as if they occured without prior notice. Instead of memorizing the subject matter, paraphrase it and integrate it into your total store of knowledge. Most people do better on tests if they do not cram.

• Be prepared. Bring several pens and pencils to the test. Arrive a few minutes early. A little excitement may improve your performance, but do not let anxiety interfere with clear thinking. Important: Self-control.

• Quickly scan the entire test, at the start. Ask the instructor immediately about any unclear phrasing. Be sure to follow all instructions exactly and to understand the criteria. Example: If a list is requested, do not compose an essay. Ask if wrong answers will be penalized. If not, guessing may improve your score slightly.

• Mentally schedule your answers and set priorities. For example, if the test lasts two hours, answer at the rate of 1% each minute. This pace gives you a little reserve time for the more difficult questions and for the all-important review.

• Study each question carefully and plan your answer. Conserve time by avoiding repetitions. Examples: Label (do not write out) each question. Give as much detail as is requested, but no more. Omit side issues, especially if they encroach on other questions. Do not write out the same answer to more than one question. Cross out wrong answers (instead of taking time to erase them). Exception: Computer-scored tests require complete erasures of mistakes.

• Avoid dogmatic presentations. In an essay on a controversial issue, give all sides before justifying your view. In an objective test, choices are usually wrong if they contain such words as always or never. A statement is false if any part of it is wrong.

• Don't belabor the obvious. For example, don't write that a company should set goals. Instead: Specify what goals are appropriate. Try to cover all bases, but briefly. Most teachers disdain padding.

• Use clear expressions. Define technical terms so that a person who is not familiar with them would understand. Example: A computer's byte equals eight bits conveys nothing at all.

• Allow time for review.

• Use the test as a springboard for further learning. Don't blame the teacher or text if the grade received is less than hoped. Pinpoint and remedy the weakness.

Source: Dr. Harold W. Fox, former professor at Ball State University, Muncie, IN, and George A. Ball, business consultant.

• Achievement test scores, not Scholastic Aptitude Test (SAT) ratings, give the best indication of freshman-year college performance, according to Harvard admissions director William Fitzsimmons. Many top schools are now relying less on the SATs than on achievement tests in specific subjects and recommendations from high schools.

DRIVER EDUCATION IN SCHOOL IS NOT ENOUGH

Driver-education programs in schools put teenagers behind the wheel for only 20–40 hours. Follow up by having one parent supervise the new driver for another 500 miles in light to medium traffic. Practice defensive maneuvers for 10–20 hours more in heavy traffic.

Source: North American Professional Driver Education Association, Chicago.

SUMMER JOBS FOR KIDS

Friends and relatives are the best source of help in finding summer jobs. Ask them for contacts or ideas.

Summer camps hire students for all sorts of jobs. Usual requirements: Camp experience, age 19 or older and at least one year of college. Send applications for review by interested camp directors to: The American Camping Association, Martinsville, IN. The Association of Independent Camps, New York. Camp Consulting Services, Huntington, NY.

The National Parks Services of the Department of the Interior provides 4,500 summer jobs (and many winter jobs) annually. Applicants must be 18, high school graduates and US citizens.

One useful approach: Advertise your services on local store and community-center bulletin boards. Two brothers kept busy painting houses (a very profitable enterprise) after putting up a note in a supermarket advertising their availability.

Many countries let foreign students work in temporary, seasonal jobs. The pay is usually low, but jobs can be interesting. Example: Working on the French grape harvest.

HERE'S HOW TO CHOOSE A SUMMER CAMP

The best time to choose a camp for your child is the summer before. This enables you to visit a number of prospective camps and see them in action. Also: This gives you the chance to apply before all positions start to fill up.

To learn about camps: Talk to friends, attend camp fairs, read advertisements and make use of the American Camping Association* (ACA) advisory/referral service.

Questions to ask yourself:

• Is my child ready for camp? If he/she cries or carries on when separated from you, or if he firmly states that he won't go, he's probably not ready for camp.

Helpful: Find out why the child doesn't want to go. Does he have false, preconceived ideas about going away to camp? (Perhaps a friend had a bad experience.) If so, you may be able to change his mind.

• What does your child want in a camp? Take stock of his interests and the kinds of things he wants to learn and accomplish at camp. Then find a camp that will satisfy his interests, not yours.

Example: If you love sports, don't pick a highly competitive sports camp unless your child also likes athletics.

• What is wanted in a camp? Determine your child's needs, what he will tolerate and what he would be willing to give up.

Example: If your child won't swim in a lake, don't pick a camp without a pool. If your child will tolerate a lake and the camp has everything else, keep it on your possibility list.

• How long will your child stay? Pick the longest time period you can afford. Reason: A child adjusts better, and learns and grows more the longer he is away.

• Should your child go to camp with friends . . . or alone? If you are considering sending your child with a friend, make sure both of them have the same interests—and that you and the other child's parents have the same criteria. Otherwise one child will be unhappy. If your child wants to go alone, let him.

What to ask prospective camps:

It's important to talk to camp directors before picking a camp to be sure it's a good match for your child. Eliminate a camp if any answers don't make sense or seem suspicious.

• What kinds of programs are available? Parents who want their kids to have a fun, relaxing summer may prefer a recreational program. Those who want their children to learn something they can't during the winter may prefer an instructional program.

Example: On the tennis court at an instructional camp, campers are drilled on strokes and the emphasis is on proper form. At a recreational program, the emphasis is more on play than on drills.

• What is a typical day like? Have someone talk you through the program, including evening events. Find out: How much instruction is private and how much is in groups . . . which activities are required and which are elective . . . if your child can get as much as he likes of any one activity . . . who makes sure he gets to each activity . . . what types of trips might he take?

• How many counselors and children are in each group? Warning: The camper-to-staff ratio can be deceiving because it may include support staff—kitchen workers, etc. Also ask: How do you recruit new counselors . . . what are your selection criteria . . . how old are the counselors?

Source: Adele Selik, director of placement services, American Camping Association, New York Section.

*The 1989 Guide to Accredited Camps, published by the ACA, Bradford Woods, 5000 State Rd. 67N, Martinsville, IN 46151, provides details about more than 2,000 accredited camps in the US.

HELPING CHILDREN GAIN INDEPENDENCE

Having the family all together for the holiday season may be cheerful. But togetherness can pall if it is overdone. And low starting salaries, high rents and a scarcity of apartments are keeping many young people at home and economically dependent on their parents well beyond graduation from college.

While some families welcome a return to lifestyles in which adult children, as well as grandparents, live together, Dr. Clifford J. Sager thinks the trend is potentially dangerous. Among other hazards, he says, children fail to develop independence quickly enough when they live at home as adults. And the household and life-cycle rhythms are off.

Financial dependency on parents through the schooling period is directly proportionate to the slower maturing of young people today.

To encourage independence, parents should:
• Supplement their children's income at the outset so that they can live in their own quarters. There is no substitute for the experience of having to manage a household.
• Charge for room and board if children must live home. Some parents put this money aside as a stake for the child's marriage or business.
• Put a time limit on living at home: Six months, a year or until the first salary raise. Whatever the arrangement, make it clear that independence is the goal.

Grown children's social lives often present problems to parents who matured in a different type of society. But parents should not be afraid to set standards:

• If they are not comfortable when their children bring sex partners home, they should say so. Making their feelings clear before a guest arrives avoids unpleasantness later.

• Parents should not be afraid to ask grown children under their roof to help with chores and with family obligations such as visiting relatives.

• After children mature, some parents want to simplify their lives by moving into a smaller house or apartment or nearer to work. Do not be deterred by sentimental arguments of the children. Independent parents foster independent children.

Source: Dr. Clifford J. Sager, director of family psychiatry for the Jewish Board of Family & Children's Services, New York.

HOW TO IMPROVE SCORES ON STANDARDIZED TESTS

No matter how smart you are, no matter how well-prepared, there are strategies you can use to improve your scores on any standardized test, including the SAT, GRE and MCAT. What to do:

• Get to know the test beforehand. Every standardized test is different. Important: Read the test booklet provided by the testing firm to find out what subjects will be covered, the precise form questions will take and the directions. If you have to spend two minutes reading the directions when the test is in progress, you're losing two minutes of valuable test-taking time.

• Review the subjects that will be covered. If the test you're planning to take has a mathematicals section, bone up on math beforehand. Likewise with logical reasoning, science and so on. Start reviewing basic skills three or four months in advance.

• Take practice tests. Sample exams prepared and distributed by the testing organizations themselves are best. They will familiarize you with the material and give a fair indication of your actual exam score. If you are unhappy with your projected score, delay taking the exam until you have improved and are satisfied you can do well.

• Come prepared. Bring your admission ticket, personal identification and six No. 2 pencils with dull points—they let you fill in the circles faster than sharp points and they don't break as easily. If you're prone to headaches, bring an aspirin or your favorite analgesic.

Arrive an hour in advance. If you're unfamiliar with the test site, make a trial run a few days beforehand.

• Keep anxiety in check. Cramming the night before the exam encourages anxiety. If you become anxious during the exam, breathe slowly and deeply. Get up and walk around during the break.

• Use strategies. Answer the short or easy questions first. Save the long reading passages for last.

If you have trouble with one question, put a mark by it in the test book and go on to the next question. Then come back if you have time.

In reading comprehension sections, some find it easier to scan the questions before reading the passage. This will clue you in on what to look for as you read.

If you finish the test early, go back over your answers.

• Mark answers carefully. Make sure the circle you're marking corresponds to the question you intend to answer. Many students mark column after column of circles only to discover they're ahead or behind where they should be.

Self-check: Every five questions, make sure that the question and answer numbers correspond.

• Know when—and when not—to guess. A few tests penalize you for wrong answers (the SAT, for instance), others don't. Find out beforehand whether your test does.

On tests where there is no penalty for wrong answers, fill in every blank—no matter how unsure of the answer you are. On tests where there is a penalty, guess only if you can rule out at least one of the possible choices.

In some exams, the SAT for instance, questions at the beginning of each section are usually easier than those toward the back. Thus, if on an early question you arrive at a quick, easy answer, and that answer is listed among the multiple choices, chances are you have the right answer. But if you come up with a quick, easy answer on a question deep into the exam, and that answer is among the multiple choices, watch out. There are no easy answers at the end of the test.

• Don't let difficult questions rattle you. If one section seems harder or less clear than the others, it could be an experimental section, being used to try out new questions, and will not count toward your score. Just do your best.

• Don't panic! If you think you bombed the test, notify the testing organization immediately (use overnight mail). For most tests you have a few days following the exam to ask that your test not be scored. You can take it again without penalty, although your record will show that you cancelled a previous test.

If your test is scored, and your performance falls shy of what you had hoped for, you can always take the test again. Most schools look only at the higher score. Exception: Most law schools average your scores.

Source: Stanley H. Kaplan, founder of Stanley H. Kaplan Educational Center, Ltd., 131 W. 56 St., New York 10019.

COLLEGE APPLICATIONS

The pressures and anxieties of first finding the right colleges and then filling out all the forms make a child's senior year in high school a difficult time for the whole family. Parents can offer support and assistance without adding to the turmoil if they are discreet.

• Learn from your friends. People who have gone through the application process recently have practical, first-hand information that is valuable. Find out what books they found most helpful (for example, *Comparative Guide to American Colleges* by James Cass and Max Birnbaum or *Selective Guide to Colleges* by Edward B. Fiske), and provide them for your child. Don't worry about your friends' personal biases about particular schools. Just pass on factual information about the housing crunch for freshmen at an urban college or the attitudes toward women at a formerly all-male campus.

• Encourage an early deadline for finishing applications. Thanksgiving is a good target date. Then the child can concentrate on his schoolwork before the end of the semester and keep his grades up. First-term senior-year grades are important to the colleges that will be considering him.

• Make copies of all the finished applications and correspondence. Most colleges acknowledge the receipt of completed papers with a postcard, so you will know if anything is missing. If too much time passes without such an acknowledgment, you can call and check. Having a copy on hand will save time and trauma.

• Consider early-action applications or at least one or two schools with rolling admissions to get early decisions. Neither admissions policy commits your child to that particular campus, but knowing before April 15 that at least one school wants him can take the pressure off.

• Talk to the high school guidance counselor. Be sure your child is applying to schools where he has a better than average chance of being accepted. One or two long shots are reasonable, but young egos are badly damaged by a series of rejections. Find out what the counselor can and will do if the worst happens and your child is not accepted anywhere. (It does occur—even to good students.)

• Budget for campus visits to potential colleges. If time and money are a consideration, save the visits for after the acceptances come in and real choices have to be made. Be sure your youngster sees the college while it is in session. Admissions offices will arrange for dormitory stays and opportunities for going to class if your child doesn't know anyone at the school.

• Don't be arbitrary. A youngster's first choice may not work out, or it may prove to be a mistake. Let him know now that he can transfer from one college to another with no loss of face. In fact, some colleges are easier to get into as a transfer student than as a freshman.

Source: Florence Janovic, writer and partner in Sensible Solutions, Inc., book marketing consultants.

Subscribe to the newspaper published by the students at the colleges in which your child may be interested. Tune in to both the problems and the good points.

INTERVIEWING FOR COLLEGE

An unfavorable interview may work against a prospective college applicant. Alternative: Group-information sessions. These are best for the student who does not have detailed questions about the college. Reminder: The student should have a personal interview if one is "recommended" but not required. Group-information sessions should be considered only when the personal interview is optional.

HOW TO VISIT COLLEGES

High school seniors who are touring colleges should make sure that their visits pay off. Here's how:

They should find out as much as they can about the colleges they want to visit and check their high school guidance office for information. Some of it will probably be out of date, but even a two- or three-year-old catalog will tell a lot about the school.

They should write to the colleges to request a view book, a freshman class profile and other descriptive material. (Catalogs are expensive to publish, and most colleges distribute them sparingly.)

They should look for what the college doesn't tell them as well as what it does. The college literature is promotional material designed to "sell" the institution. In this period of declining enrollments, many colleges are as image-conscious as Madison Avenue.

Seniors should talk with graduates of their high school who are attending the colleges they're interested in and call neighboring high schools for the names of graduates attending these colleges. After a senior has written to a college for materials, a local representative of the college may call—usually an alumnus. Many representatives remain close to their alma mater and can be very helpful. Applicants should watch out for the occasional ones whose main source of information is a romantic memory of their own undergraduate years.

If possible, high school students should visit colleges during the summer after their junior year. It will help them to cut down their list. The admissions director will have more time to talk then than he will in the fall or winter, and visitors will find out how they react to the physical environment.

The two or three colleges at the top of the list should be visited in the fall or winter, preferably on a Friday, so a few classes can be attended. The admissions office will arrange overnight stays in an undergraduate's room, as well as a complete tour of the campus with a student guide.

At the interview, applicants should be open and candid. They shouldn't try to impress the interviewer with a long list of questions that they should already have answered for themselves ("Is this a coed school?"). They should concentrate on crucial questions to which they have no way of knowing the answers: "Are freshmen classes much larger than classes for upperclassmen?" "What happens on weekends —do most students stay or leave?" "Is the library crowded?"

If the applicant knows the field in which he wants to major, he should go to that department and talk with the professors. They can give him a sure sense of what will be expected.

Most important: a visitor should spend an hour or more sitting in the student union building or some other gathering place where he can talk to students and ask them what they like best about the school—and what they think is wrong with it. This way, he can find out about social mores as well as courses and professors.

STATE UNIVERSITIES THAT WELCOME OUT-OF-STATERS

State universities and colleges were founded primarily to provide low-cost higher education for residents of the state. Since tuition and fees do not cover the costs of maintaining these institutions, they are subsidized by state taxpayers, and admission to them is usually limited for out-of-state students. However, a number of top-flight state universities and colleges recognize the educational value of a diverse student body and welcome students from all over the country. Out-of-state students are charged higher tuition than residents of the state, but frequently the total still represents a higher-education bargain.

Some first-class institutions that welcome out-of-state students:

• College of William and Mary, Williamsburg, VA. This is the second oldest institution of higher learning in the country. Located in historic Williamsburg, the college admits about 30% of its student body from out of state.

• Indiana University, Bloomington, IN. Founded in 1820, the university draws a fifth of its students from out of state. This campus was the setting for the film Breaking Away.

• New College of the University of South Florida, Sarasota, FL. Founded in 1960 as a private liberal arts college, it is now an honors-type campus of the university. Nearly half of its students are from outside the South.

• University of Michigan, Ann Arbor, MI. One of the most prestigious state universities, it has long been popular with students from around the country.

• University of North Carolina at Chapel Hill, Chapel Hill, NC. It's the nation's first state university. Most of its students come from the South, but it's also popular with students from other parts of the country, particularly the Northeast.

• University of Virginia, Charlottesville, VA. Thomas Jefferson founded it and also designed its campus. Unlike most state universities, it has considerable social prestige—its admirers claim that Princeton is the University of Virginia of the North.

• University of Wisconsin, Madison, WI. Long popular with students from the Eastern seaboard, it has always been generous in its acceptance of students from neighboring states in the Midwest.

• Virginia Polytechnic Institute and State University, Blacksburg, VA. This is a rarity—a land-grant university that seeks a national student body. Although the majority of its students come from the South, substantial numbers are attracted from the Northeast, especially to its school of engineering.

Some other high-quality universities, such as the campuses of the University of California at Berkeley and Santa Cruz, do not actively seek a national student body, but do admit substantial numbers of out-of-state students.

GETTING INTO A TOP COLLEGE WITH ORDINARY GRADES

Perfect grades and board scores are no guarantee of admission to top schools. A student with board scores in the 500s and a B average can get in anywhere, if he promotes himself correctly.

Specific things a student can do to improve his chances.

• Give the admissions office a reason to vote for you. Emphasize work or volunteer experience, interesting sports or hobbies, unusual interests, anything you're really good at.

• Don't feel you have to be the well-rounded kid. Most good colleges are looking for the well-rounded class. It's much better to do really well at one thing than to be mediocre at a dozen things.

• Go prepared to the interview.

• Don't waste the essay. If your essay is dull or contains misspellings or grammatical errors, you've killed your chances.

• Ask only teachers and employers for recommendations. Positive comments from anyone who hasn't taught or supervised you will be considered padding.

• Take the right courses in high school. Grades are more important than board scores, but the quality and level of courses count more than grades. It's better to get a B in an advanced placement or honors course than an A in a regular course.

• Don't take the college boards more than twice. More than that shows you're a little bit too neurotic and pushy. Read the review books and take review courses. If you show improvement on your second score, that helps.

• Take advantage of colleges' desire for diversity. A good student from a small Midwestern town has a better chance of getting into Harvard than one from a big city. All the schools look for geographic diversity.

• Apply to unlikely schools. One Catholic school looked very favorably on Jewish students because so few applied.

• Don't dismiss a school just because your parents went there. It helps admission chances considerably to have an alumnus parent.

Source: Steve Cohen, author of *Getting In! The First Comprehensive Step-by-Step Strategy Guide to Acceptance at the College of Your Choice,* Workman Publishing, New York.

BARGAINS IN HIGHER EDUCATION

Despite skyrocketing costs in higher education during recent decades—with tuition and fees alone well over $10,000 per year at the more prestigious institutions—there are still some bargains among both private and public colleges and universities for those who are motivated to seek them out.

Typically, the private colleges are small, liberal arts institutions in the South and Midwest, founded by religious denominations. Many of them have become independent of church control in recent years. Although they retain some ties with the founding church, none of those listed below make any religious demands on their students.

All seek a geographically diverse student body, offer academic programs of substantial quality and attract capable students. The percentage of students receiving financial aid varies from 44% to 90%. They're grouped here by the level of tuition and fees from least to most expensive. (Room, board and books are extra.) The figures in parentheses indicate the size of the undergraduate student body.

• Birmingham-Southern College, Birmingham, AL. A church-related (United Methodist) institution regionally famous for its strong liberal arts program (1750–1800).

• Drury College, Springfield, MO. A liberal arts college founded by Congregationalists. It is now independent, but it maintains ties with the United Church of Christ (1100).

• University of Dallas, Irving, TX. A church-related (Roman Catholic) liberal arts institu-tion conducted by the Diocese of Dallas/Fort Worth. Nearly one-third of its students are non-Catholic (1100).

• Hanover College, Hanover, IN. An independent liberal arts college that maintains some ties with the United Presbyterian Church. It has been providing quality education for students in the Midwest for generations (1075).

• Hendrix College, Conway, AR. A church-related (United Methodist) institution that attracts its student body largely from the South but welcomes students from other parts of the country (1,030).

• Oglethorpe University, Atlanta, GA. An independent liberal arts college that attracts about 25% of its students form the Middle Atlantic region (1100).

• Wesleyan College, Macon, GA. A liberal arts and fine arts college for women. Although independent, it maintains ties with the United Methodist Church (350).

• Austin College, Sherman, TX. A church-related (Presbyterian) liberal arts college. Students choose a relatively structured academic program or considerable freedom in planning their own courses of study (1200).

• Butler University, Indianapolis, IN. Founded by the Disciples of Christ, Butler is now an independent liberal arts institution that places considerable emphasis on career-oriented programs (4000).

• Furman University Greenville, SC. A high-quality, church-related (Southern Baptist) liberal arts institution that offers a highly successful work/study program (2500).

• Guilford College, Greensboro, NC. A church-related (Friends) institution. It has a four-day academic week. Wednesdays are for activities such as independent study (1200).

• Nebraska Wesleyan, Lincoln, NE. An independent liberal arts college that maintains ties with the United Methodist Church. It places considerable emphasis on career-oriented courses of study (1500).

• Rockford College, Rockford, IL, as an independent liberal arts college whose students are evenly divided between those pursuing intellectual/academic interests and those concerned with developing marketable skills (1100).

• Rosary College, River Forest, IL. Founded

by the Dominican Sisters of Sinsinawa as a Roman Catholic liberal arts college for women. Now coed (1100).

● Trinity University, San Antonio, TX. Founded by Presbyterians more than 100 years ago. It is now independent but retains ties with the church. It currently sends nearly half of its students on to graduate and professional school (1,700).

Land-grant colleges and state universities were founded primarily to provide low-cost higher education for residents of the state. Therefore, out-of-state students are charged an additional premium for tuition and fees. With the very low resident tuition, however, the higher charges for out-of-state students still are a bargain. The universities listed below all welcome students from out of state. They are grouped by the out-of-state total of tuition and fees. The first group listed is the least expensive.

● University of Florida, Gainesville, FL. Limits out-of-state enrollment to 10% of the entering class. Nearly half of its students enter careers in business and industry after graduation (27,500).

● Kansas State University, Manhattan, KS. A land-grant institution that places no limit on out-of-state students. The large majority of students are drawn from Kansas and neighboring states (20,500).

● University of Kentucky, Lexington, KY. Attracts students who are interested primarily in career-oriented fields (24,000).

● University of Louisville, Louisville, KY. Founded as the nation's first municipal university. It became a state institution in 1970. It has a large number of commuting students but welcomes students from other parts of the country (25,000).

● Texas A&M at Galveston, Galveston, TX. An independent campus of Texas A&M University. This campus attracts substantial numbers of students from New England and the Middle Atlantic states (29,625).

● Mary Washington College, Fredericksburg, VA. For many years the coordinate women's college of the University of Virignia. It is now an autonomous, coeducational liberal arts college (3000).

● University of Arizona, Tucson, AZ. Has an unusually cosmopolitan student body. It is located in a residential area of Tucson (23,250).

● Georgia Institute of Technology, Atlanta, GA. A prestigious Southern engineering school. It attracts substantial numbers of students from the Northeast and Midwest (9,925).

● University of Idaho, Moscow, ID. Includes seven colleges, of which the College of Letters and Science is the largest (6,875).

● Michigan State University, East Lansing, MI. Founded in 1855 as the nation's first land-grant college. It now ranks as a major academic institution (37,450).

BEST LITTLE-KNOWN COLLEGES

When academic researchers assess the quality of colleges, the same few institutions usually top the list. However, many lesser-known colleges also merit attention.

A recent study by the Higher Education Research Institute of Los Angeles rated the quality of individual undergraduate departments. Since the study excluded those departments that also had "distinguished graduate programs" whose prestige might reflect on the undergraduate program, the undergraduate departments of some prestigious schools were not assessed.

Six rating criteria were used in the assessment:

● Overall quality of undergraduate education.

● Preparation of student for graduate school.

● Preparation of student for employment.

● Faculty commitment to undergraduate teaching.

● Scholarly accomplishment of faculty.

● Innovativeness of curriculum.

The colleges listed below all ranked among the top ten on one or more of the rating criteria for the department cited. Most scored highest on faculty commitment to undergraduate teaching and/or innovativeness of curriculum. They are all small (under 2,000 students), liberal arts institutions with strong academic reputations in their own regions. All have substantial percentages of their students accepted by graduate and professional schools immediately after graduation. Most are independent. Four of them are church-related, but these require minimal or no religious studies or practices.

• Beloit College, Beloit, WI, sociology.

• Bowdoin College, Brunswick, ME, biology.

• Carroll College, Colorado Springs, CO, biology.

• Denison University, Granville, OH, economics.

• Grinnell College, Grinnell, IA, chemistry.

• Hamline University, St. Paul, MN, chemistry.

• MacAlester College, St. Paul, MN, economics.

• Ripon College, Ripon, WI, chemistry and sociology.

• St. Lawrence University, Appleton, WI, chemistry.

BEST GRADUATE SCHOOLS

The graduate school with the best overall academic reputation is the University of California at Berkeley. Here are the graduate schools that rank first in the subjects listed, as determined by a survey of US faculties.

• California Institute of Technology: Chemistry, geoscience, physics.

• U. of California, Davis: Botany.

• U. of California, San Francisco: Physiology.

• U. of Chicago: Sociology.

• Harvard: Classics, philosophy, Spanish language and literature, zoology.

• MIT: Biochemistry, cellular and molecular biology, economics, electrical engineering, linguistics, mechanical engineering, microbiology.

• U. of Minnesota: Chemical engineering, geography.

• New York University: Art history.

• Princeton: German language and literature, mathematics.

• Stanford: Computer sciences, psychology.

• Yale: English and French language and literature, political science.

Source: A study by The Conference Board of Associated Research Councils.

COLLEGE HOUSING: NEW INVESTMENT OPPORTUNITY

On many college campuses where housing is in short supply, parents are finding they can save money by spending money—investing in a condominium for their student children.

For middle-class families who can afford the down payment, the tax advantages and appreciation pay off even in the short term of a four-year education. Example of how it works:

Parents of a university student in New York City wanted a safe apartment near the campus for their daughter. They found a studio for $60,000. With a down payment of $15,000 and a $45,000 mortgage at 12% for 30 years, the monthly loan payment was $463. Adding on the $300 maintenance fee, the monthly total was $763. Tax break: Initially, all the mortgage payment and half the maintenance fee ($613 total) were deductible. Since the family was in the 28% tax bracket, the net after-tax cost per month worked out to $591. Bonus: The child finds a roommate to share the apartment for $400 a month, which brings the monthly cost to $191. After four years of school, the apartment is sold at (or above) the original price, and the initial investment is recouped—usually with a profit.

If several students share your child's condominium, the rental income may be high enough for the apartment to be treated as ordinary investment rental property, with big deductions for depreciation. The test is whether income from the other students represents fair market value for rent.

Considerations:

Dormitory costs: The average cost of college housing runs upward of $1,500 a year. Obviously, the higher the cost, the more incentive there is to find an alternative.

Campus restrictions: Some colleges have sufficient housing for their students, so the need for off-campus housing is minimal, making the condominium alternative riskier. However, many institutions cannot put up all their students, and the demand for housing in the area is acute. Cornell, for example, can house only 40% of its student body. Parents of students in the Ithaca area are investing in houses as well as in apartments.

Student responsibility: Investment real estate must be maintained to keep its value. Your child's willingness and ability to take care of an apartment full of other students should be a factor in your decision. The responsibility might be more appropriate for graduate school than for the undergraduate years, when campus social life is more important.

PARENT'S GUIDE TO CORPORATE TRAINING PROGRAMS

What can you do to help your child land the right job offer?

A corporate training program may be the answer, especially for liberal arts students, because it permits recent graduates to earn while they learn. Such programs give in-depth training in a specific industry while also offering a practical view of the corporate world. This hands-on training is useful in whatever field the student finally picks. Best of all, most corporate training programs pay well. Starting annual salaries for trainees range from $15,000 to more than $30,000.

Competition for corporate training programs is fierce. The applicant usually has to face a number of rejections before he's offered a job he wants.

How to prepare: There is no such thing as too much preparation for a job interview. Encourage your graduate first to learn about the industry that interests him. Then, once he understands the industry and the key players, he can zero in on particular companies. He should study their annual reports and recruitment materials, and articles written about them. (Articles can be obtained by telephoning a company's public relations department to request a press kit.)

Information interviews in advance of a job interview can also be helpful. Alumni from your son's or daughter's alma mater who are already working for that company or industry are often willing to take a few minutes—either over the phone or in person—to offer insights into what it's like to work there. Your own business contacts and friends may also be able to serve as informal career advisers.

Questions the job hunter should ask: What are the most satisfying aspects of your job? What are your priorities in an average work week? What do you wish you had known about this career field before you entered it? What about this employer?

Although there are no best management training programs, there are some truly outstanding ones that have earned national reputations. (Note: All are open to liberal arts graduates as well as to more specialized degree holders.) Among them:

• R.H. Macy & Co., Inc. Macy's is considered the retail industry's top performer. Its training program has been lauded as "the Harvard of retailing" by *The Wall Street Journal*. The management training program begins with a couple of months in the classroom. During that time trainees learn everything anyone ever wanted to know about a complex organization engaged in the department store business. The sales manager's job is the first permanent placement, and sales managers often run businesses with annual sales of over $2 million.

• The May Department Stores. May offers the highest starting salaries in the retail industry (more than $25,000 to the best and brightest BAs). After a number of weeks in the classroom, trainees spend several months honing their management skills in the first permanent job assignment—department manager of group sales managers.

• Grey Advertising. New York's largest advertising agency offers a unique, flexible training program. There is constant dialogue between trainees and their supervisors. In the account management area, new hires are immediately given real work that involves considerable responsibility.

• Ogilvy & Mather. Each year this advertising agency hires a small number of assistant account executives for a comprehensive and rigorous training program. "It's a friendly place, not at all the way I envisioned Madison Avenue," says an Ogilvy account executive.

• Procter & Gamble. This manufacturer and distributor of more than 300 consumer products has a reputation for promoting from within. Its reputation as a trainer is stellar. Many believe four years in brand management at P&G has more value than an MBA for those who intend to spend their careers in advertising and marketing.

• SmithKline Beckman. The company's centralized training program, which consists of four assignments over the course of 18-28 months, is clearly the fast track to management careers in this health-care and high-technology company. SmithKline is particularly enjoyable because the work environment is intellectually stimulating.

• Morgan Guaranty. Formal classroom instruction lasts six months for BA hires and includes accounting, international finance and corporate finance. The bank's emphasis is on wholesale banking. Following the classroom training, hires spend three months crunching numbers in the financial analysis department, working on companies that the lending officers serve. Compensation is generous (starting salaries are $25,000 +). For Morgan bankers there is a free lunch, which is served daily to promote comradeship among executives at various stages of their careers.

• First National Bank of Chicago. The First Scholar Program, the bank's most prestigious career offering, is a 30-month general management training program that combines employment at the bank with evening graduate programs at the University of Chicago or Northwestern University. First Scholars are required to take two courses per quarter. They get experience in a wide range of the bank's departments through periodic rotations.

• McKinsey & Co. There's no real training for consulting firm research associates. From day one, hires are expected to be able to execute whatever assignments are passed their

way. The associates get an insider's view of big business and complicated problem-solving—and fat paychecks (total compensation for year one on the job is upwards of $33,000). The expectation: Top BAs are hired, work for two years, and then leave the firm to return to school for an MBA or JD.

Source: Marian Salzman, author, with Deidre Sullivan, *Inside Management Training: The Career Guide to Training Programs for College Graduates,* New American Library, New York.

COPING WITH ELDERLY PARENTS

Getting along better with elderly parents isn't easy.

Basic strategy: Avoid criticizing, making demands or challenging their ideas. Instead: Demonstrate support and concern.

To communicate more effectively: Do not bombard them with direct questions. Instead, search gently for their true feelings. Parents listen to you only if they are heard in return. The parent says: My friend hears from her son almost every day. Wrong response: Don't expect me to call every day. The right way: Is something bothering you that you haven't told me about?

Tell parents directly when they hurt your feelings.

Parents are more likely to help if you give them a choice. Wrong way: Mother, I need you to come over and baby-sit tomorrow night. Right way: I have an important meeting tomorrow night, which I really must attend, and I can't find a baby-sitter. Point: Enlist her help in trying to find a solution.

Source: *Mother, Father, You: The Adult's Guide for Getting Along Great with Parents and In-Laws* by Carol C. Flax and Earl Ubell, Wyden Books, Ridgefield, CT.

50TH ANNIVERSARY GREETINGS

White House greetings for anniversaries of couples married at least 50 years or for birthdays of people 80 years old or older can be arranged. Send name, address and date of event six weeks in advance to Greetings Office, White House, Washington, DC 20500. *Free.*

FOSTER GRANDPARENTS: SUPPORT FOR TROUBLED CHILDREN

The inspired matching up of retired older Americans who have time on their hands with handicapped children who need patient, regular companionship and guidance is a legacy of the 1960's federal poverty program.

Volunteer citizens bring their tender, loving care and attention to young clients—who need it as much as medicine, food and shelter. This fills an urgent need at short-staffed institutions, whether for the mentally retarded and emotionally disturbed, the pediatric wards of general hospitals, rehabilitation centers for the physically handicapped or correctional facilities, day-care centers or schools.

Many of these volunteer efforts are organized by the institutions themselves or by local social-service agencies. Volunteers receive orientation and training before they start, and supervision and counseling are available on the job. Tasks vary from feeding and dressing a child, playing games, reading stories and working on specific physical therapies to simply offering unthreatening companionship for a few hours a week.

For many of the children served, the foster grandparent represents the only meaningful adult relationship in a troubled life. Watching a youngster learn to trust another human being or master a skill can be very rewarding.

The government-sponsored Foster Grandparents Program, offers financial assistance to low-income senior citizens who sign up. Eligible people must be at least 60, in good health, and below a particular income level (around $5,000) that differs from state to state. For 20 hours of "grandparenting" per week, each volunteer receives a small stipend, transportation, a daily meal, an annual physical examination and some insurance coverage. Administered by ACTION, the federal volunteer service agency, the program reaches almost 55,000 children.

NURSING HOME ALTERNATIVES

Home health care for the elderly is proving to be a happy and often more economical alternative to nursing-home care in a number of experimental programs.

Benefits to the patient: (1) Greater resiliency in recovering from physical setbacks, even severe ones such as amputations. (2) A greater sense of independence and mental alertness. (3) Increased longevity.

How the programs work: An evaluation of a patient's medical problems is made through a visit to a clinic. A therapy is prescribed, and regular home doctor and nurse visits are arranged. Social workers keep watch over non-medical problems and enlist help from other agencies for needs such as shopping or hot meals.

Cost benefits: The facts are not all in, but in at least one program (St. Vincent's Hospital in New York City), the cost is about 60% of the care in an institution. However, the doctors there donate their time, and a similar program elsewhere might be more costly.

Medicaid has approved home-care experiments in about 20 states.

HOW TO SELECT A NURSING HOME

Placing a troubled, dependent relative in a nursing home is a heart-wrenching ordeal. To ease the way, know when a nursing home is the only answer. Deciding factors: When there is a loss of control of body functions, a loss of memory or an inability to perform the basic activities of daily life such as shopping, cleaning and dressing. People do not age physically and emotionally at the same rate.

Never coerce a person into a nursing home. Rather, open the decision for discussion. When possible, have the person accompany you when you shop for the proper home.

The nursing homes with the best reputations, highest staff-to-patient ratios and longest waiting lists are nonprofit. That is, they are run by churches, fraternal orders and charities. Hitch: Only about 25% of all homes are nonprofit.

The majority of nursing homes are for profit, or proprietary. Other differences among homes:

• Health-related facilities emphasize personal, not medical, care. These are generally nonprofit homes.

• Skilled nursing facilities are for patients with serious mental and physical disabilities. Most of these places are proprietary.

Nonprofit homes usually charge a flat, high monthly fee with no extras for added services. Proprietary homes ask a lower monthly fee with extra payments for services. Always be certain that you understand the rates and service charges.

Many proprietary homes don't take Medicaid patients. The amounts paid by the state and federal health plans aren't always enough to cover the costs. Patients without any money should be placed in a nonprofit home.

To select a home, start by asking the patient's physician, relatives and friends who have gone through a similar experience for information. Also, get information from the state departments of health and social services.

Begin the search long before it becomes necessary to find a home. Caution: Many emotional problems among the elderly occur during the waiting period because of the stress of being in limbo.

Since this is an emotional experience, take a close friend with you when you inspect nursing homes. The person will look for things that you forget.

What to seek in a home:

• Good location. The right home is close enough for convenient visits. Avoid places in run-down or dangerous neighborhoods. Best: A residential area with gardens and benches.

• Well-lit, cheery environment. Doors to the room shouldn't have windows. This is a home, not a hospital.

• The home's affiliations with hospitals and associations. Find out how many patients are on Medicaid. If the number exceeds 50%, the home is not likely to provide adequate care.

• A professional staff. There should be a full-time or regularly visiting doctor with specialized knowledge in geriatrics. The total number of registered nurses, licensed practical nurses and nurses' aides should be at least 40% of the number of beds.

• The residents. Nothing speaks better for a nursing home than active, vital patients. Observe the staff to see if they treat residents with respect. Talk to the residents and ask for their complaints. Bad signs: If more than 3% of the residents are in the hospital at one time. If patients are still in bed or in bedclothes at 11 am. If many residents are catheterized to avoid linen changing. Ask what happens when a patient is hospitalized. Is the nursing home bed still available afterwards?

• Handrails in hallways and bathrooms.

• Smoke alarms in public areas and each room. Ask to see the latest fire inspection report and note the date.

• The dining room should be clean, bright and inviting, with no dirty trays around. Are special diets adhered to?

• The residents' rooms should be comfortable and attractively furnished. Be sure the room can be personalized with pictures, plants, knick-knacks. Drawers should be lockable.

• Happy patients are those plugged into the outside world. Newspapers and large-print books should be readily available. The home should show movies, bring in entertainers and provide outside trips. Other necessary activities: Gardening, workshops, education courses, lecture series and discussion groups. Find out about religious services and provisions for voting.

• Special services should include visits by a licensed physical therapist and workable therapy equipment that the patients can use. Visits by other specialists: Speech therapists for stroke victims, audiologists, dentists, psychiatrists, optometrists and podiatrists.

What to watch out for:

• Patients who are sedated to keep them quiet.

• The home asks for a large sum of money up front.

• Doctors who hold gang visits (they see 40–50 patients during each call).

• You are denied visiting rights to the kitchen, laundry and library.

• The Patient's Bill of Rights isn't displayed.

2. Sex

Sex

DATING FOR MATURE AND SUCCESSFUL SINGLES

Four years ago Abby Hirsch started a dating service, The Godmothers, for achievers whose lives are full of options, the kind you would think have no problems meeting all the right people. Not so.

Singles now settle into comfortable friendships with a peer group and have no way of getting out of it. Everyone is afraid of dating people from the office. Women are working and don't have time to give the dinner parties that used to introduce people.

The 500 or so Godmothers clients in each city (New York, Washington, Philadelphia) range in age from 18 to 67. Most women are in their 20s and early 30s, and most men are in their 30s and 40s. Second largest group: Men in their 50s and women in their early 40s. They have a wide spectrum of working credentials and interests. For a fee, each gets three different introductions.

Selection process:

Prospects send in autobiographical, professional and personal data, information on what worked and what did not work in their most recent relationships and what kind of person they would like to meet now. From this material the staff determines those who have a chance of being successfully matched up. The preliminary screening is followed by a 45-minute interview.

Who is rejected? People who ask for much more than they have to offer. Those who are too rigid and make requests the service cannot fill. People who are extremely overweight (no one will go out with them). Anyone whose only goal is marriage risks disappointment and is not encouraged. Acceptable: Those who would like to find a mate eventually but are aware that there can and should be many pleasurable experiences on the road to permanence.

What's hot, what's not:

• Highest priority: Nonsmokers.
• Second highest priority in Washington: Someone not connected with politics (no one wants to talk about politics at night).

Women: Most are making reasonable amounts of money. You don't hear ''Find me a man who is going to be able to support me'' but rather ''Find me a man who's going to be loving and sharing and wants to spend time with me.''

Men: It's not the prettiest girl on the block that they want. The demand is for a woman who really likes her work but who has time for a man in her life.

The staff tries to redirect unrealistic requests. Example: If you're interested in someone who plays tennis but you play only one hour a week, maybe there are other issues that are more important.

There is often a wide difference between what people ask for and what they respond to. Example: A woman whose last relationship had been with a photo-journalist who was almost always away on assignment asked for a solid Brooks Brothers type. She liked the stockbroker she was introduced to but soon became bored. What she really wanted was someone dependable but more adventurous. They found her an attorney whose hobby is ballooning. They're planning to marry.

Dating tips:

• Avoid talking too much about a former spouse.
• Re-examine your priorities, and try to be more flexible.
• Don't judge another person in the first ten minutes of a date. Stay open.
• Keep a sense of humor.

• Listen to what the other person is saying. Be interested, not only interesting.

Those who have the toughest time finding acceptable dates: (1) Very beautiful women. Men are afraid to approach them. When they do, it's usually not for the right reasons. (2) Very successful men. Women stay away from them because they feel such men have so many other choices, creating too much competition.

Success: Although a number of Godmothers matches have resulted in marriage, the percentage is low. But 35% have dated for six months or longer.

Availability: Whether or not you will date successfully depends a great deal on whether you are really available for a relationship.

Advice to those who want to become more available. Think through why you are asking for particular qualities in another person and why you are responding as you are. Re-examine your priorities.

Source: Abby Hirsch, founder of The Godmothers, New York.

SINGLES MEET IN HEALTH CLUBS

Health clubs now vie with singles bars as a place for people to meet. While most members of fitness centers really want to exercise, they also realize the places provide a good opportunity to connect with people who have similar interests.

WHAT MEN LOVE IN WOMEN

Brunettes come in first with 36% of the men, 29% go for blondes and 32% are indifferent to hair color. Favorite eye color: 44% select blue, 21% like brown and 20% prefer green.

By two to one, men choose curly hair over straight.

The trait men first associate with a beautiful woman: 42% say personality, 23% think of the smile, 13% say eyes and only 6% zero in on the body.

Their favorite look: Striking and sophisti-

cated is first, with 32%. Least favored: The preppy look, preferred by only 3%.

Biggest turnoffs: Heavy makeup, 26%; excess weight, 15%; arrogance, 14%.

Source: Poll of 100 men age 18–40 conducted by *Glamour.*

BEAUTIFUL WOMEN FRIGHTEN MEN

An exquisite woman is a daunting—even frightening—prospect for many men.

A man is much more likely to be impotent with a beautiful woman. Many men have no potency problem with women of ordinary looks, or even with those who are downright unattractive. But if the woman is a great beauty, the man feels he has lost control of the situation. Knowing his partner could have her pick of men, he feels he must live up to her expectations. A beautiful woman arouses feelings of envy and inadequacy in some men. This is true even if she is loving, giving and not the least aggressive.

Source: Dr. Helen Singer Kaplan, director, Human Sexuality Teaching Program, New York Hospital.

SEXUAL HABITS OF AMERICAN WOMEN

• Extramarital affairs. In a *Cosmopolitan* poll, 54% said they fooled around, 21% in the *Ladies' Home Journal,* 34% in *Playboy* and 43% in a survey by the Institute for Advanced Study of Human Sexuality. *Playboy's* poll also showed that almost 65% of wives have had affairs by age 50.

• Skill. A majority of women think they are good at sex. *Playboy* found 80% who claimed they were skilled. Some 65% of those polled in the *Journal* rated themselves good to excellent. And 64% in the Institute poll admitted they were "great."

• Frequency. Most polls say that married women make love two or three times a week.

• Orgasms. Roughly half the women questioned said they had orgasms regularly.

• Oral sex is practiced by more than 85% of

the women questioned by *Cosmopolitan* and 95% of those by *Playboy.* About one-half of married women incorporate it into their love-making.

• Sex in public places is indulged in by about one-third of those polled by *Playboy.*

• *Family Circle* found that 85% of wives are satisfied with their sex lives.

• One-third of the women polled by the Institute have had venereal disease or herpes. About 91% use sex lotions or gadgets.

• *Playboy* discovered that among young married couples, wives play around more than husbands.

EXTRAMARITAL SEX TODAY

The dramatic shift in economic and social conditions in the second half of the 20th century has led many successful men and women to have extramarital lovers.

The modern concept of this arrangement stretches back to the European aristocrats, whose marriages were land and power contracts, not romantic liaisons. Personal unions took place outside the marriage. Indeed, the romantic side of chivalry was concerned with extramarital affairs.

Attitudes changed with the rise of the mercantile middle class. A tremendous cultural and religious force was directed against anything that interfered with the marital bond. Reasons: The family was the primary economic unit. Marriages united families to facilitate the orderly transfer of acquired wealth as an inheritance to offspring. In addition, the emerging middle class had not yet acquired the cynicism and decadence of the aristocrats. They felt morally bound by the strictures that reinforce their marriage vows.

After World War II, with the help of Hollywood movies, marriage came to be regarded as an institution inspired by romantic love that could be reevaluated periodically. People began to place more emphasis on individual satisfaction. If needs were not being met in the marital relationship, alternatives were seriously entertained. Key: Economic success no longer depended on class, land holdings and family achievement. It was based on individual ability. One person became the economic unit. Each successful person had the time, finances and opportunities to form relationships apart from the marriage.

This liberation spawned many new concepts. One was the open marriage, which tries to combine outside sexual relationships with marriage. Statistics show that marriages under these contracts seldom survive for more than three years. Usually, the desire for an open contract is only an attempt to ameliorate serious troubles between spouses.

Others have followed the aristocratic patterns. Some are extramaritally promiscuous. Others are serially monogamous—true to each new love until a newer one appears. Some even have a monogamous relationship with both a lover and a spouse. Example: A busy executive has a spouse at home and a colleague/lover who is a constant companion on business trips.

What is the attitude of friends and colleagues toward this extramarital lover? It's tricky. Necessary ingredient for all parties: Tact and diplomacy.

Example: A friend, without clearing it with you in advance, shows up at your party with the lover rather than the spouse. The guest is committing a gross indiscretion. Any lover is potentially an unwanted guest. Minimum courtesy: The guest should call the host to explain that the spouse is indisposed and ask permission to bring the friend. People who flaunt their indiscretions are both rude and foolish.

Insight about etiquette: Close friends of a woman support her affairs. A man's friends ignore his affairs or offer support from a distance. Prime reason: Women tend to talk about these relationships much more. Men are usually not as involved in sharing details of their personal lives. Exception: Locker-room braggarts. They are also the ones who bring a lover to a party without prior clearance with the host, especially if they are squiring younger consorts.

Bottom line: In general, marriages do not survive a series of extramarital relationships unless they are temporary transitional crises of adult life.

Source: Martin G. Groder, M.D., psychiatrist and business consultant, Durham, NC.

MOST COMMON SEXUAL CONCERNS

Among men:

• Premature ejaculation. The answer to this problem lies in learning to control the timing of ejaculation. This is easier than you think. You have to find the point at which you can no longer stop yourself from ejaculating. During masturbation, practice ways in which you can decrease or increase feelings of arousal. Discover which fantasies or behavior triggers your excitement and what diminishes it, and learn how to focus on the latter, in order to postpone ejaculation. It's not a good idea to use the old-fashioned trick of thinking about baseball scores or work. Thinking about such totally nonsensual experiences is destructive to sexuality. Instead, focus attention on any sensation in your body, or minimal sensual thoughts, which at least keeps you in the realm of being sensual (but not at the peak of being excited).

• Sexual deviations and fetishes. Men are very much concerned with what they consider unnatural desires, such as the wish to be spanked by women. It arises from the need to be punished for feeling sexual, and also they need to be forced into sexuality as a way of avoiding responsibility for engaging in it. ("The devil made me do it.") Cross-dressing is the desire to put on women's clothes. Husbands and lovers who do this may keep the practice hidden or may be indulged by their partners until it becomes disturbing. A desire to put on women's clothes usually reflects sexual problems related to a desire, left over from childhood, to be "close to Mommy." (Mommy may not be near forever, but her clothes can be.) It may also be a sign of difficulty in integrating the passive "feminine" side of a man's nature with the active "masculine" side. Example: A man who has trouble expressing his passive side, as evidenced in the inability to cry, may find it easier to do so by putting on women's clothes.

• A desire for more sexual aggressiveness from female partners. A great many men wish that their wives or lovers would take the sexual initiative and behave less passively. There is a strong possibility that if women were less sexually passive, some men might be less inclined to homosexuality. Theory: If women could act out the more masculine side of themselves and thus come across to men in a more familiar way, physically and emotionally, far fewer men would have difficulties relating sexually to women. (This is borne out by homosexuals, who explain that what they get from relationships with men is missing from relationships with women.)

• Erection problems (failure to get or maintain erections). This is much more complex than premature ejaculation and harder to deal with. It is often complicated by emotional problems, such as insecurity or hostility to the partner, so psychological treatment, rather than special physical exercises, is usually required.

• Penis size. A very common concern, disguised with euphemisms such as "I have a handicap." (Translation: I think my penis is too small.) The solution is to understand that physiologically the small penis is not a deterrent to sexual pleasure. It is important to find out what penis size means to you or your partner and the ways it affects your desire and pleasure.

Among women:

• Not having orgasms. The first part of the solution is to learn not to focus on the missing orgasm—if it is missing. Studies show that at least half the women who think they don't have orgasms in fact do have them. The dynamics: They're looking for some ideal of an orgasm that they've heard about. For the genuinely nonorgasmic: This is relatively easy to overcome, often within a brief period of treatment which involves learning to achieve orgasm by yourself via masturbation. Goal: To learn to accept that sexual pleasure is for you, too, not just for men, as so many women have been brought up to think. After acquiring the capacity to accept the sexual pleasure she has learned to give herself, a woman can usually go on to the next step, the pleasure of orgasm with a male partner.

• Conflict over the way they're treated in relationships with men. Men are much more concerned with sexual performance and physical fears than are women. Women care far more about the psychological and emotional aspects of relationships than do men. Most common conflict: The still very common tendency among women to settle for "half a loaf" in a relationship, usually out of the mistaken belief that "That's all you can hope to get, so make do." The first step out of this trap is to refuse to accept such reasoning and to reject the false security of relationships that offer so little satisfaction.

• Problems integrating the role of parent and lover. It isn't only men who suffer from the madonna-prostitute complex (separating women into categories such as the "pure madonna" and the "sexy enticer"). Women also suffer from this syndrome. Example: The women who has a child and thus comes to feel she isn't sexy and shouldn't feel sexy because she is now a mother. Usual symptoms of the problem: Avoiding sex on the grounds of fatigue, a problem with the baby, concern over money.

Frequently asked by both sexes: Whether it's healthy to get involved in a sexual relationship with someone much older or much younger. Answer: There usually isn't a great deal wrong with this sort of thing. Such couplings are often a holdover from incestuous childhood desires. When such desires are acted out by two adults, it can be taken as psychological information, but nothing else.

Source: Dr. Judith Kuriansky, clinical psychologist and sex therapist, New York.

SEX IN LONG-LASTING MARRIAGES

The importance of physical intimacy in long-term marriages depends on each couple. Sex is great and enjoyable, but in this country, it's been overrated.

Many people like holding, cuddling and sleeping together but not intercourse. However, sex can be a matter of substantial importance if one partner (or both) doesn't find pleasure in sexual activity with a mate.

Some women want sex only to have children. And some men have sex with their wives only for children and go elsewhere for pleasure.

Many women used to feel that their sex lives were over after menopause. And an astounding number of men used to give up sex after 60. Today we know it doesn't have to be that way. Men may need more stimulation and more time before having another erection or ejaculation. But sexual pleasure for both men and women can go on and on.

It's not unusual for married couples in their late fifties or early sixties who haven't had sex together for several years to say, "We're happy, we enjoy each other and love each other, but maybe we're missing something."

If they have a desire for more sexual expression, physical causes for lack of sexual desire should be checked, and then psychological causes.

Many men and women are turned on by other lovers but not by a spouse. Familiarity is one cause. Outside partners always have an advantage because they don't have to deal with day-to-day problems. Sex is important to a person having affairs, but is it important in the marriage? If it is, the big problem is how to redirect it to the marriage. It is not always possible.

Example: A man of 73 with a wife of 65 couldn't get an erection with his wife, even though he wanted to. But with a woman friend two years older than his wife he had excellent sex a couple of times a week on a regular basis.

After a number of unsuccessful therapy sessions, the problem was discovered. His abrasive, cold wife wanted sex only because she thought her husband was neglecting her. The other woman, who was warm and had a zest for life, really enjoyed sex.

What to do:

More and more people in long-term marriages want to do something about the lack of sexual desire in their marriage. Those who've been married 20 years may not know how to cope with changes and may be drifting apart. But they don't want to run out on the relationship.

It is important to determine whether the cause or causes of reduced sexual interest are interactional (routinizing of sex, depression or other emotional problems) or organic in nature (arterial sclerosis of the arteries to the penis, postmenopausal problems in women, low levels of testosterone in men). A small number of partners are aware of the fact that over time their sexual desire has shifted from heterosexual to homosexual. Outside relationships also preempt the interest of one or both partners.

There is a virtuous attitude toward extramarital affairs in this country, and until recently, it was a major cause of divorce. We can learn from other countries, where married people have a love relationship with somebody else but still maintain the family structure without bitterness, whether or not there is sex between husband and wife.

Example: A French patient and her husband both had lovers they talked about openly. The married couple had problems between themselves, and their seeing other people was part of their annoyance with each other. They wanted to improve their own relationship. They did get closer, but they had no intention of giving up the other partners.

Very often, people with sexual problems also have problems being open about other feelings. Increasing openness about sex helps. Suggestion: Talk about fantasies and try to incorporate them into your sex life.

Executives in high-powered jobs want to come home to a loving, relaxing place. They are impatient if their needs aren't understood, making them turn off sexually. So they look for sex outside (where they can find it quickly and easily on a short-term basis) rather than working out the problem at home.

Source: Clifford J. Sager, M.D., director of family psychiatry, Jewish Board of Family and Children's Services, New York.

SEX AFTER FIFTY

Middle age can be an opportunity to make sex better and more satisfying than ever before. Basic reasons: People of mature years have had more experience in lovemaking. (Research shows that many women don't experience a climax until they are in their thirties, though this is beginning to change as men learn more about orgasm.) The pressures of career building are less frantic, leaving couples with more time to share. The children have grown up and left home, giving adults more privacy and fewer demands on their

time. And as men age, they lose the pressure to get right to intercourse and a quick climax. They can concentrate on a fuller sensual and sexual experience in lovemaking.

Most common mistakes about age and sex:

• Believing that your sex life is essentially over by the time you're in your fifties. Society tends to reinforce this notion with its emphasis on youth—the absence of advertisements showing older people as objects of sexual interest. People behave according to the expectations that the culture sets for them and begin to give up on their sexual lives at middle age. This is, in many ways, the equivalent of giving up on life itself.

• Failing to understand that the physiological changes affecting sexual function are normal and can be adapted to without the loss of sex life. Middle-aged men suppose that these changes are signals that sex is (and is supposed to be) over for them. They become fearful that they can't function any longer. Once this fear sets in, sexual function really is affected seriously. Example: Many men age 55–60 or over worry when they don't get a spontaneous erection seeing their partner undress as they did when they were 20 or 30. But this does not mean sexual function is over for them. It means only that they now require more direct stimulation. Many men put off having intercourse until they get a spontaneous erection for fear their wives will think they have some sexual problem. Sex in these circumstances becomes less and less frequent, and this is what causes wives to be fearful that their husbands are no longer interested in them.

• Believing that sex requires a climax every time. As men get older, they need longer and longer periods between ejaculations. A man in his sixties may require a full day or even several days between ejaculations. This does not mean that he cannot enjoy intercourse and lovemaking in between. Sex partners get into serious trouble when they think climaxes are essential and that the male, particularly, must have one. (The man feels he must because his partner expects it. The woman feels that if he doesn't, he no longer cares for her.) You can enjoy all the sensations of sexual arousal without climax. Remember how pleasurable it was just to neck in the back of a car in your younger days, when sex was less permissive?

Lack of lubrication, the problem for aging women: Estrogen, cycled with doses of progesterone, will alleviate this condition. The fear that estrogen might cause cancer of the uterus has prevented many women receiving this treatment. Recent studies have shown that estrogen, when given with progesterone in cycles, is not only safe, but probably offers some protection against cancer of the uterus. Another benefit: Women taking such medication show a much decreased incidence of osteoporosis (the condition that causes bones to break easily). Several times as many aging women die of fractured hips every year as die of cancer of the uterus. There is also evidence that estrogen may decrease the incidence of heart disease. And there is no clear evidence showing a relationship between estrogen therapy and the incidence of breast cancer in women.

The problem of impotence: Many factors can cause impotence. Contrary to the opinion that has prevailed since Masters and Johnson did their research, not all impotence is caused by psychological problems. New research shows that a variety of physical problems can cause impotence and that these are treatable. (Included are hormonal problems and vascular and neurological conditions.)

Impotence may be being caused by medical or organic factors (rather than psychological ones) if:

• medications are being taken to lower blood pressure, or antidepressants, tranquilizers, antihistamines or decongestants are being used.

• alcohol is being overused. Alcohol has very strong negative effects on sexual functions, including possible long-term problems such as reduced production of the male hormone, decreased sperm production and reduced sex drive.

• a major illness, especially diabetes, thyroid disease or arteriosclerosis, is experienced. Illness doesn't dictate erection problems but should be considered as a possible cause.

• the man has lost his sexual desire (as well as capacity).

Impotence is likely caused by psychological factors if:

• there are firm erections under some circumstances (waking at night or in the morning, during masturbation, etc.). This indicates that the physical mechanism is in good working order and that emotional factors are the more likely cause of impotence.

• firm erections are lost just before or after entry. The odds here greatly favor an emotional cause.

• the problem started suddenly, over a period of a month or less. More likely this is an emotionally caused impotence, since physical problems affect sexual function more gradually. Caution: There are exceptions. Emotional causes are not always sudden in their effect. And medical causes can be sudden in their effect, especially if a drug is prescribed.

• the problem started after a very stressful emotional experience (the death of a spouse, the loss of a job, a divorce, rejection by a partner).

Source: Saul H. Rosenthal, M.D., editor of *Sex Over Forty.*

SEX THERAPY

It isn't easy for couples who have sexual problems to seek professional help. They're embarrassed. They believe that therapy takes years, costs more than they can afford and might not work. Sex therapy isn't cheap. But if you do have sexual difficulties with a loving partner, there's a good chance new techniques can help in a matter of months.

The most common problems: Lack of interest. Trouble with erections and orgasms. Pain, real or imaginary.

When to consider therapy:

When the problem becomes so great it jeopardizes the relationship, when preoccupation with the problem becomes so overwhelming that work suffers and enjoyment of life wanes.

One spouse often knows instinctively when a problem reaches a critical point. When you say to yourself, I can't go on like this anymore, you're usually telling the truth. Especially dangerous to a relationship: Trying to avoid the problem by drinking, abstaining from sex or turning to extramarital partners.

Another self-deception: Believing that only

one partner has a problem. It may originate with the man or woman, but once one has a problem, both have a problem.

Finding a therapist:

Since sex therapists are not licensed, anyone can claim the title. Occasionally, unethical persons do. To find a reputable therapist, ask your physician or county medical society for a recommendation. The American Association of Sex Educators, Counselors and Therapists publishes a directory of its members, for whom it sets education and training standards.

Most qualified therapists have degrees in a behavioral science (psychology, psychiatry) as well as training in sex therapy. Although sex therapy focuses primarily on sexual problems, a knowledge of psychology is essential because sexuality is so connected with total personality and life events.

Important first step: Get a medical examination to find out whether the problem is a physical one. Many times it is, especially when the problem is pain during intercourse or difficulties during erection. If a sex therapist doesn't ask at the first visit if you've had a medical exam, or refer you for one, find another therapist.

Facts and myths:

In some states, therapists often use a surrogate partner (a paid partner) during treatment. A person with sexual difficulty is taught how to overcome it during supervised foreplay and other sexual activities with the surrogate. But many therapists consider the use of a surrogate inappropriate.

If you're married, it's more effective to undergo therapy as a couple. Reasons: Since successful therapy may mean a change in sexual practices, your spouse will inevitably be involved. Moreover, many sex difficulties, such as lack of interest and failure to be aroused, are often the result of a breakdown in communication between partners.

A typical session lasts one hour, and therapists usually recommend one session per week. Most difficulties can be successfully treated in three to six months.

Some people are helped significantly in a single session because they only think they have a problem. Example: A woman who fails to have an orgasm during sexual intercourse.

Or a man who feels guilty when his partner fails to have an orgasm during intercourse. The fact: Most women do not have orgasms during intercourse.

Emotional reasons for problems:

Lack of sexual interest, the most common problem, takes longer to treat. Therapists now recognize that although some declining interest is normal during a relationship, it's often aggravated by depression, stress or emotions that build up at home.

The new technique of sex therapists is to deal with these outside causes, with the specific goal of increasing sexual interest. The therapist may also recommend that a couple experiment at home with activities designed to heighten sexual interest. Examples: Different kinds of foreplay, verbal excitement, different positions during intercourse. Lack of interest often develops because a couple haven't been communicating their preferences in sexual activity to each other.

The most common mistake couples make is assuming that sex must always be spontaneous. Few things in life really are. Most couples don't think twice about making reservations at a restaurant, but they wince at the idea of scheduling sex. It works, say the therapists. And it's one of the simplest and most effective ways out of the problem.

Source: Dr. Shirley Zussman, president, American Association of Sex Educators, Counselors and Therapists. Washington, DC.

APHRODISIAC BREAKTHROUGH

Scientists seem to be closing in on a safe and effective treatment for human sexual (libido) dysfunction in men and women. Research focus: Yohimbine hydrochloride, a compound derived from the sap of certain evergreen trees. Human tests with the drug are just beginning, but recent studies in laboratory rats yielded remarkable results. Animals injected with the drug displayed intense sexual arousal and performance. They sought to mate twice as frequently as untreated animals. Although researchers aren't sure how the drug produces its miraculous effects, recent findings seem to indicate that it stimulates the production of *norepinephrine* (a naturally occurring brain chemical that mediates the body's response to pleasure).

Source: Research leader: Dr. John T. Clark, department of physiology, Stanford University, Stanford, CA.

DOES RUNNING AFFECT SEX?

Running can improve a man's sex life if he doesn't take it too seriously, according to recent surveys of runners. Those who clocked less than 35 miles a week reported increased sexual desire, more frequent sexual activity and greater sexual satisfaction. However, more than half the runners training for marathons and covering more than 35 miles a week admitted to sometimes feeling too tired for sex.

Source: *The Runner.*

SEXUAL FULFILLMENT FOR WOMEN

An experienced orgasmic woman takes 10–20 minutes to climax once sexual stimulation begins. Hitch: The act of intercourse itself lasts only between two and five minutes on average. Conclusion: Effective sexual foreplay is essential for the fulfillment of the female partner.

Source: Patricia W. D'Encarnacao, M.D., writing in *Medical Aspects of Human Sexuality.*

HEART ATTACKS DON'T END YOUR SEX LIFE

Older heart attack and stroke victims can usually resume sexual activity in three to four months without risk. Doing so may actually cut the chance of another attack.

Source: *Sexuality in Later Life.*

SENSUAL STIMULATION MISCONCEPTIONS

A woman's breasts may not be erogenous, and she should not feel sexually inadequate if her partner's fondling of them is not exciting or satisfying to her. Alfred C. Kinsey found in his early sex studies that nearly half the women he interviewed were not sexually stimulated by having their breasts stroked. More recent studies have confirmed that women vary widely in the parts of their bodies that give them the greatest sexual satisfaction.

Source: Dr. Michael Carrera, Hunter College School of Health Sciences, New York.

DELAYED DESIRE

A minority of women feel their greatest sexual drive right before menstruation, rather than midcycle. Doctors suggest both physical and psychological reasons. Physically, estrogen/progesterone stimulation may excite them. Psychologically, relief from worry about conception and an emotional need for affection may make them more open to sex.

Source: Dr. Ewa Radwanska, writing in *Medical Aspects of Human Sexuality.*

NOT NECESSARILY DULL

The missionary position for intercourse (woman on her back, man on top) doesn't deserve its reputation for being boring and staid. Some men and women can't reach orgasm any other way. It rarely causes anxiety, since most people are very used to it. It permits a lot of face-to-face, torso-to-torso contact. It gives many men an intense orgasm.

Source: Merle Kroop, M.D., NY Hospital-Cornell Medical Center, and Debora Phillips, author of *Sexual Confidence,* quoted in *Self.*

SLEEPING AFTER SEX

Sleep following sex comes much more quickly to men than to women. A woman's body takes longer than a man's to return to a nonaroused state (10–15 minutes). If a woman has had no orgasm, the problem of getting to sleep can be even worse. Studies show a strong correlation between sexual frustration and insomnia. Solution: Patience, communication and trust between sexual partners.

Source: Dr. Samuel Dunkell, director of the Insomnia Clinic, Payne Whitney Psychiatric Institute, New York.

ORGASMS DON'T MEAN BETTER SLEEP

It's commonly believed that satisfactory sex with orgasm leads to better sleep for both partners. But a recent experiment did not prove it. The sleep of volunteers who deprived themselves of sex with their wives for one week was compared with the sleep of those same volunteers following sexual satiation. Result: No difference in the quality of sleep, nor in how rested each person felt on awakening. Upshot: There are widespread individual differences in response to orgasm. Some people even feel more energetic after sex.

Source: Charles Fisher, M.D., writing in *Medical Aspects of Human Sexuality.*

DRUGS EASE PAINFUL ORGASMS

Pelvic pain that radiates to the inner thigh, bladder or rectum in the period preceding and during orgasm is experienced by many older men. Their ejaculatory intensity diminishes, and the time required until the next orgasm increases (in some cases, up to several days). Small doses of testosterone (via prescription pills or shots) are often effective.

Source: *Medical Aspects of Human Sexuality.*

HEADACHES DURING SEX CAN BE TREATED

Orgasmic headaches are caused by sudden reduced blood flow to the brain during intercourse. They may be related to sudden sexual excitement or to outside factors such as extreme heat, drugs or alcohol. A history of migraine attacks frequently contributes. Not related: Age or gender. Pattern: Headaches usually don't occur often. Pain, which may be severe, lasts only a short time. Preventive measures: Avoid alcohol and hot showers before intercourse. Take an aspirin an hour before sexual activity. Change sexual positions, or try activity that produces less physical stress. Important: See your doctor if orgasmic headaches occur often.

Source: George W. Paulson, M.D., Ohio State University College of Medicine.

DOUCHE WARNING

Women who use diaphragms with spermicide jelly should not douche until the contraceptive has been removed (six to eight hours after intercourse). This forcible entry of water into the vagina can undermine the sperm-killing effects of the jelly. (Swimming or bathing immediately after coitus is safe because the soft folds of the vagina walls keep out the pool or tub water.)

Source: Armando DeMoya, M.D., writing in *RN.*

HOW LONG IS IT SAFE TO WEAR A DIAPHRAGM?

Wearing a diaphragm for 24 hours or more can increase the risk of toxic shock syndrome for susceptible women. The bacteria linked to the disease (staphylococcus aureus) are normally removed from the body by menstruation and other vaginal secretions. When this natural flushing is blocked by a diaphragm (or tampon), the bacteria multiply. The poisons created by the bacteria increase and, because they are not channeled out of the body, they can enter the bloodstream and bring on the disease. Women who use diaphragms should not wear them for more than 12-18 consecutive hours.

Source: Dr. Elizabeth Baehler, resident physician in obstetrics and gynecology, State University of New York at Buffalo, Buffalo.

CONDOMS LESSEN VD RISK

Men who are exposed just once to a woman with gonorrhea have a 22–40% chance of catching the disease. But some men won't catch it even after repeated exposure. Why: They have anitgonococci organisms in their urethras or residual immunity from previous infections. To decrease risk: A condom.

WHEN CONDOMS PREVENT DISEASE AND WHEN THEY DON'T

Condoms offer protection against some venereal diseases (gonorrhea, nongonococcal urethritis and yeast infections). They are less effective against herpes, venereal warts and chlamydia, which are small enough to pass through the pores of the condom. If either partner has an active urethral infection or genital lesion, the only safe course is sexual abstinence.

Source: Dr. Michael Carrera, professor of health sciences, Hunter College School of Health Sciences, City University of New York, New York.

CONTRACEPTIVE UPDATE

New intrauterine devices (IUDs) are small. Some are impregnated with minute amounts of copper and progesterone to enhance efficiency. But they can still cause side effects, some serious. Examples: Cramping, pelvic infection and painful intercourse. Women who want children later in life are discouraged from using IUDs because, in some cases, they can lead to sterility.

Source: International Fertility Research Program, Research Triangle Park, NC 27709, and the National Center for Health Statistics, 3700 East West Highway, Hyattsville, MD 20782.

ANTIBIOTICS THAT DEFEAT BIRTH CONTROL PILLS

Women who use oral contraceptives should be aware that their effectiveness is neutralized by some antibiotics. Contraceptive failure has been linked with tetracycline (Achromycin, Panmycin, Sumycin), ampicillin (Amcill, Omnipen, Pensyn), chloramphenicol (Chloromycetin), sulfamethoxypyridazine (Midicel) and

rifampin (Rifamate, Rifadin and Rimactane). Particularly susceptible: Low-dose estrogen contraceptives like Brevicon, Demulen 1/35 and Modicon.

Source: *RN.*

SEXUAL SIDE EFFECTS OF WIDELY-USED MEDICINES

Many illnesses can themselves cause lack of libido and impotence, but in other cases it is the medication that brings on changes in sexual desire and capability. Research in this area is scanty, and the sexual side effects of many drugs are not universal. Discuss your own situation with your doctor. However, the following drugs are known to have affected the sex lives of many who take them regularly:

High blood pressure medicines:

• Esimil and Ismelin (guanethidine) may cause impaired ejaculation and lack of potency in men.

• Aldomet, Aldoclor and Aldoril (methyldopa) can decrease sexual desire and make holding an erection difficult for men. In rare cases, they cause a man's breasts to develop.

• Diupres, Exna-R, Rau-Sed, Regroton, Salutensin, Ser-Ap-Es and Serpasil (reserpine) can cause reduced libido and potency, delayed ejaculation and enlarged breasts.

• Catapres (clonidine) may produce impotence in men and failure to achieve orgasm in women.

• Eutonyl and Eutron (pargyline) may bring on impotence, delayed ejaculation or delayed orgasm.

• Inderal and Inderide (propranolol) rarely cause side effects, although difficulty with erections has been reported.

Digestive-tract drugs:

Many of the older, commonly prescribed ulcer drugs such as Banthine, Bentyl, Donnagel, Donnatal, Pamine, Pathibamate and Pro Banthine have been associated with sexual problems. The more recent medication Tagamet (cimetidine) has been reported to reduce male potency and enlarge breasts when given in very high doses.

Tranquilizers:

Librium and Valium have quite opposite effects on different individuals. For some, these drugs reduce inhibitions and increase sexual desire. In other cases, they decrease libido.

Birth control pills:

Regardless of brand, the sexual effects vary among women. Many report increased libido, which may simply be a release from the fear of pregnancy. Some women claim decreased sexual desire on the Pill, which may be caused by the drug's effect on hormonal regulation.

Antidepressant drugs:

Depression itself often causes a lack of interest in sex. Antidepressant drugs sometimes increase libido and sometimes decrease it. Other sexual side effects vary widely and are not well recorded. Possible problems include impotence, testicular swelling, breast enlargement and milk secretion, impaired ejaculation in men and delayed orgasm in women.

Antipsychotic drugs:

Many medications used to treat mental illness have adverse sexual side effects that have not been fully documented. Among the symptoms are impotence, difficulty in ejaculation, irregular menstruation, abnormal lactation, increased and decreased sexual desire and even false positive pregnancy tests.

Source: Joe Graedon, pharmacologist and author of *The People's Pharmacy* and *The People's Pharmacy-2,* Avon Books, New York.

Sleeping pills reduce the desire for sex. As administered in therapy, barbiturates often diminish sexual inhibitions, which raises sexual enjoyment. But chronic use of sleeping pills causes difficulty in reaching orgasm. More dangers: Men can become impotent, and women may suffer menstrual problems.

Source: Dorothy DeMoya, RN, and Dr. Armando DeMoya, both of Georgetown University, writing in *RN,* Oradell, NJ.

THE PILL HALVES CANCER RISKS

Women who use the Pill are only about half as likely to develop cancer of the ovaries as those who do not. Best odds: Those who take the combination oral contraceptive that contain both the natural sex hormone estrogen and the synthetic hormone progestin. Among these women, the risk of epithelial ovarian cancer decreases by almost 50%. There are 11,400 deaths among American women every year from ovarian cancer. Epithelial ovarian cancer is the most common type of the disease.

JOCKEY SHORTS LOWER SPERM COUNTS

Athletic briefs may lower the sperm counts of men who wear them. The form-fitting underwear increases scrotal temperatures, which often leads to a reduction of sperm production. Men with impaired fertility sometimes try to avoid things that raise scrotal temperatures, like hot baths. Note: Even if the shorts lower sperm counts slightly, there is no evidence that they affect male fertility.

Source: Stanley A. Brosman, M.D., writing in *Medical Aspects of Human Sexuality.*

Sperm count is reduced by poor health but not by aging. A recent study showed that healthy men between 60 and 88 had higher counts, with comparable fertilizing capacity, than a group aged 24–37.

Source: *Journal of Clinical Endocrinology and Metabolism.*

MALE FERTILITY BOOSTER

Pergonal, a drug recently approved by the FDA, is a stimulant to the testes to increase sperm count. It is especially useful in reversing the impotence caused by drugs used to treat other diseases. Drawbacks: The drug must be injected by a doctor two to three times a week for up to four months to be effective. It also increases the size of the male breasts.

JOGGING MAKES SOME WOMEN INFERTILE

Regular jogging causes infertility in some women. Running lowers the levels of estradiol and estrone, hormones that are needed for the

reproductive process.
Source: *New England Journal of Medicine.*

WOMEN'S INFERTILITY CAN BE PREDICTED

Infertility in women can now be predicted with 95% certainty by chemical analysis, tests and a physical exam. Point: A woman need not have a baby just to see if she can. When the tests determine her childbearing status, she and her husband are then free to delay having children, should they decide to do so.
Source: Dr. Stanley T. West, gynecologist, New York.

TESTICLES MAY CAUSE INFERTILITY

Infertility in men is often caused by varicocele, an enlarged vein in the testicles. Corrective procedure: A varicocelectomy. Done with local anesthetic, sometimes on an out-patient basis, the operation ties off the enlarged vein to reroute the blood flow. Result: About 70% recovery rate (men able to impregnate their wives). No one knows why this vein causes infertility. But it can affect the fertility of men in their 30s and 40s who were fertile in their 20s.

EVERYTHING THAT YOU COULD WANT TO KNOW ABOUT SPERM BANKS

Sperm banks store human semen in deep freeze for future use in artificial insemination. Today, sperm banks create possibilities for family planning unimagined 20 years ago.

One in seven married couples in the United States is infertile. These couples, as well as single women who want to have children, can turn to a sperm bank for semen from an anonymous donor. The world's largest sperm bank pays its donors (often medical students) $25 for each specimen deposited. It charges its clients $35–$45 for each specimen ordered. A woman may need to be inseminated several times before a pregnancy results.

For those considering artificial insemination, the first step is selecting a doctor they really trust. The doctor then coordinates with the sperm bank and performs the artificial insemination. Some sperm banks are not subject to federal regulation, and state laws vary widely. Since many physicians are unaware of the disparity between various facilities, it is important to know what to look for in a sperm bank.

• Does the bank have a full-time medical director, and is he a pathologist?

• Is there an affiliation with a university or hospital?

• Is the bank a member of the American Association of Tissue Banks? Does it follow the recommendatons of the association's Reproductive Council?

• How are the donors screened? A complete physical description, personal and genetic histories, medical evaluation and laboratory analysis of the semen should be standard. the donor should be tested for such things as genetic disorders, damage resulting from environmental conditons, diseases such as AIDS and hepatitis, and sperm count and motility (ability to move). Some sperm banks subjedt a donor's semen to over 40 different tests. A blood donor, by contrast, is subjected to only three tests.

• Will you or your doctor receive a detailed description of the donor, including general information about his education, background and interests? Some banks supply only very limited information of questionable accuracy.

• Although donor anonymity should be scrupulously maintained, is there a coding system that allows you to check to see if sperm from the same donor will be available should you plan to have a second child?

• What is the bank's minimum acceptable sperm count? The average American sperm count is about 60 million motile sperm per milliliter. Banks vary in their criteria, and donor sperm may contain from 65 million to over 100 million sperm per milliliter.

Some men arrange for long-term storage of semen before a vasectomy, chemotherapy or exposure to hazardous waste, or numerous other situations. Essentially, they are purchasing fertility insurance, putting aside a deposit of sperm on the chance that they may want to father a child at a time when they are no longer fertile. Pregnancies have results from sperm stored for over 10 years.

A complete deposit of three to five cubic centimeters of semen may take two to three days of abstinence to accumulate.

ABORTION IS SAFER THAN CHILDBIRTH

Legal abortion is safer for women than childbirth, according to new studies. Death rates after elective abortion have fallen to .9 per 100,000 while maternal death rates run 9.3 per 100,000 live births. Abortions are safest for women 19 or younger and most risky for those over 35.

Source: *Journal of the American Medical Association.*

VAGINAL DELIVERY IS POSSIBLE AFTER A CESAREAN

Cesarean deliveries need not necessarily be repeated for subsequent births. New guidelines adopted by the American College of Obstetricians and Gynecologists give conditions for allowing women to choose vaginal delivery after an earlier Cesarean. Among them: A low transverse type of incision in the earlier operation. A single fetus with head-first presentation, weighing less than eight pounds. A delivery room with equipment to monitor fetal heart rate and the uterus. Nonrepeating reasons for the earlier surgical delivery. However, in case of difficulties, the mother may have to have another Cesarean.

CHOOSING THE SEX OF YOUR CHILD

When nature takes its course, slightly more than half of all newborns are male. Now, parents have new ways to tip the odds in favor of one sex or the other. The new methods, however, have still not received the full support of the medical establishment, chiefly because it is not known how effective they are.

For couples who want to increase the chances of having a boy, Dr. Ronald Ericsson, a California reproductive physiologist, has developed a means of separating sperm bearing the Y, or male, chromosome, and then using artificial insemination.

Improving the odds:

According to Ericsson, the odds of having a boy are improved to about 75%. Recent tests by licensed sperm centers have confirmed these odds. Ericsson's company, Gametrics Ltd.,* has licensed 11 clinics and hospitals around the country to use the procedure.

Dr. Ervin Nichols of the American College of Obstetricians and Gynecologists says that controlled studies have not yet been performed in sufficiently large numbers to make certain that the procedure is really effective.

Ericsson's organization is currently conducting clinical trials on a method that seems to put the odds of having a girl at about 75%. How it works: The same as the artificial-insemination process for boys, except the mother takes Clomid (clomiphene citrate), a drug used for many years to enhance fertility.

Less certain method:

For some reason, Ericsson says, women who are artificially inseminated with the filtered sperm after they take Clomid have a disproportionate number of girls. However, although Gametrics-licensed clinics are also offering this technique, Ericsson cautions that there are not yet enough data to pinpoint the odds exactly.

Home methods that rely on the timing of intercourse and changing the chemical environment of the vagina to increase odds for either a boy or a girl are rejected by the medical community as ineffective. Example: Planning intercourse at the time of ovulation and douching with an alkaline solution to increase the chances of conceiving a boy.

* Sausalito, CA.

3. Staying Well

Staying Well

MAKING A PLAN FOR WELLNESS

Passing an annual physical exam was once enough to satisfy most people about their health. But today an increasing number strive beyond that—for optimal health or the condition of "wellness," as it is known. Essential to achieving wellness is a plan that is both personal and practical. How to set one up for yourself:

• Try to clarify your most important reasons for living, and write them down in a clear and concise fashion.
• With these in mind, identify the health goals that bolster the chances of living longer and healthier. Be specific: Do not plan to lose weight but to lose 20 pounds in six months. Other possible goals: Lowering blood pressure by a specific amount, accomplishing a dramatic feat, such as riding the Snake River rapids or completing a marathon.
• List supportive actions for each goal. Example: Joining a fitness club, training for long-distance running.
• Also identify the barriers to each goal and how they can be overcome.
• List the payoffs for each goal, whether they are new energy at the office or more fun at the beach.

Virtually no one, however, can hope to stay on a wellness plan without support from friends or a system of benchmarks. Before starting the program, list the network of friends you can rely on for bicycle rides, tennis or other activities in the plan.

Once the plan is under way, set realistic quarterly benchmarks to track your achievements. A log or diary is usually helpful. Pitfall: Do not become so involved in the plan that you are serving it rather than the reverse.

Source: *14 Days to a Wellness Lifestyle,* Donald B. Ardell, Whatever Publishing, Inc., Mill Valley, CA.

HEALTH PROGRAMS WORK

Seventy three male and female employees at Xerox Corporation joined a 14-week health and fitness program. They exercised as often as they liked, using cycling, etc. to raise their heart rates to a target level for 20-minute sessions. At the end of the study, significant improvements were found in the subjects' self-image, anxiety level, heart rate, triglyceride and cholesterol levels and oxygen intake.

Source: *Journal of Occupational Medicine.*

BEST EXERCISE MACHINE

The stationary bicycle is safe, aerobic and noncompetitive. You can ride it rain or shine, and because you work out continuously without pauses, you can work off more calories per minute than in a stop-and-start sport.

Source: *Spring,* 33 E. Minor St., Emmaus, PA 18049.

Selecting a stationary bike:
• Durability is an important feature. The more plastic in a bike, the less durable it is.
• Besides a quality calibration component, a good bike has a speedometer and odometer.
• The seat and handlebars should be adjustable. Correct seat height: When the leg is comfortably extended, with the ball of the foot on the down pedal.

Undertaking the program:
• Start each exercise period with stretching exercises to warm up.
• Take an easy work load for the first three to five weeks.
• Monitor your pulse rate. It dictates when to increase the exercise level. Example: As you condition yourself to a given work load, your pulse rate will drop. That's the signal to step up

the load by adjusting the calibration component.

• Make up a workout schedule. Three to five workouts a week is satisfactory.

• Ignore the handlebars when pedaling the bike. Sit upright with your arms folded or hanging down. If you have to grasp the handlebars when pedaling, it means you're working too hard. Bonus: When working out, you are free to read or watch TV.

• Elevate your legs on the leg posts of the bike after completion of the exercise period. Alternative: Lie down with legs raised. Or walk around the house for 5–10 minutes. Caution: Without the cool-down period, you risk dizziness or worse.

Source: Jerome Zuckerman, Ph.D., president of Cardio-Fitness Systems, 345 Park Ave., New York.

BEST EXERCISES FOR ELDERLY PEOPLE

Exercise keeps the joints from becoming stiff and immobile and may even strengthen the bones themselves. Reason: The pull of muscles on bones often stimulates the bones to acquire calcium. Best exercises: Flexing and stretching. Gently bend, extend or rotate the neck, shoulders, elbows, back, hips, knees and ankles. Best aerobic exercise: Walking. Also beneficial: Swimming, dancing, riding and using an exercise bicycle.

Muscles shrink only from disease or disuse, not from age. Any healthy muscle responds to exercise, no matter what the age of the person. Point: Exercise will maintain musculature, and even expand it, after the age of 50.

Source: The Health Letter.

IS EXERCISE AN APHRODISIAC?

Researchers and common sense have long held that exercise enhances health and makes people feel better about themselves and their bodies. This, in turn, makes them more sexually attractive and responsive. Now studies are suggesting that exercise is a potent stimulus to

hormone production in both men and women. It may, in fact, chemically increase basic libido by stepping up the levels of such hormones as testosterone.

Source: Whole Body Healing by Carl Lowe, Rodale Press, PA.

OUTDOOR EXERCISE BUILDS BONES

Exercising outdoors helps prevent osteoporosis (softening of the bones) in people over 40. Reason: Both physical activity and sunlight reduce calcium loss, which weakens bones.

Source: RN.

THE TRUTH ABOUT STEROIDS

Steroids used to treat asthma do not build muscles. They may actually weaken muscles when used for a long time. Reason: The steroids taken by weight lifters contain male testicular hormones. Those taken for asthma contain adrenal hormones.

Source: Allergy Relief, 33 E. Minor St., Emmaus, PA 18098.

"SPACE-AGE" EXERCISE EQUIPMENT: FACTS AND FANTASIES

The sophisticated machinery that has turned old-fashioned gyms into today's health clubs is designed to offer continuous resistance during each of the movement exercises you use it for. This is a much faster, more efficient way to build muscle strength than using weights, for example.

If you do all the exercises for all the muscle groups on a regular basis, would you be perfectly fit?

No. Strength and fitness are not equivalent. Although muscle strength is a component of fitness, you also need flexibility and heart-lung capacity. Stretching exercises make you flexible, and aerobic exercises such as running and bike riding build up your heart muscle and your lung capacity.

Can working out on these machines help you lose weight?

There is a common myth that strengthening exercises turn fat into muscle. It doesn't work that way. People who are overweight need to follow a calorie-restricted diet and do aerobic exercises, which trigger the body to use up fat. Working out on machines only builds up muscle under the fat layer. However, combining a weight-loss program with strengthening exercises can improve body tone as the weight comes off.

Are these machines safe to use?

You need to learn the proper technique for using each machine, including proper breathing, before you are allowed on the equipment alone. On the Nautilus, for example, all the straps must be secured before you start. If one is broken or missing, don't use the machine. Poor form on the machines can lead to serious injuries. So can using the wrong weight settings.

Good rule of thumb: Use a weight setting that lets you do 8–12 repetitions comfortably. If you must struggle to get beyond five, the setting is too heavy. If you complete 10 without feeling any fatigue at all, it is too light. You will have to experiment with each machine to get the right setting. Then, from time to time, you can adjust the weights upward. But be cautious. Pushing yourself too hard not only invites injury, it also discourages you from sticking to the program on a regular basis.

WALKING MISTAKES

Although we've all been walking since we were toddlers, at least 30% of all people still don't know how to walk *correctly.*

Whether you're walking for pleasure, walking for exercise or just walking to get from one place to another, it's important to do it right.

• Mistake: Not maintaining proper posture. Poor posture puts extra stress on joints, vertebrae and muscles, causing pain.

Correct: Tuck your chin into your neck so your ear, shoulder, hip and ankle form a straight line perpendicular to the ground when you're standing still. Then hold this position as closely as possible when you walk. This avoids unduly stressing any one joint or part of your body.

Avoid arching the back. This causes lower back pain and shortens the length of your steps.

Correct: Do a *pelvic tilt.* Tuck your buttocks under your body and hold in your stomach while you walk. This will take conscious effort at first, but after a while, your stomach and buttocks will stay in automatically. Walking this way strengthens the back and the stomach muscles, which redistributes weight away from the lower vertebrae, eliminating back pain.

• Mistake: Keeping your arms still. You lose almost half the exercise value of walking—increasing your heart rate and working your shoulder, back and arm muscles—by not moving your arms.

Correct: Pump your arms. Bend your elbows slightly for regular walking, and 90° for aerobic walking.

Guide the arms straight forward and back, hands rising as far as the chest—at least to the waist. Let the inside of your arms rub the sides of your body—you should hear your clothing rubbing.

Pumping your arms is an upper-body calisthenic—your shoulders, upper back and chest all get exercised. If you pump your arms during brisk or aerobic walking, it doubles the exercise value.

• Mistake: Walking duck-footed (with the knees pointed out) or pigeon-toed (with the knees pointed in). This puts stress on the knees and ankles. They are hinge joints—made for forward, not side-to-side motion. Stress causes knee and ankle pain.

Correct: Walk with your feet parallel. And use the *heel-toe roll.* Land heel first and turn the ankle out slightly (the width of a finger). Then roll on the outer edge of the foot until you reach the toe. This aligns the lower and upper leg.

• Mistake: Walking with your feet too close together. This makes it easy to trip and fall.

Correct: Keep your feet hip-width to shoulder-width apart.

• Mistake: Taking short steps. This also reduces the exercise value of walking, and it causes the leg and hip muscles to tighten.

Correct: By reaching further with each step—and using arm pumping and the heel-toe roll—most people can lengthen their average step three to eight inches. Longer steps burn more calories. . .work leg muscles. . .raise heart rate. . . increase circulation. . .make you feel more energetic. . .and increase walking speed.

Source: *Gary Yanker, author of many books and audiotapes about walking. He is the founder of Walking World, a publishing and marketing company that specializes in walking. Yanker's book is* Walking Medicine: The Lifetime Guide to Preventive and Therapeutic Exercise Walking, *McGraw-Hill, 1221 Ave. of the Americas, New York 10020.*

WALKING CAN CAUSE INJURIES, TOO

Bunions and heel spurs can be aggravated—see a podiatrist to correct these problems before you begin a fitness-walking program. *Pinched nerves* on the ball of the foot can develop if walking shoes are too tight or cushioned inadequately. *Knee or hip pain* can occur from poor posture or body alignment—so make sure your stride is even, head is held erect, shoulders are level, upper body is relaxed. *Shin splints* can occur if you do too much too soon—don't increase intensity more than 10% per week.

Source: *Roundup of walking and sports medicine experts in* The Walking Magazine, *711 Boylston St., Boston 02116.*

WALKING FOR YOUR IMMUNE SYSTEM

Brisk walks strengthen your immune system—but too-strenuous workouts can lower immunity to colds and flu. Exercising near your maximum capacity for just 45 minutes—or more—produces a six-hour "window" of vulnerability afterward. *Better:* Exercise at a moderate level—the equivalent of a brisk walk—if not training for competition.

Source: *David Nieman, DrPH, is professor of health, department of health and science, Appalachian State University, Boone, North Carolina.*

EASY EXERCISES TO STRENGTHEN YOUR BACK

Stengthening the back and stomach muscles is the best protection against a back injury.

Flexed-knee sit-ups. Lie on your back, with knees bent and arms at your side. Sit up slowly by rolling forward, starting with the head.

Bent-knee leg lifts. In the same position as the sit-ups, bring one knee as close as you can to your chest, while extending the other leg. Alternate the legs.

Knee-chest leg lifts. Work from the bent-knee sit-up position, but put a small pillow under your head. Use your hands to bring both knees up to the chest, tighten the stomach muscles and hold that position for a count of 10.

Back flattening. Lie on your back, flex the knees, and put your arms above your head. Tighten your stomach and buttock muscles and press the lower back hard against the floor. Hold this position for a count of 10, relax and repeat.

Cautions: Don't overdo the exercises. Soreness is a sign to cut back. Never do these exercises with the legs straight. If you have back trouble, consult your doctor before starting this, or any, exercise program.

Source: *American Journal of Nursing, New York.*

WALK FOR GOOD HEALTH

Exercise doesn't have to be strenuous or punishing to be effective. Despite its economy of muscle use, walking is considered by most experts to be one of the best exercises. Benefits:
- Preventative and remedy for respiratory, heart and circulation disorders.
- Weight control. Walking won't take off pounds, but it keeps weight at a desirable level. (Particularly effective in keeping excess pounds from coming back, once they have been dieted off.)
- Aids digestion, elimination and sleep.
- Antidote to physical and psychological tensions.

Walking works as a second heart. Expanding and contracting foot muscles, calves, thighs and buttocks help pump blood back to the heart. This aid is crucial. The heart can propel blood very well on its own, but the body's muscles are essential to the return flow from lower regions (legs, feet, stomach).

When the blood transportation system becomes sluggish because of lack of exercise, the heart compensates by doing more work. Heart rate and blood pressure rise. (Elevated pressure can be helped to return to normal by a regimen of walking.)

Best daily routine:

• Time. Whenever it can be fitted into daily routine. (A mile takes only 20 minutes.) People doing sedentary office work usually average a mile and a half in a normal day. Stretch that by choosing to walk down the hall to a colleague instead of picking up the interoffice phone.

• Place. Wherever it's pleasant and convenient to daily tasks. Walk at least part way to work. If a commuter, walk to the train. Walk, not to the nearest, but to the second or third bus or subway stop from the house. Get off a stop or two from the usual one. Park the car 10 blocks farther away. Walk 10 blocks to and from lunch. Walk after dinner, before sitting down to a book, TV or work.

• Clothes. Comfortable and seasonal, light rather than heavy. Avoid thin-soled shoes when walking city pavements. It may be desirable to use metatarsal pads or cushioned soles. (The impact on concrete weakens metatarsal arches and causes calluses.)

• Length. Walk modest distances at first. In the city, the number of streets tells you how far you've gone. But in the country, you can walk farther than you realize. Consequences: Fatigue on the return trip. Instead: Use a good pedometer.

• Pace. Walking for exercise should feel different from other kinds of walking. Some suggestions:

• Set out at a good pace. Use the longest stride that's comfortable. Let arms swing and muscles stretch. Strike a rhythm and keep to it.

• Don't saunter. It's tiring. Walking at a good pace allows the momentum of each stride to carry over into the next.

• Lengthen the customary stride by swinging the foot a little farther ahead than usual. Lengthening the stride speeds the walking pace with no additional expenditure of energy. It also loosens tense muscles, puts other neglected muscles to work and provides continuous momentum that puts less weight on feet.

• Most comfortable pace: Three miles per hour. It generally suits the average male and is the U.S. Army pace for long hikes. With the right shoes and unconfining clothes, most women will be comfortable at that pace, too.

Source: Aaron Sussman and Ruth Goode, authors of *The Magic of Walking,* Simon and Schuster, New York.

WALKING OFF ANXIETY

Walking is an excellent technique to drain off panic and dangerous impulses and to work toward solutions to difficult problems. The steady, rhythmic action of walking helps thinking, both conscious and unconscious. (This is not true of more strenuous exercise.)

How to encourage problem-solving while walking: Prior to the walk, clearly identify the problem. Then begin walking and put the problem aside. Think of anything else—or preferably nothing. Well into a walk, a fresh solution to the problem may spring to mind.

SHAPE UP SAFELY

Swimming and walking are still the safest ways to shape up. Swimming tops running because it puts less strain on the heart and the pace is easier to set. Brisk walking tones the body without risk of injury. Popularity of exercise: Half the population exercises on any given day, according to a national survey. Contrast: In 1960, less than 25% of all Americans exercised on a given day.

EXERCISES FOR DESK-BOUND WORKERS

Exercises to do at your desk to keep mentally alert, tone sagging muscles and relieve muscle strain:

• Tummy slimmer. Sit erect, hands on knees. Exhale, pulling abdominal muscles in as far as possible. Relax. Inhale. Exhale as you draw in stomach again. Repeat 10–20 times.

• Head circles. Drop head forward, chin on chest, shoulders relaxed. Slowly move head in large circle. Reverse direction. Do 5–6 times each side.

• Torso twist. Raise elbows to shoulder level. Slowly twist around as far right as possible, then reverse. Do 10–12 turns each way.

• Heel and toe lift. Lean forward, hands on knees. Lift both heels off floor, strongly contracting calf muscles. Lower heels, lift toes high toward shins. Do 10–15 complete movements.

Source: Doug MacLennon, The Fitness Institute, Willowdale, Ontario, quoted in *Creative Selling.*

BEER VS. JOGGING

Three beers a day may control cholesterol as effectively as jogging, according to recent research. Moderate beer imbibing seems to increase the body's high-density lipo-protein (HDL), the type of cholesterol linked with reduced heart disease risk. Moderate exercise also raises HDL levels. The benefits apppear to be either/or: Joggers who take up beer drinking do not register higher HDL.

Source: Study at Baylor College of Medicine, Houston, reported in *Journal of the American Medical Association.*

JOGGING AND ACHILLES TENDINITIS

The repetitive impact of running frequently causes inflammation, degeneration and small tears in the heel tendons. Orthopedists from Boston University Medical School suggest these preventive steps:

• Decrease weekly mileage.

• Cut down on uphill workouts.

• Prepare for running by stretching the tendons. With heels flat and knees straight, lean forward against a wall and hold for 30 seconds.

• Warm heels and tendons with a heating pad before running. After running, apply ice for 10–12 minutes.

• Elevate heels by placing small felt pads inside running shoes. They relieve tension on the Achilles tendon and contiguous structures.

• Monitor wear on outer sides of shoes. Tendons are stressed when shoe sides give no support.

• If these measures fail, consult a physician about immobilization and anti-inflammatory drugs.

Source: *American Journal of Sports Medicine.*

RUNNING FIGHTS DISEASE

New research suggests that jogging does more than build up your heart muscles and improve circulation. It raises body temperature, which in turn starts a chemical reaction that helps fight infections and slows the reproduction of bacteria and viruses. After a good workout, athletes' temperatures may run three degrees above normal. Their bodies stay heated much longer than the time needed to simply dissipate the excess heat caused by their activity. Researchers think early humans developed this ability to turn on the immune system through heavy exercise as a way of dealing with the injuries often associated with flight from danger.

Source: Joseph Cannon, physiologist, quoted in *Science 82.*

RIGHT AND WRONG WAYS TO JOG

Running on the balls of the feet causes an estimated 60% of all injuries suffered by distance runners. When the front of the foot rather than the heel absorbs the shock of each stride, the calf muscles tighten. This, in turn, leads to a variety of ailments such as runner's sciatica, hamstring pulls, pains in the Achilles tendon, shin splints and assorted ankle and foot strains. Treatment: Run so that the heels make contact first. But don't force this stride if it does not come naturally—the results of forcing can be as bad as running on the balls of your feet. Always stretch the muscles in the backs of the legs before running. Also, try running shoes with higher heels, or use heel inserts.

Source: Dr. Richard Schuster, writing in *The Runner.*

"Runner's knee" sometimes can be eliminated by a shift in breathing patterns. Most of us are "footed," meaning we lead off consistently with the same foot. We also exhale consistently either on the right foot or the left one. Left-footed breathers occasionally experience pain in the right leg, and vice versa. Why? Exhalation helps absorb shocks better than inhalation. If you have a painful leg: Try exhaling on the other foot.

Source: Dennis Bramble and David Carter, University of Utah.

Swimming half a mile equals two miles of running. Bonus: No jarring side effects. Ideal workout: 30 minutes three times per week. Good performance time: Three-quarters of a mile in half an hour.

STOMACH MUSCLES: THE KEY TO EXERCISE

The muscles of the mid-torso should be the focal point of any exercise program. Strong midsection or stomach muscles allow you to better control all your movements (to bend without flopping, for example) and increase your stretch. They also improve your posture and take strain off your lower back. Problem: Most people are hardly aware of these important muscles and must be taught to use them.

Good first exercise: Lie on your back on the floor. Bend your knees, keeping your feet flat on the floor. Clasp your hands behind your head. Slowly curl up (don't jerk up) from your head forward and see how far you can get. (Don't worry if it's only five or six inches.) Hold the position until you feel strain in the midriff. You have just found the muscles you need to strengthen. Repeat the exercise four times, very slowly.

Note: Traditional sit-ups, with straight legs held down under the couch and arms raised overhead, are dangerous for beginners, who tend to use lower back muscles rather than stomach muscles. Putting hands behind the head keeps the novices from using the momentum of flailing arms to lift themselves.

Second exercise. Lie on your back on the floor. Raise your head and shoulders, put your elbows behind you and rest your upper body on your forearms. Keep your lower back (from just above the waist down) pressed against the floor. With feet together and knees bent, raise your legs four, five or six inches without allowing your lower back off the floor. Variations: Raise bent legs, stretch them out, return them to bent position and lower them to the floor. Raise both legs and kick vertically, one leg at a time. Raise bent legs together, open and stretch, return to original position and lower both. Raise bent legs, stretch them out and scissor-kick. Work up to 50 leg movements in four or five minutes.

Standing stomach exercise. This sexy workout uses a combination of leg and stomach muscles to improve lower back flexibility. Stand with legs apart and slightly bent, and do rhythmic bumps (no grinds). With head and shoulders stationary, alternately arch and curl your back, throwing your pelvis back as you arch and forward as you curl. Use music with a strong beat. Start slowly, and work up to double time.

Exercise regimen. Try to work out twice a day. Morning exercises loosen up your muscles and get you going. Later sessions accomplish more in building strength and flexibility because you are already warmed up.

Source: Pamela Francis, personal consultant and dance teacher, New York.

SAUNA, STEAM ROOM AND HOT TUB HAZARDS

Use a sauna or steam room only about once a week, on a nonexercise day or after the week's final workout. Shower before entering, and go in wet. You hair should also be wet or covered. Protect your nasal membranes by breathing through a cool, damp cloth. Drape a cool, wet towel over your neck and shoulders to help maintain normal blood temperature. Go in and out of the room frequently, showering between heat sessions to cool yourself down and build heat tolerance slowly. If you feel dizzy when leaving, shower right away with warm (not cold) water, wrap yourself in towels or get dressed, and lie down until you feel better.

Soaking in a communal hot tub contaminates the water with two to three pints of perspiration per hour per person. The salt, ammonia, etc., in perspiration must be neutralized after each use to keep the water clean and clear. Required: A sophisticated kit that tests pH, water hardness and chlorine levels.
Source: *New Shelter.*

Infections from hot tubs are becoming more common because of a bacterium that thrives in the wood of which some are made. The germ causes skin rash and other infections that are painful but treatable. Prevention: Put larger-than-normal amounts of chlorine in the water. Better: A vinyl liner in the tub.
Source: Center for Disease Control, Atlanta.

SAUNA WARNING

Saunas have never been proven to promote health or fitness and pose many dangers—including fainting, stroke, heart attack caused by a sudden drop in blood pressure, and, after a long period in the sauna, dehydration.

Also, exposure to extreme cold immediately after the sauna causes a sharp rise in blood pressure and strain on the heart. Most at risk: People with heart conditions and the elderly.

Precautions: Don't drink alcohol before going in, remain no longer than 10–15 minutes, if you feel thirsty, leave immediately, and get up slowly as you leave.
Source: Dr. Gerald Bernstein, principal investigator at the University of Southern California Medical School.

TOILET SEAT DANGER

Toilet seats (and locker room benches) can be dangerous to women. Problem: The contagious vaginal infection, *Trichomoniasis*, (trich) can be spread from surfaces that come in contact with the perineum.
Source: *RN*, 680 Kinderkamack Rd., Oradell, NJ 07649.

SLEEP NEEDS DIFFER

Requiring as much as eight or nine hours of sleep a night can be as normal as needing six or seven. According to one survey, more than 6% of American adults regularly sleep nine to 10 hours, with only about 1% sleeping more than 10 hours. Excessive sleeping can be a symptom of such disorders as narcolepsy, which causes people to become uncontrollably sleepy in the daytime. Key to healthy sleep: The quality of the wakeful hours. If you're rested and energetic when you rise, chances are that you needed all that sleep.
Source: Dr. Merrill M. Mitler, Association of Sleep Disorders Centers, Del Mar, CA.

WHAT YOUR DREAMS MEAN

Dreams provide us with a useful commentary from our inner selves. They put us in touch with an incredibly constructive and intricate source of intelligence that we have very little access to when we're awake.

Dreams don't draw conclusions or make assessments, they locate us, connecting us with our essential position in the world at any given moment. When we're faced with a decision or predicament, dreams can be a helpful resource, often shining a new light on old problems.

Dreams speak to us in the language of images and symbols. The psyche dreams in picture language because pictures tell stories which, if put in narrative, would fill volumes. *Dreams can be interpreted on three different levels:*

• The personal unconscious. Dreams pick up the literal content of your day. We dream about incidents from the past, or current problems ...usually about incidents that caused some tension. Wish-fulfillment dreams fall in this category.

• The collective unconscious. There are patterns of behavior and experience that have been recounted in fairy tales and folklore throughout the ages. These universal patterns of human experience, known as archetypes, can be found in common dream themes that turn up throughout human history.

• World unconscious. This level includes a sense of connectedness to everything in the world.

Recurring dreams are the psyche trying to get a message across. Like someone tugging on a shirtsleeve, a recurring dream tries to get our attention by presenting us with the same theme, over and over. If a dream repeats, there's bound to be something of tremendous value in it. *Helpful:* Look back to when you've had repetitive dreams. Did they signal something that was happening at that time?

Dreams speak indirectly in poetic metaphors and symbols. You need to think symbolically to figure out what the images mean. *Reassuring:* No expert knows better than you what your dreams mean. *Caution:* Don't be too literal about the translation. *How do you know you've made the right interpretation?* You get a tingle...a sense of perfect fit.

• Losing teeth. First check out the obvious. Are any of your teeth actually loose or decayed? At the second level of meaning, losing teeth is connected to the loss of something valuable, often associated with appearance. *Metaphors:* Loss of face, of attractiveness, of self-esteem or power. Also, a lost tooth *could* indicate the loss or death of a loved one.

• Going back to school. Usually people have this dream when they're frightened or unprepared. They feel under scrutiny—either at work or in a relationship—or they're being critical of themselves.

Look at: Where you landed in the dream. Was it in elementary school, high school, college? Explore that. When you were in that school, what were you afraid of? What is being unprepared? How does that relate to what you're going through now?

• Bathrooms and feces. Feces are one of the most engaging of images. Feces are manure, manure means seeds, seeds mean growth. When feces appear in dreams I get hopeful. Right around the corner there's fertile ground for growth, new possibilities.

• Nudity. Usually embarrassment at finding yourself nude in public has to do with feeling vulnerable or exposed. In a second level of interpretation it's being without a persona... not having your clothes, your mask, that which mediates between you and the world.

This is a very important dream. The vulnerability of it signals openness, availability, willingness to drop defenses and take chances. It usually comes after a time of change in career or relationships. This type of dream may also be compensatory. If you're in a position that requires a rigid persona, such as in politics or a conservative law firm, your dreams may be compensating by presenting you as a vulnerable human being.

• Flying. The flying motif has something to do with a discovery, a transcendent perspective. *Metaphors:* Flying high, flying off the handle. Sometimes when we're caught in a predicament, flying above it all gives us an overview, allowing us to see something new we couldn't see before.

Downside: If we don't have our feet on the ground, we're somehow disconnected. Sometimes flying is a signal of inflation, being too carried away with yourself, or flying too high without a lifeline.

• Falling. Similar to flying dreams, falling dreams are especially terrifying for children. What catastrophic fear does the fall represent? What's the horrible consequence of falling? *Metaphors:* Falling in esteem, falling down on the job, falling from grace, a fear of dying.

How to deal with falling dreams: Tell yourself each night before going to sleep that when you have the dream you'll continue the fall and allow yourself to land safely. And that when you land you'll find something of value, put it in your dream pocket and take it back to your awake life. That's how primitive tribes worked with this dream.

• Finding valuables. Children often dream of finding money. This can be a wish-fulfillment dream. Or it can compensate for a fear of not having wealth. It can also be a *reminder* dream, reminding you that you're out of touch with what's valuable in your life. *Ask yourself:* What is there of value in me that I need to treasure even more? What is it I'm out of touch with in myself or am just beginning to value?

• Sex. Being sexual in a dream usually has little to do with actual sex. Flying dreams are probably more connected with libido than sex dreams are. Sex dreams can be wish-fulfillment . . .you can have lusty feelings for someone that can't be acted on in real life. The dream allows you to compensate. Like active sexual fantasies, these kinds of dreams are quite healthy.

Useful: What we do in dreams we can often do when we're awake. If you're a timid lover who becomes a magnificent lover in your dreams, you can translate this dream technique into real life.

A dream about intercourse is the most efficient way of suggesting intimate contact. It may have nothing to do with sex—it may be about wanting a relationship. Or, if you find yourself having sex with someone you'd never be attracted to in real life, it may have to do with getting in touch with the aspects of you that that person represents.

Sex is also a metaphor for creativity. There may be an aspect of your personality that's being repressed, causing you to be depressed or sad. Because the creative libido is yearning for expression, the sexual partner represents your hidden creativity.

Source: Psychotherapist Stephen Aizenstat, PhD, president of the Human Relations Institute in Santa Barbara, CA. Dr. Aizenstat is working on a book about dreams and teaches courses on dreaming all over the country, including Esalen in California and The Open Center in New York.

NATURAL SLEEPING PILL

The body chemical that puts people to sleep has been isolated in the laboratory by researchers at Harvard Medical School. In time, it will be available in a pill to give natural sleep. Serious hitches: The substance, factor S, is extracted from human urine. It takes 4½ tons of urine to produce 30 micrograms (roughly the weight of a few grains of sugar) of factor S. However, a minuscule amount puts animals to sleep in laboratory tests. Years of testing lie ahead before the chemical is made available to humans.

HOW BAD IS INSOMNIA?

Just lying awake without moving can be up to 70% as restful as sleeping, so you can emerge from a sleepless night fairly well restored. In addition, sleep-lab experiments show that insomniacs doze off for half-hour and hour-long snatches, though they insist they just closed their eyes for a moment. Many even sleep half the night without realizing it. Bottom line on insomnia: It's often not as serious as you think.

Source: *Dr. David Reuben's Mental First-Aid Manual,* Macmillan, New York.

THINGS THAT CAN DISRUPT SLEEP

Only about one-third of people wake up refreshed. While many sleep problems for the other two-thirds are caused by anxiety, these factors can also reduce the quality of sleep:

• Alcohol. Can affect both dream and deepest-sleep stage. Best: Make your drink with dinner the last of the evening.
• Room temperature. A cold room does not make you sleep better. Ideal: 60–65°.
• Exercise. Aches and pains from strenuous exercise can keep you awake.
• Sex. Unless it is both physically and mentally rewarding, it can inhibit sleep.
• Caffeine. Effects linger 6–7 hours.
• Smoking. Nicotine is a strong central-nervous-system stimulant. Heavy smokers who quit usually sleep dramatically better within days.
• Irregular schedule. The body functions on a regular rhythm.

Source: *Executive Fitness Newsletter.*

HELPING YOURSELF TO SLEEP BETTER

As the stress of doing business under unsettled conditions continues month after month, the sleeping patterns of executives with top responsibilities become more and more unraveled. Late meetings, travel and racing thoughts that produce late-night or morning insomnia result in irritability, poor work performance and lethargy at times when key decisions must be made.

Improving sleep quality:

Researchers cannot easily determine how much sleep is optimum for a specific person. But they have determined that, on average, people need seven or eight hours of sleep a day.

Evidence is clear, however, that psychological and physical health improves as the quality of sleep is enhanced. To sleep better, you should:

• Determine the right amount of sleep. How: Keep a diary of sleeping patterns for at least 10–14 days. If you feel productive and alert, the average sleep time during that period is probably the amount you need.

• Establish a regular bedtime and wakeup schedule. Stick to it, even on weekends and holidays.

• Avoid trying to make up for loss of sleep one night by sleeping more the next. Sleep deprivation of two to four hours does not severely affect performance. Having the normal amount of sleep the next night compensates for the loss without changing the regular sleep pattern. And that has long-term benefits.

• Relax before bedtime. Good ways to unwind. Take a bath, read, have a weak nightcap or snack (milk is ideal for many people), engage in sex. Avoid late-night exercise, work, arguments and activities that cause tension.

Fighting insomnia:

Knowing the reason for insomnia is the only way to start overcoming it. If the cause is not quickly obvious, see a doctor. Many emotional and physical disorders express themselves as sleep disturbances.

Avoid sleeping pills. On a long-term basis, they are useless and sometimes dangerous. And when taken infrequently, they may produce a drug hangover the next day.

Catnaps:

Avoid naps in the middle of the day to compensate for lack of sleep the previous night.

Take them only if you do it regularly and feel refreshed, instead of groggy, after a nap. Test: If you dream during a catnap, it is likely to delay sleep that evening or to cause insomnia.

Tampering with nature:

Deliberate attempts to reduce the total amount of sleep you need have a dangerous appeal to hard-pressed executives who think they never have enough time to work. Fact: Carefully researched evidence from monitoring subjects in sleep laboratories indicates these schemes are not only ineffective but unhealthful. Why: The daily biological cycle cannot be changed by gradually cutting back sleep over a period of months. Older persons apparently need slightly less sleep, but even here the exact difference is not yet known.

Hard-to-take but essential advice: Do not cut down on sleep in order to meet the clamoring and sometimes conflicting demands of a job, family and friends. You may pay a penalty of spending less time with family and friends or losing the edge at work that compulsive workaholism may provide. But the payoff is better health performance.

Source: Dr. Charles P. Pollak, codirector, of Sleep-Wake Disorders Center, Montefiore Hospital, New York.

HOW TO FALL BACK ASLEEP

Agony: Awakening in the middle of the night and not being able to fall back to sleep. Prime cause: Advancing age. People over 50 have middle insomnia. Those under 50 often have difficulty falling to sleep.

How to cope: Do not become angry when you find yourself awake at 3 am. Anger only excites you, preventing sleep. Instead, fix your mind on a single relaxing image. Example: Visualize a flickering candle. If you are still awake after 30 minutes, go to another room. Watch an old movie on TV, or read a book or magazine. When you feel sleepy, return to bed. If sleep still eludes you, go back to the other room and read some more. Frustrating and useless: Tossing and turning in bed, waiting for sleep to arrive.

Preventive steps:

- Eliminate daytime naps if they have been a habit.
- Do not go to bed too early. This only increases the chances of middle insomnia.
- Set your alarm an hour earlier than usual. This makes you more tired for the following night. Advance the alarm by 15-minute increments until you are sleeping through the night. Then slowly extend your sleep period until you are back on a normal schedule.

Source: *A Good Night's Sleep* by Jerrold S. Maxmen, Contemporary Books, Chicago.

POOR SLEEP IN HIGH ACHIEVERS

Middle-aged, high-achieving men occasionally complain of long periods of fatigue, irritability and poor sleep. Diagnosis has been difficult because there's no reason for depression and no increased source of anxiety. Often they wonder if there's a medical reason for their problems. Now, a group of patients has been identified who complained that they're "tired of being depended upon." At times, almost everyone needs to be dependent and, in many cases, this syndrome may represent a subconscious, temporary effort to acheive that passive position.

Source: *Journal of Florida Medical Association.*

EAT RIGHT—AND LIVE LONGER

It's not too late to change the eating habits of a lifetime when you reach middle age. As a matter of fact, it's probably a necessity because of the changes the body is going through at that time. Most obvious change: Slowing of the metabolic rate. Individuals who don't reduce their caloric intake after age 45 commonly gain 10 pounds a year, regardless of the amount of exercise they do. It takes 12 hours of tennis to burn off 3,500 calories, roughly equivalent to one pound.

Unfortunately, a fine steak is often associated with success and reward. Steak, though, is highly caloric, and its fat content has been linked to coronary disease and colon cancer, two potentially fatal disorders that plague older people. Chicken and fish are more healthful alternative sources of proteins.

Bones begin to grow progressively brittle after age 30. To counteract the condition, the body needs more calcium. But this important mineral can be absorbed effectively only by reducing the intake of protein (from meats) and phosphorous (from carbonated soft drinks). To prevent the brittle-bone problem, a calcium supplement of one gram a day is recommended by most nutritionists.

Because many older people secrete less hydrochloric acid, they have difficulty absorbing iron and, therefore, are more vulnerable to pernicious anemia. The best source of iron is meat, especially liver. But to avoid eating too much meat, you should turn to iron-fortified foods, especially cereals. Absorption of iron is helped by intakes of vitamin C, which is abundant in citrus fruits, broccoli, kale, red peppers and brussels sprouts. For some older people, taking an iron supplement may be necessary.

The bodies of older people also have trouble absorbing vitamin B-12, which can actually be destroyed in the body by large doses of vitamin C. B-12 deficiency can lead to anemia, particularly among vegetarians, because the vitamin is found exclusively in animal products (especially liver) and shellfish. Multivitamin supplements may be needed to insure that you are getting the right amount of each vitamin.

Caution: Although all the evidence is not yet in, most nutritionists advise against taking vitamin megadoses containing several hundred times the recommended daily allowance. In the case of vitamins A and D, megadoses are highly dangerous.

Exception: Vitamin E, large doses of which may help with several disorders, including colon cancer and the painful blood vessel spasms in the legs that older people often experience. Even with this vitamin, consult a physician before considering taking megadoses of any vitamin.

Digestive problems associated with aging make fiber especially important to persons over 45. Sources: Whole grains, fruits, vegetables.

Older people generally use more drugs than others, but their doctors often overlook the interaction of medication and nutrition.

Chronic aspirin users can suffer microscopic bleeding of the gastrointestinal tract, a condition that also causes loss of iron. Aspirin can also increase requirements for vitamin C and folic acid. Laxatives may deplete vitamin D, and antacids can lead to a phosphate deficiency. The diuretics prescribed for hypertension can promote the loss of potassium. In all these cases, vitamin and mineral supplements may be the solution.

Source: Dr. Brian Morgan, Institute of Human Nutrition, Columbia University College of Physicians & Surgeons.

AGING BODIES NEED MORE WATER

An aging body needs at least six glasses of water every day. Reason: A young adult's body is 60% water, but this amount decreases with age. Results: Skin dries out, and the kidneys do not flush wastes as well. Drinking more water means the skin has less chance of becoming dry. And the water dilutes the salts and minerals that pass through the kidneys, helping to prevent formation of kidney stones. Suggestion: Have a glass of water with every meal and another before going to bed. Take the other two glasses during breaktime. Substitute water for that second and third cup of coffee.

THE DIET/BEHAVIOR CONNECTION

Diet probably does affect behavior, but not always in the expected way. Example: Refined sugar and carbohydrates supposedly make children hyperactive and incite criminals to act aggressively. Fact: People who eat a high-carbohydrate meal are sleepier two hours later than those who have eaten a high-protein meal.
Source: MIT research reported in *Science.*

HEARTBURN REMEDY

Heartburn is a common malady. Causes: Fatty or fried foods, processed meats, alcohol, coffee, spiced foods, chocolate and tobacco. Lying down, bending over or exercising after eating can lead to heartburn. It occurs when acids back up into the sensitive tissues of the esophagus, which carries food to the stomach. Helpful hints: Eat frequent small meals. Do not eat before bedtime. Sleep with the head of the bed elevated. Avoid tight clothing. Best medicine is the old standby: Liquid antacid.

SALT AND HIGH BLOOD PRESSURE

For about 30% of people with hypertension, cutting down on salt is a therapeutic necessity: For other victims of high blood pressure and for the general population, salt reduction may be an unnecessary hardship with possible risks. New research suggests that many factors other than salt are linked to hypertension. Obesity is one. Calcium deficiency is another. Problem: Reducing sodium in the diet may adversely affect the body's ability to absorb and use other necessary nutrients.
Source: Dr. John Laragh, New York Hospital-Cornell Medical Center, and Dr. David A. McCarron, Oregon Health Sciences University.

BEWARE THE "SALT FREE" LABEL

Absence of the word salt on a list of ingredients does not necessarily guarantee something is salt-free. Other "salty" substances commonly used in food preparations include brine, disodium phosphate, sodium glutamate, baking powder, baking soda.

SIMPLE WAY TO CUT SALT INTAKE

Reducing salt in the diet may be as easy as changing salt shakers. The reason: Putting salt on food is often a procedure that is a ritual, not an actual decision. (More than 75% of the subjects in a test salted their food before even tasting it.) For habitual salt shaker users, using a salt shaker with smaller holes reduces the amount of salt used.

Source: H. Greenfield, University of New South Wales, quoted in *Nature.*

RELIEVING EXCESS GAS

To relieve the problem of too much gas in the digestive tract, try simethicone. It breaks up the large bubbles of gas. Anticholinergic drugs and carbonated water encourage belching. Irony: Fizzy water helps cause gas in the first place. Peppermints relax the system to make it easier for trapped gas to escape. When the problem is flatus, no drug helps. Best: Remove from the diet such classic incitants as beans, broccoli, onions, cauliflower, cabbage, radishes, raw apples.

Source: Dr. Stephen Goldfinger, writing in the *Harvard Medical School Health Letter.*

HOW MUCH CAFFEINE IS TOO MUCH?

Americans are suddenly adding caffeine to their growing list of health worries. Decaffeinated colas now join decaffeinated coffees in luring the public away from the caffeine habit. Some facts about caffeine:

• Low doses can increase alertness and motor ability, reduce drowsiness and lessen fatigue. Small to moderate amounts of caffeine pose no health danger, according to the Clinical Nutrition Section of Boston's University Hospital. Heavy doses produce ill effects—nervousness, anxiety, irritability, headache, muscle twitch and insomnia.
• Tolerance to caffeine varies widely from person to person. Two cups of caffeine-rich coffee make some of them nervous. Others cannot survive the day without several cups. Most sensitive to caffeine's effects: Children and the elderly.
• How much is too much: Four cups of coffee

a day (500 milligrams of caffeine) is a heavy dose for most people. Note: The caffeine quantity in coffee depends on how it is brewed. The drip method produces a higher caffeine content than the percolator. Instant coffee contains much less caffeine than brewed coffee. Tea contains half as much caffeine as coffee, and cola drinks have even less.

Irony. Most of the caffeine taken from coffee in the decaffeinization process is bought by the soft-drink industry and added to soda.

While cola drinks have far less caffeine than coffee, they are still the best-selling drink among Americans. Americans consume an average of 33 gallons of soft drinks yearly. Comparison: 28 gallons of coffee.

Caffeine has been linked to many health problems, but there are questions about its adverse effects. Examples:
• There is no evidence that caffeine is a causal factor in either arteriosclerosis or heart attacks.
• It does not increase the blood pressure of regular users.
• Caffeine does not seem to be a cancer hazard, but other compounds (found in negligible amounts) in beverage coffee are known carcinogens in animals.
• Caffeine is a much less important factor than cigarette smoking in heart disease, hypertension, bladder cancer, peptic ulcers and cystic breast disease.
• It does stimulate the central nervous system and can help reduce boredom from repetitive tasks, increase the body's muscle strength and relieve certain types of headaches by dilating blood vessels and reducing muscle tension.

Source: American Council of Science and Health, Summit, NJ.

CAFFEINE COUNT

A five-ounce cup of drip-brewed coffee contains 146 milligrams of caffeine. (Regular instant has 53; decaffeinated only 2.) Surprise: Soft drinks aren't as caffeine-laden as most of us think. The majority range between 33 and 44 milligrams. (Diet citrus drinks, root beer, ginger ale and tonic water contain little or no caffeine.) Tea: Make it quickly. A one-minute brew has half the caffeine of a five-minute brew.

WHAT VITAMIN MANUFACTURERS DON'T TELL YOU

• Vitamin poisoning. Those one-gram B-6 tablets sold in health stores can be dangerous. The body needs only one or two milligrams of B-6 a day. Overdoses may lead to loss of sensory and motor control.
Source: *New England Journal of Medicine.*

• Vitamin E should be used with restraint. High doses can cause blood clots, phlebitis, hypertension, severe fatigue, breast tumors and disturbances of reproduction. How much is too much? Dr. H. Roberts of Florida's Palm Beach Institute for Medical Research suggests that daily intake of more than 100–300 units of "active tocopherol" is excessive.
Source: *Journal of the American Medical Association.*

• Too much vitamin A and D. Unlike some vitamins (the Bs and C) that are passed out of the body through the kidneys when taken in excess, vitamins A and D are stored in fat and the liver, where they can do damage. Problems from overdoses: Cirrhosis of the liver. Dry, itchy skin. Fatigue. Painful muscles. Loss of body hair. Note: A deficiency of vitamin A is believed related to the onset of cancer. But there is no evidence that increased amounts help prevent this disease. Best: Eat a balanced diet. Limit supplementary intake to the recommended daily dietary allowances.
Source: *The Health Letter.*

• Niacin is not a tranquilizer, despite the stories about is calming effects. Taking niacin tablets in search of tranquillity can cause niacin toxicity. Symptoms: Flushed face and blotchy skin on arms. Point: Niacin pills are only for a niacin deficiency.

OVERDOSING ON VITAMINS

Vitamin E research on E's toxic effects is sketchy, but the findings suggest some problems: Headaches, nausea, fatigue and giddiness, blurred vision, chapped lips and mouth inflammation, low blood sugar, increased tendency to bleed, reduced sexual function. Ironically, one of the claims of Vitamin E proponents is that it heightens sexual potency.
Source: Victor Herbert, *Nutrition Cultism: Facts and Fictions*, George F. Stickley Co., Philadelphia.

TWO GOOD THINGS THAT DON'T GO TOGETHER

Vitamin C and aspirin should not be taken together. Studies at the University of Southern Illinois indicate that combined heavy doses produce excessive stomach irritations which could lead to ulcers (especially for those with a history of stomach problems).

VITAMIN A CANCER RISK

Eating carrots, broccoli and other vitamin A sources may reduce risk of lung cancer, say Northwestern University researchers. They report that high dietary intake of carotene (a compound converted into vitamin A in the body) reduces lung-cancer risk, even among long-term smokers. Other sources of carotene: Apples, squash, tomatoes and leafy green vegetables. Caution: Too much carotene can yellow the skin.

MICROWAVE OVEN TRAP

Cooking chicken in microwave ovens won't kill harmful salmonella and other bacteria. Reason: Microwave ovens heat food through molecular friction, leaving surface temperatures too uneven to kill the contaminants. Solution: Cook chicken in conventional ovens at 350° F, until the meat thermometer reads 185° F in both the breast and thigh areas or until the juices run clear.

Source: Ruth E. Lindsay, nutritionist, Georgia Southern College.

SALMONELLA ALERT

Studies have shown that much of the chicken we eat carries salmonella bacteria. To reduce the risk of ingesting live salmonella bacteria from any poultry, cook the bird until the internal temperature reaches at least 180°. You can check this with a meat thermometer. After handling raw poultry, wash your hands and any utensils and surfaces that have come in contact with the bird.

In a Centers for Disease Control study of salmonella poisoning outbreaks from 1973 through 1984, 33 outbreaks were caused as a result of eating turkey. This compares with 19 outbreaks as a result of eating chicken.

For more information, call the Meat and Poultry Hotline, (800) 535-4555, from 10 a.m. to 4 p.m. Eastern Time.

Source: Sharon Sachs, a representative of the Food Safety and Inspection Service's Information and Legislative Affairs Division, US Dept. of Agriculture, 1165 South Building, Washington, DC 20250.

CLEANING UP YOUR DRINKING WATER

Pure drinking water piped into the home can no longer be taken for granted. Problems: Toxic chemicals such as nitrates, asbestos, arsenic, lead, trihalomethanes (THM). Also: High sodium levels are dangerous for people on sodium-restricted diets. Statistic: 55% of the American population lives in areas with inadequate water-treatment plants.

Signs of possible contamination: Water has an odd taste, color or smell. Possible problems: Heavy construction or sewer installation in the area, a change in pesticide use, antiquated water-treatment facilities of wells. What to do: Have the water department or board of health test the water. If they won't: Consult the Yellow Pages under "Laboratories—Testing" for a lab that handles water samples. Cost: Up to $175.

How to get cleaner drinking water:

• Bottled water. Hitch: There are no standards for purity. Some do contain traces of harmful substances. Labels do not indicate this. In one New York City test several years ago, two brands that scored cleanest were Great Bear and Deer Park.

• Water filters. The only effective ones contain granules of activated carbon (GAC). Useful: Only against THM, not lead or arsenic. Never use filters that fit over the faucet. The water runs through too quickly to be properly filtered. Note: Filtered water is not necessary for such functions as dish washing. The filter should have a bypass valve.

More information: *Water Fit to Drink* by Carol Keough, Rodale Press, Emmaus, PA.

COLD HANDS SIGNAL STRESS

Cold hands are often a sign of stress if you are indoors and there's no reason for them to be chilled. Biofeedback research indicates that techniques to warm hands can also reduce the stress load. What works: Close your eyes and imagine yourself holding and playing with something soft and warm. Touch your cheeks, which are usually warm, and imagine the warmth flowing into your fingers. Interlock fingers, squeeze gently for one second, release for one second. Repeat sequence several times.

Source: Robert Hall, president, Futurehealth, Inc., Bensalem, PA.

DIET TIPS TO COMBAT STRESS

For short-term periods of stress: A high-carbohydrate, low-protein diet. The carbohydrates deliver energy to the body. For longer stressful periods: Reverse the diet—that is, more protein and fewer carbohydrates. Example: Lean meats, eggs, fish, skinless poultry and low-fat milk. Other foods that fight stress: Those rich in vitamin C and in vitamin

A. Try raw carrots, peppers and broccoli.

Bonus: Chewing crunchy foods helps dissipate the tension.

MUSIC RELIEVES STRESS

Baroque music increases concentration by reducing stress and fatigue in the listener. Insight: A composed mind absorbs information about two and one-half times faster than one blocked by anxiety. The Baroque rhythm of about one beat per second seems to be just right for setting the mind at ease. Upshot: When you need to concentrate, play the music of Vivaldi, Bach or Handel.

HAPPY PEOPLE LIVE LONGER

Happiness is the key to long life. People who suffer from anxiety and depression often age quickly and die prematurely, several studies show. This has a greater effect on longevity than being overweight, smoking or drinking. Key to positive mental health: Sociability. Friendly people tend to live longer than those who are always lonely.

How to achieve happiness: Satisfaction with love means more than satisfaction with money, health, job, being a parent, social life or sex. Happily married people are the happiest people. Contrast: Divorced people are often the unhappiest. Insight: Unmarried women are usually happier than unmarried men. Job satisfaction follows love and marriage as the most important factor in attaining happiness.

Source: George E. Vaillant, M.D., reported in *Spring.*

BEING HAPPY IS SIMPLE

Set realistic goals. The more unattainable the goals, the greater the chance of unhappiness. Don't exaggerate your emotions. Never compare your current life with pleasant days gone by. Help your children—don't burden them with lofty goals of your design. Simply encour-

age them to do their best at whatever they choose.

Source: Allen Parducci, psychology professor, UCLA.

HOW TO FIGURE OUT WHAT TO DO WITH THE REST OF YOUR LIFE

Not two people in 1,000 are happy with their careers. But it takes so little to get on the right track. Here's how. . .

First, you have to recognize that something isn't right. If you feel like you are always swimming against the current at work, then you *do* have a conflict.

Ask yourself: Am I the problem? Or, is the company the problem? Or, is it both of us?

In a period of corporate consolidations and streamlining, the first employees to be fired are those who don't quite fit. If you stay productive in spite of your unhappiness, you will be in conflict with yourself and your body will rebel with stress diseases—ulcers, high blood pressure. . .

Once you recognize that there is a problem, take a probing look at yourself. The answer to *Who am I?* is the key to productive change.

Have patience with yourself while you search for who you are. Give yourself time and *don't let anyone else do it for you.*

Think about the most successful and rewarding experiences you have had in your work life and in your non-work life—currently and in the past. Some of your happiest accomplishments may come from childhood memories or from volunteer activities. Your most enlightening exploits may have had nothing to do with your work history.

Write precise accounts of your best experiences because analyzing them will help you see where your real strengths and abilities are. This should be a rewarding exercise, full of discovery about yourself. You should begin to see what you are good at—your skills—and what kinds of jobs you really like to do.

Once you have some personal insights, you can ask the second most important question: *What direction do I want my life to take?*

For many people, this is no easier to answer than *Who am I?* because they have been pressured all their lives by parents, counselors and other "experts" to set specific goals—*get a degree* or *get a job* or *save money for a down payment.*

There is no such thing in our society as the status quo. Those kinds of goals assume there is. The direction you want your life to take will involve satisfying work that you believe in and are good at. Your task is to survey the marketplace for the opportunity or need that lets you do that kind of work.

Your goal is not a static title or position, but getting involved creatively in a project you believe in and care about.

A tough, honest support person is a great asset in your career search. A third-party perspective can be very useful in sorting out your views. You can attend a career-counseling workshop or you can ask a friend or colleague to act as a sounding board for you.

Important: Pick someone who is happy and fulfilled by his own work. Unhappy people lose their objectivity and your discussions will turn into unproductive gripe sessions.

In the same way, you want an outside opinion about why some of your job-hunting efforts go well—and some don't. It is as important to understand what *is* succeeding as what is not. Beware of the friend who is dedicated to giving answers rather than analysis. You have to make your own decisions.

Make regular appointments with your support person to go over what you have done since the last meeting. It will keep you moving forward and the steady feedback will keep you on track.

When you are clear about what kind of work you are good at and what you want to accomplish with it, you will have become, in effect, your own enterprise and you will be ready to negotiate "mergers" for yourself.

Now is the time to survey the marketplace for a fit. You know your assets, the direction you want to go in and your values. Who needs what you have to offer? Who will benefit from your particular mix of skills and aspirations? Your research will help you modify how you present yourself to your market. Manufacturers, after all, also must refine their products to meet the needs of their customers.

You may find the job you want in your present company or in a lateral move to another company. Or you may find it in a different kind of profession altogether.

Most of us must learn to overcome the conditioning we have had at the hands of authoritative adults in our lives.

Example: You are told that if you get a good job you will be rewarded. That is not necessarily true. If the job doesn't use your talents or if it conflicts with your basic values, it will make you miserable.

Many experts will tell you that the first step in making a job change is to write a good resume. Research figures show that only one job offer is made for every 1,470 resumes that are put into circulation. Those are pretty daunting odds.

Resumes are about the past. Interviewers often use them as a point of departure simply because they are given nothing more interesting to work with when they meet a job applicant.

When you are marketing yourself and what you want to accomplish for an employer, you are making deals about the future. You should have something more compelling to talk about than dates and titles from the past.

Bottom line: You know you are making good changes when you are excited by your work and involvement rather than by your titles on a piece of paper.

Source: Nella Barkley, president of the Crystal-Barkley Corp., 111 E. 31 St., New York 10016.

COINCIDENCE AND THE SMALL WORLD

Many so-called coincidences actually have a sound mathematical basis.

Example: When as few as 23 people come together, the chances that at least one pair has the same birthday is one in two.

Even more astounding (and quite a bit more useful) is the *small-world phenomenon:* The fact that the vast majority of people in this country are linked by no more than two intermediaries —that is, by friends of friends. *Point:* We are linked more closely to other people than we realize. The implications are vast—for our social lives, our job-hunting, our work performance and our attempts to influence public policy.

Assuming that each person has 1,000 acquaintances, we determined that 1% of people living in the United States know at least one person in common—and that 99% are linked by a friend of a friend (or, strictly speaking, an acquaintance of an acquaintance).

At its extreme, the small-world phenomenon seems to defy rational explanation.

Example: In a small-town hospital in Illinois, one patient, a telephone lineman, said to a Chinese patient in the next bed, *You know, I've only known one Chinese person before in my life. He was a ------ from Shanghai.* His neighbor replied, *Why, that's my uncle.*

But in its more ordinary guises, the phenomenon shapes our lives every day:

• Networking, in this light, is neither a fad nor a buzzword, but an essential strategy for any career-minded person. Whether you're looking for venture capital or a better job, you can probably find it through your personal contacts. At most, you are two people removed from financial support or a key manager in *any* company which interests you.

Prediction: Today's business cards will be replaced by computer-readable cards with magnetic strips on their backs. Instead of storing the cards you collect in a business-card file or Rolodex, you'll feed the data into your computer. Then, when you need a contact in a given field, department or location, your computer will spit out the information.

• If you want to meet someone you find attractive, there is a good chance you know someone who could arrange an introduction. The small-world phenomenon is a friendlier, more natural alternative to the singles bar.

• When salespeople need entree into another organization, they often assume that the odds are against them knowing anyone in the other company, let alone an influential executive. *Result:* They make a cold call to the company's purchasing department, with erratic results. But if they understand the small-world phenomenon, salespeople will exploit their contacts to gain a more personal—and effec-tive—introduction.

Example: A salesperson who joins the Detroit chapter of the Society of Automotive Engineers will gain direct contact with hundreds of specialists at Ford, GM and Chrysler.

The same strategy will work in marketing, sales, purchasing, executive recruitment or any other aspect of business.

• Congress is usually seen as a decision-making body—a selector of public opinions which are somehow already diffused across the country. But viewed within the small-world phenomenon, we see Congress primarily as a communication node—the place where private messages come from all corners, and where public opinion is *created* through a confrontation of attitudes.

Because of its size and geographic representation, Congress is normally within two easy links of everyone in the country. A body of 500 welds a mass of 100 million adults into a nation.

Bottom line: By using personal contacts, you can probably gain access to your congress-person—and through him, to any other congressperson who deals with a matter which concerns you or your business.

In using the small-world phenomenon, it makes no difference if you last contact with an acquaintance was 10 years ago. If you still recognize each other, our cultural norms allow you to call on one another to forge a link to someone else—without being considered rude.

All that is required is an *awareness* of the contacts you have and a willingness to put them to work.

Source: Manfred Kochen, a professor of information sciences at the University of Michigan, Medical School and adjunct professor of computer information systems at the School of Business Administration. He is also the editor and author of *The Small World,* which will be published in the near future by Ablex Publishing Corp., 355 Chestnut St., Norwood, NJ 07648.

HEADING OFF THE HOLIDAY BLUES

The holidays close in fast, and there's no time to do all the things that you've planned. Pressure builds up, finances go down. The holiday blues seem so inescapable that the joy of the season is all but forgotten.

The scenario is familiar, but you can take counter-measures, say management consultant Gisele Richardson and psychologist Marilyn Machlowitz.

How can we handle high holiday expectations?

Richardson: The culture we live in makes so much of year-end holidays that expectations run excessively high, largely induced by the media playing on the magical expectations of childhood for commercial purposes. When the magic fairy fails to materialize, we experience resentment, self-pity, guilt, disappointment. Instead, visualize a realistic scenario for the season and help those around you to do likewise. The period can be unusually rich or difficult, depending on how it's handled.

Common trap: Believing New Year's Eve is an omen. The illusion: If I'm happy (sad, loved, unloved, alone) at the New Year, I'll be that way for the next 12 months.

Machlowitz: When you finally decide which in-laws to visit and then drive or fly for hours to get there, expectations build unrealistically. To prevent a letdown: Set your sights lower. Don't expect a Norman Rockwell scene. The meal may be catered and not home-cooked. The turkey may dry out. After all, the people you're visiting have to face the same holiday problems that you do, so learn to tolerate a few frowns.

What about the temptation to spend too much?

Richardson: You're asking for a post-holiday letdown if you don't plan your holiday expenses to meet your budget. Going all out on presents and entertaining can be emotionally costly, too. Those who spend more than they can afford often are consciously or unconsciously hoping to be paid back with a like amount of love or appreciation. And they are often disappointed.

Machlowitz: Many people strain their budgets by throwing lavish parties or buying extravagant gifts. Sometimes they do it in an effort to make up for some of the rough spots in the previous year. But in the end, it just adds to the holiday blues instead of relieving them.

What to do about too much family?

Richardson: People who are most prone to holiday blues are those who have inadequate emotional support from family and friends, who live (unhappily) alone or have had painful holiday experiences as a child. If you fall into any of these categories, recognize your vulnerability. Take the initiative to ensure that you're doing something you want to do. Don't dwell on negative past experiences. Try something different. Do something for others that you enjoy, such as offering your services to an orphanage or cheering up residents in a senior citizens' home.

Machlowitz: My colleague, New York psychiatrist Dr. George Wing, has some good insights in this area. His advice: Accept your family, flaws and all. Be tolerant of in-laws who still treat you like an outsider even though you've been part of their extended family for 25 years. Don't be surprised if you quickly run out of things to say to a relative whose life is now far different from yours, even if you were once very close. Expect attitudes to change: Maybe Dad has become more liberal now that he's retired and watches Phil Donahue.

And how about all the partying?

Richardson: Monitor yourself closely during the holidays, when emotions may be more volatile than usual. Turn down invitations from people you really don't enjoy. Avoid obligations that are energy drainers. If sending cards is a burden, don't send them, and don't feel guilty about it. Instead, phone greetings to a few close friends, and charge your battery with the contact. Don't be afraid to switch plans at the last minute by booking a cruise to the Bahamas. Remember that the holidays are only a small part of your life.

Machlowitz: Stick to a sane schedule. Staying out late one night after another and overindulging in food and drink don't contribute to merriment but to hangovers. If you entertain at home, consider hiring a caterer and a clean-up crew.

Source: Gisele Richardson, Richardson Management Co., and Dr. Marilyn Machlowitz, consulting psychologist, New York.

HOW TO READ NUTRITION LABELS

Cutting down on cholesterol, sugar and salt requires a close reading of nutritional labels.

A simplified guide to understanding the fine print:

• Ingredients: They are listed in descending order, according to their weight.

• Sugar: Whether it's called sugar, dextrose, sucrose, corn sweetener, corn syrup, invert sugar, honey or molasses, the food has little nutritive value if it's among the first three ingredients. When listed as a minor ingredient, a combination of two or more sugars may mean a hefty sugar content.

• Cholesterol: Avoid coconut and palm oil. They are more saturated than animal fats. Nonspecified vegetable oils frequently mean palm or coconut. When purchasing margarine, choose the brand with liquid vegetable oil as the primary ingredient. It contains less saturated fat.

• Salt: While sodium levels are not shown on many ingredient lists, look for brands that list sodium by milligrams. Rule of thumb: No one should consume much over 4,000 milligrams of sodium daily. Those on restricted diets should have considerably less than that amount.

MISLEADING FOOD LABELS

Labels on food packages are nothing more than another form of advertising designed to sell the product. They're not there to help you make informed choices about the foods you eat. They're not a promise that what you're buying is nutritious. And unless a food claims in its advertising or on the label that it has a particular nutritive benefit, there's no law mandating that nutrients be listed on the label.

Federal law specifies only that label information be truthful . . . and truthful can sometimes mean misleading.

What labels mean:

• Natural. Nothing more than "anything occurring in nature." That includes artificial additives, fats and sugars. (Even strychnine is natural.) Natural doesn't necessarily mean healthy.

• Servings per container. The determination of serving size is completely at the discretion of the manufacturer. Because it's an arbitrary measure, comparing different brands for calories per serving is a meaningless exercise. As a rule, serving sizes are slightly smaller than an average person's appetite. This makes calorie and fat counts appear lighter than they really are.

• Lean . . . or low-fat. Defined as 25% less fat than the manufacturer's standard form of the same food, which very well could be loaded with fat.

BEFORE YOU BUY "LIGHT" FOODS

Light foods have no legal definition. By federal law, low-calorie means a food has 40 fewer calories per serving than the regular version of the product. Reduced-calorie foods legally must be one-third lower in calories than the standard. Some so-called light foods are simply marketed as low-calorie as a sales pitch. Example: A soup once sold as a hearty meal, now touted as light, has always had 90 calories per serving. Good news: Some light products such as beer and wine do cut down on calories by one-third. (They also reduce the alcoholic content.) Bottom line: To find the lowest-calorie products, read the calorie content on the label, not in the headline.

POULTRY CONFIDENTIAL

• Poultry is a low-fat, low-calorie food if you eat it "skinless" (the skin adds up to 100 calories per serving) . . . stick to white meat (dark meat adds up to 50 calories) . . . cook by roasting, broiling or poaching (deep-frying can add 240 calories).

Source: Angelica T. Cantlon, a Connecticut-based nutrition consultant, in *Self* magazine, New York.

• Chicken is still one of the cheapest (and best) sources of protein. It is virtually the same price now as 10 years ago.

TRAPS IN "NATURAL" INGREDIENTS

• Some "natural" soup mixes actually contain a number of additives, despite labeling that claims "no artificial ingredients." Unnatural additives: Hydrolyzed vegetable protein (HVP), caramel powder, and enzyme-modified blue cheese (Campbell's dry soup mixes), Mono sodium glutamate, caramel color, and HVP (Lipton's dry soup mixes), Xanthan gum (Lipton's International Soup Classics).

Source: Michael Jacobson, director, Center for Science in the Public Interest, 1501 16 St. NW, Washington, DC 20036.

• The word natural on many food packages is meaningless. The Food & Drug Administration, which regulates the labeling of most food except meat and poultry, doesn't have rules on the use of the word on food labels. Manufacturers can claim that anything is natural, whether or not it is. Natural meats and poultry, however, contain no artificial additives, in accordance with the US Department of Agriculture regulations.

Source: Center for Science in the Public Interest, 1501 16 St. NW, Washington, DC 20036.

FISH OIL DANGER FOR DIABETICS

The Omega-3 fatty acids in fish oils actually increase LDL cholesterol. Risk: Major metabolic problems.

Source: *Annals of Internal Medicine*, American College of Physicians, 4200 Pine St., Philadelphia 19104.

DANGEROUS CONDIMENT

Wasabi, the green and fiery-hot horseradish accompaniment to sushi, should be eaten only a dab at a time. One man who gulped a large amount began sweating heavily, became confused and took a full day to recover. This reaction could be fatal in a person with a heart condition or a tendency to strokes.

Source: Dr. Daniel Spitzer, cited in *East West*, 838 Grant Ave., San Francisco 94108.

MILK TIP

Supermarket milk retains its nutrition better in fiberboard cartons than in clear plastic containers. Reason: When exposed to fluorescent lights, low-fat or skim milk loses 90% of its vitamin A in 24 hours.

Source: Research at Cornell University, Ithaca, NY.

REMOVING PESTICIDES FROM PRODUCE

Pesticides cling to fruits and vegetables even after a water washing. Best: Scrub the produce with a vegetable brush under running water. To be extra sure, use a mild detergent. Soak apples and pears in water containing one-fourth cup of vinegar before scrubbing.

Source: *The Practical Gourmet*, Middle Island, NY.

CALCIUM VS. MEMORY

Memory impairment may be caused by too much calcium. Calcium is involved in the transmission of messages along brain neurons in the portion of the brain thought to direct memory functions. As rats age, calcium flow into nerve cells increases, impairing the flow of messages. Implications: If similar results occur in humans, calcium-blocking drugs might be used to prevent memory loss ... calcium supplements may contribute to memory loss.

Source: Philip Landfield, MD, professor of physiology, Bowman Gray School of Medicine, Wake Forest University, Winston-Salem, NC.

NON STICK PAN ALERT

Non stick pans (such as Teflon® or SilverStone®) can be dangerous if allowed to boil dry. At 400°F, the pans may release toxic fumes after 20 minutes—enough to make a person sick. Especially susceptible: birds and other pets.

Source: *Glamour*, New York.

PERILS OF CRASH DIETS

Crash diets actually make people fatter in the long run. Reason: When dieters consume fewer than 1,200 calories a day, they lose muscle tissue as well as fat. If they go far enough below that level, their percentage of body fat will increase, even though their weight may go down.

Source: *Berkeley Wellness Letter*, Berkeley, CA.

• Repeated crash dieting can increase the chance of heart disease. The faster weight is lost from the body, the faster it tends to go back on. It is this rapid accumulation of weight that results in higher levels of blood cholesterol. Quick weight gain also accelerates the rate at which cholesterol is deposited in the blood vessels.

Source: *The 100% Natural, Purely Organic, Cholesterol Free, Megavitamin, Low-Carbohydrate Nutrition Hoax* by E. Whalen and F. Stare, Atheneum, NY.

• Crash diets impair the immune system response and make dieters more vulnerable to infection. Special danger: Surgery patients with poor nutrition have a much higher rate of postoperative infections.

Source: Peter Lindner, MD, director of continuing medical education, American Society of Bariatric Physicians, in *Prevention*, Emmaus, PA.

WHAT THE FAD DIET PROMOTERS DON'T TELL YOU

Some of the fad diets are basically harmless, but others can do a great deal of harm if followed for very long. To protect yourself, it pays to know what each of the fad diets is all about.

• The Cambridge Diet is an extremely low-calorie liquid diet. (The FDA has issued a warning about it.) Whether there's any difference between 300 calories a day and starvation is a matter of debate. The Cambridge resembles the previously popular liquid protein diet, which caused some unexplained deaths. There's no doubt you'll lose weight on the Cambridge, but the evidence so far suggests that it's not entirely safe.

• The Scarsdale Diet isn't so bad. It's a reasonably low-calorie diet—though quite expensive. It has more protein than you need, making it more palatable than a lot of other diets. If you stick to it, it will work, because it comes to about 1,000 calories a day.

• The Atkins Diet is a very high-fat, high-protein, low-carbohydrate diet. The objective is to produce ketosis, a bodily state that may be dangerous to normal people and is dangerous to diabetics. Ketosis will probably inhibit your appetite and make you feel somewhat ill. If you follow the Atkins, you'll almost certainly lose weight. But the diet's high fat content will increase your susceptibility to atherosclerosis and other diseases. This diet is not recommended.

• The Pritikin Diet is essentially a vegetarian diet, very low in fat, sugar and salt. Originally designed to treat heart patients, it's reasonably well balanced and would decrease your risk of heart disease, cancer and hypertension. Problem: It's very extreme.

Source: D.M. Hegsted, professor emeritus of nutrition, Harvard School of Public Health.

• The first week of a diet often makes the dieter feel weak, tired, even slightly nauseated. This passes by the second week. To help you through the bad time: Be sure the diet has sufficient salt (lack of salt causes depression) and potassium. If your diet is salt-free to speed off the pounds, add a pinch. You may lose weight more slowly. But you have a better chance of staying on the diet.

Source: *How to Eat Like a Thin Person,* by L. Dusky and J.J. Leedy, M.D., Simon & Schuster.

• Cellulite is not a special fat that resists diet and exercise. It is simply the dimpled fat found on the hips and thighs of many women. Since it is ordinary fat, it can be reduced as part of any respectable weight-loss program.

Source: *Vitamins and "Health" Foods: The Great American Hustle,* by Victor Herbert, M.D., and Stephen Barrett, M.D., Stickley Publishing.

CHALLENGES TO YOUR DIET

• Carrots, corn flakes, and white bread increase your appetite for two to three hours. These foods stimulate the secretion of insulin, which inhibits appetite control.

Source: *Take Charge of Your Health* by Peter Ways, MD, Stephen Greene Press, Lexington, MA.

• Despite what you may have heard, artificial sweeteners can actually make your dieting much more difficult. Background: Any sweet taste signals the liver to shift into a food-storing mode. Artificial sweeteners provide no calories to burn, so your body craves food to satisfy its metabolism—and you end up even hungrier than if you had consumed a sugary sweet...or nothing at all.

Source: Dr. Mike Tordoff, Monell Chemical Senses Center, Philadelphia.

SAVE YOUR LIFE THE PRITIKIN WAY

If Nathan Pritikin had anything to do with it, Americans would switch to the Pritikin diet and exercise program and possibly live 20–30 years longer, enjoy better health and get more out of life. The program has scored successes with permanent weight loss, with restoring sufferers of degenerative diseases (atherosclerosis, angina, hypertension, diabetes) to normal function, and with getting athletes and people already in good physical condition into better physical condition.

Caution: Anyone on prescription drugs should consult with a physician before going on the diet or modifying drug requirements.

Exercise:
Walk one hour every day, all at one time or divided into two half hours or three 20-minute walks. Walk at a comfortable rate. If you want to jog or run, check with your doctor first.

The nutrition/health connection:
Doctors are taught drug and surgical therapies. They often don't understand how nutrition affects health.

Pritikin history:
Pritikin, an inventor whose hobby was nutrition, thought that heart disease was a result of heredity and stress. Then he saw the link to diet in England where the incidence of heart disease dropped during World War II when the high-fat/high-cholesterol diet was disrupted and then went back to usual levels when people resumed their old diet.

When Pritikin learned in 1955 that he had a serious heart condition, he developed a diet for himself using the dietary basis of underdeveloped countries, where heart disease and other degenerative diseases (epidemic in countries on an American-type diet) are almost unknown. He turned his condition around.

Pritikin diet:
Low in:
• Fats (animal and vegetable)—butter, oil, margarine, hard cheeses, pork, nonlean meats, dark meat and skin of poultry, cholesterol (no egg yolks, organ meats).

• Animal protein.

• Refined carbohydrates—brown and white sugar, molasses, corn syrup and the like.

• Salt—no salt added to foods.
High in:

• Complex, mostly unrefined carbohydrates rich in starch and fiber—grains, brown rice, whole-wheat flour.

• Fresh fruits and vegetables.
Forbidden: Cigarettes, caffeine, alcohol (an occasional glass of wine is okay), vitamin supplements.
Balance is important. Diet should be 5–10% fat, 10–15% protein and 80% complex carbohydrates.
Treatment of disease: The Pritikin in-hospital centers and the longevity centers in Santa Monica and Miami offer the Pritikin diet with medical supervision for the treatment of disease. For seven years, Pritikin and Dr. James Anderson, who uses the Pritikin diet at the Kentucky Medical Center in Lexington, have recorded and published their findings.
Results: 50% of all diabetics are off insulin in four weeks. The diet is equally effective with

heart disease and hypertension. Patients have a significant drop in serum cholesterol and triglyceride levels. Blood pressure and uric acid levels decrease.

Many patients try the program as a last resort, after surgery and drugs fail. Example: Former astronaut James B. Irwin suffered a heart attack, underwent a triple bypass operation, and then had another heart attack. The turning point: The Pritikin diet. Now NASA doctors say he's in better condition than most of the current crop of astronauts.

Who should be on the program?

• Children should go on the diet when they are weaned.

• Those under medication for disease should proceed only under medical supervision.

• Many athletes report more stamina, less fatigue and better performance.

• ''Well'' people find it successful for weight loss and weight maintenance. It may prevent breast and colon cancer and other degenerative diseases. Those on the program say they feel better, think more clearly, concentrate better, experience less fatigue and often sleep less.

Relearning eating habits:

Myths of ''health'' foods: Some foods we have been taught are good for us are actually harmful, including eggs, raw milk, cheeses, most soybean products, granola. Honey and brown sugar are no better than white sugar . . . and that's bad. Seeds and nuts have high fat levels. The American Heart Association's 1961 diet recommends polyunsaturated fat. Studies show that the AHA diet causes gallstones to grow faster than any other diet by as much as three to one. The American Cancer Institute found (in animal studies) polyunsaturates double the incidence of colon cancer.

Other popular foods to avoid: Processed foods, steaks, chops, ice cream, soda (including diet sodas), whole milk. Substitute: Water with a lemon wedge in it, pita bread and whole-grain breads, products made from skim milk, fresh fruit and salads.

Side effects: Flatulence can last for some time while intestinal flora adapt to the new nutritional environment.

Source: Interview with Nathan Pritikin, author of *The Pritikin Permanent Weight Loss Manual* and *The Pritikin Program for Diet and Exercise,* Grosset and Dunlap, New York.

PRITIKIN'S PROPER NUTRITION FORMULA

• Raw vegetable salad and raw or cooked green or yellow vegetables.
• A piece of citrus fruit and up to three additional pieces of fresh fruit daily.
• Two grains daily (wheat, oats, barley, brown rice, buckwheat).*
• Add beans or peas one to three times a week.
• Six ounces to 1½ pounds of low-fat, low-cholesterol animal protein per week.
• Add unprocessed wheat-bran flakes if bowel elimination is not normal.
• Three full meals daily and snacks (whole-grain bread or crackers, fruit, raw salad vegetables) if hungry. Maintain your ideal weight by adding or subtracting permissible foods according to their caloric values.

*Choose from breakfast cereals like oatmeal, Wheatena, Grape Nuts and shredded wheat; side dishes of pastas made without eggs, brown and wild rices, kasha (buckwheat groats) or bulgar; bread and crackers like pita bread, tortillas, sour dough, Rye-Krisp, matzos and Scandinavian flatbread.

WHAT'S GOOD FOR YOU CAN BE BAD FOR YOU

• Fruit juice can be hazardous to health. Six ounces of apple juice contain the equivalent of more than five teaspoonfuls of sugar—40% more sugar than a chocolate bar and more sugar per ounce than cola. Blood-sugar-sensitive types who experience a temporary lift from sugar followed by fatigue should be cautious about fruit-juice intake. Recommended: Eat a whole apple or orange instead of drinking juice. The fiber dilutes the sugar impact. Alternative: Eat cheese, nuts or other protein with juice.

• Nondairy cream substitutes, often used by those on low-fat diets, usually contain coconut oil and have a higher fat content than the dairy product for which they're substituting.

• Decaffeinated coffee leads to significant stomach acid secretion, causing heartburn and indigestion in many persons. Caffeine was assumed to be the culprit. A new study shows that decaffeinated coffee is even worse. The effect is seen in doses as small as a half cup of decaffeinated coffee. People experiencing ulcer symptoms, heartburn and dyspepsia should avoid decaffeinated as well as regular coffee.

Source: *Journal of the American Medical Association,* Chicago.

• Most commercial products billed as alternatives to salt are based on potassium chloride. Problem: Although potassium chloride does enhance flavor, it leaves a slightly bitter or metallic taste. And excessive potassium may be as bad for your health as too much salt. Alternatives to the alternatives . . . Mrs. Dash, a commercial blend of 14 herbs and spices. Lite Salt, a half-sodium, half-potassium blend. Or try adding parsley, a delightful herb that enhances flavor all by itself.

• One of the few proven substances that can bring on flare-ups of acne is iodine. Excessive, long-term intake of iodine (a natural ingredient of many foods) can bring on acne in anyone, but for people who are already prone to the condition, iodine is especially damaging. Once iodine hits the bloodstream, any excess is excreted through the oil glands of the skin. This process irritates the pores and causes eruptions and inflammation. Major sources of iodine in the diet: Iodized table salt, kelp, beef liver, asparagus, turkey, and vitamin and mineral supplements. For chronic acne sufferers, cutting down on these high-iodine foods and looking for vitamins without iodine may bring relief.

Source: *Dr. Fulton's Step-by-Step Program for Clearing Acne* by J.E. Fulton Jr. M.D., and E. Black, Harper & Row, New York.

• Chronic diarrhea, gas and other stomach complaints are often linked to lactose intolerance the inability to digest milk. One of every four adults suffers from this problem. Reason: Their bodies don't make enough lactase, the enzyme that breaks down milk sugar in the intestinal tract. Among the offending foods: Milk, ice cream, chocolate, soft cheese, some yogurts, and sherbet. Lactose is also used as a filler in gum, candies and many canned goods.

• People on low-sodium diets should check out tap water as a source of salt intake. Some local water systems have eight times the amount of sodium (20 milligrams per quart) that people with heart problems or hypertension should use.

Source: *The Sodium Content of Your Food,* Consumer Information Center, CO.

• Health-food candy is really no better for you than traditional chocolates. Comparison: Health-food candy contains about the same number of calories. The fat content is as high or higher. Bars made of carob are caffeine free, but the amount of caffeine in chocolate is negligible. And the natural sugars in health bars have no nutritional advantage over refined sugars.

WHAT'S BAD FOR YOU CAN BE GOOD FOR YOU

• Chocolate lovers will be pleased to know that chocolate is not as dangerous to teeth as other candies. Antidecay factors in cocoa counter the damaging action of the sugar. Cocoa tannins seem to inhibit plaque formation, and the fat in cocoa may protect teeth by forming an antibacterial coating.

Source: National Institute for Dental Research.

• Treat a cold with booze fumes. A California general practitioner* swears by this cold remedy: Take a thick mug and fill it with boiling water. After about two minutes, throw the water away. Put in two ounces of brandy or bourbon, and then fill the mug almost to the top with boiling water. Cup your hands over the top of the mug to make a nose cone. Place your mouth and nose inside the cone. Blow on the surface and inhale the fumes for 15 minutes. You should feel the vapor penetrating your sinuses. Drink the mixture if you want to. Take a cold pill to keep your sinuses open overnight, and repeat the treatment in the morning. If you start this at the first signs of a cold (before nasal passages are blocked), your cold should vanish in 24 hours.

*Dr. Robert K. Julien, Turlock, CA.

HOW TO GET DOCTORS TO TALK TO YOU ON THE PHONE

It's generally very hard to find out whether a doctor treats your particular problem or uses the procedure you need until you visit the office—a waste of your time and money, since you'll probably have to wait for the appointment and pay for the visit.

Instead: Try to get the information on the telephone. Obstacle: Most office staffs tend to overprotect doctors from such calls—even, on occasion, contrary to the doctor's inclination.

Trick: Refer to yourself on the phone as "doctor." It's amazing how that can open doors with medical professionals. Not all people feel comfortable with such deception, but given the payoff, it should be considered.

Source: Interview with Susan G. Cole, editor of *The Practical Guide to Cancer Care*, Health Improvement Research Corp., New York.

HYPNOSIS AND SELF-HYPNOSIS POWER

Hypnosis can give you greater control over your life than you ever had before. You can use it to quit smoking, to cure insomnia, and to overcome pain, among other things. And the best thing about it is that you can be taught quickly and easily to do it for yourself.

As a matter of fact, you've probably been in a state of spontaneous, self-induced hypnotic trance many times and just not realized it. Remember the last time you were so deeply absorbed in a train of thought that you were barely aware of what was going on around you. Suddenly, the voice of your boss or spouse startled you with. . ."You haven't heard a word I've said." Only then did your attention return to the room and the speaker.

That state of mind is very much like an actual hypnotic trance. It's a state of aroused, intense concentration—the exact opposite of sleep. Your awareness of peripheral activity is reduced and you are able to focus your attention entirely on a single issue.

Hypnosis as practiced by health-care professionals is nothing more than the formal use of this natural capacity for attentive receptive concentration. In a sense, all hypnosis is self-hypnosis. The hypnotist doesn't have any power over the patient. He simply guides the patient into a state of hypnosis. . .something you can do yourself. The patient then translates the message the practitioner gives and makes it a self-hypnotic induction.

Hypnosis increases a person's responsiveness to suggestion, whether the messages are directed by a hypnotist or later reinforced through self-hypnosis. During hypnosis treatment, patients are taught to enlist their inner strengths and resources in their own healing or betterment. They are taught how to *restructure* their point of view toward their body so that the focus is positive rather than negative.

Depending on who the person is, what his problem is, and his level of motivation, there's tremendous leeway to change perspectives that can alleviate a problem. This change of attitude, or *restructuring*, is the key to successful treatment through hypnosis. During hypnosis, the patient is given a set of self-hypnosis exercises to do regularly each day.

Hypnosis has been particularly successful in the following areas:

- Overcoming phobias—such as fear of flying.
- Controlling pain. This is one of the most useful applications of hypnosis. You learn how to renegotiate pain.
- Eliminating undesirable habits. Symptoms such as hair-pulling, teeth-grinding, and nail-biting can be overcome through hypnosis.
- Mastering insomnia and anxiety.
- Conquering addictions—such as those to cigarettes, food, and caffeine.

One session of hypnosis should be enough for weight control, quitting smoking, and treatment of phobias. *Ripple effect:* As a person gains control over one problem through hypnosis, his self-respect is increased, and most may gain control in other areas.

Source: Herbert Spiegel, MD, faculty, Department of Psychiatry, Columbia University's College of Physicians and Surgeons and in private practice at 19 E. 88 St., New York 10128. He is the foremost medical authority on hypnosis and a pioneer in measuring trance capacity. Dr. Spiegel is the author (with David Spiegel) of *Trance and Treatment*, Basic Books, 10 E. 53 St., New York 10022.

4. Medical Solutions

Medical Solutions

HEALTH SECRETS ONLY THE INSURANCE INDUSTRY KNOWS

Actuarial tables prepared by the life insurance industry to predict mortality rates show that:

• A larger abdomen than chest (when expanded) is the most dangerous type of obesity.

• Death rates at all ages are more than twice as high among smokers.

• The death of both parents before they reach age 60 increases the mortality risk in children up to one-third.

• Overweight people have a markedly lower suicide rate. Being underweight generally leads to a longer life.

• It is much more dangerous to your health to live alone than in a stable relationship.

• The wealthy live longer, in large part because they get the best medical care, hygiene and nutrition.

• A stroke before age 60 becomes less and less of a mortality factor the longer the person lives uneventfully after it. Getting insurance is virtually impossible for those who have a stroke after 60.

• The nearsighted are unusually prone to anxiety.

• Obsessive personality types (compulsively neat and thorough) are especially likely to become depressed and kill themselves in later life.

• Severe drunkenness once a month doubles the risk of mortality. So does getting boisterously drunk every weekend.

• Those involved in kinky sex are much more likely to die violently or to kill themselves.

• Susceptibility to fear seems to correlate with blood coagulation associated with phlebitis.

• About one insurance applicant in 10,000 is denied coverage because of a hazardous occupation. About one in 250 has to pay a surcharge because of occupation.

• Farmers, college teachers and Anglican ministers are extremely good risks.

Source: *The Invisible Bankers: Everything the Insurance Industry Never Wanted You to Know* by Andrew Tobias, Simon & Schuster, New York.

IS YOUR OFFICE HAZARDOUS TO YOUR HEALTH?

Your office environment might be hazardous to your health. Watch out for: Excess noise, air pollutants, chemically treated paper, badly heated or cooled rooms, uncomfortable chairs. Related ailments: bad back, varicose veins, failing eyesight, hypertension, migraine headaches, respiratory and digestive problems, heart disease. What to do: Keep records of where and when a problem occurs and all the people affected. List possible causes: Smokers, office machines, etc. Present a plan of action to your employer.

MOST DANGEROUS TIME OF YEAR TO BE IN A HOSPITAL

If you need competent care, put off non-emergency surgery and medical tests until late fall if you can. Reason: In the cycles of medical education, new residents—the least experienced doctors on a hospital staff—take up their duties on July 1. Senior staff physicians often take summer vacations. Bottom line: The hospital is more likely to run smoothly after the new residents have worked into the routine .

Source: Jo Ann Friedman, president, Health Marketing Systems, New York.

PATIENT'S RIGHTS

People who are asked to sign medical consent forms are often in the worst possible psychological shape to make a decision about anything. Serious illness is a terrible shock. It brings out the part of human nature that wants to abdicate responsibility and put fate in the hands of an omnipotent being—in this case, the doctor. It's important to understand before you get sick what your rights as a patient are and what medical consent actually means.

The law in this country guarantees the patient an informed consent. That means the patient must be thoroughly informed in advance about all significant aspects of the proposed treatment. Consent is necessary in all non-emergency situations in which there are invasive* procedures or treatments involving risks unknown to most lay people. This includes not only surgery but also more minor procedures such as invasive diagnostic tests or injections of any substance with negative side effects.

Since making a decision about treatment of a serious illness is so traumatic, there are things you should do to be sure your decision is the right one:

• Some hospitals provide patient representatives. Ask for one to sit in on the informed-consent procedure.

• Write down all your questions in advance. Take notes or use a tape recorder for the answers.

• Ask the doctor for recommended reading about your illness and its treatment.

• Get second (or third) opinions.

• Take a friend or relative with you. Someone uninvolved will be cool-headed enough to get more information.

• Don't agree to anything just to get it over with. Listen closely to the alternatives and risks.

The essence of informed consent is what takes place between the patient and the doctor. A consent form signed by the patient doe snot in itself constitute informed consent. The form is simply evidence collected by doctors and hospitals as protection in case of an eventual lawsuit. In all states the patient has the right to an explanation and must understand the procedure. And in some states the informed consent must be obtained by the procedure. Example: The risks of anesthesia must be explained by the anesthesiologist. The explanation must be in simple language the patient can understand. Basics:

• Consent for a medical procedure on a child or unconscious adult can be given over the telephone, but hospitals and doctors will want it confirmed in writing.

• Consent can be revoked at any time prior to the procedure. Medical consents are not legallyh binding prior to the procedure, and you don't give up any rights when you sign a form and then change your mind.

• Consent must be to a specific procedure. A general consent form is not evidence of consent for those specific procedures which require that specific information be imparted to the patient to make him "informed." Recommended: Sign general consent forms for basic hospital care. After you're admitted, it's still the hospital's and doctor's responsibility to explain any specific procedures in order to obtain consent that's informed.

• Consent is not necessary for an emergency procedure where the patient is incompetent or unconscious and no one authorized can be located to consent. Emergency: Any procedure that is medically necessary to treat a condition dangerous to life or health.

Source: Natalie J. Kaplan, a former hospital legal consultant, now in private practice in New York.

WHAT DOCTORS AND HOSPITALS DON'T TELL YOU

• Always count the pills in the bottle you get and check the total against the prescription. Discrepancies between the number of pills the doctor prescribes and the number the pharmacist gives you are quite common.

Source: *Medical Economics*.

• Physicians routinely neglect to inform their patients about the possible side effects of the drugs they prescribe. About three-quarters of patients do not receive these briefings, according to the FDA. And 35% of all patients get no information at all about prescribed drugs. Protection: Question your doctor until you know all about the drug you are to take.

• Diagnostic error. Poor bite is often misdiagnosed as a migraine or pinched nerve. People with faulty bite often unconsciously grind their teeth to align them better. Result: Headaches, earaches and pains in the jaw, neck and shoulders. Treatments: Spot grinding by a dentist to even the bite. Exercises to relax the jaw muscles. A plastic device that fits over the upper and lower teeth to protect them from grinding, help readjust the bite and ease pressure on jaw muscles.

• Doctors who operate frequently have better safety records because they maintain their skills. Guideline: A minimum of 40–50 operations a year, even more for heart surgery. Aim for a hospital that does many similar operations. Best bets: Teaching and specialty hospitals. A good one substantially improves the chances of avoiding serious complications or death.

• Postoperative delirium is a short-lived but frightening phenomenon common to patients who have undergone serious surgery. Some become disoriented or lose touch. Others suffer hallucinations. Patients who are warned about this possibility before an operation are much less likely to experience it. If they do, the effects are much less severe.
Source: *Nursing Research.*

• Keep your medical records private. Never sign a blanket medical release form. The only medical release forms you sign should specifically identify the following: Information to be released, who is releasing the information and who is to receive it. Releases are not self-limiting as to time. A form you signed 10 years ago can still be used to obtain information. A period of one year is suggested.

• Many hospital procedures can be managed at home effectively and efficiently to spare the patient's pocketbook. A home chemotherapy program run by M.D. Anderson Hospital in Houston saved an average of $1,500 per patient. Home recipients of intravenous feedings through a Cleveland Clinic project cut an estimated $100 a day from their bills. In Nashua, NH, patients who took intravenous antibiotic therapy at home instead of in the hospital saved $286 a day. Bottom line: Check with your doctor about local home-care programs the next time a family member is hospitalized.

Source: A study conducted by *Voluntary Effort Quarterly* reported in *Physician's Management,* Harcourt Brace Jovanovich, New York.

• Wrong pills in hospitals. Since 1962, when a study of hospital medication practices uncovered an error in every six doses given to patients by nurses, the handling of drugs in U.S. hospitals has changed appreciably. A majority now have central pharmacies that make up unit doses to be dispensed by nurses and/or technicians in most of their departments. Where unit dose systems are in place, errors average only three per 100. However, that 3% can be fatal, and the number of errors in departments and hospitals not served by the central pharmacy is still very high (8%–20%). The problem: Overworked nurses, confusing and similar drug names and packaging, and illegibly written prescriptions. How to protect yourself: Be sure you know exactly which drugs and what dosages your doctor has ordered for you. Never accept medication without knowing what it is and what it is for.

• Blood pressure readings taken in a doctor's office may not be accurate because of the anxiety of being there. Better: Using portable devices, patients can measure their own pressures during the day while continuing their normal activities. These measurements are particularly helpful in deciding whether to start medication in patients who have borderline hypertension.

Source: *Journal of the American Medical Association.*

• Doctor's handwriting. When doctors write the names of drugs on prescription slips, a misreading by the pharmacist can be disastrous. A drug for arthritis, Tolectin, has been mistaken for Tolinase, which lowers blood sugar in diabetics. Coumadin, a drug that thins blood in heart disease patients, was confused with Kemadrin, which is for Parkinson's disease. Useful: Tell the pharmacist the disease the medicine is for. The pharmacist can check it.

PROTECT YOURSELF AGAINST HOSPITAL ERRORS

When the mechanic hands you a bill for $500, it's unlikely that you'd pay it without a glance at the charges. But when given a hospital bill for $5,000, most people tend to do just that.

As it turns out, hospitals and doctors are far from infallible when it comes to billing. According to the New York Life Insurance Company, which has been auditing hospital bills for several years, the average hospital bill contains $600 worth of erroneous charges. This money comes not only out of the insurance company's pocket, but also out of yours. You can save money by knowing how the system works and how to spot billing errors.

With the rising costs of health care, the current trend in the insurance industry is to have the insured employee share in the cost of health care. Under major medical plans, employees are usually responsible for a fixed dollar amount, termed out-of-pocket expenses, which includes deductibles and coinsurance. In addition, many employees pay a portion of their health-care premium, so it is to their advantage to keep health-care costs down to avoid unnecessary increases in premiums.

How it works: Let's say the out-of-pocket limit is $1,000. The insurance company usually pays 80% (and the patient 20%) of all non-room-and-board charges until the $1,000 out-of-pocket expense limit is reached. After that, insurance takes over 100%. However, most patients don't reach the out-of-pocket limit, since they'd have to run up at least $5,000 worth of non-room-and-board hospital expenses or other health-care costs to do so. Therefore, while your contribution to out-of-pocket is still adding up, it clearly pays to keep costs down.

There are many billing errors for the simple reason that many hospitals have inefficient billing systems. Major problem: Hospitals are geared to making sure that patients are billed for services provided and not toward verifying charges.

Typical mistake: Because of a clerical error, a $50 electrocardiogram is entered onto your bill at a $500 charge. Since you may not know the typical cost of an EKG, the error goes undetected.

Another example: A lab technician comes in to draw blood and finds that the patient is no longer there. However, he's still charged. Reason: Billing starts from the day the charges are entered in the book, and his charges are never canceled.

Similar mistakes occur with drug prescriptions. Example: The doctor might order 10 days of penicillin and then switch to tetracycline after seven days. If the unused three days' worth of penicillin is not returned, the patient is billed for it.

The four major mistake areas:

• Respiratory therapy. Equipment such as oxygen tanks and breathing masks isn't credited when it's discontinued. Sometimes it's not even removed promptly from the room.

• Pharmacy charges. Credit isn't given for drugs that were returned, or unused drugs are not returned.

• Lab tests. Cancellations of tests aren't noted.

• Central supply items. Hospital staff or nurses may run out of something and borrow it from another patient. They intend to give credit or return the item, but often they don't get around to it.

What you can do:

• Keep track of the most basic things, such as how many times your blood was drawn. Suggestion: If you're able, jot down what happens daily. Note: If the patient is too sick to keep track of services rendered, a family member should try to keep track of the charges. Although it may be difficult to know how many routine things such as blood counts or X rays were done, someone who visits regularly is likely to know about nonroutine services, such as barium enemas or cardiac catheterizations.

• Ask questions. Ask the doctor to be specific about tests. If he orders X rays, ask him what type of X rays. If he doesn't answer the question to your satisfaction, ask the nurse. Always ask. It's the most important thing a health-care consumer can do. Reassuring change: The newer generation of doctors is more willing to involve the patient in his own care.

• Insist on an itemized bill, not just a summary of charges.

• Check room and board charges. Count the days you were in the hospital and in what kind of room. Are you being charged for a private room, even though you were in a semiprivate? Some hospitals have different semiprivate rates for two-bed and four-bed rooms. Check your rate.

• Review the charges for TV rental and phone.

• Be equally careful with doctor bills. Often these bills are made out by the doctor's assistant, who may not be sure of what was done. Most common errors: Charges for services in the doctor's office, such as a chest X ray or an injection, that weren't actually performed. Charges for routine hospital physician visits on days that the doctor was not in attendance.

Source: Janice Spillane, manager of cost containment in the group insurance department of New York Life Insurance Co., New York.

HIGH-TECH MEDICAL DANGERS

The medical profession is more sophisticated and high-tech than ever before. It can effect treatments and cures that would have been considered miracles only 10 years ago.

But the health-care system is also more dangerous than ever.

With more diagnostic tools and surgical options available, many more opportunities exist for physicians to make mistakes or to act on incomplete knowledge. The wrong doctor—or the wrong lab test or the wrong surgery—is dangerous and even deadly. More than 200,000 Americans die each year, according to authoritative estimates, because of their doctors' negligence.

To survive the modern health-care system, patients must be assertive, informed, and ready to protect themselves from myriad hazards, including...

• Misdiagnosis. It happens more than you think. A study of 1,800 autopsies from 32 hospitals found a diagnosis error rate of 20%. Half the errors—180 cases in all—led to the patients' deaths. Most commonly overlooked: Pulmonary embolisms, peritonitis, and pulmonary abscesses ... all life-threatening conditions.

• Laboratory errors. More and more doctors do lab work at their offices these days. It's a big money-maker for them ... and it's also hazardous to your health. Doctor-operated labs have double the error rates of independent or hospital laboratories, which are monitored far more tightly by the state. And even these are not failsafe. As many as 35% of pap smears produce false positives or false negatives. The former can lead to an unneeded hysterectomy, the latter to an untreated cancer.

• Hospital infections and errors. A hospital is the most dangerous place in the world for sick people. One out of every 10 patients gets a new infection inside the hospital. Many of these are fatal ... and 80% are preventable. In addition, a good hospital will have a 2%–3% error rate in medicating their patients. On average, one patient in this country every minute gets either the wrong medicine, too much or too little or is dosed at the wrong time. This problem has worsened with the recent nursing shortage, since more nurses come out of "pools" and there is less continuity of care.

• Alcoholic, drug-addicted or incompetent doctors. The local medical society knows who they are ... but they keep the information confidential. You'll know, too, if your doctor shows up bleary-eyed, mumbling or wobbly. The problem is that many impaired doctors—and particularly surgeons—are not as obvious.

Source: Charles Inlander, president of the People's Medical Society in Emmaus, PA, and co-author of *Medicine on Trial*.

CHOOSING THE RIGHT ANESTHESIOLOGIST

It is common knowledge that patients should consult more than one doctor before proceeding with any kind of surgery. But when it comes to the selection of an anesthesiologist, we tend to be much more passive. However, the quality of the care we receive from our anesthesiologist is as important—or more so—as the quality of surgical care. Anesthesiologists' work involves not only the administration of potentially lethal drugs but also the monitoring of the patient's vital signs during the surgery.

Typically, the first contact with the anesthesiologist is in the hospital, the night before the operation. Better: Ask your surgeon for the name of the anesthesiologist he plans to use when the operation itself is discussed. Meet the proposed anesthesiologist well before the operation.

Ask your surgeon how often he has worked with this anesthesiologist. Ask your family doctor if he knows him and what he thinks of him. Ask anyone you know who works at the hospital—nurses, volunteers, etc.—for the hospital grapevine's assessment of the anesthesiologist.

Unless someone volunteers the information, you won't be able to find out whether anyone has ever sued this anesthesiologist for malpractice. However, you can call the licensing board of your state and ask if any complaints have been made against him and how they were resolved.

The fact that one complaint has been made does not necessarily mean the doctor is guilty of any misconduct. But if the doctor has inspired a number of complaints, this should tell you something. Make sure the doctor is board certified. Look up his credentials (in any medical-specialist book at any public library) to find out where he trained and how long he has been practicing.

The hospital may want to assign a nurse anesthetist. An individual nurse anesthetist may be well qualified to administer anesthesia.

Interview the proposed anesthesiologist. Ask him to explain the options available to you and to tell you why he recommends a particular course. There is greater risk in general anesthesia than in local anesthesia. Can the operation you are having be done with local

anesthesia? Feel free to discuss anything that bothers you.

If you are at all dissatisfied with the proposed anesthesiologist's qualifications or competence, request another one...and check him out. If that can't be arranged, seriously consider changing to another surgeon and/or hospital. The choice is always the patient's.

Source: Leonard Glantz, associate professor of health law, Boston University School of Public Health, Boston.

PRECAUTIONS WHEN YOU NEED BLOOD

Companies cannot set up exclusive blood banks for employee use because of blood's perishability. Blood properties begin to break down within the first 24 hours after donation. The maximum shelf life for blood is five weeks.

But there are certain precautions individuals can take to insure against getting contaminated blood in hospitals:

Prior to surgery, make a specific request of your physician to use only volunteer-donor blood. Volunteer blood does not cost any more than commercial blood. And commercial (paid-donor) blood has a much higher incidence of hepatitis contamination.

The big limitation: Hospitals cannot be held liable if they have no volunteer-donor blood and must, in an emergency, give paid-donor blood to a patient who requested volunteer-donor blood only. The worst risk is in public hospitals, where both commercial and volunteer blood are used.

DRUGS VS. PSYCHOTHERAPY FOR ANXIETY AND NEUROSIS

Drugs affect psychological symptoms and emotional distress. Therapy affects relationships with others and social adjustments.

Drugs start acting more quickly, but wear off sooner. The results of therapy are slower to appear, but last longer. Drugs are useful for temporary disorders, therapy for deep and long-lasting personality trait disorders.

Source: Toksoz Karasu, Albert Einstein College of Medicine, writing in *American Journal of Psychiatry*.

NEW DRUG THEORY— LESS IS MORE

Virtually all drugs are administered with the common assumption that the higher the dose—and the more often the dose is repeated—the greater and longer-lasting the effect.

But it turns out that the opposite may be true—according to research done with animals.

The drugs grow more potent as the intervals between doses are lengthened. In other words, weekly doses have more impact than daily doses. Monthly doses provoke an even greater response. The longer you wait between doses, the more quickly the medicine works.

In addition, we have found that a drug continues to exert effects long after all traces of it have disappeared from the body.

This time-dependent sensitization theory, now being tested with humans, holds dramatic potential for patients now taking stimulants, anti-depressants, anti-anxiety drugs and anti-psychotics. It offers a possible solution to the common problem of tolerance—the body's tendency to respond less and less to a drug the more often it is taken. At the same time, greater intervals between doses would reduce—if not eliminate—undesirable side effects.

The hold-up:

Despite the publication of several papers in top scientific journals supporting these findings, there is little funding for further experiments. Reason: The theory may represent a radical change in the way drugs should be prescribed. It goes against the long-held views of both academia and the pharmaceutical industry.

How it works:

The body is pushed to respond to a drug because of its foreignness. The body recognizes the medicine as an unfamiliar substance, and therefore as a stressor and potential threat.

But if the drug is introduced repeatedly within a short period, and to no ill effect, the body begins to make peace with the intruder. The drug's potency is muted. This is the phenomenon of tolerance.

If, on the other hand, the drug is administered intermittently—with several weeks or months between doses—the body will still respond to each dose as if it were the first dose. The drug will still work with full force each time.

When a person begins to take anti-depressants, weeks often go by before any benefit is observed. According to conventional wisdom, the drug must be given continually until it accumulates to a certain level in the body, at which point it begins to take effect.

Another possibility: The body may need several weeks after the first dose to "learn" to respond to a second dose. The intervening doses will not accelerate that process. They only decrease sensitivity and build tolerance.

Much more testing is, of course, necessary, and our findings may not be applicable in all cases. There is, however, strong reason to believe that the theory could lead to a reduction in expense and complications in many, many cases.

Source: Seymour M. Antelman, PhD, associate professor of psychiatry at the University of Pittsburgh.

PRESCRIPTION-DRUG ADDICTION

For every person addicted to heroin in the US, there are 10 hooked on prescription drugs. And withdrawal can be as painful as from any in the illicit-drug world.

Why addiction happens: The doctor prescribes a psychoactive drug (one that affects the mind or behavior) to relieve a physical ailment.

By altering your moods, psychoactive drugs can affect your ability to make judgments and decisions. Some drugs mask the symptoms of serious ailments or can impair your physical activity. These drugs have their place among useful medications (generally for short-term relief), but they do not cure physical ailments.

Most commonly abused psychoactive drugs: Codeine, Valium, Librium, Demerol, Dalmane and Nembutol. Worse: Mixing drugs or combining a drug with alcohol.

If your physician is reluctant to make a specific diagnosis or refuses to explain the effects of drugs, find another doctor. Question every prescription you're given: Will it cure the ailment or will it just relieve the symptoms?

Before accepting a drug for an emotional problem, seek another solution: a vacation, exercise, counseling. If the problem is physical, ask why this drug is being prescribed rather than another treatment.

Cut drug dependency gradually, under a doctor's supervision. Stopping the pills immediately is sometimes possible. But it is often accompanied by insomnia, muscle twitches, a burning sensation of the skin or even seizures. Withdrawal symptoms often occur days after the individual stops taking the drug. When they occur, many people are convinced that they are overstressed and resume taking the drug that caused the problem in the first place.

Source: *Weathering* by Stephen Rosen, M. Evans & Co., New York.

ADVANTAGES OF BUYING DRUGS OVERSEAS

Many drugs that require a prescription in the US are sold over the counter in other countries. Example: Cough syrup with codeine.

Even when a medication requires a prescription overseas, most foreign doctors will give you one if you say you have a prescription in the US.

Prescription drugs that are commonly sold over the counter outside the US:

- Amoxicillin *antibiotic*
- Digoxin *cardiac regulator*
- Erythromycin *antibiotic*
- Lasix *diuretic*
- Megistrole *codeine analgesic*
- Metronidazole *antifungal*
- Motrin *analgesic*
- Penicillin *antibiotic*
- Prednisone *steroid*
- Propranolol *cardiac regulator*

Rules about prescriptions are much looser overseas. In Latin America, for instance, doctors commonly write large-quantity (100 tablets plus), *refillable* prescriptions for drugs that in the US require a new prescription each time the drug is dispensed.

Outside the US you can buy some medications that aren't available here, even with a prescription.

Also more readily available overseas: Experimental drugs.

Many people who suffer from fatal and very serious diseases are turned down for experimental treatment in the US. Reasons: Manufacturers' restrictions on which patients are eligible for experimentation and the potential for enormous losses from lawsuits.

The most publicized example is the use of AZT (azidothymidine) for the treatment of AIDS. Because AZT is a new treatment, not all AIDS patients can receive AZT therapy in the US. Treatment is more readily available in France, where researchers at the Pasteur Institute have extensively studied AIDS, and at Caribbean and Mexican clinics set up solely to administer the drug.

Treatment using interferon for malignant forms of leukemia and melanoma are also available overseas.

The risks: Side effects and proper dosages of experimental medications aren't fully known. That's one of the reasons the Food & Drug Administration hasn't approved them for general use.

Source: Cynthia Ronan, MD, a pharmacologist at Griffin Hospital, 130 Division St., Derby, CT 06718.

BEST PAINKILLERS

Despite the recent innovations in pain relief, the best drug for most pain is still aspirin. It works as well as or better than many pills that claim to be stronger, including Darvon (propoxyphene), Clinoril (sulindac) and Motrin (ibuprofen).

We know by now that all aspirin, whether buffered or not, works the same. (In fact, nearly all brands are made by one of two manufacturers: Dow or Monsanto.) Most brands, whether popular or generic, dissolve at about the same rate. Most brands, whether buffered or not, can severely damage the stomach lining if taken in excess. If aspirin works for you but bothers your stomach, you might try an enteric-coated tablet, such as Encaprin or Ecotrin. They are designed to dissolve in the small intestine rather than in the stomach.

Brand names can make a difference. One study found that up to one-third of aspirin's pain relief is the result of the placebo effect, based on the patient's seeing a familiar name on the tablet. Bottom line: If you have a favorite nonprescription pain reliever, keep using it. If you believe in it, it's probably worth the premium.

Acetaminophen (Tylenol, Datril, Anacin-3) is about as good as aspirin for relieving pain and fever. This drug is also useful for avoiding stomach irritations and ulcers. (Aspirin works better with arthritis, however.)

Drawback: Heavy long-term use of acetaminophens can result in liver damage. Tylenol may be a liver hazard if it's mixed with barbiturates, antianxiety agents (Valium and Librium) or alcohol.

Most potentially dangerous: Combination painkillers, such as Vanquish or Extra-Strength Excedrin, which include more than one analgesic. These may increase the risk of kidney damage, and combination painkillers have been banned in several countries.

Source: Joe Graedon, author of *The New People's Pharmacy,* Bantam Books, New York.

NEW MEDICINES AND YOU

Many drugs and medications not yet approved by the Food and Drug Administration (FDA) are available abroad. You can legally bring a three-month supply into the US (or have it sent). Examples: Losec for ulcers, Dipentum for inflammatory bowel disease. You need a letter or prescription from your doctor, who may also be able to help you find a foreign pharmacist, doctor or manufacturer to fill the order.

MEDICINES NOT TO GIVE YOUR CHILD

Alcohol-based medicines can make children nauseated, confused or sluggish. If taken intensively for an extended period, they can even lead to heart and respiratory problems. Trap: Alcohol is an unlabeled ingredient in many liquid antihistamines, cough syrups and anti-colic medicines. Advice: Ask your pediatrician to prescribe a nonalcohol-based alternative.

Source: Dr. Jean Lcokhart, director of the American Academy of Pediatrics, in *New Age Journal.*

DANGEROUS MIXES

Citrus fruits and juices (orange, grapefruit) and aluminum-containing medications . . . or medications that contain aluminum *and* citrates. Reason: Too much aluminum in the system increases one's risk of brain damage, brittle bones and senile dementia. Citrus increases aluminum absorption by as much as 50-fold. Even safer precaution: Avoid ingesting aluminum in any form.

Source: *The Lancet,* Little, Brown & Co., 34 Beacon St., Boston 02108.

MEDICINES AND WINTER

The weather affects both the body and the mind. And winter, the most extreme season of all, elicits the most extreme effects. Drug potency changes in the winter. Digitalis, the heart drug, becomes more toxic as barometric pressure drops. And diabetics respond more slowly to insulin. Important: Discuss dosage adjustment with your doctor.

Source: Maria Simonson, PhD, ScD, director of the Health, Weight and Stress Clinic, Johns Hopkins Medical Institution, Baltimore.

THE ABC'S OF ANTACIDS

Most stomachs produce acid 24 hours a day in intermittent bursts (usually after meals). As part of the evolutionary refinement of the human physiology, this process probably served our prehistoric ancestors well. The acid acted as a built-in food sterilizer. Although that function is not crucial today, most people live comfortably with their stomach acid and suffer only brief upsets now and then. However, for about 10% of the population this acid causes chronic problems because their systems make too much of it or don't drain it away fast enough or because the linings of their stomachs are very sensitive to it. The result may be frequent and painful irritation of the stomach, the upper intestine or the esophagus (heartburn). Worst problem: Ulcers.

The classic treatment for these acid-related digestive problems is antacids to neutralize the gastric juices and diet to prevent excessive irritation. (Spicy foods, alcohol, coffee, tobacco, aspirin and stress can all be irritants.)

Ulcer treatment: A breakthrough for ulcer treatment has been the development of Tagamet, a drug that stops the production of stomach acid. On the market since 1976, Tagamet has revolutionized the care of ulcer victims. Ranitidine is even more potent and has few side effects. Another new ulcer drug, Sucralfate, sticks to raw areas like a bandage, protecting the sores from irritation as they heal. Its side effects are minimal.

For indigestion: Short of ulcers, most stomach upsets can be treated with simple antacids. The basic neutralizers are sodium bicarbonate, calcium, magnesium and aluminum salts.

Sodium bicarbonate—the baking soda your grandmother used to take—is found in such over-the-counter antacids as Alka-Seltzer. The problem for people with high blood pressure is the high sodium content of these products. Alka-Seltzer combines sodium bicarbonate with aspirin, which is fine for many people. It can be counterproductive, however, for those whose stomachs are irritated by aspirin.

The calcium-based antacids (Tums, Equilet and Titralac) are best for occasional mild indigestion.

In general, liquid antacids are more potent and quicker acting than antacid tablets. However, magnesium-based antacids (such as Phil-

lips Milk of Magnesia) have a laxative effect and are not terribly effective for stomach upsets.

Aluminum-based antacids (Amphojel, Alternagel, Basaljel and Robolate) are also mild, but they have a binding action (good for people who tend to diarrhea).

Combination antacids, the obvious compromise, make up the majority of products on the market. Maalox and Mylanta have more magnesium and tend to cause loose stools. Aludrox, Gelusil and Riopan, heavier on aluminum, are weaker, but they cause less diarrhea. Gaviscon, a magnesium-aluminum combination, has a special foaming action. It floats on stomach juices and prevents the acid from coming into contact with tender digestive linings. Gaviscon is especially useful in stopping heartburn.

Some antacids also contain simethicone, an antiflatulent (Simeco, Maalox Plus, etc.).

The most potent antacids are extra-strength preparations such as Maalox T.C. and Mylanta II. Doctors use these products to treat severe digestive-tract problems because patients may need as much as seven ounces of antacid a day. When such heavy doses are called for, taste becomes important. If someone really gags on the medicine, he won't take it regularly. Antacids now come in various flavors such as peach, watermelon and mint. Suggestion: Chilling them helps to inhibit the taste.

Chronic use of antacids can interfere with the body's absorption of minerals and other medications. People with persistent stomach problems—or those over 40 who suddenly develop digestive upsets—should be under a doctor's supervision.

Source: Dr. Bruce H. Yaffe, a gastroenterologist in private practice in New York.

WORST DAYS FOR HEART ATTACKS

Fatal heart attacks happen most frequently on Saturdays, according to new research. (Too much "living it up" Saturday night?) Other studies have pinpointed Monday as the worst day for sudden deaths from heart attacks. These researchers suggest that job-related stress may be the precipitator.

Source: The Mayo Clinic.

ANGER MAY CAUSE HEART DISEASE

Angry people are more prone to heart disease than less hostile personality types. After calculating the ''hostility scores'' for 255 male doctors who took the Minnesota Multiphasic Personality Inventory 25 years ago, a researcher compared the results with current health records of the subjects, who are now between 45 and 50. More than 12% of those who had high hostility ratings now suffer from heart disease. Less than 3% of those with low hostility ratings are heart patients.

Source: Redford B. Williams Jr., M.D., Duke University.

VIRUSES CAN DAMAGE THE HEART

Serious viral infections may cause coronary damage that facilitates a heart attack. The viral infections are those that commonly bring on bad colds. If they persist, they could inflame the heart muscle, making the patient susceptible to attacks.

Source: The Harvard Medical School.

LOW CHOLESTEROL MAY PREVENT HEART ATTACKS

Reducing blood cholesterol levels may cut the odds of having a heart attack, but the connection between the two is not definite, says Dr. Basil Rifkind, chief of the Lipid Metabolism-Atherogenesis Branch of the National Heart, Lung & Blood Institute, Bethesda, MD.

A diet low in saturated fats can reduce cholesterol levels and may also raise high-density lipoproteins (HDL). These are thought to protect against heart attack. The body offsets cholesterol eaten in food by decreasing its own

production to some extent, but the higher your intake, the higher your blood cholesterol level. Efforts to reduce cholesterol when it is high are valuable. Helpful: Exercising regularly. And eating food with less animal fat to reduce intake of saturated fat and cholesterol.

Those who inherit high cholesterol from one parent often fail to reach age 50.

TIME-RELEASE MEDICATION FOR HEART PROBLEMS

Skin patches are replacing tablets as a way for people with heart problems to take nitroglycerin. When placed on the skin, the patches gradually release the drug, creating a constant level for 24 hours. Though more expensive than tablets, the patches are safer and have fewer significant side effects. The patches are for people who have angina pectoris or congestive heart failure.

Source: *Therapaeia.*

EXERCISE AND DIET INSTEAD OF HEART SURGERY

Men who had been considered candidates for coronary bypass surgery were put on a diet, drug and exercise regimen for between 20 months and 12 years. The annual death rate among the group was 1.4%, about the same as the death rate of survivors of successful coronary bypass surgery. Significant advantage of the regimen: The patients were not exposed to the 2–3% risk of dying on the operating table.

Source: Report from the Harvard School of Public Health in *New England Journal of Medicine.*

CROWDING CAUSES HYPERTENSION

Cramped living conditions cause significant increases in systolic blood-pressure levels, according to research at Yale University School of Medicine.

Source: *Psychosomatic Medicine.*

CRAVING FOR SALT CAN SIGNAL HYPERTENSION

Hypertensive craving for salt may be a symptom of the disease rather than a cause. Reason: Researchers speculate that hypertensives have a diminished taste for salt and thus use more.

CLIMATE AFFECTS BLOOD PRESSURE

Blood pressure medication may have to be adjusted as the seasons change. As a result of new studies, researchers believe that warm weather may cause pressure to decline, especially if you perspire excessively. The opposite occurs in cold weather.
Source: *British Medical Journal.*

BLOOD-PRESSURE DRUGS MAY DISTURB SLEEP

High-blood-pressure drugs can cause insomnia and nightmares as well as daytime drowsiness. For those who develop sleep disturbances, taking the medication in the morning may help. Others may do better taking the medication at bedtime. Consult your doctor before changing the schedule.
Source: *RN.*

RAPID BLOOD-PRESSURE DROP MAY SIGNAL DANGER

Low blood pressure, if it is your normal reading, is a healthy sign. Actuarial data show that people with low blood pressure tend to live longest. But any sudden drop in blood pressure may be dangerous, signaling rapid bleeding, fluid loss or possibly a heart attack or other serious illness. Prompt emergency treatment is imperative if blood pressure ever falls precipitously.

DIABETES AND BLINDNESS

Diabetics should have regular eye exams by an ophthalmologist knowledgeable about problems of the retina—the main cause of blindness in diabetics if not spotted early. Problem: Nonophthalmologic doctors, even those who specialize in diabetics, often miss the early symptoms.

DON'T READ IN THE DARK

Reading in the dark may not ruin your eyes, but it will hasten the development of nearsightedness and can cause eyestrain. Adequate lighting: 150 watts three feet from the page. Greater distances require higher wattages.
Source: *Total Vision* by Richard Kavner, A&W Publishers, New York.

CONTACT LENS UPDATE

Disposable contact lenses are becoming the treatment of choice for lens wearers. Advantages: They are thrown away before deposits build up and make them uncomfortable . . . patients save time and money spent disinfecting lenses . . . fewer eye infections from dirty lens cases. Daily safety check for disposables: Blink six to eight times and make sure eyes feel well . . . check for redness or discharge . . . check clarity of vision in each eye—and both eyes together.
Source: Stanley Yamane, OD, contact-lens specialist, Honolulu.

HELPING OUT A BLIND PERSON

If you encounter a blind person whom you think needs help, introduce yourself by name first, and then offer to help. Let him/her instruct you on how to help: Some prefer to take the arm of a helper . . . others prefer to have the helper take their arm. Orient the person with specific information: Say we're four feet from the curb and allow him to set the pace. Avoid: Revolving doors and escalators, whenever possible. People with guide dogs: They may need help, too. Ask. Important: Never walk away without letting the person know that you're leaving.

Source: *Good Housekeeping,* 959 Eighth Ave., New York 10019.

CONTACT-LENS SWIMMING DANGER

Don't wear soft contact lenses in a pool, lake or hot tub. Soft-lens wearers are susceptible to a corneal infection caused by acanthamoeba, a parasite found in water. Routine levels of chlorination do not kill this organism. It can cause a serious, extremely painful corneal infection resulting in partial or total blindness.

Source: *Good Times Almanac* by the editors of Rodale Press, 33 E. Minor St., Emmaus, Pennsylvania 18098.

GETTING RID OF BAD BREATH

Mouthwash does not kill the germs that cause bad breath, according to the Federal Drug Administration. What does improve bad breath: Brushing your teeth and tongue often and using dental floss to clean between the teeth and under the gums. If halitosis persists, see a doctor.

Source: Dr. E. L. Attia, otolaryngologist, quoted in *American Health.*

HOW TO TREAT CANKERS

Canker sores, those painful irritants that attack the lining of the mouth, are usually started by a scratch from a hard-bristled toothbrush, a sharp utensil or even sharp-cornered foods like peanut brittle or nuts. However, recurring canker sores may be a reflection of an iron, vitamin B-12 or folic acid deficiency. In that case, correcting the deficiency clears up the sores.

Source: Dr. Abner L. Notkins and Dr. David Wray, National Institute of Dental Research.

BRACE WEARERS NEED CALCIUM

People who wear braces on their teeth may need more calcium. When teeth are moved, it creates gaps in the jawbone that must be filled. New bone requires calcium. Sources: Green leafy vegetables such as asparagus, broccoli and turnip greens, milk, calcium supplements.

Source: Dr. David Ostreicher, orthodontist, Columbia University.

NATURAL TOOTHACHE RELIEF

Oil of cloves gives temporary relief of persistent tooth pain. (It is the only active ingredient in other effective dental-pain killers.) Next step: Consult your dentist.

SAVING A KNOCKED-OUT TOOTH

When a tooth is knocked out, there is a 90% chance it can be successfully replanted if you get the tooth and the patient to a dentist within 30 minutes. Procedure: Wrap the tooth in a damp cloth, without cleaning it, and get to a dentist's office as quickly as possible. After two hours, the odds on being able to save the tooth drop to only 10%.

Source: J.O. Andreasen, DDS, University Hospital, Copenhagen, Denmark.

Another way: Replace the tooth in its socket and hurry to the dentist. Next best: Pop it in a glass of milk for the trip.

Source: Dr. Frank Courts, Gainesville, FL.

EVERYTHING YOU SHOULD KNOW ABOUT DENTURES

One-third of all Americans end up losing all their teeth in an arch requiring a full denture. This is a horrible statistic since people need not lose all their teeth. Anyone who has some teeth left should consider saving them, not getting dentures. That is especially important for lower teeth. Upper dentures can be worn satisfactorily and comfortably. Lower dentures always pose much more severe and continuous problems than do uppers.

Why: Uppers hold much better because they rest on a palate and a wide ridge. Lowers have only a very thin ridge to adhere to, and the tongue tends to displace the dentures.

Also important: Eye teeth (canines), the large, pointed teeth on either side of the upper jaw. They are strong teeth, the cornerstone of the mouth's arch, and are essential to maintaining the ridge of the mouth. Other important teeth: Front teeth. When they are removed, they cause a collapsed-looking mouth, particularly in areas of the lips and nose. (When any teeth are removed, the bony structure around them shrinks up and inward.)

Before allowing teeth to be removed: If teeth are painful, loose and continually troublesome, and a dentist advises removing any or all of them, get two other dentists' opinions before consenting. It is important to try to keep teeth even if it is obvious they can last only a few years more. The only reason to consider teeth hopeless: When the bone around them has been lost to a degree that it cannot hold the teeth. Nonvalid reasons for extracting teeth: Abscesses, decay, pain. These conditions can be corrected with treatment.

What to expect with full dentures:

An immediate denture is a prosthesis inserted at the same time the teeth are extracted. This is done to avoid going without teeth for any period of time. Usual effects: Swelling and discomfort for a few days.

Within the first six weeks to three months of the time teeth have been pulled, shrinkage of bone and gums in that area accelerates rapidly. Significance: The original denture no longer fits and must be relined with acrylic to fill in areas that have shrunk.

At the end of the first year, an entirely new denture (or dentures) should be made. This second denture has a better fit and appearance than the original, which had to be molded while real teeth were still in the mouth.

People prone to problems with dentures:

• Diabetics or people with poor general health. They tend to have more bone disap-

pearance after their teeth have been pulled.
• People with a very high palate (tapered arch), a result of thumb-sucking in childhood or of genetic inheritance. They tend to have trouble retaining even an upper denture.
• People whose psychological approach or sensitivity to the feel of dentures is so negative that they can never adjust to them properly.
• People with bony projections sticking out from the palate. Most people who have them are not aware of them. They can be removed surgically, before the denture is fitted.

Main error denture wearers should avoid: Thinking that, as long as dentures are comfortable and giving no trouble, nothing more needs to be done about them. Fact: Bone shrinkage, after teeth are lost, goes on continually. Denture wearers should be checked by a dentist at least once a year, and their dentures regularly relined, even if the denture does not feel loose. Why this is important: The better the denture fits, the less the bone around it will shrink away.

How denture teeth should look: As natural and individual as possible, not perfectly symmetrical. It is a mistake to insist on completely even picket fence or piano key teeth.

How to get high-quality dentures:

Look for a dentist who stresses natural and individual-looking teeth and who gives detailed attention to planning aesthetic appearance and proper balance of dentures. Another guide: Cost. A bargain-basement price usually yields less carefully planned and executed dentures. Point: The materials used in dentures do not vary much or cost much. What does vary from dentist to dentist is expertise, time and attention to aesthetic considerations.

Cost of a denture: Prices vary. Lowers tend to be more expensive because they are more difficult to make.

Signs of problem dentures:

• Teeth touching each other when mouth is in normal, relaxed position. This means the teeth are too long.
• Teeth may click when talking.
• Jaw may ache.
• Deep lines or collapsed-looking area around the mouth, or sores at the corners of the mouth. Dentures are not providing proper

support. They have settled into the gums too much and need to be relined or replaced with new ones.

• Soreness or bleeding gums. Neither should exist as a chronic condition. (The same holds true of any dentistry, such as partial bridges.)

• A denture that keeps breaking every few months. The denture is not stable and does not sit right. Bite is wrong.

Dentures pastes: Should not be substituted for relining of dentures that no longer fit.

Bottom line: People should make every effort to maintain their own teeth. There's nothing like the real thing.

Source: Dr. Arthur S. Brisman, dentist, New York.

FACTS ABOUT HERPES

Genital herpes is transmitted by direct contact with individuals. The infection has not been demonstrated to be transmitted from toilet seats or from other inanimate objects. No case reports exist in which a family member with herpes has spread the infection through the household. Despite what you hear to the contrary, herpes appears to be transmitted only when there are open lesions. (They look like cold sores.)

How herpes spreads:

Contact must occur between the sores of an infected person and an open wound on another person. This phenomenon is related to basic factors:

• The organism's ability to survive. Herpes is a virus. Viruses can survive and multiply only within a living cell. Recent articles suggesting that herpes can survive for several hours on a toilet seat suspect. The investigators in the study actually painted the toilet seat with an infectious dose of herpes that quite possibly contained far more organisms than would ever come from one or two lesions on a single individual with active herpes.

• The ability of the organism to get inside another body. This must be accomplished through a break in the skin or through contact with certain body mucosa. The skin itself provides a barrier against the herpes organism.

There are now unfounded fears about toilet seats and public facilities. Examples: Quite unnecessarily, people have given up using public swimming pools. Employers are asking about herpes in job interviews. Others are requiring employees with a history of herpes to be isolated at work and to be given sick leave during active bouts of the disease. These precautions are absurd.

Sensible precautions:

Family members who have any kind of herpes —genital or the cold-sore variety—should not permit those lesions to come in direct contact with other body surfaces. Individuals with open genital herpes lesions or herpes lip lesions should not participate in oral-genital sex.

If a family member has herpes, follow the basic rules of hygiene around the house. Wash your hands after touching the lesions, whether the lesions are yours or someone else's.

If family members with a history of genital herpes have sores present, they must avoid transmitting the infection to their sexual partners. Patients with active lesions should avoid sex while lesions are present. Abstinence may seem extreme, but genital herpes has serious consequences.

Infants passing through an infected mother's birth canal are at high risk. There appears to be a high correlation between cervical cancer and genital herpes. It can be extremely painful.

It is possible for women and some men to have an active infection and not be aware of it because there are no obvious symptoms such as visible surface sores. A woman, for example, could have an active lesion on the cervix. If you suspect an infection, check with your doctor.

Source: Dr. Eugene Washington, Center for Disease Control, Atlanta, GA.

FULL BLADDER RISKS INFECTION

Urinary-tract infections decrease significantly when the bladder is emptied often. A full bladder restricts blood flow to itself. This delays the arrival of white blood cells to combat infections. Point: When the bladder signals a visit to the bathrroom, go immediately. Antidote to a very mild urinary infection: Cranberry juice and Vitamin C. They create an acidic environment that inhibits bacterial growth.

ALL ABOUT COLDS

People pick up relatively few cold viruses from their associates at work. An office may have many people nursing colds, but chances are few of them have the same virus strain.

The majority of colds are caught at home. And the main carriers are children, who are exposed to the most viruses through close association and direct physical contact with their playmates. The parents then catch the cold from the sick child.

Current research indicates that most colds are probably spread by direct physical contact. Large droplets in the air in the immediate vicinity of a cough or sneeze are a likely source, too.

The viruses grow in the nose and eyes (but not the mouth). When infected people wipe or blow their noses sloppily, some of the cold virus can get onto their hands. Outside the body, the virus can survive as long as a day. Result: Unless washed off, it spreads to toys, furniture, drinking cups and other people's hands. Shaking hands with someone who has a cold and then rubbing your eyes can be riskier than standing directly in front of a sneezing person.

Colds are contagious, beginning with the onset of symptoms until the symptoms vanish. Worst period: The first two to three days. Children and adults with colds should avoid physical contact with other people at the workplace and at home as much as is practical.

Advice to snifflers: Use a tissue or handkerchief when covering coughs and sneezes. Bare hands pick up the virus and spread the cold.

Defensive tactics:

• Wash your hands frequently when around people who have colds, especially after touching things they have handled.

• Keep hands away from noses and eyes.

• Do not rely on household sprays to disinfect objects. Their value is unproven.

Source: Dr. Jack Gwaltney, Jr., professor of internal medicine, University of Virginia Medical School.

ASPIRIN WON'T HELP YOUR COLD

Taking aspirin to bring down a fever when you have a virus actually weakens your body's defenses. Interferon, a protein produced by the body to fight off the virus, works less effectively when the fever is brought down.

Source: American Physical Fitness Research Institute.

ANTIHISTAMINES CAN PROLONG A COLD

Discontinue antihistamines when a cold shifts to the chest. They help relieve upper respiratory conditions, but can aggravate lower respiratory ones, such as bronchitis and asthma. By reducing mucus production, antihistamines make bronchial secretions stickier. This plugs the bronchial tubes more and makes it harder to clear them with coughing.

Source: John H. Dirckx, M.D., writing in *Consultant.*

TLC FIGHTS THE COMMON COLD

Hot chicken soup is beloved by sick people. Yet the tender loving care that usually accompanies it may be at least as helpful to the patient. Levels of agents in the immune system that fight colds and viruses rose when subjects in a test saw a movie about Mother Teresa as she worked with the poor in India. Levels of these agents stayed high as the viewers later recalled times when they had been cared for by others.

Source: Research by Harvard University psychologists David McClelland and Carol Kirshnit reported in *Psychology Today.*

WINE AS A COLD REMEDY

It acts as a short-term antibiotic, particularly after the first signs of a cold. Remedy recipe: Pour a bottle of red wine into a double boiler and heat to 140°. Add a slice of lemon or orange peel and a tablespoonful of cinnamon. Simmer for three minutes. Drink one glassful twice a day for three days.

Source: *Stay Healthy With Wine* by Marjorie Michaels, Doubleday, New York.

COUGH MEDICINES THAT DON'T DO WHAT THEY ADVERTISE

The Federal Drug Administration is beginning to agree with an increasing number of independent doctors who say commercial cough remedies are of little benefit. Basic Drawback: Virtually all commercial medications interfere with the body's natural way of clearing the respiratory tract, which is coughing. Doctors are especially concerned with:

• Antihistamines, which they say work by thickening, not thinning, lung secretions. Good only for allergies.
• Decongestants, which might be good for extreme stuffiness but are otherwise of doubtful effectiveness.
• Expectorants, which drug companies say loosen mucus and phlegm, although the evidence is scanty.
• Suppressants, which suppress the brain's cough reflex. They are especially hazardous for people with asthma or bronchitis who rely on coughing to breathe when their lungs are not clear.

Skeptics of cough medications say home remedies may be more effective and less risky. Chicken soup and fruit juices may work as well as an expectorant. Vaporizers and humidifiers offer relief, as does a drop of honey on the back of the tongue.

Source: Dr. Sidney Wolfe, M.D., and others, quoted in *Executive Fitness*.

MEASLES VACCINE ALERT

A measles vaccine should be given to any adult born after 1956 who has not had either a documented case of the disease or an injection with live-virus vaccine. (A medical study of blood samples has shown that most people born before 1956 either have had the disease or are immune to it.) Caution: The killed-virus vaccines available between 1963 and 1967 are ineffective. If you're unsure if you're protected, it is advisable to have a live-virus vaccine administered.

Source: Interview with Steven Wassilak, MD, medical epidemiologist, division of immunization, Centers for Disease Control, Atlanta.

NOSEDROP WARNING

Nasal decongestants can make your stuffy nose worse. They may give temporary relief—but when they wear off, the tissues become more congested. Continual use can cause formation of skin folds (polyps) or thickening of the nose lining. Both inhibit breathing. Cilia (the microscopic hairs lining the nose) need some mucus to lubricate them and to help them filter dust. Constant drying up of the mucus by decongestants causes the cilia to become irritated and inflamed. Other side effects: The chemicals used in the drops can cause blood pressure problems (especially under anesthesia) and reduction of the adrenaline needed to handle stress. Also, fluid can drip into the lungs from the nasal passages, causing pneumonia.

Source: *Prevention.*

SOOTHING A SORE THROAT

Gargling is soothing to an inflamed throat, and it also helps the healing process along by cleaning the infected area and stimulating circulation. Effective home solutions: One-fourth teaspoonful of salt dissolved in eight ounces of warm (not hot) water. Dose: Gently gargle the full glass of salt water (about 10 swizzles) every two to four hours.

EATING SMART TO BEAT A VIRUS

Your body has to fight viral infections by itself. Antibiotics won't do a thing for colds, flu or stomach virus or for the sore throats and diarrhea that often accompany them. You can help your system recover by watching carefully what you eat and drink.

In general, when a virus strikes, you should eat simply. Avoid foods that are hard to digest, like fried dishes, rich sauces, gravy and heavy desserts. Extra vitamins are not necessary during a short illness (four or five days). If you are not hungry, don't force yourself to eat. A day or two without food won't hurt you, but you do need liquids. As you recover, your appetite will pick up, and you can work back to your normal diet.

Specifically, how you should eat depends upon where the virus strikes and what your symptoms are. The same virus can cause different reactions in each of its victims.

Fever. High fever makes you sweat. The dangers are dehydration and loss of salt. Make yourself drink liquids with a high salt content, like Gatorade, tomato juice or lemonade with a pinch of salt. If you are hot, treat yourself to cool drinks. In the chills stage, drink hot soup or tea (although tea alone can increase urine output and cause further dehydration). Fever burns up extra calories. But weight loss from a virus is usually due more to water loss and dehydration than to fat loss. Keep it plain: Toast, soup, cottage cheese and yogurt.

Grandma was right.

Stuffy nose. There's some evidence that chicken soup actually does help clear nasal passages.

Headache: When headaches are brought on by fever and sinus congestion, caffeine can bring relief because it constricts blood vessels. Drink tea, coffee or colas, as well as aspirin preparations that include caffeine. It is important to treat sinus headaches with decongestants.

Upset stomach. Nausea and vomiting can cause dehydration, as well as a lack of desire to eat or drink. You don't have to eat, but liquids are important. Chew on ice chips or sip water or soda. Milk is often hard for adults to digest. When the stomach is unsettled, milk should be avoided for several days. Coffee and alcohol also irritate the stomach. Some people cannot tolerate citrus juice because of the acid. When the nausea is over, start eating light foods such as unbuttered toast, yogurt and cottage cheese. Avoid fats and spicy foods for several days.

Diarrhea. Replacing lost fluids, potassium and sodium, with juice or broth is necessary with severe diarrhea. Best: Sweet lemonade or Gatorade. When you are feeling better, you can begin eating simple foods with slightly constipating properties: rice, bananas and mild cheeses.

Preventive eating. A healthy diet for keeping fit and staving off infections is high in fiber and complex carbohydrates (whole grains, fresh fruits and vegetables), with adequate protein (meat, fish and dairy products) and low in fats (particularly saturated ones like butter and cheese) and simple carbohydrates (sweets).

Source: Bruce H. Yaffe, M.D., New York.

HAY FEVER REMEDIES

For mild, occasional cases, over-the-counter antihistamines will give relief. If one kind doesn't work, another may. Caution: All antihistamines tend to make you drowsy (don't drive), and all interact dangerously with alcohol (don't drink). For more severe and longer-lasting cases, professional help is needed. New steroid nasal sprays, available only by prescription, give quick relief with few side effects. For seasonal sufferers: Wash your hair before bed to keep pollen off your pillow. Keep the shoes you wear outdoors out of the bedroom. Keep windows closed until 9 pm. Use the car air conditioner while driving. Don't go outside in early morning or late evening, when cool air puts more pollen at nose level.

Source: Dr. Stanley Wolf, The Allergy Center, Silver Spring, MD.

SINUS REMEDIES THAT BACKFIRE

The sinuses are four pairs of spaces in the human skull, each lined with mucous membranes. When these membranes swell, the drainage of mucus slows or stops, bringing painful discomfort. Causes: Primarily viral infections, such as a cold or flu. But sinus membranes also swell from pressure changes during air flights, from swimming or diving in chlorinated water, or from sudden changes of temperature, such as going from the hot sun to an air-conditioned room.

Over-the-counter drug tablets and capsules work only temporarily. When this medicine wears off, it leaves the patient with more pain, which requires more medication. The same is true for nosedrops and nasal spray.

Best: Apply hot-water compresses to the affected areas. Drink extra fluids. Use a humidifier or vaporizer in your room. If bacteria are the cause of the problem, try a week or 10 days of antibiotics prescribed by a physician.

HAVING YOUR TONSILS OUT

Tonsillectomies, while almost never recommended for healthy children today, may be necessary for those who have recurring throat infections, snore during sleep or pause in breathing, or breathe through their mouths.
Source: *Journal of the American Medical Association.*

HOW TO TREAT STUTTERING

Stuttering, usually regarded as an emotional problem, may actually result from faulty neuromuscular control of the larynx. Many stutterers become fluent when singing or whispering, which involve movements of the larynx that differ from those required for normal speech. Of six stutterers who recently underwent laryngectomies for cancer, four are now totally fluent and the other two have improved to some degree.
Source: *Science News.*

WHAT CAUSES CHOKING?

An estimated 9,000 Americans choke to death every year, most frequently while dining out.

Researchers at the Swallowing Center at Johns Hopkins Medical Institutions in Baltimore now suspect that muscle and nerve disorders of the throat are at fault in many cases. Swallowing problems can appear at any age, but stroke victims seem to be particularly susceptible. Symptoms include difficulty in swallowing, coughing, a lump-in-the-throat sensation, voice changes and occasional choking episodes. Treatment ranges from surgery to swallow-safe diets. People with swallowing disorders can choke in their sleep. But a restaurant seems to distract many sufferers from the normal swallowing process and to stimulate choking episodes. Precaution: Always sit up straight while eating and keep your head erect. Never tilt your head back or eat while lying down.

SAVE YOURSELF FROM CHOKING

A choking person can save himself by falling so that a table or a chair hits his diaphragm, thrusting it up against the lungs. It is the forced expulsion of air from the lungs that blows out the obstruction.
Source: Dr. Henry J. Heimlich, originator of the "Heimlich maneuver" (whereby a second person saves the choker).

IF TONGUE DEPRESSORS MAKE YOU GAG

If you gag when the doctor applies a tongue depressor, it helps to sing "Ah" in falsetto. You may feel silly, but you'll avoid the scary gagging reflex.

HEARING LOSS FROM STEREOS

Portable stereocassette players can impair hearing if they're used for lengthy periods of time at high volumes. A survey of Manhattan wearers found that people using the sets to block out street noise had the volume at dangerously high levels. Recommended: Avoid continuous use. Give the nerve fibers in your ears a break from it.

For information: Better Hearing Institute (800) 424-8576.

HOW TO TREAT FEVER

When you have a fever, take aspirin or acetaminophen only when your temperature is over 102° and you're uncomfortable. Dress lightly enough so that body heat can escape. Sponge with tepid water, not alcohol (the vapors can be dangerous). Take a bath and wash your hair if you feel like it—the evaporating water may lower your temperature. Drink eight to twelve glasses of liquid a day to avoid dehydration.

Take your temperature first thing in the morning for the most accurate reading. Wait 30 minutes after eating, drinking, smoking or exercising so your mouth will be neither cooled down nor heated up. Shake down the thermometer to below normal—mercury rises from the last reading. Relax. Hold the thermometer under the back of your tongue for four minutes. Don't move your tongue, breathe through your mouth or talk. Rectal thermometers: When using a rectal thermometer on an infant, lubricate it with water-soluble jelly and hold the baby's legs so a quick movement won't dislodge it or break the glass. Leave it in at least two minutes. New disposable thermometers are not very accurate. Better: The old-fashioned kind.

Call the doctor for a fever when: (1) A child's temperature goes above 102° or an adult's over 101°. (2) The fever persists for more than 24 hours with no obvious cause. (3) The fever lasts for more than 72 hours even if there's an obvious cause. (4) An infant under three months old has any temperature elevation. (5) There is a serious disease involved. Bottom line: Call the doctor when you feel really sick, even if you haven't got a fever.

SIMPLE CAUSES OF BACKACHE

Backache may be caused by discomfort and tension arising from poor everyday living hab-its. Examples: Gobbling food, sleeping on a sagging mattress, wearing uncomfortable clothing, using appliances in a restrictive way or simply sitting too long.

Tips to avoid backaches:
• Clothing should never be tight. This applies to pajamas and nightgowns as well as to everyday dress.
• Avoid narrow-toed shoes. They tense the leg muscles, which in turn affect the back. Heels should not be too loose or too tight. Either extreme produces ankle sway, which works its way up to the back and neck. Women's high-heeled shoes shorten the hamstring and calf muscles, causing the tension that frequently leads to backache.
• Toes of socks and stockings should not be tight. You should be able to wiggle your toes freely.
• Too high or too tight a collar can cause a stiff neck. Wear collars half a size larger and, if your neck is short, stick to soft, narrow collars.
• Narrow shoulder straps of brassieres can cause shoulder and upper back pain, especially if they are pulled too tight.
• Wide shoulders require bigger pillows for those who sleep on their sides.
• Foam rubber pillows force the neck into a rigid position. Use a feather pillow.
• Never sit in one position for more than an hour or two. Get up and move around.
• On car trips, stop frequently to limber up.
• While reading, avoid strain by keeping the page at a comfortable distance. It's also important to have enough light.
• To use muscles more evenly, office workers should shift the telephone from one side of the desk to the other each day.
• Instead of tensing when the phone rings, make it a practice to shrug the shoulders before reaching out to pick up the receiver.

Source: *Backache, Stress and Tension* by Hans Krause, M.D., Pocket Books, New York.

GOOD NEWS FOR DISK SUFFERERS

Slipped-disk sufferers who don't respond to bed rest or traction now have another alternative to surgery. It's a medication derived from papayas called Chymodiactin. The injected drug dissolves protruding disk tissue to ease pain-causing pressure on surrounding nerves. When it's effective, positive results are usually apparent within a week, though patients may experience temporary lower-back stiffness and possibly muscle soreness.

Source: *Medical World News.*

WHY YOU HAVE A HEADACHE

Usually, headaches aren't serious. Tension headache: Pressure is equal on both sides of the head, but may come from front or back. Tight neck muscles or emotion could be the cause. Migraine or vascular headache: Throbbing is stronger on one side. The sides may alternate during an attack. Warning symptoms (flashing lights, blind spots) occur for one-fifth of sufferers. Cigarette smoke, chocolate or cheese can trigger attacks. Hangovers: The throbbing on both sides of the head has several causes. Complex flavorings (i.e., brandies) are toxic, and dehydration interferes with the body's water levels. Surprise: Allergies and sinus congestion are rarely the cause of headaches.

FOOD THAT GIVES YOU HEADACHES

• MSG is not the *only* culprit. Look out for tyramine-containing foods like chicken livers, chocolate and pickled herring. Drinks that have it include beer, champagne, red wine and sherry.

• Ice-cream headache is a brief, but intense, pain in the throat, head or face that results from biting into ice cream. The pain is a physiological response of the warm tissues of the mouth to the sudden assault by cold. The pain is sometimes felt throughout the head because cranial nerve branches in the area spread the pain impulse along a broad path. Prevention: Allow small amounts of ice cream to melt in the mouth before eating successive large bites.

Source: *Freedom from Headaches* by Joel R. Saper, M.D., and Kenneth R. Magee, M.D., Simon & Schuster, New York.

TREATING PAIN WITH ICE

Ice rather than heat (the traditional method) may be the best long-term treatment for muscle and joint aches caused by overexercising. Apply the ice for 10–15 minutes before and after gently exercising the sore area. It has a mild anesthetic effect that minimizes exercising pain. Prolonged use of heat can actually increase swelling.

Source: Rob Roy McGregor, M.D.

EASE THOSE ACHING KNEES

Arthritic pains in the knees are effectively relieved with bags of ice water. This simple, drug-free treatment consists of application of the ice bags above and below the knee for 20 minutes three times daily. Bonus: The relief enables many sufferers of rheumatoid arthritis to cut back on doses of potentially harmful pain-killing drugs. To make an ice bag: Put six cubes of ice in a plastic bag and add a quart of cold water.

Source: Dr. Peter D. Utsinger, Germantown Medical Center, Philadelphia, PA.

QUICK FIX FOR LEG CRAMPS

Leg cramps can usually be alleviated by firmly pinching your upper lip for 20-30 seconds.

Source: Dr. Donald Cooper, former US Olympics team doctor, in New York.

DANGERS OF POORLY FITTING GLASSES

Poorly fitting eyeglasses that tilt to one side or slide down the nose can cause an unconscious imbalance of the head and the neck. This may result in compensation by the shoulders, hips and spine in order to maintain balance, causing both pain and stiffness in the muscles, tendons and joints.

Source: Lionel A. Walpin, M.D.

QUICK FIXES THAT REALLY WORK

• Muscle trick to relieve cramps and spasms: Contract the muscles in the muscle group opposite the one that is cramped. This confuses the troubled muscle, making it relax. (Example: If your calf cramps, tighten the muscles in the front of your lower leg to relieve the discomfort.)
Source: *American Health.*

• To cure hiccups, swallow a teaspoonful of granulated sugar or eat crackers. The slight irritation in the back of the throat interrupts the hiccup cycle. Alternatives: Suck on a lemon wedge soaked in Angostura bitters. Or induce sneezing by sniffing pepper. Or take a sniff of something with a strong aroma, such as vinegar.

• Instant ice pack. Try a bag of frozen vegetables (like peas or corn niblets). The bag is clean, watertight and pliable enough to fit almost any part of the body.
Source: *Harvard Medical School Health Letter.*

• Drugless headache cures: (1) Eat a cheese sandwich. (2) Take a hot shower, followed by a cold one—until you shiver. (3) Place crushed ice in the mouth and throat (not for the elderly or ill). (4) Massage the lower part of the big toe and beneath all the toes. (5) Breathe into a paper bag (stops hyperventilation). (6) Ask a partner to press your "trigger" points (temples, back of the neck, below your shoulder blades). (7) Rotate a hairbrush in small circles, starting above your temples, and working it down over your ears to your neck.
Source: *Spring.*

• Mosquito-bite relief. Turn your hair dryer on the bite for a minute. The warm, dry air dulls the itch.

• Bad-tasting medicine goes down more easily when you rub an ice cube over the youngster's tongue first. This temporarily "freezes" the taste buds to make the medication more palatable.
Source: *Practical Parenting Tips* by Vicki Lansky, Meadowbrook Press, Deephaven, MN.

• Pills slide down the throat more easily if the patient swallows some water before taking the medicine. The water moistens the mucus membranes, which facilitates the swallowing of pills with water. This works best for someone whose mouth is dry from sleeping and for those who are dehydrated, such as the elderly.
Source: Joan Durbak, RN, Newark, OH, writing in *RN.*

• Avoid the natural inclination to bend your head back when swallowing a capsule. It's better to tilt your head or upper body forward. Then the lighter-than-water capsule can float toward the throat.
Source: *Modern Maturity.*

• Stop fingernail loss that usually occurs after you hit your fingertip with a hammer or crush it in a door. Squeeze the nail steadily for about five minutes. Start immediately after you hit it. Nail loss results because a bruise forms under the nail bed and displaces it. Squeezing prevents blood from leaking out to form the bruise.

HAZARDOUS SUNGLASSES

Ordinary dark sunglasses may actually be harmful to your eyes. Reason: By causing the pupils to dilate, the glasses allow even greater amounts of harmful ultraviolet light to penetrate the eyes. Better: Lenses that screen out at least 75% (and ideally 95%) of ultraviolet rays (available from opticians).

Source: Skin Cancer Foundation, New York.

EYE DROPS CAN MAKE YOUR EYES REDDER

Overusing eye drops can trigger a rebound effect, causing your eyes to stay red with drops or without.

Best: Apply a saline solution known as artificial tears as often as you like. But avoid daily use of *vasoconstrictors*, which shrink surface blood vessels. Your pharmacist can help you distinguish between the two varieties.

Source: *Cosmopolitan*, 224 W. 57 St., New York 10019.

SKIN CANCERS ARE ON THE RISE

Contributing factor: The thinning ozone layer. Without this natural shield around the earth, more ultraviolet radiation penetrates the atmosphere. These rays cause melanomas and other skin cancers. Why the ozone layer is thinning: Widespread use of chlorofluorocarbons used in aerosol sprays, refrigeration and air-conditioning systems, insulation-blowing devices and liquid fast-freezing of food. Prognosis: Today, one in three melanomas is diagnosed too late to save the patient's life. One reason: Patients often do not disrobe completely during physical exams, leaving areas of skin unexamined.
Source: *RN.*

Malignant melanoma (skin cancer characterized by a black molelike growth) can now often be cured if caught early. Finding: Survival rate after eight years is about 99% when the lesion is cut out while still very thin. Advice: Ask your doctor to check for melanomas at every visit. The cancer appears to be related to sun exposure.
Source: *Medical World News.*

THE BEST SOAP FOR YOUR SKIN TYPE

Soft soap. Contrary to traditional wisdom, a soap with a high pH content, or high alkalinity, does not irritate normal skin. It does cause soap film, especially in hard-water areas. Who should be cautious in choosing a soap: The elderly if they have sun-damaged skin. Women who have overused makeup and soaps. People with very dry skin. Best for these skin types: A petroleum-based, synthetic imitation soap. This type has gentler ingredients as well as added moisturizers.

DANGERS OF "UNSCENTED" COSMETICS

Cosmetics labeled "unscented" can still cause the itchy, swollen skin known as dermatitis because they contain masking perfumes. *Best bet:* Look for "fragrance free" labels on makeup and creams. Dab perfume only on clothes or hair.
Source: American Academy of Dermatology, cited in *Women's Health.*

DANDRUFF SHAMPOOS THAT DON'T WORK

Antidandruff shampoos can actually cause the condition, a study shows. Reason: The harsh solutions irritate the scalp. Simply switching to a milder shampoo may control the problem. It's also a good idea to discontinue the use of hair oils. Suggestion: Visit a dermatologist, who can prescribe a topical antibacterial agent.
Source: *International Journal of Dermatology.*

LASERS FOR SKIN PROBLEMS

They can remove dilated blood vessels, birthmarks and tattoos. The blue-green argon laser is absorbed by red and brown pigment; the carbon-dioxide laser, used to fade tattoos, is not color-dependent. The bloodless procedures are performed in short sessions under local anesthetic. Several treatments may be needed. Cost: $125 per treatment. Availability: At centers located in most large cities in the US.* A pioneer laser dermatologist, Dr. Elizabeth McBurney, 1538 Front St., Slidell, LA 70459 is training many more doctors in laser use.

*To find the center nearest you, contact American Society for Laser Medicine & Surgery, 813 Second St., Wausau, WI 54401.

DEODORANTS VS. ANTIPERSPIRANTS

Deodorants cut down on bacteria but do not halt perspiration. Antiperspirants reduce perspiration by shrinking the openings of the sweat glands. They also control odor by fighting bacteria. Neither deodorants nor antiperspirants are toxic. But people with sensitive skin may find antiperspirants an irritant. (Such people should use unscented deodorants, which are less apt to cause allergic-type reactions.) Best underarm protection: Either roll-ons or creams. Because they are water-based, they are less irritating.

EXCESSIVE SWEATING MAY SIGNAL A PROBLEM

Unexplained sweating can be a symptom of serious disease. Exertion, excitement, anxiety and ingestion of spicy foods may all cause increased perspiration. But excessive sweating may also be symptomatic of hyperthyroidism, undiagnosed infections with chronic fever and rheumatoid arthritis. Other causes: Some painkillers (Dalmane, Demerol and Talwin), heart drugs (Isordil and Peritrate).

Source: *RN.*

PREVENTING SMELLY FEET

Smelly feet can be prevented quite easily by keeping the feet dry and cool to minimize bacteria growth. Strategy: Wear leather shoes (leather breathes), and alternate pairs so they can dry out. Avoid socks or stockings of synthetic fibers. Best: Light cotton. Use ordinary talcum powder. For special problems: Prescription antiperspirants are available.

Source: *The Harvard Medical School Health Letter.*

ATHLETE'S FOOT IS HEREDITARY

People do inherit a vulnerability to this fungus infection. Patients with incurable athlete's foot were tissue typed. Result: The patients matched in one linked group of genes. This suggests a shared genetic predisposition to the problem.

Source: Study by Dr. A. Razzaque Ahmed, dermatologist, UCLA School of Medicine.

HOW TO CHOOSE THE RIGHT SUN LOTION

You can now determine which sun screen is best for you, thanks to sophisticated tests that have established the degree of protection given by various sun-screen brands. The measure of protection a sun screen affords is its SPF number. This number tells the length of time it takes the sun's rays to penetrate the screen and burn your skin. The higher the SPF number, the longer you can stay in the sun without burning. Example: If you're going sailing for four hours, you'll want a screen with the highest available SPF—15. The lowest SPF number is 2, virtually no protection against the sun's rays.

In addition to giving protection against the sun, a sun screen should be durable. It should not "wash off" as soon as you begin to perspire. Other important properties: It should not be toxic to your skin, smell bad, feel offensive or stain.

To find the best screens: Look for the Skin Cancer Foundation seal of approval when choosing a screen. The foundation conducted tests of the leading sun screens to determine their actual effectiveness outdoors and the degree to which they have all the other important properties (durability, lack of toxicity, etc.). Their seal of approval was assigned to the brands that met these standards. The seal appears on the container.

Brands that don't have the seal of approval aren't necessarily ineffective. They may simply not have been included in the tests.

So-called "alternate" sun screens of aloe or coconut compounds are worthless as protection.

Tan gradually. Don't sit in the sun until you get red. Redness means it's too late—the sun's rays have already damaged your skin.

Source: Dr. Perry Robins, associate professor of dermatology, New York University Medical Center.

How sun-screen number is determined: The time it takes the skin to arrive at the state of minimal redness, unprotected, is divided into the time it takes for the skin to reach that condition with a sun screen. This gives the screen's SPF number. Example: If it takes 10 minutes under a bright sun to become slightly red, and it takes 90 minutes wearing a screen to arrive at that same condition, the screen had the SPF number of 9.

SUNSCREEN DANGER

Discolored sunscreens are dangerous to your health. Old sunscreens separate and lose their effectiveness at screening out harmful ultra-violet rays. Discard sunscreens that have lost their creamy consistency, avoid buying sunscreens packaged in discolored, smudged or beaten-up bottles, and mark new sunscreens with date of purchase.

Source: Dr. Madhu Pathak, senior associate in dermatology at Massachusetts General Hospital.

ASPIRIN CAN RELIEVE SUNBURN

Minimize sunburn inflammation by taking two aspirin three to four times daily as soon as you notice you're turning red. Aspirin's main component, acetylsalicylic acid, cuts down on the inflammation caused by dilation of surface blood vessels (sunburn symptom). The aspirin also relieves sunburn pain. Caution: Aspirin in these dosages also can cause stomach upset.

Source: Dr. Harvey Blank, dermatologist, quoted in *Self.*

MEDICATIONS AND SUN DON'T MIX

Many common drugs can make your skin more susceptible to burning. Major ones: Tetracyclines (antibiotics), sulfa drugs (antibacterials), phenothiazine derivatives (major tranquilizers), griseofulvins (antifungals), sulfonylureas (anti-diabetics) and thiazides (diuretics).

Source: Maureen Poh-Fitzpatrick, Columbia University College of Physicians and Surgeons, writing in *Self.*

Sun rash or a quick burn can result when people with sensitive skin put cologne or perfume on areas of the body exposed to the sun. (Some soaps and deodorants may also produce this effect.) The ailment: Photodermatitis. Remedy: Apply colognes and perfume to clothing, not to skin.

SMOKING AND SURGERY DON'T MIX

Smoking produces carboxyhemoglobin (nonoxygen carrier) in the blood, which takes space away from hemoglobin (an oxygen carrier). The reduced amount of oxygen carried to the tissues affects the body like anemia, greatly reducing the body's ability to withstand the trauma of surgery. Helpful: Stop smoking at least 12 hours before surgery to give your body time to get rid of the carboxyhemoglobin buildup.

SMOKING MAY CAUSE IMPOTENCE

Even a single cigarette causes enough constriction of peripheral blood vessels that a thermographic camera shows a drop in hand temperature before and after the smoke. In men particularly sensitive to tobacco, an evening of smoking can so constrict the flow of blood to the penis that a full erection is impossible. While this phenomenon is temporary, long-term smoking can have a permanent adverse effect on potency by inducing arteriosclerosis.

Source: Arne M. Olsson, University of Lund, Sweden, writing in *Medical Aspects of Human Sexuality.*

SMOKING AND ALZHEIMER'S

In a health study conducted by Harvard University, it was observed that individuals who smoked more than one pack of cigarettes a day were four times as likely to develop Alzheimer's disease as those who smoked less. Reason: Unknown.

Source: Stuart L. Shalat, ScD, assistant professor of epidemiology and medicine, Yale University School of Medicine.

LOW-TAR CIGARETTES AREN'T SO HEALTHY

Smoking low-tar cigarettes increases exposure to other toxic substances in the tobacco and paper. Reason: Since low-tar cigarettes are milder than those high in tar, smokers generally inhale them more deeply and more often.
Source: *The Lancet.*

Danger comes not only from tar, nicotine and carbon monoxide but from unknown chemicals added to cigarettes. Tobacco companies have refused to reveal voluntarily the hundreds of chemicals added to cigarettes. Thus far, the FDA has chosen not to force them to do so, despite requests from the American Cancer Society and the American Lung Association. Low-tar/low-nicotine brands don't seem to reduce the risk of heart disease. Highest heart-attack risk: Filter cigarettes without perforations in their filters. They have a higher carbon-monoxide content than unfiltered cigarettes.
Source: *The Harvard Medical School Health Letter.*

A SAFER CIGARETTE

A cigarette with an additive to protect smokers from lung cancer was developed in the 1970s by tobacco products manufacturer Liggett & Meyers, but never marketed. Reason: The company's attorneys warned that marketing the safer cigarette would be admitting that Liggett's other tobacco products were destructive.

MOST FORMER SMOKERS START AGAIN

Readdicted former smokers. Three-fourths of the hard-core smokers who kick the habit begin smoking again within six months. Their moments of vulnerability: (1) Parties where the ex-smoker is having a good time with people who are smoking. (2) Periods of stress. (3) Times of relaxation.
Source: University of South Florida study cited in *Monitor.*

SMOKING WHILE DRINKING CAN KILL

Cigarette smoke and alcohol are a lethal mixture, especially when held together in the mouth. New finding: When subjects drink and smoke simultaneously, a chemical called ethyl nitrite appears in detectable amounts in the breath. This chemical produces mutations, often carcinogenic, in living cells. Heaviest concentrations of the chemical: When the subject holds the alcohol drink and the smoke in the mouth together for as long as 10 seconds.

Source: A study by Dr. John MacDonald of Fairfield University and Anders Jonsson of the University of Stockholm.

ACCURATE RADON TESTING

Radon testing isn't conclusive the first time unless the reading is very low—below four picocuries per liter. But if you get a reading higher than that, don't panic. It may be a temporary wave of radon, not a permanent condition. You need at least a year of follow-up testing to get a conclusive picture of high radon content. Recommended: If your area is reported to have a high incidence of radon, contact your state environmental agency for a copy of the Environmental Protection Agency's listing of companies that provide reliable long-term radon testing kits.

MODERATE DRINKING CAN BE HARMFUL

Even moderate drinking may be bad news for some people (susceptibility varies widely). Serious mental and physical disabilities can sometimes result from intake of three to four drinks a day (or fewer if alcohol content is high)

Sleep disorders. Sleeplessness, and awakening early. Reason: Alcohol depresses body functions for four to six hours. So an evening drinker may awaken at 4 am or 5 am, as the body begins to rebound. (Similarly, lunch-time drinkers may get nervous by late day and decide to have another drink.)

Source: Dr. Robert Millman, psychiatrist, New York Hospital.

ALCOHOL LINKED TO HEART DISEASE

Researchers have discovered chemical compounds, called fatty acid ethyl esters, in the hearts of people who died while intoxicated. These may explain the connection between alcohol and heart disease. Potential effect: Discovery of the role these compounds play in heart disease could lead to the development of drugs to counteract them.

Source: Study by Washington University School of Medicine.

ALCOHOL MAY CAUSE VITAMIN DEFICIENCY

Vitamin B_1 deficiency often leads to neurological ailments such as loss of memory or muscle coordination. Background: Vitamin B_1 (thiamine) helps the brain use glucose as a food. Without thiamine, the brain risks death by starvation. Signs of vitamin B_1 deficiency: Behavior changes, depression, insomnia, chest pain and chronic fatigue. Cause: Excessive drinking.

THE ALCOHOL/ACCIDENT CONNECTION

Alcohol causes more than just auto accidents. High alcohol levels are found in 25% of home-accident victims. Half of fatal falls and 75% of fatalities from choking, drowning, burns and assault are also alcohol-related.

Source: Internal Medicine News.

DON'T WALK WHILE DRINKING

Walking in traffic when tipsy can be as dangerous as driving after drinking. Finding: Over one-third of adult pedestrians killed by a vehicle had been drinking. In 72% of the cases, they —not the driver—were to blame. Most dangerous time: 1:00 am–3:00 am, when bars close.

Source: Journal of American Insurance.

HANGOVER HELP

There is no cure for inebriation nor any magic formula to prevent the headache and general malaise that follow an evening of drinking too much alcohol too quickly. However, some measures can keep a night on the town from being a total disaster.

• Eat fatty or oily food before you have the first drink. That lines your stomach and slows the body's absorption of alcohol. (Cheese and nuts are good choices.)

• Eat starches while you drink to soak up the alcohol. (Bread or crackers work.)

• Avoid spirits with high levels of cogeners (additives that can cause toxic effects). Brandy, red wine, dark rum and sherry are the worst. Vodka and white wine are the least adulterated.

If you wake up with a hangover, you can only try to treat the symptoms and help bring back to normal all the bodily functions disrupted by alcohol. Some suggestions:

• A dry mouth is a sign of dehydration. Drink plenty of water to replace the lost fluid.

• Alcohol depletes the system of many nutrients, particularly vitamins A, B, B6 and C and minerals such as niacin, calcium, magnesium and potassium. Take a multivitamin that includes minerals.

• Take charcoal tablets to speed up the removal of the cogeners (four tablets if you are small and up to six for large people). Cabbage and vitamin C are reputed to help in this area as well.

• To work the alcohol out of your system (actually to metabolize it), a little exercise is useful. It increases your intake of oxygen, and oxygen speeds up this process. So does the fructose found in honey and fruit juices.

• For pain or nausea, over-the-counter analgesics or antacids are the antidote.

• "A little hair of the dog that bit you" is an old cure that has some basis in reality. The brain cells affected by alcohol can return to normal quite suddenly. This explains the supersensitivity to noise and smells associated with hangover. A small amount of alcohol (one to one-and-a-half ounces) can ease your brain back into awareness. Recommended: If you try this panacea, mix the spirits with something nutritious like cream. Other possibilities: A can of beer. A Fernet Branca, a packaged alcoholic mixture that includes herbs and folk-medicine standbys like camomile and aloe.

Source: *The Hangover Handbook* by David Outerbridge, Harmony Books, New York.

The highest rating for morning-after headaches goes to brandy, with red wine running a close second. In descending order of toxicity: Dark rum, sherry, scotch, whiskey, beer, white wine, gin and vodka.

Source: Study by Dr. Gaston Pawan, Middlesex Hospital, London.

YOU CAN'T SOBER UP FAST

Hard stuff. It takes the body one hour or more to get rid of one shot of whiskey, four ounces of wine or 12 ounces of beer. Exercise, black coffee or a cold shower don't reduce the alcohol levels in the bloodstream.

Source: New York State Department of Motor Vehicles.

Drunk-driving remedies due on the market soon should be eyed with suspicion. The combinations of minerals and vitamins are said to provide quick sobering up, but the FDA warns that none of the compounds is yet proved to be effective.

WOMEN AND ALCOHOL: SPECIAL CONCERNS

Heavy alcohol consumption just a few weeks into pregnancy can apparently harm the fetus, even before the woman is aware that she is pregnant.

Source: *Executive Fitness Newsletter.*

WATCH THAT WINTER DRINKING

Extremely cold weather is more dangerous if you have been drinking. Reasons: Alcohol impairs judgment, making it harder to tell when you are dangerously cold or frostbitten. Alcohol also dilates the superficial blood vessels of the skin, which allows you to lose heat more rapidly. Biggest danger: Hypothermia (body temperature drops below 94°), which can be fatal.

ONLY ABSTINENCE HELPS ALCOHOLICS

Controlled drinking for recovered alcoholics was the controversial goal of a recent, understandably well-publicized study of the problem. But follow-up analysis now indicates that alcoholics are better off when they remain abstemious. Statistics: Of those original 20 persons who tried the controlled-drinking experiment, only one remained a controlled drinker. Eight went on to drink excessively. Four died from alcohol-related causes. One is missing after becoming disabled by drinking. Six abandoned the program to swear off completely.

Source: UCLA research study reported in *Science.*

YOU AND YOUR HORMONES

Common misconception: That an underactive thyroid can cause obesity. This is virtually impossible. Reason: The thyroid regulates the interaction of body metabolism and appetite. If the thyroid is underactive, appetite will not be great enough to create obesity. About 99% of people with an underactive thyroid are not overweight. Dangerous: Thyroid hormone to treat obesity. An excessive amount can induce hyperthyroidism, causing severe side effects such as an overworked heart, muscle breakdown and psychological changes.

Source: Norbert Freinkel, MD, Kettering professor of medicine and director of the Center for Endocrinology, Metabolism and Nutrition at Northwestern University Medical School.

• Older men who have trouble attaining erections at night can do better with morning sex. Testosterone levels are higher earlier in the day. **Source:** *Medical Aspects of Human Sexuality,* New York.

• Alcohol affects a woman most on the days just before and at the start of her period. Why: Hormones influence the way alcohol is metabolized and absorbed into the body.

SHOULD GALLSTONES BE REMOVED?

Gallstones may best be left alone until they act up. Current practice: To remove them as soon as they are detected. A recent long-term study of 123 males with gallstones showed that over a 15-year period, only 16 developed problems and only 14 required surgery. About 15 million people have gallstones.
Source: William A. Gracie, M.D., reporting in *The New England Journal of Medicine.*

HOW TO TREAT VARICOSE VEINS

Varicose vein sufferers should consider surgery only as a last resort. Before surgery: Change your diet to include a high proportion of whole grains, seeds, nuts, vegetables and fruit. Avoid: Constipation, too much sitting with crossed legs, too much standing, tight clothing. Use a slant-board and elevate the foot of your bed. Walk and swim. Use elastic support stockings if the condition is severe. Surgery is not a permanent solution. The condition will reappear unless the underlying causes are corrected.
More information: *Every Woman's Book* by Paavo Airola, Health Plus, Phoenix, AZ.

FALSE ALARM ON LOW BLOOD SUGAR

Chronic hypoglycemia (low blood sugar) is extremely rare, contrary to popular opinion. Poor eating habits, though, can produce temporary cases of it. Symptoms: Trembling, sweating, weakness, heart palpitations. Typical causes of false hypoglycemia: Skipping a meal. Drinking alcohol instead of eating lunch. Going on a high-carbohydrate binge.
Source: American Council of Science and Health.

SENILITY MAY BE CURABLE

Medications can bring on reactions that resemble senility. Drugs seniors should watch: Sedatives, tranquilizers, even antihistamines.

Point: Senility is not an inevitable product of aging. Its symptoms are often induced by curable ailments. The cure might be as simple as a change of medication. Best: A physician skilled in geriatrics.
Source: National Institute of Aging, Bethesda, MD.

QUESTIONS TO ASK YOUR PLASTIC SURGEON

Plastic surgery for cosmetic reasons is surrounded by a lot of hype. The fantasy that your life will be magically transformed by surgery can play into the hands of the unscrupulous. Although the overwhelming majority of plastic surgeons are competent and ethical, there are a few bad apples.

If you know what questions to ask both yourself and your doctor before you make a commitment to surgery, you'll save heartache—to say nothing of money.

What to ask yourself:

Do I really need plastic surgery? You must be objective when you look in the mirror. Some people want surgery for a couple of wrinkles that are barely noticeable to anyone but themselves. Their vulnerability to the power of perfection may make them easy marks. How it can happen: Someone who thinks he needs a face lift begs the surgeon to "just give me a little tuck." An unethical surgeon who is pushed, instead of refusing, may put the patient under general anesthesia, make a couple of incisions and sew him up. The patient then wakes up with two healing incision lines near his ears and thinks he looks great. In reality, he has paid up to $8,000 for virtually nothing.

Criteria to follow: Would repair of an imperfection that bothers you enhance your well-being? Does that imperfection actually exist?

What do I want done. . . what will it accomplish for me? Although the psychological factor in cosmetic surgery cannot be overlooked, it must be approached realistically. Cosmetic surgery can improve your state of well-being—for some people, how they feel depends on how they look—but it usually does not change anyone's life. Many people blame all their difficulties on a particular physical defect. They delude themselves into believing that their difficulties will instantly be overcome if their physical defect is corrected.

How did you find your plastic surgeon? Did you fall prey to advertisements for low-cost surgery (with limousine service thrown in)? Like anything else—you get what you pay for. Stay away from high-pressure advertising. Best: Referral from other satisfied patients. If you don't know anyone who has had the type of surgery you want, ask your family doctor or internist for a recommendation. If you have a good relationship with your primary physician, there will be quality control. Your doctor can't afford to have his name smeared by a shlock doctor.

Have I asked for a second opinion? There's no other area where second opinions are more valuable. Only another doctor can confirm that you actually need the surgery and that the particular procedure your surgeon wants to do is reasonable for the result you seek.

What to ask your plastic surgeon:

Realistically, what will be done? Not what can be done, or what you can hope for, but what you can expect. You also want to know what will happen if you don't get the result the doctor promises. How will he remedy that situation? Will you have to pay for the unsatisfactory job? Will he do a corrective procedure at no cost? Or will he say, "Sorry, I can't help you"? Crucial: Preoperative and post-operative pictures taken by the same photographer. Only with photos can you prove that you didn't get the promised result.

What is the chance of real damage, and, if it happens, what might the extent of it be? Plastic surgeons aren't gods. They are physicians who have had extensive training in delicate repair of skin; but nobody can break the integrity of normal skin without leaving a mark. Plastic surgeons are only a bit like magicians. They leave marks in areas that are less conspicuous. But if you have a big growth in the middle of your cheek, you can't expect the doctor to cut it out without leaving a mark. Other areas of concern: The chances of infection and other complications.

Where will the surgery be done? Although many reputable plastic surgeons operate out of their own offices, surgery done in a hospital inevitably offers more quality control. There's much less room for nonprofessionalism in a hospital, where nurses and operating room teams are provided by the institution and there is peer review of a surgeon's work. Generally safest bet: A doctor who is university affiliated and teaches in a hospital or medical school.

May I see your book of before and after pictures? You may want to speak to a surgeon's other patients, but since this might violate confidentiality, he may only be willing to show you before and after pictures. If he offers you a whole book of good results, you can feel confident.

Can the surgery be done in stages? A male model had a bad result on facial moles that a plastic surgeon had treated with liquid nitrogen. His skin had darkened, and there were brown spots and scars. The surgeon hadn't done a trial on one mole, but had treated them all at one session. Suggestion: If you have many of the same defects, have one corrected first to see if you like the result.

Is there a less serious procedure that will produce a similar result? Very effective collagen and silicone injections available today eliminate both wrinkles and acne scars. Suction lipectomy can remove fat pockets. Look into such lesser procedures before undergoing full-scale surgery.

How much will it cost? How much time will it take? How long will I be out of work or away from home? Ask whatever other questions concern you. Prepare a written list. No matter how many questions you have or how trivial you feel they are. . . ask!

Source: Neal B. Schultz, MD, clinical assistant dermatologist. Mount Sinai Hospital, New York City.

FACTS ABOUT FACE-LIFTS

Each year, half a million Americans choose face-lift operations as a way to turn back the clock.

Factors that hasten this decline: Hereditary tendencies (some faces age faster than others). Cigarette smoking, which decreases blood flow to the skin. Excessive use of alcohol, poor nutrition, lack of sleep and exercise. Main culprit: Sunlight. To keep skin smooth, stay out of the sun. When exposed, apply sun-screen lotion.

A face-lift is major surgery. What is done: The facial and neck skin are literally lifted from the underlying tissue and set back in place. This gives the face a smoothed-out appearance. Possible complications: Blood clots, hemorrhages under the skin, facial-nerve injuries, abnormal scarring.

Payoff: The operation removes wrinkles and restores firmness. But at best it makes the face look 10 years younger.

Avoid: A minilift in which the skin is pulled tight rather than lifted off the face.

Note: Most insurance policies do not cover elective cosmetic surgery.

More information: *Beauty By Design: A Complete Look At Cosmetic Surgery* by Dr. Kurt J. Wagner, McGraw-Hill, New York.

AIDS AND HETEROSEXUAL SEX

Contrary to popular belief, AIDS is not spreading in the heterosexual world through ordinary sexual intercourse (penis/vagina intercourse where there are no open lesions on the genitals). Based on my studies, I believe that the only way AIDS can be transmitted is by introducing a whopping dose of the AIDS virus directly into the bloodstream. The only realistic ways this can happen are through blood transfusions (basically safe now, due to careful screening techniques), sharing of needles by users of intravenous drugs, and anal intercourse (which often involves abrasions, bleeding and lacerations).

Important: This does not mean AIDS is a "gay" disease. If gay men engage in sex other than anal intercourse, they are as risk-free as any heterosexual.

It is very difficult to become infected with AIDS, because it is a fragile virus that dies quickly outside of a cell and in the air. It is considered several thousand times less infectious than the hepatitis B virus, with which it is often compared. *Common mistake:* Confusing its deadliness with its degree of infectiousness.

Many men who say they contracted AIDS through sex with a prostitute aren't telling the truth. They are bisexual married men who find it more palatable to blame something other than anal intercourse with another man. In the study where this common falsehood was discovered, one man did not admit his bisexuality until the fourth in-depth interview. Most HIV-positive men are not studied in such depth.

Women who say they contracted AIDS through heterosexual intercourse were not asked, in most cases, if they had engaged in anal intercourse. In the one study that did ask this question, 50% of the women admitted that they had. The number may even be higher than that, because women who have been persuaded against their desire to have anal intercourse may feel embarrassed afterwards and deny the truth.

Similarly, a partner of an intravenous-drug user who is persuaded to share a needle (this is psychologically important to an addict, who will often say "Do it just once . . . if you love me") and contracts AIDS will say she is not an IV-drug user. She can believe this because she didn't do it regularly.

Bottom line: You are far more likely to die in a plane crash than from AIDS contracted through ordinary heterosexual sex. Nevertheless, medical authorities still think we should err on the side of caution when dealing with AIDS transmission.

Source: Robert E. Gould, MD, clinical professor of psychiatry at New York Medical College, a member of the Committee on AIDS of the American Psychiatric Association.

5. Improving Your Appearance

Improving Your Appearance

HOW TO BUY CLOTHES THAT MAKE YOU LOOK GOOD

Mistake: Choosing color to "go with" your hair and eyes. It's your skin tone that matters most crucially in your choice of color. That's what determines how a particular color looks on you. Mistake: The idea that black will make you look slimmer. Black will make you stand out, particularly against any light background. (The walls of most rooms are light.) The more intense and dark your clothing, the larger you'll appear and the less likely to blend into the environment. Another problem: Black is usually draining, especially on men, who don't have the help of makeup to offset the pasty look that black gives. Most men should beware of very dark or black suits. Similar problem color: White, which tends to wash out the face and yellow the teeth. Soft ivory tones are somewhat better, but look good on relatively few people.

• Mistake: Sticking to one or two color groups that you think are good for you. Most people can wear many different color groups. It's the shade that's important. (There are some shades of your favorite color that can look deadly on you.) The point: Don't rule out whole color groups—all blues or all greens. Most people can wear certain shades of most color groups. Exceptions: The few color groups, such as orange and purple, that are really not good for many people in any shade.

• Mistake: Failing to pay attention to pattern or weave. People who are short or small-boned should not wear big prints or checks. They can wear a small true tweed. Slender, smallish men and women are overwhelmed by heavy fabrics. Light wools are better for them than heavy worsteds.

• Mistake: Not considering aging skin in choosing colors. Wrinkled skin is minimized by softer shades. Hard, dark, intense colors maximize the evidence of aging.

• Mistake: Not allowing for the way environment affects your physical appearance. The colors and textures of your office or living room can affect your looks for better or worse, especially in a small room. The colors surrounding you determine the way in which the eye perceives your skin and even your features. Some colors will produce deep shadows, enlarge certain features or produce deep facial lines because of the way they interact with your skin tone.

• Women's mistake: Changing makeup to "go with" clothes. Makeup should be chosen according to skin tone only. Using the wrong color makeup is worse than wearing the wrong color clothing.

• Men's mistake: Misplaced affection for plaid and madras in sports clothes. Men tend to think they look terrific in these patterns. Fact: Most men can't wear them. Reason for the disastrous choices men make in their sports wardrobe: They are restricted, or restrict themselves, to conservative business clothes. A man rarely lets himself wear, say, a green suit to the office. Result: When men choose sports clothes, they go wild in the other direction, having had little practice in choosing dramatic colors that are suitable.

• Mistake: Ignoring the effect of graying hair on complexion. Few men have the sort of skin that takes graying hair well. Men whose skin looks sallow next to graying hair should think of covering the gray.

• Mistake: Thinking you can wear colors you ordinarily don't look good in because you have a tan. Tan does make you look healthier, but it doesn't change the basic effect of certain colors on your skin. With a tan, wearing colors you normally look good in is important, because that's when those colors look better than ever. Point: Neither season nor fashion should dictate the colors of your clothing.

Source: Adrienne Gold and Anne Herman, partners in Colorconscious, Inc., Larchmont, NY.

WHAT WOMEN HATE ABOUT WHAT MEN WEAR

No matter how differently women dress from one another, they are surprisingly unanimous about what looks good on men.

To verify that hypothesis, an informal survey across the female stylistic spectrum was conducted. The survey included all types of women: preppies in gray flannel Bermudas, ladies who wore gold lame to lunch, dress-for-success executives in skirt suits, Soho trend setters flashing blue nail polish, dignified disciples of designer labels, overaged hippies with feathered headbands and no-nonsense types in polyester pantsuits with matching vinyl shoes and bags.

The result of this survey is a ten-point program:

• Socks. These were by far the most frequently mentioned item of annoyance. Socks, women say, must be long enough to cover the calf or ''it's death to a woman's libido.'' Nothing is less titillating than a glimpse of hairy skin below the trouser cuff when a man wearing short socks crosses his legs (except maybe wearing socks to bed when otherwise naked). Also ''out'' are socks with clogs, black socks with tennis sneakers, white cotton socks with business shoes and socks with holes in the heels.

• Comb-overs. Although not strictly a dress item, the habit of letting hair grow long at the side and combing it over a bald head was high on women's list of loathing. ''Who does he think he's kidding?'' they ask. ''And when the wind blows, oh brother, if he could see himself!'' Pulses may quicken over young men with full heads of hair, but women don't dislike baldness per se. They do dislike comb-overs and other compensatory acts of denial and bravado. They like men who like themselves.

• Miami Beach macho. Those who sold men on exposing five buttons' worth of chest and a medallion should be hanged at dawn by their own gold chains. Women hate that look. Even women who think men are nifty in manicures and pinky rings hate that look.

• Misfits: Women say clothes that don't fit advertise poor character traits. Either the guy doesn't really see himself, which means he is probably oblivious to all his other flaws, too, or he doesn't like himself enough to care how he looks, which means a woman will spend her life shoring up his self-image. Or he's got the Alexander Haig syndrome, choosing the pigeon-breasted tight-jacket look to give the impression that he's too big for clothing to contain him. Or he blames his buttons bursting in midair on shirt shrinkage (his wife's fault), not calories. Whatever the analysis, most women conclude that a man in poorly fitting clothes bodes ill for women.

• Textures. Passions run high. ''Men shouldn't wear velour; it's like being with a stuffed animal.'' ''Silk is arrogant. If a man has to wear a robe, only terry cloth is forgivable.'' Corduroy, yes! Rayon, no! Camel's hair, yes! Double knit, no! Eventually one rule emerges: Men shouldn't shine. Anything synthetic that glistens is too glitzy and anything naturally shiny is ''pseudo-regal.'' Or, as one woman put it, ''Men need a matte finish.''

• Affectations. Women opt for simplicity. They like their men unadorned, not gimmicky. ''Playboy rabbit insignia drive me wiggo,'' said a normally subdued woman. ''Full-dress fully grown cowboys look ludicrous on Lake Shore Drive,'' said another. Also contemptible: Men wearing one earring (not to mention two); ''MCP'' printed on anything; initials on shirts; tie clips or lapel pins promoting a lodge, Lions Club, PT-109, the American flag or God; sweaters with reindeer (''I thought of establishing a moth colony to get rid of it''); leprechaun hats; and ''anything Tyrolean.''

• Shoes. This is an easy one. Whether women were partial to men in Guccis or Adidas, cordovans or bucks, glove-leather wing tips or crepe-sole Hush Puppies, nobody loves tassel loafers.

• Color. Anything goes—except the too-bright tones. For instance, heather green is great in a sport jacket, kelly green ghastly. For a sweater, buttercup yellow is warm and friendly, chartreuse off-putting. If it stops traffic...stop wearing it.

• Gestures. If women understand the power of clothing better than men, it is because traditional female socialization teaches them to gain approval through their appearance. Women also know that clothing inspires attitudes in the wearer. An elegant gown can inspire even a child to act aristocratic. And women say certain items of clothing inspire annoying gestures in men. The worst: "Shooting cuffs"—the almost spastic movement with which a man pushes his arms out so that his sleeves show more of his shirt cuffs (usually monogrammed and affixed with ostentatious cuff links). "The mirror sneak"—checking and rearranging his tie in every looking glass "The hoist"—the unceremonious, vaguely obscene lifting of the waistband of loose trousers. Women's advice on the subject: Stop posturing, sit still and pay more attention to us.

• Underwear. Questions about boxer shorts versus jockey shorts and T-shirts versus sleeveless undershirts produced another quick consensus. The issue is settled by body type. The man with a "good bottom" and tight belly should wear jockeys. The well-muscled-shoulder man should wear sleeveless undershirts. Everyone else shouldn't. And if boxer shorts are what a man wants, women prefer that the ones with pictures and slogans be left to the little boys.

Source: Letty Cottin Pogrebin, writer and *Ms.* Magazine editor.

PROPER PANTS FIT

It's not the waist size but the rise (the measurement from waistband to crotch) that determines the way a man's pants fit, according to the head tailor at Brooks Brothers. A man 5 feet 6 inches or shorter needs a short rise. Regular: 5 feet 6 inches up to 5 feet 9 inches. Long: 5 feet 9 inches to 6 feet 3 inches.

ACCENTUATE THE POSITIVE, ELIMINATE THE NEGATIVE

Women's figure flaws can be minimized in summer.

Top-heavy: Wear tunics that glide over the problem areas, V-neck blouses to make shoulders and bosom appear smaller, a diagonal-wrap one-piece bathing suit in contrasting colors, blousy tops (gathered at the waist).

Chunky: To suggest curviness, wear nipped-in waists and eye-catching belts, a blouson dress or drop-waist dress, a one-piece bathing suit with vertical or diagonal stripes.

Bottom-heavy: Pants that end below the knees to show shapely calves, classic pantsuit that falls smoothly in a straight line without pleats or cuffs, vertically striped wraparound dress, one-piece bathing suit with a colorful bra top and darker color below.

THE BEST PERFUMES

The best perfumes for women to wear in the office are the lighter scents. This is particularly true for those with dry skin. Reason: Dry skin makes any perfume more pungent. Avoid Oriental scents such as musk and heavy jasmines. Reason: Too strong.

STOCK UP ON TOILET BASICS

Basic personal items that are essential to your life, such as shaving cream and toothpaste, should be stocked. Keep a back-up supply. These items are inexpensive, but have the power to ruin your day if you run out of them.
Source: *Time Talk.*

BEST TIME TO USE AN ANTIPERSPIRANT

To stay dry all day, it helps to put on antiperspirant at bedtime. The main ingredient (aluminum chlorhydrate) works by plugging sweat glands, and it does that best when they're dry as long as possible. You're dry longest when you're asleep. To build up sweat protection, it's best to use antiperspirant every day. It takes up to eight days for an antiperspirant to reach maximum effectiveness.

Source: Kenneth Hiller, Ph.D., coordinator, Procter & Gamble Beauty Care Council.

HAIR CARE SECRETS

Baby shampoos are not as mild as special-formula shampoos for dry or damaged hair. Their detergents and pH levels put baby shampoos into the middle range of hair cleansers, which makes them right for normal hair. People with oily hair need a stronger shampoo especially made for that condition.

Wet hair should be combed, not brushed. Hair is weakest when wet and can be easily damaged then. Use a wide-tooth comb to reduce the chance of breaking your hair.

Hair care: Twenty-five brush strokes a day is optimal for best distribution of natural oils in the hair. More brushing can cause damage.

DANDRUFF SIGNALS STRESS

Dandruff is a warning that your body is unhappy about something. A chemical reaction triggered by stress speeds up the process of flaking skin at the scalp, which is dandruff. Most susceptible scalps: Those that are excessively oily, not dry as is commonly believed. Dandruff scales are actually flakes of skin secured by oil. Cure: The application of any anti-dandruff lotion. Avoid: Harsh anti-dandruff shampoos.

More information: *The Complete Hair Book* by Philip Kingsley, Grove Press, New York.

THE BETTER WAY TO BEAT BALDNESS

Now there's a better way to treat baldness. New

tool: Tissue expanders—balloon-like rubber implants used to stretch the skin.

How they work: The bladder is implanted under the skin in the problem area, then injected with a salt-water solution. This produces a slight tension in the overlying skin. Once or twice a week, more solution is added to maintain tension as the skin begins to stretch.

After one to two months, the bladder is removed, and the skin manipulated to cover the defect.

Tissue expanders have virtually limitless potential for reconstructive surgery. Essentially, they give surgeons new skin to work with without the need for skin grafts.

Male pattern baldness. By removing a portion of hairless scalp and expanding hair-covered areas, doctors can redistribute hairs to cover the whole head. Tissue expander treatment works better than hair plugs or skin grafts. Drawback: Patients undergoing tissue expansion of the scalp look odd during the two-month process. Privacy is essential.

Source: Andrew Kleinman, MD, United Hospital Medical Center and New Rochelle Hospital Medical Center, New Rochelle, NY.

WHY WOMEN GO BALD

About 30 million men and 30 million women in the United States are bald by natural causes. Surprising: Genetic malfunctions, illness, medication and stress can cause more women than men to go bald—sometimes irreversibly.

Causes of Hair Loss

● Temporary loss: Women can suffer hair loss for weeks or months due to physiological stress and hormonal changes caused by any of these factors:

1) Ingestion of particular prescription drugs, such as beta-blockers, vitamin A analogs (taken for acne) and thyroid supplements.

2) Changes in hormonal levels—occurring, for instance, when a woman has a baby or stops taking birth control pills.

3) Overuse of cosmetic treatments such as dyes, permanents, etc.

4) Severe illness and high fever.

5) General anesthesia.

6) Underactive thyroid.

• Permanent loss: This can be caused by the following conditions:

1) Androgenetic alopecia, the most common cause of female balding, is thought to be a genetically predisposed oversensitivity to the male hormones active in every female. Background: The small amounts of male hormones can cause hair follicles to shrink, first making hairs grow finer and then preventing hair growth altogether. Result: Diffuse balding.

2) Alopecia areata (a localized patch of hair loss) is an autoimmune disease in which antibodies damage hair cells. Sometimes helpful: Steroid treatments.

Making Hair Look Fuller

• Surgery: Small sections of hairbearing scalp can be transplanted to bald spots. Caution: These procedures are less effective for female balding than for the larger unified patterns typical of male balding. Also: Costs are high at $1,000–$5,000.

• Minoxidil: The lotion form of this drug—still awaiting approval from the Food and Drug Administration—appears to be the most promising treatment. The drug enlarges hair follicles so that thick hair grows instead of thin, a particularly effective approach for diffuse balding.

Drawbacks: Minoxidil works on only 25% of those who use it . . . if treatment is halted, gains are reversed . . . one year's supply costs as much as $1,000.

• Hairpieces and wigs: These are still the safest and easiest way to cover baldness. Custom-made pieces of real hair are virtually undetectable.

Source: Dr. Arthur Bertolino, assistant professor of dermatology and director of the Hair Consultation Unit at New York University School of Medicine.

THE SECRETS OF A GREAT SHAVE

A good shave with a blade demands the best possible equipment and proper preparation of the beard. It is false economy to buy anything less than the best, since the entire annual cost of shaving seldom exceeds $40. Also, blades and shaving creams are constantly being improved. Treat your face to the most up-to-date equipment.

Shaving cream: All types of cream (lather, brushless and aerosol in either lather or gel form) are equally efficient. Brushless shaving cream is recommended for dry skin.

If you like, buy three or four different kinds of shaving cream. Use different ones for different moods.

Blades: Modern technology makes the current stainless-steel blades a real pleasure to use. The best type: The double-track blade.

Proper preparation. Wash your face with soap at least twice before shaving. This helps soften the skin, saturate the beard and remove facial oils. Best: Shave after a warm shower.

The secret of shaving cream is its ability to hold water on the hairs of the beard, which allows them to absorb the moisture. Thus, any cream is more effective if left on the face for a few minutes prior to actual shaving. This saturation causes the facial hairs to expand by about one-third, which enhances the cutting ability of the blade. One routine: With the lather on your face, brush your teeth and then set up your razor and other equipment. Do other minor tasks while allowing the lather to soak the beard.

Except on the warmest days, preheat lather in the can or tube by immersion in hot water.

The art of shaving: The manufacturing process leaves a slight oil residue on the edge of the new blade. This can catch and pull the tender facial skin during the first couple of strokes. So start by trimming the sideburns, a painless way of breaking in the new blade. Always shave the upper lip and chin last. Why: The coarsest hairs grow here. You skin will benefit from the extra minutes of saturation and wetness.

When you have finished shaving, rinse the blade and shake the razor dry. Never wipe dry a blade; this dulls the edge. When rinsing the blade, hold it low in the water stream for quicker results.

After shaving: Save money by skipping the highly advertised aftershave lotions. Use witch hazel instead. It is odorless, less astringent, leaves no residue and is better for your skin than most of the aftershave lotions.

WHAT DRY CLEANERS DON'T TELL YOU

The dry cleaning process is not mysterious, but it is highly technical. After marking and sorting your clothes on the basis of color and material type, the cleaner puts them into a dry cleaning machine. This operates like a washing machine except that it uses special solvents instead of water. After the clothes have gone through the dryer, the operator removes stains from them.

A good dry cleaner will use just the right chemical to remove a stain without damaging the fabric. Pressing correctly is next—also a matter of skill. With some fabrics, the garment is put on a form and steamed from the inside to preserve the finish. After pressing, the clothing is bagged.

What to look for:
• Suits should be put on shoulder shapers.
• Fancy dresses and gowns should be on torso dummies.
• Blouses and shirts should be stuffed with tissue paper at the shoulders.
• Except for pants and plain skirts, each piece should be bagged separately.

Taking precautions:
• Bring in together all parts of a suit to be cleaned. Colors may undergo subtle change in the dry cleaning process.
• Check all pockets before bringing in your clothing. A pen left in a pocket can ruin the garment.
• Read care labels carefully. Many clothes cannot be dry cleaned at all. Do not dry clean clothing with printed lettering or with rubber, nylon or plastic parts. If in doubt, ask your dry cleaner.
• Make sure your dry cleaner is insured if you intend to store a large amount of clothing during the winter or summer months.
• Examine your clothes before leaving them with the cleaner. Point out stains and ask whether or not you can expect their removal.

For best results, tell the cleaner what caused the stain.

Getting your money's worth:
• Don't wash clothes and then bring them to the cleaner's for pressing. The saving is minimal.
• Don't try to remove stains yourself. You may only make them worse. Bring stained clothing to the cleaner as soon as possible. Old stains are harder to remove.
• Ask if the cleaner will make minor repairs as part of the cleaning cost. Many cleaners offer such service free.
• Don't request same-day service unless absolutely necessary. Rushed cleaners do a sloppy job.

Damage or loss:
• If your cleaner loses or ruins a garment, you should be reimbursed or given a credit. Most dry cleaners are neighborhood businesses where reputation is vital. You can hurt a cleaner's reputation by giving the cleaner bad word-of-mouth. You might remind the store of this fact if there is resistance to satisfying your complaint.
• If your cleaner fails to remove a stain you were told could be removed, you still have to pay for the cleaning job.
• If your cleaner dry cleans a garment with a "do not dry clean" label, the store is responsible for ruining the garment.
• If your cleaner ruins a garment that should not be dry cleaned but lacks the "do not dry clean" label, responsibility is a matter of opinion. The cleaner may reimburse you to keep your goodwill, or you may have to complain to an outside agency.
• The amount you will be reimbursed is always up for bargaining. You will have to consider original value and depreciation, and whether you have a receipt.

Making complaints:
If you cannot get satisfaction from your cleaner voluntarily, most states have dry cleaners associations to arbitrate complaints. These associations go under various names in different states, so check with your local Department of Consumer Affairs. Make sure to keep all dry cleaning receipts and other relevant information to substantiate your complaint.

Source: Joseph Boms, former assistant manager, Kless dry cleaning chain, Brooklyn, NY.

CARING FOR DOWN

Down is almost spongelike in its ability to absorb moisture, oils and dirt, its worst enemies. But cleaning is hard on down and even harder on its owner. Some maintenance tips for staving off cleanings:

• Sponge off the shell fabric, as soon as possible after spotting, with mild soap and water.

• Enclose comforters in removable sheet casings that can be washed frequently. (These are available in most department stores.)

• Let garments air-dry away from steam pipes, sun or other heat sources before putting them in the closet. (Or put them in a large drier at low heat with a clean sneaker.)

• Patch tears, rips or holes in the shell with the pressure-sensitive tapes sold in sporting-goods stores until you can make a permanent repair with a fine needle and thread or have a professional make a "hot spot" repair.

• Hang vertically channeled coats upside down occasionally to redistribute the down.

• Store clean down flat or loosely folded. Wrap it in a breathable covering such as a sheet to protect it from dust, light and rodents.

Washing down:

Care labels frequently recommend washing. (Gore-Tex, for example, is destroyed by dry cleaning.) Smaller items can be easily washed in a front-loading, tumble-type machine. Empty the pockets and close all the zippers, snaps and Velcro tabs.

Run the washer on medium cycle with warm water. Use half the amount of nonphosphorated soap or detergent recommended. Rinse twice to be sure the soap is all out.

Never use a top-loading agitator machine. It will take apart seams, fray internal edges and diminish the life of the garment by 75%.

For larger items, use the bathtub. Dissolve mild soap or detergent in warm water first. Then submerge the jacket or coat completely. Let it soak no more than 15 minutes. Let the water drain out without disturbing the article, and rinse several times until the water runs clear. Don't twist or wring, but compress out the excess water before hanging the garment over a rack or several lines to dry. Be extra careful with comforters or you will tear the baffling, which is irreplaceable.

Drying down:

Never a fast process, air-drying can take several days even in perfect weather. Be patient, and turn the article often. Home driers are good only for small items such as vests and children's jackets. Larger items don't have room to fluff properly. Hot driers can melt nylon zippers and even some fabrics. Best: Commercial drier with a low heat cycle. Add a couple of clean sneakers (laces removed) or clean tennis balls and a large towel to break up the wet down clumps. Take plenty of change; the process requires several hours.

Dry-cleaning down:

Professional dry cleaning may be the easiest way to restore good down clothing and bedding. However, there are traps in this. The best solvent for cleaning is a non-chlorinated petroleum product that is banned from most city cleaning establishments because of its flammability. Two companies* specialize in this preferred type of cleaning and take care of customers through United Parcel Service. Both also handle repairs and restylings.

Conventional dry cleaning, which is harder on the product, necessitates careful airing afterward to allow toxic fumes to evaporate.

Always spray clean garments with silicone water repellent (such as Scotchguard or Zepel) yourself. Professional waterproofing is a dip that soaks the down. (Nylon shells will not take silicone spray or dip.)

COSMETIC SURGERY

Every year, thousands of Americans try the latest plastic surgery techniques designed to keep them looking younger longer. Problem: Each new procedure is only as good as the surgeon who administers it. And not being aware of the risks ahead of time could leave you emotionally as well as physically scarred.

How to decide if you should have surgery done: Consider your emotional need to have the procedure done, as well as the problems that may result from it. Then try to balance the two to determine what you want to do.

*Down East, New York, Down Depot, San Francisco.

• Liposuction, removing fat cells from the body to produce smoother contours, has been around for a few years. We're now discovering more of its many risks.

Problems: If too much fat and fluid are removed, you can go into shock, bleed internally—or die. Bottom line: This is a cosmetic procedure that, in the wrong hands, can end in disaster. And even when it's performed correctly, it can cause dimpled or sagging skin.

• Retin A is a wonderful drug that replaces a sallow color with some pinkness . . . causes blood vessels beneath the surface to proliferate (improving skin texture) . . . promotes collagen formation (thereby plumping up the skin and filling out fine wrinkles). It is used topically at bedtime in very small quantities. Net results: Removal of very fine crosshatch wrinkles . . . evening and removal of brown mottling that often results from prolonged skin exposure . . . refreshment of scaly dull skin while plumping it up and restoring some of its pinkness.

Problems: Treatment leaves you much more susceptible to sunburn. And too much Retin A can cause redness and peeling.

Choosing a good surgeon:

The success of any cosmetic procedure depends on the skill of the surgeon. To find a good one:

• Call a teaching hospital in your area and ask for recommendations from the staff. Reason: Teaching hospitals offer much higher quality control and peer review.

• Talk to people who have had the type of surgery that you are considering. See if they are happy with it. And find out who their doctors are.

• Choose a board-certified plastic surgeon. Note: Although this is a form of quality control, it does not necessarily mean you will get the best surgeon. Reason: Plastic surgery is an art . . . and to become board-certified, all you have to do is pass an exam. Better: A recommendation from someone who has had successful surgery.

• Make sure the surgeon you choose has performed the procedure hundreds—if not thousands—of times. And he should be able to give you the names of at least three satisfied patients you can call to verify results.

Source: Neal Schultz, MD, a dermatologist in private practice at 1040 Park Ave., New York 10028.

HOW TO READ COSMETICS LABELS

The strange-sounding additives in grooming aids are harmless. . .unlesss you have sensitive skin or an allergy. FDA regulations prohibit using dangerous additives in US-produced cosmetics. Hidden dangers: "Counterfeit" cosmetics, usually foreign-produced and marketed to look like a high priced designer brand, may contain harmful chemicals. To protect yourself: Read labels carefully, and, if you have sensitive skin, test a new product on a small patch of skin and wait 24 hours for any reaction.

What additives do:

• Acacia: Thickens hair products and helps control unmanageable hair.

• Allantoin: Skin-soothing agent that helps heal abrasions. Used in lotions and shaving products.

• Benzethonium chloride: Preserves cosmetics and keeps germs from growing.

• Candelilla wax: Used to harden lipsticks.

• Cetyl alcohol: Smooths and softens skin. Used in creams, foundations, depilatories, deodorants, lotions.

• Isopropyl alcohol: Used to dissolve colorants or other ingredients into hair color rinses, lotions, other cosmetics.

• Para-aminobenzoic acid (PABA): Sunscreen used in tanning lotions, sun blocks, foundations.

• Petrolatum: Known as petroleum jelly—acts to seal moisture into skin with protective film. Used in cold creams, eye shadows and pencils, some depilatories.

• Polysorbates: Keeps oil and water from separating. On a label, the word is usually followed by a number. Found in lotions, deodorants, baby products.

• Propylene glycol: A humectant (helps retain skin's moisture) found in foundations, mascaras, shaving lotions, spray deodorants.

• Sorbitol: Smooths skin and prevents moisture loss. Found in beauty masks, deodorants, hair sprays.

• Triethanolamine stearate: Emulsifies oil and water in hair mousse and gel, cleansing creams, foundations.

Source: Dr. Leon Lichtin, director of cosmetic science at the University of Cincinnati, and Jo Ann Nickatacus of the Cosmetic, Toiletry and Fragrance Association.

DANGERS IN PERSONAL-CARE PRODUCTS

Many beauty and hygiene products contain chemicals that can make you sick—or even kill you.

Cosmetics often are made from harmful substances. Lipstick may contain PVP (poly-vinylpyrrolidonne plastic), saccharin, and mineral oil, all of which have caused cancer in animals. Formaldehyde,, alcohol, and plastic resins in mascara can cause irritation, burning and swelling of the eyes.

Solution: Use a natural lip gloss. If you must have color, stain your lips with beet or berry juice and brush colored clays (available at most natural-food stores) on cheeks and eyelids. Buy unscented, hypoallergenic mascara.

Source: Debra Lynn Dodd, author of *The Non-toxic Home,* Jeremy P. Tarcher, 9110 Sunset Blvd., Los Angeles, 90069.

HAIR-CREAM WARNING

Prolonged use of hair creams and lotions containing estrogen has caused breast enlarge-ment in men and young children. Also: One hair product led to vaginal bleeding in women as old as 82.

Source: *The Harvard Medical School Health Letter,* Cambridge, MA.

ELECTROLYSIS ALERT

When having electrolysis to remove unwanted hair, be certain that careful attention is paid to hygiene. Reason: Hepatitis, and even AIDS, can be transmitted by contaminated needles.

Source: *Saving Face: A Dermatologist's Guide to Maintaining a Healthier and Younger-Looking Face* by Nelson Lee Novick, MD, Franklin Watts, New York.

FINGER BEAUTY DANGER

Nail-wrapping, glue-on false nails, and nail augmentation can cause rashes, redness, scaling, and swelling of the skin surrounding the nail . . . or worse, infection of the nail bed (skin beneath the nail) and even permanent loss of nails. Problems: Cyanoacrylates, and ingredient in nail glues, trigger allergic reac-tions . . . infection-causing bacteria, fungi, and yeast get trapped in the nail bed by waterproof nail-wrappings . . . longer nails increase the chance of tearing the nail plate from the nail bed.

Solution: Halt use of products. Recom-mended: Keep nails a reasonable length and if a problem develops, dispense with enhance-ment techniques.,

Source: Dr. Paul Kechijian, chief of the nail section at New York University Medical Center.

6. Your Home

Your Home

INSPECT YOUR PROSPECTIVE NEIGHBORHOOD

When a real estate agent takes you to see a house, don't stop immediately at the property. Drive on for a while to see how neighboring properties are maintained. They will affect the long-term value of the house you will be looking at.

Source: *Inspection of a Single-Family Dwelling* by Sol Sherman, American Association of Certified Appraisers, Cincinnati, OH.

HOME BUYING MONEY TIPS

Your main financial goals should be to: (1) Minimize the cash you pay out now. (2) Keep all payments, including balloon payments, in line with your ability to meet them. (3) Not borrow unless the cost of money is less than the return you expect from it.

Source: *Real Estate Investing Letter.*

HOW TO BUY A HOUSE WITH NO MONEY DOWN

As real estate prices skyrocket in many areas, the concern of most hopeful buyers is, ''How are we going to scrape together the down payment?'' As hard as it is to believe, however, it's not only possible to buy property with no money down, it's not even that hard to do—provided you have the right fundamental information.

Note: No money down doesn't mean the seller receives no down payment. It means the down payment doesn't come from your pocket.

• Paying the real estate agent. If a seller uses a real estate agent on the sale, he's obligated to pay the agent's commission. At the average commission of 6%, that can involve a substantial sum of money. The sale of a $100,000 home, for example, would return to the agent at least $6,000.

Strategy: You, the buyer, pay the commission, but not up front. You approach the agent and offer a deal. Instead of immediate payment, suggest that the agent lend you part of the commission. In return, you offer a personal note guaranteeing to pay the money at some future date, with interest. If you make it clear that the sale depends on such an arrangement, the agent will probably go along with the plan. If he balks, be flexible. Negotiate a small monthly amount, perhaps with a balloon payment at the end. You then subtract the agent's commission from the expected down payment.

• Assuming the seller's debts. Let's say, as so often happens, that the seller is under financial pressure with overwhelming outstanding obligations.

Strategy: With the seller's cooperation, contact all his creditors and explain that you, not the seller, are going to make good on the outstanding debts. In some cases, the relieved creditors will either extend the due dates, or, if you can come up with some cash, they'll likely agree to a discount. Deduct the face amount of the debts you'll be assuming, pocketing any discounts from the down payment.

• Prepaid rent. Sometimes you, the buyer, are in no rush to move in and the seller would like more time to find a new place to live—but you'd both like to close as soon as possible. Or, if it's a multi-apartment building and the seller lives there, he may want more time in the apartment.

Strategy: Offer to let the seller remain in the house or apartment, setting a fixed date for vacating. Then, instead of the seller paying the buyer a monthly rent, you subtract from the down payment the full amount of the rent for the entire time the seller will be living there.

• Satisfying the seller's needs. During conversations with the seller, you learn that he must buy some appliances and furniture for a home he's moving into.

Strategy: Offer to buy those things—using credit cards or store credit to delay payment—and deduct the lump sum from the down payment.

• Using rent and deposits. If it's a multi-apartment building, you can use the rent from tenants to cover part of the down payment.

Strategy: Generally, if you close on the first of the month, you are entitled to all rent normally due from tenants for that month. Therefore, you can collect the rent and apply the sum toward the down payment.

• Using balloon down payments. Arrange to give part of the down payment immediately and the rest in one or several balloon payments at later, fixed dates.

Strategy: This technique gives you breathing room to: (1) Search for the rest of the down payment; and/or (2) Improve the property and put it back on the market for a quick profit.

• Caveat: This move can be risky if you don't make sure you have a fall-back source of cash in the event that time runs out.

• Using talent, not cash. In some cases you may be able to trade some of your personal resources if you are in a business or have a hobby through which you can provide services useful to the seller in lieu of cash.

Strategy: Trading services for cash is, among other things, very tax-wise. Many working people can provide services in exchange for down payment cash. Most obvious: Doctors, dentists, lawyers, accountants. Less obvious: Carpenters, artists, wholesalers, entertainers, gardeners. Note, however, that bartering produces taxable income, and taxes have to be paid on the value of such services.

• Raising the price, lowering the terms. Best applied when the seller is more interested in the price than in the terms of the deal.

Strategy: By playing with the numbers, you might find that you save a considerable sum of money if you agree to a higher price in return for a lower—or even no—down payment.

• High monthly down payments. If you have high cash flow, this could be a persuasive tactic to delay immediate payment.

Strategy: It's not unusual for a seller to be more anxious for steady cash flow after the sale than for immediate cash in hand. An anxious seller might bite at this offer because it gives him the full price. It also offers you the prospect of turning around and quickly selling the property—since you aren't tying up ready cash.

• Splitting the property. If the property contains a separate sellable element, plan to sell off that element and apply the proceeds to the down payment.

Strategy: Perhaps a portion of the land can be sold separately. Or there may be antiques that are sellable. . . the proceeds of which can be applied to the down payment.

Source: Robert G. Allen, a real estate insider and author of the bestseller, *Nothing Down.* He's also publisher of the monthly newsletter, *The Real Estate Advisor.*

CO-OWNERSHIP CONTRACTS

About 200,000 households, both couples and singles, doubled up last year to buy a house or condominium. 10–20% of the single-family housing units in some areas of the country have been converted to accommodate these new arrangements. Important: The co-buyers should have an attorney draw up a legal agreement detailing each owner's responsibilities and documenting who paid what and who owns what. Co-buyers should be specific as tenants in common, rather than joint tenants, to avoid inheritance problems.

DOCUMENTING THE DEED

Your house deed will be recorded among the land records in the jurisdiction where your house is located, so don't worry if you find you have lost it when it comes time to sell the house. The title attorney handling the sale of the house will be able to prepare a new deed from these records. Alternative: The attorney or title company that conducted your settlement. Either might have the original recorded deed in their company files.

House documents to keep (in addition to the deed to the house): The settlement sheet (for future tax purposes), the deed of trust and the promissory note that you sign with your lender.

WHAT CONDOMINIUM SALESPEOPLE DON'T TELL YOU

Don't buy on impulse. Experience in buying a single-family house doesn't alert you to all the things to look for in a good condo deal.

Your lawyer must read the covenant of condominium (also called the master deed or declaration of condominium). Clauses in a covenant are non-negotiable: all participants must have the same wording. There are traps that could make it more desirable to walk away from the whole deal.

• Resale restrictions. The condo association (the governing body of owner representatives that owns and maintains common areas such as hallways, parking lots and swimming pools) may have a 30-, 60-, or 90-day right of first refusal. That delay could cost you a sale. Be advised that Federal Housing Administration, Veterans Administration, and other government-insured mortgages are not available when there are certain resale restrictions. Your resale market could be cut significantly.

• Use restrictions. Does the covenant permit owners to rent their units? If you are buying the condo as an investment, you must be able to rent. If you are planning to live in a unit, you may want this restriction. Other use restrictions may concern children, pets, window decorations, even the type of mailbox you can put up.

• Sweetheart deals. The most common one is when the developer owns the common areas and leases them back to the association. Such leases are usually long term and include escalator clauses and pass-alongs that could cause big jumps in your monthly association fees. In other cases, the developer does not own the common areas, but has a long-term contract to manage them. The best deal for the buyer is when the condo association owns all the common areas. All management agreements with the condo association should strictly control costs and contain termination provisions.

Potential problems that won't show up in the covenant:

• Subsidized fees. Developers of newly built condos often manage common areas for a fee until most of the new units are sold. To speed sales, the developer may keep the management fee below cost. Then, when the condo association assumes management, the owners' monthly costs soar. It is prudent to check fees charged by similar condo associations in the same area.

• Construction problems. Before you buy, have an engineer inspect the condition of the entire property, if feasible, not just your unit. Reason: If the condo association has to make repairs, you will be assessed for the cost. If you are buying a unit in a converted building, ask the condo salesperson for the engineer's report. Most converted buildings need one to obtain financing.

The best times to buy are when prices are lowest during the pre-construction sale of new units, or early in the conversion of a building. But if you buy too soon, you could end up as one of the few owners. As long as units remain unsold, your investment will not appreciate. Check the price and demand for similar units in the area.

Source: Thomas L. O'Dea, O'Dea and Co., Inc., Winston-Salem, NC.

SELF-DEFENSE FOR TENANTS

Tenants are rapidly becoming a beleaguered species as rents skyrocket and vacancies plummet in desirable urban areas. Confronted with a booming seller's market, landlords often become greedy and take advantage of tenant desperation. Most states with major populated areas now have some form of protection for tenants, however. Tenant remedies vary according to state or local laws. But there is one power that a tenant anywhere has and should use when circumstances warrant it—the power to withhold the rent. If you understand the basic concepts of tenant law, you will know when and how to use your ultimate weapon.

Your apartment must be suitable for habitation by a human being. If it's not, the law in most states requires the landlord to do whatever is necessary to make it habitable. The following must be provided:

• Heat, hot and cold water.

• Electricity, or a facility for it if it's metered through a public utility.

• Air conditioning, if it's in your lease.

• Absence of roaches and vermin.

• Clean public areas (lobbies, halls) in the building.

• No dangerous health conditions in the apartment. Examples: Falling plaster, peeling lead-based paint.

The warranty of habitability deals mainly with health, not with cosmetics. If your bathtub is cracked, it isn't a violation of the warranty unless water is leaking. The crack might be a violation of the local tenant protection act, however, which varies from state to state.

The question of unfair leases came up because landlords were taking advantage of the scarce housing situation to force tenants into signing leases with unconscionable provisions. Examples: Clauses saying the landlord doesn't have to provide heat and hot water; clauses waiving a tenant's right to trial by jury in a landlord/tenant conflict; clauses giving the landlord the right to change a tenant's locks if he doesn't pay the rent—all without going through the court system.

Recommended: Sign whatever lease the landlord offers. Then take him to court if some of the provisions prove unconscionable.

The best way to find out the law in your area is to call your local Congressman. Many local legislators have a hotline or an open evening for community residents to come in with their problems. At the least, a local legislator can head you in the right direction—a community group or a tenant organization in your area.

Don't run immediately to a lawyer. Try a community group first. If you do decide to hire a lawyer, make sure he's a specialist in landlord/tenant law. This is a very specialized and volatile area. Laws change frequently. An amateur can do you more harm than good.

The most effective method of confronting the landlord is through a tenant organization. If you are having problems with your landlord, the other tenants in your building probably are, too. If you approach the problem as a group, your chances of success improve immeasurably.

How to go about it:

• Speak with the tenants in your building, and distribute flyers calling a meeting. At the meeting, elect a committee of tenants to lead the group.

• Pass out questionnaires to all tenants, asking them to list needed repairs in their apartments.

• When the questionnaires have been collected, a member of the committee should call the landlord and suggest a meeting with him to negotiate complaints. Many landlords will comply with this request, since the specter of all their tenants withholding rent can be a frightening prospect. Negotiation is always preferable to litigation. It is a very effective tool. Also: Negotiation can be desirable for a landlord who is not getting his rent on time. Tenants can emphasize that they are willing to improve the landlord's cash flow problems by paying on the first of the month if he is willing to make repairs.

• If negotiation fails, organize a rent strike. That's a procedure whereby tenants withold rent collectively, depositing the money each month in an escrow fund or with the court until repairs are made. If your tenant organization is forced to go this route, you will need a good lawyer. Be prepared for a long court battle.

If the other tenants won't cooperate, you can withhold your rent as an individual. Reasonable grounds: Lack of services (heat, hot water, garbage collection, elevator). Don't withhold rent without a good reason. If you lose, you'll be liable for the landlord's attorney's fee plus court costs. Advantage of withholding: You'll get your day in court and the opportunity to explain to a judge what the problem is. Even if you lose, you will be allowed to pay rent up to date and not be evicted. The harassment value of forcing your landlord to take you to court is likely to make him more compliant in the future. Get a lawyer to represent you if the problem is severe.

Tenant versus tenant. If a tenant in your building is involved in a crime or drugs or is excessively noisy, there are a number of possibilities:

• Take out a summons, claiming harassment or assault. Probable result: The court will admonish the tenant to stop causing a disturbance (which may or may not have any effect).

• Sue for damages in civil court. You may win (although collecting the judgment is another story).

• Try to persuade your landlord to evict the undesirable tenant. Best way: Put pressure on him through your tenant organization. A landlord can't be forced to evict anyone. He has the right to rent to whomever he chooses. But if your association has a decent relationship with the landlord, he might comply, especially if the tenant is causing a dangerous condition or destroying property.

• You do have the right to break your lease if you're being harassed by another tenant, but this may not be much comfort if apartments are scarce in your area.

MOVING FRAGILE OBJECTS

When moving valuables, consider carriers other than household movers. Special handling is important for irreplaceable and fragile objects and for jewelry, collections and currency. Options: Air freight, UPS, armored service, registered U.S. mail, yourself.

CHOOSING AN INTERSTATE COMPANY

If you plan to move to another state, you should get an estimate from several movers and check it against their latest interstate performance report. A company's interstate performance report (required by the US Interstate Commerce Commission) shows how often a mover's estimate was accurate, whether the delivery was on time and the number of damage claims made by customers. Your best bet: The mover whose performance report comes closest to the estimate given.

MAKING THE MOST OF YOUR HOUSE

With today's tight economic conditions, many owners are taking long looks at their houses with an eye toward ''adjusting'' to them—either extending and upgrading through additions and renovations, or constricting living space for greater efficiencies.

Procedure for additions or renovations: The architect compiles a set of preliminary drawings to obtain a rough idea of costs from contractors. Next, a complete set of drawings makes closer estimates possible.

For small jobs, rely on the cost estimate of a reputable local contractor. For more complex work, get estimates from two or three contractors. No estimate is reliable unless based on a complete set of drawings.

Costs: Per square foot, a new bathroom is the most costly room in the house. Next most expensive: The kitchen. Least expensive: A bedroom.

Planning: Try to have all the outside work done during the fair-weather months. Save the interior finishing for winter.

Problem: Kitchen renovation. No matter what time of the year this work is done, you end up with sawdust in the scrambled eggs. Best: Take a vacation while the kitchen is being rebuilt. More realistically: See that as much work as possible is done outside the kitchen. Then have the actual installation of items such as cabinets, counters and appliances concentrated in one burst of activity. This might take as little as one week.

In the search for more living space, many owners convert an attached garage into a family room. A new, level floor should be installed over the existing concrete slab, which is often pitched. Important: Insulate the space under this new floor. Slip new windows and doors into the old openings. Convenience: A new bathroom for this area. If the plumbing is properly prepared, a kitchenette can be added later. Thus the family room can be quickly converted into a rental apartment for added income when the kids have grown up and moved out, assuming local zoning allows for accessory apartments in residential neighborhoods.

Parents whose children no longer live at home often adopt a country-kitchen style of living. The couple centers its activities around the kitchen, even sleeping in a nearby room. Aim: To conserve heat by warming only the core of the house in winter.

New source of heat and comfort: An old-fashioned woodburning stove. Warning: Charming as these stoves are, they can cause fires if not properly installed.

Other things to know before altering your house:
• Zoning and building permits are required before the construction of most additions. Key word: Setbacks. These are the hypothetical lines on your property beyond which you are not allowed to build without a variance.
• No addition may encroach on an existing water well, septic tank or septic field. Find out locations of these and plan accordingly.
• Know the capacity of your present electrical service. An older house may receive only 60–100 amps. You may have to push service to 200 amps to meet the demands of the newly finished space.

Source: Charles Jacob of Irving & Jacob Architects, Norwalk, CT.

CHOOSING A BUILDING CONTRACTOR

• Get bids from three contractors that you have picked by looking at their work or through friends' recommendations.
• Make sure your job specifications are the same for each contractor, so all the bids will be for exactly the same requirements.
• Watch out for low bids. They may presage shoddy workmanship or bad materials.
• Thoroughly check out the contractor you decide to use (credit, bonding references, insurance, etc.).

• Be specific about every detail of the job, leaving nothing in doubt in the final agreement.
• Pay one-third up front, one-third when the job is almost done, and the balance at the conclusion of the job. . . if you are satisfied.
• If you make changes during construction that are not in the contract, be sure to get all the costs in writing before the alterations are made.

GETTING YOUR MONEY'S WORTH FROM A HOME IMPROVEMENT CONTRACTOR

Plunging ahead with major improvements or additions to your home without a carefully thought-out contract is asking for trouble. What to get in writing?
• Material specifications, including brand names, and a work completion schedule.
• All details of the contractor's guarantees, including the expiration dates. Procedures to be followed if materials or workmanship should prove defective. Trap: Do not confuse manufacturers' guarantees with the contractor's guarantees of proper installation.
• An automatic arbitration clause. This provides that an impartial board will mediate if problems of excessive cost overruns arise.
• A clause holding the contractor responsible for negligence on the part of subcontractors. Check with your lawyer for specifics.
• A cleanup provision, specifying that all debris be moved.

Do's and dont's of a contract job:
• Do consult a lawyer before signing a complex contract.
• Don't sign a contract with any blank spaces. Write void across them.
• Don't sign a work completion certificate without proof that the contractor has paid all subcontractors and suppliers of materials.
• Don't pay in full until you are completely satisfied.
• Don't pay cash.

BEWARE OF CERTAIN HOME IMPROVEMENTS

Big problem for today's home owner . . . the house you bought for $50,000 in the 1960s is now worth $200,000, and you'd like to put some of the profit in your pocket. But the housing market is soft. In many areas, home prices are falling.

If you can't wait for the market to turn around, there are effective steps you can take now to enhance the value of your house for sale . . . or you can get cash from it by renting or mortgaging.

Most people are now aware that when they sell a house, they never recoup the value of swimming pools, finished basements and most other major improvements.

But what many people don't know is that these additions can actually decrease the value of the home.

Reason: Some prospective buyers don't like swimming pools, and others have their own ideas about finishing the basement. By making these improvements yourself, you simply lose these prospects.

Even if you were lucky enough to find a would-be buyer who wants a pool, you won't get your money back, because the price of your house is largely determined by the average home price in your neighborhood. If a prospective buyer is looking for a more expensive house, he'll look in a neighborhood that has many houses in that price range.

Exceptions: Good bathrooms and kitchens do help to sell a house. If yours are in bad shape, fix them up. It pays to consult an agent if you're in doubt about fixing up a room. Tell the agent you're selling in a year, making it in the agent's interest to give you free advice.

Ironically, the improvements that really help sell a house are basically cosmetic and inexpensive. In today's slow market, they can be very important. Some of the easy, and inexpensive, improvements you can make . . .

- Trim the lawns and shrubs.
- Paint the front entrance, and put a couple of pots of geraniums by the door.
- Make sure the porch light and bell are in working order.

- Clean the house thoroughly, and keep the windows clean. If this isn't your forte, hire a cleaning service.
- If rooms are even the slightest bit cluttered, move out some of the furniture.
- No matter what you have in your closets, take at least half of it out. Remove at least half of what you have on your kitchen counter.
- Tighten any knobs or faucets that are loose.

Before the agent shows the house, be sure you . . .

- Close the garage door.
- Park the kids and the pets with a neighbor.
- Put away the kids' toys.
- Remove all conspicuous personal items such as awards, souvenirs and religious items. (They might make you more interesting, but not the house.)
- Turn on all the lights, and open all the curtains. Exception: Leave the curtains drawn if the window looks out on a used car lot.
- If there's a smoker in the house, remove ashtrays and all other evidence of tobacco.
- Use an air freshener if the house doesn't already smell fresh. But don't bother if there's a nice cooking aroma coming from the kitchen.
- Turn off appliances. It's okay, however, to have very soft music playing in the background.

Source: Edith Lank is a real estate broker who writes *House Calls*, a nationally syndicated column of the Los Angeles Times Syndicate. She is also author of *The Complete Home Seller's Kit* and *The Complete Home Buyer's Kit*, Longman Financial Services Publishing Co., 500 N. Dearborn St., Chicago 60610.

BEFORE YOU BUILD A SWIMMING POOL

What kind of pool should I build?

Most in-ground pools today are either concrete or vinyl-lined. Not as common: Fiberglass.

Concrete: Either poured or pneumatically sprayed (Gunite or Shotcrete). Gunite has largely replaced poured concrete for residential use because it is less expensive and can be made into any shape. Poured concrete is limited to simple rectangles and circles.

Vinyl-lined: The plastic is hung on a wall system of aluminum, steel, plastic, wood, masonry or fiberglass. Vinyl pools have become increasingly popular because they are faster to install and cost substantially less. The savings are greatest in the Northeast and Midwest because of the difficulties of building with concrete in colder climates.

What about pool maintenance?

All pools require regular cleaning and purifying. Vinyl-lined pools are easier to clean. Concrete can roughen, and algae can grow more easily.

Concrete pools that are closed every winter have to be drained once a year. Pools in year-round use need draining every few years.

Concrete pools have to be painted every three years or re-marble dusted every five or six years. Vinyl liners must be replaced every 10 years or so.

What other costs will there be?

Accessories (ladders, lights, diving board), heater, cover, decking or patio, planting, fencing, housing for equipment and support systems will vary considerably.

Utilities: Heating costs depend on the degree of warmth and how long you heat the pool. In most areas, costs of gas and oil are similar, but gas is favored because it is quieter and cleaner. Solar heat is also becoming popular.

Filtration and pump.

Cleaning: You can keep your own pool clean or use a maintenance service. Cost varies with frequency and what's included (opening and closing pool, chemicals, vacuuming, etc.).

Increased real estate taxes.

Insurance: Most homeowners' policies cover pools, but it might be necessary to add a rider at a slight charge.

Bottom line: Build the kind of pool you want, and don't try to economize on the pool itself. Instead, hold off on decking, landscaping and other things you can add later.

How do you site a pool?

The first consideration is a sunny location. The second is privacy. Your contractor will know about codes, restrictions and zoning regulations on setbacks, fencing, etc. Alternate: Call the building department yourself.

The builder will need a 10-foot wide access for equipment.

When is a good time to build?

In the Northeast, and Midwest, most pools are put in in May. You can get a better price in late fall and early spring, when contractors are less busy. Allow enough time for construction. Averages: Two weeks for vinyl, six weeks for Gunite. Advice: Plan now for next season. Don't wait until you want to swim in the pool.

How should you select a contractor?

There are a lot of fly-by-nights in this business. It isn't a good idea to make your choice on the basis of low bid. Unreliable operators who undercut on price might not be around long enough to make good on the work.

Get referrals from people you know, or ask a contractor for names of customers to call. Be sure you deal with someone who has a good reputation. With a pool, you don't know what you're getting until you use it over a period of time.

Source: Gregory Gordon, pool contractor, Easthampton, NY.

BUILDING A TENNIS COURT

There are four types of tennis courts: Clay, Har-Tru (pulverized clay with a gypsum binder), asphalt and concrete. Clay and Har-Tru are soft and need daily maintenance. Asphalt and concrete are hard courts that require little upkeep.

Choosing the right court. Soil and rock conditions can dictate the best type for your yard as much as your playing preference. Sandy soil with good drainage makes an ideal base for any kind of court. Heavy clay soil holds an all-weather court easily but requires additional excavation and filling for a soft court. Rocky areas may need blasting to create a proper base for any kind of court.

Construction time. A tennis court needs time to settle, particularly the hard surfaces (asphalt and concrete) that might crack if the base were to heave. In the northern part of the country, where winters are severe, the ideal building schedule for hard courts is to excavate in the fall, let the base settle over the winter and finish the surfacing in the late spring or early summer. With soft courts, settling is less of a problem because cracks can be filled in with more clay or Har-Tru. A soft court can be built in six to eight weeks, with three weeks for settling.

Zoning and permits. Property owners must provide an up-to-date survey of their property and be sure that the proposed court fits within the set-back requirements—or get zoning variances if necessary. Contractors obtain the building permits. Many communities require fencing.

Costs. Prices vary considerably from one part of the country to another. Special excavating problems create only one of the price variables. In general, however, a clay court with sprinkler system and fencing is less expensive than a similar Har-Tru court. All-weather courts (asphalt in the East, concrete in the West) are the least expensive of all.

Maintenance. Soft courts must be swept and relined daily, sprinkled and rolled periodically and refurbished annually (or oftener in climates where they get year-round use). Hard courts must be resurfaced every five to seven years. Many builders offer maintenance-service contracts.

Source: Ray Babij, tennis-court builder, Remsenberg, NY.

Home tennis courts require much more space than commonly believed. While the actual playing area of a court is relatively small (36 by 78 feet), adding the out-of-bounds areas pushes the total required to 60 by 120 feet, about one-sixth of an acre.

ALL-WEATHER SPEAKERS

All-weather speakers of good quality can pipe your favorite music outdoors. Designed for all temperatures and impervious to rain, the speakers can be mounted in trees or tucked around the pool. Permanent installation requires heavy cable like that used for outdoor lights. (It can be bought by the foot at hardware stores.)

SAFER HOME CHEMICALS

Combustible liquids—gasoline, kerosene for backyard torches and charcoal lighter fluid—cause more deaths and injuries than all other summer chemicals combined. Trap: The combustible liquid could spill near a person who is smoking, or near an open flame, and ignite.

Another way people get hurt is by adding an extra dose of lighter fluid to boost an already-lit fire. Result: The can may explode, scattering burning lighter fluid all over. Recommended: Put plenty of lighter fluid on the first time. If the fire doesn't catch, douse the whole thing with water and start over with fresh charcoal.

Paint. In the warm summer months, many people paint or varnish furniture, decks, etc. Caution: If the labels says, "use with adequate ventilation," do the project outdoors. Opening windows and doors in the house does not provide enough ventilation. If you can't take the project outdoors (you're painting a room, for instance), use water-based paint, which doesn't require as much ventilation during use.

Source: Jay Young, chemical health and safety consultant in Silver Spring, MD.

KEEPING YOUR HOME SAFE

• A multipurpose dry chemical unit is the best home fire extinguisher. Check the label to see what kinds of fires it's effective against. It should cover Class A (ordinary combustibles like wood and cloth), Class B (gases, greases, flammable liquids) and Class C (electrical fires)

• Smoke detectors work best in a two-units system. Place an ionization detector in the hallway outside your bedroom for a quick alert on a racing fire. Then install a photoelectric model downstairs in the general living area or in the main stairway that will detect smoke from smoldering upholstery or rugs.

Aluminum wiring, which was used in two million homes and apartments built between 1965 and 1973 has caused more than 500 home fires in the last 10 years. To check: Ask the original electrical contractor, or look for an "AL" stamp on exposed wires in your basement. If you do have aluminum wiring, a qualified electrician may be able to make your house safe at a moderate cost. Never attempt repairs (even simple ones) on your own.

Source: *Consumer Adviser*, Reader's Digest Association, Inc., Pleasantville, NY 10570.

OIL-VS. WATER-BASED PAINT

Water-based paint has many distinct advantages over oil-based. It dries in less than an hour, has no paint-like smell, doesn't show brush or roller lap marks as openly and makes for an easy soap-and-water cleanup. It also wears longer, is washable and holds color best. Overwhelming choice: Water-based paint (also known as latex or acrylic).

Stick with oil-based paint if the exterior surface is already painted with an oil-based paint (alkyd resin). Reason: Latex expands and contracts more easily than oil during the freeze-thaw weather cycle. This action may pull off any underlayers of oil-based that aren't locked onto the surface.

Latex exterior paints are ideal for surfaces that have never been painted. Why: They allow the surface to breathe. And their flexibility during the freeze-thaw cycle enables them to adhere better to the surface. (If you have latex over an oil-based layer that is holding, continue with water-based.)

When painting over an already painted exterior surface, first rough up the gloss with sandpaper or a wire brush. This gives the smooth surface some tooth, on which the fresh paint can grip and bond.

Before painting, scrub under the eaves and in protected spots with a solution of detergent and water. Reason: Salts from the air collect in these areas that are not washed clean by the rains. Exterior paints won't hold.

Use latex paint for any interior jobs, even if it means covering existing oil-based layers. Exception: When there is a water-soluble substance underneath the oil. The water in latex softens these substances, which leads to peeling. Enough coats of oil-based paint usually shield the underlying calcimines or sizers from

the water in the latex. Test: Paint a small area with latex. If there is no peeling within a couple of hours, continue with latex.

Source: Neil Janovic's grandfather founded the family paint and paper concern, Janovic Plaza in 1888 in New York.

PAINTING TROUBLE AREAS

Often, paint peels in one section of a wall or ceiling. Causes:
• A leak making its way through the walls from a plumbing break or an opening to the outside.
• The plaster is giving out in that area due to age or wear and tear.
• The layers of paint may be so thick that the force of gravity plus vibrations from outside make the paint pop and peel in the weakest spot.

Fix: If it's a leak, find and correct it. Otherwise, remove as much of the existing paint as you can. Scrape away any loose, damp or crumbling plaster. Spackle and smooth the area. Prime and paint it.

For real problem areas: Spackle, then paste on a thin layer of canvas. Apply it as though it were wallpaper. Smooth it out so it becomes part of the surface. Then prime and paint it.

BEST COLOR TO PAINT A HOUSE

Yellow houses have the most "curb appeal" and sell faster than those of any other color. Most people associate yellow with sunshine, optimism and warmth.

Source: Leatrice Eiseman, color consultant and educator in Tarzana, CA, in *Consumers Digest*.

CHOOSING INTERIOR PAINT COLORS

Paint the rooms of your home in colors that best flatter you and fit your lifestyle. Make a list of the colors you like and that look best on you. Then think about your lifestyle, and decide whether you want a peaceful effect or a dramatic one. It can vary from room to room. Choose appropriate colors from your list. If you are unsure of your choice, put on a wall a large piece of paper painted in the color you plan to use. Keep it there for a week or so to see whether you really like it before you make a final decision.

PAINTING PADS

Originally made for coating wood shingles, pads are coming into general use. They are now available in a number of sizes and shapes for jobs such as edges and window trim or whole walls, indoors and out. Once the basic stroke is mastered, most home painters find pads faster and neater than either rollers or brushes. Made of nylon fiber pile, pads leave a smoother finish than other applicators with both oil-based and water-based paints.

LEAD-PAINT ALERT

When renovating your home, beware of scraping and sanding. Problem: These activities may liberate dangerous flakes of lead paint, especially in homes built before 1960, when lead-based paints were used frequently. Keep children away from areas of the house where work is being done.

LATEX TEST

Latex exterior paint should be checked out on the house to be sure all the chalk from the existing coat has been removed. Paint a small area of the house with two coats of the latex. After the paint has dried for two or three days, scratch a straight line through the new paint. Press a strip of cellophane tape over the scratch, and then pull the tape off quickly. If more than a few specks of paint stick to the tape, the new paint is not adhering correctly. Remedies: Try again to clean off all the chalked paint sur-

faces. Or switch to an alkyd paint, which covers chalk better.

PATCHING CRACKS WITH CEMENT

Chip out the inside of the crack with a cold chisel to make the crack wider at its base than at the surface. This keeps the patching cement locked into position. After the crack is prepared, brush out loose pieces of concrete and dust. Add water to ready-mix patching cement. Blend until its consistency is like cake icing (not crumbly and not soupy). Wet down the crack with a fine spray from a garden hose or a paintbrush dipped in water. Pack the mixed cement into the crack with a small trowel. Poke the trowel into the crack frequently to prevent air pockets. Overfill the crack, and then trim off the excess with the trowel edge. To cure the cement properly, keep it damp for 48 hours by spraying it periodically.

AVERT STRUCTURAL DAMAGE

Repair cracks in concrete as soon as you spot them. Look for them in the warm months, before the troublesome weather hits. The action of water, especially as it freezes and thaws, can quickly turn a small crack into a major one, possibly even resulting in structural damage. Essential: First investigate and correct the cause of the crack.

Source: *New Shelter.*

PROTECTION FOR STORM WINDOWS

See-through plastic windowpanes guard against breakage in hazardous locations such as storm and garage doors and basement windows. Use acrylic plastic one-eighth inch or one-quarter inch thick. Cut with a power saw fitted with a fine-toothed blade. Or cut by hand, using a scribing tool.

ROOF LONGEVITY

Slate or tiled roofs should last a human lifetime, as should terne (lead and tin) or copper sheeting. Asphalt shingles ought to hold out for 15–25 years. Good precaution: After a roof is 15 years old, have a roofer inspect and repair it annually.

SKYLIGHTS

Skylights are now available in sizes ranging from 16 inches square to 10 feet square. Modest-sized skylights can be installed in one day.

MODERNIZE YOUR HOME HEATING

Heating systems that are more than a few years old need modernizing. Gas: Install a stack damper and electric ignition to produce an average gas saving of 10%. Oil: Older systems don't have a flame retention head burner, which saves 15%. Both systems pay for themselves in about three years.

ELEVEN WAYS TO CONSERVE HOME HEATING FUEL

1. Buy a new heating system. Reason: Systems more than 20 years old operate in the 65% efficiency range. New ones average at least 80% efficiency. Increasing efficiency from 65% to 80% saves $255 a year in a house using 1,700 gallons of heating fuel at $1 a gallon.

2. Service heating systems annually. Point: A 2% increase in efficiency will pay for tests and adjustments.

3. Reduce the hot-water heater setting to 120°F or lower. (Average settings range from 140° to 160°F.)

4. Minimize use of hot-water appliances.

5. Install automatic flue stack dampers on hot-water and steam-heating systems. They conserve heat by closing the flue pipe when the oil burner is off. Potential saving: 5–10%.

6. Put in clock thermostats that automatically reduce heat at certain times during the day or night. Potential saving: If the clock thermostat is set to reduce the temperature from 70°F to 65°F for 16 hours a day, heating bills will drop 10%.

7. Use spot heating when needed.

8. Use draperies, shades and blinds to prevent heat from escaping. Minimize use of exhaust fans.

9. Insulate.

10. Use trees and shrubs as windbreakers.

11. Use humidifiers. Reason: Rooms with less than 30% humidity will feel chilly even when well heated.

Source: Frank C. Capozza, manager of Frank's Fuel, a fuel distributor, N. Tarrytown, NY.

Heating and cooling use 70% of the energy. Water heating takes 20%. Cooking, refrigeration, lighting, etc. total only 10% of use.

INSULATING YOUR HOME

The best time to insulate is spring when contractors are not as busy as in the fall. Your first saving can come on air-conditioning bills. Biggest saving: Heat bills next winter.

The estimate should include:

• The exact areas to be insulated.

• The specific type and brand of product to be installed in each area (including the number of packages or bags that will be needed).

• The R-value (resistance to heat loss) of the products, which is the most important measurement.

• The total cost broken down into materials, labor, clean-up, service charges and taxes.

Materials: The most common insulation products are mineral wool (fiberglass and rock wool) and cellulose. Urea formaldehyde foam is no longer recommended. Any of these can be blown into sidewalls. Mineral wool and cellulose are used for open areas such as attics. Be sure the brand you contract for carries the seal of the Underwriters' Laboratories (UL). Insist on written guarantees for claims concerning R-value, inflammability, moisture absorption, shrinkage or settling, odor and soundproofing.

Attic insulation: A good contractor will provide proper ventilation above the attic insulation to prevent water condensation and moisture damage. (Attic insulation should never be applied directly to the underside of the roof.) A vapor barrier should be applied on the warm side of the insulation.

Sidewall insulation: Holes for blowing the insulation in should be drilled between all studs and above and below every window. The contractor should drop a weighted string through each hole to check for obstacles in the wall. (Holes should be drilled below an obstacle as well.) Require a thermograph (heat picture) to check the finished sidewall insulation. X-ray guns do not give an accurate picture of total insulation.

Important contract provisions:
• Written guarantees of product claims.
• An adjusted-cost clause that gives you the savings if less than the estimated amount of materials is needed.
• A written guarantee of workmanship, including the contractor's responsibility for any future damage caused by the insulation.

Source: John D. Constance, licensed engineer specializing in home maintenance, Cliffside Park, NJ.

WEATHER STRIPPING

To test the airtightness of a window or door, move a lighted candle along its frame. If there is enough draft to make the flame dance, then caulk or weather-strip it. For a door, add weather stripping if you can slip a quarter underneath it.

IS HOME SIDING ECONOMICAL?

New home siding of vinyl, aluminum or steel beautifies but does not save energy. The FTC has warned about advertising that claims adding siding helps lower fuel bills. Exception: Some insulating effect occurs when the siding is installed over sheets of formed plastic.

SPECIAL NEW TELEPHONE SECRET

A network interface is a special telephone jack that allows *you* to determine which wires are faulty when your phone goes dead—outside wires, which the phone company must repair at no cost to you, or inside, which the phone company may charge to repair.

Installation: If you want to install your own interface, buy the materials at a phone-supply store. If your phone repairman installs it, you must purchase the materials from him. *Tip:* To avoid charges for the visit, have the repairman install the interface when he is at your house doing other phone work.

How the interface works: When your wires go dead, simply plug a phone into the network interface. If you hear a dial tone, the problem is in the wiring on your premises. If there is no dial tone, something is wrong with the wires leading to your house. *Extra benefit:* If the problem is internal, the phone plugged into the interface will provide phone service until repairs are made.

Cost advantages: You are no longer susceptible to billing tricks of the phone company.

Example of such a trick: If you don't pay inside wire maintenance fees, phone repairmen often claim that the problem is in the wiring on your premises—when it's really in outside wiring. *Result:* The phone company charges you for the repairs and visit, which should be free.

Also: You can repair an internal problem yourself or have an electrician do the job, which is often cheaper than the phone company's work. And you no longer have to pay inside wire maintenance fees, which cover the cost of any service call the phone company makes on the wires inside your house. Since these wires almost never break you can save up to $60/year for maintenance you don't need.

Source: Carl Oppedahl, a New York City lawyer and author of *The Telephone Book*, Weber Systems Inc., Chesterland, OH.

CAPPING THE CHIMNEY FLUE

Chimney problems. Warm air leaks out, and birds nest in the flue. Solution: A Keeper Kap that closes off the chimney flue at the roof. A long chain hangs down into the fireplace. To open the flue, pull the chain to release the spring loaded cover. A tug on the chain closes the flue.

EASY ENERGY-SAVING OPPORTUNITIES

Most homeowners know that insulation prevents heat loss and saves on energy bills. But the cold air that still sneaks into the house through cracks and other openings is the chief cause of wasted energy. If you add up all the air leaks in the average house, you'd have a hole about three feet in diameter.

There are, however, some simple and inexpensive ways to protect your home from infiltration.

To test for infiltration spots: Walk through your house with a lit candle or burning incense. You can tell where the drafts are by the amount of the smoke or flame—and the direction.

To protect against infiltration

• Repair or insulate obvious heat-loss sites. Broken shingles . . . holes in the foundation . . . openings around air vents, water pipes, utility meters, etc. . . . damaged glass.

• Use caulking* to fill in cracks. This should be done around doors, window frames and base boards . . . in exterior seams between different materials (bricks, wood, etc.), corners, aluminum- or vinyl-siding joints.

• Don't use your fireplace unless it is a new model that obtains its oxygen supply from outside the house. Most fireplaces use already-heated interior air to fuel the fire, then send the twice-heated air up the chimney. It may be warm in front of the fire . . . but your furnace has to work harder to replace lost air.

• Install an electronic set-back thermostat. This automatically lowers and raises house temperatures when you want. Example: It can be set to lower the temperature while you're at work and raise it before you get home in the evening. Then, lower it again while you sleep . . . and raise it before you wake.

• Make your water heater more efficient.

Source: Gary Mayk, acting managing editor, and David Sellers, research engineer, *Practical Homeowner,* 33 E. Minor St., Emmaus, PA 18098.

HOME ENERGY HINTS

• Draft resistance. Before winter sets in, trace drafts. A $\frac{1}{16}$-inch crack beneath a door lets out as much warm air as a 4-inch-square hole in the wall. Check with your utility about local energy audit services to help find leaks and stop heat losses.

• Cut kitchen heat loss by covering the range hood's vent (when not in use, of course). Use a piece of ¾-inch Styrofoam encased in aluminum foil. Attach it to the hood with springs, or by fastening temporarily with duct tape.

• Solar protection. Keep insurance in mind when converting a home to even partial solar power. Among the hazards: Rooftop storage tanks too heavy for present structural supports. Vulnerability of collection panels to hail, lightning, falling objects and vandalism. Potential bursting of pipes of liquid freezes in heat-transfer systems.

DO-IT-YOURSELF HEAT SAVER

Homemade reflectors placed behind your radiators give more efficient heating. Directions: Cut radiator-size sheets of quarter-inch-thick Styrofoam and cover one side with heavy-gauge aluminum foil. (Tape or staple it in place on the reverse side.) Slip the reflector behind the radiator, with the foil facing the room. The Styrofoam keeps the cold wall from absorbing heat, and the foil directs the heat out into the room.

For best circulation of radiator heat, keep the radiator fins well dusted and make sure that there is a free flow of air above and below the radiator. Drapes and furniture should be at a distance, and radiator covers should have ample holes at the top and bottom.

COOLING THE HOUSE WITHOUT AIR CONDITIONING

Ventilating fans can cool a whole house—or a single room—at a fraction (about 10%) of the cost of air conditioning. The trick is knowing how to use them.

Unlike oscillating fans, which simply move air around, ventilating fans exhaust hot air while pulling in cooler air. You control the source of the cooler air by manipulating windows. During the day, for example, downstairs windows on the shady northern or eastern side of the house are most likely to provide cool air. All other windows should be closed and shaded from direct sun with blinds and drapes.

At night, lower-floor windows can be shut for security while upstairs windows provide cool air. The very motion of air, like a light breeze, has a cooling effect.

Types of ventilating fans:

Attic fans are permanent installations above the upper floor. They are powerful enough to cool a whole house. The opening to the outside must be as large as the fan-blade frame in order to handle the air flow properly. Louvers, bird screening and (particularly) insect screening all reduce the exhaust capacity of a fan. A doorway or other opening must allow the fan to pull cool air directly up from the rest of the house. Direct-connected fans are quieter than belt-driven fans. Some attic fans have thermometers that automatically turn them off and on when the attic temperature reaches a certain degree of heat.

Window fans have adjustable screw-on panels to fit different window sizes. Less powerful than attic fans, they serve more limited spaces.

Box fans are portable and can be moved from room to room to cool smaller areas.

Picking the right size fan:

Ventilating fans are rated by the cubic feet per minute (CFM) of air that they can exhaust. For effective cooling, engineers recommend an air-change rate of 20 per hour (the entire volume of air in the area to be cooled is changed 20 times every 60 minutes). To calculate the required CFM rating for a particular room, calculate its volume in cubic feet. Then multiply this figure by $\frac{20}{60}$ ($\frac{1}{3}$). Example: A room 20 feet by 15 feet with an eight-foot ceiling contains 2,400 cubic feet of air. This multiplied by $\frac{1}{3}$ gives a CFM rating of 800 for a proper-size fan.

The CFM rating of an attic fan is done the same way. Total the cubic feet of the rooms and hallways you want cooled before multiplying by $\frac{1}{3}$.

Source: John Constance, licensed engineer, specializing in home maintenance, Cliffside Park, NJ.

AIR CONDITIONING SECRETS

Room air conditioners mounted in a window or through the wall are ideal for keeping small, comfortable havens against the worst of summer's hot spells. They can be more economical than central air conditioning because they are flexible—you cool only the rooms you are using. But even a single unit can be expensive.

Buy for economy. Suit the size of the unit to the room. Oversized air conditioners cool a room so fast that they don't have time to dehumidify the air properly. Slightly undersized units are more efficient (and cost less to begin with). Check the energy-efficiency tags on different models for lowest operating costs.

To keep a room cool with minimum use of the air conditioner:

• Limit the use of the air conditioner in the "open vent" setting—it brings in hot outside air that the machine must work hard to keep cooling.

• Protect the room from the direct heat of the sun with awnings, drapes or blinds.

• Close off rooms that you are air-conditioning.

• Turn off unnecessary lights. They add extra heat (fluorescent lights are coolest).

• Turn off the unit if you will be out of the room more than 30 minutes.

• Service room air conditioners annually to keep them efficient. Replace filters, keep condensers clean and lubricate the moving parts.

Buying too large an air conditioner is uneconomical. To find the most efficient machine:

Divide the BTU rating by the watts rating (also on the label). If the resulting number (the energy-efficiency rating) is eight or more, it won't run up your electric bill unduly.

Compare prices. Energy-efficient air conditioners cost more initially. Where use is heavy (the South) or electric rates are high (the Northeast), the price difference is probably worth the investment. Bonus: Energy-efficient air conditioners cool rooms faster.

Supplement central air conditioning with a room air conditioner in the most-used room. Greatest saving is when only one person is home and the excess cooling isn't needed.

Source: John D. Constance, licensed engineer specializing in home maintenance, Cliffside Park, NJ.

HOME EMERGENCY CHECKLIST

Vital information about the house should be known by everyone in the family in case of emergency. Key items: The location of the fuse box or circuit-breaker panel. Placement of the main shutoff valves for the water and gas lines. The location of the septic tank or the line to the main sewer. Also keep easily accessible: Records of the brands, ages and model numbers of the stove, refrigerator, freezer, dishwasher, furnace, washer and dryer.

Source: *Woman's Day.*

VISIBLE ADDRESS MAY SAVE YOUR LIFE

A clear address outside your house helps emergency vehicles (and visitors) locate you easily. Complaint of firemen and ambulance drivers: Most street addresses are difficult to find and hard to read. Solution: Put large figures where they are easily read from the center of the street at night during poor visibility.

BUYING A BURGLAR ALARM

Home alarm systems, once mainly for the rich, are coming into widespread use. Reason:

Locks aren't deterring burglars. Recent FBI figures show that 82% of the time, illegal entrance is gained through home doors, most often the front door.

Burglars just break open the door with their shoulders. Faced with a deadbolt or double lock, the burglar will use a heavy tool to take out the frame.

Best type of alarm: One that sounds off (not a silent alarm), so that the burglar is aware of it and alarm central (a security company office of the local police) is alerted. This makes sense, since most burglars are youngsters age 12–24 who live within an eight-block radius of the target.

Select a system with sensors on vulnerable doors and windows. The inexpensive alarm promoted at many electronics stores is not worthwhile. Good systems need a complex electrical tie-in in the basement as well as a control panel installed away from prying eyes and little children. Good systems can also switch on lights and TV sets and alert alarm central by automatic telephone dialing or a radio signal.

Have a secondary line of defense. This can be a few thin electronic pressure pads under rugs in high-traffic areas, or strategically placed photoelectric cells.

Choose a reputable, well-tested system. The brand names are American District Telegraph (ADT, the biggest alarm company), Honeywell, Silent Knight and ADEMCO.

Drawbacks: The greatest is the danger of continual false alarms. The police may ticket you if the family is to blame. Also, an alarm system needs regular testing and a routine for setting at night or when you're away.

Alarm systems can provide a false sense of security. The homeowner may not take all necessary precautions with locks or may leave the garage door partially open.

SECRETS OF A PROFESSIONAL BURGLAR

From my own experience as a successful burglar, and also from talking with hundreds of fellow inmates in prison for burglary, I've concluded that burglary is a psychological game. The only real deterrent is the realization that there is immediate danger to him, the burglar. Locks don't do this. Alarms don't do it. Hardcore doors don't do it. Only mind games really work. I'm not against good locks, sturdy doors and alarm systems. But if you rely 70% on mind games and 30% on hardware, you'll do much better in the end.

If a burglar sees warning signs, no matter how outlandish, on your house, he will think twice before breaking in. These signs should be handwritten, in large, clear print, on 6-inch by 8-inch cards posted above each doorknob. Don't put them on the street or in your yard where passersby can see them. You don't want to give a burglar a reason to case your place and find out they are not true. You can make up your own wording. Just be sure the signs look fresh and new. Some suggestions:

• Danger: Extremely vicious, barkless German Dobermans. In his nervous frame of mind, a burglar probably isn't going to wonder if there is such a thing. He won't want to take the chance.

• Knock all you want. We don't answer the door. Most burglars check to see if anyone's home before breaking in. About 95% of those questioned said they'd pass up a house with that sign.

• Carpenter: Please do not enter through this door. My son's three rattlesnakes have gotten out of the cage and we've closed them off in this room until he returns, hopefully in a few days. We're sorry for this inconvenience, but we don't want another person bitten. The first is still in the hospital.

• Please stop! We've already been forced to kill one burglar who was trying to get in while we weren't home. Please don't become the second. Like the barkless dog sign, this one seems outlandish. But a jittery burglar isn't going to stick around thinking up ways you could kill him while you're not home.

• Attack dogs trained and sold here. Again, 95% said they'd be gone like a shot if they saw this sign. Suggestion: Have one engraved, and post it on your front door (so it can't be seen from the street).

• Leave extremely large bones and two-foot wide dog dishes near all entrances. A person

up to no good will think a very large dog lives there.

• Paste stickers on the windows indicating that you have an alarm system. Try motion detector alarm: This building is equipped with laser-type motion detector devices. Bodily movement inside will set off audible or silent alarm. Some 85% of inmates questioned said they'd pass up a house with this notice. Also: Paste alarm foil along windows. Put suction cups on the inside of windows and alarm-type bells on the outside walls.

• Put fine gravel in your driveway or in gardens surrounding the house. This makes a lot of noise that burglars won't want to chance.

• When you go on vacation, don't tell anybody except the local police. Ask a neighbor to pick up your mail and newspapers and occasionally empty a small can of junk into your trash can. Close all curtains. Leave at least one, preferably two, radios on. Have your outside lights on a light-sensitive switch and inside ones on an alternating timer. Take your phone off the hook. Put up your deterrent signs.

• Buy an air horn (the kind small-boat owners use). If someone breaks in while you're at home, go to the opposite window and squeeze the horn. These horns can be heard for a mile over water. Everyone said this tactic would scare them off.

Common lock and alarm mistakes:

• Putting a deadbolt or other expensive lock on a flimsy door that can be kicked in. Also: Thinking that this lock will do the trick—but the burglar simply uses a bigger crowbar.

• Not locking the door when you're home.

• Positioning a lock on a door with a glass window in such a way that, if the window is broken, the burglar can reach in and unlock the door.

• Installing the burglar alarm on/off switch outside the house, not inside it.

• Forgetting to turn on your alarm.

Some burglar-survey results:

• 85% were deterred by hearing a TV or radio in the house.

• 75% were more likely to go through windows than doors. (Sliding glass doors are easier to open than wooden ones.) Remedy:

Storm windows. None surveyed would bother with them at all.

• 85% cased out a house before hitting it. Recommended: If you see a stranger hanging around, call the police.

• Only 20% picked locks or tried to pick them. Why: It takes too much skill. There are so many faster ways into a house.

• 63% cut the phone lines before entering. Remedy: A sign saying that the police will be notified automatically if the phone lines are cut.

• 65% said that a large, unfriendly dog would scare them away. Most frightening: Dobermans.

• 80% looked in garage windows to see if a homeowner's car was there. Remedy: Cover your garage windows.

• 50% said that neighborhood security guards didn't deter them.

• 72% made their entrance from the back.

• 56% continued to burglarize if they were already inside when they realized people were home sleeping.

BURGLARY PREVENTION

Do:

• Secure all windows and doors.

• Leave drapes open to a normal position.

• Engrave your Social Security number on all valuables that can be removed from the house.

• Arrange to have the lawn mowed and the newspapers and mail rerouted or stopped when you go on vacation.

• Trim shrubbery to eliminate hiding spots for prowlers.

• Leave your car lights on until you have opened the garage door.

• Have a house key ready when you arrive home.

• Instruct family members about these security precautions and procedures.

Don't:

• Let the telephone go unanswered or give any inviting information over the phone, such as the fact that you are not at home during the day.

• Advertise valuables by making them easily visible through your windows.

• Leave a key outside the house.

• Leave notes on doors.

• Leave a porch or front foyer light on. It advertises that you are probably not home.

• Leave a ladder outside.

• Enter your home if anything appears suspicious. Call the police from a neighbor's telephone. Don't lose your life trying to save items that can be replaced.

Source: Vertronix, manufacturer of electric burglar-detection systems, Larchmont, NY.

RECOMMENDATIONS OF A MASTER LOCKSMITH

Traditional wisdom says there's no point in putting a good lock on a flimsy door. This is not true. In most cases you must prove forcible entry to collect insurance. If you have a poor lock, your cylinder can be picked in seconds. You're inviting your insurance company to give you a hard time.

The best strategies:

• If you have a wooden door, get what the industry calls a police lock. This is a brace lock with a bar that goes from the lock into the floor about 30 inches away from the base of the door. Our favorite: Magic Eye. Its new model can be locked from the inside like the old model, but you can get out easily in an emergency. Also: Get a police lock if your door frame is weak. It keeps the door from giving because of the brace in the floor. Even the best regular locks won't protect you if the whole frame gives.

• If you're buying a door, buy a metal flush door without panels, and get an equally strong frame to match it. What makes a good frame: A hollow metal construction, same as the door.

• On a metal door, I like a Segal lock on the inside and a Medeco on the outside with a Medeco Bodyguard cylinder guard plate. If it's a tubular lock, get Medeco's D-11. It gives you the option of a key on the inside, and you don't need a guard plate.

• If your door opens out instead of in, get a

double bar lock—one that extends horizontally on each side. With a door that opens out, the hinges are often exposed on the outside, allowing a burglar to remove the door from its hinges. With a double bar lock he can't pull the door out.

Other important devices:

Plates: Pulling out the lock cylinder is the burglar's easiest and most effective way of getting in. Most people put a plate over their lock and think that will take care of it. But most plates have bolts that are exposed on the outside. With a hollow metal door, the burglar can pull that plate away from the door with a wedge and simply cut the bolts. If the head of the bolt is exposed, he can pull it out slightly with pliers and snap it right off. Remedy: Medeco's Bodyguard. A cylinder and plate combination, it's a drill-resistant, one-piece unit with no exposed bolts, a sleeve to prevent burglars from chiseling the bolts, and a hardened plate to protect the keyhole.

• Jimmy bars: Don't bother with them. They're psychological protection only. If you have a metal door, a good lock is sufficient protection. With a metal door, we recommend a jimmy bar only if the door has been damaged through a forcible break-in and is separated from the frame. In this case, the bar will straighten out the door and hide some of the light shining through. If you have a wooden door, a jimmy bar can actually help a burglar by giving him leverage. He can put a crowbar up against it, dig into the wood and break through the door.

• Peepholes: Get one that's as small as possible. Large peepholes use a one-way mirror that doesn't permit you to see around corners. And if someone hits that mirror while you're looking through, it could damage your eye. Small peepholes use a double lens, making it possible to see around corners. And if the small peephole is knocked off the door, it won't benefit the burglar. If a big one is knocked off, it creates a weakness in your security. Recommended: If you already have a large peephole, remove it. Have the locksmith bolt two plates on the door, with a smaller hole in the center to accommodate a small peephole.

• Closets: Let's say you want to protect a closet—not necessarily against burglars, but against someone who might have a key to your house or apartment. Locking the closet isn't sufficient, because most closets open out and have hinges on the outside, making it easy to remove the door. Remedy: A door pin. This involves putting the pin on the hinge side of the door and through a receiving hole in the frame. Anyone who cut the hinges off or removed the pins couldn't lift the door out.

• Window locks: The best window locks use a key, which makes them difficult to manipulate from the outside. Without a key, any window lock is vulnerable. Best: One with a heavy pin that allows you to drill holes for either complete locking or three- or six-inch ventilation. Our favorite: Lok Safe.

• Window gates: In New York and other cities, the fire laws prohibit window gates that lock with a key. Remedy: Gates with keyless locks. They allow you to get out easily, but a burglar can't put his hand through the gate to open it. Our favorite: P-A-G window gates.

Choosing a locksmith:

Go to locksmiths' shops to size them up. Make sure the store is devoted exclusively to the locksmith business and isn't just doing locksmithing on the side. Ask to see the locksmith's license if it's not displayed. There are a lot of unlicensed people doing business illegally. Best: Locksmiths who belong to an association. They are keeping up with the latest developments. Look for a sticker in the window indicating membership in a local or national locksmiths' association.

Source: Sal Schillizzi of All-Over Locksmiths, Inc. 1189 Lexington Ave., New York.

BEST PLACE IN YOUR HOUSE TO HIDE VALUABLES

Even if you have a safe, you still need a good hiding place for the safe key or combination. It should not be hidden anywhere near the safe. And if you don't have a safe, you should hide your jewelry and other valuables where they won't be found.

Recommendations:

• Don't hide things in any piece of furniture with drawers. Drawers are the first place burglars will ransack.

• Don't hide anything in the bedroom. Thieves tend to be most thorough in checking out bedrooms. Find hiding places in the attic, basement or other out-of-the-way areas. Best: The kitchen. In 90% of burglaries the kitchen is untouched.

• Don't be paranoid. If you have thought up a good location, relax. A burglar can't read your mind.

Good hiding places:

• Inside the phony wall switches and generic-label cans sold by mail-order houses.

• In a book, if you have a large book collection. So you don't forget which book you chose, use the title to remind you (for example, *The Golden Treasury of Science Fiction*). Or buy a hollowed-out book for this purpose.

• Inside zippered couch cushions.

• In the back of a console TV or stereo speakers (thieves usually steal only receivers, not speakers) or in the type of speakers that look like books.

• Under the dirt in a plant. Put non-paper valuables in a plastic bag and bury them.

• Under the carpet.

• In between stacks of pots in the kitchen, or wrapped up and labeled as food in the refrigerator or freezer.

Source: John Littlejohn, manager of Abbey Locksmith, Inc., New York.

The best hiding places for household valuables are those that look completely innocent and, preferably, would be inconvenient to take apart. Examples: Inside an old, out-of-order TV or vacuum cleaner in the basement. In a pile of scrap wood beneath the workbench. In the middle of a sack of grass seed.

Source: *How to Hide Your Valuables* by Linda Cain, Beehive Communications, Medfield, MA.

BEST SAFES

Valuable items require a safe that's protected on all six sides. Such safes carry the Underwriters Laboratories rating TRTL30x6. The most common safes on the market, usually labeled TL15, TL30 or TRTL30, are protected only on the front face and door.

Source: *Security World.*

SECURE WINDOWS

Glass blocks appear in more and more dwellings as replacements for windows. Reason: They are good protection from burglars, since they are very difficult to break. Typical uses: In basement windows and other ground-level openings that are susceptible to break-ins. Bonus: The insulating capacity of the blocks equals that of a regular window-with-storm combination. Three styles: Fully transparent, wavy surface that obscures vision, diamond pattern for prismatic effect.

BIGGEST HOUSE-FIRE DANGER SPOT

Not the kitchen, as commonly believed, but the living room. Fires there account for the largest number of deaths year after year. Safety measure: Install a smoke detector in the living room.

Source: *Journal of American Insurance.*

One smoke alarm isn't enough. Recommended: An alarm on each level of your home and in each bedroom.

Source: International Association of Fire Chiefs, Washington, DC.

EASY WAYS TO DO HARD THINGS

• Keep aluminum windows and doors in working order with simple maintenance procedures when you switch from screens to storm panels. (1) Clean the channels where window panels slide up and down with the crevice nozzle of the vacuum cleaner or a tiny stiff brush. Spray with silicone lubricant. (2) Spray stiff spring locks with a moisture-displacing penetrating lubricant (WD-40, for example). (3) To prevent oxidation and pitting on frames, scrub with a detergent solution, rinse and coat with a good grade of automobile wax.

• To unclog a sink drain, first place a basin below the trap (the U-shaped drainpipe beneath the sink). The basin will catch water that runs from the trap. Then use a wrench to unscrew the plug at the bottom of the trap. Slip on a rubber glove and move a finger into the open trap to loosen any blockages. To complete the job, run a stiff wire into either side of the trap. Screw in the plug and tighten it with the wrench.

• Sluggish sink drains respond to one of these treatments: Remove the strainer. Pour several pots of boiling-hot water down the drain. Then run hot tap water down the drain for a couple of minutes. If this does not bring results, pour one cup of baking soda into the drain. Follow this with one cup of vinegar.

Cover the drain opening tightly for 20 minutes. Then run hot tap water down the drain. Last resort: A commercial preparation.

• Prevent clogged drains by replacing the S-trap in the drainpipe with a squeezable trap. One hard squeeze sends a drain block on its way. Available from hardware and plumbing-supply stores. Easily connected with a screwdriver.

• To clean a burned pot, first dampen it. Sprinkle baking soda on the charred area, and add a little vinegar. Let it stand for 20 minutes. The pot should then wash clean.

• Alcohol stains on tabletops. To remove white rings, rub gently in one direction with moistened cigar ash or superfine steel wool dipped in mineral oil.

• Furniture scratches. For small blemishes: Try toothpaste—its mild abrasive action is effective on minor scratches. Deeper scratches or wide areas: Use a blend stick, crayon, liquid shoe polish or paste boot polish. Apply toothpaste to even out the finish after coloring.

Then wax with furniture polish and buff with a clean cloth.

• Sticky drawers. Rub the bottom rails with soap. If the rails are rough or worn, rub chalk on the drawer runners or sides or on the chest's rails or guides. Put the drawer back in and move it until it sticks. That spot will be marked by chalk. Sand or plane the sticky spot and then rub the area with soap.

• Cutting down on dust. Spray your home furnace filter with a no-wax dusting product that attracts and holds circulating particles. Then, clean the filter regularly. Do the same with the air-conditioner filter.

• Contact lenses lost in a carpet: Place a nylon stocking over the nozzle of a vacuum cleaner and carefully vacuum the area. The lens will be pulled up onto the stocking.

BEST TOILET BOWL CLEANER

In-tank toilet bowl cleaners containing calcium hypochlorite corrode the flushing mechanism. Moreover, cleaners are of little use. All toilet bowls get dirty, and the best way to clean them is with a sponge or brush and a liquid cleaner. Nonhypochlorite cleaners, which are okay to use: Automatic Liquid and Solid Vanish, Blu-Boy, Automatic Blue Sani-Flush, Dependo, Ty-D-Bol.

HOW TO NOISE-PROOF YOUR HOME

Noise intrusion is a constant and nagging problem in many buildings because of thin walls and badly insulated floors and ceilings. Some solutions:

Walls: Hang sound-absorbing materials such as quilts, decorative rugs or blankets. Note: Cork board and heavy window draperies absorb sound within a room but do not help much with noise from outside. Unique step: Carpeted walls provide excellent soundproofing. Some brands of carpet can be attached to the wall with adhesive. Alternative: A frame that attaches to the wall. Insulation goes on the wall within the frame, and then a fabric is affixed to the frame.

Ceilings: Acoustical tile may be applied directly to the ceiling with adhesive. Best: A dropped ceiling of acoustical tile with about six inches of insulation between the new and existing ceiling.

Floors: A thick plush carpet over a dense sponge rubber padding works well. Key: The padding must be dense, at least three-eighths of an inch thick. Your foot should not press down to the floor when you step on the padding.

VERSATILE VINEGAR

This safe, natural and inexpensive product is a handy thing to have around the house, aside from its obvious usefulness in the kitchen. It can be used as: A cleanser and deoxidizer. An antiseptic for minor first-aid needs. A fluid (three parts vinegar and one part water) that keeps windshields both ice and frost free.

ANTIQUE FURNITURE CARE

Use a room humidifier when central heating is on. (Dryness causes cracks and splits.) Keep furniture away from heat sources such as radiators, working fireplaces and direct sunlight. (Excessive heat will make it warp.) Use a clear, hard wax once a year, but avoid liquid or spray waxes containing silicon, which damages wood. Don't worry about any tiny bumps or scratches; they're signs of authenticity.
Source: *Diversion.*

WHEN YOU NEED AN EXTERMINATOR AND WHEN YOU DON'T

Bug problems can usually be solved without an exterminator. Keys: Careful prevention techniques, basic supermarket products and apartment-building cooperation.

Roaches are persistent pests that are the bane of apartment dwellers. The problem is not that roaches are so difficult to kill but that the effort has to be made collectively, by every tenant in a particular building. Roaches cannot be exterminated effectively from an individual apartment. If one apartment has them, they'll quickly spread throughout the building.

Most landlords hire exterminating services that visit during daytime hours when most tenants are at work. They wind up spraying just a few apartments, which is totally ineffective. Recommended:

• Apartment dwellers have to get together, contact their landlord and arrange for all apartments to be exterminated at the same time. If the landlord is uncooperative, the Board of Health should be notified. If you live in a co-op, the co-op board should make arrangements for building extermination. Best: A superintendent or member of the building staff should perform the regular exterminations, since he can get into apartments at odd hours when the tenants are not home. A professional exterminator should be called only as a backup, in case of a severe problem in a particular apartment.

• Incinerators that no longer burn garbage are a major infestation source in large buildings. Many cities, to cut down on air pollution, have ordered the compacting rather than the burning of garbage. Garbage is still thrown down the old brick chutes, which have been cracked from heat, to be compacted in the basement. Roaches breed in these cracks, fed by the wet garbage that comes down the chute, and travel to tenants' apartments. Remedy: Replacement of the brick chutes with smooth metal chutes which don't provide breeding places. Also: Compactors must be cleaned at least once a week.

• Homeowners do not need regular extermination for roaches. Since a house is a separate unit, a one-time extermination should do the job. Food stores are the major source of roach infestation in private homes. People bring roaches home with the groceries. Check your paper grocery bags for roaches before you store them.

• Ants and silverfish can be controlled by the homeowner himself, unless there is a major infestation. Don't call the exterminator for a half-dozen ants or silverfish. Try a store-bought spray first. Exception: Carpenter ants and grease-eating ants must be exterminated professionally.

• Clover mites come from cutting the grass. They look like little red dots. The mites land on windowsills after the lawn is mowed and then travel into the house. Remedy: Spray your grass with miticide before cutting.

• Spiders don't require an exterminator. Any aerosol will get rid of them.

• Termite control is a major job that needs specialized chemicals and equipment. Call an exterminator.

• Bees, wasps and hornets should be dealt with professionally. Their nests must be located and attacked after dusk, when the insects have returned to them. If the nest is not destroyed properly, damage to your home could result. Also: Many people are allergic to stings and don't know it until they are stung.

• Clothes moths can be eliminated by hanging a no-pest strip in your closet and keeping the door tightly closed.

• Flies can be minimized with an aerosol or sticky strip. An exterminator is of no help getting rid of flies. Best: Screens on all the windows and doors.

• Weevils and meal moths can be prevented by storing cereals, rice and grains in sealed containers. Also: Cereals are treated with bromides to repel infestation. The bromides eventually break down. Throw out old cereals.

There is no 100% effective solution to exterminating mice. Try these alternatives:

• Trapping is effective unless you have small children or pets.

• Poison should be placed behind the stove or refrigerator where children and pets can't get at it.

• Glue boards (available in supermarkets) placed along the walls can be very effective. Mice tend to run along the walls due to poor eyesight.

Many of the residual (long-lasting) sprays have been outlawed because they don't break down and disappear in the environment. The old favorites, DDT and Chlordane, are no longer permitted except for particular problems like termite control. What to use:

• Baygon, Diazanon and Dursban are general-purpose, toxic organo-phosphates meant for residual use in wet areas. They're recommended for all indoor insects, including roaches.

• Drione is a nontoxic silica gel, which dries up the membranes in insects. Recommended for indoor use in dry areas only, it is especially effective on roaches.

• Malathion is helpful in gardens, but it should not be used indoors.

• Pyrethrin is highly recommended, since it is made from flowers and is nontoxic. It has no residual effect, but is good for on-contact spraying of roaches and other insects. If there is a baby in the house, Pyrethrin is especially useful, since children under three months should never be exposed to toxic chemicals. Don't use it around hay-fever or asthma sufferers.

When buying products in the store, look at the label to determine the percentage of active ingredients. Solutions vary from 5% to 15%. The stronger the solution, the better the results.

Prevention is synonymous with sanitation. If you are not scrupulous about cleanliness, you will be wasting your money on sprays or exterminators.

Moisture is the main attractor of insects. If you live in a moist climate, you must be especially vigilant. Coffee spills, plumbing leaks, fish tanks, pet litter and pet food all attract bugs. Clean up after your pets, and take care of leaks and spills immediately. If puddles tend to collect around your house after it rains, improve the drainage.

• Word of mouth is the best way to choose a good exterminator. Don't rely on the *Yellow Pages*.

• Contracts for regular service, which many exterminators try to promote, are not recommended for private homes. A one-time extermination should do the trick, but apartment dwellers must exterminate buildingwide on a regular basis.

Source: Tom Heffernan, president of the Ozane Exterminating Co., Bayside, NY.

• Rout roaches without poisoning your kitchen. Boric acid or crumbled bay leaves will keep your cupboards pest-free. Another benign repellent: Chopped cucumbers.

Source: Clifton Meloan, chemist, Kansas State University, writing in *Science.*

• Wood storage and insects. Firewood kept in the house becomes a refuge and breeding ground for insects. Risky solution: Spraying the logs with insecticides. (When the sprayed wood burns, dangerous fumes could be emitted.) Better: Stack the wood (under plastic) outside and carry in only the amount needed.

• To remove a bat from your house at night, confine it to a single room, open the window and leave the bat alone. Chances are it will fly right out. Otherwise, during the day when the bat is torpid, flick it into a coffee can or other container. (Use gloves if you are squeamish.) Release it outdoors. Bats are really very valuable. A single brown bat can eat 3,000 mosquitoes a night. Note: Bats, like other mammals, can carry rabies. If you find a downed bat or you are scratched or bitten by one, call your local animal control agency and keep the animal for testing. However, very few people have contracted rabies directly from bats. More likely source: Skunks.

PLANT POISONING

Plant poisoning among adults has increased alarmingly in the last decade. For children under five, plants are second only to medicines as a cause of poisoning. Prime sources: Common houseplants, garden flowers and shrubs, as well as wild mushrooms, weeds and berries.

Most important rule: Never eat anything that you are not absolutely sure is safe. More than 700 US plants have been identified as poisonous when eaten, causing violent illness and sometimes death. If you suspect someone has eaten a poisonous plant: Call the nearest poison control center and your doctor. Try to collect samples of the plant for identification.

Among the most common poisonous plants:

Garden flowers: Bleeding heart, daffodils, delphinium, foxglove, hens and chickens, lantana, lily of the valley, lupine, sweet pea.

Houseplants: Caladium, dieffenbachia, philodendron.

Garden shrubs: Azalea, mountain laurel, oleander, privet, rhododendron, yew.

Wildflowers: Autumn crocus, buttercups, jimson weed, mayapple, moonseed berries, poison hemlock, water hemlock, wild mushrooms.

INDOOR PLANT CARE

Spider plants are the champion indoor plant for fast growing, catchy looks and long life with little care. The leaf colors range from solid deep green to green and white stripes. Fastest growers: Plants with all-green leaves. A small plant fills out in four months. Hang it in a north window (flowers form faster in low light). Keep the soil damp. Fertilize once a month.

Self-watering planters can tend your indoor garden while you are on vacation or simply save you time in regular maintenance. Based on the principle of capillary action, these non-mechanical pots come in a variety of sizes, shapes and finishes. They can be bought at garden centers or at florist shops. Foliage plants with modest demands will stay sufficiently moist for as long as three months. Names to look for: Akvamatic, Grosfillex and Natural Spring.

HOME REMEDIES FOR HOUSEPLANT PESTS

• Red spider mites. Four tablespoons of dishwashing liquid or one-half cake of yellow soap dissolved in one gallon of water. Spray weekly until mites are gone, then monthly.

• Hardshell scale. One-fourth teaspoon olive oil, two tablespoons baking soda, one teaspoon Dove liquid soap in two gallons of water. Spray or wipe on once a week for three weeks; repeat if necessary.

• Mold on soil. One tablespoon of vinegar in two quarts of water. Water weekly with solution until mold disappears.

• Mealybugs. Wipe with cotton swabs dipped in alcohol. Spray larger plants weekly with a solution of one part alcohol to three parts water until bugs no longer hatch.

Source: Decora Interior Plantscapes, Greenwich, CT.

TEN FOOLPROOF HOUSEPLANTS

These hardy species will survive almost anywhere and are a good choice for timid beginners without a lot of sunny windows.

• Aspidistra (cast-iron plant). This Victorian favorite, known as ''The Spittoon Plant,'' survived the implied indignity in many a tavern.

• Rubber plant. Likes a dim, cool interior (like a hallway). If given sun, it grows like crazy.

• Century (Kentia) palm. A long-lived, slow-growing plant that needs uniform moisture. Give it an occasional shower to dust it.

• Philodendrons. They like medium to low light and even moisture, but will tolerate dryness and poor light.

• Dumb cane. Tolerates a dry interior and low light, but responds to better conditions. Don't chew the foliage or your tongue will swell.

• Bromeliads. Exotic and slow-growing, they like frequent misting, but are practically immune to neglect and will flower even in subdued light.

• Corn plant (dracaena). Good for hot, dry apartments.

• Snake plant. Will survive almost anything.

• Spider plant. A tough, low-light plant that makes a great trailer and endures neglect.

• Nephthytis. Will flourish in poor light and survive the forgetful waterer.

Source: Edmond O. Moulin, director of horticulture, Brooklyn Botanic Garden, Brooklyn.

SECRET OF A GREAT LAWN

Less work makes a grassier lawn. Mowing: Set the blades to a height of 2–2½ inches, and cut the grass only once a week. When the weather gets really hot, every other week is fine. Benefits of taller grass: Less mowing, stronger and healthier plants that spread faster, more shade to discourage weeds. Bonus: Let the clippings lie. They will return nutrients to the soil.

Other work- and lawn-saving tips:

• Water only when there has been no significant rain for three or four weeks. Then give a one-inch soak. (Use a cup under the sprinkler pattern to measure—it takes longer than you think.) Frequent shallow watering keeps roots close to the surface, where they are vulnerable to drought and fungus disease.

• Use herbicides and insecticides only for specific problems. Routine use weakens the grass and kills earthworms.

• Sow bare spots with rye grass for a quick fix. Proper reseeding should be done in late August or early September, when the ground is cooler and moister.

• Apply fertilizer twice a year, but not in the Spring. September and November are the right months.

GARDENING FOR FUN AND FOOD

Growing your own produce can save money. Even when it does not, you still get exercise, fresh air, tension release and vitamin-packed harvests.

Home gardeners feel deep satisfaction in making the salad or seasoning the casserole with freshly picked plants. The taste is incomparable. It also works more fresh vegetables into meals. Surplus may be frozen, given as gifts or sold by the children.

Where space is limited, grow a minigarden, indoors or out. Windowsills, balconies and doorstep areas can be used, as well as milk cartons, pails, plastic buckets and cans.

Gear planting to local weather conditions. Summer planting can still be done in June in most regions. Planning for fall crops can be started in early summer.

Proper spacing is very important. One sturdy plant is better than several weak ones. Crowding chokes root systems, causing spindly growth and poor production. Save packet directions for referral.

Look for hybrid bush seeds rather than vining ones to save space.

Seeds do not always have to be bought. Reasonably fresh dill, anise, fennel, coriander and other seeds already on the spice rack should grow. If not, they are too old to add much to food anyway and should be replaced. Plant sprouting garlic cloves, ginger eyes, onions and potato eyes.

Scoop out seeds from vegetables you've bought. Dry them a week or so before planting. Zucchini, summer squash, beans and peas are among the easiest. Or try tomato seeds, especially cherry tomatoes.

Buy seeds for growing vegetables that don't contain seeds—beets, radishes, carrots, swiss chard, mustard greens, scallions, celery, shallots, endive, brussels sprouts, kale.

Ruffled-leaf lettuces grow more easily and are much more nutritious than iceberg. Sprouting (stalk) broccoli is easier than head broccoli.

Consider grapes and berries. Though some take a while to get established, they bear more each year.

Gardening offers a change from the monotony of the supermarket. You can grow yellow tomatoes, ornamental purple kale, scalloped squash—all interesting variations.

Soil preparation is crucial for good results. Have the soil tested annually. Every state has a land-grant college that will test soil for a small fee. It will give abundant basic gardening advice, largely free, through its Cooperative Extension arm. Check state or federal government listings under Agriculture. There are even offices in some large urban centers. Many have helpful USDA home and garden bulletins available. No. 202, *Growing Vegetables in the Home Garden,* and No. 163, *Minigardens for Vegetables,* are good starters. Some offices publish newsletters that give local planting suggestions plus listings of courses or talks about gardening. Get on mailing lists. Always be guided by local experts on the specifics, since weather can vary greatly even within a few miles.

Planting suggestions:

• Minimize weeding with mulch (hay or black plastic surrounding plants). It also helps retain soil moisture.

• Companion planting can help insect control. Example: Basil with tomatoes. (See organic gardening publications.)

• Look into raised-bed or hill planting when space or soil is limited.

• Where light is limited, put the smallest plants in front of the sun's arc, larger ones behind it.

• Harvest often. Many vegetables stop producing if allowed to fully mature.

• Don't expect instant results.

Source: Sally Sherwin, editor of *Investment Cooking.*

Vegetable seeds' life span: One to three years: Hybrid tomatoes, leeks, onions, corn. Three years: Beans, carrots, peas. Four years: Chard, fennel, beets, standard tomatoes. Five years: Brussels sprouts, broccoli, cantaloupe, radishes. To store seeds: Seal packet with freezer tape. Mark with date, and freeze in container.

BEST GARDEN CATALOGS

• Armstrong Nurseries, Box 614, Stevensville, MI 49127. Colorado blue spruce, pines, wonderful new hybrid peaches.

• Breck's, Peoria, IL 61632. Dutch tulips, crocus, etc.

• Brittingham Plant Farms, Box 2538, Salisbury, MD 21801. Twenty-seven varieties of strawberries.

• W. Atlee Burpee Co., 2103 Burpee Building, Warminster, PA 19874. Many varieties of vegetables and flowers.

• Henry Field's Seed & Nursery, 1008 Oak St., Shenandoah, IA 51602. A hundred pages of fruits and vegetables.

• Gurney's Seed Co., 1304 Buffalo Rd., Ro-

*Catalogs are free unless a price is indicated.

chester, NY 14264. Bicolor corn, cucumbers, melons and flowers.

• Inter-State Nurseries, 113 E St., Hamburg, IA 51640. All varieties of gladiolas.

• Jackson & Perkins Co., Medford, OR 97501. Bulbs, trees, wide variety of roses.

• J.W. Jung Seed Co., Randolf, WI 53956. Trees, flowers, vegetables.

• Kelly Bros., 281 Maple St., Dansville, NY 14437. Fruit trees, fruit plants, etc.

• Liberty Seed Co., Box 806-A, New Philadelphia, OH 44664. All kinds of garden seeds. Small charge.

• Earl May Seed Co., Shenandoah, IA 51603. Tomatoes, midget vegetables.

• J.E. Miller Nurseries, 510 West Lake Rd., Canandaigua, NY 14424. Fruit trees, vines, berries.

• Musser, Box 53N-A, Indiana, PA 15701. Fine-quality tree seedlings.

• Olds Seed Co., Box 7790, Madison, WI 53707. Flowers from A to Z.

• George W. Park Seed Co., 410 Cokesbury Rd., Greenwood, SC 29647. Complete garden supplies.

• Rex Bulb Farms, Box 774-E, Port Townsend, WA 98369. Lilies, etc. Small charge.

• Spring Hill Nurseries, 110 West Elm St., Tipp City, OH 45371. Widest variety of fruits, vegetables and plants. Small charge.

• Stokes' Seed Catalog, 1733 Stokes Building, Buffalo, NY 14240. Everything.

• Van Bourgondien & Sons, Route 109, Babylon, NY 11702. Finest domestic and imported bulbs and plants.

• Vermont Bean Seed Co., Garden Lane, Bomoseen, VT 05732. All kinds of vegetables.

• Wayside Gardens, 422 Garden Lane, Hodges, SC 29695. Over 1,000 varieties of garden plants. Small charge.

• White Flower Farm, Litchfield 3503, CT 06759. Everything for the garden. Small charge.

FLOWERS THAT ARE GOOD TO EAT

Many common flowers also make gourmet dishes. Calendula (pot marigold): Add minced petals to rice, omelets, chicken soup, clam chowder or stew. Nasturtium: Serve leaves like watercress on sandwiches, or stuff flowers with basic- and tarragon-seasoned rice, then simmer in chicken stock and sherry. Squash blossom: Pick blossoms as they are opening, dip in a flour-and-egg mixture seasoned with salt, pepper and tarragon, then deep-fry until golden brown. Camomile: Dry the flowers on a screen in a dark place to make tea. Borage: Toss with salad for a cucumberlike taste, or use fresh for tea.

Source: *House & Garden.*

BEST FOR BIRD FEEDERS

Mix your own seed. What birds like most: Niger seed (thistledown), sunflower seeds (particularly the thin-shelled oilseed), white proso millet and finely cracked corn. Avoid: Milo and red millet, which are used as filler in commercial mixes and are not attractive to birds. Peanut hearts attract starlings, which you may want to avoid. Requirements of a good feeder: It should keep the seed dry (mold by-products are toxic to birds) and be squirrel resistant (baffles above and below are good protection). For winter feeding of insect-eating birds (woodpeckers, chickadees, titmice and nuthatches), string up chunks of beef suet.

Source: Aelred D. Geis, Patuxent Wildlife Research Center of the US Fish and Wildlife Service, Laurel, MD.

7. Your Car

Your Car

FIXING YOUR PRESENT CAR VS. BUYING A NEW ONE

Some drivers run their cars into the ground and put them on the scrap heap long before their time. If you're considering trading your present car for a new one, you may want to reconsider. Most older cars can be refurbished—and in fact be made as good as new—for far less than the cost of a brand new car. The key: Determining the break-even point of the deal.

Let's say your present car is worth only $3,000, and the car you want to buy stickers for $10,000. The dealer will give you $3,000, and you're looking at carrying $7,000. By the time the car is paid off, you'll have spent close to $10,000 anyway.

To figure fix-up costs, first have a competent mechanic take a hard look at the car. Ask for a detailed list of everything that's wrong and costs to fix it up. Even if the car needs major work such as rebuilt transmission ($400), new tires ($300), new paint and minor body work ($500), new upholstery ($200), new brakes all around ($100), that would add up to $1,600. With that kind of renovation, a car should be good for another five years with no major repair expenses. Even if the car needed a complete new engine ($2,000), it would still be cheaper to repair the old car than to buy a brand new one.

Gas mileage is not a key consideration. Assume that a new car would get 50% better gas mileage than the older car. It would still take at least 10 years to break even on mileage alone. Example: Your present car gets 15 MPG, and a new car would get 30 MPG. You buy 1,000 gallons of fuel per year (15,000 miles of driving) and it costs $1.40 per gallon. Your present gas bill is $1,400 per year. The 30 MPG car would cost you $700 per year. At that rate, dis-regarding all the other expenses of the new car, it would take 14 years for a payback on the improved mileage.

On the other hand, if your car is worth less than $1,000 and is rusting, rebuilding is not recommended. Mechanical problems with an engine and power train can usually be solved fairly easily and are cost-effective in the long run. Severe rusting, however, can't be fixed.

Source: Tony Assenza, editor of *Motor Trend.*

BEST AND WORST FOUR-WHEEL DRIVE CARS

Four-wheel drive is the new wave in auto manufacturing—and not only for sporty luxury cars. Within five to 10 years, every auto manufacturer will have at least one four-wheel-drive passenger line suitable for family use.

The reason is twofold. For one thing, horsepower is back in fashion. Car owners are now willing to sacrifice marginal gains in fuel economy for peppier performance.

But the new fashion comes on the heels of the switch to front-wheel-drive cars. Problem: Heavy horsepower and front-wheel drive don't mix. When you pour too much power through two front wheels, you get "torque steer." The car wants to turn where traction is best...and the driver feels as though the steering wheel is being pulled from his hand. The result isn't actually dangerous, but it's worrisome. It makes handling unsatisfying and less precise.

Obvious solution: Divide the power among all four wheels. Besides preventing torque steer, four-wheel drive offers several other advantages:

• Traction is far superior—not only on

snow and ice, but on rainy and oil-slick roads, which can be just as treacherous.

• Handling is surer and more powerful, since the car's load is more evenly distributed. Sharp turns are more safely negotiated, especially at higher speeds.

• Acceleration is smoother, if not faster, with no spinning of wheels.

• Tire wear is relatively even.

You get all of this for an added cost of only about $500 (a figure that is bound to go down as more units are manufactured).

There are few disadvantages to four-wheel drive. You may lose a little passenger room because of the added drive shaft. And you'll add 50-100 pounds to the weight of a given car, which means a slight reduction in economy. But in a good design, neither of these factors will be significant.

Current choices: Today's elite four-wheel-drive cars are the Audi Quattro 4000 (about $18,000) and the 500 ($24,000). They lead the pack for both performance and safety features.

For less money, you can do very well with any Subaru. All its four-wheel-drive models can be switched to front-wheel drive in good weather (for a fuel saving of a couple of miles per gallon). All are durable and reliable. If you want to add some dash, try Subaru's new top-of-the-line XT coupe ($14,000 base).

A unique contender is the Dodge Colt Vista, a seven-passenger hybrid between a van and a station wagon. At only $10,000, it makes a lot of sense for any large family.

The model to avoid is the AMC Eagle. It's mechanically antiquated and unwieldy, with truck components bolted to a station-wagon body.

At least five other automakers are expected to enter the four-wheel-drive market, including BMW, Merkur (by Ford of Europe), Volkswagen (in its Golf line) and domestic Ford.

Bottom line: Four-wheel drive has obvious benefits in the Snow Belt. But it's also a plus for anyone who has a steep driveway or who rolls up heavy mileage, regardless of climate.

Source: Tony Assenza, an associate editor of *Motor Trend.*

HOW TO BUY A CAR WITHOUT GETTING TAKEN FOR A RIDE

There's more to buying a car than price. Where you buy it counts, too. Take the time to evaluate different dealerships. Go to a few and walk around. When a salesperson comes up to you and one will—say, "I'm just looking around. I'll come to you when I'm ready." Don't let any of them intimidate you.

Walk through the service area and sit down. Stay for about a half hour. Observe:

Is it orderly and run efficiently?

Is the manager there and working?

Are the customers treated with respect?

Proceed into the service lot and look at the license plate frames. In a good dealership you'll see frames from competing dealerships, too.

Don't choose a dealership that's out of the way. The salespeople know that they have just one chance to make a sale, and they lean hard on you. Also avoid multifranchise dealerships. Too many people run different parts of the operation, causing confusion in service.

Choose your salespeople—don't let them choose you. Speak with several. Ask:

• How long have you been at this dealership? (The longer, the better.)

• Where else have you worked? For how long?

• May I get the name and number of a recent customer? (Follow up with a phone call.)

If there's a lot of turnover, leave—the dealership is unstable. Trap: Looking for a salesperson who's a member of your ethnic group because you think you'll get special treatment. You won't, and you'll be letting your guard down.

Educate yourself. Get as much information as possible about a car before you sit down with the salesperson. Collect brochures (dealers don't usually keep them on display, because they want you to approach the salespeople) and read consumer magazines that rate autos.

Don't let salespeople woo you into trusting them with their "impressive" knowledge of a car. That's how they try to establish authority and take control of the sale.

Know the competition, too. If you say that you're considering a competing brand, the salesperson will knock it and be very convincing if you're uninformed.

If you're not firm about what you want, you could easily end up with what the salesperson wants to sell you—the most expensive model, with the most extravagant options, at the highest price.

Once you show serious intentions of buying, the salesperson will offer you a test drive, during which he will talk glowingly about the car to get you to take mental ownership of it. He is seducing you. Resist.

Trap: Negotiating to buy when you're tired of shopping. Salespeople are attracted to this kind of customer like bees to honey. They know that if they promise you what you've been looking for—whether they have it or not—you'll probably buy on the spot. Buy only in an energetic mood.

Few salespeople ask idle questions. Seemingly irrelevant questions are actually attempts to find out about your lifestyle, income, driving habits, etc. Avoid answering these questions.

Options are where dealers make their money. Common tactic: The dealer says, "Sorry, but all the cars arrive with power windows. If you don't want them, I'll have to make a special order. It could take several months." Result: You end up paying for an option that you don't want. But if you stand firm, he'll work something out—he wants the sale.

Another trick: Cars for the lot are ordered without carpeting, and customers are told that carpeting is extra, when it's really standard. Read the dealer's brochure carefully. It lists every standard option and every extra.

Also make sure every option has the car's name on it: That means the dealership is responsible for it if it breaks. For example, Honda uses Alpine brand radios, but Honda's name is on the faceplate—which means Honda is responsible.

To get the best price, get a range of prices from several dealerships, and write them down. When you're at the first one, don't let the salesperson know it. When he asks what other dealers have quoted, say, "Why don't you give me your best deal and we'll take it from there."

Read this sticker carefully: D.A.P. stands for Dealer Added Profit. Locator Cost means the dealer located the car. Procurement Cost means the dealer procured the car. All these charges are negotiable.

Take particular note of a common price-padding tactic: A prep fee of $100 or more (whatever the dealership thinks it can get away with). The cost of preparing your car for delivery is already included in the manufacturer's sticker price.

Salespeople's trick: Constantly consulting with the manager and pretending that they're on your side. They aren't—they work on commission.

Don't shop for price by phone because salespeople will quote anything just to get you into the dealership. Shop for financing in advance so you'll know a good deal when you hear one. Don't believe salespeople who claim that they can get you good insurance rates—they can't.

Trap: Accepting a trade-in price for your old car that you know is too high. The dealership will make up the difference on the price of the new car or on the options.

Don't let yourself get "turned over." If a salesperson feels that he's not in control of the sale, he'll say that he's going on a coffee break and will "turn you over" to another salesperson. In a high-pressure operation, this could happen three or four times, until they wear you down. How to resist: Go out for a walk, have a cup of coffee at a nearby diner, say that you need to think about it. Get away from the salespeople so you can think clearly.

When the deed is done, inspect your new car thoroughly before you leave the dealership. Make sure everything is working correctly.

Final dirty trick: The car was dented in transport, so the dealer parks it close to a wall to hide the damage—which greets you when you arrive home.

Source: Two veteran car salesmen who asked to remain anonymous.

BEST TIME OF YEAR TO GET A GOOD DEAL ON A CAR

The best car-buying time is shortly before Christmas, when business tends to be slow and dealers are willing to take smaller profits. Also good: The post-holiday period into February, especially in cold-winter climates. Best day: A rainy Monday.

Source: *Consumer Adviser,* Reader's Digest Association, Inc., Pleasantville, NY.

LEASING VS. BUYING

Leasing a car costs an average 15% more than buying, but it pays off in some situations. Lease if you: Keep a car for only two or three years, don't like to deal with auto maintenance, want to use the auto down-payment money for other investments, drive your car for business purposes, are a high-mileage driver, prefer a medium- or high-priced vehicle.

HOW TO PLAY THE CAR-BUYING GAME TO WIN

Remar Sutton rocked the auto establishment by telling the inside story on how new and used cars are sold.

Must buying a car always be a duel with the salesman?

To save money, you have to learn to play the game. Salesmen thrive on confusion. They bombard you with questions and numbers to divert your attention from simple issues.

Go shopping armed with specific information. Remember that you're not there to fall in love with a car or to make a friend of the salesman. Get answers you can understand.

Strategic suggestions: Be indecisive. The salesman will think there's a car you like better down the road. That means he must give you his best shot.

Best times to shop: If you know what you are doing, you can get the same price any time. But there are times when it is easier to get the best deal. Examples: the last day of the month, when dealers close their books and want good sales figures, and very late in the day, when the sales staff is exhausted.

During red tag sales, dealers' profits are higher than at any other time. Customers mistakenly assume they will save money during special sales. Really, they are fantasies that draw you away from reality. Stay with black-and-white issues you can control.

Decide what you can afford. This is determined by two things: How much cash your trade-in gives you towards the down payment and how much you can shell out each month.

Find out the true wholesale value of your present car. Tell dealers you are interested in selling your car for cash. Their figures will give you a better idea of what your car is worth than a blue book. Selling your old car is one transaction, and buying the new or used car is another. Don't mix the two.

It's best to sell your car privately. A dealer will only give you the wholesale price so the car can be resold at a profit. If you sell it yourself, get the retail price and pocket the profit yourself.

Buy the latest edition of *Edmund's New Car Prices.* It lists the base costs of each car and accessories such as air conditioning and automatic transmission. Thus armed, go to the showrooms. When you find the car you like, copy down all pricing information from the manufacturer's sticker on the window. Compare the sticker prices with those in *Edmund's* to determine the dealer's profit. This gives you real bargaining ammunition.

Tell the dealer you want a car without undercoating, rust-proofing, glazing and fabric protectors. Unfortunately, many cars come with those extras already in place. If so, negotiate on the basis of the car price without the add-ons. Then offer 50% of what the dealer is asking for those extras.

Source: Remar Sutton, car dealer and author of *Don't Get Taken Every Time: The Insider's Guide to Buying Your Next Car,* Penguin Books, New York, is also consumer commentator for cable and TV networks.

NEW-CAR OPTIONS

Select your options carefully. They can quickly inflate the purchase price of your car. There are two categories of options:

• Performance. Includes disc brakes, radial tires and manual transmission. The cost of these options is cheaper when ordered with a new car than if bought separately. The dealer's profit (and your bargaining margin) on performance options is about 20%.

• Luxury. Includes air conditioning, power

seats, power windows, cruise control and sun roof. These options are very expensive for what you get. Worse: They have a high frequency-of-failure rate. You'll probably have to pay for repairs. The dealer's profit on these options is about 30%.

COLORS THAT INCREASE A CARS RESALE VALUE AND SAFETY

Other things being equal, color can be a crucial factor, affecting safety and resale value. Safety: White is the most visible color in most situations. Yellow and orange are best when driving in heavy snow or white sand. Under adverse conditions, the most difficult colors to detect are gray, red, blue, brown or black. The least visible color in general is dark green. Resale value: Red and beige are the most popular colors. Blue cars also sell well (unless they're a very light shade of blue). But yellow, white and metallics are not much in demand. **Source:** National Association of Fleet Administrators.

TOP-OF-THE-LINE CAR STEREOS

For the serious music lover who spends a lot of time in a car, first-rate radio and tape systems are available—at a price. Although most factory-installed stereos are mediocre, a number of audio companies make good sound systems for cars.

Like home stereo systems, car stereos are bought in components:
• Radio/tape decks: Alpine, Kenwood and Sony.
• Speakers: Sound to rival home units... B and W and ADS.
• Amplifiers: High-powered units with low distortion and good reliability are made by ADS and Alpine.

Essential: Professional installation with a warranty. Proper mounting and wiring of the components affect not only the sound but also the system's longevity.

TAKING DELIVERY

Before accepting your car from the dealer, allow him enough time to "prepare" the car. Before you buy, find out what the dealer's preparation includes. Engine tune-up? Emission checks? Installation of optional equipment and a test drive? Some automobile dealers charge extra for every step of the preparation.

Inspect the car yourself. Check paint and body moldings. Examine the car in daylight. Look for imperfections and mismatched colors. The car may have been damaged in transit and repainted.

Compare the list of options on your bill of sale with those actually on the car. Be sure they are the options you ordered and not inferior substitutes.

Examine doors, latches and windows to see that they are operating properly. Inspect tires for cuts and bulges. Look at the interior finish. Test the heater, the radio and the air conditioner.

During the first week of ownership, test drive the car under as many conditions as possible. If the car does not perform satisfactorily, then you will have a better chance of getting the car dealer to make adjustments than if you wait a month or two before complaining.

HOW TO BUY A USED CAR

Before looking for a used car, decide the exact make, model and price you want (just as you would if you were buying a new car). Most important: Determine whether you want to use the car for extensive traveling, for weekends and summer travel, or just for getting to the train station and back. This helps you decide whether you want a three- to five-year-old car (extensive travel) or one five to seven years old (suitable for weekend use and summer travel). For trips to the train station in the morning, or for equivalent use, a car that is seven to 10 years old will do.

To choose the right car:
• Choose a popular make in its most successful and long-lasting model. These are easy to

find, if you go to a trusted car mechanic. He knows from experience which cars are sturdy and relatively trouble free. Repair parts are also easier to find.

• Get the local paper with the most advertising for used merchandise. It will offer a large selection of privately owned, often very well maintained cars, at prices much lower than those being offered by dealers.

• Look for the deluxe model of the popular make you've chosen. Since it cost a lot more when it was new, there's a better chance it was well cared for than the economy-class version. It's worth paying the few dollars' difference to get a deluxe secondhand car. The same principle applies when you're deciding what kind of car to look for. The difference in price between a new Cadillac and a new Chevrolet is substantial. As used cars, the difference is slight.

The gas question: Although the deluxe model is usually large and heavier and can be a gas guzzler, you'll still save more, in the long run, with a deluxe model than with a smaller car. Reason: You pay a premium for smaller, more gas-efficient cars, without getting much in return. The annual gas expense of a second car is not high to begin with, since the car tends to be driven less. Another factor: The larger, more expensive, well-built cars will last longer and require fewer repairs. Even though the repairs themselves may be somewhat more expensive, the overall costs of repair may end up much lower than those for the cheaper model. Bonuses: The larger car provides a much higher margin of safety in an accident. And deluxe models come with all sorts of extras.

• Search for the going price of your desired make and model. Then select only those cars offered at above the average price. Owners of the better-cared-for cars usually demand a premium. That premium will usually be very small, considering what a well-maintained deluxe model will save you in the future. Advantage of dealing with a private owner: You can get the true history of the car. A professional is much more likely to give you a slick story.

• The car should require no repair of any kind. One in need of work when sold indicates a lack of ongoing maintenance. Don't worry about high mileage or body dents. A high-mileage, well-maintained car is a better buy than a low-mileage car that has been driven hard.

Best time to buy: In the winter. Car buying increases in spring and summer, when people are more interested in travel. It's easier to get a good buy in winter, when customers are fewer.
Source: Dr. Peter Shaw, used car expert.

You don't have to be an expert to decide whether a used car is worth paying a mechanic to check out. Even if you can't tell a carburetor from a drive shaft, you can make an inspection that will be valuable to you in negotiating your final price with a dealer. The key steps:

• Get the name and telephone number of the previous owner. If the dealer won't give you this information from the title, pass up the car. (It could be stolen.)

• Call the former owner and ask what the car's major problems were (not if it had any problems). Also, get the mileage on the car when it was sold. If the speedometer now reads less, it has been tampered with. Go elsewhere.

• Inspect it yourself. Even a superficial look can reveal some signs that will warn you off or will be worth getting repair estimates for before you settle on a price.

• Check the car for signs of fresh undercoating. There is only one incentive for a dealer to undercoat an old car—to hide rust. Check this with a knife or screwdriver (with the dealer's permission). If you find rust, forget the car.

• Rub your finger inside the tailpipe. If it comes out oily, the car is burning oil, and your mechanic should find out why.

• Kneel down by each front fender and look down the length of the car. Ripples in the metal or patches of slightly mismatched paint can indicate bodywork. If a rippled or unmatched area is more than a foot square, ask the mechanic to look at the frame carefully. (Ask the former owner how bad the wreck was.)

• Open and close all the doors. A door that has to be forced is another sign of a possible wreck.

• Rust can mean expensive body replacements are needed. Check around moldings, under the bumper, at the bottom of doors, in the trunk, under floor mats and around windows. Lumps in vinyl tops are usually a sign of rust. Rust and corrosion on the radiator mean leaks.

• Check the tires. Are they all the same type? Does the spare match? If there is excessive wear on the edges of any single tire, the car is probably out of alignment.

• Check the brakes by applying strong pressure to the pedal and holding it for 30 seconds. If it continues to the floor, it needs work.

• Test-drive the car, and note anything that doesn't work, from the air conditioner to the windshield wipers. Listen for knocks in the engine and grinding or humming in the gears. Check the brakes and the steering. Drive over bumpy terrain to check the shock absorbers.

Source: *Don't Get Taken Every Time: The Insider's Guide to Buying Your Next Car* by Remar Sutton, Penguin Books, New York.

HOW TO SELL YOUR CAR

Body: Wash and wax your car, and touch up small nicks and scratches. If major bodywork or repainting is required, determine whether you would do better by making the investment or by selling the car as is.

Interior: Vacuum and dust, cover worn carpeting with mats, oil squeaky hinges. If necessary, replace pedal pads.

Engine: Remove oil and grease with products made for that purpose. Use a baking-soda solution to clean battery terminals. If it's needed, get a tune-up.

What price? Look up your car's value in the *NADA Official Used-Car Guide* or the *Red Book* at your library, bank, auto club or auto dealership. Either book guides you in allowing for accessories, condition and mileage. You will arrive at the wholesale (trade-in or loan) value and the retail value (normally charged by dealers).

Ask a couple of dealers what they would offer you for the car. Compare that with your wholesale value. Look at the prices of comparable cars advertised in your newspaper.

By now, you should have a good idea of the price you can expect. It will be somewhere between wholesale and retail. Determine your

asking price and the minimum amount you would accept. Now you're all ready to go to market.

Your best bet is to advertise in your local newspaper on Friday, Saturday and Sunday, when most people are looking to buy. Use positive phrases like "one owner," "low mileage" and "excellent condition," if they truly apply. There is debate about the wisdom of stating price, but if you do, you will eliminate shoppers looking for giveaways. Suggest negotiability. Example: Asking $2,000.

Precautions: Most people will want to road test the car they are considering buying and perhaps to have a mechanic inspect it. However, be wary of car thieves and irresponsible drivers. Join the prospective buyer on the test drive. If that's not possible, protect yourself by asking to see the driver's license and other identification. Record the information. Agree to a reasonable amount of time for the excursion, but no more than an hour. It is reassuring if the person arrives by car and leaves that vehicle while testing yours.

Payment: Accept only cash or a certified check. If it is a personal check, go with the buyer to the bank to have it cashed. Do not transfer title until you have been fully paid.

Notifications: Let your state's motor vehicles department know of the sale so that you won't be held responsible for the new owner's traffic violations. Also notify your insurance company.

Source: Sal Nuccio, president of the Nuccio Organization, financial consultants, Yonkers, NY, and author of *The New York Times Guide to Personal Finance*.

Used cars sell fastest when they're bright red or beige. Next best: Blue, if not too light. Less desirable: Yellow, white and metallic colors. Hardest to unload: Green cars.

Source: Runzheimer & Co., Rochester, WI.

WHAT AUTOMAKERS WON'T TELL YOU

One of the best-kept secrets of the automobile industry is the existence of informal warranties. How they work: When a significant number of new-model cars are reported to have the same mechanical problem, the manufacturer may inform regional sales offices and car dealers that it will cover the cost of repair—beyond the standard warranty.

Problem: Neither manufacturers nor dealers publicize these warranties.

Solution: If your car has a malfunction that may be covered under one of these warranties, write to the Center for Auto Safety (2001 S St. NW Washington, DC 20009), an auto-complaint clearinghouse that tracks corporate memoranda, bulletins to regional offices and dealers, and car-owner complaints to deduce which components are likely to fall under informal warranties. Tell the Center the automobile's year, model, and problem, and you'll be sent pertinent information.

If the malfunctioning component appears to be covered, speak with the dealer's service manager for repairs. . .and if he or she won't fix the problem, contact the factory's regional office and ask the factory representative to mediate.

Last resort: Take the dealer to small-claims court or seek arbitration through the Better Business Bureau. You'll have a good chance of winning if you're armed with documentation.

Source: Robert Dewey of the vehicle safety division, Center for Auto Safety.

MOST DANGEROUS TIME OF DAY TO DRIVE

The worst time to drive is between midnight and 3 AM. You're 13 times more likely to have a fatal car accident than between 6 AM and 6 PM. Most dangerous hour: From 2 AM to 3 AM on Sunday morning (after the bars close)—your chance of a fatal accident then is 22 times higher.

Source: Study by Sherman Stein, professor of mathematics, University of California at Davis.

CAR SAFETY SECRETS

Small, two-door cars have the worst accident records. The safest vehicles are the larger, four-door cars and all sizes of station wagons.

Worst overall injury record: Datsun 200 SX, Subaru DL, Plymouth Sapporo, Dodge Challenger.

Worst collision-loss record in the high-priced sports-specialty category: Chevrolet Corvette, BMW320i, Datsun 280ZX.

Best record: Mercury Marquis, Oldsmobile Cutlass wagon, Buick Le Sabre, Oldsmobile Delta 88.

More information: Highway Loss Data Institute, Washington, DC.

Don't pump the brakes if your car has the increasingly popular disk variety. The danger: When you pump disk brakes, there's a chance they might not release at all. Occasionally, they lock. Right method: Apply slow, steady pressure. Then ease up and slowly repeat the procedure.

Source: Peterson, Howell & Heather, fleet management consultants, Baltimore, MD.

Front-wheel vehicles: (1) Don't take your foot off the gas too suddenly when going into a skid. Better: Step lightly on the gas pedal. If the road is too narrow for that, shift into neutral and continue to steer. (2) Never put extra weight in the rear trunk compartment. It reduces traction rather than improves it.

• Driving on ice. The warmer the temperature, the more hazardous the driving on icy surfaces. Ice at 30°F is twice as slippery as ice at 0°F.

• Skidding. For front-wheel-drive cars: If rear wheels lose traction, step lightly on the gas. (The front wheels pull the car forward, and the rear wheels follow.) Don't do this when front wheels lose traction. That could make matters worse.

• Stuck in snow. Turn the auto's wheels from side to side to clear snow away. Then gently ease forward with wheels kept as straight as possible. Rocking back and forth can be helpful, as long as you swing higher in each move.

• Windshield freeze-up. The washer fluid must be correct for the outdoor temperature. Before using the fluid, prepare the windshield by heating it with a full blast from the defroster.

• Fog and mist. Use all lights, including four-way flashers.

• Braking distance. For rear-wheel vehicles

moving at 20 mph, use of snow tires will not result in any improvement over regular tires. But studded types and reinforced chains (under the same conditions) yield 20% and 50% improvements, respectively. Snow tires do help when driving on loosely packed snow. Estimated improvement: 13%. But again, reinforced chains (with a 37% improvement) are a lot better.

Source: *National Association of Fleet Administrators (NAFA) Bulletin.*

WINTERIZING CHECKLIST

• Radiator coolant: Read the label on your antifreeze to be sure you make the right blend of water and antifreeze. The antifreeze keeps your radiator from freezing and cracking; the water, even in winter, keeps your car from overheating.

• Battery condition: You car needs three to four times more starting power in winter than in summer. Have a mechanic do a complete battery draw and load test. If your battery fails, a recharge may save it for another year. Otherwise, invest in a new one.

• Windshield washer fluid: Frozen fluid in the washer tank is dangerous. Use a premixed commercial fluid. Check that the hoses are clear, and clean the washer nozzles out with a thin piece of wire.

• Electrical system: Make sure the distributor cap, points, condenser, ignition coil, spark plugs, and spark-plug cables are in good shape. Borderline components that still function in summer will give out in cold weather.

• Hoses and belts: If they are cracking or fraying, replace them.

• Tires: If you have all-season tires, be sure the tread is still good enough to give you traction on slippery roads. Otherwise, put on snow tires. Important: If you have a front-wheel drive car, the snow tires go on the front. Store summer tires on their sides, not on the tread. (Storing on the tread causes a flat spot and an unbalanced tire.) Inflate stored tires to only 50% of their operating pressure.

• Windshield: Apply antifogging compound to the inside.

• Cleaning: Clear dead bugs off the radiator by hosing it from the inside of the engine compartment. Pick out dead leaves and debris from the fresh-air intake box of the ventilation system.

• Stock up: Buy flares, an aerosol wire-drying agent, a scraper and brush, chains and a military-style collapsible trench tool for emergencies. Keep a lock de-icer at home and/or at the office for getting into the car in freezing weather.

WINTER WINDSHIELD WIPERS

Snow Belt drivers may want to shift to windshield wiper blades specially designed to handle snow and ice. A rubber boot completely covers the blade, preventing ice buildup on the connectors. This maintains the flexing action needed when the wiper moves over the curved surface of the windshield.

ALL ABOUT SPEEDING TICKETS

The best way to avoid speeding tickets is, of course, to avoid speeding. But all of us drive over the limit occasionally.

Here are some suggestions to help you avoid tickets:

• Know the limits. It's no illusion that police officers generally ignore cars driving just slightly over the posted speed. In fact, many departments set threshold speeds (for example, six miles an hour above the limit) at which officers are to take no action. You might be able to slip by at 65 mph in a 55 mph zone, but you're unlikely to do the same at 70 mph.

• Be selective. Most speeding tickets are written during the morning and evening rush hours, when there are more motorists and more police officers on the road. Late night and very early morning traffic are not watched nearly as carefully.

• Drive unobtrusively. Flashy cars attract attention, something to keep in mind if you drive a red Maserati. The same applies to flashy driving styles. Don't tailgate slower cars to force them aside. Don't weave in and out of traffic.

• Be vigilant. The likeliest spot to get nabbed on the highway is just beyond a blind curve or the crest of a hill, the best hiding places for patrol cars. Learn to recognize probable traps, and reduce your speed whenever appropriate.

• Remember that police officers can nab speeders from virtually any position—the rear, the front, the side, or even from aircraft. Be on the lookout at all times. An unmarked car with its trunk open on the side of the road is especially suspect. (A radar device may be inside.)

• Fight back. Radar guns can be foiled occasionally. What to do: Position your car close to other cars whenever possible. Police officers generally cannot match your speed with the speed indicated on their guns unless they have an unobstructed view of your car. In most states, motorists also can make use of radar detectors, devices designed to alert drivers to radar early enough for them to slow down before police officers can get a good reading. If you do a lot of driving, a detector is a sensible investment if it is legal in your area.

• Use psychology. All is not lost even if you are pulled over. Police officers feel vulnerable when stopping speeders. You could be speeding away from a murder for all they know, and consequently they are usually nervous. Put them at ease. Sit still, keep your hands in plain view (on the steering wheel is a good place). Be courteous and respectful. Above all, be honest. If you have a good excuse for going over the limit, state it. Otherwise, admit guilt and apologize. Police officers can be surprisingly lenient if you're cordial.

RUSTPROOFING CAUTION

Don't assume your car has really been protected. Reasons: Many new-car buyers pay upward of $200 for rustproofing that later turns out to be a botch job. Worst offender:

New-car dealers. They do about 70% of all rustproofing.

More information. *Rust Never Sleeps,* Consumer and Antitrust Division, Maine Attorney General's Office, State House, Augusta, ME.

BEWARE OF CAR WAXES

Nearly all car waxes contain abrasives, which are needed to remove the effects of oxidation in older cars—but can destroy new car finishes. Tip-off: A wax labeled as a cleaner and polisher will scratch. *To protect your car during the first year:* Use silicone, available at paint supply stores, instead of wax. Regularly wash the car using car soap and non abrasive towels, such as diapers. Don't go to a car wash that uses brushes—they scratch the paint. After a year, choose mildly abrasive waxes to remove built-up debris.

Source: Dré Brungardt, editor of *Nutz & Boltz,* Box 123, Butler, MD 21023.

SIMPLE CAR CARE

Half the cars checked in a recent survey had dirty air filters. One third had more than one underinflated tire and were more than one quart low on oil. Almost half had corroded batteries, were low on coolant and lacked windshield-wiper fluid.

Source: Survey by Car Care Council.

HOT WEATHER CHECKLIST

• Inspect the radiator for leaks, and check the fluid level.

• Check all hoses for possible cracks or sponginess. Make sure all connections are tight and leak free.

• Test the thermostat for proper operation. If it does not operate at the proper temperature, overheating could occur.

• Inspect the fan belt for cracks and proper tension. Belt slippage is a common cause of boilovers. It also drains electrical power.

• If loss of coolant has been a problem, check for water seepage on the water pump around the engine block.

Emergency road action:

• Don't turn off the engine when the temperature warning light goes on. If stuck in traffic, shift to neutral, and race the engine moderately for 30 seconds at two-minute intervals.

• Shut off the air conditioner to avoid further overtaxing of the cooling system.

• Turn on the heater for a few minutes. It may help.

• If the radiator continues to overheat, drive the car off the road, turn off the engine and raise the hood.

• Wait at least a half hour before removing the radiator cap. Then do it very slowly and carefully, with the help of a towel or thick rag. Keep your face turned away from the radiator.

• If your car has the see-through overflow catch tank, replace any loss of coolant. Don't touch the radiator.

• If the fluid level is low, restart the engine while adding cool or warm water as the engine idles.

Source: Automobile Association of America.

CAR MAINTENANCE SECRETS

• Replace brake fluid at least once a year. This isn't a common practice, and few owner's manuals mention it, but brake fluid attracts water (from condensation and humidity in the air), often causing corrosion in the master and wheel cylinders, shortening their lives. Replacing brake fluid regularly saves the more costly replacement of cylinders.

Source: *The Durability Factor*, edited by Roger B. Yepsen Jr., Rodale Press, Emmaus, PA.

• Cold weather probably means your tires need more air. A tire which may have lost a few pounds of pressure during the summer and fall driving season could easily become 8–10 pounds underinflated on a freezing day. This is enough to cut tire life by 25%. Rule of thumb: For every 10-degree drop in the ambi-

ent temperature, the air pressure in a tire decreases by one-half pound to one pound.

• Average life expectancy for some vital parts of your car. Suspension system: 15,000 miles. Ignition wires: 25,000 miles: Water pump: 30,000 miles. Starter: 40,000 miles. Brake master cylinder, carburetor and steering mechanism (ball joints): 50,000 miles. Fuel pump: 75,000 miles. Clutch, timing gear chain/belt, universal joints: Up to 100,000 miles.

• Average recommended service intervals (in miles) under both normal and severe driving conditions, from a survey of mechanics:

	Normal	Severe
Oil & oil filter change	4,155	2,880
Replace air filter	10,363	5,927
Replace fuel filter	11,597	8,591
Replace spark plugs	14,185	11,298
Tune-up	14,254	11,245
Replace PCV valve	16,202	14,288
Flush & change coolant	22,848	18,049
Replace V-belts	24,853 or when necessary	20,610 or when necessary
Replace radiator and heater hoses	29,031 or when necessary	24,679 or when necessary
Change auto-transmission fluid	25,862	18,994
Adjust auto-transmission bands	26,591	19,141
Chassis lubrication	5,550	4,701
Repack wheel bearings	21,580	16,414
Rotate tires	9,003	7,929
Replace windshield-wiper blades	15,534 or when necessary	11,750 or when necessary

Source: *National Association of Fleet Administrators Bulletin.*

• The oil-pressure warning light on the dashboard is not a foolproof system. By the time the light flashes, the engine has been without oil long enough to harm the machinery.

• Car-scratch repair. When the scratch hasn't penetrated to the metal: Sand with fine sandpaper (400–600 grit) until it disappears. Wipe the area clean with a soft cloth. Paint it carefully, and let the paint dry for a few days. Then apply rubbing compound according to the directions in the package. When the scratch has penetrated to the metal: After sanding with fine paper, apply a primer. After the primer dries, sand again with 320–400 grit sandpaper. Paint and let dry. Apply rubbing compound. Buy materials at an auto-supply store.

• Use vinegar to clean dirt from chipped exterior car surfaces. Then, when the spot is dry, restore with touch-up paint.

• Idling the car doesn't warm up all the car's systems, such as lubricants, steering fluid or even all the drive train. Better: Keep speeds under 30 mph for the first quarter mile and not much over that for the next several miles.
Source: *National Association of Fleet Administrators Bulletin.*

• Replace radials whenever the tread is worn down to $\frac{1}{16}$ inch from the bottom of the tire groove. At that point, the grooves are too shallow to take water away, and hydroplaning may occur at higher speeds.
Source: National Association of Fleet Administrators.

• Do not "cross-switch" radials. Always exchange the left front with the left rear and right front with the right rear. Radials should never be remounted in a manner that will change the direction of rotation.

• If your car is shaking and vibrating, wheels may need aligning. Improper alignment causes excessive tire wear and increases fuel consumption.

• Wax your car at least twice a year. . . more often if it is exposed to salt air, road salt or industrial air or if it's parked ouside. Clue: If water doesn't bead up on the car's surface after rain, waxing is needed.

• Car-washing damages the luster and finish if laundry detergents are used. Best: Stay with products designed to clean auto finishes. Brand names: Dupont Carwash Concentrate, Poly Wash, Simoniz Super Poly Car Wash, Star Brite Car Wash. Next best: Mild liquid dishwashing detergents. A car cannot be washed too often with the proper cleansers. Procedure: Work in the shade. Flood the car's surface with a hose before applying suds. Rinse before drying. When washing the outside, spray the wheel wells and also the underside of the car to clean out corrosive agents.

BEST CAR BATTERY FOR COLD CLIMATES

When buying a car battery, get a cold-cranking amperage (CCA) at least equal to the engine size in cubic inches. Choose a CCA of at least 250, no matter how small the engine. The best for cold climates: The Sears Incredicell, with a CCA of 650.
Source: *The Family Handyman.*

ENGINE OIL ALERT

For long auto life, the single most important maintenance procedure is to change your oil every 3,000–4,000 miles, regardless of operating manual instructions. Reason: The acids caused by combustion break down the additives now found in all modern lubricating oils. These acids can begin to corrode engine parts.
Source: *The Durability Factor,* edited by Roger B. Yepsen Jr., Rodale Press, Emmaus, PA.

Change the oil filter with each oil change. Synthetic oil, although far more expensive than petroleum, lasts longer and may, in some instances, increase gas mileage.

WHEN YOUR WARRANTY EXPIRES

Auto repairs will sometimes be covered by the manufacturer even after the car is off warranty, especially for problems that began before the warranty expired. Essential: The original receipts of the paid invoices for all previous repairs must be presented. This means getting originals (not copies) for all repairs, even those that were done after the warranty period expired.
Source: *The Road Ahead.*

KEY TO UNLOCKING DOORS

When the car door key won't insert, try flushing the lock with a spray lubricant. Dirt usually causes the jam-up. Don't use oil. It will mix with the dirt and worsen the clog.

ADDITIVES THAT REALLY GIVE BETTER MILEAGE

There are two that have been shown to work consistently: Tufoil and Slick 50. Both these products use PTFE (poly tetra fluoro ethylene), a compound similar to DuPont's Teflon, but not Teflon. Teflon, though excellent for other low-friction applications, is harmful to your automobile engine. Under heat and pressure such as an engine produces, Teflon particles clump into long, stringy molecules that eventually clog your engine. Beware of any additives that claim to have Teflon as an active ingredient. (DuPont has stopped Teflon micropowders to manufacturers for auto engine applications and has prosecuted others who put Teflon labels on their gas-saving preparations.)

How much mileage you gain from using Tufoil or Slick 50 depends on the age of your car, the condition of its engine and your driving habits. Improvements can range from a meager 2% to as much as 30%. The greatest potential saving: Using additives in older cars with big displacement engines. Smaller cars with smaller engines are more fuel-efficient in their design, so additives can't improve mileage by very much.

Source: Tony Assenza, editor of *Motor Trend.*

BEST AUTO MECHANICS

Find one who's been certified in your area of concern (front end, brakes, etc.) by the National Institute for Automotive Service Excellence. Certified mechanics wear a gear-shaped shoulder patch on their workshirts. Bar-shaped patches underneath list their specialties. Best: A double-gear patch. It indicates that the mechanic has passed all eight tests.

Source: *Popular Mechanics.*

VERY BEST TIRES

The most durable automobile tire is the Michelin XH, according to the National Highway Traffic Safety Administration. The XH beat 133 other tires. It lasted 66,000 miles in average driving. Least durable: Bridgestone's 174V-70, with 16,000 miles. Lesson: More money doesn't necessarily buy a better tire.

FLAT TIRE DO'S AND DON'TS

• Repair a tire only when the puncture in the tread area is ¼ inch in diameter or smaller. This puncture must be at least 15 inches away from a prior one, and tread depth must be more than $\frac{1}{16}$ inch.

• It's important that the mechanic remove the tire from the wheel. A permanent repair can be made only from inside the tire. Another reason: An internal inspection is a "must," for driving on a flat (even a short distance at low speeds) can damage the crucial inner surface.

• After repair, have the tire and wheel assembly rebalanced. This will more than pay for itself in a smoother ride and longer tire life.

• Avoid the use of instant tire sealants. They camouflage the slow loss of air that signals a punctured tire.

TIRE PRESSURE IS IMPORTANT

Test your car's tires weekly with a dial-type gauge (gauges without dials are often inaccurate). Studies show that most cars have two or more tires that have low air pressure, causing poor fuel mileage, unsafe handling, excessive wear and heat buildup. All these problems can cause early tire failure.

Source: *The Durability Factor,* edited by Roger B. Yepsen Jr., Rodale Press, Emmaus, PA.

Correcting tire pressure before taking off on that long summer trip can knock as much as 3% off fuel bills.

CAR STEREO THEFT

Theft of car stereos is reaching epidemic proportions—one is taken every few seconds in the US. These thefts occur in shopping centers, on city streets and even when the cars are parked in driveways at home. Most vulnerable: The expensive European systems, such as Blaupunkt or Alpine that come in high-priced foreign cars like the BMW and Audi. These units are easily pulled from the dashboard. Some remedies: An alarm that sounds when the stereo is attacked. The *Decoy*, a false front that slips over a stereo to make it look like a cheap AM radio.

BEST CAR BURGLAR ALARMS

Briefly, the features of a good alarm should be:
1. Passively armed system. That is, it should require nothing more of the driver than shutting off the motor and removing the ignition key, without complicated setup procedures.
2. Instant "on" at all openings. That means the alarm should trigger as soon as any door, the hood or the trunk is opened.
3. Remotely disarmed by a code, instead of by means of a switch or a key. A lock can be picked. A code is impossible to break.
4. Hood lock. Denying a thief access to your engine, battery and siren is a major deterrent.
5. Backup battery to prevent a thief from crawling under your car, cutting the car's main battery and killing the entire electrical system and therefore the alarm system.
6. Motion detector. The best kind are the electronic motion detectors that sense a car's spatial attitude at the time the alarm is armed whether it's on a hill, on uneven ground, etc. (Also least prone to false alarms.)

Beyond these essentials, extras like pressure-sensitive pads in the seats and under carpeting, glass-breakage detectors, paging systems and air horns are available and can be added to all systems. Wheel locks are a good item to have on your car if you own expensive optional wheels.

Most insurance companies will give you a discount if your car is so equipped. Generally, it's 10% off the premium—each year.

Don't put stickers in the window announcing to the world what type of burglar alarm system you have. Most experts feel that this removes the element of surprise and can even help the thief.

Cheap alarms provide little more than a false sense of security for a car owner. A good thief can foil them easily. A completely unprotected car can be stolen in less than 30 seconds.

CAR THEFT PATTERNS

An auto is most likely to be stolen on a Monday or Friday night when it's parked on the street at home. Most thieves enter through an unlocked door and pull out the ignition lock cylinder. What makes the job even easier: Alarm systems that aren't in use or don't function 25% of the time.

Source: Survey by General Motors and auto insurers, reported in *Journal of American Insurance*.

OUT-THINKING CAR THIEVES

• To prevent being towed away: Put the car in park or gear, depending upon whether it is an automatic or a standard. Then apply the emergency brake.

• To prevent entrance into the car with a coat hanger: Purchase a tapered button for each door.

• To prevent steering: Buy a Kokloc—a hook that attaches the steering wheel to the brake pedal.

• To prevent theft at airports and other long-term parking lots: Remove the coil wire from under the hood. It is impossible to start the car without that connecting wire, unless your thief is particularly knowledgeable and has brought an extra coil wire with him. Extra precaution: Replace the coil wire with a broken one. This way, the thief will not know why the car isn't starting up.

• To prevent theft in your driveway: Back in rather than driving straight in. The thief will then be forced to do his suspicious tinkering in full view of neighbors.

Source: National Association of Fleet Administrators, New York.

44 WAYS TO FOIL A CAR THIEF

Make your car hard to steal:

- Take your keys.
- Lock your car.
- Park in well-lighted areas.
- Park in attended lots.
- Install a burglar alarm.
- Don't put the alarm decal on your car.
- Install a secondary ignition switch.
- Park with wheels turned toward the curb.
- Remove coil wire from distributor cap.
- Replace T-shaped locks with straight ones.
- Use your steering-wheel lock.
- Install a steering-wheel lock, and use it.
- Close car windows when parking.
- Don't hide a second set of keys in car.
- Never leave your car running.
- Don't let a potential buyer "test drive" alone.
- Install an armored collar around the steering column to cover the ignition.
- Activate burglar alarm or antitheft device when parking.
- For front-wheel-drive cars, put on emergency brake and put in park.
- Back your car into your driveway.
- Lock your garage door.
- Lock your car in your garage.

- Install a special antitheft device that you have created.
- Remove rotor from distributor.
- Install a fuel-shut-off device.

  Be sure your car can be identified:
- Etch an identifying mark on your car.
- Drop a business card into door frame.
- Keep a record of your car's vehicle identification number (VIN).

  Don't encourage a second crime:
- Don't leave valuables in view.
- Don't keep license and registration in car.
- When parking in a public garage, leave only ignition key with attendant.
- Leave nothing in car with your address on it.
- Don't put identification on your car key ring.

  Don't unwittingly buy a stolen car.
- Deal only with a reputable used-car dealer.
- If you buy from an individual, be sure he is who he says he is.
- Be sure you can locate seller after the sale.
- Ask the seller about past financing and insurance on the car, and verify it.
- See if the VIN has been tampered with.
- See if the VIN matches the number of the seller's title.
- Be suspicious of a fresh paint job on a late-model car.
- Be sure inspection sticker and license tag are current and were issued by the same state.
- Ask for the manufacturer's keys.
- Be suspicious if the seller gives you replacement keys for a late-model car.
- Complete all paper work at time of sale. Titles are frequently counterfeited.

Source: Aetna Life and Casualty.

8. Travel & Vacations

Travel and Vacations

SECRETS OF FLYING SAFELY IN UNSAFE TIMES

Despite new technology, there's no evidence that airlines are appreciably safer than they were a decade ago. Over the last 10 years, US airlines have averaged one fatal accident for every 2,000,000 departures.

Part of the problem is an unintentional consequence of deregulation. During the era of federal control, many airlines exceeded minimum safety requirements. But today, fewer airlines exceed the standards because deregulation has toughened competition, thereby creating financial problems that have forced some airlines to divert resources away from safety.

But ... more information about airline performance is now available, and it gives passengers new ways to choose safer airlines and increase their chances of surviving a crash. How to choose safer airlines:

• *Rule #1:* If possible, don't fly an airline that's in financial difficulty. There's no certainty that a money-troubled airline will be less safe. But the FAA itself increases safety surveillance of such airlines on the assumption that they're under pressure to cut corners on safety and maintenance.

For similar reasons, think twice about flying an airline with severe labor problems, especially those that may disrupt maintenance operations.

Right now, American, Delta and United seem to be in excellent financial shape and have no major labor problems. Continental, Pan American and TWA appear less healthy. Eastern still has serious labor trouble.

• *Rule #2:* Avoid small regional airlines whenever possible. While some regionals have good safety records, statistics show that you're three times more likely to die in a crash on a plane with 30 seats or fewer than a larger craft.

Among other problems, regionals often use small airports that aren't as well-equipped to guide planes in at night and in bad weather as larger airports are. Also, small airplanes often lack the more sophisticated instrumentation for bad-weather flying, and regional pilots are generally not as experienced as those who fly for major carriers.

Trap: Airlines don't always tell passengers that they're routed on a regional carrier for a particular leg of their trip. For that reason, always ask which airline you'll be flying on each leg. You may find that another major airline will fly directly to your destination or that you can rent a car and drive from a nearby major city.

Safest planes... safest seats:

The National Transportation Safety Board* keeps records on accidents of specific planes, and these are available to the public. Challenge: The accident data are difficult to interpret because problems may originate with the different kinds of engines that a single type of aircraft may use. And some aircraft that are flown over more dangerous routes may appear statistically less safe than others when they're really not.

Nevertheless, if for no other reason than peace of mind, travelers can avoid specific types of planes, particularly the DC-10 that's been involved in several recent disasters. And, avoiding a certain type of plane is easier than most passengers realize.

When you make reservations, ask the ticket agents or travel agents what kind of plane is scheduled on your flight. If they balk, be insistent. Agents virtually always have that information. If you have qualms about the plane, ask for another flight or make reservations with another airline.

Before you leave for the airport, check again with the airline to see if there's been a change in planes. If there has been, and if you don't want to fly on the craft, you again have the option of making other travel arrangements (unless you have a nonrefundable ticket).

Even with a nonrefundable ticket, don't give up. Go to the airport and use persuasion on the ticket agent. Unfortunately, you have no other power to ask him to switch your flight.

Agents are under no obligation to help travelers in that situation. But if you make it clear that the only reason you want to switch is to fly on another type of aircraft, the agent may accommodate you to earn goodwill for the airline.

Choosing the safest seats:

Myth: That the safest seats on all commercial aircraft are those next to emergency exits.

Reality: Aisle seats close to the over-wing emergency exits are safer. These seats are commonly in the mid-front section of the plane. If you sit in the window seat next to an emergency exit, you may be worse off in the event of a crash that jams the exit. Aisle seats near several exits give you more escape options in a crash.

Lifesaving precaution: When you take your seat in the plane, count and memorize the number of rows to the nearest exits. Reason: If smoke fills the cabin after a crash, you may have to feel your way in the dark to an exit. This precaution is based on the tactics that crash survivors actually have used to get out of a plane.

• For some protection against fire, wear full-length clothing, suits or dresses, made of wool or cotton, sturdy shoes and eyeglasses with an attachable lanyard. Avoid wearing shorts or clothing made of synthetics like polyester which can melt to your body in a fire.

• Women should not wear high-heeled shoes on a plane. They can cause you to trip, and they can snag on the emergency exit slide.

• If the plane fills with smoke, stay low, even if you have to crawl. Two or three breaths of toxic smoke can kill you. If there's enough warning before a crash, place a damp cloth over your mouth in order to breathe through smoke.

• Get as far away from the plane as possible if you're lucky enough to escape it after a crash. People on the ground are often killed when a downed plane explodes.

• Learn how to open the exits by reading the emergency instructions soon after you get on the plane. That's something you don't want to learn as the aircraft bursts into flames.

*800 Independence Ave. SW, Washington, DC 20594. Phone: 202-382-6600.

Source: Chris Witkowski, director, Aviation Consumer Action Project, an advocacy group for airline safety and passenger rights, 2000 P St. NW, Washington, DC 20036. The organization also publishes *Facts and Advice for Airline Passengers*, a booklet that gives more information on safety and consumer rights, ACAP, Box 19029, Washington, DC 20036.

HOW TO GET A PASSPORT FASTER

Go to the passport office in person. Bring: Your airline ticket, two passport pictures, proof of citizenship (an old passport, voter registration or birth certificate), a piece of identification with your photo on it and the $35 fee. Give the passport office a good reason why you are rushed. Result: A few days' versus weeks' wait.

If your passport is lost or stolen when you're traveling abroad, immediately notify the local police and the US embassy or consulate. Good news: An overnight replacement is sometimes possible in an emergency. To hasten the process: Know your passport number. This speeds up verification of the original application. Next best: Have a valid identification document with you. Shrewd: Take a photostat of your passport on the trip.

Source: *Travel Smart.*

OVERLOOKED AIRFARE SAVER

Many airlines will reimburse you for the amount of any drop in the price of an airline ticket that occurs after you buy it but before you use it. But you won't get a reimbursement if you don't ask. Advice: Before getting on your flight, ask the ticket agent to check his computer for the current price of your ticket, and see if you are entitled to a refund.

Source: *The Wall Street Journal.*

CHEAPER AIRFARES

Airfares are usually cheapest on Tuesdays and Wednesdays, highest on Mondays and Fridays. Rates are discounted most often on midday and late-night flights, rarely during morning and evening business commuting hours.

Source: *Travel & Leisure*, 1120 Ave. of the Americas, New York 10036.

OVERSEAS PRECAUTIONS

On a trip abroad you can encounter problems you might never have thought of. It's important to make adequate preparation and to be aware of how American embassies abroad operate.

Before you leave:

• Check your health and accident insurance to see if you're covered for illness or injury abroad. Also: Will your policy pay for transportation home if you're on a litter and need more than one airplane seat? Although a number of companies will pay for treatment, transportation is rarely covered. Recommended: section provided in your passport for a contact in case of emergency. Keep it accurate and up to date for each trip. Don't list your spouse if he/she is going with you. It can delay notification of your next of kin by the Department of State.

• Carry a copy of the prescriptions for any medications you're carrying. Don't take large amounts of any prescription drug, as you might come under suspicion by foreign Customs.

If something happens:

US embassies or consulates all have consular sections to assist American travelers who encounter emergencies abroad. If you're in any trouble don't hesitate to use their services. Call or visit the embassy. Consuls are responsive to the needs of Americans traveling or residing abroad. However, they must devote the majority of their priority time and energy to those Americans who are in serious trouble (legal, medical, etc.).

Lost passports and credit cards:

If your passport is lost or stolen, contact the nearest embassy or consulate immediately. A consul will interview you and, if he is satisfied of your US citizenship and identity, a new passport can be quickly issued. Will he believe you? Most Americans are able to satisfy the consular officer on the basis of a personal interview and presentation of identification that was not stolen or lost with the passport. In some cases, however, the consul may find it necessary to wire the Department of State to verify that you had been issued a previous passport.

The consul will be able to refer you to any local offices of the major credit cards and travelers checks for reporting loss of credit cards or travelers checks. If you lose all your money, the embassy will assist you in having funds transferred from a friend or relative in the US through State Department channels. What it won't do: Lend you money.

Missing persons:

The State Department often receives emergency requests to locate a friend or relative who has disappeared abroad. If you're worried about someone abroad, call the Citizens Emergency Center in Washington. It maintains a 24-hour line at (202) 632-5225. The center will provide a liaison between the concerned person in the States and the appropriate embassy, which will try to locate the missing traveler. If you contact the Department of State for assistance in locating someone abroad, provide as much information as possible about the itinerary of the person you wish to locate. (This is one reason to leave a detailed itinerary with a relative. Note: Under the Privacy Act of 1974, the consul cannot provide information about a US citizen without the authorization of that person.)

Medical care:

The embassy or consulate has lists of local English-speaking doctors, some of whom were trained in the US, and lists of the better local hospitals.

Source: John P. Caulfield, Bureau of Consular Affairs, Department of State, Washington, DC.

IF YOU ARE ARRESTED OVERSEAS

In a sample year, 3,000 Americans were arrested in 97 foreign countries for offenses ranging from narcotics and disorderly conduct to murder. If arrested, you should ask to contact your embassy. Be polite but persistent in making this request. American embassies are usually informed when Americans are arrested in foreign countries. A consular officer will visit an American in prison as soon as possible and provide him with a list of local attorneys, including their specialties and qualifications. The consul can also call an attorney for the American if he isn't able to make a call, notify his friends or relatives at home, help him wire for funds, make sure his basic health and safety needs are being met and make sure he's not being discriminated against because he's an American. What the embassy can't do: Get someone out of jail. Americans are subject to the laws of the country where they are residing or visiting.

Dangers:

• Auto accidents. In many foreign countries, you can be arrested or imprisoned for driving while intoxicated or held criminally liable for an accident in which someone is injured. Drive carefully!

• Narcotics. Those convicted of possession or trafficking in drugs usually spend from two to 10 years in jail, often with long waits in jail for a trial. Bail is generally not possible for narcotics offenses or other serious offenses in most foreign countries. Important: If you get a call from abroad saying your youngster has been arrested, confirm the arrest with the Citizens Emergency Center before sending money. The call might be an extortion attempt.

• Black marketeering. This is a very serious offense in many countries and is often punished by a prison term. Also: Beware of black-market currency transactions. You could be robbed or wind up with counterfeit currency.
Source: John P. Caulfield, Bureau of Consular Affairs, Department of State, Washington, DC.

CLEARING CUSTOMS

Personal exemption: $300 ($600 from Guam, American Samoa or the Virgin Islands). The next $600: A flat rate of 10% duty (5% from the U.S. islands). Above this: Individual assessments are made on goods.

Sending gifts: Duty-free, if marked unsolicited gift, value under $25. Gifts cannot be sent to yourself or to a traveling companion.

Sending goods home: Duty must be paid on major items. They do not count as part of a personal exemption.

Liquor and tobacco: You are allowed one liter of alcohol, 100 cigars, and 200 cigarettes. (State laws take precedence over federal regulations.)

Drugs: Medications obtained abroad could be seized.

HOW TO FLY ON COMMUTER AIRLINES

Most of the big catastrophes involving major airlines have been attributed to either poor weather conditions or air traffic controller errors. But most commuter airline crashes stem from pilot error. According to the watchdogs at the Aviation Consumer Action Project, you are three times more likely to be in a fatal accident on a commuter airline than on a large trunk carrier.

Scary reasons: Many commuter pilots are inexperienced, hired fresh out of flight school with very little—and sometimes no—bad weather or emergency training. For economic reasons, these pilots get most of their hands-on training late at night or on weekends . . . after they've already put in a full day of flying. Most of them are never trained in simulators—standard for the big airlines—because the commuter lines operate on a shoestring budget.

What's in your control:

Even seasoned travelers often don't realize that commuter airline passengers have much more control over flight operations than do passengers on the big trunk carriers. Strategy: Assume that you and the pilot are the only ones on the plane . . . even if you're surrounded by other passengers. Commuter pilots have more leeway than you'd think and, according to our sources, are often willing to act on passenger suggestions . . . as long as they're reasonable and don't jeopardize safety.

Whether you're flying in a 20-seat jet or a two-seat air taxi, there are a few things you can do to increase your personal safety. Some of these steps might cost you time or money, but they can save your life.

• Watch that the pilot checks the plane thoroughly before takeoff. For example, does the pilot take fuel samples?

• Ask about weather conditions. If the skies are cloudy, ask whether the pilot is instrument-rated, whether he is up-to-date on the navigation equipment and whether a flight plan has been filed to allow the plane to be navigated based on instrument readings rather than on visual information. If the answer to any of these questions is no, you are in great peril . . . especially at night. If at all possible, skip this flight.

• If every seat is full, ask if the plane is too heavy for takeoff . . . especially on a warm day or when you're taking off from a short runway. Many smaller planes are dangerous if every seat is full.

• Once in the plane, watch the pilot get ready for departure. He should be using a checklist and checking everything methodically. Don't trust anything to his memory.

• Once aloft, watch weather. If you hear the pilot talking about thunderstorms with an air traffic controller and the plane's not equipped with radar or a Stormscope, tell the pilot that you're in no hurry. He can take a longer—and safer—route.

• If you see ice forming on the plane, suggest that the pilot take a restroom stop. (It sounds odd, but it's more common than most people think.)

• If the pilot is flying visually (by sight, not instruments), and it appears that he can't see a good distance, tell the pilot that you'd prefer to discontinue this flight. Other reasons to discontinue: Clouds below the plane . . . rain . . . snow . . . flying low.

• If the pilot tries to entertain you by flying low, making steep bank turns or pulling the plane in for a closer look at something on the ground, insist calmly that he take you back to the airport.

• If an approach and landing are being tried in bad weather, tell the pilot that it's OK with you to land at another airport.

• If fuel gauges appear low or the pilot says he's stretching it, suggest a refueling stop . . . sooner, not later.

Warning: Commuter airlines are not governed by the same stringent rules as the large trunk carriers. If your trip requires a change of plane, the second leg of your journey could be on a commuter plane. Option: Consider renting a car or taking a train or bus.

Source: Privileged information from our conversations with pilots, air traffic controllers, consumer protectionists and government officials.

BEWARE OF AIRLINES USING OLD JETS

US airline carriers are flying older jets than European and Far Eastern carriers. Percentage of US jets over 15 years old: Pan Am and TWA, 65% each . . . Northwest, 57% . . . United, 52% . . . Delta, 22%. A comparison of foreign carriers: Japan Air Lines, 22% . . . Lufthansa, 18% . . . Swissair, 9%.

REDUCE AIRLINE LUGGAGE LOSSES

Buy extra baggage insurance when you check in at the airport. It's called excess valuation. Estimate the value of your bags and their contents. For 50¢–$1.00 per $100 of value, you're insured in case of total loss. You must provide receipts of the contents to collect on a loss. However, the chances of loss are reduced because airlines take extra care in handling bags covered by excess valuation.

Source: *Travel Smart*, 40 Beechdale Rd., Dobbs Ferry, NY 10522.

TRAVEL TIMESAVERS

At the airport: Arrive at least 45 minutes early to check your luggage and obtain your boarding pass. This gives you time to take care of any booking problems early and lowers your chance of being bumped from an overbooked flight. If you have a rental car, allow another 15 minutes to return it.

Source: Dr. Barbara Pletcher, National Association for Professional Saleswomen, Sacramento, CA.

BEST CREDIT CARD TO USE ABROAD

Frequent international travelers can save money by using their American Express cards more than other cards. The company generally takes longer than others to process foreign bills. In effect, that is an interest-free loan to you.

Source: Travel Smart for Business.

HOW TO GET BEST FOREIGN EXCHANGE RATES

To get the most for your dollar while traveling, change your money in commercial banks, not in hotels and restaurants. Make sure you take some local currency in case you reach a country after banking hours. Find out the bank closing times and holidays when you arrive so you won't be caught short.

TRAVELERS' HEALTH SECRETS

• Motion-sickness cure. By taking your mind off the motion, you can help your body restore equilibrium without drugs. How to do it: Close your eyes, or concentrate on a spot in front of you, and hold your head as steady as possible. Then focus your attention on your breathing or on alternately tensing and relaxing your muscles. Continue to concentrate until the nausea has vanished.

• Traveler's diarrhea aid: Get a prescription for the antibiotic doxycycline. One tablet a day generally prevents the problem. Limitation: Not recommended for children or pregnant women, since it can discolor developing teeth.

Source: Healthwise.

• Congested sinuses and airplanes don't mix. Reason: Aircraft cabins are pressurized below atmospheric pressure. If a sinus is blocked, the trapped air inside expands and can lead to serious infection, including brain infections. Advice: Don't fly with a serious sinus problem. Improve drainage prior to ascent and descent with decongestants or nose drops.

HOW TO MINIMIZE EAR PAIN WHEN FLYING

To minimize ear pain when flying:
• Don't fly with a cold or nasal congestion.
• If you must fly with a stuffy head, take nose drops and an antihistamine a half hour before takeoff and a half hour before landing. Drink plenty of nonalcoholic liquids.
• Don't have more than one or two alcoholic drinks. (Reason: Alcohol dilates the veins and dries up infection fighting mucus.)
• Don't sleep during landing (you won't swallow as much to relieve the pressure in your ears).
• Chew candy or gum to make yourself swallow during landing.

Source: Travel and Leisure.

QUICKEST WAY TO FIND ALL-NIGHT DRUG STORE IN A STRANGE CITY

Call the police. They know which pharmacies are open late. Many people waste precious time calling every drugstore in the Yellow Pages or running all over town in a frantic search.

MID-DAY HOTELS

If your schedule permits, nap for several hours between connecting flights when traveling out of town. A growing number of hotels rent rooms for day use at only about half the regular rate.

Source: OAG/Frequent Flyer.

HOW TO AVOID TRAVEL ANXIETY

Pretrip jitters hit many travelers, even veterans. Remedies: Since the cause of jitters is often anxiety over things left undone, pack a few days early and make checklists. Always allow plenty of time prior to leaving. Extreme solution: Pretend your departure is an hour earlier than it actually is. Arrive at the airport an hour early, and you will have time for a leisurely glass of wine or a cup of coffee before the trip.

When you travel, avoid putting pressure on yourself: Don't rush to the boarding gate the moment your flight is announced. Relax in the waiting room until the rush is over—your seat is reserved. Similarly, wait in your seat after the plane lands. Those who push for the exits end up standing for long periods. Unless absolutely necessary, don't run to catch a bus, cab or subway. When commuting by car, occasionally take the less traveled routes.

Source: *Time Is Money* by Ross A. Webber, The Free Press, New York.

LOWER HOTEL RATES

When visiting a company in another city, ask whether that company has a special deal with one of the hotels in town. Most hotels offer a rate to local companies that's even lower than the corporate rate for other firms. If that's the case, ask the local company to make the reservation.

Source: *Travel Smart for Business.*

HOW TO CANCEL NONCANCELABLE TICKETS

Problem: "Super Saver" tickets cost as little as 30% of regular airfares, but airlines say you can't get a refund if you change travel plans. Solution: A cooperative travel agent.

When you buy a ticket from an agent, the agent makes your reservation immediately. But it doesn't forward your money to the airline for a few days—in some cases not until a week later. That's because agents pay airlines only once a week. During the time gap a friendly travel agent will let you cancel the reservation and get your money back.

Caution: Travel agents don't have to accomodate you. But if you're a good customer and the agent wants to keep your business, chances are good that you can get a refund.

Helpful: Check with your agent to see if two round-trip, non-cancelable discount fares cost less than one full round-trip ticket. Even if you use only half of each of the discount tickets, the cost for both may be less than a full fare ticket.

Source: Harold Seligman, president, Management Alternatives, travel management consultants, Box 8119, Stamford, CT 06905.

BEST HOTELS IN THE WORLD

The world's premier travel accommodations, according to a poll of leading bankers, are (in order of preference):

1. Bangkok, *The Oriental.*
2. Hong Kong, *The Mandarin.*
3. Tokyo, *Hotel Okura.*
4. Zurich, *Dolder Grand Hotel.*
5. Singapore, *Shangri-La Hotel.*
6. Paris, *Hotel Ritz.*
7. Hamburg, *Hotel Vier Jahreszeiten.*
8. Hong Kong, *The Peninsula.*
9. Madrid, *Ritz Hotel.*
10. London, *Claridge.*
11. New York, *The Hotel Carlyle.*
12. Paris, *Hotel Plaza Athenee.*
13. Zurich, *Baur au Lac.*
14. London, *The Connaught Hotel.*
15. Rome, *Hotel Hassler Villa Medici.*
16. Munich, *Hotel Vier Jahreszeiten.*
17. London, *The Berkeley.*
18. Washington, DC, *Four Seasons Hotel.*
19. Vienna, *Hotel Imperial.*
20. Washington, DC, *The Madison.*
21. Manila, *The Manila Hotel.*
22. Chicago, *The Ritz-Carlton.*
23. Toronto, *Four Seasons Hotel.*
24. Tokyo, *Imperial Hotel.*

25. Paris, *Hotel Meurice.*
26. Geneva, *Le Richmond.*
27. New York, *The Pierre.*
28. Paris, *Hotel George V.*
29. London, *Inn on the Park.*
30. Vienna, *Hotel Sacher.*
31. Los Angeles, *Beverly Wilshire Hotel.*
32. Sydney, *Sheraton Wentworth.*
33. Stockholm, *Grand Hotel.*
34. New York, *The Park Lane Hotel.*
35. Mexico, *Camino Real.*
36. Geneva, *Hotel des Bergues.*
37. Montreal, *Ritz-Carlton.*
38. San Fransciso, *The Mark Hopkins Hotel.*
39. London, *The Savoy.*
40. New York, *The Regency Hotel.*

Source: *Institutional Investor.*

EIGHT GRAND OLD HOTELS THAT ARE STILL MAGNIFICENT

A stay in a gracious hotel reminiscent of an earlier era can be the highlight of a vacation or can turn a run-of-the-mill business trip into a decided pleasure.

Some great old hotels have never lost their luster, and an increasing number of formerly faded dowagers have recently had facelifts, restoring them to their original beauty. Here are a few special places.

• Adolphus Hotel, Dallas. Texans used to describe this turreted pile of stone as ''early beer baron,'' but their laughter turned to admiration when this Gothic revival hotel reopened in 1980 after four years of careful restoration to its original 1912 magnificence.

• Burgenstock Hotel Estate, Switzerland. A splendid aerie 1,500 feet above Lake Lucerne. It artfully mixes modern meeting facilities featuring the latest electronic gadgetry with truly baronial accommodations. The guest rooms are luxurious, and the public spaces resemble museums. Open May–October.

• The Connaught, London. This landmark in the perennially stylish Mayfair district is elegance itself, and the service is as impeccable as only the finest English establishment could make it.

• Four Seasons Olympic, Seattle. This eclectic hotel in the center of Seattle had its ups and downs between its construction in 1924 and its renovation in 1982. The World War II blackout paint is now off the ballroom windows, the lobby is grandly furnished, and the rooms are modern yet luxurious.

• Hotel Imperial, Vienna. Built in 1867 on a fashionable boulevard as the home of the Duke of Wurttemburg, it has been a sumptuous hotel since 1873. Personalized service in the tradition of the Hapsburg empire still reigns supreme.

• Hotel Inter-Continental, Paris. Built for the 1878 World's Fair, it was taken over by Inter-Continental in 1968. Its public spaces gleam, and its guest rooms are sybaritic retreats with extras like hair dryers, minibars, bathroom scales and color TV with in-room movies. The Salon Imperial is a stately banquet hall, and the recently restored Garden Court is a tranquil oasis in the busy heart of Paris.

• The Mandarin, Hong Kong. Classic hotel in the center of Hong Kong's business district. All other hotels in the Orient are ultimately judged by this one. Lovely and luxurious, it sets the standard for impeccable service, superb cuisine and Oriental ambience combined with Occidental efficiency.

• Hotel Seelbach, Louisville. It was built in 1905 and hit a long, slow decline before closing in the early 1970s. The restorers (rather than the wreckers) took over, embarking on a three-year refurbishment to its original glory. This Louisville landmark reopened to rave reviews in March 1982.

BED AND BREAKFAST BARGAINS

A fine old British institution has finally arrived in America. Now you can rent a room with breakfast in a private home (apartments, too) for much less than the cost of a hotel room. They range from the luxurious to the merely adequate. Recommended: Book as far in advance as possible. Paperback books, with information on bed and breakfasts are available in most bookstores and libraries.

RESOLVING TAXI DRIVER QUARRELS

To settle a dispute with a taxi driver abroad, ask the driver to take you to your hotel, where the bell captain can straighten it out. You are unlikely to succeed arguing the issue out alone with the driver.

HOTEL ROBBERY PREVENTION

Hotel thieves have a favorite technique. They strike up a conversation with their victim on the hotel elevator. They step off at the same floor and pretend to be otherwise occupied. Then, when the victim has opened his or her door, the robbers push in and go to work.

Source: Andrea Forrest, president, Preventive Security Services, New York.

AIRPORT CRIMES

Most persistent airport crime: Pickpocketing. Favorite targets: First-class-ticket buyers, travelers on foreign carriers, anyone who keeps a billfold in an accessible place, particularly in a back trouser pocket.

LUGGAGE IDENTIFICATION WARNING

Luggage identification tags properly filled out will return that lost bag to you. However, your name and office address, not home address, should be on the tag. With the economy breeding crime, don't advertise that you will be out of town. When you make your travel reservations, a phone contact is always requested. Leave your office number (or a friend's), not your home number.

Source: Judith Preston, travel consultant, Park Ridge, IL.

MOTEL LIABILITY

A motel clerk handed out a room key to the wrong person, who used it to rob a guest of a large sum of money. The motel claimed that its posted notice of a safe available for guests' property limited its liability to $100 by state law. The Louisiana Supreme Court held that the $100 limit referred only to contractual liability as a depository. There was no limitation when the loss was caused by negligence of the motel or its employees.

Source: *Kraaz* v. *LaQuinta Motor Inns, Inc.,* 410 So. 1048.

A motel's liability for guests' property applies to a guest's vehicle and its contents while on a parking lot provided for guests and under the care of the motel keepers.

Source: *Vilella* v. *Sabine, Inc.,* Okla. S. Ct., 5-27-82.

BEST INTERNATIONAL AIRLINES

Frequent air travelers generally believe Lufthansa and Scandinavian Airlines are tops for their adherence to schedule and their excellent service. But truly seasoned travelers know that Asian airlines are also great on price and service. Recommended are Taiwan's China Airlines, Philippine Airlines and Singapore Airlines.

These three have in-cabin service that's superb. Flight attendants go all out to put the passengers at ease and to make the flight as pleasant as possible. Cabins are clean and comfortable. Food is excellent. Flights usually depart on time, and luggage is handled smoothly.

Source: Herbert J. Teison, Publisher of *Travel Smart for Business.*

WHAT THE AIRLINES DON'T TELL YOU

• Never accept the first fare quoted. Half the time, some other airline's flight within hours of the one you booked has a special, less expensive deal.

• Take advantage of ''illegal'' connections. These are connecting flights usually less than 45 minutes apart—too close for airlines to feel safe in making them connect. Result: These flights usually do not even show up on the computer when your trip is being routed. Solution: Have your agent write up your flight in two separate tickets. The second is for the illegal connection that originates at your transfer point.

Example: You arrive at O'Hare in Chicago on the way to San Francisco. Instead of waiting three hours for the safe connecting flight, you already have a separate ticket from O'Hare to San Francisco on an illegal connection. If you miss the connection, you turn that ticket in for the next available flight. Cost for two separate tickets: No more than one through ticket. Baggage: Waiting for it to be unloaded can cost you valuable time on this tight schedule. Best: Travel with carry-on luggage.

Source: Martin G. Blinder, M.D., San Francisco.

• Use do-it-yourself searches with a CRT. Plug into the Official Airlines Guide data base and retrieve all information needed on alternative flights and fares. How the electronic data base works: First, search out the flights available at the desired time. Using another code, find out what fares are available on each airline for the time period. At this point, if no asterisk is shown, it's possible to book the flight right up to the last minute. If there is an asterisk next to the airline flight number, ask the system what the restrictions are.

Source: Harold Seligman, president, Management Alternatives, Stamford, CT.

• Be imaginative, and do a little calculating. Some supersaver fares are low enough that even if you can't stay as long as their requirements (usually seven days) you will save by buying two round trip tickets—one from your home to your destination for the day you want to *leave* and one from your destination to your home for the day you want to *return*. The total may be less than the regular round-trip fare.

Source: *Your Money and Your Life* by Robert Z. Aliber, Basic Books, New York.

• If you miss your flight and there's just time

to catch another, go right to the other airline's departure gate instead of to its ticket counter. If it has an empty seat, the second airline will usually honor the ticket for the flight you missed.
Source: Dr. Barbara Pletcher, president, National Association for Professional Saleswomen.

• Best seat in the plane. After first class, the choices center on your priorities. For comfort and a smooth ride, pick a seat over the wings. For silence, sit as far forward as possible, but avoid the galley and rest rooms for leg room, try the first row or seats beside the emergency exits.

• Best way to get standby seat. Reserve a coach seat for your flight. Arrive at the airport the day you are to leave and see if you can get a standby ticket (Monday, Tuesday and Wednesday are the best standby days). If you do get a standby seat, become a no-show on your reservation (it's built into the price of your ticket) for a full refund. You may win. You can't lose.

Source: *Your Money and Your Life* by Robert Z. Aliber, Basic Books, New York.

• Airport X-rays and film. Studies show that one pass through a normal low-dose airport x-ray machine causes no visible change in photo images. But two passes cause fogging, and six passes make pictures uneven and/or overexposed. More serious: Damage by high-dose X-rays used at all departure points for the Concorde, throughout the Soviet Union, at London's Heathrow Airport, at Cathay Pacific in Hong Kong and at Philippine Airways in the Philippines. Best bet: Carry film in a transparent plastic bag and give it to the X-ray operator for hand inspection. Warning: Japan and Italy refuse to hand inspect. To take film through these countries, you will need a lead pouch to protect it.

Source: *Travel and Leisure.*

• Airport duty-free shops are not always bargains. Know prices before you buy. Even without state and local taxes and import duties, prices can be higher. Trap: The owners of such shops pay high rents for the privilege of being monopoly sellers and pass these costs on.

Source: *Your Money and Your Life* by Robert Z. Aliber, Basic Books, New York.

• International round-trip tickets. Travel one way, then change dollars into local currency to buy the return ticket. To check on your trip, ask the reservationist to quote the ticket price in local currency bought at destination.
Source: *Travel Smart for Business.*

SAVE ON FOREIGN TRAVEL

Save air fare by buying return tickets in the currency of the country you're visiting. (Your travel agent may be able to do this for you before you leave the US.) Example: Coach fare on Air France, Los Angeles to Paris, is $939... the return trip costs $602 if bought in French francs. Sometimes it pays to buy a "throwaway leg" from a country with cheaper money. Example: Return fare on Swissair, Geneva to New York, is $1,287 in Swiss francs. However, a ticket from Milan to New York via Geneva, bought with Italian lire, is only $1,044. Buy the Milan ticket and don't use the Milan-Geneva coupon.
Source: *Travel for Smart Business.*

FLIGHT-PLAN

Carry an airline guide (or photo copies of specific pages) on trips so you can look up schedules if you need to change reservations. Don't rely on the airlines to tell you the next flight out on any airline. They will usually tell you when their next flight is.
Source: *Execu-Time.*

CONFIRMING RESERVATIONS

Confirm airline reservations on international flights at least 72 hours prior to departure. For the return flight: Confirm on arrival at your destination. Do it at the airport. Or consult your airline ticket envelope for the local phone number. Backup: Note the date and time of your confirmation call and the name of the airline person with whom you speak.

BAGS FOR AIRLINE TRAVEL

American carriers now measure bags in total inches—that is, length plus height plus width. For international economy flights, the two checked pieces may add up to 106 inches, with neither bag exceeding 62 total inches. First-class passengers are allowed a total of 124 inches. In any class, a carryon that adds up to 45 inches is acceptable.

Some foreign lines limit luggage by weight —44 pounds for economy class and 66 pounds for first class.

For domestic flights, the allowance is two checked bags, one no larger than 62 total inches and the other not exceeding 55 total inches, plus a 45-inch carryon.

To help spot your bags quickly, place a sticker, ribbon or special tag on the outside. Always put identification inside the luggage in case the outside tags are lost.
Source: American Society of Travel Agents, Washington, DC.

Air travel with only a duffel bag eliminates the need to check baggage through. Size of bag that can be taken aboard: One with total dimensions of 40–45 inches. Example: A duffel 7 inches high, 16 inches wide and 21 inches long totals 44 inches. The flexible duffel contours to fit into the space under the seat. Pick a smooth-surface bag for easy sliding. To pack a duffel: Do not roll clothes. Fold them. Wear the bulkiest clothes, including boots. Segregate commonly used items such as toiletries, vitamins and prescriptions into small vinyl bags so they will be more readily available without emptying the contents of the large bag.

WHAT CAR RENTAL AGENCIES DON'T TELL YOU

• Give a rented car the once-over before driving away in it. Check the headlights, turn signals and brakes. Squirt the windshield washer to be sure that there is fluid. Check the oil level. Drive it around the block before taking it on the expressway.

• Don't pay for more insurance than you need on a rented car. Rental agents routinely encourage customers to pay around $5 a day for optional collision coverage. Chances are, however, that your own personal-car policy may extend coverage to a rented car. Check the insurance policy before signing up for unnecessary coverage.

• Automatic drop-off can be a rip-off on late-night rented-car returns. Unlike normal rental-car check-in, where the clerk totals up the costs and gives you a copy of the bill, automatic drop-offs require you to return all copies. You often don't get a copy until your credit-card company has billed you. Protection alternatives: Return your rental car during business hours. Make a copy of the rental form before returning it, noting your entry of the final mileage. Don't pay your credit-card bill until you get the car-rental bill and make sure their figures agree with yours. If they have overcharged you, dispute the bill and let the credit-card company know about the problem.

Source: *Travel Smart for Business.*

DRIVING VS. FLYING

Driving rather than flying is often simpler for distances under 200 miles, avoiding ticket lines, flight delays and airline food. Driving time can be spent profitably by listening to tapes on management, selling, and so on, or to tape-recorded reports from subordinates.

Source: *Manage Your Time, Manage Your Work, Manage Yourself* by Merrill Douglass, AMACOM, New York.

LONG-DISTANCE DRIVING

For a safe, healthy trip when you're driving long distance, do most of your driving during daytime hours. Visual acuity is lessened at night. Be particularly careful to check out your car's exhaust system before leaving—a leak can send odorless but deadly gases into the car. To insure sufficient fresh air inside the car, leave both a front and a back window open, and keep the tailgate window (if you have one) closed. Use your air conditioner. It provides fresh air and quiet inside the car. Although it reduces gas mileage, the loss is not much more than the loss from open windows' drag.

Use seat belts and shoulder harnesses to relieve fatigue as well as to boost safety. Take 20- to 30-minute rest breaks after every one and a half or two hours of driving. Exercise during your breaks. Have frequent high-protein snacks for improved driving performance. Don't stare straight ahead, even if you're the only car on the road. Keep your eyes moving.

CAR GAMES

To make the ride less tedious, here are some games to play:

Educational games:

• Spelling Bee. Take along a dictionary.

• Discover America. As someone keeps score, riders name the states of the union and their capitals.

• Add a Letter. Start with a single letter and go around building a word.

• I'm a Famous Person. Pretend to be a celebrity—living or dead. Give clues to your personality as others try to guess who you are.

• Quiz Kids. Before the trip, collect an assortment of difficult questions and answers.

• Words. Select a long word, such as separation, and then see how many words can be made from its letters. Have pencil and paper handy.

Silly games:

• Famous Pairs. Within a given period of time, perhaps half an hour, reel off the names of famous couples. Examples: George and Martha, Ron and Nancy, Jimmy and Rosalynn.

• Don't Say That Word. Prohibit certain words from the conversation, such as it, no, yes. Try to maintain a dialog without using them.

• What Time Do We Arrive? Each person guesses the time of arrival at various places along the route—the next big city on the map, when you stop for lunch or gasoline.

• **Animals.** See who can spot the most cows, horses, etc. in the fields by the side of the road.

• **Name That License Plate.** Look for funny personal license plates that have names, initials or unusual numerical combinations.

• **Sign Games.** Think up lines to rhyme with interesting billboards or signs.

• **Let's Find It.** Agree to look for one special thing—a covered bridge, a bright red automobile. The first one to spot it wins and then selects the next thing to look for.

• **If I Were a Millionaire.** Ask what people would want if they were millionaires. Then ask them for second wishes.

• **Favorite Books and Movies.** Review the books and movies you have liked best. Tell what makes them enjoyable.

• **Sports Favorites.** Prepare a series of questions about sports events and stars before you depart. Then quiz sports fans while on the trip.

• **Where Am I Going?** Mentally select a place that you are headed for. Give hints about your imaginary destination, and let the other passengers guess where you are going.

Song games:

• **Sing-Along.** See how many songs you can sing by different composers—Cole Porter, Irving Berlin, Billy Joel, The Beatles.

• **Sing Along With Me.** Bring a book of popular songs and lead the car in an old-fashioned sing-along.

• **Tap-a-Song.** Tap out the rhythm of a famous song. Give each person three guesses.

Semi-serious games:

• **Personal History.** Spin tales of family remembrances—a time spent with grandparents, a favorite birthday, a lovely trip taken in the past. Give each person a chance to share an experience.

• **Play Psychiatrist.** Ask everyone what bothers them most about their lives. Try to help them resolve their problems.

BEST PLACES TO EAT ON THE ROAD

• Don't simply follow the truck drivers.

Their first priority is a huge parking lot, not the best food.

• **Avoid restaurants on or very near major highways and in shopping centers.** You'll likely do better downtown. Good bets: College or university towns.

• **Best authorities:** Book store managers, fancy kitchenware and gourmet food store's personnel. Worst: Tollbooth or gas-station attendants.

• **Check out the parking lot.** Too many out-of-state license plates suggests a tourist trap. Good sign: A high proportion of foreign cars (especially European ones).

Source: *Travel & Leisure.*

TRANSPORTING YOUR CAR

Drive-away services drive your car to a destination if you don't want to do it yourself. It takes about 7–10 days to go cross country. Drawbacks: Insurance, gas and maintenance for the trip are usually extra. Your car also suffers the strains of a long trip. Alternative: Send your car by truck or train. Although the price is higher, it includes insurance.

INTERNATIONAL DRIVING PERMITS

US residents may drive in most foreign countries with a valid driver's license from their home state. An American International Driving Permit is required in Austria, Greece and Spain. Ask your travel agent where to buy one. In Italy and Germany, you need a translation of your American license or an American International Driving Permit. Drive on the left in Great Britain, Ireland, Cyprus, Australia and in some Caribbean islands.

Source: American Society of Travel Agents, Washington, DC.

UNIQUE WAYS TO PLAN YOUR TRIPS

If you're the type who finds the sameness of Holiday Inns comforting or prefers to have dinner at McDonald's—in Paris—this article isn't for you. But if you love country inns, a pot of coffee brewing in your room, four-poster beds, claw-legged bathtubs, lunch beside a swan pond, discovering the best wine cellar in Vermont or the trail that isn't on a map, then you might want to plan your vacations differently.

Consult the guidebooks and travel agent last. Before that, in fact the year round, collect information on all kinds of interesting vacation possibilities. Then, whether the trip is for summer or winter, a weekend or longer, a family vacation or a getaway for two, the research accumulated over the months allows you to make a choice based on a highly personalized and selective array of options. Here is how you can do it:

Keep files. Keep geographical files labeled Caribbean, West Coast, The South, New England, Europe, Israel, Japan and Exotic Places, for example. You can make your own headings and add new folders when the catch-all category gets too full to be manageable. Subdivide your files into subject files labeled Ski Vacations, Tennis Vacations, Club Med Locations, Charming Inns/Elegant Small Hotels, Houses for Rent or Exchange and Great Restaurants in Other Places (to distinguish it from your home town restaurant file).

It doesn't matter what categories head each folder as long as you remember what you meant. To start planning, decide on a location or a specific type of vacation, reach into the appropriate folder for articles and tips on things to do and see in that place, and then choose just the right lodging. Finally, make a list of restaurants you mustn't miss while you're there. Voila! A retrieval system without computer assistance. But how do you fill the files in the first place?

Articles from airline magazines, newsletters and the travel section of your newspaper are the obvious resources. Some less obvious resources:

Interview friends: When you agree with your friends' taste in food, furnishings, theater or painting, chances are you can trust their vacation advice. Don't wait for them to show their home movies. Ask where they have been lately that they've loved and why, what it looked like, what's to do there, and whether it's a good place for kids, a lovers' retreat, a flake-out resort or a center for sports and night-life. Jot it all down and put it in the files.

Go beyond your closest circle. Talk with neighbors, clients, tradespeople, friends at work. The more people you talk with, the more information you'll gather.

Friends you meet on one vacation can become hosts on another.

People who really "know how to live" can become splendid sources of vacation ideas because you can save the picture postcards they send you from wherever they travel.

Eavesdrop. This quirky information source is surprisingly fertile for first leads. In an airport or restaurant, on the bus or train to work, if you hear a total stranger describe a perfect meal she had in Kansas City, or a rustic lodge in the Adirondacks with a gorgeous view of the sunset, jot it down. You can check out the details later. That's where guidebooks and travel agents come in handy.

If you tune in on the middle of a conversation, and missed the name of the place under discussion, interrupt the stranger and ask for it. People are flattered to be seen as authorities in wining, dining or travel.

Books, movies, magazines. In vacation terms, life can imitate art. You'll want to visit Big Sur if you've read Henry Miller or seen where Elizabeth Taylor's breathtaking house is set in the movie *The Sandpiper.* Hemingway and Gertrude Stein make you eager to retrace their steps all over Paris. If you're an antique car buff and you've seen the British movie *Genevieve,* why not meander around the same English countryside where the automobiles rally?

In a *Fortune* profile of a business tycoon, he mentions his favorite beachfront refuge in Antigua; clip the page and file it. A fashion layout is photographed on a verdant Scottish golf course surrounded by charming cottages; you can track its identity through the ad agency. You can even dope out the names of the resort where Richard Burton and Ava Gardner carried on in the film *Night of the Iguana,* or the one in which Dudley Moore and Bo Derek made a mockery of the libido in *10.*

It's not hard to notice beautiful or intriguing locations in books or movies. What's hard is to realize that they're not always the most expensive vacation spots. Harder still is recording the information and putting it where you can find it when you're ready to act on it.

Business trips as fieldwork. When traveling for business, ask the people you meet where you should stay if you ever come back to their city for pure fun. If you're meeting over lunch or dinner, ask them to pick a restaurant they love, instead of your hotel's dining room. That's how you can discover the best hush puppies in Atlanta, the best Tex-Mex restaurant in Dallas and the best ice cream in Vancouver— and that's how the list of ''bests'' gets into your files for your next pleasure trip to those territories.

If you're invited someplace to lecture, ask to be put up not in a motel with a pool overlooking the Interstate but at a guest house, inn or bed-and-breakfast place, on the chance it will turn out to be special enough to come back with your family.

Source: Letty Cottin Pogrebin, an editor at *Ms.* magazine.

HOW TO GET THE BEST TABLES IN RESTAURANTS

You can get better restaurant tables by making reservations through a hotel concierge. Reason: The restaurant wants the hotel to continue to recommend it to customers, so it keeps the hotel guests happy by giving them the best seats.

RELUCTANT VACATIONERS

Not all executives love to get away from it all on a vacation. Many really prefer to work. But families need vacations, and so do workaholics occasionally.

How to take yourself away successfully:

• Make vacations somewhat similar to your year-round life, so that they offer continuity as well as contrast. If you enjoy a daily swim at the gym, be sure to pick a vacation spot with a pool. If you never step into art museums at home, don't feel you have to drag yourself to them when you're away.

• Leave your calculator, beeper, dictating device and briefcase at home. (One person planned camping or cross-country skiing trips chiefly to keep a workaholic spouse from bringing along a briefcase.)

• Avoid finishing lots of work at the last minute. It can leave you feeling frantic. And it could make it hard to plunge back into work when you return.

• Don't drive your staff crazy by leaving lots of lists and memos or calling continually. Things probably won't fall apart in your absence. Limit yourself to two calls the first day and one a day thereafter.

• Take enough time off to recharge your energy. Two weeks may feel too long, but three days is too short.

Source: Dr. Marilyn Machlowitz, a New York organizational psychologist and consultant.

TIPPING GUIDE FOR TRAVELERS

In a restaurant: Maitre d', $1–$15 every few visits (if you get special treatment). Waiter, 15%. Captain, 5%. Sommelier, 7% of the liquor bill or $2 for each bottle. Cloakroom, 50¢–$1 per coat. Doorman, $1 if he hails a cab.

The above tips are applicable at deluxe and top restaurants only. In other restaurants, the waiters get a 10%–15% tip and coat check is usually 25¢–50¢.

At a hotel: Chambermaid, $1–$1.25 per room per night, or $7 a week. Dining room (American Plan), waiter gets 15% of the food bill for the total stay and the maitre d' a flat $10 for a stay of five to seven days. Room service, if service charge is not added, 10%–15%, depending on the amount of service given. Pool attendant, $1 per day. Waiter (snack bar, golf club, beach or tennis club), 15% of the bill. Locker attendant, 50¢–$1 a day. Bartender, 15% of bill. Doorman, 25¢–$1 unless baggage is handled, then 50¢–$1. Baggage handler, 50¢

per bag. Bellman, 50¢-$1 per errand. Taxi driver, 15% of bill, 25¢ minimum for small bill.

In Europe and the Orient, tips are usually included in the form of a service charge of 10%-15% of the bill. Be sure to check your bill before leaving additional money.

On a cruise (two in a cabin): Cabin steward or stewardess, $3-$4 per day. Dining room steward, $3-$3.50 per day. Shoe cleaner, $5 at end of trip. Cabin boys, $1 per errand. Wine steward, 15% of total bill. Night steward, $2 per night if services are used. Deck steward, $10-$15 for the whole cruise. Bar steward, 15% of the total tab.

Barber or hairdresser: Hairdresser, 15%-20% of his or her services (but do not tip the owner of a salon). Shampooer, $2. Manicurist, $2. Pedicurist, $4. Coat check, $1.

Caterer: Party supervisor, $20. Head waiter, $10. Head cook, $10-$15. Others, $5 each.

Miscellaneous tips: Garage attendant, 50¢-$1. Valet parking, $1. Redcap, 50¢ per bag. Washroom attendant, 25¢-$1. Strolling musicians, $1-$2/single, $5/group.

BEST RESTAURANTS IN WASHINGTON, DC

• Cantina, 3251 Prospect St., NW, 20007, (202) 337-5130. Informal, with first-rate Italian food.
• Dominique's, 1900 Pennsylvania Ave. NW, (202) 452-1126. A smallish restaurant with unusual nouvelle food.
• Germaine's, 2400 Wisconsin Ave. NW, (202) 965-1185. Interesting specialties from both the Orient and the Occident.
• Jean-Louis, 2650 Virginia Ave. NW, (202) 298-4488. Elegant, with distinctive Continental food and superb service.
• Jean Pierre, 1835 K St. NW, (202) 466-2022. Still one of the city's most respected French restaurants.
• Jockey Club, 2100 Massachusetts Ave. NW, (202) 659-8000. A favorite of the current administration. Dark paneled and masculine, with a hearty menu.

• Le Lion d'Or, 1150 Connecticut Ave. NW, (202) 296-7972. Classic French food served with style.
• Tiberio, 1915 K St. NW, (202) 452-1915. Chic and fun, good Northern Italian food.
• Washington Palm, 1225 19 St. NW, (202) 293-9091. A sturdy steakhouse.

BEST RESTAURANTS IN PHILADELPHIA

No other city has experienced the recent spectacular change in fine dining that Philadelphia boasts. Among the top restaurants:
• Le Beau Lieu, Barclay Hotel, Rittenhouse Square, (215) 545-0300. Elegant eatery in one of the city's most chic hotels. The Continental cuisine is served to perfection.
• Le Bec-Fin, 1523 Walnut St., (215) 567-1000. The best dining in Philadelphia. Owner George Perrier features the freshest foie gras and truffles, and quenelles as light as a feather. Try the Bec-Fin cake.

• Cafe Royal, Palace Hotel, 18 St. and the Parkway, (215) 963-2244. Chef Jean-Pierre Petit serves prix-fixe dinners only. His style of cooking is inventive, with terrine of salmon, fricassee of snails and rare lamb in fresh thyme sauce.
• Fountain Restaurant, Four Seasons Hotel, 1 Logan Square, (215) 963-1500. Glorious restaurant in a lavish new hotel just recently opened. Here you will find old favorites cooked to perfection.
• Frog, 1524 Locust St., (215) 735-8882. Innovative cuisine served in a modern setting. The food is an unusual mingling of American, French and Asian specialties.
• The Garden, 1617 Spruce St., (215) 546-4455. Charming restaurant with outdoor dining in fine weather. The pub-like Oyster Bar is favored for its clubby atmosphere. Try the pasta primavera.
• La Truffe, 10 S. Front St., (215) 925-5062. The food combines classic French with a touch of the nouvelle. The sauces are light and the presentations perfect. The sweetbreads and

assorted salads are unusual. The terrine of two fishes succeeds where others have failed.

Here are two old favorites, once the best that the city had to offer. Both are large busy and old-style, with excellent plain seafood, steaks, chops and classic American food.
- Bookbinders–Old Original, 125 Walnut St., (215) 925-7027.
- Bookbinders Classic Seafood Center City, 215 S. 15 St., (215) 545-1137.

BEST RESTAURANTS IN BOSTON

Boston is an old city where seafaring and a diverse population affect local cuisine. Both seafood and ethnic restaurants abound. Here are some of the best:

- Tuscan Grill, 361 Moody St., Waltham, (617) 891-5486. Sophisticated northern Italian food, with fresh pasta, fine veal dishes and perfect espresso.
- Cricket's, Faneuil Hall Marketplace, South Market Building, (617) 720-5570. A relaxed spot to enjoy unusual food, from lunch to after-theater. Specialties: Scallops Rockefeller and chicken William III.
- The Empress, Hyatt Regency Hotel, 575 Memorial Dr., Cambridge, (617) 492-1234. The view is stunning. Specialties: Continental, Mandarin and Szechuan cuisines, including Peking duck, Hong Kong steak, and veal with mushrooms.
- Joseph's Restaurant, 729 Dartmouth St., (617) 266-1502. Elegant surroundings in Boston's Back Bay area combine here with traditional Continental fare. Expect to find rare roast beef, sole Marguery and lovely rack of lamb.
- The Julien, Meridien Hotel, 250 Franklin St., (617) 451-1900. A wide selection of nouvelle cuisine.
- Locke-Ober Cafe, 3 & 4 Winter Place (617) 542-1340. A revered tradition in Boston. Authentic Victorian atmosphere, with hearty but elegant fare. Try the clams Winter Place, lobster Savannah, filet mignon and lusty desserts.

- Maison Robert, Old City Hall, 45 School St., (617) 227-3370. Old World elegance and ambience grace the two Maison Robert restaurants—BonHomme Richard and Ben's Cafe, both in the same building and both serving fine French food. Best: Mignon de veau Orloff, lobster in champagne, tarte de pomme.

- Ritz Carlton Main Dining Room, Ritz Carlton Hotel, 15 Arlington St., (617) 536-5700. Overlooks Boston's Public Garden. This elegant restaurant is the place to see all Boston's first families dining spendidly on simple, classic fare. Examples: A clear broth without a hint of fat, fine grilled sole, a simple lamb chop. Fine wines. Great desserts, too.

Uniquely Boston:
- Durgin Park, Faneuil Hall Marketplace, North Market Building, (617) 227-2038. A Boston landmark, with hearty food and lots of hungry diners.

- Legal Sea Foods, 43 Boylston St., Chestnut Hill, (617) 277-7300. This simple, informal restaurant is known for its excellent fresh seafoods.

- Ye Old Union Oyster House, 41 Union St., (617) 227-2750. Boston's oldest restaurant, specializing in freshly shucked oysters, Yankee-style seafood, shore dinners, and char-broiled steaks.

BEST RESTAURANTS IN CHICAGO

- Ambria, 2300 N. Lincoln Park West, (312) 472-5959. Expect to find excellent, original recipes with a French bias.
- Berghoff, 17 W. Adams, (312) 427-3170. A big, friendly German restaurant with huge portions of excellent, hearty food.
- Biggs, 11 50 N. Dearborn, (312) 787-0900. A handsome, Continental dining spot with international cusine. The seven-course prix fixe menu is one of the city's best values.

• Cricket's, 100 E. Chestnut, (312) 280-2100. A cozy, clubby restaurant with Continental cuisine.

• L'Escargot, 140 E. Huron, (312) 337-1717. Bright and airy, with French food, particularly from Provence.

• Le Francais, 269 S. Milwaukee, (708) 541-7470. Superb—as good as you would find in France. And while it does require some driving to get there, it is worth the effort. Reservations must be made weeks in advance.

• The Ninety-Fifth, John Hancock Center, (312) 787-9596. For the best views in Chicago, try this 95th-floor restaurant. The food is international cuisine.

• Le Perroquet, 70 E. Walton St., (312) 944-7990. Lovely atmosphere, excellent fresh fish. Fowl receives special treatment.

• Trader Vic's, 17 E. Monroe St. (the Palmer House), (312) 726-7500. Just like all the others, but very reliable when you feel like good Polynesian food.

• Truffles, 151 E. Wacker Drive, (312) 565-1000. A lovely French eatery.

LOS ANGELES RESTAURANTS

• Avenue Saloon, 2040 Ave. of the Stars, Century City. Casual lunches, dinners and after-theater suppers.

• Bernard's, Biltmore Hotel, 506 S. Grand Ave. Nouvelle cuisine in a glorious setting.

• Bistro Garden, 176 N. Canon Dr., Beverly Hills. Anyone who is anyone lunches here.

• Chasen's, 9039 Beverly Blvd., Beverly Hills. More like a club than a restaurant, Chasen's has a faithful clientele of many years' standing.

• Coterie, Beverly Hills Hotel, 9641 Sunset Blvd., Beverly Hills. An elegant restaurant with a Continental menu.

• Carol O'Connors, 369 N. Bedford Dr., Beverly Hills. Simple fare, ample portions and a friendly atmosphere.

• Harry's Bar and American Grill, 2020 Ave. of the Stars, Century City. A replica of the Venice original, with simple, straightforward food.

• Jimmy's, 201 Moreno Dr., Beverly Hills. A favorite of the movie moguls.

• La Scala, 410 N. Canon Dr., Beverly Hills. Classy Italian, with fresh pastas and delectable veal.

• L'Escoffier Room, Beverly Hilton Hotel, 9876 Wilshire Blvd., Beverly Hills. Very French.

• L'Orangerie, 903 N. La Cienega Blvd., Hollywood. First-rate French food.

• Madame Wu's Garden, 2201 Wilshire Blvd., Santa Monica. Worth the trip for remarkable Chinese food.

• Ma Maison, 8555 Beverly Blvd., West Hollywood. Fine French food and lots of movie stars.

• Mandarin, 430 N. Camden Dr., Beverly Hills. Unusual Mandarin cuisine.

• Mr. Chow, 344 N. Camden Dr., Beverly Hills. Chinese specialties combined with a Continental menu. The service hasn't improved, however.

• Morton's, 8800 Melrose Ave., Beverly Hills. A trendy spot for star-gazing, with good nouveau cuisine.

• Rangoon Racquet Club, 9474 Santa Monica Blvd., Beverly Hills. Specialties include such diverse food as chili and hot curries.

• Spago, 8795 Sunset Blvd., Hollywood. New American cuisine. American goat cheese, fresh pastas and a variety of pizzas are among the specialties.

FOUR-STAR DINING IN DALLAS

• Arthur's, 1000 Campbell Centre, 8350 N. Central Expressway. Steaks that are the pride of Texas, and a remarkable wine list.

• Les Saisons, 165 Turtle Creek Village. Elegant atmosphere and a Continental menu.

• 650 North, Plaza of the Americas Hotel, 650 N. Pearl Blvd. A sophisticated menu of both classic French and nouvelle cuisines. Rack of lamb is a specialty.

• Cafe Royal, Plaza of the Americas Hotel, 650 N. Pearl Blvd. A sophisticated menu of both classic French and nouvelle cuisines. Rack of lamb is a specialty.

• Cafe Pacific, 24 Highland Park Shopping Village. Stylish setting for an eclectic bill of fare. Try Sunday brunch.

• Enjolie, Omni Mandalay Hotel, 221 E. Las Colinas Blvd. Very European in feeling and food.

• French Room, Adolphus Hotel, 1321 Commerce. Turn-of-the-century rococo decor and a menu supervised by Jean Banchet, chef-owner of Le Francais in Wheeling, IL.

• The Mansion on Turtle Creek, 2821 Turtle Creek Blvd. The restaurant of an elegant hotel that attracts businessmen. The cuisine is haute-Texas.

• Old Warsaw, 2610 Maple Ave. Old-fashioned flavor and Continental dishes.

• Pyramid Room, Fairmont Hotel, 1717 N. Akard St. International cuisine in a festive setting.

• Ruth's Chris Steak House, 5922 Cedar Springs Rd. Great steaks.

BEST BREAKFAST SPOTS IN THE BIG APPLE

Business meetings over bacon and eggs or croissants and espresso give New Yorkers a head start. Favorite rooms for mixing work with the most important meal of the day:

• Carlyle Hotel (Carlyle Restaurant). Fresh brioche and croissant served elegantly in a quiet Continental atmosphere. Madison Ave. at 76 St., (212) 744-1600, opens at 7.

• Drake Hotel (Wellington Grill). Very British. Park Ave. at 56 St., (212) 421-0900, opens at 7.

• New York Helmsley. Fine selection of imported jams embellishes breakfast breads. 212 E. 42 St., (212) 490-8900, opens at 7.

• New York Palace (Trianon Room). Good food in a sumptuous atmosphere. 455 Madison Ave., (212) 888-7000, opens at 6:30.

• Hotel Inter-Continental (Barclay Restaurant). A popular spot for diplomats. Good food. Good service. 111 E. 48 St., (212) 755-5900, opens at 7.

• Mayfair Regent Hotel (Lobby Lounge). Very European, elegant and homey. 610 Park Ave., (212) 288-0800, opens at 7.

• Helmsley Park Lane Hotel (Park Room). A wonderful view of Central Park accompanies the meal. 36 Central Park South, (212) 371-4000, opens at 7.

• Hotel Pierre (Cafe Pierre). Elegant decor, perfect service and fine food. Fifth Ave. at 61 St., (212) 838-8000, opens at 6:30.

• Plaza Hotel (Edwardian Room). English breakfasts in a handsome setting. Fifth Ave. at 59 St., (212) 759-3000, opens at 7.

• Regency Hotel (Le Restaurant). First-rate food and service for a power-broker clientele. 540 Park Ave., (212) 759-4100, opens at 7.

• Ritz Carlton Hotel (The Jockey Club). A favorite of politicians. 112 Central Park South, (212) 757-1900, opens at 6:30.

• UN Plaza Hotel (Ambassador Grill). Modern, mirrored elegance with an international flavor. 1 United National Plaza at 44 St., (212) 355-3400, opens at 7.

• Vista Hotel (Greenhouse). A harbor view, close to Wall Street. 3 World Trade Center, (212) 938-9100 opens at 6:30.

BEST RESTAURANTS IN GREENWICH VILLAGE, SOHO AND TRIBECA

Greenwich Village:

• Da Silvano, 260 Ave. of the Americas. Florentine food served up by one of the most impressive Italian kitchens in New York. Very expensive. (No credit cards.)

• El Rincon de Espana, 226 Thompson St. Small and crowded, with the top Spanish cooking in New York. Exceptional octopus. Medium priced.

• Il Mulino, 86 W. Third St. Hearty food and pleasant service. One of the Village's most popular Italian restaurants. Expensive.

• The Jane Street Seafood Cafe, 31 Eighth Ave. Straightforward American-style seafood with good, fresh fish. Medium-priced.

• La Metairie, 189 W. 10 St. Hearty French cooking with a North African accent. Try the couscous. Expensive.

• La Tulipe, 104 W. 13 St. Classic French cooking with a delicate hand. Very expensive.

• Texarkana, 64 W. 10 St. Good cooking from the American Southwest. Roast suckling pig can be ordered in advance. Expensive.

Soho:

• Chanterelle, 2 Harrison St. French food prepared in a personal style by an owner chef and served in a small, graceful setting. Very expensive.

• Omen, 113 Thompson St. Japanese food with a great variety of individually prepared vegetable dishes. Meat and fish are also available. Inexpensive.

• Raoul's, 180 Prince St. French country cooking served in a converted New York bar. Expensive.

• SoHo Charcuterie, 195 Spring St. Well-prepared fancy French food. Exceptional Sunday brunch. Very expensive.

Tribeca:

• Le St. Jean des Pres, 112 Duane St. One of the few Belgian restaurants in the US. Big brasserie serves light meals as well as full formal dinners. Expensive.

• Le Zinc, 139 Duane St. A popular artists' hangout with old-fashioned French bistro food. Medium priced.

• Odeon, 145 W. Broadway. Best food south of Canal St. in Manhattan. The cooking is modern, French and expensive.

• Sheba, 151 Hudson St. Spicy Ethiopian food that is not at all hard on American palates. Small and unpretentious (you can use your bread to scoop instead of a fork). Inexpensive.

Source: Seymour Britchky, publisher of *Seymour Britchky's Restaurant Letter.*

BEST NEW YORK BARS

• Cafe des Artistes, 1 W. 67 St. Drink under the sylvan murals of Howard Chandler Christy. (And be sure to visit the restrooms.)

• Le Cirque, 58 E. 65 St. View all the beautiful people who gather here.

• Elaine's, 1703 Second Ave. Stargaze a while at the fresh new crop of theatrical and literary geniuses.

• The Four Seasons, 99 E. 52 St. Manhattan's most beautiful bar and probably the best place to capture the feeling of the city. Very convenient, too.

• The Ginger Man, 51 W. 64 St. Near Lincoln Center. Busy, friendly and noisy, with generous drinks.

• Harper, 1304 Third Ave. Mingle with young, beautiful models and their escorts.

• Jack's, 1022 Lexington Ave. New to the scene, friendly and trendy.

• Jim McMullen's, 1341 Third Ave. A long, cheerful bar, always crowded with happy people.

• Maxwell's Plum, First Ave. at 64 St. It's fun to people-watch the singles crowd at this beautiful bar.

• Michael's Pub, 211 E. 55 St. Crowded and lively (especially on Monday night, when Woody Allen often plays along with the resident jazz orchestra).

• Mortimer's, 1057 Lexington Ave. One of the city's most fashionable spots. You may spot England's Princess Margaret.

• Tavern on the Green, 67 St. at Central Park. Extremely beautiful...right in Central Park.

• Windows on the World Hors d'Oeuvrerie, World Trade Center Tower. WOW!

Hotel Bars:

• The Bar, United Nations Plaza Hotel, First Ave. at 44 St. Right across from the UN, and filled with the diplomatic crowd.

• Bemelmans Bar, Hotel Carlyle, Madison Ave. at 76 St. Lovely bar with good background music.

• Cafe Pierre, Pierre Hotel, Fifth Ave. at 61 St. Loved by the international set.

• Harry's Bar, Helmsley Palace Hotel, 455 Madison Ave. Always a pleasant spot to view the rest of the New York crowd.

• Jockey Club, Ritz Carlton Hotel, 112 Central Park South. The city's newest bar, and certainly one of the most elegant.

• The Rendezvous, Berkshire Place Hotel, Madison Ave. at 52 St. Excellent midtown location. A crowded, handsome bar with fine drinks.

BEST DISHES AT GREAT NEW YORK RESTAURANTS

Appetizers and side dishes:

• Black bean soup. Coach House, 110 Waverly Place.

• Blini with red caviar, Russian Tea Room, 150 W. 57 St.

• Eggplant salad, Sammy's Rumanian Jewish Restaurant, 157 Chrystie St.

• Fishhead soup, Woo Lae Oak of Seoul, 77 W. 46 St.

• Kale, Woods, 148 W. 37 St.

• Linguine with clam sauce, Zinno, 126 W. 13 St.

• Onion tart, Lutece, 249 E. 50 St.

• Panzanella (bread salad), Da Silvano, 260 Ave. of the Americas.

• Paratha, poori and pulka (Indian breads), Madras Woodlands, 308 E. 49 St.

• Ravioli malfatti, Il Nido, 251 E. 53 St.

• Spaghetti primavera, Le Cirque, 58 E. 65 St.

• Sushi, nuta (raw fluke and scallions in a soybean paste, lemon and saki sauce) and chawanmushi (hot custard with greens, mushrooms, fish, shrimp, gingko nuts and lemon rind), Hatsuhana, 17 E. 48 St.

Main courses:

• Cassoulet Toulousain, La Cote Basque, 5 E. 55 St.

• Chicken scarpara, Parma, 1404 Third Ave.

• Choucroute garni, Lutece, 249 E. 50 St.

• Double steak, Joe & Rose, 747 Third Ave.

• Fettuccini filetto de pomadoro (green noodles with tomato, onion, prosciutto), Gargiulo's, 2911 W. 15 St., Brooklyn.

• Frog's legs provencale, La Grenouille, 3 E. 52 St.

• Lemon chicken, Rao V, 455 E. 114 St.

• Peking duck, Peking Duck House, 22 Mott St.

• Oyster pan roast, Oyster Bar and Restaurant, Grand Central Station.

• Roast chicken with herbs, Lutece, 249 E. 50 St.

• Roast striped bass with dill, Coach House, 110 Waverly Place.

• Roast suckling pig, Texarkana, 64 W. 10 St.

• Steak or lobster, Palm, 837 Second Ave.

Supper dishes:

• Hamburgers, Diane's, 249 Columbus Ave.

• Pastrami sandwich, Carnegie Delicatessen and Restaurant, 854 Seventh Ave.

Desserts:

• Lemon tart, John Clancy's Restaurant, 181 W. 10th St.

• Oeufs a la neige, La Grenouille, 3 E. 52 St.

Source: Mimi Sheraton, author of *New York Times Guide to New York Restaurants*, Times Books, New York.

HOW TO GET A GREAT MEAL AT A GREAT RESTAURANT

Restaurateurs, like other business people, are dependent on their regular customers and give them special attention. However, few people can afford to be regulars at very expensive establishments. Most save their visits for special events or, if they live out of town, for infrequent trips to that city. Such celebratory meals can be doubly disappointing if the service is poor or the choice of food is not what the kitchen does best.

Mimi Sheraton's practical suggestions for making a rare visit to a special restaurant the event you had hoped for:

• Avoid Friday and (particularly) Saturday nights if you can. That's when restaurants are at their busiest and have the least time to give you the special attention that you want.

• Do your homework. Read up on the restaurant to find out its strengths and weaknesses so you can order the best it has to offer.

• Make a reservation well in advance. Explain how you have looked forward to coming, and ask for some help in choosing your menu. This may not be necessary at a steak house where you know what the bill of fare is, but in more elaborate places, the management will appreciate your interest and really put themselves out to accommodate you.

• Confirm your reservation by telephone that day. Even the best-run places have an occasional slip-up. (If the number of people in your party changes, be sure to notify the restaurant. It does make a difference.)

• Check out ahead of time what credit cards the restaurant takes and any dress requirements so there will be no embarrassment at the door.

BEST SHOPPING BARGAINS IN NEW YORK

Tucked away in a corner of lower Manhattan is a shoppers' paradise, the Lower East Side. Historically, the area was a way station for the immigrants who came to America in the late 19th and early 20th centuries. It's not history, though, that brings people to the Lower East Side these days. It is bargains on some of the finest merchandise available anywhere!

Everything is closed on Saturday but is open all day Sunday. Sunday is the busiest shopping day. If it's the only day you can get there, go early in the morning. Best: Shop early on a weekday. Business hours are generally 9–5, but many stores close early on Friday.

The stores listed here carry only first-quality merchandise. Discounts are at least 20%.

• Leslie's Bootery, 36 Orchard. Shoes and boots for men and women by Caressa, Jacques Cohen, Fred Braun, Clarks of England, Olaf Daughters, Bally, Johnston & Murphy, Bostonian, Bill Blass...and more.

• Haar & Knobel, 29 Orchard. Everything and anything in sports clothes and outerwear for men: Levi, Woolrich, Izod, London Fog and more. The second floor has the most extensive collection of outerwear we've seen anywhere.

• Pan Am, 50 Orchard. The best names in men's fashion. Tailoring is free. Downstairs is a dressy-clothes department for kids.

• Charlie's Place, 61 Orchard. The biggest selection of all-weather coats in the city. Also an excellent selection of men's slacks and sports clothes.

• Goldman's, 321 Grand (corner Orchard). Fine china by Wedgwood, Royal Doulton, Mikasa and many others. Sterling silver and crystal, figurines by Lladro and Limoges and just about anything else in this category you can think of.

At the corner of Orchard and Grand is the beginning of the domestic dry-goods center of the Lower East Side. Turn left on Grand Street to find store after store of designer sheets, towels and bedspreads, always at great prices. Also check out Mayfield Co. (303 Grand) for fine men's and women's underwear, hosiery and lingerie...and Kreinan's (301 Grand) for a huge selection of children's better clothing.

• Forman's, 82 Orchard. Three floors of beautiful women's clothing...dresses, separates, coats.

• Maximum, 91 Orchard. Shoes for men and women in elegant styles by Bernardo, Rosina Ferragamo and many others.

• Little Rascals, 101 Orchard. The most unusual and beautiful children's clothes and shoes imported from Europe.

• Antony, 106 Orchard. Stunning men's clothing, imported from Europe...natural fabrics only.

• Flair's Edge, 110 Orchard. Men's and women's shoes of exceptional quality and design.

• JBZ, 121 Orchard. Magnificent women's clothing by Perry Ellis, Norma Kamali, Yamamoto Kansai, Issey Miyake, Betsy Johnson and many others.

• Giselle, 143 Orchard. Three floors of

women's designer clothing. Lots of variety. Wonderful buys, especially toward the end of a season.

• Arivel, 50 Orchard. Opulent fur coats and jackets for men and women. Custom fitted and guaranteed. Also interesting clothes for women.

• Fleisher's, 186 Orchard. Tremendous variety of women's suits and coats. Abundant choices within size ranges. Top brands.

You've come to the end of Orchard Street, corner E. Houston, which is the food street of the Lower East Side. When you turn left onto Houston, you will come upon Moishe's Bakery and Ben's Cheese Shop (both at 181 E. Houston St.). The two offer delicious opportunities to refuel before you continue your shopping expedition. If you prefer to sit down and be served, walk left three blocks to Yonah Schimmel's Knish Bakery. This Lower East Side landmark has homemade apple strudel, knishes of every variety and yogurt made on the premises. Or walk one block to the right to Katz's Delicatessen (corner Houston & Ludlow) for the ultimate hot dog, french fries and a Coke. Enjoy!

Source: Ellen Telzer and Sharon Dunn Greene, authors of *The Lower East Side Shopping Guide*, The Shopping Experience, New York.

BEST RESTAURANTS IN CANADA

Calgary, Alberta:

• Cafe Danois, Chevron Plaza, (403) 263-1114. Comfortable, small and pretty, with an emphasis on Scandinavian specialties. The fried fish, liver, open-face sandwiches and vegetables are wonderful.

• La Dolce Vita, 916 First Ave. NE, (403) 263-3445. Pleasant, with prompt service and wonderful pasta. The veal and chicken dishes are authentic Italian.

• Sushi Hiro, 727 Fifth Ave. SW, (403) 233-0605. The best place to eat in this all-around great restaurant is the sushi bar.

Edmonton, Alberta:

Montreal, Quebec:

• The Beaver Club, 900 Rene Levesque West, (514) 861-3511. The atmosphere is clublike, and the cooking is nouvelle. You can be sure of the finest ingredients prepared with skill. Most fish is imported from France. Specialties include a wonderful ragout of turbot, trout with chives and flounder flamed with cider.

• Cafe de Paris, 900 Rene Levesque West, (514) 842-4212. A traditional French restaurant in the Hotel Ritz Carlton. It offers wonderful food cooked in the old manner. The hotel's garden restaurant is open for warm-weather dining, and its Maritime Bar is a delightful place for before- or after-theater dining.

• Le St. Amable, 188 Rue St. Amable, (514) 866-3471. An old stone house in the heart of charming Old Montreal. The food is excellent, with delicacies such as quail with foie gras, spring lamb and delectable desserts.

• Savini, 3820 St. Lawrence Blvd., (514) 845-3326. If you tire of French food, try Savini, a touch of Northern Italy in the heart of this French-speaking province. The small menu is crammed with authentic Italian delicacies.

Quebec City, Quebec:

• Le Biarritz, 136 Rue Ste. Anne, (418) 692-2433. Enjoy the relaxed ambience of this intimate restaurant in a lovely old house. The dishes are mostly from the Basque region of France, and the pear Helene is worth a special visit.

• Serge Bruyere, 1200 Rue St. Jean, (418) 694-0618. You must reserve well in advance. Once you arrive, plan to spend considerable time, since everything is cooked to order. The excellent food includes fresh cod, shrimp, sole, scallops, a fine filet of pork and crisp salads.

Toronto, Ontario:

• Bindi, 3241 Yonge St., (416) 487-2881. Thoroughly modern but rather small and simple. Authentic Italian food, with risotto, pasta, cannelloni and lots of delicious fresh vegetables.

• Truffles, 21 Avenue Rd., (416) 964-0411. A superb international restaurant in the Four Seasons Hotel. It offers a French menu and top-notch service.

• Winston's, 104 Adelaide St. West, (416)

363-1627. Specialties: Game birds and imaginative desserts.

Vancouver, British Columbia:

• Cafe de Paris, 751 Denman St., (604) 687-1418. A delightful restaurant, with a glorious wine cellar and a fine menu of fresh fish prepared by a first-class chef.

• Maxim's, 257 Keefer St., (604) 688-6281. The finest Chinese restaurant in a city of good ones. Try the sweet dough wrapped around barbecued pork.

Victoria, British Columbia:

• Chez Daniel, 2522 Estevan Ave., (604) 592-7424. A thoroughly Continental owner-chef restaurant in British Columbia's capital on Vancouver Island. Wonderful salmon, noisettes of lamb, rabbit and coquilles.

THERE ARE A VARIETY OF EXCITING WAYS TO SEE THIS WONDERFUL WORLD

Too many people think that foreign travel is an expensive option open only to the well-to-do. They may long to see other parts of the world and meet people from other cultures, but they can't seem to put aside enough money for the big trip.

Fact: You don't need a lot of money to go abroad if you really want to do it. You can use your own enthusiasm and interests to pay for part of your trip—and you can custom-design the itinerary to your own specifications. Or you can—with even less effort-cut your costs to a minimum by getting free transportation or lodging.

Putting a group together:

There are several ways to get free trips by organizing your own travel group...

• Tour company representative. Several tour groups, for example, will give you a complimentary package tour (including transportation and lodging) if you act as their representative (part-time)—and sell their packages. When you meet their quota of five or six paid-up travelers, they'll award you a free package trip. If you double the quota, you can get a free package trip for your spouse as well.

• Tour organizer. You can get a free trip by becoming the designated organizer for a tour put together by many of the national travel companies like American Express or Thomas Cook and Son. Your obligation is to bring in 15 or more paying customers for one of their nationally advertised travel packages. Look at affinity groups you belong to. An art history lecturer, for example, put together her quota from students who valued her judgment in choosing an art tour. A minister attracted participants for a trip to the Holy Land from his congregation.

Chaperone students. If you work with young people—as a teacher, coach or Scout leader, for example—you can get a free trip by recruiting and chaperoning a group of paying students to almost anywhere in the world.

Not everyone enjoys such a "busman's holiday," but my wife and I have found sharing young people's delight in discovering another culture to be quite rewarding in itself.

• Lead a special-interest tour. A lawyer we know planned a two-week legal-eagle tour of London with his travel agent—and recruited enough colleagues and spouses to pay for his and his wife's fares and lodgings. He made arrangements for the group to hear trials at Old Baily and at the Royal Courts of Justice. They visited the Inns of Court and met with solicitors and barristers.

If you have a passion for art, theater, photography, wine, food or architecture, you can use your knowledge to design a trip that will be special to you and your friends.

• Design your own adventure vacation. If you are an experienced outdoors person, you can put together the challenge trip of your dreams with a travel agent and attract your own group of adventurers. You can organize a camelback trek with the Ruaregs out of Timbuktu, climb the Himalayas or balloon over French vineyards and chateaus.

Free lodging:

• If you don't have the time or inclination to package your entire trip, you can still cut down on your travel expenses appreciably by joining a home or hospitality exchange.

Source: Robert William Kirk is author of *You Can Travel Free*, Pelican Books, 1101 Monroe St., Graetna, Louisiana 70053, and is a college professor in Northern California who has logged more than 250,000 miles of free travel over the last 19 years.

BEST MONTHS AT 42 TOP TOURIST SPOTS ON SIX CONTINENTS

Europe:

- Greece. March–May, October and November.
- London. April–June, October and November.
- Paris. April–June, October and November.
- Riviera (Monaco, France, Italy). Christmas, New Year's and Easter holidays. Also: June–August.
- Rome. March–May, October–December.
- Scandinavia. May–September. Winter sports: February and March.
- Switzerland. Winter sports: December–April. Summer activities: May–August.
- USSR. April–June, September and October. Summers are torrid, with no air conditioning. Winters are harsh.
- Venice. March–June.

Africa:

- Egypt. Always hot and humid. Best: March–May, October–December.
- Kenya. Seasons are reversed. June, July and August are coolest. December, January, February and March are hot and dry.
- Morocco. The sun shines 300 days a year. In the south around Agadir and in Marrakesh: December–March. Avoid visiting in August or September.
- South Africa. There are no extremes of climate. Capetown: January–March. Kruger National Park: June–September. Johannesburg: May–August.

Middle East:

- Israel. Tel-Aviv: April–June, October–December. Jerusalem: January–June, October and November.
- Jordan. Hot and dry all year. Best: March–May, November and December.
- Saudi Arabia. December–March.

Orient:

- China. The country is vast, with a wide-ranging climate. The most visited cities are Peking, Tientsin, Nankin, Hangchow, Shanghai and Canton, where summers are hot and humid and winters are relatively mild. Best: April–June and October.
- Japan. April–June, October and November.

Asia and the Pacific:

- Australia. Seasons are reversed. Melbourne, Sydney, Canberra: October–February. Darwin: June–August.
- India. The climate varies greatly. Best: November, December, February and March. Monsoons: June–September.
- Malaysia. March–July and September.
- Nepal (Himalayas). September–November.
- New Zealand. The weather is always cool and temperate.
- Philippines. November–March.
- Singapore. Always hot, with little variation in rainfall.
- South Korea. March–May, October and November.
- Tahiti. May–October.
- Thailand. November–April.

South America:

- Argentina. October–March.
- Brazil. March–October.
- Chile. October–February.
- Peru. Lima: January–March. Mountains: June–September.
- Venezuela. December–March.

Closer to Home:

- Bermuda. May–October. Also: Easter week.
- Canada. Winter sports: November–April. Summer sports and city vacations: May–September.
- Caribbean. November–April.
- Florida. December–April.
- Hawaii. Ideal all year.
- Mexico. October–April.
- Puerto Rico. November–April.

BEST UNCROWDED RESORTS IN MEXICO

For the cheapest prices and probably the most exciting vacations, stay away from well-known, overcrowded resorts like Acapulco and Taxco.

Other resorts, many of them favored by Mexican business executives and bankers, are now sometimes so hungry for business that prices for those who spend dollars are drastically reduced. Travelers who know Mexico well say they especially like:

• Ixtapa, 150 miles north of Acapulco on the Pacific. Warm, dry and uncrowded, the resort has one of the most luxurious new hotels in Mexico, the Ixtapa Camino Real. The slightly less plush Krystal is usually more expensive.

• Merida, the capital of Yucatan, is old, exotic and cheap. Tourists in Yucatan, unlike some other places in Mexico, are unlikely to be victims of rip-offs or petty crimes. The elegant Montejo Palace costs much more than other hotels. Merida is the takeoff point for excursions to nearby Mayan ruins, where hotels are similarly priced.

• Oaxaca is near the site of some of the most beautiful pre-Columbian ruins. A 16th-century convent has been converted into El Presidente hotel.

• Vera Cruz, not touted by Mexico's tourist officials, is a picturesque old city on the Gulf of Mexico with some of the best food in the country. The six-hour drive from 7,200-foot-high Mexico City to sea-level Vera Cruz is spectacular. The beachside Mocambo hotel is reasonably priced.

Because of the county's volatile economy, prices can change fast.

Once you decide on a destination, you can either rely on a travel agent or make travel and hotel arrangements yourself. In either case, it pays to compare package deals offered by Mexicana and several US airlines to find out what it would cost to book flights and hotels separately.

Unless you book a package tour, it's best to ask the hotel for a telex (sent to your agent or company) confirming the reservation. Asking for confirmation of the price is a gamble. By the time you get there, it could be lower.

Caution: If you take US currency to convert in Mexico, don't take bills larger than $20 and make sure they're in perfect condition. Many hotels and even some banks won't accept foreign money that has even the slightest tear. Savvy travelers to Mexico generally bring in a moderate amount of pesos, a few US dollars for emergencies and otherwise rely on credit cards.

CHOOSING A CARIBBEAN HOTEL

The windward side of the island is best—the breeze will cool you at night and keep the bugs away. Caribbean-side beaches are less dramatic than those on the Atlantic, but safer for swimming and superior for snorkeling or sailing. Upstairs rooms get better views and breezes. Best of all: A corner room. Be sure your room has air conditioning.

Source: *Travel & Leisure.*

WHERE TO EAT AND SHOP IN JERUSALEM

Where to eat: Try eating as the natives do. Israeli vegetables and dairy products are outstanding. Recommended: Take a hotel bed-and-breakfast plan. The hotels all serve extravagant Israeli breakfasts of numerous salads, cheese, yogurts, rolls, breads, tea and coffee. Eat breakfast at your hotel and your other meals out.

Good lunch spots:
• Heppner's, 4 Luntz St., in downtown Jerusalem, offers good Jewish deli-type food at very reasonable prices.
• Cafe Atara, 7 Ben Yehuda St., is an outdoor cafe on the "midrahot," a pedestrian promenade where you can people-watch while eating. It serves sandwiches, pastries, ice cream, waffles, fish and chips, and soup.
• Hahoma Restaurant, 128 Hayehudim St., Jewish quarter, Old City, is a quiet, elegant spot for a relaxing lunch, which you'll need after sightseeing. It serves delicious Moroccan and Continental food, including steak, osso bucco, wiener schnitzel, shish-kebob, lamb chops, couscous and filet mignon.
• Eilon Tower, corner of Ben Yehuda and King George, is a hotel with a restaurant on the 21st floor with a spectacular view of all Jerusalem. It caters to American tastes with good fried chicken, turkey, steak, french fries and a generous salad bar.

Recommended for dinner:
• National Palace Hotel, Al Zahar St., East

Jerusalem, serves gourmet Arab cuisine on a charming roof garden with a view of Old Jerusalem. Be sure to order "Mazzas," a spectacular variety of exotic Middle Eastern appetizers, including stuffed zucchini, stuffed grape leaves, tahina (sesame paste), hommos (chickpea paste), pickles, olives, eggplant and more. Try the shish-kebob with french fries as a main course.

• Maharajah, 11 Shlomzion Hamlka St., is a good kosher Indian restaurant. Traditional Indian curries, masalas, ghunas and parathas are served.

• Alla Gondola, 14 King George St., serves excellent Italian food including pastas, veal in cream or marsala sauce, and filet mignon.

• Mandy's is at 3 Horkenos St. If you ever wondered what happened to Mandy Rice-Davies (of the British Profumo scandal), she started a chain of Chinese restaurants in Israel and Greece. Her Jerusalem branch serves good Chinese food at reasonable prices.

• Mishkenot Sha'ananim, Yemin Moshe St. near the King David Hotel, is a fine restaurant in the historic Moses Montefiore house, the first house built outside the walls of the Old City in the 1860s. It serves outstanding kosher Middle Eastern versions of gourmet French cuisine.

Where to shop:

• Arab market. A traditional "shuk" or Arab bazaar, this market is one of Jerusalem's main attractions. Noisy, colorful and exciting, it has hundreds of tiny open-air shops lining the narrow cobbled streets of the Old City. A huge variety of goods is sold, from souvenirs to spices and sandals. Be prepared to move aside quickly for passing Arab boys on donkeys, which are used to transport merchandise through streets too narrow for cars. You'll find great buys, especially if you get into the spirit of the market and aren't too shy to bargain. The merchants here expect it. But don't buy anything until you comparison shop. Best buys: Palestinian pottery, hand-tooled leather bags, costume jewelry, "kefiyahs" (Arab scarves), Bedouin copperware, olivewood sculptures, embroidered dresses. Pass up: Antiquities (their authenticity is questionable here) and Indian clothing (the same goods are imported to the US).

• Maskit, 12 Harav Kook St., was founded by Ruth Dayan to promote Arab and Israeli home handicrafts. The prices, though high, are good values. The exquisite and unusual items include glassware, jewelry, embroidered and handwoven fabrics and clothing, enamels and ceramics. Good buys: Heavy woolen coats and capes, Roman glass jewelry set in silver, handwoven bedspreads.

• Jerusalem House of Quality, 12 Hebron Rd., is a center for artisans. Watch artists making enamelware, pottery, woodwork, glassware, jewelry and metal religious articles. Don't miss the glassblower who makes tiny, delicate vases. Prices vary from $5 for an ashtray to hundreds of dollars.

• Yakov Heller, 22 King David St., offers handmade silver jewelry and statuettes depicting biblical scenes. Heller's beautiful work has been presented by Israel to political leaders around the world. Prices are reasonable.

• Mea Shearim is the religious Jewish section of Jerusalem. You'll feel transported to an 18th-century Eastern European ghetto. A variety of shops on the main street sell religious articles, jewelry and souvenirs. The prices are good, and the merchants are trustworthy. Don't miss Shlomo Ohana, 20 Ein Yakov St. He makes "davening Hassidim," whimsical little figurines that move in a breeze and seem to be praying.

Source: Ahuva Aharon, Israel Ministry of Tourism, Jerusalem, and Jacob Shoshan, private tour guide and dedicated gourmet, Jerusalem.

THE WORLD'S BEST SPAS

American spas are fitness-oriented. The best ones offer massages and sybaritic treatments of all kinds, but the emphasis is on vigorous exercise and rigid diet. They usually include some behavior modification, so that the dropped pounds stay dropped and the stress-reducing techniques pay off.

California:

• La Costa. Complimentary championship golf and tennis are part of three programs. The original spa plan has daily massage, facial, herbal wrap and exercise classes.

Minimum: Four nights. Carlsbad, CA 92008, (800) 854-6564.

• The Golden Door. Highly structured program with a compulsory Sunday-to-Sunday stay. Wake-up at 6 AM, lights-out at 9 PM. Maximum: Two weeks. Escondido, CA 92025, (619) 744-5777.

• Sonoma Mission Inn Spa. Gourmet spa food, mineral water, health and beauty treatments, and fitness routines using equipment that ranges from very basic to advanced. Costs less after mid-October. Also daily and monthly rates. Boyes Hot Springs, CA 95476, (800) 358-9022.

Florida:

• Bonaventure Hotel and Spa. After medical evaluation, clients learn new fitness and nutrition habits and use the superb facilities, which include outdoor exercise pools, gyms with Paramount equipment, and golf, tennis and horseback riding. Fort Lauderdale, FL 33326, (800) 327-8090.

• The World of Palm-Aire. Specializes in weight loss (Elizabeth Taylor shed 20 pounds in three weeks). Athletic facilities include championship 18-hole golf courses, 37 all-weather tennis courts, five racquetball courts, Olympic-size pool and Nautilus. Seven-day/six-night package includes medical exam, fitness tests, daily facials and massages. Pompano Beach, FL 33069, (800) 327-4960.

Texas:

• The Greenhouse. Very structured program from 8:30 AM to 5:30 PM. Features an 850-calorie gourmet diet and heavy emphasis on beauty, with Yves Saint Laurent and Charles of the Ritz programs. Minimum stay: One week. Maximum: Three weeks. Arlington, TX 76010, (817) 640-4000.

• The Phoenix. Specializes in individualized treatment—only 13 women at a time. There are occasional men's weeks. Promises a permanent lifestyle change and weight-control program in one week. Strenuous workouts and a full program from 6:30 AM to 9 PM. Houston, TX 77024, (800) 548-4700.

Europe:

European spas emphasize water and mud cures as treatments for a variety of diseases rather than vigorous athletics or weight loss through stringent diet. They are oases for relaxation, where you can get your back problem or tennis elbow treated and lower your stress level and blood pressure.

Britain:

In orientation, British health spas fall somewhere between the American and European styles. Although there are sports and athletic facilities, exercise classes and organized hikes, there isn't as much emphasis on workouts as at American spas. For good diet food, British and American spas are about equal. British spas are places to lose weight, relax, get some exercise, succumb to the hedonistic pleasures of daily massage and use as a base for antiquing forays. British spas cost only a fraction of what their American counterparts do—usually less than $100 a day. If you're planning to stay a week or two, you'll save enough money for your air fare plus a week in London.

• Champneys at Tring. Less than an hour north of London, this former Rothschild mansion is surrounded by 170 acres of gardens and parkland. It offers 1,000- and 500-calorie diets, massage, seaweed and salt baths, and back-mobility exercises. Guests must arrive on Sunday for a five- or seven-day program and on Friday for a two-day program. Tring, Hertfordshire HP23 6HY, Berkhamsted, (04427) 3351.

• Grayshott Hall. This beautiful 83-room mansion, former home of Alfred Lord Tennyson, is an hour southwest of London. Athletic facilities include a nine-hole golf course, tennis, badminton, croquet, an indoor swimming pool and a Jacuzzi with a panoramic view of the garden and grounds. In addition to conventional massage and facials, Grayshott features aromatherapy, a massage that uses fragrant oils on different parts of the body. Grayshott Near Hindhead, Surrey GU26 6JJ, (042873) 4331.

Italy:

Italy's spa tradition goes back 3,000 years. Mineral-water and thermal-mud springs occur primarily from Florence northward and from Rome southwest along the "boot." Most hotels have swimming pools, and many of them have tennis courts.

• Abano. You can take the cure mornings and tour Venice in the afternoon and evening.

Abano and its neighbor, the Montegrotto Spa, are two of the most important mud-therapy centers in the world. The hotels themselves have treatment facilities. Best hotels: Royal Orologio, Bristol Buja, La Residence and Trieste e Victoria.

• Fiuggi. Situated 50 miles west of Rome, it offers Etruscan ruins, a summer theater and nightclubs. Mineral water—praised by Michelangelo—is everywhere. The baths are located in the enlarged, modernized Fonte Bonifacio Ottavo and the new Fonte Anticolana. Best hotels: Palazzo della Fonte, Silva Splendid, Vallombroso & Majestic.

• Montecatini Terme. This spa is an hour away from Florence, Pisa, Lucca, Siena, Pistoia and Arezzo. Among its sports and entertainment facilities are a race course, tennis courts, trap shooting, miniature golf, a theater, a concert hall and a cinema. The spa itself is a group of 12 buildings set among gardens and completely cut off from motor traffic. The waters of five of the springs are for drinking; two others are used for therapy and one in the preparation of thermal mud. Best hotels: Grand Hotel & La Pace, Ambasciatori Grand Hotel e Cristallo, Bellavista-Palace & Golf and Cristallino.

Source: Judith H. McQuown is the author of five investment books and writes about shopping, antiques and travel as well.

BEST DUDE RANCHES

Dude ranches offer attractive, offbeat vacations. They're particularly appropriate for families with children and those interested in the outdoors (especially horseback riding and fishing). Our list includes some of the best dude ranches in the country. They are, understandably, all in the West.

California:
• Quarter Circle U-Rankin Ranch, Box 36-A, Caliente 93518. (805) 867-2511. Rate includes meals and horses. Easter through Thanksgiving.

Colorado:

• Vista-Verde Ranch, Steamboat Springs 80428. (303) 879-3858. Rate includes everything. Summer for horses; winter for skiing.

New Mexico:
• Rancho Encantada, Santa Fe 87501. (505) 982-3537. Room only. Easter through Christmas.

Oregon:
• Donna Gill's Rock Springs Guest Ranch, 64201 Tyler Rd., Bend 97701. (503) 382-1957. Rate includes meals and horses. June 23 to Labor Day.

Wyoming:
• A-BA-A Encampment 82325. (307) 327-5454. Rate includes meals and horses. June to October.

• Eaton's Ranch, Wolf 82844. (307) 655-9285. Rate includes meals and horses. June to October 15.

GREAT GOLF VACATIONS

A superior golf resort provides comfortable accommodations and special courses that offer unusual scenery, challenges and/or history. The following ones are exceptional:
• Casa de Campo, La Romana, Dominican Republic. One of the best of the tropical golf resorts. Contact your travel agent for information and reservations.
• Doral Hotel and Country Club, 4400 Northwest 87 Ave., Miami, FL 33178, (800) 327-6334. Features four 18-hole golf courses and one nine-hole par-three course. The Blue Course is the home of the Doral Rider Open event.
• Gleneagles Hotel, Perthshire Scotland. One of the great manor houses of the United Kingdom. There are three 18-hole championship courses, and a fourth course is presently under construction. Open April through October only. Call our travel agent for information.
• The Greenbriar, White Sulphur Springs, WV 24986, (800) 624-6070. Has three golf courses, one of them designed by Jack Nicklaus.
• The Lodge at Pebble Beach, 17-Mile Drive, Pebble Beach, CA 93953, (408) 624-3811. Home of the Bing Crosby Pro-Am. Pebble Beach also features two famous golf holes (the seventh and the 18th) that are known for their difficulty.

• Sawgrass, Box 600, Porte Vedura Beach, FL 32082, (800) 457-4653. This resort is home to the PGA's Tournament Championship, the richest purse on the tour.

• Seapines Plantation, Hilton Head Island, SC 29928, (800) 845-6131. Three courses are available. One, the Harbor Town Links, is world class and is the site of the Heritage Golf Classic.
Source: Stephen Birnbaum, editorial director, *Diversion.*

HOW TO GET A CRUISE SHIP'S BEST PRICE

Don't rely solely on travel agents. Not all of them are knowledgeable about cruises, and some promote only one or two lines. Better: Read the latest issues of *Travel Weekly* (published by Ziff-Davis), especially the issues with a cruise guide.

After choosing several possible cruises, go to a few travel agents to see which can get you the best price. Surprisingly, these often vary because of the many promotion gimmicks of the cruise lines. Ask about cash rebates, free air fare to the port of departure, flat rates for inside and outside cabins, free passage for third and fourth persons. Frequently, the steamship company itself can get you an even better deal.
Source: Daniel A. Nesbett, travel marketing consultant, Darien, CT.

FREIGHTER AND CARGO CRUISES

These cruises are becoming increasingly popular, but they can be taken only by people who can be away from business for long periods of time and have flexible schedules. They're very good for retirees.

There is no assurance that a ship scheduled to depart on a particular day will indeed leave that day. The first consideration of such ships is their cargo, and they will stay in port until they are completely loaded, even if that means waiting for weeks. The same holds true all along the route. You are protected on price, however. The longer the voyage, the lower the per diem costs.

Some advantages of these cruises:
• The costs are considerably lower than for other types of cruises. Everything is included in the price.
• Most ships carry only 8–12 pasengers, so you have an excellent opportunity to get to know your fellow cruisers. (However, you might travel with people you don't care for.)
• You get more port time than with regular ships.
• The quarters are usually first-rate. The food is simple and good. Larger ships sometimes have their own swimming pools.

There are certain restrictions on age and health on the smaller ships. On those with 12 or more passengers, a doctor is required, so they are more lenient about health restrictions.

When you make your reservation, you pay a deposit. The balance of the cost must be paid by a month before scheduled sailing time. Cancellations are refundable if the ship company is able to resell your space.

Although all the freighter lines do have individuals who book trips directly, it is recommended that you work through a travel agency familiar with this type of ship. A travel agency can help you with the many documents to be filed. It often will charter an entire ship and hold all the bookable space. It can assist you in the event a refund is necessary. Travel agencies that specialize in freighter and cargo cruises are also well aware of the conditions on the various ships and can direct you to the one best suited to your own needs.

Most popular freight and cargo lines:
• American President, 61 Broadway, New York 10006.
• Bergen Line, 505 Fifth Ave., New York, 10017.
• Delta Steamship, 1 World Trade Center, New York 10048.
• Farrell Line, 1 Whitehall, New York 10004.
• Ivaran Lines, 17 Battery Place, New York 10004.

- Moore McCormack, 2 Broadway, New York 10004.
- Naura Pacific, 100 California St., San Francisco 94111.

BEST CRUISES

- American Hawaii Cruises, 550 Kearny St., San Francisco, CA 94108, (415) 392-9400. The SS Independence and SS Constitution cruise the Hawaiian Islands. Incentives: Low one-way air fares home from Hawaii. Two nights free at a Waikiki hotel.
- Bahama Cruise Lines, is a part of Bahama Tourist Office (212) 758-2777. Bahama Tourist Office 150 E 52nd St., NY NY 10022. Week-long cruises on the SS Veracruz from Tampa, Fl, to Cancun, Cozumel and Key West. Incentives: Free parking in Tampa if you drive to Florida. Special rates at a Tampa hotel before the cruise. Discounted round-trip air fares from New York City.
- Carnival Cruises, 3915 Biscayne Blvd., Miami 33137, (305) 576-9220. Three ships sail weekly from Miami to the Caribbean. Incentives: Free round-trip air fare from principal US cities to Miami. Hotel accommodations for passengers from west of the Rocky Mountains.
- Paquet French Cruises, 1370 Ave. of the Caribbean cruises go out of Miami and San Juan. Incentives: Free round-trip air fare from 60 US cities to point of embarkation. Free wine aboard.
- Queen Elizabeth II, Cunard Lines, 555 Fifth Ave., New York 10017, (212) 880-7531. One of the most palatial ships afloat, this grand ocean liner makes regular transatlantic crossings, a few trips through the Panama Canal and one around-the-world tour each year. Incentives: Free flight home on British Airways from transatlantic trips. Reduced rates at Cunard hotels in London (one night free and others 50% off). Free passage for one when you buy a single outside cabin accommodation.
- Royal Cruise Lines, 1 Maritime Plaza, San Francisco 94111, (415) 788-0610. Its ships cruise the Panama Canal, the Caribbean and European ports. Incentives: Passengers on winter Panama Canal and Caribbean trips get bonuses for summer Scandinavian or Mediterranean cruises. Free wine with meals, free shore trips. European passengers get two free nights in a London hotel and free theater tickets.
- Royal Viking Line, 1 Embarcadero Center, San Francisco 94111. (800) 422-8000. Deluxe ships cruise around the world. Incentive: Free air fare to embarkation points.

GETTING VIP TREATMENT ON A CRUISE SHIP

First, get the word to the shipping line that you rate A-1 treatment. This can be done by your travel agent writing the shipping line. Or you might have the public relations director of your firm write with the same message. This one-two attack is bound to get your name starred for VIP treatment when you come aboard. That could include dinner at the captain's table, an invitation to the captain's special cocktail party, or perhaps flowers and assorted gifts in your cabin. Also, of course, the more expensive your cabin accommodations are, the better treatment you will generally get.

Make sure to get a good seat in the dining room. Usually, that means in the center, close to the captain's table. Go over the dining room plan in advance of your trip with your travel agent and pick out the two or three tables you want. Then ask the agent to see if he or she can reserve the table for you in advance. If that can't be done, make sure that as soon as you go aboard ship, you visit the maitre d' and tell him what you want—with a tip.

It's desirable to have an early talk with your dining room captain and waiter. Ask them what the chef's specialties are. Order those far in advance for your dinners later on the cruise. See if you can order such items as Chateaubriand, crepes suzette, special souffles, scampi, lobster, Caesar salad. These items usually can be ordered on most cruise ships. The trick is to know what the kitchen is good at; give the chef time to prepare them.

Tip the dining room captain and let him

know there's more for him if the service is excellent. Also give the dining room waiter, in advance, half the amount you would normally tip him at the end of the cruise and indicate he'll get at least as much more for top-notch service.

Your room steward is the man who can get you all sorts of snacks, like fruit, cheeses, sandwiches, iced tea, and ice cream—almost any time of day or night. Ask him what is available, and if there is a best time to order these items for your cabin. If you want ice cream at 11 pm every night, tell him in advance, so he can plan accordingly. Also, give him half the tip in advance and let him know that good service will bring a reward.

If you want to impress your friends, invite them to the ship for a bon voyage party. It can be quite elegant but remain inexpensive. Make all the arrangements through the shipping company. The ship will usually supply setups, soda, and hors d'oeuvres at a very modest price. Expect to bring your own liquor when the ship is in port, but you can easily buy a few bottles from a local liquor store and bring them aboard.

The steward can serve drinks and other items to your guests in your cabin. If your crowd is large enough, ask for a section of one of the public rooms.

You can play expansive host by holding nightly parties while cruising, and it won't be too costly. The ship's staff will help you with parties in your room or in a public room at a fraction of the cost of a party in a hotel ashore. The liquor costs are minimal. Setups and other items often come free, as do canapes and other party snacks. You also usually get the service of waiters and bartenders at no cost (but you provide the tips).

Book the second sitting for meals when on a cruise. That leaves you more time to get ready for dinner after a day of touring, a longer cocktail hour and less time to kill until the evening activities begin.

BEST AFRICAN SAFARIS

Seeing the great animals of East Africa in their natural habitat is one of the most exciting and exhilarating vacation possibilities of all for city dwellers.

Modern safaris are well organized and comfortable, even for novice campers. Accommodations can be luxurious or basic and simple, but the food is usually universally good and dress is always casual.

Two prerequisites: You must be willing to get up early that is when the animals are most active and fun to watch. And you must bring a camera—because the opportunities for photography will be irresistible.

Keyna and Tanzania are the major safari countries.

A selection of safaris from the pampered to the robust follows. These sponsors offer safaris on a regular basis. If you miss this year's trip, inquire about next year's. Make reservations at least two months ahead.

• Overseas Adventure Travel: 349 Broadway, Cambridge, MA 02139. (617) 876-0533.

Camping safaris in Tanzania for the fit and active. Serengeti Plains region: 19 days. Departures: All months except April and November. Selous: 17 days of bush camping and river boating in the game reserve, plus two days visiting Zanzibar. Departures: August, September, October.

• Questers: 257 Park Ave. South, New York 10010. (212) 673-3120.

Unhurried travel by minibus. Comfortable stays in lodges or safari camps. Time: 23 days. Departures: July, October, February.

• Mountain Travel: 6420 Fairmount, Cerrito CA 94530. (510) 527-8100.

All trips are for the adventurous and the athletic. A hiking safari in Kenya explores Mount Kenya and Tsavo National Park. Time: 20 days. Departures: June, July, August, September and December. A camping safari in Kenya combines horseback riding with game-viewing drives by Land Rover. Time: 18 days. Departures: June and December. A high-altitude hiking trip of Mount Kenya (five days) includes pauses for viewing game. Total time: 21 days. Departures: June and September. Mountain Travel also offers a less rigorous family safari in Kenya especially planned to include children. Time: 14 days.

BIKE TOURS

Bike from inn to inn while traveling along rustic New England back roads. On these special tours, you pedal until midafternoon, then dismount for cocktails, dinner and a night's sleep at a country inn. Baggage is carried in a support van. Daily rate includes breakfast, supper and lodgings.

More information: Vermont Bicycle Touring, RD 3, Bristol, VT 05443.

Bike tours of the Heartland: The Wisconsin Bikeway covers nearly 600 miles of lightly traveled roads. Along the route are campsites, hostelries, swimming holes and fishing streams. Details: Wisconsin Division of Tourism, Box 7606, Madison 53707. Other trails: (1) A 500-mile run through the Ozarks. Details: Arkansas Dept. of Parks, 1 Capitol Mall, Little Rock 72201. (2) Levee-Bluffs Trail and Cairo Bike Trail. Details: Illinois Travel Information, 208 N. Michigan Ave., Chicago 60601. (3) Leisurely tours through Iowa. Details: Quad Cities Bicycle Club, Box 3575, Davenport 52808.

BEST BICYCLE TOURS

More than 200 companies are organizing bicycle tours* these days, making it tough for potential travelers to make a confident choice. No matter what the destination, good tours start with reputable tour companies and skilled guides. The tours listed below fit that description.

Family tours:

• Chesapeake Cycle & Sail. Two days' cycling on Maryland's eastern shore, plus a full day aboard a Chesapeake Bay skipjack.

Country Cycling Tours, 140 W. 83 St., New York 10024, (212) 874-5151.

*More information: Bicycle USA, Suite 209, 6707 Whitestone Rd., Baltimore, MD 21207. Directory of 150 tour operators. Bikecentennial (The Bicycle Travel Association), Box 8308, Missoula, MT 59807. Distributes information on bicycle touring. Bicycle Touring Network, Inc., Box 7069, Ann Arbor, MI 48107. Clearinghouse for travel information.

• Historic Vermont. Weekend excursion along the Black River. Dinner and accommodations at The Inn at Weathersfield, a landmark built in 1795.

Vermont Bicycle Touring, Box 711, Bristol, VT 05443, (802) 453-4811.

• Puget Sound International. Eight-day tour of Washington's Puget Sound area, including Widbey, San Juan and Vancouver (Canada) islands. Accommodations in historic inns.

Tailwind, 4130 SW 117 Ave., Suite G, Beaverton, OR 97005, (503) 641-2582.

• Williamsburg. Five-day tour of historic Tidewater Virginia. Takes in Yorktown, Jamestown Island and Colonial Williamsburg (where it starts and finishes).

Bike Virginia, Inc., Box 203, Williamsburg, VA 23187, (804) 253-2985.

Teenage tours:

• Cape Cod and the Islands. Twenty-day trek takes riders from Provincetown down the Cape Cod National Seashore. Side trips to Nantucket and Martha's Vineyard, and whale watching in Plymouth.

The Biking Expedition, Box 547, Maple St., Henniker, NH 03242, (603) 428-7500.

• Coastal Oregon. Strenuous nine-day trip from Portland to the mouth of the Columbia River at Astoria and down the coast. Beachcombing, whale watching.

American Youth Hostels, National Administrative Offices, 1332 I St. NW, Suite 800, Washington, DC 20005, (202) 783-6161.

• Rocky Mountains. Group learns bike maintenance and safety during three-day stay in Steamboat Springs, CO, before five-day, 180-mile biking/camping trip to Denver.

Timberline Bicycle Tours, 3261 S. Oneida Way, Denver, CO 80224, (303) 759-3804.

Adult Adventures:

• Catalina at Little Harbor. Weekend mountain bike tour of this tropical island from base camp on the beach at Little Harbor.

Wilderness Bicycle Tours, Box 692, Topanga, CA 90290, (310) 455-2544.

• Coast of Maine. Five-day tour along the rocky coast of Penobscot Bay. Lodging and fine dining in country inns along the way.

BCC 4-Seasons Cycling, Box 145, Waterbury Center, VT 05677, (802) 244-5215.

• Rio Grande Detour. Fairly strenuous six-day trek through northern New Mexico. Includes one-day raft trip on the Rio Grande and off-road cycling in the San Juans.

Bicycle Detours, Box 44078, Tucson, AZ 85733, (800) 223-5369, ext. 267.

Source: Don Alexander, editor of *Bicycle Rider*, T.L. Enterprises, Agoura, CA 91301.

BEST FAMILY CAMPING TENTS

A tent for camping should allow about 25 square feet of floor space for each adult and half that for each child. For a family of four: At least 80 square feet. Best: An umbrella tent. It folds up neatly to fit into a car trunk. And it weighs only 24–40 pounds. Best material: Nylon. Features to look for: Good cross-ventilation. Openings with sturdy mesh to keep out insects. Windows that close during a storm. Seams double-stitched with 8–10 stitches per inch. Also: Seams should be lap-felled (the material folded back on itself for extra strength and waterproofing). Good tents have extra stitching at points of stress. Before taking the tent on a trip, set it up in the yard and douse it with a hose. Check for leaks (particularly at the seams).

TRAVEL ACCESSORIES

Convenient containers for travel and backpacking are empty *Squeeze Parkay* holders. They nest together, have pour spouts and can be made watertight. How: Place a double piece of foil over the opening before replacing the top. Liquids such as syrup, honey and cooking oil can be kept without leaking. Or the containers can be used for nonliquids like dry milk or sugar.

CANADIAN TRAVELING

Our neighbor to the north still offers cool, convenient and varied summer-vacation possibilities, from mountains and seashore to historic cities and arts festivals. Bonus: An advantageous exchange rate for Americans. Exchange your travel money at Canadian banks for the best deal. No passport or visa is needed, but good identification will ease your way back into the US.

AMERICA'S BEST MUSEUMS

California:
• J. Paul Getty Museum, 17985 Pacific Coast Highway, Malibu. Extraordinary private art collection from Greek and Roman to 20th century.
• Huntington Library, Art Gallery and Botanical Gardens, 1151 Oxford Rd., San Marino. Gainsborough's Blue Boy, 18th-century British and European art.
• Los Angeles County Museum of Art, 5905 Wilshire Blvd., Los Angeles. Outstanding collection from antiquities to 20th-century art.
• San Franciso Museum of Art, 401 Van Ness Ave., San Francisco. Fine collection fo 20th-century European and American art.
• Asian Art Museum of San Francisco, Golden Gate Park, San Francisco. Finest collection of Oriental art in the Western world.
  Colorado:
• Denver Art Museum, 100 West 14 Ave., Bannock, Denver. North and South American Indian collections.
  Connecticut:
• Wadsworth Atheneum, 600 Main St., Hartford. The oldest art museum in the United States and one of the best.
• Yale University Art Gallery, 1111 Chapel St., New Haven. John Trumbull's paintings of the American Revolution and much more.

District of Columbia:

- Corcoran Gallery of Art, 17 St. and New York Ave. NW, Washington. Historic American paintings, European art.
- Freer Gallery of Art, 12 St. and Jefferson Drive SW, Washington. Far and Near Eastern art; Whistler's works.
- Hirshhorn Museum and Sculpture Garden, Independence Ave. at 8 St. SW, Washington. The entire collection—sculpture and modern art—of millionaire Joseph Hirshhorn.
- National Gallery of Art, 4 St. and Constitution Ave. NW, Washington. A jewel of a museum with a brilliant new wing by I.M. Pei. General European and American art collection.
- National Portrait Gallery, 8 St. at F St., Washington. Portraits of all the American presidents displayed in an 1840 Greek Revival building, the former US Patent Office.

Georgia:

- The High Museum of Art, 1280 Peachtree NE, Atlanta. Renaissance of 20th-century American and European paintings, sculpture and decorative arts.

Illinois:

- The Art Institute, Michigan Ave. & Adams St., Chicago. Outstanding Impressionists and post-Impressionists in a first-rate collection.

Maryland:

- Baltimore Museum of Fine Arts, Art Museum Drive (near N. Charles and 31 St.), Baltimore. Fine French post-Impressionist works; mosaics from Antioch.

Massachusetts:

- Boston Museum of Fine Arts, 465 Huntington Ave. Boston. The new I.M. Pei wing is impressive.
- Fogg Museum, 32 Quincy St., Cambridge. Harvard's extensive art collection.

Michigan:

- Detroit Institute of Arts, 5200 Woodward, Detroit. Great masters and moderns.

Minnesota:

- Walker Art Center, 725 Vineland Place, Minneapolis. Post-Impressionist and contemporary art.

New York:

- Albright-Knox Art Gallery, 1285 Elmwood Ave., Buffalo. Splendid modern collection, as well as general collection.
- Brooklyn Museum, 188 Eastern Parkway, Brooklyn. Fine general collection with strong Egyptian art and American paintings.
- The Frick Collection, Fifth Ave. at 70 St., New York. One of the best private collections.
- The Solomon R. Guggenheim Museum, 1701 Fifth Ave. at 88 St., New York. Modern art and sculpture in a circular building designed by Frank Lloyd Wright.
- Metropolitan Museum of Art, Fifth Ave., at 82 St., New York. Probably the finest general collection in the US.
- Museum of Modern Art, 11 W. 53 St., New York. First US museum devoted to 20th-century art—from paintings and sculpture to design and film.
- The Pierpont Morgan Library, 29 E. 36 St., New York. Illuminated Bibles, Rembrandts and other superb art.
- Whitney Museum of American Art, 945 Madison Ave. at 75 St., New York. 20th-century US art.

Ohio:

- Cleveland Museum of Art, 11150 East Blvd. at University Circle, Cleveland. All cultures. Strong on medieval and Oriental art.

Oregon:

- Portland Art Museum, 1219 SW Park Ave., Portland. Appealing outdoor sculpture, mall, general collection.

Pennsylvania:

- The Frick Art Museum, 7227 Reynolds St., Pittsburgh. Eclectic collection of Russian, Chinese, Flemish and French art and artifacts.
- Philadelphia Museum of Art, 26 St. and Benjamin Franklin Parkway, Philadelphia. Magnificent general collection.
- Rodin Museum, 22 St. and Benjamin Franklin Parkway, Philadelphia. Sculpture, sketches and drawings by this famous French artist.

Texas:

- Amon Carter Museum of Western Art, 3501 Camp Bowie Blvd., Fort Worth. Extensive collection of Frederic Remington's and Charles Russell's work.
- Houston Museum of Fine Arts, 1001 Bissonnet, Houston. Fine general collection.

RENTING A SUMMER PLACE

If you rent a place for the summer, you'll make a substantial investment of time and money. With some planning you can avoid disappointments.

Draw up a lease:

If you don't go through a real estate broker, draw up a complete contract with the owner of the home. Do not make a friendly verbal agreement or scribble your contract on a paper napkin. Stationery stores sell standard leases (Blumberg's is most commonly available) that cover summer rentals. Have the lease witnessed and notarized, preferably by a lawyer or real estate agent. Go through the lease form to make sure all clauses in it are acceptable to you.

• Most important lease item: A list of all household property and the specific condition of each. Specify items such as: Pale green carpet in fine condition.

• A normal-wear-and-tear clause is reasonable. The lessee won't be held responsible for each minor thing like sand in the rug.

• Improvements. If you plan to make any improvements on the house or property, these must be noted in the lease, along with the owner's approval and any reimbursement agreement.

Expenses and responsibilities:

• The renter should expect to pay for heat, hot water, electricity and telephone for the rental period. You may be asked to install a phone in your own name.

• The renter is generally responsible for the care and watering of the plants and lawn, raking the beach, keeping the place reasonably clean and other standard household maintenance. Responsibility for expensive or highly technical maintenance, such as pool cleaning or skilled gardening, should be discussed and outlined in the lease. Owners often include items such as pool maintenance as part of the rental price.

• The owner must tell the renter about climatic changes (such as summer floods), insect or rodent infestation or anything else that affects the house's habitability. Failure to do so is grounds for breaking the lease and getting your money back.

• The owner must repair any essential items that break down in midseason (such as the refrigerator or the plumbing). If he is unavailable, you can pay for repairs and bill him.

• The owner must return your remaining rent, plus security, if an act of God makes the house uninhabitable during the season.

Damages:

The house must be left in the same condition you found it in. If you damage something, you must replace it with a similar item. Recommended: Attempt to work things out amicably with the owner. Offer to pay for anything you have broken before the owner discovers the problem.

Rent and security:

• Expect to pay all the rent plus the security (which is as much as half the rent) in advance. Installment payments are generally unacceptable.

• Your security will be returned when the outstanding bills have been paid. The best way to insure that you will get your security back in full is to check the house thoroughly before the lease is signed. Make sure everything is listed so you can't be accused of taking something that wasn't there.

What to look for:

When you're inspecting a summer house, check out the plumbing, kitchen equipment, water pressure, availability of heat and climate problems. Ask the owner what the neighborhood is like.

Insurance:

• Your summer house should be covered by your landlord's homeowners policy for burglary, accident, damage to the house and grounds, fire and flood. However, if *you* caused the damage, *you* can be held responsible.

Example: If the house is burglarized, and the police find that the door was left unlocked, you can be held liable. Get a rider on your own homeowners policy to cover the rental.

• Insure your own property. Your jewelry and other valuables will not be covered by your landlord's homeowners policy.

References:

Be prepared to give business and personal references when you rent a summer place. As more owners have harrowing experiences, they are becoming more careful about whom they rent to. Example: An elderly European man rented his apartment for the summer without asking for references from the two "nice-looking young men wearing suits and ties" who said they were schoolteachers. At the end of the summer, he discovered that they had fled, leaving a sacrificial altar in the middle of the living-room floor. It had burned right through the floorboards to the apartment below.

References commonly requested: Your place of business and length of time employed. A current or former landlord as a personal reference. Your phone and utility account numbers (to check your payment record). A credit reference (some owners are now subscribing to services that check the credit rating of prospective tenants).

Source: Jacqueline Kyle Kall, City Island, NY, realtor specializing in resort properties in the United States and worldwide.

BETTER SUMMER WEEKENDS

The most desirable thing to look for in a weekend house is ease of maintenance. Get rid of rugs in the summer. Ask the landlord to remove his accumulations of dustcatching peacock feathers and other decorator touches. And keep your own importations to a minimum. In a summer house, bare is beautiful.

Cut down on weekend cleaning chores and outdoor work with hired help. In some communities, this is relatively simple, especially with the guidance of a neighbor who is a year-round resident. Or the rental agent may have a network of people willing to help out.

You might expand on leisure time by commuting with the laundry. That's cumbersome, but better than hours in a laundromat on a sunny afternoon.

Almost as important to a relaxed summer is the fine art of list-making. Shopping and menu planning can be almost painless if the list is done right. One couple owns an island where everything, including drinking water, has to be brought in. And they haven't run out of anything in years.

If you're planning a Saturday dinner party, don't rely on the local supermarket for the perfect roast unless you've ordered (and confirmed) in advance. It's far safer to bring the main course with you and to shop locally for the fresh produce. The accompanying wines might be better purchased at home, too, unless you're sure of your local supplier.

It's a good idea to take the same precautions as you would for a trip—extra reading glasses and copies of prescriptions might save you an unwanted journey home.

BUYING TIME-SHARE IN VACATION CONDO

Watch out for abuses. Time-sharing (purchasing rights to a hotel or apartment unit at a resort for a specific week or two each year) has been subject to incidents of fraud and deception. Example: 2,100 people bought time shares in Colorado resort condominiums before the developers went bankrupt. Two men were jailed in South Carolina for selling shares in a nonexistent resort. Protection: Consult a lawyer before buying. Study all documents carefully. Call the Better Business Bureau or Department of Consumer Affairs for information about the project and developer. Go to inspect the resort. Resist high-pressure sales techniques.

Vacation time-shares can be more of a burden than a bargain. Problems: Time-share vacations are very expensive. The same place every year is boring. The money invested does not earn interest. Resale of used time-shares can be very difficult. The real cost of a time-share is much higher than its selling price. Financing involves payment of 16–17% interest. Few banks give loans for time-sharing.

If you buy a time-share vacation home: (1) Pick a place you are sure to love year after year. (2) Don't pay more than 10 times the going rate for comparable time in a rental unit in the same area. (3) Buy early—prices are lower. (4) Buy where geography and/or zoning prevent overbuilding. (5) Buy from an experienced builder. To enhance your selling/swapping prospects: Buy a one- or two-bedroom unit in a place easy to reach during the peak season.

HOUSE-SITTING CHECKLIST

To decide what kind of sitter you need (to live in or to visit regularly, long term or short term), determine your requirements. Typically, sitters should:

• Make the house look lived in so it won't be burglarized.

• Care for plants, pets and grounds.

• Make sure the pipes won't freeze.

• Discourage squatters.

• Guard the house and its possessions against natural disasters.

Where to find help: Some communities have sitting services or employment agencies that can fill the job. Better: Someone you know—the teenage child of a friend, a cleaning woman, a retired neighbor. Also: Placement services at colleges.

Important: When interviewing, test the resourcefulness and intelligence of the candidate. Check references.

Barter: If you find a writer looking for a place to stay or a person from the place you are heading to who would like to exchange houses, you might make a deal without any money changing hands.

Before you leave:

• Walk through every sequence of duties with the sitter.

• Put all duties in writing.

• List repair, supply and emergency telephone numbers and your own telephone number or instructions on how to reach you.

• Make clear that no one is to be admitted to the house or given a key without your prior consent.

VACATION LIKE A MULTIMILLIONAIRE FOR A WEEK: $2,000 AND UP

If you want to experience a magic vacation week—seven days to match your wildest fantasies—try any of these ideas. Like the super-rich you will be emulating, you should let your travel agent take care of the details.

• Travel first class by present standards and those of another age. Whip to London on the Concorde in three hours. Then settle into the new Orient Express for a leisurely trip to Venice. The legendary train (with its 1920s cars completely restored to their former polished-brass-and-crystal glory) makes the London-Paris-Milan-Venice run twice a week. Base your Venetian sight-seeing at the Hotel Cipriani before returning to London and flying home. Upwards of $12,000 for two.

• Lose weight in luxury with the Lancaster Farm program at Brenner's Park Hotel in Baden-Baden, Germany. (The main building was a residence of Napoleon III.) Do water exercises in a Pompeiian pool. Have a daily massage, facial, body wrap and beautiful meals that add up to only 1,000 calories a day. Makeup, manicures and pedicures are part of the program. Baden-Baden has colonnaded shops and a famous casino. One week with first-class air fare from New York costs upwards of $7,500 for two.

• See Burgundy by balloon. View the chateaus and vineyards of southeastern France from the gondola of a flowered hot-air balloon (between terrestrial tours of the region by car). Stay in the Hotels de la Poste in Beaune and Vezelay, sampling the local wines. The great French Balloon Adventure leaves every Sunday from Paris starting in May and is organized by the Bombard Society in San Francisco. Upwards of $2,980 per person. Air fare to Paris is extra.

• Charter a yacht—with crew—and cruise the Caribbean. Captain, cook, hands and provisions are included. Upwards of $7,750 for two. Air fare from New York to the Virgin Islands is extra.

• Try a villa or a castle for a week. With air fare, ground transportation, staff and food, two can enjoy Dromoland Castle in Ireland for upwards of $4,750. An Acapulco villa is upwards of $7,750 for two.

• Entertain like a king (or a Comstock Lode heiress) in San Francisco by renting the penthouse suite of the Fairmont Hotel. Designed in the 1920s for Maude Flood, a gold and silver baroness, the suite has a walnut-paneled living room, a dining room that seats 50, a domed library, a mosaic-walled gameroom complete with pool table, three bedrooms and baths with gold fixtures. The kitchen is fully equipped. The bar is stocked. Dinnerware, silver and linens are included, as well as a vault, a baby-grand piano, books, artwork, a butler and a maid. Food is extra. Upwards of $2,500 a night.

• Great hotels. Pick a city you want to explore and put yourself in the hands of a master innkeeper for a week. Some suggestions:
• California wine country, Sonoma Mission Inn.
• Colorado Springs, The Broadmoor Hotel.
• Paris, The Plaza Athenee.
• Palm Beach, The Colony Hotel.
• Beverly Hills, The Beverly Hills Hotel.
• New York, The Helmsley Palace.
• London, The Savoy.
• Dallas, The Mansion at Turtle Creek.
• Rio de Janeiro, The Meridien Hotel.

VACATIONS OF THE STARS

Letitia Baldrige, etiquette adviser and businesswoman:

In 1947, I went for an Easter trip with a group of six friends (American and Swedish) from the University of Geneva to the Isle of Capri. There we ran into a group of students from England (Cambridge and Oxford). We were Capri's first tourists after World War II, and we spent 10 enchanted days. From our hotel on the top of Anacapri we saw the island at its most glorious best. Each night musicians serenaded us, and we ate, drank, and were very, very merry.

Jimmy Breslin, syndicated columnist for *The New York Daily News:*

Once I went to Saratoga and "hit" a lot of horses. I think anything planned and organized is no fun. Perhaps your first real vacation is when you send the *kids* away. Then you can stay home and enjoy yourself and relax!

Keith Carradine, actor:

My best vacation? I guess it's a toss-up between a three-week vacation in China with my wife (actress Sandra Will) and a 12-day ski trip to Switzerland with Sandra.

Oleg Cassini, fashion designer:

Skiing in St. Anton in Austria. But then, St. Moritz, Cortina, Gstaad and Aspen were also wonderful. I have good times in the Caribbean, but I really prefer skiing in the winter. I have good vacations. In the summer, I prefer to stay in my house in the country, because this is the time the whole world is topsy turvy, with everyone on the move.

Craig Claiborne, food editor of *The New York Times:*

Each year at Christmas I go to St. Barthelemy in the French West Indies. I consider it the area's most civilized island. (I also love to be at my house in Easthampton, but I have to leave it for a real vacation because of the telephones.) I love the friendly civilization and the availability of everything at St. Bart. One year, on very short notice, I had to cook a very special dinner. Right in St. Jean I found chickens from Bresse, wonderful imported prosciutto and all sorts of other delicacies. I also love Tuscany in Italy for vacations.

Leona Helmsley, corporate officer of the Helmsley Hotels:

My favorite vacation is wherever Harry is —no kidding, that's true.

Judith Krantz, author of three best-selling novels—*Scruples, Princess Daisy* and *Mistral's Daughter:*

I was looking around for the setting for my next novel and came upon it recently when we went back to Provence for a glorious trip. This whole area is so special, with its southern French magic. Everywhere you look you see a splendid village perched upon a hill, and the sun and the wind beat down upon the entire landscape. But then again, I really love to go to Venice, a city of theatrical excitement.

Jerry Rubin, former Yippie leader and current president of Business Networking Salons:

I enjoy my work so much that I consider my work a daily vacation, but I did enjoy my vacation/honeymoon to Morocco. We had no contact with the outside world—no telephones, no mail. What was exhilarating was the total immersion in another culture. The same feeling came to me years ago, when I spent six months in China, India and Japan. It was ego-reducing.

John Weitz, fashion designer:

My favorite vacation was really three vacations spent with my wife on the super-yacht *La Belle Simone*. We were guests of Bill Levitt in the Mediterranean, the Aegean and the Caribbean. After years of visiting the world's top spots, to me nothing rivals these three trips.

Joe Granville, president of Granville Market Letter:

My favorite vacation, I guess, was going back to Virginia to work on my new book, a novel. It's my first novel. It's going to be called *Bagholders,* and it's set in Virginia. I love working vacations where I can play a lot of golf but still spend time writing.

Arnold Bernhard, publisher of Value Line:

My favorite spot is the island I own in the Bahamas, Hummingbird Cay.

Vidal Sassoon, chairman of Vidal Sassoon, Inc:

Once a year I take my children to Israel. We visit Jerusalem, Tel Aviv, the Golan Heights and Elat.

Gisele Richardson, president of Richardson Management, Montreal:

There are two types of vactions that I have enjoyed particularly—either discovering something new and exotic, like a trip to Nepal, or a thoroughly laid-back vacation where I can boat or ski and come in contact with nature. There is something nourishing about a vacation of the sort where you change your environment entirely. Two vacations stand out. One was a trip to Petra, a city in Jordan, which could be reached only by horseback. And once I rented a crewless boat and sailed the Caribbean.

HOW TO ENJOY A DAY AT THE RACES WITHOUT GOING BROKE

The aim of a day at the track should be to enjoy every race while controlling your losses. Fifty dollars lost out of a hundred dollars played with could be considered a highly satisfactory day.

Strategy for betting:

• Begin with the choices of the handicappers. Handicapping—the prediction of likely winners —is done by a track official who assigns odds to the horses in the morning races. Handicapping is also done by bettors in the course of the day (which causes the odds to change). Both kinds of handicappers represent a well-informed consensus of serious students of racing. One-third of the favorites chosen by handicappers win their races.

• Decide on the amount of money you are willing to lose. Set aside one-fifth of it for entertainment betting. The rest should be spent on serious betting. For about $20 you can bet on every race plus the daily double. Then you have continuous action. Avoid the tendency of most bettors to increase bets when losing in order to catch up. Also avoid the trap of betting more when winning to try to make a killing. To control spending: Bet just 20% of your remaining capital each time you bet, whether your capital goes up or down.

To pick horses for fun betting: Choose horse by name, jockey, appearance or any means you wish. You may get lucky and win one out of ten bets this way. Plan to make four serious bets in the course of a day. Most important requirements:

• Pick the appropriate races to bet on. Always eliminate the following races for serious betting: Maiden races (the horse's first year of racing), two-year-old races and races where it's indicated that the horses chosen won no race but their maiden race. These are all races in which handicapping is not effective, and there is too much uncertainty. Use these for fun bets.

• Picking the two or three likeliest winners in the race. To do this, see handicappers' choices in local newspapers, racing forms and tip sheets sold at the track. Look especially for handicappers who predict in great detail how the race will be run (in addition to giving their pick). Look for the handicapper who tells you the front runners, the come-from-behind horse and the outcome. On the basis of the predictions of several of these tipping sources (they tend to agree), choose the likeliest horses.

• Combine this intelligence with local conditions, easily observable changing factors that can influence the outcome of a race. (This is one advantage of actually being at the track.) Be alert to late scratches (the elimination of contenders), which can very much change the projected script of a race. If one of the two predicted front-runners is scratched, the remaining front-runner's chance is increased. That makes a good bet.

Also pay attention to rain. In the racing form, "mudders" (horses that have a history of doing well in the rain) are indicated with an asterisk. As the track is progressively softened by rain, the chances of mudders improve. Most adversely affected by rain-softened tracks are the horses closest to the rail at the outset (post-position horses 1, 2 and 3). Reason: Those positions are where most of the running takes place, so the track gets especially muddy there. The horse in the most adverse position on a rain-sodden track is a speed horse—a front-runner in the post position.

Another local condition to watch for: Shifts in odds. Lengthening (higher) odds on a horse increase your chance of a good return. Watch for obvious reasons for a drop in popularity in the course of a day. The physical condition of the horse can be observed during the viewing ritual, when the horses are paraded at the rear of the track before each race. This is one of the best parts of the event. Watch for negative signs so that you can eliminate horses.

• Front-leg bandages.
• A prolonged struggle as the jockey attempts to mount. A bit of liveliness and fight against the jockey is a good sign, but a prolonged struggle can exhaust a horse.
• Sweats and tremors. Sweat shows as a yellow lather around the haunches, rectum and genitals.

Kinds of bets you can place: There are win bets (they pay only if the horse wins), place bets (they pay if the horse comes in first or second) and show bets (paying if the horse comes in first, second or third). If you choose win bets alone, you can usually hope for at least one win out of four. A combination of bets, such as a win and place or a win and a show, increases your chances of a payoff. But the return will be smaller.

Shortcut method of choosing horses: Gather all the racing forms and tip sheets. Look at all the choices in a given race. Then bet on a horse mentioned by at least one handicapper on which the odds offered are greater than the number of horses in the field. (However, don't pick any horse going at odds greater than fifty to one.)

The point: To bet a long shot in each race, hoping to win once in the day at a very large payoff. The horse you're choosing is assured of having some kind of chance if it is mentioned by at least one handicapper.

Source: Peter Shaw, cultural critic, historian, college professor and occasional bettor.

SECRETS OF PICKING HARNESS WINNERS

Harness racing is far easier to handicap than thoroughbred ("flat") racing. Reason: The bettor has fewer variables to take into consideration.

Harness races are almost always at a mile and on the dirt. The fields are more manageable, with rarely more than nine entries. And, since the horses carry no weight on their backs, there are no weight differences to compensate for. (Thanks to some complex law of physics, the sulky pulled by the horse actually adds momentum, rather than drag.)

Standardbred harness horses are calmer, tougher and more dependable than thoroughbreds. The favorites win more often than thoroughbred favorites—about 36% of the time. Still, most bettors are chronic losers, in part because they ignore the most important betting factors.

Most decisive of all is post position, especially on short half-mile or five-eighths-mile tracks. The nearer the rail, the less distance the horse must travel, both at the start and around a turn. The horse in the number one post (at the far inside) has a tremendous advantage. Since he's already at the rail, he doesn't need to spend energy to get there. Even if he doesn't make the lead, he will likely be close enough to make a move in the stretch.

Conversely, if a horse draws an outside post (six or higher), the driver will either have to "park" outside other horses while contending for the lead or take back to the rear. Later on, he may be boxed in with no racing room. To mount a stretch drive, he will have to return outside, losing at least one and a half lengths around the final turn. And given the width of the other sulkies, there may be no convenient holes to burst through. All in all, it's tough to catch the leader.

Post positions are also a key to interpreting past performances. Example: In his last outing, Armbro Gold raced from the eight post and finished a distant sixth. But in the race before that, starting from the one post, he led the way and won handily. If he's returning to an inside post, you can expect Armbro Gold to improve, perhaps at good odds.

The other underrated factor: The driver's ability. Every track has a few leading drivers; check their names in your program and remember them. Steer clear of any driver who fails to win at least 10% of his starts. And you should never bet on a novice or provisional driver.

Postive sign: A switch from a trainer-driver to a leading full-time driver. This often means the trainer believes the horse is now at his best, ready to win.

But even the best driver can't help a slow starter from an outside post. Good advice: Check each race (consult the track program) for horses with good early speed. There are no Silky Sullivans in harness racing—no champions who consistently come from last place to take the purse. You'll find that the winner is usually among the first four horses at the half-mile.

In weighing past performances, the horse's time in the final quarter mile is more revealing than his overall time. Most promising: A fast final quarter (under 31 seconds) following a fast first half-mile.

It's also positive if the horse:

Won his last race (unless he won by a small margin that was less than the last time).

Is going off at lower odds than in his last race.

Raced steadily last time while parked (indicated by a small "o" in the program) for one or more calls. (Parked means outside one or more other horses.)

But don't bet heavily if the horse:

Is moving up steeply in class (signified by purse money or claiming price).

Hasn't been in a race for more than two weeks.

Seems clearly superior in the program but is going off at odds of five to two or greater. (The horse's handlers don't think he can win.)

Broke stride in his last race (check in your track program).

Has pinned ears (ears are back flat against his head) or is nervous or sweating in prerace warmups.

Source: Don Valliere, manager of the Ontario Jockey Club's track in Fort Erie and author of *Betting Winners: A Guide for the Harness Fan,* Gambling Book Club Press, Las Vegas, NV.

GAMBLING TRAP

Never accept a check to cover a gambling debt. If the check bounces, the amount is not collectible in a court of law. This is true even in states where gambling is legal.

HOW TO WIN AT POKER

Not so many years ago, every poker book told you the same thing: Play tight (fold bad hands). This is still good advice as far as it goes. In a typical home game, the players who win the most pots wind up as losers because they throw too much money away on all the pots they play—but don't win. You can beat these games to death simply by contesting 20% fewer hands than anyone else.

Be selective but aggressive. Ideally, you should end a hand by either folding or raising. Avoid calling bets with vulnerable hands, such as two pair.

Your goal: To own the table psychologically so that the other players are glancing at you every time they make a bet. Be friendly, but at the same time be confusing and unpredictable. Never gloat. You want your opponents to enjoy trying to beat you.

In a low-to-moderate-limit game, you can win without mathematical genius or brilliant originality. In fact, most of your profit will come from your opponents' mistakes. Their chief error: Calling for too many pots with mediocre hands.

This makes bluffing a poor strategy. First of all, unsophisticated opponents won't even understand your intended deception. Second, they're likely to call you anyway, a habit you want to encourage.

Exception: You might try a strategic bluff just once, early in the session, as an "advertisement."

Example: You can even advertise without bluffing. In a five-card draw, you call the opener and then rap pat (taking no cards) with absolute garbage, such as 10-7-6-3-2 of different suits. After the other players draw and check to you, you check as well as show your pathetic cards. You'll lose, of course, but your opponents will feel forced to call your good hands later on.

The only other time to bluff is when your legitimate hand fizzles at the end. If you calculate that pot odds (the money already in the pot versus the amount it would cost to bluff) are favorable, bluff on.

Discipline is especially crucial in a low-limit game, when you need more hands to make up losses.

You must decide in advance how you will react in each of various situations. Never play a hand out of impatience or on a "hunch." Play it for a good reason. Monitor yourself carefully. If you make a mistake, admit it to yourself and get back on track. Don't let one bad play erode your entire system.

Also avoid:

Looking for immediate revenge after an opponent burns you on a big pot. If you force the action, you're apt to get burned again.

Refusing to quit after you've already taken a beating. In fact, you should stay later when you're ahead and leave early when behind. When you're losing, you have no psychological control of the game. Opponents try to bluff you out of pots and are less likely to call your good hands. (When you're on a hot streak, they are more likely to call. If they lose, they can always console themselves by blaming it on your luck.)

Complaining about bad luck. The cards don't owe you a fair shake every session.

Of course, one of your goals will be to try to avoid getting behind in the first place.

Regardless of how your cards are running, you can gain a heavy advantage by watching for and learning to read opponents' "tells"— the mannerisms they fall into that tend to give away whether their hands are good or bad.

In general, follow the rule of opposites: Players usually act weak when their hands are strong, and they commonly act strong when their hands are weak.

The following tells are trademarks of bluffers:

Breathing shallowly or holding their breath.

Staring at their hands—or at you as you prepare to bet.

Reaching for chips out of turn.

Betting with an authoritative pronouncement.

Flinging chips into the pot with an outstretched forearm.

Showing unusual friendliness toward opponents.

Players with powerful hands have their own set of tells:

Sharing a hand with a bystander (especially a spouse).

Shaking noticeably while making a bet. (This reflects a release of tension. Most players show obvious outward nervousness only when they feel they're in little danger.)

Talking easily and naturally.

Behaving in an unusually gruff manner toward opponents.

Leaning forward in a seat.

Betting with a sigh, shrug or negative tone of voice.

Asking, "How much is it to me?" or requesting another clarification.

Glancing quickly at the player's chips after receiving a (good) card.

"Tells" can be extremely helpful, but they can also induce a player to call too many pots.

Bottom line: Look for reasons to fold just as eagerly as you look for reasons to call.

Source: Mike Caro is a gambling teacher and theorist, a columnist for *Gambling Times*. He is author of *Caro on Gambling* and *Mike Caro's Book of Tells—The Body Language of Poker*, both published by *Gambling Times*, Hollywood, CA.

INSIDER'S GUIDE TO CASINO GAMBLING

As a weekend gambler, you're basically out for a good time. The odds are you won't break the bank. But you can enhance your enjoyment—and maybe even take home some house money—if you follow a few general rules.

• Go in with a game plan and stick to it. Decide in advance how much money you're going to take, how much you can afford to lose and at what point you will quit.

• Limit each bet to 1% of your original stake. That may be as little as $5 (the weekend minimum in Atlantic City). Up your bets only when you are ahead. Never bet more than 10% of the stake. If you start chasing money you have lost, the odds of going broke are much higher. That's the wrong approach to gambling.

• Don't push your luck. If you have won $100 with a given dealer and then lose $20 of your profits, back off. Take a deep breath or break for dinner. In any case, find a new table.

• Pass up the free drinks. Casinos offer them for a reason. If you lose your inhibitions, you may desert your strategy and change your betting patterns. You want to keep a clear head.

Blackjack is the best casino game—the only one in which a skilled player can beat the house over time. Overall, of course, the casinos make a nice profit because their edge against the average "hunch" player runs from 6% to 15%.

However, with an advanced card-counting system, the odds are turned around. The experienced player has a 2% advantage. Mastery of the counting system takes time and practice. A simplified version gives the player a 1.5% edge, but it still requires instruction and some dedicated use.

For the recreational gambler, a basic blackjack strategy—with no counting—can cut the house edge to only .4%. Given those odds, you'd lose about $2 in an average hour if you bet $5 per hand—not a bad entertainment value.

Rules for the no-count system:

• Never split pairs of 4s, 5s or 10s. Always split aces and 8s. Split other pairs if the dealer's up card is 2 through 6.

• Double your bet on 11 unless the dealer shows an ace. Double on 10 unless the dealer shows an ace or 10. Double on 9 if the dealer shows 3 through 6 and on soft hands (hands with an ace that can be counted as 11 without going over 21) of 13 through 18 if the dealer shows 4 through 6.

• Always stand on hard hands (hands with no ace or an ace that must be counted as 1) of 17 and up. Stand on hands of 12 through 16 if the dealer shows 2 through 6. (Otherwise, hit.) Always stand on soft hands of 18 and up. Always hit on soft hands of 17 or less if it is too late to double.

These rules will keep you out of serious trouble. But human nature being what it is, you will naturally want to play an occasional hunch against the odds. Best hunch bet: An "insurance" bet on the dealer's hand when you have been dealt a blackjack. Reason: When you have a blackjack, the only thing that can keep you from winning is the dealer also having a blackjack. An insurance bet on his cards assures you of getting at least something on the hand.

Craps: This is the most emotional casino game. Fast and noisy, it can sweep you into making more bets per hour than other games—as many as 150. Result: The money turns over faster and you can lose more. However, if you stick to the most favorable bets, you concede an edge of only .8% to the house.

Bets to make: Pass line. Don't pass. Come. Don't come. In each case, always make the maximum accompanying "odds" bets (these offer the best percentage of all). The only other acceptable wagers are "place" bets on 6 or 8 (the house edge is 1.4% on these).

Avoid all long-shot and one-roll bets like "hardway 4." The stickman will encourage this action because it makes money for the casino. The odds against you are enormous because the house advantage runs from 10% to 16%.

Under the laws of probability, there is no true number system to help the craps gambler. Each roll of the dice is independent. But there are useful betting strategies. A good one: After the roller has thrown two passes (winning rolls), up your bet 50% every other pass thereafter.

Roulette:

Number systems will do you no good in roulette. The general house edge is high: 5.3%. To halve your disadvantage, stick to "outside" even-money bets: Red-black. Odd-even. High-low. If 0 or 00 comes up, you lose only half of these wagers. Other bets are lost in full.

Baccarat:

Although the house edge is only 1.1%, this "upper crust" game gives the player no control. You make only two decisions: How much you want to put down and whether you choose the banker or the player.

Baccarat players tend to be superstitious, and they are notorious for being streak players.

Warning: The baccarat minimum is generally pretty high—$20–25. This makes it an expensive game to play.

Slot machines:

Casinos make more than half their profit on slot machines. The house edge is 17%. If you must play, find a "progressive" machine that increases its jackpot as money is pumped through it. Some $1 machines pay as high as $250,000.

The ultimate sucker bet is the big wheel, a giant circle where numbered sections pay various odds. The house take approaches 25%.

Final shot:

Let's say you've doubled your initial stake, and you have time for one more session before the weekend is over. Don't be greedy. Just as you set a strict loss limit (say, 20% of your stake) and stop at it, you should quit while you are ahead, too. Enjoy the sights and the shows, and go home with your profit. If everyone did that, the casinos would be in trouble.

Source: Jerry L. Patterson, author of *Casino Gambling*, Perigee Books, New York.

BEST GAMBLING CASINOS IN THE WORLD

Gambling is an international passion. Some gambling is done at casinos and hotels, depending on local regulations. We offer here the very best places to gamble, along with their best hotels.

Rates vary according to the season. It's best to book through a travel agent, since gambling packages are usually available at lower costs than the average room rates.

United States:
• Atlantic City, NJ: Trump Plaza, Trump's Castle, Caesar's Palace, Claridge, Bally's Grand, Harrah's, Sands, Trop World.
• Las Vegas, NV: Caesar's Palace, Las Vegas Hilton, Bally's, Riviera, Circus Circus, Four Queens, El Cortez, Flamingo Hilton, Golden Nugget, The Mirage, Stardust.
• Reno, NV (Lake Tahoe): Circus Circus, Clarion, Eldorado, Bally's, Riverboat, Club Cal-Neva.
• Laughlin, NV: Ramada Express, Golden Nugget, Riverside, Harrah's, Colorado Belle.

Caribbean:
• Antigua: Curtain Bluff, Halcyon Beach Cove Resort.
• Aruba: Americana Aruba, Aruba Concorde, Aruba Sheraton.
• Curacao: Curacao Hilton, Curacao Plaza.
• Dominican Republic: Casa de Campo at La Romana, Hotel Santo Domingo, Plaza Dominicana, Santo Domingo Sheraton.
• Guadeloupe: Meridien, PLM Arawak.
• Haiti: Habitation LeClerc (Port au Prince).
• Martinique: Meridien, PLM La Bataliere.
• Nassau/Cable Beach: Nassau Beach Hotel.
• Paradise Island: Bahamas Princess, Paradise Island Hotel, Princess Tower.
• Puerto Rico: Caribe Hilton, Cerromar Beach Hotel (Dorado Beach), Condado Beach Hotel, El Convento.
• St. Kitts: Royal St. Kitts.

Europe:
• Baden Baden, Germany: Brenner's Park Hotel.
• Cannes, France: Carlton, Majestic.
• Deauville, France: Normandie.
• Estoril, Portugal: Palacio, Ritz (in Lisbon, half an hour away).
• Marbella, Spain: Marbella Club, Los Monteros.
• Monte Carlo, Monacao: Hotel de Paris,

Hotel Hermitage, Loew's Monte Carlo.

- Sveti Stefan, Yugoslavia: Milocci, Sveti Stefan.

- Venice, Italy: Excelsior (Lido Beach), Gritti Palace, Royal, Royal Danieli.

Elsewhere:

- Macao: Hyatt Regency Macao, Lisboa, Royal. (Macao is a Portuguese territory on the tip of mainland China, 40 miles from Hong Kong by jetfoil.)

- Marrakesh, Morocco: Hotel de la Mamounia.

STATE LOTTERY WINNING STRATEGY

When playing a state lottery, it's a good idea to choose at least one number higher than 31. Reason: Many lottery players use number combinations based on birthdays, anniversaries, and other dates. Since this group concentrates on numbers of 31 or lower, a winning combination with one or more higher numbers will likely be shared by fewer people.

Source: Dr. Jim Maxwell, American Mathematics Society.

WINNING CRAPS STRATEGY

While craps is the most exciting and emotional casino game, it has always had one major drawback—it appears to be unbeatable. It differs from blackjack, where card-counters could gain an edge against the house in certain situations.

New way: Using systems I've learned from a professional gambler known as the Captain, who has won consistently at craps for the last 10 years, I've found that the casinos can indeed be beaten.

The key to winning at craps is to capitalize on a "hot" roll. You need to be betting when a shooter establishes a "point" (4, 5, 6, 8, 9 or 10) . . . and then throws the dice a dozen or more times before rolling a 7 ("sevening out").

Problem: Craps players are routinely devastated by a series of "cold" shooters, who seven out within a few rolls of establishing a point.

By the time a hot shooter comes along, they have lost so much money that they don't have enough left to invest and recoup.

The Captain observed that craps games tended to run in streaks . . . long, cold periods would be interspersed with briefer hot ones. If players oculd conserve their money by not betting during the cold steaks, he reasoned, they could come out ahead over the long haul.

This principle led him to the *5-Count*. It's a very simple strategy that would prove more effective than any previous craps system.

The 5-Count automatically eliminates the horrendous rolls that can swallow a player's stake. It allows you to stay afloat while you wait for the "wave" of a hot roll to bring you a profit.

Even if that wave fails to arrive at a given session, the "5-Count" will keep you from drowning.

How the 5-Count works:

When a shooter takes the dice for his/her first "come-out" roll, you do not place any bets. Instead, you wait for the shooter to complete five successful rolls of the dice, as follows:

- On the first roll, the shooter must hit a point number—4, 5, 6, 8, 9, or 10—for the 5-Count to start. If the shooter rolls 2, 3, 7, 11, or 12 on the come-out, the count has not begun.

- On the second, third, and fourth rolls, any number except 7 is included toward the 5-Count. (As soon as the shooter sevens out, the count is terminated and begins again at zero.)

- On the fifth roll, the shooter must again roll a point number for the 5-Count to be completed. Your betting begins only after the successful completion of this sequence.

The easiest way to win:

In his own play, the Captain uses his "Supersystem." While this method requires no special mathematical skills, it is too intricate to describe within the confines of this article.*

There is, however, a simpler variant that has also proven successful—the Limited Bankroll System. More conservative than the Supersystem, it can still produce a steady profit.

Assuming you play at a $5-minimum table (the cheapest available in Atlantic City or Las

*A full description is in *Beat the Craps Out of the Casinos.*

Vegas), that System calls for you to "place"** $6 on the 6 and $6 on the 8 after the "5-Count" is completed.

The play:

- Unless the shooter rolls 7—in which case you'd lose, and would start a new 5-Count—you keep both of your place bets working for five rolls.

- If neither the 6 nor the 8 hits within five rolls, tell the dealer that your bets are off, and keep them off for two rolls. Then put both bets on again for three rolls. If you still fail to win, take your bets off for the next two rolls, and maintain this pattern.

- As soon as either the 6 or the 8 hits, give yourself five more rolls for either one to hit again.

- After your numbers have hit a total of six times on the same roll, you must "press" (double) your bet on the number that represents your seventh win. Example: After you've won four times on the 6 and twice on the 8, the shooter rolls another 8. At that point you increase your bet on the 8 from $6 to $12.

- After the eighth hit, you must press your bet to $12 on the opposite number—in this case, the 6.

**In a "place" bet, you're wagering that the number you've bet on will be rolled before the shooter sevens out. A winning place bet on the 6 or 8 pays $7 for every $6 wagered.

- From that point on, you press your bets on the 6 and 8 after the fifth and sixth hits—to $24 on each, and then (on the rare occasion that you hit another six times before the shooter sevens out) to $48.

One advantage of *The Limited Bankroll System* is that you can play comfortably with a stake as small as $150. Another plus is that you're highly unlikely to get wiped out in a hurry—a common hazard for more conventional craps players.

Worst-case scenario: There are times when the shooter will repeatedly seven out on the sixth, seventh or eighth rolls—a deadly sequence for anyone playing the 5-Count.

How to handle it: If you lose one-third of your stake ($50, if you start with $150) within 20 to 30 minutes, change tables, If you quickly lose another one-third at the next table, call it quits for that session. As with any system, there are days when it just doesn't pay to play.

Both the *Supersystem* and *The Limited Bankroll System* are designed to "grind" out modest but profitable results. They are not get-rich-quick schemes. They reward patience and discipline —and players who stay within their strict guidelines.

Source: Frank Scoblete, a regular contributor to *Win* magazine, and author of *Beat the Craps Out of the Casinos*, Paone Press, Box 610, Lynbrook, New York 11563.

9. Sports and Recreation

Sports and Recreation

FISHING A NEW LAKE

If you know where to start looking, you can fish any lake successfully.

Where bass congregate:
- Near trees that have recently fallen into the water.
- In hot weather: Under lily pads, especially in the only shallow spots around.
- In consistently mild weather: In backwater ponds and coves off the main lake. Best: Good weed or brush cover, with a creek running in.
- Any time at all: In sunken moss beds near the shore.

Source: *Outdoor Life.*

FISHING AROUND A FALLEN TREE

Start at the top, using deep-running lures. Along the sides, use medium-running lures. Toward the base of the tree, change to shallow and surface lures.

Source: *Sports Afield.*

GOOD YEAR-ROUND FISHING

Florida's east coast from Melbourne Beach to Fort Pierce. Fall and spring: Runs of snook, the delicious saltwater gamefish that weighs up to 30 pounds. Winter: Surf fishing for blues, big whiting and pompano, which many think is the best-tasting of all the saltwater fish. The nearby Indian River also provides good year-round fishing with light tackle.

BEST OFFSHORE FISHING

Face it: You've always wanted to play Ernest Hemingway for a day, your muscles straining, your face stinging from salt and sun, hair lashed by the wind, hooting and hollering in pain, exultation and glory as you engage in mortal combat with a colossus of the deep—man versus marlin.

Fact: Offshore fishing for big game fish requires the least amount of previous experience of any type of sport-fishing. You don't have to rig your tackle, bait a hook, cast a line or navigate. All you need is a good boat, a good captain, a competent crew and a strong back!

Once known as "deep-sea fishing" (a term now seen only in the brochures of tropical resorts), offshore fishing refers to sport-fishing for larger species: The billfish (marlin, sailfish and swordfish), tuna, tarpon, cobia and shark. The US offers excellent fishing off all three coasts.

Chartering a Boat: The procedure is similar everywhere. If time permits, visit the boat docks at sunset when charters return. See what kinds of fish are being brought in. Talk with the passengers: Were their previous fishing experience and their expectations similar to yours? Did they have fun? Are they satisfied with their day's trip? Would they do it again?

Talk to the mates. Are they pleasant? Enthusiastic about the captain?

Next, inspect the boat. Is it clean and well maintained? Does it appear to have proper radio and safety equipment? Naturally, a boat will not look its best on its return from a day's fishing—but are the running gear and fishing tackle well kept? Or is tackle randomly stowed, paint chipped, hardware corroded?

Many fishermen prefer an owner-operated boat to a vessel run by a salaried captain. In either case, check to see if the captain has been licensed by the Coast Guard.

Boats that carry six passengers or fewer are not required to pass an annual Coast Guard inspection, but they must carry mandatory safety equipment. Boats that have undergone a voluntary inspection will display a Coast Guard sticker. If you're planning to bring a child along, ask if junior-size life preservers are available.

If you expect to be able to keep your catch, check with the captain beforehand to avoid a dispute at the end of the day.

Expect to pay $300-$400 a day for a private charter. In some areas, $600-$800 is not uncommon.

Variations in costs depend largely on how far the boat must travel to reach prime fishing waters. In Boothbay, Maine, for example, you may have to travel only three to 10 miles offshore, while from Montauk, NY, 60 or 70 miles is not unusual.

Although some areas may offer half-day charters if the travel distance is not too great, it is more common for a good fishing trip to take a whole day.

Regardless of whether fish are caught, it is customary to tip the mate at the end of the day (and also the captain, especially if he is salaried and not the owner of the boat). The going rate is about 10% of the cost of the trip. Of course, as in any service business, a good catch and/or good service may inspire a more generous tip.

Party Boats: For a less costly trip, though not necessarily a less enjoyable one, try a "party boat" or "head boat." These big, stable boats, equipped for a large number of passengers, range in cost from $15 or so for half a day to $20-$30 and up for a longer trip. Such boats are a great introduction for a beginning angler or for a fisherman who is new to an area. They offer wide variety and often concentrate on "good-eating" fish. Disadvantages: The equipment may be worn from continuous use. (Don't hesitate to request another pole if you don't think yours is working right.) And you can't ask to go home if you're not having a good time.

On the Pacific Coast, some boats offer three-day to three-week trips for about $100/day. They fish for numerous species along the Mexican coast. Passengers may keep their catch.

Most boats let you keep most or all of what you catch. The mate is usually happy to clean and fillet your fish for a small fee. But it is in very poor taste to ask the captain or the mate to clean your fish and then try to sell it on the dock. Take what you plan to eat and offer the rest to the boat. Keep your fish on ice in a cooler, being careful not to let your fillets come into contact with fresh water or ice.

Etiquette:

• Dress appropriately. Bring extra layers of clothing, even if you are in the Florida Keys. It can be a lot cooler on the water than on land, and mornings are often chilly. Wear soft-soled boat shoes, polarized sunglasses and a hat, and bring a sunscreen.

• Take precautions against seasickness. Ask your doctor for medication ahead of time if you think you'll need it and begin to take it at least 24 hours before your departure. (This allows you to sleep off the early, drowsy part and be fully alert for your trip.) Medications for seasickness do not help if you wait until you are already queasy.

• Bring plenty of nonalcoholic beverages. It is easy to get dehydrated while you are on the water. Also, bring any food you may want (it's a good idea to include a salty snack). Most charter boats do not supply food or drink, although many party boats have snack bars. Note: Although it is not in poor taste to enjoy a few beers over the course of a day's fishing, it is downright boorish, and frequently dangerous, to become drunk while on the water.

• Limit the number of passengers. Many people make the mistake of overloading a boat, hoping to split the costs. But on a charter boat with only one or two "fighting chairs," passengers take turns fishing. The more people on board, the fewer your turns to fish actively. As a general rule, a 28- to 30-foot boat accommodates four passengers comfortably. A 35-foot or larger boat can handle six.

• Listen to the instructions of your captain and mate. They have spent years studying an area, and they want you to catch fish. There are many differences in tackle, bait and techniques, and your favorite walleye lure may not be appetizing to a yellowfin tuna.

• If you are a novice, say so. Not only will the captain and mate appreciate your honesty, but they will best be able to help you if they have some idea of your previous experience.

• Fish with an open mind. The vacation

day you have allocated for fishing may turn out to be a day fish are not feeding. Your guide isn't holding out on you.

Long-Distance Chartering: Many people don't have time to explore the docks of an area before they choose a boat. For recommendations by telephone, try calling a local tackle shop or the editors of a major outdoor magazine. (Resort hotels usually limit their referrals to the guides who service the hotel.)

Several travel agencies specialize (at no cost) in arranging fishing trips. Two good ones: Fishing International, Santa Rosa, CA, (707) 542-4242, and PanAngling Travel Service, Chicago, (312) 263-0328.

A few other pointers: Many captains will take "split charters." If you are traveling in a small group and would like to divide the cost of a charter, inquire at the dock for similar parties. It is not polite, however, to ask a captain to find five other people to share your trip.

If you plan to take children, choose a charter geared toward variety fishing. Try a half-day charter first, and stay away from hard-core game fishing—it is boring just to watch Daddy fish all day!

Many of the favorite captains are booked solid a year in advance. Scout around early if you plan to fish in a new area.

Seasonal suggestions:

• April and May: It's long-range party-boat season in Southern California. San Diego is the biggest port. Party boats in New York and New Jersey venture out for flounder, cod and other bottom fishing. Party boats and skiff guides are active in the Florida Keys.

• June: Head for the Gulf Stream from the Outer Banks of North Carolina for tuna and white marlin. It's big-game billfish season offshore in the Gulf of Mexico from Louisiana to Texas.

• July, August, early September: In New York through New Engalnd, fish for giant tuna (up to 1,000 pounds!). It's peak season for white and blue marlin in North Carolina. There's excellent fishing in the Florida Keys (not crowded) for sailfish, bonefish and permit. Party and charter boats fish for salmon in the Pacific Northwest through Alaska.

• September and October: Catch bluefin tuna off Prince Edward Island before they migrate south.

• October and November: Big game fishing is winding down in the North and in the Gulf. But it's great for bluefish from Massachusetts through Chesapeake Bay.

• September through November: For a more glamorous trip, the black marlin fishing is tremendous off the Great Barrier Reef in Australia or New Zealand.

• December and January: Winter is winter, even in the Florida Keys, but sailfish like the cold, rough seas. (Dress warmly.)

• February and March: The weather is very changeable in southern waters, so allow at least three to five days for a fishing trip. You may thus get one or two good days of fishing. There is still plenty of good fishing in the Caribbean, even though it is not peak season. Try for marlin and billfish in the Bahamas.

• November through March: Cabo San Lucas, Mexico, is prime for marlin, sails, dolphin (the fish, not the mammal) and roosterfish.

Good fishing! Once you try it, you'll be hooked!

Source: Barry Gibson, editor, *Salt Water Sportsman* and John F. Klein, a charter captain out of Sarasota, FL. Phone: (813) 923-4415.

HOW TO GET INTO SHAPE FOR SKIING

Being physically fit makes skiing more fun and helps prevent soreness and injuries. Getting ready for the slopes can be like your regular exercise regimen.

Muscle tone and flexibility. Stretching exercises keep your muscles long and pliable. They also warm muscles up for strenuous sports and help relax them afterwards. Always stretch slowly. Hold the extended position for 20–30 seconds. Don't bounce. Simple stretches. Rotate your head. Bend from side to side. Touch your toes. Lunge forward while keeping the back foot flat on the floor. Do sit-ups with your knees bent to strengthen abdominal muscles (they can take stress off the back).

Endurance and strength. Practicing any active sport, from swimming to tennis, for three one-hour sessions a week will get you into shape. Jogging builds up the muscles of the lower torso and legs. Running downhill strengthens the front thigh muscles, essential to skiing. Running on uneven terrain promotes strong and flexible ankles. Biking builds strong legs and improves balance.

BEST PLACES TO SKI

California

• Squaw Valley. Developed for the Olympics, it includes an 8,200-foot tram. (916) 583-0121. Stay at: Squaw Valley Lodge.

Colorado

• Aspen. Ski Aspen Mountain, Ruthie's Run, Snowmass or Aspen Highlands. (303) 925-9000. Stay at: Aspen Inn, Aspen Lodge, The Gant or Hotel Jerome.

• Vail. A wide variety of runs is available in this movie-star ski capital. Alternate: Beaver Creek, just 12 miles farther on Interstate 70. (303) 476-5677. Stay at: Inn at West Vail, Sunbird Lodge, Vail Village Inn.

Idaho

• Sun Valley. An old-timer, but still going strong. Experienced skiers enjoy Mount Baldy and Dollar Mountain. (208) 622-4111. Stay at: Sun Valley Lodge.

Utah

• Alta. Experienced skiers attempt the High Rustler Run, with 40-degree slope, no trees and frequent avalanches. (801) 742-2040. Stay at: Alta Lodge.

• Snowbird. Known for powder skiing. Hidden Peak is 11,000 feet high. There are also runs for beginners. (801) 742-2000. Stay at: The Lodge.

Vermont

• Killington. Highest lift-served summit in New England. (802) 422-3333. Stay at: Mountain Inn, Summit Lodge.

• Stowe. Ski the demanding sectors of Mount Mansfield, Spruce Peak, Sterling Mountain. (802) 253-7321. Stay at: Green Mountain Inn, Stowehof, Topnotch.

• Warren. Excellent skiing is available at Mount Allen, Mount Lincoln Peak or Sugarbush Valley. (802) 583-2381. Stay at: Sugarbush Inn.

Western Canada

• Vancouver area. Ski the Black Comb and Whistler Mountains, with the highest vertical drop in North America. Heli-skiing is also available. (604) 932-3434 for Whistler Mountain Ski Corporation. Stay at: Bayshore or Four Seasons.

Eastern Canada

• Mount Tremblant. 90 miles north of Montreal, in the Laurentians. (819) 425-8711. Stay at: Gray Rocks Inn, Mount Tremblant Lodge.

Europe

Austria

• Innsbruck. Twice an Olympic site, this 800-year-old city is surrounded by excellent ski areas. Austrian National Tourist office, 500 5th Ave., NY 10110 20th Floor. Stay at: The Europe, Goldener Adler, Sporthotel.

• Kitzbuhl. A favored, more chic ski spot in the lofty Austrian Alps. Stay at: Grand, Goldener Graf, Hirzingerhof.

France

• Chamonix, Courcheval, Val d'Isere. Ski the Haute Savoie chain of mountains, including Mont Blanc. French Government Tourist Office, 610 Fifth Ave., New York 10020, (212) 757-1125. Stay at: Carlton, Croix Blanche or Mont Blanc in Chamonix. Carlina, LeLana or Pralong 2000 in Courcheval. Christiania or Grandes Parades in Val d'Isere.

Italy

• Cortina d'Ampezzo. Downhill skiers are enthusiastic about the spectacular Dolomites, just north of Venice. Italian Government Travel Office, 630 Fifth Ave., New York 10111, (212) 245-4822. Stay at: Hotel Cristallo, Hotel de la Poste, Miramonti Majestic.

Switzerland

• Swiss Alps. The finest downhill skiing. Swissair, (airport). (718) 995-8400. Stay at: Belvedere, Derby or Schiezerhof in Davos. Palace, Park or Residence Palace in Gstaad. Badrutt's Palace, Kulm or Suvretta House in St. Moritz. Monte Rosa or Mount Cervin in Zermatt.

Phone numbers in the US and Canadian sections are for area-information services that can take your reservation.

WHEN SHARPENING IS BAD FOR SKIS

Sharpening skis frequently to remove nicks and restore the edges can change their performance. Flat filing the bottom reduces the thickness of the plastic base and makes skis more flexible. Side filing can narrow skis and change the turning radius. For experts, this may be a problem, but most recreational skiers won't notice a difference.

Source: *Skiing.*

HOW TO BUY SKI BOOTS

First rule: If a boot is not comfortable in the store, it will be worse on the slopes. Proper fit: Toes should be able to wiggle while the heel, instep and ball of the foot are effectively, but not painfully, immobilized. An experienced shop technician can expand the shell and modify the footbed and heel wedge. Forward flex: When you bend your foot, you should feel no pressure points on your shin or upper ankle. Boot height: A high boot spreads flexing loads across a wider shin area than low boots. Most recreational skiers are at ease in a high boot with a soft forward flex. Low, stiff boots concentrate loads just above the ankle, which can be painful for the occasional skier.

Source: *Ski.*

HOW TO PLAY BETTER GOLF

I studied every prominent golfer who ever played the game and listed the techniques they shared. From this, I distilled my system, *Ultimate Golf Swing Fundamentals.* Within nine months, at the age of 70, I reduced my handicap from 28 to scratch.

How it works:

The backbone of this system is a *stairstep* program. The principle is simple. I believe that the foundation of every sound golf game resides in putting.

The fundamentals for every succeeding swing —from the chip and pitch, through the irons, to the woods and driver—are the same. The only difference is that the golfer's stroke becomes successively longer.

According to the stairstep principle, the golfer must perfect every shot possible with a particular club before moving on to the next club, up the stairstep.

More advice:

In addition to practicing on the course's practice area (and doing it *right*), I recommend the following steps for any golfers intent on sharpening their game:

• *Play regularly.* In my turn-around year, I increased my frequency of play from once a month to once a week. I finally got to *know* my golf course, and could begin to aim my shots to areas where the following shots would be easier.

• *Do your golf exercises in front of a mirror.* I achieved a major breakthrough while swinging a 5 iron before a full-length mirror. *Don't be modest:* Dressed only in my shorts, I soon isolated my problem—a quivering of my right knee during my backswing, the source of my frequently errant iron shots. With proper exercise I developed control of my knee—and with it my iron game.

• *Never rush on the golf course.* Allow time upon arrival for your practice shots and putts. Once on the tee, visualize the shot to be made and the spot where you expect it to land. Concentrate on this spot—and *not* on anyone who may be watching you—as you stroke the ball.

• *Skip practice swings just before you hit for real.* Most people tend to tighten up with extra swings. It's better to relax and fire away.

• *Don't overswing.* Use a three-quarter backswing with your irons—and only a one-half backswing for your chips and pitches. You'll more than gain in control and accuracy anything you might lose in distance.

Source: John Youngblood, author of *How I Went from 28 to Scratch in One Year Playing Once a Week,* Price Stern Sloan, 360 La Cienega Blvd., Los Angeles 90048.

ALL ABOUT IN-LINE ROLLER SKATES

In-line roller skates—skates with their wheels all in a row—have become very popular. More than a million pairs have been sold in the US, and sales are doubling each year.

Often called rollerblades, after the manufacturer Rollerblade, Inc., these skates:

• Ride faster and more smoothly than conventional roller skates. Because the wheels are in a straight line, the rubber is making less contact with the ground—avoiding more surface bumps and other obstructions. And because the wheels are under each boot, rather than at the four corners, they can't hit each other if your feet come close together.

• Provide better ankle support than most conventional roller skates. In-line skates have a polyurethane boot with an inner liner—much like a ski boot.

• Provide excellent exercise. Skaters burn up to 450 calories in 30 minutes.

In-line skates cost $50 to $400 a pair—the same as conventional skates. Plan to spend at least $200. Cheaper models are less comfortable and have inferior wheels and bearings, which can slow down your progress in learning. Learning how:

The biggest risk is falling . . . usually from not knowing how to stop, or because of surface hazards—gravel, oil, etc. Self-defense: Wear knee and elbow pads, wrist guards and a lightweight bicycle helmet.

I also advise people to take a lesson or two before trying to skate on their own. Find an instructor through the shop where you buy your skates.

Warning: Good instructors are hard to find. In-line skating, long popular in Europe, is only 10 years old in the US.

Protection: Find out how qualified the instructor is. Ask . . . How long have they been in-line skating . . . What type of training have they received from other in-line instructors . . . Do they have any related training and background in similar areas such as ice skating, skiing or roller skating?

Source: Joel Rappelfeld, an in-line-skating instructor and author of *The Complete Blader*, St. Martin's Press, 175 Fifth Ave., New York 10010.

TENNIS PRO SECRETS

Psyching yourself for a big point on the tennis court means employing a normal physiological mechanism—the adrenaline response. When adrenaline is pumped into our systems, we are stronger, faster and quicker for a brief period. How to trigger the response: Open your eyes wide and fix them on a nearby object. Breathe deeply and forcefully. Think of yourself as a powerful, aggressive individual. Exhort yourself with phrases like "Fight!" Try to raise goose bumps on your skin—they signal a high point. Note: Save this response for a key moment toward the end of the match. Psyching yourself too often will leave you drained.
Source: *Tennis.*

Tennis players often have trouble switching from one type of playing surface to another. Ease transitions by preparing. If you're moving to fast cement from slow clay, for example, practice charging the net before the switch. If it's the other way around, spend extra time on your groundstrokes. Tactical adjustments also should be made in advance.
Source: *World Tennis.*

When you're facing a superior tennis player:
• Suspend all expectations. Avoid thinking about the situation. Watch the ball, not the opponent.
• Play your game. Don't try to impress your opponent with difficult shots you normally never try.
• Hit the ball deep and down the middle. The more chances for your opponent to return your shot the more chances for him to err.
• Concentrate on your serve. No matter how outgunned you may be, you can stay in the match if you hold your serve.

CHOOSING THE RIGHT TENNIS BALL

Tennis balls come in four varieties: Heavy duty, regular, high altitude and pressureless. Difference between heavy duty and regular: The felt cover. Heavy-duty balls have additional nylon to resist wear on hard courts. Regulars have more wool in the covering for play on clay courts. Note: Do not use heavy-duty balls on clay. They become slower as the nylon in the cover picks up dirt. High-altitude balls are for courts more than 5,000 feet above sea level.

Pressureless balls are long-lasting. But they are heavier than most American players are accustomed to.

Save the slightly fluffier tennis ball for your second serve. The fluff lets the ball take the spin more easily than a fresh, new ball or an old, bare one. Until the nap is fluffed, a new ball flies faster, skids farther and has less bounce.
Source: *Tennis.*

HOW TO PLAY GOOD TENNIS AFTER 40

Older tennis players can win and avoid injuries by using the right strategies and techniques. In his new book,* Pancho Gonzales, the former champion who is now a leading Seniors player, advises playing a "thinking man's" game.

Pancho's practical pointers:

With age, it becomes harder to concentrate on the ball. Recommended: When hitting, watch the ball right up to the point where it hits the strings of the racket.

Aim for consistency rather than winners. Common error made by older players: Hitting too hard. For power and pace, shift your body weight forward on every stroke. At impact, the weight should be completely on the front foot.

Anticipate your opponent. Example: If you have hit a shot to your right, it will probably be returned to your left. Be ready to move left, but don't commit yourself until the ball has been hit.

Back swing: The "how" (straight back or a looping motion) doesn't matter as much as getting the racket back quickly and all the way.

Better strategy:

Try to swing the same way on every shot, both for consistency and for deception. Your opponent shouldn't be able to tell from the swing if the shot is hard or soft. Not recommended: The underspin slice. Reason: The ball travels more slowly, giving older players a better chance to reach it. Better: Flat shots deep to the corners.

Always change a losing game. Lob fre-

Tennis Begins at Forty, Pancho Gonzales, Dial Press, New York.

quently against opponents who are dominating plays, especially if they have a winning net game. Against winning base line players, hit drop shots to force them to come in and play the net.

Save energy. Take plenty of time between points and before serving. Don't go all out in a game that you are losing by a score of 0–40.

The serve! The serve!!

Work on a consistent second serve. The resulting gain of confidence will lead to improvement of the first serve.

When practicing the serve, spend time on the toss. Suggestion: Practice with a bucket placed where a perfect toss should fall.

Beware of the topspin serve. Though effective, it is hard on the back muscles.

Return serves as early as possible, and keep them low.

Health and conditioning:

Playing tennis twice a week or so isn't enough to keep in shape. Weekly running and exercises are a must. Squeezing an old tennis ball a few minutes a day builds up arm muscles, and rope jumping improves footwork.

Rest before and after playing. Use a warm-up jacket to speed the loosening of the muscles before play. During play, run with bent knees to reduce shock to knees. After play, apply lotion to the palm of your racket hand to keep it from scaling and blistering.

Equipment:

The flexible wood racket probably jars the arm less than a metal racket. Older players will likely be more comfortable with lighter-weight rackets, and they may improve their game by using a racket that has been loosely strung.

Doubles strategy:

A doubles team should agree on strategy and signals before playing. Most important signal: Net players must let their partners know when they plan to cross over to intercept the return of a serve. (A clenched fist behind the back is often used.) During this move and all other moves, both partners should be in motion. . . one to make the shot and the other to cover the exposed part of the court.

The weaker player should take the forehand court. This player should be assigned to serve when the wind and sun are behind the server. The weaker player should play closer to the net. Reason: It is easier to volley in this position.

In doubles, one player normally concentrates on setting up shots. The job is to hit the ball low in order to force the opponents at the net to hit up on the ball. The second player has the job of making the put-aways.

PICKING THE RIGHT RUNNING SHOES

The choices seem endless. Where do your feet fit in the race for the perfect pair?

There are five things to look for in running shoes:

• A heel counter still enough to hold your heel in place and keep it from rolling in and out.
• Flexibility in the forefoot area so the shoe bends easily with your foot. (If the shoe is stiff, you leg and foot muscles will have to work too hard.)
• An arch support to keep the foot stable and minimize rolling inside.
• A fairly wide base for stability and balance. The bottom of the heel, for example, should be as wide as the top of the shoe.
• Cushioning that compresses easily. (Several different materials are used now.) The midsole area absorbs the most shock and should have the greatest amount of padding. However, the heel (which particularly for women should be three-quarters of an inch higher than the sole) needs padding, too. Too much causes fatigue, and too little causes bruising.

Running shoes do not need to be broken in. They should feel good the moment you try them on.

Fitting:

• Start with manufacturers' least costly shoes and keep trying until you find the one that feels best.
• Try on running shoes with the same kind of thick socks you will be wearing with them.
• Light people need less cushioning than heavier people.
• If you have a low arch or tend to flat feet, pick a more stable shoe with more rear foot control, called a "cement"-lasted or boarded shoe. ("Last" is the foot shape that the shoe is built around.)
• For a high arch, try a softer, more curved last (called a "slip" last).
• Be sure you have adequate toe room (at least one-half inch of clearance). Running shoes, particularly in women's sizes, run small, and women often need a half-size or whole-size larger running shoe than street shoe.

Source: Gary Muhrcke, proprietor of the Super Runners Shop, 1337 Lexington Ave., New York 10028.

HOW TO BUY THE RIGHT BIKE

Commuters have special biking requirements. If you're in the suit-and-tie crowd, you'll want fenders to keep yourself clean. You may want a rack on the back for a newspaper or side racks for your briefcase. They're making bicycle sacks (panniers) of heavier nylon now, with stiffeners to retain their briefcase shape. Although rubber pedals are less durable than steel, they'll help preserve your leather soles. Finally, every city rider needs a topnotch lock. The U-bolt models by Kryptonite and Citadel are among the best ones.

What kind to buy:

Touring bikes are right for most people. They have a longer wheel base for a "Cadillac" ride. Racing bikes offer a "Fiat" ride. With their shorter wheelbase, you feel the road more, but you get better handling and efficiency.

The Japanese have learned how to make bikes better and more cheaply. A European bike of equivalent quality will cost at least 20% more. Although there are 30 different Japanese makes, they're all produced by one of two corporate families, so they're about the same.

The best American bikes offer better frames, with superior materials and hand-craftsmanship. But you sacrifice quality on components.

Choosing parts:

A good frame design for women is the mixte (pronounced mix-tay). Two parts run from the head tube to the rear axle for added stability. With longer skirts, many women can use a man's 10-speed, and they do. The men's models are lighter and stronger.

For those who find bicycles uncomfortable to sit on, a new anatomically designed saddle may be the answer. These seats, made of leather with foam padding, feature two ridges to support the pelvic bones, with a valley in between to avoid pinching and sciatic nerve.

Mixte handlebars, which project almost perpendicularly to the frame, are good for all-around cycling, as are racing (or drop) bars. The traditional curved bars are not recommended for city riding. They keep you sitting erect, so your spine is jolted by each bump. And foam grips will absorb more road shock than standard cloth tape grips.

In buying a helmet, look for a low-impact plastic shell. In a typical biking accident, this will protect the head better than a high-impact motorcycle helmet.

Padded bike gloves make good shock absorbers. Sheepskin bike shorts provide added comfort. Bike jerseys with rear pockets will keep your keys from digging into your leg with each push of the pedal.
Source: Charles McCorkell, owner, Bicycle Habitat, New York.

Female bike riders should point the seat slightly downwards to avoid irritating the genital area. Men should point the seat upward, to avoid problems such as irritation of the urinary tract and injury to the testes.
Source: *Physicians and Sports Medicine.*

• Sizing up a new bike. Straddle the frame with your feet flat on the floor. There should be an inch of clearance between your crotch and the top tube. If you can't find an exact fit: Buy the next smaller size, then adjust seat and handlebar height. A frame that's too big can't be adjusted.
Source: *How to Select and Use Outdoor Equipment,* HP Books, Tucson, AZ.

BEST SKI PANTS

Stretch ski pants look great, but not all models are warm enough—especially for the novice or intermediate, who burns fewer calories and generates less heat. What to look for: High wool content (preferably with the wool floated to the inside, nearest your body). Terry lining (traps insulating dead air). For those who get cold easily: Newly marketed insulated stretch pants, with a three-layer sandwich construction.
Source: *Ski.*

FIGHTING FROSTBITE ON SKI SLOPES

For warm hands and feet, a good hat helps. Reason: If your head and torso (the body's first priorities) are kept warm, blood circulates freely to the extremities. Most versatile hat: Wool with an acrylic liner gives you warmth without itchiness.
Source: *Skiing Magazine.*

HOW TO BUY SPORTS GOGGLES

Swimmers: Some types of goggles apply pressure in the wrong places. Best: Buy the kind with soft rubber rims around the eyes.

Racquet sports, particularly squash and racquetball, can and do cause serious eye injuries if players don't wear protective goggles of some sort. Least effective: Open goggles without lenses. Best: Polycarbonate lenses that have been tested to stop a .22 bullet at 20 feet in a lab test.

HOW TO CHOOSE ICE SKATES

Most important: A stiff boot with a snug fit. Toes should reach the tip of the boot but lie flat. Lace the boot tightly through the toe area, very tightly through the instep, comfortably at the top. To check the fit: Walk. If your ankles wiggle even though the lacing is correct, ask for smaller or stiffer skates.

HOW TO CHOOSE A CANOE

Before buying a canoe, consider what you're going to use it for, where, and how many people you'll be carrying. For rocky rivers: Get an aluminum or plastic hull. Rocks destroy fiberglass hulls. Royalex ABS plastic hulls (made by Old Town) are the most popular. Disadvantages: ABS canoes are more expensive than aluminum and are vulnerable to wear and tear on bow and stern. One remedy is optional skidplates. Good starter boat: The Coleman polyethylene plastic canoe, which you can assemble yourself.

Source: *Canoe.*

BUYING AN INFLATABLE BOAT

Inflatable boats are no longer considered toys. They are now reputable crafts with a variety of functions. Inflatables perform well with much less horsepower than rigid-hulled boats. They can be stored at home, saving winter storage costs and mooring fees. They're easier to transport. What to look for: A design with several airtight compartments, an inflatable keel, self-bailers, bow handles and fitted D-rings, lifelines, heavy-duty fitted oarlocks, wooden or antislip aluminum floorboards, and bow-dodgers with windshields for added spray protection.

BACKPACKING SECRETS

To make it less draining: Do not load up with unnecessary items. Do not walk too fast (if you cannot carry on a conversation, you are walking too quickly). When climbing uphill, do the rest step. How: Walk slowly, with all your weight on your back leg. Inhale while moving your unweighted foot forward. Exhale while transferring your weight to the front foot. Trail exercise: During breaks, lean forward, with your hand and head against a tree trunk. Put one foot behind the other. The weight should be on your back foot. Drive that knee forward. Repeat with the other leg. Good camp stretch: After the day's hike, kneel on your foam pad. Then slowly lean back with your arms behind you. Each stretch should last at least one minute.

Source: *Sports Afield.*

WALKING BAREFOOT ON HOT COALS

Walking barefoot over coals with no pain or burns has been used for centuries by gurus to demonstrate the power of mind over body.

Our observation: Coals are bad conductors of heat. Although the temperature of coal cores can reach 1,500°F, you can walk quickly over them without sustaining burns. Experiment: In a study at the University of California at Los Angeles, hundreds of students walked over hot coals without serious harm—with no training.

Source: Dr. Paul Kurtz, chairman of The Committee for the Scientific Investigation of Claims of the Paranormal, Box 229, Buffalo, NY 14214.

ARE PRO BASKETBALL GAMES FIXED?

Background: As of April 8, the Washington Bullets had a home record of 28 wins and nine losses. On the road, their record was only nine wins and 26 losses. The same home/ away contrast holds true for every team in the NBA. The fix: Team owners, who want to attract crowds to their home arenas with the lure of victory, require visiting teams to take the earliest scheduled flight on game day, which often demands a 6 a.m. wake-up call . . . the home team usually has the night off before the game, while the visitors may have played several consecutive nights in different cities in different time zones.

Source: Reprinted with permission from *The Washington Monthly.* Copyright by The Washington Monthly Co., 1611 Connecticut Ave. NW, Washington, DC 20009.

BINGO NEVER WAS A GAME OF CHANCE

Most people play bingo as if it were a game of sheer chance—as if any set of cards had just as good a chance of winning as any other. They are mistaken. If you correctly choose the cards you play, you can significantly improve your odds of winning any bingo game.

My system works with straight bingo (where

you must cover five squares in a row—vertically, horizontally or diagonally), coverall (a jackpot game, in which you must cover every square on your card) or any other variation.

Key strategy: To get as many of the 75 numbers as possible on a given set of cards. There are 24 numbers printed on every bingo card. (There are 25 squares, but the center square is a non-numbered free space.) If you chose three cards at random, their 72 numbered spaces would represent only 49 different numbers—the other 23 spaces would have duplicate numbers.

It is possible, however, to find sets of three cards with no duplicates—with 72 different numbers. (Time permitting, players can choose their cards freely at the beginning of any session.) If you were to play such a set, you would be 25% more likely to win a given game than a player with a random set. Depending on the size of the prizes, that edge can translate into hundreds—or even thousands—of dollars of winnings within a few weeks.

Ironically, most players choose sets that are worse than random. They look for cards with one or two "lucky" numbers—7 or 11, for example. And they are especially drawn to cards where those lucky numbers are at the corners.

The results are devastating. In an average straight game with 1,000 cards in play, a bingo will occur after 15 numbers are called. That means that any given number—regardless of whether it is "lucky" or not—will be called in only one of five games. In those other four games, any set of cards with an uncalled "lucky" number is 25% less likely to win. (When a number is at a corner, it affects three lines—one vertical, one horizontal, one diagonal.)

Another advantage of choosing non duplicating cards is that it makes it easier to keep track of the numbers you're covering—and harder to miss one by accident.

Example: If you are playing three cards on which there are no duplicate numbers, every time a number is called, you know you will cover a space. Exception: If the number is called on the N line, you will cover a space only 80% of the time because the center square, which contains the free space, is in the N line.

There are countless statistical systems favored by bingo players, but this is the only one I've found that generates consistent profits.

The only other live variable in bingo is the proportion of money collected that is returned to the players. Most operators hold back at least 50% for overhead and revenue. (The percentage is usually posted on the bingo sheets or somewhere in the hall.)

Other games, however, return as much as 75% to the players. The more money that comes back, of course, the better your chances of coming out ahead.

Source: John "Dee" Wyrick, author of *Complete Authoritative Guide to Bingo*, Gambler's Book Club, Box 4115, Las Vegas 89127.

10. Smart Consumer's Guide

Smart Consumer's Guide

HOW TO BUY SHOES THAT REALLY FIT

Shoes should provide a lot of cushioning to match the type of surface the bare foot needs. Poor: A rigid, so-called supportive shoe. Shoes should be loose and giving. Good: The running shoe, the most physiologic shoe made. Soft and malleable, it provides cushioning and a little bit of support. (Leather ones breathe best if your feet sweat.) Women: If you wear a high-heeled, thin-soled shoe, have a thin rubber sole cemented onto the bottom to cushion the ball of the foot.

• Fit shoes with your hands, not with your feet. There should be an index finger's breadth between the tip of the toes and the front of the shoe. Tell the salesperson to start with a half-size larger than you usually wear and work down. The shoe shouldn't be pushed out of shape when you stand. The leather should not be drawn taut.

• An ideal heel height for a woman is 1½–2 inches. This is not a magic number, simply the most comfortable. If a man wore a 1½-inch heel, he'd be more comfortable than in the traditional ¾-inch heel.

• Flat feet are not bad feet. A flat, flexible foot is very functional. Most great athletes have them. Problem: The shoe industry doesn't make shoes to fit flat feet. Look for low-heeled shoes that feel balanced. They should not throw your weight forward on the balls of your feet or gap at the arches.

Source: John F. Waller, Jr., MD, chief of the foot and ankle section, Lenox Hill Hospital, New York.

• Buy shoes in the late afternoon when your feet have had a full day's workout and are slightly spread. Shoes that you try on first thing in the morning may be too tight by evening and uncomfortable for all-day wear.

GREAT FUR-BUYING OPPORTUNITIES IN MONTREAL

Buying even the best furs in Montreal costs only a fraction of the US price. Typical savings range from $2,500 to $3,000. Examples: Blackglama female mink, $2,500-$3,000 in Montreal versus $5,000-$6,000 on sale in New York; female fisher, $16,000-$24,000 versus $30,000-$50,000; or Canadian lynx, $7,000-$15,000 versus New York's $15,000-$25,000.

Here's why it works. Besides the great buying power of the American dollar, Montreal furriers can spread their overhead costs over a greater number of garments than US furriers can. Montreal, the center of Canada's fur and fashion industry, is the city with the most furs owned per capita in the world. In addition, because all Montrealers wear their furs nearly every day in winter, local furriers can shift a good percentage of their costs to the repairs that become inevitable through heavy winter wear.

Bonus: Thanks to Canadian weather, which makes the basic winter coat fur rather than cloth, men's fur design is taken seriously in Montreal. Accordingly, men's furs here are especially attractive and suitable for executives and professionals, who find an enormous selection from which to choose.

As a rule, Canadian furs are of higher quality than their US counterparts. The pelts are denser because the animals grow thicker fur as insulation from the colder climate. Best buys: Native Canadian furs like fisher, lynx (second in price and quality only to the rare Siberian variety), sheared or unsheared beaver, fox and Canadian Majestic mink (equal in quality to Blackglama, which is also available at bargain prices, but denser and warmer, in a softer

224

brown preferred so enthusiastically by Europeans).

Very special: Canadian sable, a luminous, luxurious golden color. The pelts are much lighter in weight and warmer than mink. Prices for coats average around $17,500 US (much more affordable than Siberian sable's $50,000-$60,000).

You're better off buying your fur from a furrier—especially from a member of the select professional Maitres-Fourreurs Associes (Master Furriers Association)—than from a department store. Furriers are more knowledgeable and better trained than department store personnel. And, they are more flexible on prices. In addition, a good furrier can design a garment especially for you, coming to your hotel, if desired, to measure you and make a canvas pattern. This service and design capability is very important for petite women (5'3" or under) or heavy women (size 16 or larger)—two categories that together account for 40% of adult American women. Since furs are a major investment, they should look magnificent and fit perfectly. There's no reason why purchasers should decide to settle for less.

In order to choose the best fur, think of its function. Some furs are more fragile, others more durable—a characteristic of the fur itself, independent of its price. Most durable: Mink, beaver, raccoon and fisher. More fragile (not for everyday wear): Sable, lynx, fox, broadtail and squirrel.

Educate your eye by asking to see the best garment in the fur of your choice. The quality of the skins will be your benchmark. If the price is too high, sometimes just a simpler sleeve or collar will bring the garment into your price range without your having to compromise on the quality of the skins. At any rate, you'll quickly learn—by sight and touch —the characteristics of the finest-quality furs.

Fur prices depend on the number of skins used in the garment, the quality of the skins, and the workmanship (a crucial factor, because even top Blackglama mink skins, worked badly, can look like muskrat).

In lynx, sable, mink and fisher, female skins are more desirable and expensive than male.

Since they are smaller, lighter in weight and more flexible, they adapt better to sophisticated designs. If you can't afford an all-female mink, sable, lynx or fisher, ask your furrier about female sleeves in a male coat. You'll get a more fluid and supple sleeve. The body of the coat may be closely fitted, so male skins will do very well for that. You will save at least $1,000, depending on the fur and design.

Avoid dyed furs unless you're using them as a disposable high-fashion item. Sooner or later dyed furs oxidize, turning an unforeseeable color. The skins will crack and split. Instead, choose natural (including mutation) or, at most, tip-dyed furs. There's plenty of color selection, and you'll get years of wear.

Top furriers: McComber Furs (440 boulevard de Maisonneuve Ouest); its neighbor, Grosvenor Furs (400 boulevard de Maisonneuve Ouest), which has a department in Harrods; and designer-furrier Georges Pouliot (4435 rue de la Roche), former president of the Maitres-Fourreurs Associes.

Furriers will process the necessary paperwork for US Customs. They'll also calculate whether it's better for you to take your fur with you, paying the Quebec sales tax (refunded to you by check, in two to three months) and taking advantage of your personal Customs exemption, or to ship your fur via UPS, avoiding the Quebec sales tax but losing your personal Customs exemption (available only on goods you bring back to the US).

Source: Judith H. McQuown, author of four investment books, writes about fashion, travel, shopping and antiques for many national magazines.

FUR COAT IDENTIFICATION

For fur coat safety, monogram the lining or one of the pockets. Insurers call that an "identifiable characteristic."

HOW TO RECOGNIZE QUALITY CLOTHES IN OFF-PRICE STORES

To take advantage of sales, discount designer stores or consignment shops, learn the details that signal first-class workmanship, label or no label. Look for:

- Stripes and plaids that are carefully matched at the seams.
- Finished seam edges on fabrics that fray easily (linen, loose woolens, etc.).
- Generous seams of one-half inch or more.
- Buttons made of mother-of-pearl, wood or brass.
- Neat, well-spaced buttonholes that fit the buttons tightly.
- Felt backing on wool collars to retain the shape.
- Ample, even hems.
- Straight, even stitching in colors that match the fabric.
- Good-quality linings that are not attached all around. (Loose linings wear better.)

Source: *Dress Better for Less* by Vicki Audette, Meadowbrook Press, Deephaven, MI.

DESIGNER BARGAINS FOR WOMEN IN BOYS' DEPARTMENT

Not all the smart women shopping in the boys' department have sons. Many are just looking for bargains in shirts, sweaters, pants, jackets, robes and belts for themselves. Even designer boys' clothes run 20–50% less than similar items in the women's department. How to size up boys' wear:

Women's size	Boy's size
5/6	14 top, 29/30 pants
7/8	16 top, 30/31 pants
9/10	18 top, 31/32 pants
11/12	20 top, 32/33 pants

HOW TO BUY SUNGLASSES

Be sure they are large enough. Light should not enter around the edges. Best: Frames that curve back toward the temple. Lenses: Plastic is less heavy than glass. Drawback: It scratches easily. Clean with a soft cloth, not a silicone tissue. To prevent glare: Greenish grays, neutral grays and browns are best. Other colors absorb wavelengths and upset color balance. Test: Try on the glasses. The world should appear in true color, but not as bright. Good all-around choice: Sunsensor lenses. They adjust from dark to light. For use near water, polarized lenses block reflected glare. An old pair of prescription lenses can be tinted to a desired density.

BEST EYEGLASS CLEANER

Use a piece of damp newspaper. There is less chance it will scratch the lenses than cloth or tissue.

Source: *Shortcuts* edited by T. Augello and G. Yanker, Bantam Books, New York.

PERFUME CONFIDENTIAL

Perfume lasts longer if the bottle is kept tightly closed and stored in a cool, dark place. If kept in the light, the fragrance oxidizes and loses its effectiveness within a year.

Source: *Seventeen.*

HOW TO CHOOSE THE RIGHT HAIRBRUSH

The best hairbrush bristles come from boars. Their uneven surface cleans better than smooth nylon. Stiffest: Black bristles from the back of the boar's neck. Good for thick, heavy hair, these are the rarest and most expensive bristles. White bristles are better for fine and/or thinning hair.

Source: Jan Hansum, Kent of London, quoted in *The Best Report*, New York.

BEST MOUTHWASH

Bad breath is cured best by mouthwashes containing zinc. The source of most mouth odor is sulfur compounds. The zinc mouthwashes negate these compounds for at least three hours. Contrast: Nonzinc mouthwashes attack bacteria. Point: Check the labels of mouthwashes for zinc.

Source: Joseph Tonzetich, Ph.D., professor of oral biology, University of British Columbia, Vancouver.

BEST INSECT REPELLENTS

Insect repellents vary in the amounts of active ingredients they contain and their effectiveness. Active ingredients: N, N-diethyl-meta-toluamide (deet) and ethyl hexanediol. Most effective: Deet. Spray with highest deet level: Repel (52%). Liquid with highest deet level: Muskol (95%).

BEST SLEEPING BAGS

Waterfowl down still offers the best warmth-to-weight performance as padding (or fill). But now the newer, lightweight, polyester-filled sleeping bags (in most above-freezing conditions) are preferred by campers on practical grounds. Polyester's virtues:

• It keeps two-thirds of its insulating capacity when wet (it absorbs very little moisture), and it dries much faster. Down is worthless when wet. It takes hours to dry and must be refluffed before the bag can be used again.

• It's washable, even by machine. Down bags are best dry cleaned.

• It's nonallergenic. It doesn't collect dust. Down is a magnet for dust, the real cause of suffering for those who think they are allergic to down.

• It's much cheaper than down. Most polyester-filled sleeping bags cost about 50% less than comparable down-filled ones.

HOW TO BUY A MATTRESS

The quality of sleep makes the quantity less important. To enable you to relax, your mattress must provide proper support for your body, yet be resilient enough for comfort.

The old-fashioned double bed gives each sleeper only 26 inches of space, about the same width as a baby's crib. The current most popular size—queen—is seven inches wider and five inches longer than the old double bed. King size is an additional 16 inches wider.

Mattress prices depend on the materials, quality of construction, size, number of layers of upholstery and the store's markup. (Prices may be lower in small, neighborhood stores with low overhead.)

Standard mattresses have two different kinds of construction, innerspring or foam rubber. Top-quality innerspring mattresses have covered metal coils, cushioning material and an insulator between the coils to prevent them from protruding.

Foam mattresses are made of a solid block of urethane, high-resiliency foam or laminated layers of varying density sandwiched together. A good foam mattress is at least five to six inches high and feels heavy when lifted. A high-density foam mattress should last 10–15 years. Foam mattresses can be used on a wooden platform for extra firmness or with a conventional boxspring.

When shopping for a mattress:

• Sit on the edge of the bed. The mattress should support you without feeling flimsy, and it should spring back into shape when you get up. A reinforced border increases durability.

• Lie down. (If the bed is to be used by a couple, both partners should test it lying down.) Check several different firmnesses to choose the one you're most comfortable with. Next, roll from side to side and then to the center. The mattress should not sway, jiggle or sag in the middle. If you hear creaking springs, don't buy it.

• Examine the covering. Best: Sturdy ticking with a pattern woven, not printed on.

• Check for handles on the sides for easy turning, small metal vents to disperse heat and allow air to circulate inside, and plastic corner guards.

• Up to 80% of the sleeper's weight is borne by the boxspring. The finest mattress won't be effective unless it's accompanied by a boxspring of equal quality. When a new mattress is needed, both the mattress and spring should be replaced to ensure that the support system is specifically designed for the mattress.

Queen-size innerspring sets should be used in a sturdy bed frame with a footboard or in a six-leg heavy steel support. Twin and double size can use a four-leg metal frame. A good innerspring sleep set should last 15–20 years.

There is no proven medical advantage to sleeping on a hard surface, so consider comfort the key factor. According to Dr. Hamilton Hall, an orthopedic surgeon who specializes in techniques to relieve back pain, there is no single perfect mattress. "What's perfect for one person may be uncomfortable for another."

Best advice: Only buy a sleep set made by a manufacturer with a good reputation and sold by a reputable dealer. Be very wary of advertised bargains.

TEST OF WELL-MADE WOODEN FURNITURE

Is the piece stable when you gently push down on a top corner or press against the side? Is the back panel inset and attached with screws (not nails)? Do drawers and doors fit well and move smoothly? Are corners of drawers joined with dovetail joints? Do long shelves have center braces? Are table leaves well supported? Are hinges strong and well secured?

Source: *Better Homes and Gardens,* Des Moines, IA.

TEST OF GOOD CARPETING

(1) Insist on density. Closely packed surface yarns and tightly woven backing make for carpets that wear and look good longer. Bend a piece of the carpet backward. If a lot of backing is visible through the pile, go for a higher quality. (2) Avoid soft plush textures when covering moderate-to-heavy traffic areas. (3) Invest in good padding. It absorbs shocks, lengthens carpet life and creates a more comfortable surface. (4) If cost is a factor, compromise on the amount or size of carpet, not on the quality. Or choose lesser qualities for low-traffic areas.

Source: *Better Homes and Gardens,* Des Moines, IA.

ORIENTAL-RUG TEST

Spread the pile apart. If you see knots at the bottom, the rug was made by hand. But sewn-on fringes are a clear machine-made giveaway.

Source: Pasargad Inc., rug importers and manufacturers, Washington, DC.

BEST TOILET SEAT

The standard toilet seat was the most uncomfortable of all those tested in a recent contest of designs. Winner: An elongated seat contoured to support the thighs and buttocks.

Source: Report on tests made at the University of Technology, Loughborough, England, in *New Scientist,* Commonwealth House, London.

BEST ICE-CREAM SCOOPERS

Look for the kind that resemble large spoons. The familiar metal scoops with press-in spring levers on the handle are not as effective. (They work best for scooping tuna and egg salad.) How to scoop ice cream correctly: With the scoop held vertically, dip the tip into the ice cream. Draw the scoop toward you. The ice cream will curl into the head while allowing air to enter. (The air makes the ice cream taste better.) Repeat the procedure until a ball is created. The most expensive is not necessarily the best. The shape of the scoop, not the cost, determines its efficiency.

BUYING KITCHEN KNIVES

Best steel: High-carbon stainless steel. It takes and holds a sharp edge well and resists discoloration. Good: Carbon steel. It is relatively inexpensive. Drawback: It must be kept dry or it will deteriorate. Worst: Stainless steel. It is very difficult to sharpen. Top four brands: Wusthof, Hoffritz, Henckels and Sabatier.

BEST POTS FOR POT ROAST

Pot roasts cook best in heavy cast ironware. That's one tale that happens to be true, though it is mysterious. Other iron-pot pluses: They're energy savers, since they hold heat longer. And traces of iron released chemically into food (unlike nonferrous metals) are good for you, especially for sufferers of iron-deficiency anemia. People with rare hemochromatosis (too much iron in the system) should avoid all food contact with ironware.

Source: *How Safe is Food in Your Kitchen?* by Beatrice Hunter, Scribner's, New York.

• The best potholders are mitts with elastic bands on the cuffs to prevent them from slipping off. The thicker they are, the better. A rough palm gives an extra grip.

HOW TO TRACK DOWN AN OUT-OF-PRINT BOOK

The economics of modern publishing dictate that all but the top best-sellers go out of print very fast, and bookstores cannot afford to stock a full selection of older titles.

To find that wonderful story you loved, first track down the correct title, the author's name and, if possible, the publisher and copyright date. (Your local library can help you.)

Next, check local used-book or antiquarian booksellers. New York City, the publishing capital of the country, has several famous used-book stores that are worth a visit: Donan Books, Inc., 253 E. 53rd St., New York 10022. Gotham Book Mart, 41 W. 47 St., New York 10036. Strand Book Store, 828 Broadway, New York 10003.

Last resort: Contact a book finder. Most of these services do not charge a search fee, but make their profit through the markup on books they do locate and place. Fees can run $5 per book. Most services will quote you the price of a book they have located before they buy it for you. Tracking down a book can take four to eight weeks because the book finder will check his bookstore sources and then advertise for your title in *A.B. Bookman's Weekly,* a used-book dealers' exchange paper. Don't approach more than one bookfinder at a time with the same request, because several ads for the same book will jack up its price.

Most book finders deal strictly in hardcover editions or special paperbacks. Some specialize in a particular subject matter. Their ads appear in book review sections of major papers and in other book-related publications. They are listed under *Books, retail* in the Yellow Pages. Their success rate in ferreting out old titles is close to 40%.

WHERE TO BUY HARD-TO-FIND RECORDINGS BY MAIL

• Musical Heritage Society, 14 Park Rd., Tinton Falls, NJ 07724. The best place to buy rare classical recordings.
• Andre Perrault, Old Stone House, 73 E. Allen St., Winooski, VT 05404. Another excellent source for classical music.
• Time-Life Records, 777 Duke St., Alexandria, VA 22314. Selected masters in both the classical and pop fields. Best: A collection of Mozart in 30 boxes and the Giants of Jazz series.
• Smithsonian Recordings, Box 10239, Des Moines, IA 50336. Reconstruction of old musical comedies, vintage jazz and other historical treasures.
• Book-of-the-Month Records, Camp Hill, PA 17012. Everything from great modern classical masters to songs of the Depression taken from old 78-RPM records.

BUYING A PIANO

The best sound comes from a grand piano, but new ones can cost a bundle. A smaller spinet, console, or studio upright will provide satisfactory sound for most people and costs much less. How to test a piano before purchase: Play it by running up and down the scales. High notes should be clean and crisp, low notes should resonate. If considering the purchase of a used piano, look for one ten years old or less. Don't buy one more than 20 years old. Have a piano tuner check out a used piano.

BEST CHOCOLATES IN THE WORLD

The finest chocolates in the world need be no farther than your mailbox. All the chocolatiers listed below ship throughout the US from October through May. (High temperatures are too hard on good chocolates to risk summer shipment.)

• Bissinger's French Confections, 4740 McPherson, 63108, (314) 534-2400. Chocolate-covered mints, chocolate golf balls and other specialites. Free catalog.

• Bloomingdale's Au Chocolat Shop, 1000 Third Ave., New York 10021, (212) 705-3177. Noteworthy selections include: Michel Guerard's low-calorie Nouveau Chocolat, slender chocolate leaves (14 leaves per ounce) with less sugar and more cocoa. Gaston Le Notre's delicate French caramels, pralines and fruit creams. Adrienne's assorted truffles of caramel with praline crunch, orange peel and coffee, among others. No catalog.

• Andre Bollier, Ltd. 5018 Main St., Kansas City, MO 64112, (816) 561-3440. Bold and rich Swiss-type chocolates. Catalog: price refundable with the first purchase.

• Chocolaterie Corne de la Toison d'Or, Trump Tower, New York 10022, (212) 308-4060. Elegant assortment of Belgian chocolates with butter cream and liquor-flavored fillings. Free catalog.

• Delittante Chocolates, 2300 E. Cherry St., Seattle, WA 98122, (206) 328-1530. Hand-dipped light or dark chocolates, truffles, marzipan and French butter creams. Free catalog.

• Edelweiss Chocolates, 444 North Canyon Dr., Beverly Hills, CA 90210, (213) 275-0341. Liquored truffles and brandied cherries. Free catalog.

• See's Candy Shops, 210 El Camino Real, San Francisco, CA 94082, (415) 761-2490. Old-fashioned fudge.

• Teuscher Chocolates of Switzerland, 620 Fifth Ave., New York 10020, (212) 751-8482. The newest chocolates are called rusty tools (for their shapes). They are dusted with cocoa. The champagne truffles are justly popular. Free brochure.

BEST TIME TO DRINK CHAMPAGNE

Vintage champagne should be drunk shortly after purchase. It will not improve with age, and it will deteriorate with prolonged refrigeration. For proper chilling: Use an ice bucket with ice and a little bit of water.
Source: *The Wine Spectator.*

EASY-OPENING CHAMPAGNE

Opening champagne is easier if the bottle is chilled in a bucket of ice rather than in a refrigerator. If the neck of the bottle gets too cold, the cork won't come out. Then you lose the satisfying, dramatic effect of a forceful cork-popping.
Source: *Successful Meetings.*

THE SIX BEST CHAMPAGNES

• Taittinger Comtes de Champagne—vintage only. A rose champagne that should go far to overcome Americans' prejudice towards this celestial brew. Taittinger also makes a fine blanc de blancs, and a nonvintage brut.

• Dom Perignon—vintage only. Probably the most widely acclaimed champagne and deservedly so. Elegant and light, with delicate bubbles. The producer also makes, under its Moet et Chandon name, a vintage rose champagne, a vintage champagne, and a nonvintage champagne, and a nonvintage brut.

• Perrier-Jouet Fleur de Champagne—vintage only. This house produces champagne of the highest quality in a particularly popular style. The wine is austere, yet tasteful. It is also extremely dry without being harsh or acidic. Perrier Jouet is introducing a rose champagne.

• Louis Roederer Cristal—vintage only. Cristal's magic lies in its plays with opposites: Elegant yet robust, rich taste without weightiness. Roederer also produces a sparkling rose, a vintage champagne, a nonvintage brut.

• Bollinger Vieilles Vignes—vintage only. This is the rarest of all fancy champagnes. Its vines have existed since before phylloxera (a plant louse) killed most French grapevines in the middle 1800s. The wine is robust and rich flavored. Bollinger also makes a vintage champagne, and a nonvintage brut.

• Dom Ruinart Blanc de Blancs—vintage only. Produced by Dom Perignon in Reims rather than in Epernay, it is a sleeper. It is held in low profile so as not to compete strongly with its illustrious coproduct, but is every bit as good. The wine is light (not thin), complex, very alive, yet velvety.

Source: Jack Lange, veteran of the wine business and vice president of 67 Wines and Spirits, New York.

BEST BUYS IN WHITE ZINFANDEL

Popular new wine: California's "white" Zinfandels. They are pink and semisweet, but still crisp and refreshing. Best buys: Belvedere White Zinfandel California Wine Discovery Series 1984; Buehler White Zinfandel Napa Valley 1984; Grand Cru White Zinfandel California Vin Maison 1984.

Source: The Wine Spectator.

GREATEST WHITE WINE

Alsatian white wines are among the greatest in the world, yet strangely go underappreciated,

says The Wine Advocate editor Robert M. Parker, Jr. Dry, rich and full-bodied, they are closer to white Burgundies than to German Reislings. Great bargains include the Domaine Weinbach Reserve Pinot Blanc and the F.E. Trimbach Pinot Gris (both $5.99).

Source: Connoisseur.

BEST JUG WINES

Jug wines, the inexpensive table blends that come in 1.5- or 3-liter bottles, are proliferating so fast that only an expert can keep abreast of good new choices. Ask your local wine merchant for recommendations. Or sample the house wines in your favorite restaurants and ask what the brand is when you find one you particularly like. (You still may miss some of the best!)

To deal with this problem, a panel of wine aficionados recently held a blind tasting of more than 200 jug wines at the International Wine Center in New York, rating the following 17 white wines and 15 reds as superior.

Whites:
• Alexis Lichine White Table Wine of France.
• Almaden Mountain Chablis.
• Boucheron Blanc de Blancs.
• Concha y Toro Sauvignon Blanc/Semillon 1981.
• Cuvee Saint Pierre Blanc.
• Della Scalla Soave.
• L'Epayrie Blanc de Blancs.
• Gallo Chablis Blanc.
• Gallo Sauvignon Blanc.
• Klosterkeller Siegendorf Gruner Veltliner 1980.
• Los Hermanos Chablis.
• Parducci Vintage White 1980.
• Paul Masson Chablis.
• Petternella Soave.
• Sebastiani Mountain Chablis.
• Sommeliere Blanc de Blancs.
• Villa Carasol Blanco Fino.

Reds:
• Beaudet Rouge.
• Concannon Burgundy 1979.
• Cuvee Saint Pierre Rouge.

- L'Epayrie Rouge.
- Jean Boulaine Cuvee Rouge.
- Louis Martini Burgundy.
- Monterey Vineyard Classic Red 1979.
- Moreau Rouge
- Parducci Vintage Red 1978.
- Partager Vin Rouge.
- Robert Mondavi Red 1980.
- San Martin Burgundy 1977.
- Sebastiani Country Cabernet.
- Sebastiani Mountain Burgundy.
- Villa Banfi Roman Red.

Wine is perishable. Once a jug is opened, its contents should be stored in the refrigerator. If the remainder won't be consumed within a few days, decant it into a smaller bottle to preserve the flavor. (Oxidation in a half-full container destroys the quality.)

BEST CORKSCREW

Waiter's corkscrew is 25% longer than the traditional model, resulting in greater leverage. White or black nickel finish.

Source: Delvan Co., Providence, RI.

BEST AMERICAN BEERS

The quality of beers varies almost as widely as the quality of wine...but the difference in price between the worst and the best is far narrower. Unlike wine, beer can be judged visually. Like wine, taste is the ultimate test.

How to tell a fine beer by sight: Use a tulip-shaped glass or a large brandy snifter. The beer should be at about 50° (a bit warmer than refrigerator temperature). Pour it straight down the center of the glass. Side pouring is necessary only if the beer has been jostled or insufficiently chilled. Now look for the three visual signs of excellence:

(1) Small bubbles that continue to rise for several minutes.

(2) A dense head, one and one-half to two inches high, that lasts.

(3) No trace of cloudiness.

After drinking, look for the clear "Brussels lace" tracery that should remain on the inside of the glass.

Best American regular beers:
- Anchor Steam Beer (San Francisco).
- New Amsterdam Amber Beer (New York City).

Best dark beers:
- Prior Double Dark Beer.
- Sierra Nevada Porter.
- Sierra Nevada Stout.

Best beers to go with meals:
- Kronenbourg (from France).
- Kirin (from Japan).

To buy and store beer:
- Be sure the bottles are filled to within one and one-half inches of the top.
- Buy bottles instead of cans. Avoid twist-cap bottles, if possible.
- Try to buy refrigerated beer that has not been exposed to fluorescent light.
- Store bottles upright at 40°-50°. Avoid agitating the bottles in transit or in storage. (For example, do not put them on the door shelves of a refrigerator.)
- Do not store beer for long periods.
- Do not quick-chill beer in the freezer.

Source: *The Gourmet Guide to Beer* by Howard Hillman, Pocket Books, New York.

BEST SPARKLING WATER

Connoisseurship apparently knows no limits. Many people who used to ask for whiskey by the brand do the same with sparkling water. Some may even distinguish among flavors, but not if ice cubes and limes are used. Differences are hard to spot, even when the waters are downed neat, but they do exist as the chart indicates. Brands of club soda and carbonated mineral water are ranked by preference and rated as follows: Four boxes, *excellent;* three, *very good;* two, *good;* one, *fair;* zero, *must suit tastes other than mine.*

☐☐☐☐ **San Pellegrino,** Italy: A real charmer with a lively, gentle fizz. Clear, springlike flavor is balanced and sprightly.

☐☐☐ **Saratoga,** US: There's a bracing lilt to the soft fizz. The clear, neutral flavor has a slightly dry, citric pungency.

☐☐☐ **Perrier,** France: Dependably neutral

SMART CONSUMER'S GUIDE / 233

when cold, but a mineral taste develops. Overly strong fizz softens quickly.

□□□ **White Rock,** US: Moderately strong fizz. Sunny lemon flavor is pleasantly astringent, if a bit distracting.

□□ **Poland Spring,** US: Fizz is a bit overpowering. Generally acceptable flavor with some citric-sodium aftertaste.

□□ **Canada Dry,** US: Despite an overly strong fizz, this has a fairly neutral flavor with mild saline-citric accents.

□ **Apollinaris,** West Germany: Strong, needling fizz and a warm, heavy mineral flavor that suggests bicarbonate of soda.

□ **Calistoga,** US: After the gently soft fizz, it's all downhill. Musty, earthy flavor has salt-sodium overtones.

Seagram's, US: Sugar-water sweetness is a real shocker. Citric bitterness develops later. Moderate fizz.

Schweppes, US: A prevailing citric-saline bitterness makes this dry in the mouth. Fizz is extremely strong.

Source: *Time.*

HOW TO SELECT A CIGAR

Fondle it from tip to tip. It should feel supple and soft, never hard. Avoid: Cigars that have wrapper leaves with lumps or veins. Shop only at a tobacconist's store. Favored: Unwrapped cigars that have been kept under perfect storage conditions. They have better flavor than cigars sold in metal or plastic tubes.

MILDEST SOAPS

If your skin feels dry and taut, it may be due to the harshness of the soap you're using. A number of popular soaps were rated on a scale of zero to ten. Those below a rating of one are mildest, and those above five are harsh: Dove, .5. Dial, 2.4. Neutrogena, 2.8. Ivory, 2.8. Jergens, 3.3. Irish Spring, 4.0. Zest, 6.1. Camay, 6.4.

Source: Dr. Albert Kligman, professor of dermatology, University of Pennsylvania.

EXPENSIVE SOAPS ARE WORTH THE MONEY

Luxury soaps may be worth the extra money. They contain more ingredients then normal soap to soothe skin problems while they clean. Luxury soaps come in many different shapes, sizes and scents. Prices. $3–19/bar.

HOW TO SELECT A PHONOGRAPH CARTRIDGE

Better sound doesn't necessarily come from more expensive phonograph cartridges. Despite claims of manufacturers, different types in the moderate price range ($55–125) perform similarly. Some have different audio characteristics, but none is clearly superior to the others.

Source: Hans Fantel, author of *Better Listening,* writing in *Diversion.*

STEREO SECRETS

• Record player adjustments. When the pickup arm skips across a record: First be sure the stylus is not turned to 78 RPM. This could cause skipping. Then hold the stylus under a magnifying glass to see if the point is worn, rounded or broken off. To remove the needle for replacement, hold the pickup arm as high as possible. Lift the clip, and the stylus will slide out. (Some units have a screw holding the stylus in place. Or the whole cartridge assembly may have to be removed.) If the sound is mushy or weak, the cartridge may be defective. Remove the cartridge by loosening the mounting screws or by prying it from its clips. Make a note of where each color-coded wire goes (red and green are usually on one side and black and white on the other). This makes installing the new cartridge less complicated.

Source: *The Illustrated Home Electronics Fix-It Book* by Homer L. Davidson, Tab Books, Blue Ridge Summit, PA.

• Your stereo needle needs regular cleaning to prevent sound distortion caused by dust buildup and to reduce the wear on the needle. How to do it: First moisten a needle brush with stylus cleaner (both available in stereo stores). Start cleaning around the base of the needle, and work your way up to the needle itself. Repeat the process to get all the debris.

• To withdraw a phonograph record from its cover, bow open the album by pressing it between an extended hand and your body. Grasp a corner of the inner sleeve to pull out the disk. Try not to squeeze the sleeve against the record. This presses dust caught on the record into the grooves.

• Soiled stereo records can be cleaned with soap and water as a last resort. Normally, conventional cleaning techniques should keep records clean and dust-free. If a record is so dirty that these methods don't work, however, consider giving it a bath. Procedure: Fill two plastic wash basins with about three inches of water. To one, add a drop of liquid detergent. Then dip the record into the soapy water (using a dowel inserted through the spindle hole for support) and rub it gently with a soft brush or sponge. Then rinse the record in the second basin and set it aside to dry.

Source: *High Fidelity.*

BEST EARPHONES FOR PERSONAL STEREO

Although almost all personal portable stereos come with a set of earphones, most such earphones are cheaply made and incapable of transmitting the stereo's sound quality to its full potential. A good pair of earphones boosts the sound quality enough to justify its cost.

Favorites:
• The Koss PortaPro. Very good sound and exceptionally comfortable.
• Sennheiser HD414.
• Signet TK20.
• Audio-Technica ATH Point 6. Snap on the "hear muff" option for winter wear.

Recommended: The foam-earpiece models

with a band that crosses your head. These foam earpieces are like miniature versions of regular stereo headphones. They are more comfortable and sound better than in-the-ear systems.

Source: David Drucker, editor of *Audio/Video Buyer's Guide for 1985,* Harris Publications, Inc., New York.

CARE OF VIDEOTAPES

Do not rewind videotapes after use. Wait until just before playing them the next time. This flexes the tape and sweeps away any lingering humidity.

• Store tapes in their boxes to keep dust and dirt from reaching them.
• Never touch the tape itself. Oil and acid from the fingers do damage. Also, cigarette smoke blown on the tapes does them no good.
• Avoid abrupt changes in temperature. When bringing a tape into a heated room from the cold outside, allow half an hour for the tape to adjust to the change before playing it.
• Never keep a tape in pause or still frame for more than a minute. The video heads moving back and forth will wear down that section of tape.

BEST VCR HEAD CLEANER

VCR recording heads can wear out after as little as 1,000 hours of use. Major enemies: Humidity, dust and cigarette-smoke particles. To avoid premature replacement of heads (at a cost of up to $200), use a wet-cleaning cassette after every 30 hours of use. Recommended: The system by Koss, which uses a fresh ribbon for each cleaning.

Source: Hans Fantel, writing in *The New York Times.*

HOW TO BUY BLANK VIDEOTAPES

When buying blank videotapes, you should stick to brands put out by well-known tape or electronic-equipment manufacturers. Bargain or no-name brands are likely to flake their oxide coating and gum up your player's head, an expensive component to fix. Save money by buying standard grade tape for recording shows you want to see just once. For archival storage of favorite movies or special events, invest in high-grade tape. It gives the sharpest image, best color and finest sound without jeopardizing your videocassette recorder.

BEST BLANK VIDEOTAPES

The best blank videotapes for all-around performance: Fuji's H451 Super XG, TDK's HD-Pro, and Maxell's HGX Gold. Best budget-priced tape: Scotch Standard Grade.
Source: Survey by *Video*.

WHAT VIDEOTAPE RENTAL CLUBS DON'T TELL YOU

Video rental clubs may not be the bargain they seem. Some stores offer comparably low daily rentals on cassettes without membership fees. Costly catch: The "lifetime membership," which lasts only as long as the club stays in business.

HOW TO STRAIGHTEN OUT A WARPED VIDEODISC

A warped videodisc can cause annoying "crosstalk"—a vertical bar of squiggly lines moving horizontally across the screen. Testing the warp: Place the disc on a flat surface. Then lay a nickel underneath the curved part. If the warpage exceeds the thickness of the coin, you have a problem. Treatment: Place the warped disc between two firm, flat surfaces, such as heavy plywood or glass. Load the top surface evenly with heavy weights (a few old telephone directories will do). The disc will be playable in a day or so.
Source: *Video*.

BEST SATELLITE DISH ANTENNAS

Despite the protests of some cable companies, the 1.5 million Americans who pull in their television programs with backyard earth stations (the huge Frisbee-shaped dishes that receive satellite signals) are not necessarily thieves. The issue of satellite viewing rights was settled by the passage of a federal law that says:

• It is legal to manufacture, market and use earth stations.

• Dish users are required to pay a reasonable fee to a program's owner only if the owner has provided a mechanism to receive payment from private earth station users.

• Private users in violation of the law face a maximum fine of $1,000 and six months in prison. The penalties for commercial offenders are substantially higher.

What does this mean for the private user? In effect, very little. It is virtually impossible for program owners to prove that they have been ripped off. As a result, HBO and Showtime will probably soon begin scrambling their signals. Dish owners, however, will still have free access to the many advertising-supported satellite channels whose desire for larger audiences deters them from scrambling.

The dish is a signal reflector that intercepts satellite signals and focuses them to a feed horn. Signals are then amplifed, converted and processed for your TV by a satellite receiver.

When shopping, consider:

• Type of construction. Dishes are either one piece or petalized (made up of several sections) and are solid or metal mesh. A petalized dish is easier to transport but more difficult to put together. Most dishes are made of aluminum, stainless steel or fiberglass. Although there is still no consensus, many find fiberglass dishes to be the best performers and the most durable.

• Size: The larger the dish, the more the

signal it picks up is enhanced. Larger dishes are also better able to pick up signals from one satellite while rejecting those of others, giving you stronger reception. You can tune your dish in to a single satellite or—using a remote-control device that costs between $100 and $1,000—rotate the dish to catch signals from other satellites as well.

What's available: There are about 200 manufacturers of dishes in the US. Prices range from under $900 to $6,500, about 25% less than five years ago. Price differences generally reflect the size, quality and durability of the dish. A six- or eight-foot dish might be more than adequate in the center of the country, where satellite signals are strongest, but you might need an eight- or 10-foot dish in the South or on either of the coasts. In some extreme locations a larger antenna may be required.

Although manufacturers have established suggested retail prices, competition in many areas has led to discounting. Shop around, but be skeptical. It is a young industry, and you may get better value and service if you buy from a company that has been in business for a while (Bowman Industries, Winegard or Channel Master, for example).

Once you have chosen a manufacturer, determining exactly what you need should be fairly easy. Many dealers have mobile systems that can be tested at your home before you buy. You can save $400-$700 in installation costs if you are handy enough to put in your dish yourself (mounted on a pole cemented in the ground).

The payoff: The 17 satellites orbiting the earth provide 120 channels of video programs, and a single dish can be turned to pick up programs from several satellites. For people in remote areas of the country, where commercial signals are weakest and cable is scarce, dishes offer a welcome assortment of programming from many sources: Commercial stations, cable networks, public television and even business news services.

Source: Fritz Attaway, vice president and counsel, Motion Picture Association of America, Washington, DC; Glenn Martin, manager of technical services, Channel Master, Smithfield, NC; Jerry Poyser, product evaluation manager, Comm-Tek Publishing, Hailey, ID.

HOW TO BUY A USED CAMERA WITHOUT GETTING STUNG

• Ask for a 90-day repair warranty (never less than 30 days) and a 10-day, no-risk trial period. Use the 10 days to shoot several rolls of slide film at different combinations of shutter speeds, f-stops and lighting conditions. The enlarged, projected slides will reveal whether any features are defective.

• Unneeded camera attachments: A motor drive is usually a waste of money unless you take a lot of sports or fashion pictures. Zoom lenses are good only for sports events. Their many glass elements tend to produce glare and internal reflections. Good substitute: A 250 mm telephoto that does not zoom.

BEST BINOCULARS

The consensus favorite is the West German Zeiss Dialyt 8x30B. Besides providing unmatched clarity, they're comfortable, lightweight (21.2 ounces) and compact. They also permit full-field viewing for eyeglasses wearers. Cost: About $550 at a typical discount.
Source: *Money* magazine.

ELECTRICAL APPLIANCES: REPAIR VS. REPLACE

Repairing electrical appliances is seldom worthwhile if the repair cost is more than one-third of the original price. Consider replacing the appliance with a new one under warranty. Many appliance repair shops give free estimates of repairs.

BEST CLOCK RADIO

The Proton Model 320, according to *The New York Times*'s Hans Fantel. The sound is pleasantly balanced, with separate treble and bass controls. Added features: Gentle wake-up with gradually rising volume. Capacity for two separate wake-up times.

BEST FIRE EXTINGUISHERS

Look for an extinguisher rated ABC to fight the three most common household fires. Class A fires involve paper, wood, cloth. Class B: Flammable liquids and gases. Class C: Electrical equipment. Choose the most powerful unit you can easily carry and use. Power categories: Range from 1 (low) to 10, indicating what size fire the unit can fight. Recommended: An all-purpose ABC unit having a minimum power rating of 2-A:10-B:C.

RETURNING DAMAGED GOODS

If damage is obvious, write "refused" on the unopened package, and send it back. If damage is discovered after you open the package, repack it, explain the problem in an accompanying letter and send it back by certified or insured mail.

YOUR RIGHTS WHEN YOU BUY AS IS

Buying "as is" doesn't mean the buyer has no rights at all. "As is" clauses relate to quality, not to general class or description. Example: If the buyer contracts to buy boxes of bolts as is, sight unseen, he won't be obligated if the boxes turn out to contain screws, not bolts. Also, "as is" clauses don't override express warranties. They don't bar claims for fraud or misrepresentation. And they don't stop tort claims (personal injury actions if someone's injured by a defective product).

Source: Dr. Russell Decker, professor emeritus of legal studies, Bowling Green State University, Bowling Green, OH.

HOW TO COMPLAIN EFFECTIVELY

Americans are not great defenders of their consumer rights. Two-thirds of the respondents in a major survey admitted to living with shoddy goods, incompetent services and broken promises. Only one-third of them had asked for redress.

People should complain. More than half of all consumer complaints result in some sort of satisfaction. (The psychological lift that comes with filing a protest is an added bonus.)

People don't complain because they think it won't do any good. But there are effective ways to complain an get results:

• Have your facts straight before you act. Be clear about dates, prices, payments and the exact nature of the problem.
• Be specific about what you want done—repair, replacement or refund.
• Give reasonable deadlines for action you expect to be taken: A week for store personnel to look into a problem, for example. Deadlines move the action along.
• Send copies of receipts. Keep the originals for your records. File copies of all correspondence and notes (with dates) on any telephone dealings. Those records may be the pivotal factor if negotiations are prolonged or you must take your complaint elsewhere.
• Be businesslike in your attitude and project an expectation of a businesslike response.
• Find out where you can go if the seller fails to make good, and indicate your intention to follow through. Government agencies, such as a state attorney general's office, may need the very kind of evidence that your case provides to move against chronic offenders. Licensing boards or regulatory bodies are good bets for complaints against banks, insurance companies or professionals.

Additional recourse:
• Consumer action centers sponsored by local newspapers and radio and television stations often get swift results.
• Small claims court. If you can put a monetary value on your loss, you may get a judgment by suing in small claims court. Collecting can be a problem (you must take the initiative yourself), but the law is on your side and the psychological benefits are enormous.
• Trade associations can be effective with their

member organizations but not with outside companies.

Protect yourself before making large purchases or contracting for expensive services by dealing with reputable sellers. Companies that have been in business a long time have a vested interest in keeping their customers happy. Think about what recourse you will have if something does go wrong. A company with only a post office address, for example, will be impossible to trace.

Source: Nancy Kramer, co-author with Stephen A. Newman of *Getting What You Deserve: A Handbook for the Assertive Consumer,* Doubleday, New York.

WHAT GOES ON SALE WHEN

A month-by-month schedule for dedicated bargain hunters:

January:
- After-Christmas sales.
- Appliances.
- Baby carriages.
- Books.
- Carpets and rugs.
- China and glassware.
- Christmas cards.
- Costume jewelry.
- Furniture.
- Furs.
- Lingerie.
- Men's overcoats.
- Pocketbooks.
- Preinventory sales.
- Shoes.
- Toys.
- White goods (sheets, towels, etc).
  February:
- Air conditioners.
- Art supplies.
- Bedding.
- Cars (used).
- Curtains.
- Furniture.
- Glassware and china.
- Housewares.

- Lamps.
- Men's apparel.
- Radios, TV sets and phonographs.
- Silverware.
- Sportswear and equipment.
- Storm windows.
- Toys.
  March:
- Boys' and girls' shoes.
- Garden supplies.
- Housewares.
- Ice skates.
- Infants' clothing.
- Laundry equipment.
- Luggage.
- Ski equipment.
  April:
- Fabrics.
- Hosiery.
- Lingerie.
- Painting Supplies.
- Women's shoes.
  May:
- Handbags.
- Housecoats.
- Household linens.
- Jewelry.
- Luggage.
- Mothers' Day specials.
- Outdoor furniture.
- Rugs.
- Shoes.
- Sportswear.
- Tires and auto accessories.
- TV sets.
  June:
- Bedding.
- Boys' clothing.
- Fabrics.
- Fathers' Day specials.
- Floor coverings.
- Lingerie, sleepwear and hosiery.
- Men's clothing.
- Women's shoes.
  July:
- Air conditioners and other appliances.
- Bathing suits.

- Children's clothes.
- Electronic equipment.
- Fuel.
- Furniture.
- Handbags.
- Lingerie and sleepwear.
- Luggage.
- Men's shirts.
- Men's shoes.
- Rugs.
- Sportswear.
- Summer clothes.
- Summer sports equipment.
  August:
- Back-to-school specials.
- Bathing suits.
- Carpeting.
- Cosmetics.
- Curtains and drapes.
- Electric fans and air conditioners.
- Furniture.
- Furs.
- Men's coats.
- Silver.
- Tires.
- White Goods.
- Women's coats.
  September:
- Bicycles.
- Cars (outgoing models).
- China and glassware.
- Fabrics.
- Fall fashions.
- Garden equipment.
- Hardware.
- Lamps.
- Paints.
  October:
- Cars (outgoing models).
- China and glassware.
- Fall/winter clothing.
- Fishing equipment.
- Furniture.
- Lingerie and hosiery.
- Major appliances.
- School supplies.
- Silver.

- Storewide clearances.
- Women's coats.
  November:
- Blankets and quilts.
- Boys' suits and coats.
- Cars (used).
- Lingerie.
- Major appliances
- Men's suits and coats.
- Shoes.
- White goods.
- Winter clothing.
  December:
- After-Christmas cards, gifts, toys.
- Blankets and quilts.
- Cars (used).
- Children's clothes.
- Christmas promotions.
- Coats and hats.
- Men's furnishings.
- Resort and cruise wear.
- Shoes.

A SHOPPER'S GUIDE TO BARGAINING

The biggest problem most shoppers have with bargaining is a feeling that nice people don't do it. Before you can negotiate, you have to get over this attitude. Some ammunition:

- Bargaining will not turn you into a social outcast. All a shopkeeper sees when you walk in is dollar signs. If you are willing to spend, he will probably be willing to make a deal. He knows that everybody is trying to save money these days.
- Bargaining is a business transaction. You are not trying to cheat the merchant or get something for nothing. You are trying to agree on a fair price. You expect to negotiate for a house or a car—why not for a refrigerator or a winter coat?
- You have a right to bargain, particularly in small stores that don't discount. Reasoning: Department stores, which won't bargain as a rule, mark up prices 100%–150% to cover high overhead costs. Small stores should

charge lower prices because their costs are less.

The savvy approach. Set yourself a price limit for a particular item before you approach the storekeeper. Be prepared to walk out if he doesn't meet your limit. (You can always change your mind later.) Make him believe you really won't buy unless he comes down.

Be discreet in your negotiations. If other customers can overhear your dickering, the shop owner must stay firm.

Be respectful of the merchandise and the storekeeper. Don't manhandle the goods that you inspect. Address the salesperson in a polite, friendly manner. Assume that he will want to do his best for you because he is such a nice, helpful person.

Shop at off hours. You will have more luck if business is slow.

Look for unmarked merchandise. If there is no price tag, you are invited to bargain.

Tactics that work:

• Negotiate with cash. In a store that takes credit cards, request a discount for paying in cash. (Charging entails overhead costs that the store must absorb.)

• Buy in quantity. A customer who is committed to a number of purchases has more bargaining power. When everything is picked out, approach the owner and suggest a total price about 20% less than the actual total. Variation: If you are buying more than one of an item, offer to pay full price on the first one if the owner will give you a break on the others. Storekeeper's alternative: you spent $500 on clothing and asked for a better price. The owner said he couldn't charge you less, but he threw in a belt priced at $35 as a bonus.

• Look for flawed merchandise. This is the only acceptable bargaining point in department stores, but it also can save you money in small shops. If there's a spot, a split seam or a missing button, estimate what it would cost to have the garment fixed commercially, and ask for a discount based on that figure. Variations: You find a chipped hairdryer. When you ask for a discount, the manager says he will return it to the manufacturer and find you an undamaged one. Your reply: ''Sell it to me for a little less and save yourself the trouble.''

• Adapt your haggling to the realities of the situation. A true discount house has a low profit margin and depends on volume to make its money. Don't ask for more than 5% off in such a store. A boutique that charges what the traffic will bear has more leeway. Start by asking for 25% off, and dicker from there.

• Buy at the end of the season, when new stock is being put out. Offer to buy older goods—at a discount.

• Neighborhood stores: Push the local television or appliance dealer to give you a break so you can keep your service business in the community.

Source: Sharon Dunn Greene, co-author of *The Lower East Side Shopping Guide,* Brooklyn, NY.

HATE SHOPPING?

Most big stores have employees who'll do your shopping for you. You don't even have to be there. Call the store and ask for the personal shopper. Stores that specialize in personal shopping: Bloomingdale's and Saks Fifth Avenue in New York. Woodward & Lothrop in Washington, D.C. Marshall Field in Chicago. I. Magnin in San Francisco.

BUYING FROM DOOR-TO-DOOR SALESPEOPLE

Impulse buys made from door-to-door salespeople or at houseware parties need not be binding. Under Federal Trade Commission rules, you have three business days to reconsider at-home purchases of $25 or more.

Recommended procedure. At time of purchase, always ask for two copies of a dated cancellation form that shows date of sale and a dated contract with the seller's name and address. The contract should specify your right to cancel. Note: If you have received no forms, contact the nearest office for advice within three business days.

To cancel. Sign and date one copy of the cancellation form, and keep the second copy. Hint: As insurance, send the cancellation by registered mail (receipt requested).

Sellers have 10 days to act. Their obligations: To return any signed papers, down payment and trade-in. To arrange for pickup or shipping of any goods. (Sellers pay shipping.) Pickup must be made within 20 days of your dated cancellation notice.

Reminder about picking up merchandise. You must make it available. If no pickup is made within the 20 days, the goods are yours. If you agree to ship the goods back and then fail to do so, or if you fail to make the goods available for pickup, you may be held to the original contract.

Note: The same rules apply at a hotel, restaurant or any other location off the seller's normal business premises. They do not apply to sales by mail or phone, or sales of real estate, insurance, securities or emergency home repairs.

BARGAINING WITH A MAIL-ORDER FIRM

Discounts from mail-order firms are often possible. How: Wait for the catalog to be out for three months or so. Then phone and ask if the company will give you a 25% discount off the item you want. Many won't, but some that are trying to get rid of unsold merchandise will welcome the opportunity.

Source: Sue Goldstein, author of *Underground Shopper,* SusAnn Publications, Dallas.

HOW TO AVOID JUNK MAIL

To avoid much of today's advertising mail, get in touch with the Direct Marketing Association, 6 E. 43 St., New York 10017. DMA's Mail Preference Service (including over 500 major national mailing houses) can get your name off many computerized mailing lists.

HOW TO AVOID LINES AND BEAT CROWDS

If time is scarcer than money for you, you might be willing to pay to add the equivalent of a 25th hour to your day.

Suppose your local museum offers free ad-mission from, say, 6 p.m. to 8 p.m. one evening a week. I can guarantee that you'll have the museum to yourself if you go from 5 p.m. to 6 p.m. that night. Everyone else will be waiting for the stroke of 6.

Similarly, if your watering hole reduces the price of drinks during its Happy Hour from 5 p.m. to 7 p.m., go after 7. (Unless, of course, you hope to meet someone, in which case you'll want to be there when it's most crowded.)

If you hate waiting in line, simply learn when places are least crowded and go then. Some suggestions:

• Movies are semideserted on Mondays, since most people go out over the weekend. If it's a really hot film, the showing immediately after work is less likely to be crowded than the 8 p.m. or 10 p.m. show.
• Bakeries are also almost empty on Mondays. (People start their diets promptly Monday morning and forget them by Tuesday morning.)
• Banks are least busy before payday. So go Thursdays, if Fridays are payday where you live, or on the 14th and 29th if paydays fall on the 15th and 30th.
• Post offices aren't crowded on Thursday afternoons.
• Supermarkets have long lines fifteen minutes before closing time but no lines fifteen minutes after opening.

If you're unsure as to when your health club, swimming pool, laundromat or barber shop is least crowded, just ask the manager.

Learn which days you have two opportunities to do something rather than one. Example: If your favorite restaurant offers two dinner seatings some evenings and only one on others, your best bet is to aim for a two-seating night. Similarly, you're more likely to get into an evening theater performance on a day when there's also a matinee.

Another trick is to reverse the logical sequence of things. Almost everyone buys tokens or commuter passes before boarding the train. If, instead, you line up as you exit, you'll be on your way in no time. Take some deposit tickets or air-shuttle forms with you when you leave the bank or airport. Fill them out at your convenience. Take them with you when you need them instead of struggling to complete them as you stand in line.

To minimize wasted telephone time, make your next appointment as you leave your dentist or doctor's office. Make your next reservation as you leave a restaurant. You can do the same thing with your lunch companion or golf cronies, as well.

If you hate being placed on "hold," call before 9 or after 5. This is an old journalists' trick that almost guarantees that you won't be intercepted by a protective secretary. Learn the numbers of people's private lines and their "hotlines." You can quietly copy these down when you're in the office, or you can ask. Most travel agents, for instance, know numbers the public doesn't know for reaching airlines and hotels. If all else fails, invest in a speaker phone. That way, at least, you can continue working while you hang on "hold."

Source: Dr. Marilyn Machlowitz, a New York-based organizational psychologist and consultant, and author of *Workaholics: Living With Them: Working With Them,* New American Library, New York.

HOW TO GET A BARGAIN AT A POSTAL SERVICE AUCTION

A US Postal Service auction is an exciting combination of Las Vegas and a flea market— you gamble for bargains and come out a winner or loser, depending on the effectiveness of your strategy. In the meantime, you've had lots of fun, and you just may pick up the buy of a lifetime.

The Postal Service holds regular auctions of lost, damaged or undeliverable merchandise every two or four months in all major US cities. (The New York City Postal Service has an auction once a month.) Call the main post office in your city for time and date.

The kind of merchandise available ranges from jeans and oriental furniture to bottles of dishwashing detergent and microcomputers. In fact, anything that can be sent through the mail might turn up at a post office auction. Items typically available: Stereo equipment, TVs, radios, dishes, pots and pans, tools, typewriters, clothing, books, coins.

How it works:

• Items are sold by "lot." Similar articles are often grouped together, such as a dozen jeans, or four typewriters, or three radios. The items must be purchased together. Suggestion: Bring friends who might want to share a lot with you.

• Lots are displayed the day before the auction. Inspection is not permitted on the day of the sale, and viewing is all that's allowed. Lots are in compartments or bins that are covered with netting. Nothing (except clothing on hangers) can be handled or tested. Suggestion: Many compartments are badly lighted, so bring a flashlight to get a good look.

• All lots are listed by number on a mimeographed sheet given out on the inspection day. They are auctioned off by number, and each has a minimum acceptable bid listed next to it (never less than $10). But the minimum bid is no indication of how much the lot will sell for. Some go for 10 or more times the minimum bid listed.

• All lots are sold "as is." There is no guarantee as to quality or quantity. Despite the disclaimer, the Postal Service is not trying to trick anyone into bidding high for damaged goods. It tries to mark items it recognizes as damaged. Remember: All sales are final.

• You must pay the day before the auction to obtain a paddle for bidding. Each paddle has a number on it, which the auctioneer recognizes as your bidding number. To bid, hold up your paddle until the prices being called by the auctioneer exceed what you are willing to pay. The cost of the paddle will be refunded if you don't buy anything. Otherwise, it is applied to the purchase price.

• You must deposit 50% of the purchase price in cash or certified check 30 minutes after buying a lot. It is desirable to bring several certified checks instead of one big one.

• Merchandise must be picked up a day or two after the auction. You must bring your own container.

The bidding at these auctions is extremely unpredictable and quirky. There is absolutely no way of knowing how much a lot will go for. Some lots are overbid, while others go for the minimum bid, often with no obvious relationship to actual value. Example: At a recent auction, a set of inexpensive plastic dishes went for more than the retail price, while a much more valuable and lovely set of china dishes sold for less than the plastic ones.

Prices seem to depend on who is attending a particular auction and what they are in the market for. Example: In furious bidding at the same auction, a number of dealers bid up a record-album lot to $750. But no one was interested in a number of lots of Reed & Barton silver-plated flatware, which went for the minimum bid of $5 per place setting.

Other sample prices: Sanyo cassette deck: $100. Sansui amplifier: $100. Brother electric typewriter: $120. Oriental jewelry chest (very large and ornate): $85. Hamilton Beach blender and hand mixer: $28. Persian lamb jacket with mink-trimmed sleeves (brand new): $40.

Bidding tips:
• Go through the list of lots carefully while looking at the merchandise, and write down your maximum bids. During the actual auction, bidding is confusingly fast, with prices rapidly increasing by $2 at a time as bidders drop out. Listen carefully to the bidding, and don't exceed your maximum.
• Sit in the back of the room, so you can see who is bidding against you. Why: If you're in the market for a particular item, you'll be aware of how many others are in the same market that day. Also, you can see people drop out of the bidding.
• Take someone knowledgeable to the visual inspection, especially if you're planning to bid on something like electronic equipment. Find out how much that particular piece is worth, and calculate your top bid by including the cost of repair.
• If you can't find someone who is knowledgeable, stick to bidding on lots that you can see are in good shape. Best bets: Dishes, cutlery, pots and pans, hand tools, furniture, clothing sold by the garment (much of the clothing is sold in huge bins and can't be inspected).

GEARING UP FOR AUCTIONS

Depending on the kind of auction (country, indoor) and the type of merchandise sought (bric-a-brac, tools, furniture), assemble the appropriate gear. Suggestions:
• Cash, credit cards or checkbook. (Some auctions accept only cash.)
• Pens, pencils and notebook.
• Pocket calculator.
• Rope for tying items to car roof.
• Old blankets for cushioning.
• Tape measure.
• Magnet (for detecting iron and steel under paint or plating).
• Folding chair and umbrella (if auction is outdoors).
• Picnic lunch (auction food is unpredictable).

HOW TO CHOOSE A LONG-DISTANCE PHONE SERVICE

All these services work essentially the same way. First you dial a local number into the company's computer through a pushbutton telephone (or an adapter). A signal indicates that you have reached the computer. Then you punch in your code number (five to seven digits) and finally the area code and number that you are calling. The computer sends your call via microwave or satellite equipment into the local Bell system where you're calling.

None of the private services is technologically perfect. The systems can and do fail periodically, losing calls or making bad connections. (You will be credited for such mishaps if you keep a record of the time it happened and the number you called.) If you make a mistake in dialing, all the systems allow you to redial without the nuisance of hanging up and starting over.

All the companies charge monthly fees and then offer percentage discounts off Bell rates for different times of the day during the week and for weekends.

Analyze your use of long distance. If there are only a couple of cities that you call frequently and you can make your calls in the evening, look for the company that serves those cities at the lowest rates. When you have found two services that reach your targeted cities during the times you like to call and at competitive prices, check the message-unit cost of your access calls. A number of expensive access calls could run up your regular telephone bill.

What the private telephone services can't do: Cut down the high cost of short-distance calls within a metropolitan area. Example: Calls between suburban Westchester County and Manhattan can eat up as many as five message units for the first three minutes of talk and an extra message unit for each subsequent minute.

CELLULAR PHONES

Expensive cellular phones provide no better connection than cheap ones. Power and broadcast specifications are mandated by the FCC so, for example, you can't get a phone with more power or a longer range. The great disparity in the cost of phone systems (from $500 to $3,000) results from the ignorance of consumers who don't comparison shop or research good buys . . . and the addition of expensive features that are of little value for many. For example, some models let you program in 40 or more speed-dial numbers. But this feature is likely to be of little use in a portable phone unless you can remember all the speed-dial codes.

Source: Harry Newton, publisher, *Inbound/Outbound*, 12 W. 21 St., New York 10010.

TIP-OFFS THAT PHONE BILL IS INCORRECT

Calls listed without a time or with the digits missing (5 pm, instead of 5:00 pm) more often than not have been misbilled.

Source: Alan H. Jordan, telemarketing consultant, Wayne, PA, writing in *The Office*.

HOW TO CHOOSE THE RIGHT CELLULAR PHONE

The new cellular mobile phones have one terrific advantage—they let you make and receive calls from your car as easily as you would from your home. In the near future they'll have even more advantages, but right now there are drawbacks that advertisements and salespeople don't mention. Before you buy a cellular phone, be aware that:

• They're not cheap. The average price for the basic equipment that's installed in your car is around $2,100, and options can cost as much as $3,000 more. The cost of leasing the equipment is $99-$200 a month, often with options to buy at the end of two or three years.

• Phone bills are also expensive because you're billed for incoming as well as outgoing calls. Executives who use their phones while traveling to and from work and occasionally on weekends could count on at least $100 a month in additional phone bills. A salesperson who uses it often throughout the day could easily run up $300-$400 a month in calls. And there's an access charge that typically runs $20 a month.

• Insurance costs may go up because few basic auto policies now cover the theft of cellular phones from cars. Figure on $50 a year per vehicle for additional insurance.

• Cellular phones will be available in only about 50 of the largest urban areas.

• Some equipment is being marketed by companies that may not be in business in the future as the competition gets tougher.

• Cellular phones cut down the chance that a third party can monitor your calls. But they don't eliminate the possibility altogether.

Who needs a cellular phone: Apart from the prestige value, they're useful to people who must keep in touch with clients or co-workers when they're outside the office . . . usually salespeople, service-industry personnel and professionals such as doctors and lawyers. The phone is worth the expense whenever (1) Making calls from your car actually frees you for more productive activities at the office, or (2) You can prove that the calls really result in an increase in company business.

How they work: The equipment that goes in your car consists of an outside antenna, a handset-dialer mounted inside the car and a receiver located in the trunk. When you place a call, it's handled by a network of low-power transmission stations instead of the single station that handles the traditional mobile phone calls. Result: High-quality transmission as you drive along. And since the network can handle many calls simultaneously, you don't have to wait for a free channel, as you did with the old phones.

In the future, there will be cellular phone corridors along major interstate highways so you can make calls as you drive from city to city. Today, you can't make cellular calls outside the urban areas where the transmitters are located. The first corridor that is expected to be in operation is Boston-New York-Philadelphia-Baltimore-Washington.

Also in the future: Cellular phones that are linked to the company's computer system. They'll let you send and receive data on a video display mounted in the car by a voice system.

Here's what to look for today when you buy a cellular phone:

• A speaker-phone model so you can talk without holding the handset, a valuable feature because it lets you keep both hands on the wheel except when you're dialing.

• A system that hooks into the company switchboard. Then office calls can be forwarded directly to you by the switchboard operator.

• An electronic lock that lets you dial a code number to stop calls from being made to or from the phone.

• A switch that enables you to talk on both frequencies that cellular transmitters use in cities when they're available. Phones with only one frequency occasionally lose quality when the car passes through an area where there's interference with the radio waves that carry the conversation.

• A cellular phone manufacturer that's been in existence for several years and isn't known to have financial problems.

Source: Fritz Ringling, communications research, Gartner Group, Stamford, CT.

FINDING AN APARTMENT

Networking, not brokers or real estate ads, turns up the best apartments at the lowest rents. That has been the experience of a New York executive having trouble finding what he wanted through commercial channels. A letter to 25 friends resulted in more viable possibilities in a couple of weeks than contacting newspapers or real estate dealers could have. Caveat: Not all the rentals turned up through friends were legal sublets. The magic words:

Hi, friend. I'm looking for an apartment and thought you might be able to help. This is what I'm looking for:

1. Occupancy: To begin around April 1.
2. Length of lease: One to two years.
3. Size: Large studio or one bedroom.
4. Furnished or unfurnished.
5. Location: Anywhere in Manhattan.
6. Price: Up to $1,000 per month.

If you have any leads for me, I'd be most appreciative. It's my perception that the nicest and most reasonably priced apartments are not seen by brokers. Please write or call me.

Thanks so much.

John Doe

BRINGING IN A FOREIGN HOUSEWORKER

In the "good old days," sponsoring a foreign live-in domestic was just a matter of contacting an employment agency and filling out a few forms. But now, in many parts of the US it is difficult, if not impossible, to bring in an alien as a private housekeeper. The process of obtaining Department of Labor certification and a visa from the Immigration and Naturalization Service can take two years.

In order to get work certification from the Department of Labor, it is necessary to prove that there is no available US citizen or resident alien to fill the job. You also must prove that you are not trying to undercut prevailing wages for that kind of work.

Alternatives: Some employment agencies place legal aliens already here. Others place illegal aliens with families to help get them certified. Individual employers also bring in workers or find illegals in this country. Actually, a number of illegal aliens are already working as domestics in the US. But it is against the law for anyone to work without a Green Card.

The quota system was replaced by a worldwide ceiling of 270,000 permanent immigrants per year, with a maximum of 20,000 visas for each country.

Claude Henry Kleefield, a specialist in immigration law in New York, offers the following advice on how to import a live-in domestic or how to make legal an illegal worker already here. The procedure is the same for either. It's best to work with a lawyer. One mistake can cause delays or a turndown.

Recruitment: The first step after you find a candidate is to put three ads in a general-circulation newspaper to show you tried to hire a citizen or resident alien. You must specify a live-in domestic, since day workers are usually available. Be prepared to show results of the ads.

Work experience: The candidate must have one year's full-time paid employment in this kind of work. Experience must be documented with statements from employers (with a translation if not in English) and income tax returns.

Need: You must show why you need a sleep-in domestic (children, business entertaining at night). An application may be turned down if a day worker could qualify.

Ability to pay: You must prove that you can afford this domestic.

Application: You must specify exactly what the duties are, the wages (average, not minimum wage is required), the daily work schedule, the total hours of employment a week and the amount of money to be advanced by the employer, with terms of repayment. Also: The alien must be free to leave the premises during nonwork hours or may work overtime if paid no less than the legal hourly rate.

Further responsibility of employer: To furnish a free, private room and board. To comply with income tax and Social Security tax regulations. (The employer can put payments in an escrow account until legal status is established if the alien is working without a Green Card.) To give two weeks' notice before firing.

Responsibility of employee: To come with the intention of staying on the job for a year. (But the employee can leave with two weeks' notice.) To execute all the conditions of employment. All aliens without Green Cards in the US must return to their country of origin to get a visa to enter legally. Although the employer usually advances the money for the trip, most employees pay that and legal fees out of wages.

Literacy test: After all papers are approved and the alien is ready to return, he or she must pass an oral and written literacy test in the native language that requires about a third-grade education.

HIRING A PRIVATE DETECTIVE

Times have changed for private detectives. They're no longer breaking down hotel doors to snap incriminating photos for divorce cases.

The modern private eye's bread and butter lies in serving the business world, in both security and personnel matters.

Private detectives are often effective in tracking down runaway children. A missing-persons bureau may have to worry about 30 cases at a time; a private eye can focus and coordinate the leads for a single client, giving the matter undivided attention. Caution: If the detective can't find a hard lead within three days, but is eager to continue, he may be milking the client.

For three hours' work, a detective can devise a home security plan that will satisfy any insurance company, including itemized lists, photographs, locks and alarms.

How to choose one: Before hiring a detective, interview the person for at least 20 minutes to discuss your needs and how they'd be met. Be sure that the detective is licensed and bonded. A bond larger than the minimum bond, might be advisable for a broad investigation covering several states or even a foreign country. To make certain the private eye's record is clean, check with the appropriate state division on licensing (usually the Department of State). And ask the detective for a resume. The best detectives usually have ample experience. The best gauge is frequently word of mouth. Reputations are hard-won in this business.

Source: James Casey, private investigator and former New York City police detective, East Northport, NY.

SUPERMARKET SECRETS

• Most vulnerable time for supermarket overspending is when you set out with an empty cart. Complete your shopping within half an hour. Why: Customers spend 50 cents a minute after they have been in a supermarket longer than 30 minutes.

Source: *The Household Handbook* by Tom Grady and Amy Rood, Meadowbrook Press, Deephaven, MN.

• Generic products are still gaining in popularity, with one out of every three female customers now purchasing at least one generic item per shopping trip. Most popular: Paper goods, canned fruits and vegetables, laundry products and soap, soft drinks, canned soups and canned tuna.

• Don't be taken in by advertisements pushing premium paper towels (those that are extra-strong or super-absorbent). Keep in mind: For most uses (wiping up small spills or drying your hands), the typical supermarket economy brand can probably do the job equally well.

• Bottled carbonated waters are sold everywhere today, each with a different descriptive name. However, each carbonated water fits into one of three categories: (1) Sparkling mineral water is carbonated water from an underground spring. (2) Seltzer is carbonated tap water. (3) Club soda is also carbonated tap water, usually with mineral salts added. Most popular today: Domestic seltzers. They have no added sodium, and they are less expensive than most imported mineral waters. Insight: Price seldom parallels the taste and quality of various brands. Often the least expensive have the cleanest taste.

• When buying fresh garlic, select bulbs with dry, unbroken skins. Avoid garlic that is soft, wrinkled or sprouting. To peel a clove, place it concave side down. Press firmly with your thumb or the flat side of a knife. The skin will slip off. Do not bother peeling before putting a clove in a garlic press. Add salt when chopping or mincing garlic. It keeps the pieces from sticking to the knife.

• Choosing a ripe pineapple. Look for a bright yellow-gold color on the skin, at least around the base. The higher up the yellow color goes, the more even the pineapple's flavor. The surface should be firm and gently yielding to the touch. A leaf pulled easily from the crown does not prove ripeness. Negatives: Wrinkled skin, softness, fermentation aroma, green or reddish-bronze color, leakage, mold, cracks, withered leaves. Quality signs: Well-trimmed butts, single-tuft crowns less than twice the length of the fruit.

• Milk is best when you buy it in cardboard containers, not translucent plastic jugs. Reason: When exposed to fluorescent lighting in the supermarket, milk in jugs oxidizes. It develops a flat taste and loses vitamin C.

Source: *Family Practice News.*

GET RID OF PAIN CHEAPLY

"Inexpensive aspirin works as well as the most expensive brand. So always buy the least expensive." This phrase is heard so often that it is a cliche. Surprise: It happens to be true. Findings of a new study: All brands contain the same amount of aspirin in each tablet. All dissolve at approximately the same rate. Each is absorbed into the bloodstream to start relieving pain in about the same length of time.

COFFEE-LOVER'S GUIDE

Which fruit product is most consumed by Americans? If you answered coffee, you were correct. The coffee "bean" is actually the pit of the round fruit of the coffee tree. (It's called a "cherry" by growers.)

Varieties: Two species account for most of the coffee we drink. Arabica, grown at high altitude and rich in flavor, is the larger crop. Robusta, mostly from Africa, is hardier but thinner in flavor.

Important producers:

• Brazil: The quality ranges from indifferent to good. Best: Bourbon Santos.

• Columbia: Good to superlative coffees.

• Costa Rica: Arabicas, ranging from poor to great. Costa Rican coffees are rated by the hardness of the bean. Trust your coffee merchant to provide strictly hard bean (SHB) or good hard bean (GHB), the mountain-grown best.

• Jamaica: Look for mellow, aromatic Blue Mountain.

• Java: The word java was once the slang for coffee. However, the finest trees were destroyed in World War II and replaced by robusta. Sturdy, rich, heady Indonesian arabica is now very scarce.

• Kenya: All Kenya's crop is arabica—mild, smooth and round.

Roasting: Slightly roasted beans have little taste. Overroasted ones taste burned. Variations in roasting time affect flavor, but there is no right or wrong, just personal preference. Darker roasts are not stronger. The strength of the brew depends on the amount of coffee used.

Some roasting terms:

• Light city roast: Often called cinnamon. Can be thin.

• City roast: The most popular. Makes a tasty brew.

• Full city roast: Beans are dark brown, with no show of oil. Preferred by coffee specialty shops.

• Viennese roast: Somewhere between full city and French roast.

• French roast: The beans are oily, and the color is that of semisweet chocolate. Nearing espresso, but smoother.

• Italian/espresso roast: The beans are oily and almost black. Serious coffee, drunk in small amounts.

• French/Italian roast: Dark and full flavored, but not as bitter as espresso.

Choosing coffee: Most coffees are a blend of two or more varieties. A skillful blender balances his components.

Suggestion: Start with a coffee merchant's house blend. Like house wine, it must please a broad range of tastes and demonstrate the quality of the merchant's offerings. Go on to try many blends. Most merchants sell their coffees in half-pound or even quarter-pound amounts.

Source: Lyn Stallworth, senior editor of *The Pleasures of Cooking* and author of *The Woman's Day Snack Cookbook.*

HOW TO ROAST BEANS IN YOUR OWN OVEN

Coffee beans can be roasted in any ordinary oven. Place the green beans in a perforated pan under the broiler (set at 350° F). Toss them every two minutes. For a light American roast, go for 10 minutes. For a dark Italian roast, figure 20 minutes.
Source: *The Washingtonian.*

BEST PLACE TO STORE COFFEE

For fresher coffee, store it in the freezer. (Frozen beans stay fresh longer than frozen ground.)
Source: *The Washingtonian.*

BEST AND WORST WAYS TO BREW COFFEE

Brewing the perfect cup of coffee. The drip method is best. Worst: Percolating. Reason: Boiling, oil extraction and the long eight-minute filtering cycle produce a bitter product.

HERBAL TEAS CAN BE DANGEROUS

Herbal teas sometimes counter the effects of prescription drugs or cause serious side effects. Severe diarrhea: Senna (leaves, flowers and bark), buckthorn bark, dock roots and aloe leaves. Allergic reactions: Camomile, goldenrod, marigold and yarrow. Cancer: Sassafras. Toxic (possibly fatal) reactions: Shave grass, Indian tobacco and mistletoe leaves. Hallucinations: Catnip, juniper, hydrangea, jimsonweed, lobelia, nutmeg, wormwood.

REMOVING PESTICIDES FROM PRODUCE

Pesticides cling to fruits and vegetables even after a water washing. Best: Scrub the produce with a vegetable brush under running water. To be extra sure, use a mild detergent. Soak apples and pears in water containing one-fourth cup of vinegar before scrubbing.

Source: *The Practical Gourmet.*

BEST VIDEOTAPED COOKING LESSONS

You don't need to be a master chef to profit from a cooking videotape. In some cases, you don't even have to know how to boil an egg—as long as you know how to pop a tape into your VCR. These programs suit a wide range of tastes and ambitions. A sampling of five of the most popular tapes:

• *A Guide to Good Cooking,* $49.95. Jacques Pepin (a former chef to Charles de Gaulle) runs through the basics, beginning with kitchen tips: How to buy the proper pans and knives. How to stop a cutting board from sliding (place it on a wet cloth). How to chop garlic without dicing your fingers (curl your hands and position the blade against your knuckles). Then he proceeds from simple egg breakfasts to a complete chicken dinner with sauce and a fruit salad. It's the best tape for beginners.

• *The Slim Gourmet,* $39.95. This is the program for thin wallets and bulging waistlines. Barbara Gibbons (with the hefty McLean Stevenson as housewife helper) offers a no-nonsense tour through 30 quick and typical recipes...pot roasts, veal, turkey, lasagna, filet of sole, low-fat chili. Each dish is explained in several easy-to-follow steps. You're also given calorie counts, along with appropriate side dishes and desserts. Drawback: A cloying theme song sung by a woman whose high notes could curdle milk.

• *Master Cooking Course,* $29.95. The drily efficient Craig Claiborne and peppery chef Pierre Franey put on a four-menu cooking show, with only a few incidental tips along the way. The recipes include cream of carrot soup, sauteed cucumbers, poached salmon and chicken Portuguese. To re-create one of these meals, you'll need a spacious kitchen, a food processor, and a variety of pots, pans and molds—not to mention at least one or two

hours. But if you have the spare time, it's a tempting adventure for the seasoned cook.

• *Madeleine Kamman Cooks,* $89.95. Kamman natters along like Jacques Cousteau at 78 rpm...fast, precise and amusing. ("This poor fellow!" she exclaims, while performing a poultry autopsy.) Her recipes are rich (duck in cacao sauce), expensive (shrimp and avocado salad) and time-consuming. But along the way, she dispenses a number of valuable tips...an easy route to a nice, crumbly salad topping, or the use of lime juice to keep avocados from turning brown. Kamman also has exquisite visual taste and knows just when nothing but a black plate will do to set off a particular recipe. A must for any true kitchen artist.

• *Judith Olney on Chocolate,* $39.95. These desserts are both easy and irresistible. The hardest part lies in melting down bar chocolate —the first step in each recipe. But soon you'll be duplicating Olney's fabulous dips, truffles and cake decorations. Then you'll move on to a few basic cakes and mousses, and finally to an awesome cream-filled sponge cake. Olney is unabashedly decadent. She delights in mixing raw eggs and sugar with her fingers or in rolling gooey chocolate in her hands. In the midst of all this, she informs us that chocolate contains calcium, protein and riboflavin. But who cares about nutrition at such a time? This tape is a turn-on!

Source: Ron Smith, a reviewer for *Video.*

BUYING AND STORING CHEESE

• Does it matter where you buy cheese?

Yes, it does. You should go to an experienced cheesemonger because you should buy only cheese that is fully or almost fully ripened. Getting cheese to this prime state is a specialist's job. For example, our store buys Brie and Camembert 85% ripened. Then it takes us 10 days of expert care to bring it to eating condition. Supermarkets sell potentially good cheeses, but because they can't take the time to age them properly, the shopper is often disappointed. Any cheese is at its best when it is bought from a good cheese store in a perfectly ripened state and is eaten within hours.

• How can you be sure all the different cheeses you might want for a party are at their best?

Visit your cheese shop a week or more in advance to make your choices. The proprietor can then have each variety ready at its optimal state—even pinpointed to a particular hour for serving it—on the day of the party.

• What about the leftovers? Can they be kept successfully?

We find that cheese, if kept cool and well wrapped, doesn't really need all that much care once it is ripened. We have mailed more than 5,000 packages of cheese and had only five complaints—and two of those were sent to the wrong addresses.

• How do you store leftover cheese?

Wrap cheese "like a Christmas present" in plastic wrap or aluminum foil. Be generous with the wrapping, and tuck in the sides. A chunk of well-wrapped hard cheese will keep for more than a month in the refrigerator without losing much weight or moisture. If it develops surface mold, you can just brush that off.

• Can you freeze cheese?

In most cases, yes, and the quicker you freeze it, the better. If you receive a gift wheel of Cheddar, Swiss, Muenster or Parmesan, for example, cut it into half-pound or one-pound portions. Make individual slabs, not wedges, so it will freeze evenly. Put the unwrapped slabs in the back of the freezer overnight. Take them out the next day, wrap them immediately, and put them back into the freezer. The cheese should be good for six months. Let it defrost overnight in the refrigerator before you use it.

If you want blue cheese for crumbling over salads, we recommend refrigerating it unwrapped so it dries out a little. (Wrapped blues—Stilton, Roquefort and Danish blue—will keep several weeks refrigerated.)

• Which cheeses are poor keepers?

The triple cremes, such as St. Andre and Explorateur. The higher the cream content, the greater the risk of change. When creamy cheese is frozen, crystals form.

• What about the glass cheese keepers sold in many gourmet shops?

You put vinegar and water in the bottom, supposedly to preserve the cheese. We find that it gives the cheese an unpleasant vinegar odor.

Source: Neil Hearn, proprietor of The Cheese Shop, 255 Greenwich Ave., Greenwich, CT 06830.

FOOD-STORAGE SECRETS

• Banana bulletin. For about 15 years now, it has been okay to put bananas in the refrigerator, contrary to the still popular 1940s Chiquita Banana jingle. (More sophisticated picking and shipping have speeded the ripening process.) Yellow bananas can be held at the just-ripe stage in the refrigerator for up to six days. Although the peel might discolor slightly, the fruit retains both its flavor and nutrition. Green bananas should ripen at room temperature first. Mashed banana pulp can be frozen.

• Nuts in the shell keep at room temperature for only short periods of time. Put them in a cool, dry place for prolonged storage. Shelled nuts remain fresh for several months when sealed in containers and refrigerated. For storage of up to a year, place either shelled or unshelled nuts in a tightly closed container in the freezer.

Source: *The Household Handbook* by Tom Grady and Amy Rood, Meadowbrook Press, Deephaven, MN.

• Storage times for frozen meats vary significantly. Recommended holding time in months: *Beef roast or steak, 12. Ground beef, 6. Lamb, 12. Pork roasts and chops, 8–12. Bacon and ham, 1–2. Veal cutlets and chops, 6. Veal roasts, 8–10. Chicken and turkey, 12. Duck and goose, 6. Shellfish, not over 6. Cooked meat and poultry, 1.

• Keep an accurate thermometer in your refrigerator or freezer. Optimal refrigerator temperature: 40°F for food to be kept more than three or four days. For the freezer: 0° is necessary for long-term storage. Note: Some

*Based on a freezer kept at zero degrees or lower.

parts of the freezer may be colder than other parts. Use the thermometer to determine which areas are safe for keeping foods long term.

• Freezing leftovers. Raw egg whites: Freeze them in ice cube trays. Hard cheeses: Grate them first. Soup stock: Divide it into portions. Stale bread: Turn it into crumbs in the blender. Pancakes, french toast and waffles: Freeze and reheat in the toaster oven at 375°. Whipped cream: Drop into small mounds on a cookie sheet to freeze and then store the mounds in a plastic bag. Citrus juices: Freeze in an ice cube tray.

• Freezing fish. Make a protective dip by stirring one tablespoonful of unflavored gelatin into ¼ cup lemon juice and 1¾ cups cold water. Heat over a low flame, stirring constantly, until gelatin dissolves and mixture is clear. Cool to room temperature. Dip the fish into this solution and drain. Wrap individual fish pieces in heavy-duty freezer wrap. Then place them in heavy-duty freezer bags. Use within two months.

Source: *Fish and Game Cooking* by Joan Cone, EPM Publications, McLean, VA.

• If you do your own food canning, preserve only enough food to eat within one year. After that time, its quality deteriorates.

FREEZING VEGETABLES FROM YOUR GARDEN

Tomatoes: Cut out the stems and rotten spots. Squish each tomato as you put it into a big cooking pot. Boil the tomatoes down to about half their original volume. Then put them through an old-fashioned food mill, catching the puree and discarding the skins and seeds. Pour the puree into a large, deep metal baking pan and leave the uncovered pan overnight in the freezer. The next day, run some hot water on the bottom of the pan to remove the puree, place the block of puree on a chopping board and icepick it into small pieces. Bag and freeze the chunks (a few to each bag).

Zucchini: Peel and split it and scrape the seeds out. Grate coarsely. Stir-fry until half-cooked in lots of butter. Follow the same freezing procedure as for tomatoes.

Greens: Boil, drain, squeeze the water out, chop to desired consistency and follow the same freezing process.

SECRETS OF CONTEST WINNERS

Cash, vacations, houses, cars, electronic equipment, cameras and much, much more are the dream prizes that keep millions of Americans doggedly filling out entry blanks and helping to lower the post office deficit. More than $100 million worth of prize money and goods are dispensed annually through an estimated 500 promotional competitions and drawings.

Some dedicated hobbyists have been able to win as many as 50 prizes in a single year. Lesson: There is an advantage to a planned approach to overcome the heavy odds against each entrant.

Winning strategies:
• Use your talents. If you can write, cook or take photographs, put your energy into entering contests rather than sweepstakes. Since contests take skill, fewer people are likely to compete. . . improving your chances. Photography contests have the fewest average entries.
• Follow the rules precisely. If the instructions say to print your name, don't write it in longhand. If a three-inch by five-inch piece of paper is called for, measure your entry exactly. The slightest variation can disqualify you.
• Enter often. Always be on the lookout for new sweepstakes and contests to enter. Sources: Magazines, newspapers, radio, television, store shelves and bulletin boards, product packaging.
• Make multiple entries. The more entries you send in, the more you tip the odds in your favor. A scheme for large sweepstakes: Spread out your entries over the length of the contest—one a week for five weeks, for example. When the volume of entries is big enough, they will be delivered to the judges in a number of different sacks. The theory is that judges will pick

from each sack, and your chances go up if you have an entry in each of several different mailbags. Simple logic: A second entry doubles your chances of winning...

• Keep informed. Join a local contest club or subscribe to a contest newsletter. Either source will help you to learn contest traps and problems —and solutions. They'll alert you, too, to new competitions.

• Be selective. You must pay taxes on items that you win, so be sure the prizes are appropriate for you. If you don't live near the water, winning an expensive boat could be a headache. (Some contests offer cash equivalents, but not all do.)

If you do win, check with your CPA or tax lawyer immediately. You must report the fair market value of items that you win, whether you keep them, sell them or give them away. This can be tricky. Also, if you win, you can deduct the expenses of postage, stationery, etc. that you have used to enter this and other sweepstakes and contests in the same year. These costs are not deductible if you don't win.

Most contests and sweepstakes ask you to enclose some proof of purchase or a plain piece of paper with a product name or number written on it. Obviously, since these competitions are designed to promote a product, the sponsors have a vested interest in your buying what they are selling. And many people assume that a real proof of purchase will improve their chances of winning. Fact: In a recent survey, more than half the winners of major prizes reported that they had not bought the sponsor's product.

Source: Roger Tyndall, with his wife Carolyn of the country's largest circulation newsletter, *Contest News-Letter, Fern Beach, FL.*

HOW TO BECOME A GAME-SHOW CONTESTANT

Getting an audition as a contestant on a game show is easy. But the contestants who make it onto a show—and go on to win—have special qualities. The edge: These players know how to put their best face forward, and they know their game. To get an audition:

• Target the game show. Your favorite game as a viewer may not be the game you play best. Important: Choose a vehicle for your best skills and personality traits, matching them to one of the four game show categories: Trivia/quiz, word/puzzle, personality, and kids/teens.

• Prepare diligently. Expertise at a game will compensate for almost any shortcoming. The game show producers want you to win. Game shows are popular in proportion to the excitement they generate. Winners are exciting.

Key: Watch the game regularly—daily is best. Tape it if necessary. Know all the rules and be familiar with game "lingo."

Essential: Practice, practice, practice. The best ways: (1) Play along as you watch the game. (2) Play mock games. (3) Play board games, read books and periodicals, and play video/computer/arcade games.

• Get an audition. Some shows, such as "Let's Make a Deal" or "The Price Is Right," pick directly from the studio audience, with little or no preliminary interviewing. More common: Watch for a trailer at the end of the show that supplies addresses and/or telephone numbers to contact for audition information. Best: Call rather than write. Calling is faster and you can get immediate answers to your questions.

Smart questions to ask when calling a show: I am planning a trip to Hollywood during the period of _____. When will you be interviewing during that time? Will I have time to get through all my audition interviews during that time? If I qualify, will I be able to tape my shows during that time? Will you be conducting a contestant search in or around my area in the coming months? What is your audition process?

Important: Be polite and to the point in all your conversations.

• At the audition:

Jitters are expected, but it's important to pay attention and be yourself. Guidelines:

• Play up your best qualities. Rule of thumb: Be yourself—your best self. What game show contestant coordinators look for: Someone with good eye contact, an outgoing personality, enthusiasm, a voice that projects. Turnoffs: Someone who is abrasive, who boasts of never having seen the show, who is extreme in some negative way (is constantly self-deprecating, etc.).

- Listen to who's talking to you. This includes the contestant coordinator, the show host, or your partner. Pay attention only to what relates to you.

- Don't focus on the competition. Forget the crowds.

- Don't think about prizes. It adds pressure and takes away from having fun. Better: Just relax and enjoy playing the game.

- Wear something you feel comfortable and attractive in. An all-new outfit or "new look" will distract you.

Bottom line: A game show shouldn't be a teeth-clenching endurance test. Contestant selection is tailored to pinpoint people who will enjoy themselves and give the show a good feeling.

Source: Greg Muntean, former game show contestant coordinator for "Jeopardy!" and "Wheel of Fortune."

RADIO CONTESTS: MORE THAN LUCK

Almost every popular radio station uses giveaways. Rewards include cash, cars, vacations and other prizes, ranging from record albums to TV sets. Playing the contests won't make you rich, but there's nothing like the thrill of hearing your name announced over the radio—as a winner.

Although chance plays the major role, you can greatly increase your odds of winning by understanding how call-in contests are run.

To begin: Pick a few stations that have entertaining contests and good prizes. Listen to each closely for a few hours, and phone in several times to get a feel for how the game is played.

The more contests you enter, the greater your chance of winning. The trick is to do this without spending your life on the phone. The key: Each program's disk jockey has a format that he follows closely.

Example: My prime listening time is from 11 p.m. to 1 a.m. By monitoring four stations, I have found that one holds regular contests at 42 minutes after the hour, another at either 15 or 45 minutes after the hour, another at either five or 35 minutes after the hour, and another at five of the hour. I tune in those stations only at those times.

After the contest has been announced, several factors determine how quickly you should place your call:

- The winning number: The number of the winning call often corresponds to the station's location on the dial. For example, one station, at 95.5 FM, always rewards the 95th caller. If you dial right away, you'll be about number 20 (stations generally tell you your number when your call is answered). So wait 35 seconds before dialing. By the time the call goes through and the phone rings a few times (at least five seconds per ring), you'll be pretty close to call number 95. It usually takes the station 70–75 seconds to reach that call.

- The number of lines at the station: This helps determine how quickly they get to the winning number. A station with only two phone lines moves more slowly than one with 22. If you ask, most stations will tell you how many lines they use for contests.

- The number of people answering the phones: Stations that have two or more people handling the calls move more quickly than those where it's left up to the DJ. After you've played the contests a few times, you'll get to know the voices—and the number of phone answerers at each station.

- Individual speeds: Some DJs get the contest rolling quickly, others slowly. Get to know their habits.

There's always an element of chance. The difference between being caller number 94 and caller number 95 is a split second, and there's no way you can control that. But you can greatly increase the odds of winning.

Don't give up. If you get a call through and you're five or more numbers away from winning, hang up and try again. And don't let a busy signal discourage you. Hint: Many stations have a recording telling you "Please try again later" if all the lines are busy. Stay on the line. Your call will be answered...sometimes in the middle of the recording, sometimes soon after it is completed.

Some DJs award the prize at random rather than counting through the calls to, say number 95. Others announce that caller number two will win, so they don't have to answer 95 calls (and with such a low number, it's really no contest at all). Your only recourse in such a situation is to complain to the station's management. If lazy DJs know they've been caught, they'll improve.

Source: Bob Gross, who has won more than $10,500 in cash and prizes in radio contests over the past five years.

CHRISTMAS TIPPING GUIDELINES

• Household help. The equivalent of a week's pay is standard. But much more elaborate gifts are appropriate for employees who have been in your service for a long time or to whom you are very close.

• Newspaper deliverer. $5–$10.

• Garbagemen. $5–$10 each if it is legal in your community; a bottle of liquor or fancy foodstuffs are an alternative.

• Mailmen. While it is technically illegal to tip the postman, many people give $5–$10 to their regular carrier.

• Deliverymen. $10 per person for those who come regularly to your house like the dry cleaner, the milkman or even your United Parcel Service man, if you get a lot of packages.

• Baby-sitter. A record or a book for a regular teenage sitter; a bottle of perfume or $10–$15 for an adult.

For apartment dwellers:*

• Superintendent. $25–$50.

• Doorman. $15–$25.

• Elevator operator. $15–$25.

• Concierge. $20–$25.

• Handyman. $20.

• Porter. $15.

• Garage attendant. $15–$20.

Outside the home:

• Restaurants where you are a regular customer. Maitre d', $20–$40. Bartender, $10–$15. Captain, waiter, busboy: Divide the average cost of a meal among the three of them.

• Beauty salon or barber shop. Give the owner-operator a bottle of wine or a basket of fruit. For employees who regularly attend you, $15–$25.

• Butcher. $10–$15 for regular good service.

• Tailor or seamstress. $10 or wine or perfume.

*If your building establishes a pool for tips that is divided among employees, you need only give an additional amount to those service people who have gone way beyond the call of duty for you this year.

11. Party and Entertainment Guide

Party and Entertainment Guide

HOW TO ENJOY HOLIDAY ENTERTAINING

Although everyone is supposed to look forward to the holidays, they can be a season of great strain, especially for those who are entertaining.

Everyone is likely to be overtired, overstimulated and overfed.

Children come home from college, accustomed to being on their own.

Parents arrive as houseguests.

Divorcees bring new partners.

Patterns are changed and roles are shifted, and the results can be shattering.

If you are the host or hostess there are things you can do (aside from leaving town) to minimize the strain:

• Include nonfamily in your invitations. Reason: Everyone is then on "party manners," and the snide comments, teasing or rivalries are held back. This is not the time for letting it all hang out.

• Accept help. Encourage your family and friends not only to make their favorite or best dish but to be totally responsible for it—heating or freezing or unmolding and serving. Reason: It makes everyone feel better. The afternoon or evening becomes a participatory event, rather than one where one or two people do all the work and the rest feel guilty or, worse still, awkwardly attempt to help. (The quality of the meal, by the way, improves enormously.) The one who hates to cook can supply the wine or champagne. The best baker can be responsible for dessert. A favorite pudding, a special way to prepare vegetables, a conserve—all are welcome. Even the most unaccomplished cook can wash, peel and slice a colorful assortment of raw vegetables.

• Let the table itself set a mood of fun, not formality. Use place cards wisely, and make them amusing with motifs appropriate for each guest, rather than names. Or let one of the younger children make them with a sketch of each guest or hand lettering. Set them out with forethought. Make sure a particularly squirmy youngster is nowhere near an aunt known for her fussy table manners. If there are to be helpers, seat them so they can get up and down with ease. Put the famous spiller where the disaster can be readily cleaned up. If the light is uneven, seat the older people in the brightest section.

• Put everyone around a table. It creates a warmer, more shared meal than does a buffet, and it's amazing how tables can expand. Hint: Use desk or rental chairs, which are much slimmer than dining chairs. (Avoid benches for older folks.)

• Borrowing and lending furniture, such as tables, can help you to find room for everyone. It doesn't matter if the setup is not symmetrical or everything doesn't match. A ping-pong table covered with pretty new sheets can provide plenty of room, or you can have tables jutting into hallways or living rooms. Using oversize cloths from bolts of attractive cotton can be an inexpensive way to cover your tables.

• Have some after-dinner games ready. Ping-pong, backgammon, chess and cards are among the favorites. You may want to buy the latest "in" game or a new word game. Often the games are never opened, but it is comforting to know they are there, just in case. Bringing out old family albums can be fun, too.

• Gift exchanging is really a potential hazard. Children, especially, can grump all day if something they expected hasn't been forthcoming. Grandparents often ask what is wanted, but they may be unable to do the actual buying. Do it for them. A check is not a fun package to open. If you want to be sure no one overspends, set a limit. Or set a theme. Or rule out gifts altogether, except for the children.

Source: Florence Janovic, writer and marketing consultant.

OVERCOMING THE ANXIETY OF GIVING A DINNER PARTY

Hosts who constantly worry whether everyone is "comfortable" or who fear their guests are not eating enough are suffering from the situational anxiety of a dinner party. Making the right preparations for the party will relieve these and similar anxieties.

Practical suggestions from a very useful book:*

Define the goals of this dinner party. The main purpose may be to establish a professional connection or to bring together two people likely to be attracted to each other.

Eliminate anxieties by verbalizing them. Example: Fear that the guests will not get along. Ask your spouse or a close friend to listen while you describe your worst fears. Once verbalized, the actual possibilities will appear less of a problem than when they were vague apprehensions.

Specify that the invitation is for dinner. It's not enough to say that you are having a get-together at 7:30. Let people know about dress —casual, nice but not formal, formal but not black tie. While phoning, mention one or two of the other guests, what they do and, if possible, what they are interested in. If a guest is bringing a friend, don't hesitate to ask something about the friend. Is there anything special you should mention or avoid mentioning to this person?

Do not serve a dish you have never prepared before. Guests will enjoy what you prepare best, even if it is just plain steak and potatoes or a simple fish casserole.

Have everything ready at least an hour before the party. Take a relaxing warm bath or shower. Allow extra time to dress and make up, and give yourself an additional 20 minutes to sit quietly.

Suggestion: Arrange to be free from the kitchen when the first two or three guests arrive. They need the host's help to start up conversation.

For the single host: Reduce last-minute anxieties by inviting a close friend to come over early, test the food and look over the arrangements.

Source: *Situational Anxiety* by Herbert J. Freudenberger and Gail North, Anchor Press, Doubleday & Co., Garden City, NY.

SURVIVING THE COCKTAIL PARTY GAME

In America, it's old news that everyone worships success, everyone litters and everyone lusts. But the deep, dark, dirty little secret that remains unspoken is that everyone hates cocktail parties.

Even people who give cocktail parties hate cocktail parties. They give them because it's the most efficient way to discharge a great number of social obligations in the shortest time at a cost ranging from modest to obscene. Trouble is, after you give a cocktail party, your guests owe you a reciprocal treat, and you have to go to their cocktail parties. And so it goes, year after year.

Here is a very simple plan to end the canape competition. Fight back.

You can confess that you hate standing around like an asparagus stalk, watching the waiters' trays stripped bare by the guests clustered near the kitchen door while you chew ice cubes or OD on martini olives.

You can ask the American Medical Association to issue a warning against drinking while upright and shifting weight from one foot to the other and getting a chill from the condensation dripping from your glass into your sleeve and down your arm.

You can stand up in church, synagogue or group therapy and tell the truth about cocktail-party conversation (which is to human discourse what paint-by-numbers is to fine art). And the truth is that cocktail-party conversation only suits people who have three sentences to offer on any given subject and who prefer their listener's eyes to be sweeping the room as they speak.

You can send in your check without making an appearance at the next charity cocktail party. Better still, start a trend. Ask potential donors, "How much will you pay not to have to go to a cocktail party?"

Seasoned political activists can boycott

cocktail parties and petition the great hosts and hostesses of the world to give, instead, a sit-down dinner for ten, a round-robin Scrabble tournament, an intimate tea dance, a computer game-fest, a book circle or a quilting bee —anything but the dehumanizing ritual of the cocktail party.

Admit it. Cocktail parties are like sex. Everyone believes everyone else is doing it better and having more fun. Cocktail parties are like medicine. They may be good for your career, but often the cure is worse than the illness. Cocktail parties are poor indicators of interpersonal success. People who are good at glib smiles and small talk are often lousy at life.

But suppose you can't avoid cocktail parties? How can you survive them? Five tips:

• If possible, attend with someone sociable and loquacious who will stand at your side and banter with passers-by as you think about tomorrow's headlines.

• Pick one interesting person, someone who seems to be eyeing the clock as longingly as you, and spend the next half hour getting to know that person as though you two were alone in the world. Cultivate your savior with as much energy as you would a sex partner. If you choose well, time will fly.

• Act as you would if the party were in your honor. Introduce yourself to everyone, and ask them about themselves head-on. People will be profoundly grateful for your initiative. They don't call you overbearing—they call you charming.

• Tell the host you have an injured leg. Then commandeer a comfortable chair and let people come to you. (They'll be glad for an excuse to sit down.) If no one does, find an oversized art book to browse through, or indulge in a few fantasies.

• Help the host. You'd be amazed at how overwhelmed a party giver can be and how many small tasks need doing—even with hired help. You can pass the hors d'oeuvres,

hang up coats, refresh the ice buckets and generally free the host for socializing. What's in it for you? A chance to move around (some call it "working the room"), the gratitude of your host and a nice feeling of usefulness.

Source: Letty Cottin Pogrebin, writer and editor for *Ms.*

SECRETS OF SUCCESSFUL PARTY GIVERS

The kind of entertaining you do depends on the length of your guest list and the dimensions of your house. For 10 or fewer people, a sit-down dinner is appropriate. For 25, a buffet is usually better. As the numbers grow, open houses and cocktail parties become the options. Limits are set by the size of your living space and the hours of the party. A cocktail party is traditionally scheduled for the two hours before dinner. An open house—usually 1–4 pm or 3–6 pm—can accommodate more people. If your rooms for entertaining hold 90–100 people for a party, you can invite as many as 250 to an open house. Trick: Stagger the hours you put on the invitations.

If you want to entertain several disparate groups—family, business associates and/or social friends—consider giving separate parties on succeeding nights. It takes stamina, but it does save effort and expense. You buy one order of flowers and greens for decorating the house. You assemble serving dishes and extra glasses (borrowed or rented) just once. You arrange furniture one time only. And you can consolidate food, ice and liquor orders, which, in bulk, can save money. Extra food from the first party can be served at the second.

You want people at a cocktail party to stay on their feet and circulate, so your living area probably holds more people than you think. Removing some furniture—occasional chairs and large tables—gives you space and keeps guests moving. Clear out a den or downstairs bedroom, and set up a food table or bar to attract guests to that room, too. If you have a pair of sofas facing each other in front of a fireplace, open them out so guests can easily walk around them. Use a bedroom or other out-of-the-way place for coats. (You can rent collapsible coat racks, hangers included.)

Set up different foods at different parts of the party area. If you have open bars, put different drink makings at each set-up. A group drinking a variety of cocktails will not be able to congregate for refills in the same place. Avoid bottlenecks. Don't put a bar or buffet table in a narrow hall, for example, or at the back of a tiny room. To make the most of a small space, have waiters to take drink orders and a bartender to fill the orders in the kitchen or pantry. Waiters can also pass the hors d'oeuvres in tight quarters, saving the clustering at a food table.

Count on seven hors d'oeuvres or canapes per person. Some will eat less, but it will equal out between the dieters and the hungry folks who make a meal of the party. Stick to finger foods. You'll want a variety of 8–10 canapes, but pass each separately, starting with the cold foods and bringing out the hot dishes later. Trays with a single selection look prettier and save the congestion of each guest having to make a choice. For long parties where a turnover of guests is likely, arrange two cycles of passing food, so the later guests get the same fresh selection as the earlier guests.

You know better than anyone what your guests like to drink. Chilled white wine has become increasingly popular, as have mimosas (champagne and orange juice) for brunches and for afternoon parties. Discuss amounts with your liquor dealer, and ask if you can return any unopened bottles. It is often cheaper to buy mixers by the case. Some dealers allow you to return unopened extras. A good nonalcoholic drink: Half cranberry juice and half ginger ale, garnished with a sprig of mint and a slice of orange.

Ice: For a large party, you should order ice ahead from an ice company. Figure that a 40-pound bag will provide enough cubes for 50 people. Get more if you are also chilling wine. Use a bathtub to keep the ice in. (No matter what kind of holder you devise for ice, the container will sweat and you'll have a puddle.) A bathtub full of ice and chilling champagne can be a festive sight by itself. Or you

can decant from the tub to smaller ice chests for each bar. If the nearest bathtub is too far from the party area, buy a plastic garbage can to hold the major supply.

You cannot be a good host without hired hands to take care of the food and drinks. Your job is to keep the guests happy, meeting each other and circulating from group to group. At a minimum, you need a bartender to be in charge of drinks and someone else in charge of the food. The larger the party, the more help you will need. Recommended: A bartender at each set-up, someone in charge of the kitchen and one or more waiters to pass food and replace dirty ashtrays.

Source: John Clancy, chef, teacher, restaurateur and author of several cookbooks.

• Clear ice cubes. Boil the water first. Cool and then freeze it. (Clear ice cubes last longer because they have fewer air bubbles.) To keep ice cubes separate: Store them in a dry, chilled metal container in the freezer.

• Separate the ice cubes for mixed drinks from the ice being used to cool the beer and soft drinks. For the average cocktail party, figure on two-thirds of a pound of ice per guest. For a dinner party, one pound per guest. Ice for the cooling of mixers and soft drinks should be figured separately. For cooling large quantities, a combination of block ice and cubes is best.

Source: *Entertaining* by Elizabeth Post, Harper & Row, New York.

• Best beer service. Use a spotlessly clean glass or mug (soap, grease or lint can ruin the taste). Just before pouring, rinse the glass in cold water and shake it dry, or put it in the freezer for a few minutes to frost it. Open the beer bottle or can carefully, without shaking up its contents. Tilt the glass and pour the beer down the side to start. Then straighten the glass and pour into the center. How much foam? It's a matter of taste, but you control it by the distance you hold the beer container from the glass as you pour. The greater the distance, the thicker the head.

• The fastest way to cool off a bottle of soda, beer or anything else is to hold it under running cold water. It's faster than putting it in the freezer.

• Pile the food high when laying out a party buffet. Avoid perfect rows of food. After the first attack, the rows look depleted, but piles of food retain some form. Place all the main-course food on one table. Don't allow empty spots, even if it means adding extra dishes. Put the food as high as possible, with platters or baskets on top of sturdy overturned bowls to add elevation.

Source: Mary Risley, director of Tante Marie's Cooking School, San Francisco.

PLANNING A BIG FAMILY PARTY

Are you hosting a large family gathering?

Because a reunion brings together people of all ages, it presents special challenges. Ideas to make your party more enjoyable for everyone:
• Infants and toddlers. Parents will appreciate a place to change diapers and a quiet room for naps and nursing. Let them know if you can provide high chairs, cribs, safety gates or playpens. Toys: A box of safe kitchen equipment. Food suggestions: Mild cheese, bananas, crackers, fresh bread or rolls.
• Preschool children. Set aside a play room. Best toys: Balloons, bubbles and crayons. Pay an older cousin or neighborhood teen to babysit.
• School-age children. A den or basement room and board games, felt pens and coloring books will keep them happy. Put them in charge of setting and decorating a children's dining table.
• Teenagers. Most teenagers find family reunions boring. For those who have to come, provide a room with a stereo, video games and radio. Teenagers may be shy around relatives they don't know. When they come out of hiding, give them tasks that encourage their involvement with others, such as helping out grandparents.
• Older folks. They need comfortable chairs where they can hear and see what's going on without being in the way. Some may also need easy access to a bathroom and place to rest or go to bed early. Food considerations: Ask if anyone needs a low-salt, low-cholesterol or special diabetic diet. Spicy foods are probably out. Make travel arrangements for those who can't drive so they don't worry about inconveniencing others.

Now that you've seen to individual needs, how do you bring everyone together? Common denominator: Family ties. Make an updated family tree and display it in a prominent place. If you have an instant camera, take pictures as people arrive and mount them on the appropriate branch of the tree. Special: Ask everyone to bring contributions to a family museum. Suitable objects: Old photographs, family letters, heirlooms, written family histories, old family recipes. After dinner, gather around the fire and exchange family anecdotes. You may wish to record them.

Source: *Unplug the Christmas Machine: How to Give Your Family the Simple Joys of Christmas* by Jo Robinson and Jean Staeheli, Morrow, New York.

HOT TUB ETIQUETTE

Equipment: When you're invited to a house with a hot tub, imagine it's a miniature swimming pool. Bring a towel. If it's daytime and the tub is outdoors, you might want sunglasses. Bathing caps are declasse. Bathing suits? If you have doubts, bring one. You might not wear it, but you might be sorry if you don't have one.

Options: If you're ambivalent about dress (or undress), take your cue from the host or hostess. It's like avoiding the awkwardness of using the wrong fork at a dinner party. Nudism works best with everyone doing the same thing, too.

Unlike dining, however, everyone doesn't have to participate simultaneously, or at all, so there's always an out. You don't have to go in.

Attitude: Nonchalance is absolutely de rigueur—a combination of Japanese politeness and California cool is recommended. Sustain the mood by maintaining eye contact with members of the opposite sex, especially when they are getting in and out of the tub.

Who's in charge: Part of the culture of the

hot tub is being "laid back." You might not receive a specific invitation to get in or out of the tub. The host or hostess might not be monitoring the temperature, either. If you think it's getting too hot, speak up. Better still, get out. This is one place where it's never bad manners to march to a different drummer.

HIRING PARTY HELP

Whether you call them butlers or waiters/waitresses, they help you with the fundamental chores of a cocktail or dinner party. Duties: Take coats, tend bar, prepare snacks or meals, serve and clean up. How many are needed: One helper serves a seated dinner party of 10 or a cocktail buffet for 20, if the host prepares the food. Hire two for groups of 30. For 40 or more, use four helpers. How to find them: Word of mouth. Contact a local college or bartenders' school for willing students. Payment: At the end of the party. Rates: Experienced workers earn more, with higher rates for late-night and holiday work.

CAVIAR SECRETS

Keep the tin of caviar in the refrigerator until 15 minutes before serving. Then open the lid and place the tin in a serving bowl of crushed ice. Spoon helpings carefully, since caviar takes on an oily quality if the eggs are broken. Eat with a fork. Accompany with lightly toasted triangles of bread thinly buttered. Caution: Never serve caviar with onion, sour cream or chopped egg, or squeeze lemon over it. These detract from the pure flavor. Best: Burst the eggs between the tongue and upper palate. This releases the full taste properly.

Source: Christian Petrossian, caviar importer, quoted in *Harper's Bazaar.*

CREATIVE SUMMER DRINKS

With only a bit more effort than it takes to make a vodka and tonic or to pour a soft drink over ice, you can create impressive summer drinks.

Single alcoholic drinks:

- Wine Cooler. Put 2 teaspoons of sugar and 1 teaspoon of cold water in a 10–12 ounce highball glass. Stir until sugar is dissolved. Add 1 tablespoon of orange juice and 4 or 5 ice cubes. Fill with chilled red or white wine. Garnish red wine cooler with a lemon slice and white with an orange slice.
- Bullfrog. Mix 4 tablespoons of lime juice with 1 teaspoon of sugar in a highball glass. Add 2 ounces of vodka and 3 or 4 ice cubes. Fill with club soda and stir. Garnish with a lime slice.
- Floradora. Put 1 cup of crushed ice in a highball glass. Add ½ teaspoon of sugar, 3 tablespoons of lime juice, 2 ounces of gin and 1 tablespoon of grenadine or raspberry syrup. Pour in 2 ounces of club soda or ginger ale. Stir gently.
- Iced Irish Coffee. Combine 1 cup of strong chilled coffee and 1 teaspoon of sugar. Stir. Put 2 tablespoons of whipped cream in the bottom of a glass. Pour in coffee mixture. Stir. Add 3 or 4 ice cubes and 2 ounces of Irish whiskey. Top with 2 tablespoons of whipped cream. (Regular Iced Coffee: Omit the whiskey.)

Single nonalcoholic drinks:

- Summer Delight. Put 3 or 4 ice cubes in a 10–12 ounce glass. Add 3 tablespoons of lime juice and ¾ ounce of raspberry syrup. Fill with club soda and stir. Garnish with fruit.
- Saratoga. Combine 2 tablespoons of lemon juice, ½ teaspoon of sugar and 2 dashes of Angostura bitters in a glass. Add 3 or 4 ice cubes. Fill with ginger ale.

Punches:

- Fish House Punch. Dissolve 2 cups of sugar in 3 cups of lemon juice in a punch bowl. Add a large block of ice. Add 1½ quarts of brandy, 1 pint of peach brandy, 1 pint of rum and 1 quart of club soda. Stir well. Decorate with fruit. Serve in 4-ounce punch glasses. Makes about 32 servings.
- White Wine Punch. Pour a 25-ounce bottle of white wine over a block of ice in a punch bowl. Add the juice of 1 lemon and the peel cut into strips. Sprinkle in 1 tablespoon of sugar. Stir. Add 2 ounces of brandy and 1 quart of club soda. Garnish each glass with a stick of

cucumber. Makes about 15 4-ounce servings.

Nonalcoholic punches:

• Strawberry Cooler. Blend 1 pint of fresh strawberries with ½ cup of sugar in an electric blender. Add 2 cups of vanilla ice cream and 1 cup of milk. Blend again. Pour over a block of ice in a punch bowl and combine with 1¾ quarts of milk. Makes about 15 4-ounce servings.

• Pensacola Punch. Combine 2 cups of sugar and 6 cups of water in a saucepan. Cook over low heat, stirring until sugar is dissolved. Cool. Pour one 46-ounce can of grapefruit juice and 3½ cups of lime juice over crushed ice in a punch bowl. Add the sugar syrup and 1 pound of grapefruit sections. Garnish with maraschino cherries and mint sprigs. Serve in 8-ounce goblets. Makes about 18 servings.

Bartending tips:

• Measure accurately. Use a double-ended measuring cup for pouring. One end is a jigger (1½ ounces) and the other is a pony (1 ounce). A dash is 3 drops.

• Use superfine sugar. The finest granulated sugar, superfine, dissolves quickly and easily. Confectioners powdered sugar is not as good.

• Develop your own "specialty." Experiment with recipes to create your own drinks. Important: With alcoholic drinks, don't be heavy-handed with the liquor—you'll spoil the taste and the effect of the drink.

THROWING GUESTS OUT GRACEFULLY

Close the bar. Glance at your watch occasionally. Stifle a yawn or two. Start emptying ashtrays and cleaning up. If subtle hints have no effect—tell the truth. Say you're exhausted, that you have to get up early the next morning and that the party's over.

Source: *Entertaining* by Elizabeth Post, Harper & Row, New York.

PUTTING OFF UNWANTED GUESTS

Favorite ploys of city dwellers who don't want to put up all the out-of-town relatives and friends who invite themselves: "We'd love to have you, but... The apartment is being painted. We will be out of town ourselves. The house is full of flu. My mother-in-law is visiting. The elevator is out of order. The furnace is broken and and we have no heat or hot water (winter version). The air conditioning is out, and you know how hot and humid it gets here (summer version)."

SURVIVING WEEKEND GUESTS

Weekend guests can be a drag. They leave the lights on, show up late for breakfast and expect to be waited on. But the clever host or hostess graciously but firmly takes charge and doesn't let guests become a nuisance.

Be a benevolent dictator. You can't run a house as a democracy. The host or hostess has the right not to be put upon. If someone is cadging an invitation when you'd rather be alone, suggest another time. You don't have to take a vote to decide on the dinner hour if there's a time that's most convenient for you. Some hosts post written house rules. For most households, though, verbal instructions are adequate.

If you live without servants, tell guests what you want them to do—pack the picnic lunch, bring in firewood. You'll resent them if they're having fun and you're not.

Don't let food preparation become a chore. Plan enough ahead to have options if you decide to spend the afternoon on the boat instead of in the kitchen. Have on hand a dish you can pull out of the freezer, or a fish or chicken that will cook by itself in the oven or crockpot and maybe yield leftovers for other meals.

Involve guests in preparation and cleanup. If they volunteer to bring a house gift, ask for food. If guests have special diets that vary radically from your own, try to give them the responsibility for supplying and preparing their own food.

Breakfast can be a frustrating meal to coordinate. Even if you eat all other meals together, it's a good idea to give guests a kitchen tour and coffee-making instructions so they can fend for themselves when they wake up.

Lay out plans and options early. First: present your own fixed responsibilities and activities. Don't be embarrassed to do something without your guests. Next: Present optional activities for everyone. Mention anything you expect them to participate in. Discuss availability of transportation, facilities and other amenities.

Finally a pattern for the weekend will begin to emerge. Keep it flexible. Suggest ways to communicate changes and important information (a corkboard for messages, an answering machine, etc.).

Encourage independence. Supply maps, guidebooks, extra keys. And provide alarm clocks, local newspapers, extra bicycles.

Even dictators can reward good behavior. Warm thanks, praise and other signs of appreciation go a long way toward encouraging more of the same. After all, a host or hostess can't punish bad guests. . .except by not inviting them back.

12. Collecting and Hobbies

Collecting and Hobbies

SECRETS OF A FAMOUS COLLECTOR

Over the last 60 years, Roy Neuberger, founder and senior partner of the highly respected investment management house Neuberger & Berman, has amassed a collection of outstanding American art of the 19th and (primarily) 20th century. Much of it is now in the Neuberger Museum of the State University at Purchase, NY. Here are some of Mr. Neuberger's secrets of successful collecting.

Train your eye:

• Pursue formal study. This is one way, but not the only one.

• Discover good critics and follow them. Hilton Kramer of *The New York Times* is sensitive and has a good eye.

• Look at art. This is the best way to develop your taste. Go to galleries. Look in museums, but be selective. There are too many museums today. Their experts who select what's to hang aren't infallible. Visit New York City, the current art capital of the world.

• Never stop learning. There is always more to know.

What to buy:

• Unknown artists: Buy someone you have never heard of before. That is especially good if you don't have much money. Names that are unfamiliar could turn out to be popular after a while.

• Noninvestments: I don't think of art as an investment. People should buy art because it's good for them and fulfills them. If art is meaningful to people, their judgment is likely to be sound, and then art could turn out to be a good investment.

• Individuals, not schools: Artists are individuals.

• Be skeptical: A lot of expensive, phony non-art is masquerading as art.

Where to buy finds:

• Consultants: Banks are charging 2% for their services as investment counselors on art. It's better to pay attention to an art critic whom you trust.

• Dealers: No matter how informed you become, a smart, honest dealer is important.

• Local exhibitions: There are good artists everywhere in the country.

Important: You can collect better if you're a good walker. Keep in top physical condition and get around.

Source: Roy Neuberger, Neuberger & Berman, New York.

ART AS AN INVESTMENT

Quality is the main factor at every level of the art market. It determines both purchase price and liquidity. The best items appreciate most when the economy is flush and maintain their value best in a recession.

The key to success is knowledge about art and the market. Knowledgeable collectors who follow their own intuition and buy what they like usually do better than investors who follow elaborate strategies.

Most experts agree that investors should never invest more than 10% of their assets in the art market. And art should be a long-term investment. Plan to keep an item at least five years to get the best return. To learn the market:

• Visit dealers. Prices of comparable items can vary.

• Attend auctions. Dealers usually set their prices according to current auction prices.

• Subscribe to auction catalogs. Auction houses such as Sotheby's and Christie's annually publish prices brought by major items sold during the year.

• Consult with experts. Museum curators, dealers and art scholars can be very helpful, especially in assessing the work of lesser-known artists. Most will give free advice about a specific work. Never make a major purchase without consulting an expert.

Most works of art are bought and sold at private galleries and at auction houses. A good dealer has a large selection of works preselected for their quality, whereas auction houses sometimes have to dispose of less worthy items. With a dealer, there is no waiting for a purchase time as there is for an auction, but a purchaser still can take time to reflect. A good dealer is willing to share knowledge, stands behind what is sold and often has an exchange policy. Ask a museum curator for the name of a reputable dealer.

For a knowledgeable collector, auctions present an advantage—comparable items can often be bought for less than from a dealer. Primary advice: Buy what you like, but buy quality—the best examples that you can find and afford.

Buying today:

• Because of the preference for oil paintings in today's art market, drawings and sculpture arc better buys.

• Less popular subjects—some portraits, animals, religious paintings, violent subjects—are often less expensive.

• Paintings that are under or over the most popular size (two feet by three feet to three feet by four feet) tend to cost less.

• Works that are not in an artist's most typical or mature style are usually less expensive.

• Avoid the currently stylish. Investigate the soon-to-be stylish.

• Works of western art that are not attributed or authenticated can be cheap, but they are bad investments. A work with an authentic signature and date is always worth more than one without them.

Collecting contemporary art:

At least 120,000 people in this country think of themselves as serious artists. Among them, fewer than 500 will ever see their works appreciate in value. Most of these artists are either very well known and very expensive or reasonably well known and reasonably expensive.

Works by artists who have not yet received the recognition they merit are affordable now and might appreciate in value. These artists are likely to be included in group exhibitions but may not have been shown alone. In private galleries, their paintings may sell for $5,000–$20,000 and their drawings for $250–$1,500. If the artist does not have a dealer, as the more famous artists do, you might be able to save 50%—the dealer's commission—by buying directly.

Large quality paintings by relatively unknown artists can be found for as little as $800. If you choose well, you can get a significant work of art, help support a deserving artist and, if you are very lucky, watch your work's value escalate.

Source: Steven Naifeh, author of *The Bargain Hunter's Guide to Art Collecting,* New York.

INVESTING IN YOUNG ARTISTS

The art world has its fads, fashions and passions. The evaluation of the best artists (and consequently the price tags) changes every 10 years.

Subscribe to every art publication available: *Art Forum, Art in America, Art News,* etc. Two excellent ways to use them.

• Look at the pictures, and tabulate the number of times a certain artist or work of art is mentioned. Do the same with museum catalogs for both US and European museums. (European museums are more experimental and adventurous.) If you find an artist mentioned five times and a work of art mentioned three times, buy it if you can. The art world is very different from the stock market. A stock market insider who gives someone a tip can go to jail, but a person who gives tips in the art world is feted.

• Study the critical articles. New quality art creates its own rules and violates the old rules. Look for critics who make the most sense and help you see a painting in a new way. Then take their advice.

With these rules, a computer could pick better emerging art and artists than nine out of 10 collectors.

Listen to the hype about new artists. If the hype works, believe it. Hype is derived from the Greek word meaning beyond. It implies exaggeration. Many people use the word derogatorily. However, most people in the art world are hyperenthusiastic. Few convince the public at large, so if they do, it is because the work is truly appealing.

Once an embryonic art collector identifies the best hype and the most enthusiastic reporting about art in publications, he should be ready to buy.

• Buy quickly. Get to the gallery before the show opens. (Shows are announced in the art magazines. You must be quick, because there are many, many more art patrons than there are good artists.)

• Enthuse. If you can't buy, still say the artist is sensational, and be willing to wait until a work by the artist becomes available.

• If you like an artist in a top gallery who is not a superstar, buy his work anyway. After you buy enough, the gallery owner may offer you its top artist.

• When you discuss price, ask two questions: "Is there a discount?" (Whether there is or not, say *Wonderful.*) "Can I have time to pay it off?" (Never pay cash for what the gallery owner is willing to finance.) This second tactic may lead to a buying spree. Caution: If you buy on time, always pay precisely on the agreed-upon date. Most people—even the richest—do not. And you want the gallery owner to be able to rely on you.

• If possible, have a nice home to show the work off well. A gallery owner's job is to spread the artist's name as widely as possible. If you exhibit the work in a handsome setting, you become a living advertisement for the artist and the dealers.

• Invite the artist in to look at the painting in the new setting. Ask him to bring a friend. (Usually he will bring a critic.) Ask a lot of questions, including "Who's new that you like?" (You have to be careful with this one, because the artist may suggest his/her lover.)

• When you get a quality piece of art, broadcast it. Then it will act as a magnet for others to offer you quality paintings.

• Save a great deal of your money for the sec-

ondary market. That means buying from other owners, not directly from the gallery. One great painting bought in the secondary market—which is more accessible—can attract pieces from the primary market.

• Be a sucker, and pay "too high" prices at times. Other people will then try to take advantage of you, and you will be offered a lot of quality art. In truth, dealers can't ask very much beyond a certain known range for any artist.

• Donate a piece to a museum. It gets you well-known as a collector. Besides its minor tax advantage, it also increase your reputation as a collector.

Art greats to be:

These suggestions are 100% biased. They are just one collector's idea of what might be a good gamble for people starting out.

• Cindy Sherman. Her performance-art photography is on the cover of an issue of *Art in America*. Original prints of the pictures can be purchased at Metro Pictures Gallery for as little as $300.

• John Cage. The composer does both artistic scores and magnificent drawings, all of which sell for $1,000–$3,000. Because of his historic stature, his works should appreciate in value.

• Anselm Keefer. The most important artist to come out of Europe in decades works in many media. Paintings sell for up to $150,000. Drawings sell for $3,000–$15,000 at the Marion Goodman Gallery.

• Susan Rothenberg. Her exceptionally beautiful drawings sell at the Willard Gallery for $1,800–$5,000. Some of her paintings cost $40,000 and up.

• Julian Schnabel and David Salle. Their drawings go for $1,800–$5,000. Both are already renowned artists.

More speculative options:

• Sarah Charlesworth. Her photographic work has incredible strength. It cost $1,500–$2,000 for a four-foot by five-foot work. She sells her own work from 591 Broadway, New York.

• Jack Goldstein. He is tremendously respected in Germany and other parts of Europe. His paintings are derived from pictorial images in newspapers or on television, and are realistic. Paintings run from $2,000 to $10,000.

• John Ahern. His sculptures of living people go for $4,000–$5,000 at Brooks Alexander Gallery. There is a waiting list.

• Richard Bossman. He does extremely violent paintings (also at the Brooks Alexander gallery). A 24-foot by 30-foot painting goes for $3,500. The Metropolitan Museum bought one recently.

• Adolf Benca. This young artist may be a little overinfluenced by Picasso and Gorki, but keep watching. His drawings and monographs go for $300 at the Twining Gallery.

• Bill Anastasi. He may be the most overlooked artist in America, an original whom many other artists copy. His works start at $500 and go up to $10,000. He lives on Riverside Drive, New York.

• Dove Bradshaw. She does conceptual art that is absolutely beautiful, small and delicate. It sells from $300.

• Ross Bleckner. Artists love him. He is in the best new gallery in New York—Mary Boone. His paintings are almost abstract, but figurative, and go for $4,000–$5,000.

• Troy Brauntuch. His drawings, mostly black-and-white figures, are owned by many other artists. They cost $4,000–$7,500 at Mary Boone Gallery.

• Mel Kendrick. His sculptures start at $3,000, but many of the country's best collectors own one already.

• Michael David. His heavy, encrusted, ugly paintings become beautiful when studied. Small: $1,500. Large: $10,000.

Wild cards:

• Suzanne Jolson. Her first mature painting was done only last year. Her works, at Fredericks Ordover Gallery, cost $3,000 for a six-foot-square painting.

• Bob Lobe. The artist does aluminum site sculpture. That is, he wraps aluminum around a rock and then removes it. His work is handled by the Willard Galley and goes for $2,000–$6,000.

• Ken Scharf. His paintings of cartoon characters are smiliar to early Miro. His prices have jumped fast, but you can get a small piece for $4,000.

Source: Eugene Schwartz, private collector.

COLLECTING ART DECO

Art Deco is a design style that burst onto the international scene in the 1920s. (Its name comes from the 1925 Paris *Exposition International des Arts Decoratifs et Industriels.*) The sleek modern lines of the style appeared in architecture, furniture design, fabrics, posters, book covers, silver, glass, ceramics, clocks, boxes, cases, enamelware, jewelry and even clothing. Flamboyant and optimistic in the prewar years, it came out of *Art Nouveau* and melded into *Art Moderne,* a more industrial, machine-age fascination with technology and new materials like plastics and chrome, in the 1930s. Art Deco motifs were Egyptian, Mayan, cubistic and futuristic. The craftsmanship was superb.

Art Deco was rediscovered by collectors in the late 1960s, and prices escalated in the 1970s. Then, as with many other antiques and collectibles, the market softened in the 1980s, particularly for mass-produced items in good supply. Example: A Lalique colored-glass vase that sold in the late 1970s for $15,000 fell to $6,000. When collectors and dealers sensed that Lalique was becoming cheap again, they started a new wave of buying, and the price roller coaster started up again.

Furniture by an Art Deco master like Emile Jacques Ruhlmann or lacquerwork by Jean Dunand (most famous for furnishings on the liner *Normandie)* has not weakened in price. The workmanship and rarity of such attributed pieces keep them at a premium. A record was set in Monte Carlo for a coiffeuse (dressing table) designed by Ruhlmann with Dunand lacquerwork—$200,000. You may still find chairs (and sometimes tables) for under $3,000 by Louis Sue and Andre Mare, Jules Leleu and Dominique. American names to look for are Donald Deskey (responsible for much of the Radio City Music Hall decor) and Paul Frankel.

For the beginning collector: Look for well-built wood furniture. It was properly dried and crafted in the 1920s, using rare woods like amboyna and black macasser ebony that won't be seen again.

For the serious investor-collector, only signed,

handmade pieces of great quality are safe buys for the future.

Mass-produced 20th century decorative arts may not be an investment, but they are great fun to buy and use. Charming design and good quality control make Art Deco household and personal items competitive with contemporary merchandise. Art Deco table silver, cigarette holders, ladies' compacts, perfume bottles, jewelry, boxes, lighters and other small items have great flair and affordable price tags. Some consider Art Deco low-quality art, but it has a sense of humor and great style.

Books on Art Deco:

• *The Spirit and Splendor of Art Deco* by Alain Lesieutre, Paddington Press, 1974.

• *Art Deco: A Guide for Collectors* by Katherine Morrison McClinton, Clarkson N. Potter, 1972.

• *The Art Deco Style* by Theodore Menton, Dover Publications, 1972.

Source: Alastair Duncan, Christie's; Herve Aaron, Didier Aaron, Inc.; Nicholas Dawes, Phillips; and Fred Silberman, Fred Silberman Gallery, all of New York.

COLLECTING BRONZE SCULPTURE

In the world of our grandparents and great-grandparents, no home was without its bronzes. J.P. Morgan and Henry Clay Frick collected them, and even families with modest incomes could afford these commercially produced pieces.

A recent revival of interest in sculpture of all kinds has created a lively market in old bronzes as well. They are plentiful, decorative and easy to take care of (with a feather duster).

Collecting categories:

• Academic or salon sculpture. These realistic 19th-century bronzes from Europe and America were cast in a variety of subjects—portrait busts, prancing putti of India, laboring peasants and nudes. They provide a good starting point for beginners. Important sculptors: Jean Baptiste Carpeaus, Jules Dalou, Achille d'Orsi.

• Animal Sculpture. A school of French artists led by Antoine-Louis Bayre produced sculptures of horses, dogs, lions and hunting scenes that are prized for their fine modeling and realistic movement. Important artists: Pierre-Jules Mene, Georges Gardet, Emanuel Fremiet, Alfred Dubucand. Attractive pieces are available starting at about $100, though name artists command more. Examples: A Mene bronze of two pointers sold for $1,100. A gilt-bronze, *Ostrich Hunting in the Sahara* by Dubucand brought $4,620.

• Art Nouveau and Art Deco. Popular with collectors who specialize in all designs of these periods, these styles are subject to current fashion. Art Nouveau prices have leveled off after a period of inflation. Art Deco is still *in* and expensive. Bronze and ivory figures of exotic dancers by Demetre Chiparis recently brought $30,000. More modest Art Nouveau and Art Deco pieces, particularly by American designers, can be found for $500–$5,000. Many Deco bronzes are of athletes. "Pushing men" bookends are typical and popular.

• American West sculpture. The peak of this craze has passed, but prices are still very high for this area of Americana. Frederic Remington's *The Norther* was sold for $715,000, a record price for American sculpture of any kind. But this was the last available cast of a rare edition and Remington is considered a major artist. Western sculpture by other artists is a less secure investment, but of course it is also less expensive.

• Impressionist and Early Modern. Bronzes by established artists of this era are considered fine art rather than decorative objects and are available only through auctions and galleries. Works by Rodin, Daumier, Degas, Maillol, Picasso, Henry Moore, Brancusi, etc. have proved to be sound investments, but they are extremely expensive—from $100,000 to well over a million dollars.

• Museum specialties. Medieval, renaissance, baroque, oriental and African bronzes require study and connoisseurship and attract only a few independent collectors. Expert advice is essential if you consider buying one of these.

What affects value?

• Fame of artist or founder. Signatures or foundry marks should be crisp and clear. (Fakes abound.)

• Edition. A rare and limited edition is more

valuable than a common one. Problem: Records of most 19th-century bronzes are sketchy. Many pieces were cast literally in thousands. And the records vary for established artists. Remingtons are carefully documented, including casts made by his family after his death (called estate editions). Rodins, on the other hand, were made in several different foundries, and few records exist, providing a ripe market for forgeries or pirated editions. Estate editions, though authentic, are not as valuable as those supervised by the artist.

• Condition. Original condition is preferable. However, it is acceptable to have 19th-century bronzes repatinated or repaired in a reputable foundry if necessary.

• Size. This is a matter of fashion. Currently, the demand (and prices) are greatest for very large pieces appropriate for outdoor settings.

Spotting fakes:

Valuable bronzes, even those of contemporary artists like Henry Moore, have frequently been forged. The most common method is to make a "sur-moulage" casting from the original. The fake will be slightly smaller than the original, since bronze shrinks as it cools, but the differences are minuscule. Fakes also may vary in color, weight and clarity of detail.

Danger signals: Bronzes that have been epoxied to a marble base so you can't check the hollow interior. An unnaturally even "Hershey-bar brown" color. Color that can be removed with nail-polish remover or scratched with a fingernail. A ghost impression around the signature or foundry mark. Air bubbles, bumps and craters around the base (good 19th-century craftsmen would have hand-finished such imperfections).

Seek expert advice as you learn the field. Stick to dealers and auction houses that guarantee the authenticity of the works they sell. Make sure your receipt is specific: "One bronze signed Henry Moore" says just that. It does not say the piece was made by Henry Moore.

Books on bronzes:

• *Bronzes* by Jennifer Montague, G.P. Putnam's Sons, New York, 1963 (Pleasures and Treasures series), out of print.

• *A Concise History of Bronzes* by George Sav-

age, Frederick A. Praeger, Inc., New York, 1969, out of print.

Source: Alice Levi-Duncan, Jody Greene, and Christopher Burge, Christie's, New York.

ART RENTAL

Rent a painting for a few months to see if you really want to live with it before making a permanent financial commitment. Most art museums offer this option for the works of local artists. Object: To help prospective buyers develop their taste in art, while giving artists exposure in the community. Rates: Usually 10% of the purchase price for a three-to six-month trial.

COLLECTING COLOR POSTERS

Posters caught the public's fancy in the 1880s and have retained a fascination for collectors ever since. The development of cheap color lithography led to that first wave of artistic posters, most of which were designed for advertising. From 1880 to 1900, French, Belgian, English and American artists left their mark on the medium. Best known: The French Art Nouveau artists Toulouse-Lautrec, Mucha, Cheret and Steinlen.

German artists turned out the finest posters from 1900 to World War I. Leading Light: Ludwig Hohlwein, who did posters for clothing stores and theatrical events and a famous series for the Munich zoo.

American posters came to prominence during World War I. *Uncle Sam Wants You,* the recruiting poster showing a determined Uncle Sam pointing toward the viewer, is an unforgettable image. The Artist: James Montgomery Flagg. He and Howard Chandler Christy produced many of the most famous posters of their day. Today an Uncle Sam poster can sell for $600-$700.

The work of French artist A.M. Cassandre stood out during the period between the two world wars. His most popular contributions: The *Nord Express* and other train posters done between 1925 and 1932. His widely reproduced and imposing *Normandie* was completed in 1936.

Posters of note since World War II include those of Ben Shahn and the San Francisco rock posters of the 1960s.

The categories for collectors encompass circus, theater, ballet, movies, music halls and both world wars. Best buys: Automobile posters (except those for American cars, which are not of very good quality). Star: The Peugeot poster by French artist Charles Loupot.

Posters in constant demand: Those connected to avant-garde art that combine strong typographic design with photomontage. Rare finds: Work from the 1920s associated with the Bauhaus, the Dada movement and Russian Constructivism. Constructivist film posters made in 1925–31 most often measure about 40 inches by 28 inches. Classic example: Any of the few advertising the film *The Battleship Potemkin.*

Beginners should look at Japanese posters made from the mid-1970s to the present. Also recommended: Post-World War II Swiss posters for concerts and art exhibits.

Best: Stick to recent foreign posters made in limited editions and not distributed beyond their place of origin.

Poster condition: Creases and small tears in the margin are acceptable. Faded posters are undesirable. (The quality standards are not quite as stringent for posters as they are for prints.)

Source: Robert Brown, co-owner of Reinhold Brown Gallery, New York.

GREAT ANTIQUES ARE CHEAPER THAN GOOD MODERN FURNITURE

Antique furniture is a better buy than modern reproductions. For example, a modern reproduction of a Georgian mahogany bowfront chest can cost over $5,000, yet the originals sell frequently at auction for $800-$1,000.

Antique furniture also "stores" value better than modern reproductions do. Like a new car driven out of a showroom, even expensive modern reproduction furniture becomes "used" as soon as it's delivered. Offered for resale, it generally brings one-third or less of its original cost.

In contrast, antique furniture retains its value. If you buy a Georgian mahogany chest at auction for $1,000, change your mind and consign it to the next auction, it will probably fetch around $1,000 again. Allowing for commissions at both ends, you'll have lost $200. But if you hold on to that chest for two or three years, you'll see an increase in value. And the longer you keep an antique piece—barring your buying at the top of a vogue and selling at its bottom—the more valuable it will become. It's a much better investment than its modern reproduction, which can cost you $3,000-$4,000 and bring you only $1,000-$1,200 if you should decide to resell it.

Furniture buyers should look for simple lines and consider their space limitations. Buy basic shapes. You won't get tired of looking at the pieces, and they'll be easy to sell if you move or redecorate. Some antiques are especially suitable for small apartments—for example, drop-leaf tables (often with a drawer underneath for silver and linens) and nests of tables. Very large pieces are often sold at low prices because most people don't have enough room to accommodate them. Similarly, tall chests sell for less than low chests because people can't hang pictures above them.

When buying antique furniture at auction, look closely at the catalog's glossary and definition of terms. Christie's East, for example, distinguishes between "A George III mahogany chest of drawers, mid-18th century" ("the piece is essentially of the period and has not been significantly altered or restored"), "A George II mahogany chest of drawers" (no date: "the piece is essentially of the period and has been significantly restored or altered"), and "A George II style mahogany chest of drawers" ("the piece is an intentional copy of an earlier design").

Antique furniture should be examined carefully before purchase. For chests and desks, check the drawers to see that they move properly, and check the alignment of the runners. Check tables for structural stability. Federal and Empire tables on a central pedestal are frequently top-heavy and wobbly.

Open a drop-leaf table to see whether its leaves lie flat or are warped. Are the leaves the same color? Or has the table been sitting in the sun so that one or more leaves have faded?

Inspect upholstered furniture very carefully. If the upholstery is in good shape, the rest of the piece is probably sound or has only minor damage that can be repaired easily. Keep in mind that professional reupholstering adds $500-$600 to the cost of a chair and $800-$1,200 to the cost of a couch.

Other repairs: Any reputable auction house or antique dealer can recommend a good cabinetmaker and tell you what should be repaired and approximately how many hours it should take.

Even first-timers can learn a lot by asking auction-house personnel the following questions:

Has this piece been repaired or altered?

Were the repairs done well or badly?

Will it need work? If so, what should be done?

What kind of antique furniture comes up at auction? Just about everything that was made after 1650 in the US, England, Europe and the Orient. This furniture is less than museum quality, and there is a lot of it around.

Source: Judith H. McQuown is the author of five investment books. She also writes about shopping, antiques and travel.

ANTIQUES: SPOTTING THE REAL THING

Guidelines to help you get the antique you think you're paying for:

• Wedgwood. The only way to determine if a piece of Wedgwood is old or recent (assuming it bears the impressed mark of Wedgwood) is by close examination of the raised relief molding. The earlier works have greater depth and more delicacy.

• Porcelain. The Chinese made porcelains a thousand years before anyone else. Pieces that were copied at a later date may have had the original identifying marks copied also. (The Chinese didn't do this to deceive, but rather to pay their respects to the skill of their ancestors.) Only a real expert can distinguish between the old and the very old.

• Pewter. The alloy of tin and other metals is easily identified by its color and appearance, which are more mellow and subtle than silver or silver plate. If a piece called pewter is marked Dixon or Sheffield, with a number on its underside, it is not pewter at all but Britannia metal, a substitute.

• Ironstone. Mason's ironstone, found largely in jugs made for the home and in dinner service, is the original only if the words Mason's Patent Ironstone China appear in capital letters on the bottom.

• Enamels. A dealer offering Battersea enamel does not necessarily mean a snuffbox or needle-and-thread case made at the small factory at York House, Battersea, between 1753 and 1756. The term has come to be used for old enamels made mostly in other English towns in the 18th century. However, the piece could also have been produced within recent years in a factory in Birmingham, or even in Czechoslovakia. The originals are of copper, surfaced with an opaque glass that was then hand decorated with inked paper transfers taken from copper plates.

• Silver. Old Sheffield plate will show the copper where the silver plating has worn off. This generally means that the piece was made before 1850. Once a piece has been resilvered by modern electroplating methods, it is just about impossible to differentiate it from other kinds of silver.

• China. The patterns are not always an indication of age since copyright is a relatively new idea. In years gone by, one porcelain maker cheerfully borrowed the pattern of a predecessor. The only way to cope with the resultant identification problem, say the experts, is to look carefully until you become savvy enough to recognize a Staffordshire printed earthenware plate by the flowers of its border.

• Collecting in general. When looking around, always be on the alert for items whose design is basically sound. In this way you have the best chance of picking up the so-called antiques of tomorrow. Meanwhile, since more and more Americans have become collectors, and the supply of items made before 1830 (the cutoff date between antiques and nonantiques) is limited, the value of any *good* old piece increases.

BEST ANTIQUE SHOPS IN NYC

French and English furniture:

- Arthur Ackerman & Sons, 50 E. 57 St., 753-5292.* Stunning collection of 18th-century English furniture. Strong on Chippendale, Sheraton and Queen Anne.

- Jean-Paul Beaujard, 209 E. 76 St., 249-3790. Large collection of 19th-century furniture, with emphasis on the French Empire.

Some Art Deco.

- Dalva Brothers, 44 E. 57 St., 758-2297. Mainly 18th-century French antiques, but you can also find a few fine Italian and English pieces here.

- Malcolm Franklin, 762 Madison Ave., 288-9054. Fine rare English antiques.

- Howard Kaplan's Antiques, 827 Broadway, 674-1000. A treasure trove of French, English and American pieces ... and not too expensive.

- Kentshire Galleries, 37 E. 12 St., 673-6644. The place for formal English antiques. Eight floors of first-quality English, with the emphasis on Regency.

- Malmaison Antiques, 253 E. 74th, 288-7569. Excellent collection of ormolu, parquetry and other inlays.

- Martell Antiques, 53 E. 10 St., 777-4360. The antiques have a country flavor, but the selection is fine and imposing.

- Newell Art Galleries, 425 E. 53 St., 758-1970. An eclectic collection of formal furniture and bric-a-brac from Renaissance to Art Deco.

*Area code is 212 unless otherwise noted.

- Florian Papp, 962 Madison Ave., 288-6770. In business since the turn of the century, with three floors of fine 19th-century furniture.

19th-century American furniture:

- Didier Aaron, Inc., 32 E. 67 St., 988-5248.

- Margaret B. Caldwell, 115 E. 82 St., 472-8639. By appointment only.

- Don Magner, 309 Henry St., Brooklyn, (718) 624-7296.

Other specialty shops:

- Rita Ford, 19 E. 65 St., 535-6717. Finest collection of music boxes in the city.

- Edwin Jackson, Inc., 307 E. 60th St., 759-8210. Antique fireplaces, mantels and accessories.

- Leo Kaplan Antiques, 910 Madison Ave., 249-6766. Eighteenth-century English pottery, paperweights, etc., and a large selection of French cameo glass.

- D.M. & P. Manheim, 305 E. 61 St., 758-2986. Pottery, porcelains and enamels from the 17th, 18th and 19th centuries.

- Lillian Nassau, 220 E. 57 St., 759-6062. The best place in the US to buy Tiffany glass. Also has a fine collection of Art Nouveau and Art Deco glass and accessories.

- James Robinson, 15 E. 7th, 752-6166. Antique silver, china and glass, and a fine collection of antique jewelry.

- Minna Rosenblatt, 844 Madison Ave., 288-0250. Tiffany glass and other antique glass, plus a lovely collection of French cameos.

- Philip Suval, Inc., Box 6011, New York 10022, 517-8293. Incredible collection of antique English porcelain and pottery, paintings, and porcelains from the China trade. By appointment only.

- A la Vieille Russie, 781 Fifth Ave., 752-1727. Specializes in Imperial Russian Faberge accessories and jewelry.

COLLECTING AMERICAN FOLK ART

American folk art was "discovered" in the 1920s. Although there were a few pioneer museum exhibits, and a group of collectors founded the museum that was to become the Museum of American Folk Art in 1961, it didn't take off until recent years. Folk art has become increasingly popular for many reasons, including the country-furniture boom, its compatibility with modern design and the recent rise in American appreciation for things American.

What is folk art?

Folk art is difficult to define. It ranges from three-dimensional objects, such as copper weathervanes and carved wooden decoys, to naive oil portraits and fanciful quilts. Traditionally, it was created by immigrants who continued to use inherited design motifs—the Germans in Pennsylvania, the English in New England. But artisans outside of immigrant communities produced work that falls into this category, too. Common denominators: It is created by and for common folk, and it is utilitarian but has an esthetic quality that elevates it beyond mere functionality.

Although country furniture is often classified as folk art, it really isn't. The country woodworker is a professional.

There are three kinds of collectors:
• Antiques collectors who use folk art as decoration.
• Fine-art collectors who also collect folk art.
• Those who collect folk art as an investment.
How to begin:
• Visit galleries and museum exhibits that feature your special interest.
• Go to antique shows.
• Talk with antique dealers. They are the best-informed of all those in the field and are willing to share their information.

What to buy:

Acquire quality. It's better to buy one good thing than a lot of inferior pieces that will never be esthetically pleasing and won't appreciate.

Specialize. Become knowledgeable in one particular area to be an effective competitor in the marketplace. But be flexible. It's shortsighted to say, "I don't collect that," and pass up something you really love.

Prices have skyrocketed in the last several years and are still high. At a recent Sotheby's sale, a late-19th-century Statue of Liberty weathervane went for $75,000. That was more than double the previous auction record for a weathervane. A watercolor of a whaling ship from the Barbara Johnson collection brought $02,500.

But most folk art is still accessible. Tip: Right now, 20th-century folk art is worth looking into. Ceramics, sculpture, quilts, textiles, paintings and other crafts are being produced all over the country. The problem is sorting out the quality. The trick: Look at enough good things to develop your eye.

Caveat emptor:

Anyone who is making a major purchase should ask for a written guarantee. It should include a description of the piece, the name of the maker, the period and disclosure of all restoration. The guarantee should specify that if any of the information proves to be incorrect, the piece can be returned for full refund.

Source: Robert Bishop, director of the Museum of American Folk Art, New York.

COLLECTING AMERICAN QUILTS

Appreciation of American quilts has grown greatly in recent years. Most sought after right now: Amish or Mennonite quilts. Prices start at $1,000. Many are made in somber colors (black, purple, dark blue) with a geometric design. They look striking in modern interiors. The quilters were forbidden by their religion to use flowers or other frivolous designs or decoration. However, they often tricked sterner members of the sect by backing their quilts with patterned fabrics.

Does this patterned fabric add to the value?

No. The fine stitching and the sophisticated color schemes are the spectacular features of an Amish quilt. Incidentally, you will find a deliberate mistake, such as one square in a color that clashes with the rest of the scheme, in every quilt. This illustrates that only God is perfect.

Are most Amish quilts old?

Actually, most were made in the 1920s and

early 1930s. Quilts older than that have worn out from use.

Are they entirely handmade?

No. Most borders were put on by machine. (They had sewing machines as early as 1840.)

Are the Amish and Mennonites still making quilts?

Yes, but unfortunately they now use a combination of cotton and polyester fabrics. Even the cottons aren't the same. The old ones were vegetable-dyed, which gave special richness to the colors.

What other sorts of quilts are desirable?

White brides' quilts, which are very rare. Fine patchwork with tiny pieces. (Tiny pieces, if expertly sewn, add to the value of a quilt.) Applique, in which a tulip, a basket or some other motif is cut out and sewn on separately. Trapunto, quilting with a raised effect made by outlining the design with running stitches and then filling it with cotton.

How do you judge a quilt?

By design, color harmony and needlecraft. However, mediocre design with wonderful stitching can be outstanding. So can a quilt with less fine needlework, but with marvelous pattern or colors. The ideal is to find great taste and great workmanship together.

Is it possible to find large quilts?

Once in a while you'll see one that's 100 inches wide, but most are in the 72-inch to 78-inch range, and often square. Quilts are rarely a standard size. If you have a very fine quilt, don't use it on a bed. There's too much risk of wear.

Where are quilts found now?

The best buys are in the Midwest, particularly in Ohio and Missouri, but also in upstate New York and other more remote rural communities. Search at auctions and antique fairs.

How are quilts displayed?

They are used as wall hangings, which is what most dealers advise. Dramatic colors and designs are the qualities that you should look for in a quilt you would like to use as a wall hanging.

How do you care for a quilt?

If you hang it behind glass, it must never touch the glass. To frame a quilt, treat it like a fine print, and back it with acid-free paper. Never display a quilt in direct sunlight—colors fade, especially the reds. To store, roll it (don't fold) to prevent wear cracks. Wrap it in acid-free paper. Avoid old quilts with brown materials. Something in the mordant (the dye-setter) or the dyes themselves causes the brown to disintegrate.

How do you clean a quilt?

No dry cleaning, ever. The solvents are too strong. If you must wash the quilt, do it in the bathtub with a dishwashing detergent such as *Joy.* Then rinse the quilt many, many times with distilled water. But sometimes you may have to leave it dirty. Don't fool with rust stains, or with blood stains (made by pricked fingers) which were not washed out right away.

Source: Barbara Doherty, co-owner of Pineapple Primitives, Brooklyn, NY.

COLLECTING CHINESE PORCELAIN

In recent years, fine Chinese porcelain has often outpaced stocks, bonds and the money market, with an annual appreciation of 15% or more. News was made in December of 1981, when a blue and white Ming jar auctioned at Sotheby's brought $1.3 million. This was the highest price ever paid for a Chinese porcelain.

Chinese porcelain is pottery that contains the mineral products kaolin and feldspar (for translucency) and is fired at very high temperatures. Manufacture began in the late 10th century.

Why are dynasty names, such as Ming, used?

Porcelain study is organized historically, and these names place an object in time. The dynasties: Northern Sung (960–1127); Southern Sung (1127–1279); Yuan (1280–1368); Ming (1368–1643); and Ch'ing (1644–1912). Also, names of certain rulers within dynasties are used, especially for the 17th and 18th centuries. Example: K'ang-hsi (1662–1722). K'ang-hsi blue and white ware is highly prized.

Are there ways for a beginner to identify a period by the shape or color of an object?

It is a complicated subject that demands a lot of looking. However, there are a few broad generalizations. The earliest porcelains are the white wares of the Northern Sung dynasty, termed Ting. The first blue and whites appear in the Yuan period. They are called Mohammedan blue, because both cobalt and the techniques used to fashion the wares were imported from Persia. The floral and figural decorations on porcelain with a predominant background color (Famille Rose, Famille Noire, Famille Verte, etc.) are 17th and 18th century. The monochromes (pure yellows, celadons, oxbloods, peach blooms, etc.) are basically developments of the 18th century. They were extremely popular with collectors in the early part of this century.

What is most sought after now?

The highest prices are for early Ming (15th century) blue and white pieces bearing a reign mark. Within the past eight years or so, a mania for reign marks has developed. The reign mark or seal was placed on the object as a sign of deference or good will. In Ming pieces, they are crucial. Example: A hypothetical good early Ming blue and white vase will bring $100,000 if marked. Unmarked, it will go for around $30,000.

How much do chips or cracks affect value?

Very much, in today's market. Steer clear of anything the slightest bit damaged, underfired or overfired.

Is it possible to begin collecting without paying a great deal of money?

Yes, indeed. For the new collector, transitional blue and white ware, which was made in the 17th century, between the end of the Ming and the beginning of the Ch'ing dynasties is still reasonable. A hypothetical sleeve vase (flaring and cylindrical) made between 1640 and 1650, with some nice incised decorations, should cost around $2,500 in perfect condition. That is not so much when you consider the price of other antiques of equal artistry.

Another relatively modest way to start: Export wares made for European and American markets, especially those bearing family arms or marks. They were made from the 18th century into the 19th, often as tea or dinner services. Prices would run from about $200 for a small plate up to $5,000–$8,000 for a fine tureen. It is fun to do research on the family arms and to track them down to the year the porcelain was commissioned.

Is it difficult to care for porcelain?

Just don't drop it! Porcelain is very durable, use reasonable caution, and wash it in soapy water.

What is the state of the market?

Extremely erratic. Example: A 10¾-inch dish that Christie's sold in November 1981. It was an early Ming blue and white saucer dish with a six-character Hsuan-te mark. The estimated value was $15,000–$20,000. It sold for $66,000. This is a classic example of something from the right period with the right reign mark.

What are the best reference works on Chinese porcelain?

There are hundreds of books on the subject; but the following are unequaled for the person seriously interested in the field. They can be found in good libraries.

• *Oriental Blue and White* by Sir Harry Garner, Faber and Faber, London, 1954, 1973, 1977.
• *Chinese Armorial Porcelain* by David Sanctuary Howard, Faber and Faber, London, 1974.
• *Chinese Celadon Ware* by G. Saint B.M. Compertz, Faber and Faber, London, 1958.
• *Ming Porcelain,* by Daisy Lion-Goldschmidt, Rizzoli, English edition, 1978.

Source: Andrew Kahane, Christie's, New York.

COLLECTING PEWTER

Pewter appeals to collectors for both its handsomeness and its history. Because of their classic styles and satiny, silver-gray finish, pewter pieces also lend themselves well to decorative display.

Although pewter has sometimes been called the poor man's silver, fine pewter has always been esteemed. Basically, pewter is tin alloyed with lead, copper, bismuth and sometimes antimony. The proportions of metals vary according to the maker, but generally a lower proportion of lead (and subsequently lightness) means higher quality.

Today the most sought-after pewter in the US is American pre-19th-century, both for its scarcity and the general fever to collect Americana. American craftsmen melted down damaged or badly worn pewter for recasting into new pieces. Constant remelting, heavy use and eventual discarding left little to survive.

Since so few 17th-century and early 18th-century American pieces are available, most collectors concentrate on post-Revolutionary War pewter.

The great scarcity has escalated prices. A rare 1740 tankard sold for $15,000 at a recent auction. (Auctions with sizable collections of 18th-century pewter are also infrequent.) A late 18th-century plate or a small liquid tavern measure, however, might be found for $300–$500.

Pewter was still made in the early 19th century, but in order to compete with the growing popularity of pottery and glass, some makers began adding antimony to their alloy. The result was a harder metal, adaptable to the refined patterns of silver. Called Britannia metal, this pewter was extremely popular until the mid-19th-century. To a purist pewter collector, though, it lacks the attraction of the traditional pewter.

By the mid-19th-century, mass-production methods and the process of electroplating made silverplate more affordable, and pewter production died out. A collector might find pewter that was once silverplated with the plate later removed, but it is not as desirable as the original pewter.

Twentieth century pewter pieces are not valued by collectors.

Beyond American shores, pewter has a truly ancient history that goes back to the Bronze Age. Pewter production has thrived in England since the Middle Ages. An astute collector may manage to find English pewter from as early as the 16th-century. Imported by American dealers, 17th- and 18th-century English pewter is far more available than its American counterpart. It also commands about half the price of comparable American pieces, even when the English piece is as much as 75 years older. As American pewter becomes rarer, the urge for collecting English pewter seems likely to increase. Off-the-beaten-path antique stores in England are a source of bargains for the knowledgeable collector. So far, most European pewter is valued at only a fraction of English pewter's worth.

Design, good condition and an absence of discoloration are important considerations in evaluating pewter. The most important factors are age and origin. Touch marks im-printed on pewter are highly prized. Such symbols make it possible to date pieces and to determine if they are American (sometimes even the region is identified), English or Continental. However, early American craftsmen often copied British symbols or stamped "London" on their wares to mislead the public. And some early pewter was not marked at all. The multitude of signs, hallmarks and makers' signatures makes reference-book research a necessity for the serious collector. Since fakes and forgeries are common, experts advise buying only from a very reputable dealer.

Early pewter was cast in heavy molds and then finished on a lathe. The finishing left shallow grooves called skimming marks on the pewter. When a handle was attached, the linen support placed under the handle left the impression of its weave. Hammer marks on the underside of a plate rim also indicate early craftsmanship. **Learning:** Most museums with Early American collections have displays of pewter that a beginner can learn from.

Source: Price Glover, antique dealer and specialist in pewter, New York.

COLLECTING ANTIQUE AMERICAN CLOCKS

Clock collecting goes back to 15th-century Europe, when royal patrons commissioned ornately jeweled timepieces. In America, quality clockmaking began in colonial times, and collecting by the affluent got an early start. A major display at the Columbian Exposition of 1893 was of colonial clocks.

Major collecting categories:

Tall-case clocks. The earliest American-made clocks are over seven feet high and are popularly known as grandfather clocks. (Collectors call them tall-case clocks.) The earliest had square dials. Later versions have arched dials, often with pictures or moving figures that show the phases of the moon. Late 18th-century clocks may have wooden works. Names to look for: William Claggart, Peter Stretch and Simon & Aaron Willard. Prices for tall clocks range from the low thousands to over $80,000.

Banjo clocks. In the late 18th century,

banjo-shaped wall clocks were created. The earliest ones are now as valuable as tall-case clocks made in the same years. At a recent auction, an elaborate early-19th-century banjo clock by Lemuel Curtis sold for $15,000. One of uncertifiable make sold for $2,000.

Shelf clocks. In the early 19th century, these more affordable clocks appeared. About two feet high, they fit comfortably on the mantel. Their mass-production methods, devised by Eli Terry and Seth Thomas, were America's main contribution to the clock industry. A good shelf clock can cost from $200 to several thousands of dollars.

What makes clocks valuable?
• The best clocks have, besides age and beauty, all their original parts in good working order. Cases must also be in good condition.
• Replacements or repairs should have been expertly done with methods and materials of the clock's period. With proper restoration, a clock maintains its quality.
• Signatures and labels of esteemed clockmakers enhance value. But fine unsigned clocks also get good prices.
• Embellishments to conform to a current fashion detract from a clock's worth.
• Scarcity is not synonymous with value. Some fine clockmakers made many clocks, which all command high prices because of quality, not rarity.

Starting out:
Veteran clock collectors have been described as one of the most canny groups of collectors. Fortunately, the novice can acquire information easily. Many good books are available in public libraries. Museum collections are a useful guide to variety and high quality. The National Association of Watch and Clock Collectors has 125 chapters, a bimonthly journal and research services.

For the serious beginner, the best way to buy is through a reliable dealer who gives a written guarantee that the clock can be returned.

Clocks are no longer a good high-return, short-term investment. But quality clocks, especially tall-case clocks, will retain their value and grow with inflation. Even some pre-World War II clocks may be of collecting value. Two contemporary American clock companies, Chelsea and Howard, are still making limited quantities of high-quality clocks that may turn out to be the desirable antiques of the future.

Source: Chris Bailey, curator of the American Clock and Watch Museum, Bristol, CT.

COLLECTING OLD WATCHES

Clocks were reduced to portable size in the early 1500s, when the first watches, highly decorated pendants, were proudly worn as fine jewelry. Technical advances in the 1870s, coupled with the newly chic long waistcoat (watches were slipped into convenient pockets), led to more practical timepieces. Two hundred years of innovations and refinements culminated in the precision instruments beloved by collectors today—primarily European, handcrafted mechanical watches made between 1700 and 1900.

European watches:
• Decorative watches have decorative cases with lids that close (called hunting cases) or unusual shapes and scenes or designs in engraved or repousse gold, enamel or jewels.
• Complicated watches have intricate technical mechanisms for functions other than telling time. Some tell the month, day, year, phase of the moon, international times or even sidereal time. Others have alarms, timers or musical chimes. Watches were made with chronographs, thermometers and compasses—and one, sold recently for $1,350, had a built-in roulette wheel. A most popular type of watch, called a repeater, strikes on the hour, quarter hour, or even minute, when a button is activated. Automata have moving figures that perform on the hour or quarter hour on demand. An erotic version was offered recently for almost $8,000. Always popular are skeletonized watches, whose movements are visible through clear cases. Some of these may sell for under $1,000.
• The rarest of the rare. It is the dream of every serious collector to own a watch by Abraham-Louis Breguet, an innovative French watchmaker of the late 18th to mid-19th centuries. Every watch he made is unique and distinc-

tive. Only a small percentage of his known output has been accounted for. In 1895, a Breguet watch cost the equivalent of about 20 houses. Today, one would sell for $20,000–$150,000, and many fakes are around.

• Other names to look for: Patek-Philippe ("the Rolls-Royce of watches"), Frodsham, Rolex and Audemars Piguet.

American watches:

• Railroad watches. Conductors and engineers of the late 19th century were dependent on their watches to keep to their timetables. These are the most popular collectible type in America. Often large and plain, and always accurate, they were expensive a century ago. Names: Waltham, Elgin, Howard, Illinois "Bunn Special," Hamilton and Ball.

• Dollar watches. Inexpensive, mass-produced pocket watches from the 1920s and 1930s are still inexpensive and easy to find. With few exceptions, dollar watches will probably never be highly valued, but they can be lots of fun for the beginning collector. Exceptions: Watches made for the World's Fairs (Chicago 1893, New York 1939 and others) or novelty watches like *Mickey Mouse* or *Buck Rogers*, now selling for hundreds of dollars.

• Top of the line. Before 1915, many American watch companies made a "top of the line" model in limited quantities, numbered and inscribed which rivaled or even outshone contemporary European models. Collectors can learn to recognize these through reading and research.

• Recent watches. While the new quartz watches hold little interest (so far) for collectors, early electric watches—the first Hamilton electric, for example—are sought, as are watches from Cartier or Tiffany made through the 1940s.

What adds value?

A famous maker or model. Degree of complication. Amount of purity of gold (or silver). Number of jewels. A low serial number (look inside). The beauty of case and movement. Condition. (Watches should be in working condition or repairable. Repairs must be done in the style of the original.)

Watches as an investment:

Six or seven years ago, "investment fever"

began to push prices out of the range of collectors of fine antique watches. These inflated values have dropped, and it is currently a buyer's market. Prices for even the rarest watches are about half what they were. A Patek-Philippe perpetual calendar minute repeater that brought $110,000 two years ago was recently sold in France for $45,000. American watches have held their values because they are collected only in the US. They are expected to slowly increase in value over the next 15–20 years. The classic European watches by master watchmakers will always be valuable, but they are no longer a short-term investment with high yield.

Inexpensive watches are available wherever old jewelry is sold. When you consider purchasing an expensive watch, however, be sure to consult an expert. Estate auctions are generally good sources. General auctions, even at major houses, are questionable. They may offer watches that are unrepairable.

For the beginner:

Membership in the National Association of Watch and Clock Collectors includes two publications: *The Bulletin* and *The Mart* (in which members buy, sell and trade watches—a wonderful source). The association also maintains a museum, a lending library and a new computerized "horological data bank."

Source: Dr. Walter D. Bundens, former president of the National Association of Watch and Clock Collectors, and William Scolnik, dealer in antique watches, New York.

COLLECTING NATIVE AMERICAN SILVER JEWELRY

In the late 1960s and early 1970s, Native American Indian silver jewelry, previously collected by a small coterie, began to capture the interest of the general public. Count on a 10–15% annual appreciation on the value of fine old and contemporary pieces.

Learning the ropes. Look at photographs, go to museums, read. Expect to make a few mistakes. You have to do some impulse buying, then go home, study what you bought and profit from the experience.

Background. Indians of the Southwest are the major producers of silver jewelry. Most talented and prolific: Navajo and Zuni. Also on the market: Limited amounts of Hopi (known for overlay work) and Santo Domingo (turquoise and shell, sometimes combined with silver or gold).

Navajo first-phase jewelry. The Navajos were the first Indians in the Southwest to work with silver. They learned the craft from the Spanish-Mexicans in the mid-1860s. Ornaments made for their own use or for trading with other Indians: Concha belts, najas (bridal decorations), bracelets, squash-blossom necklaces. Characteristics: Primitive, simple design with Spanish influence. The quality of silver is often not good, and hairline cracks may be visible. Cost: Very expensive.

Navajo second phase. Starting about 1890–1900, they began to use ingots. They embellished traditional designs and used more turquoise. Coral from Europe was introduced around 1910–1920.

Early tourist jewelry. This covers 1910–1940. Produced for barter with white traders, it included belts, bracelets, boxes, lipstick cases, ashtrays and cigarette holders.

Zuni. After the 1920s, the Zuni began to make silver inlaid with coral, turquoise, mother-of-pearl and jet. They developed the cluster style (clusters of symmetrically shaped stones). They also devised channel work, which is silver strips, typically with beading, outlining shapes in which turquoises are inserted. Generally, Zuni jewelry is more delicate than Navajo.

Since there is very little jewelry on the market from the 1800s, start by buying early tourist jewelry. Secret: Buy what can be worn by you or someone close to you unself-consciously. Reason to choose: Because you love the piece.

Most popular right now. Concha belts. One recently sold for $25,000.

What to look for. Quality of stones, weight of silver, stamping, craftsmanship and soul. Problem: It is difficult to find outstanding examples of all these elements in one piece.

Contemporary silver. If the artist is well known, you often pay more for a new piece than for an old one.

Sources. Flea markets, antique shows, local art and craft galleries. Best possibilities: Indian sidewalk markets on the plazas in Santa Fe and Albuquerque. Shops in pueblos and trading posts on reservations.

Recommended books:

Indian Silver Jewelry of the Southwest 1868–1880 by Larry Frank, New York Graphic Society, Boston.

Collecting Southwestern Native American Jewelry by Mark Bahti, David McKay, New York.

The Navajo and Pueblo Silversmith by John Adair, University of Oklahoma Press, Norman, OK.

Indian Silverwork of the Southwest, Volume One by Harry P. Mera, Dale Stuart King, Globe, AZ.

Source: Teal McKibben, collector and owner of La Bodega de Rael, Santa Fe, NM, and Carl Druckman, researcher and consultant in Indian jewelry, Santa Fe, NM.

COLLECTING ANTIQUE JEWELRY

Antique jewelry satisfies a love of the past and the appreciation of fine craftsmanship. It fulfills the expectation that quality jewelry should give pleasure for a long time. In addition, some of the most beautiful and unusual gems and designs can be found in antique pieces.

Investment: new versus old:

Despite the fact that the markup on new jewelry is as much as 100%, resale value declines the minute a piece is purchased. Unless a new piece has gemstones that at least double in value, its worth will decrease drastically in a short time.

Antique jewelry is, of course, also marked up for retail. However, other factors besides gemstones help stabilize and increase its value. Setting, workmanship, style, rarity and history all determine price. The passing of time enhances rather than diminishes value. Excellent antique jewelry nearly always rises in value.

Buying:

Knowledge is essential. Many antique dealers are not well informed about jewelry. Look for a dealer who is long established, and seek personal recommendations from other jewelry collectors.

Browsing to compare prices and learning what you can from books are basic. Auctions can be instructive, but novices are better off out of the bidding until they have some expertise.

Periods of design:

Jewelry styles may overlap decades or be so classic that they are repeated from one era to another. However, one of the most important things to learn is the dominant periods of design. Pieces made before the 18th century are extremely scarce, very expensive and usually impractical to wear. The following historical periods are the major sources of available antiques.

Georgian: Jewelry from the early 1700s to approximately 1830 looks different from any other style in history. Its characteristics are well worth studying. Comparative rarity and esthetic appeal keep its prices high.

Although Georgian gold jewelry appears substantial, it is light in weight. Stones were often foiled (backed with colored metal) to enhance their hue. Glass gems, cut and polished as carefully as real ones, were often set in silver. The brilliant-cut diamond was new to the era and popular, but all precious and semiprecious stones were used, as well as natural oriental pearls, coral and ivory.

Victorian: From 1830 to the turn of the century, a great deal of jewelry was made, and much of it still survives. Victorian jewelry is characterized by massive pieces of heavy gold and silver. Colorful stones and impressive parures (matched sets) were common. Jewelry with sentimental messages was highly popular.

Most available Victorian jewelry is English-made. American-made jewelry, though simpler in design, is scarce and apt to be higher in price.

Art Nouveau: At the end of the Victorian era, the flowing, sensuous lines of Art Nouveau emerged to dominate design. Jewelry became graceful, slender and feminine. Sterling silver was often used, and popular stones were muted in color or even colorless. Many odd stones were also used, and iridescence was highly regarded. Opals, mother-of-pearl, horn and shell were common. Craftsmen aimed for unique designs. Fakes and reproductions are common.

Art Deco: From World War I to about 1940, the angular, shiny designs of Art Deco came into vogue. Its clean geometric lines and contrasts of black and white are still appealing and very wearable. Onyx, enamel, white gold, crystal, diamonds and jade are characteristic. Although such jewelry is not old enough to qualify as truly antique, the continuing popularity of Art Deco has escalated prices.

Condition:

Never buy a piece solely because it is old. Antique jewelry should be in good or perfect condition. Damaged jewelry has little resale value.

A 10-power jeweler's loupe is essential for the serious collector. Check for glued-in stones, thin ring shanks and poorly mended or broken parts. Signs of repair or alteration are drawbacks. The jewelry should be very close to its original state. Avoid jewelry that has been put together from various pieces, such as earrings from bits of a necklace.

Caring for jewelry:

If a piece breaks or wears out, it should be repaired by a jeweler who is an expert on antiques. Generally, the less repair the better.

For cleaning, be gentle. When in doubt, do nothing. Avoid over-zealous polishing or electronic cleaning. It can be damaging, and it destroys the wonderful patina of age. Soapy water will do for most pieces, but read up on the care and composition of a piece before trying anything.

Real or reproduction?

Honest reproductions are acceptable—but be alert for deception. A reproduction is apt to show signs of haste in its construction. Modern touches such as safety catches are often giveaways. If more than one sample of a certain piece is on display, be leery—few identical pieces survive.

Source: Rose Leiman Goldemberg, author of *Antique Jewelry, A Practical and Passionate Guide,* Crown Publishers (out of print but available in almost all libraries), and *All About Jewelry,* Arbor House, New York.

HOW TO BUY JEWELRY AT AUCTION AND SAVE

Clearly, "cutting out the middleman" can save jewelry shoppers thousands of dollars on just one purchase. This is especially true of single diamonds. D color,[*] internally flawless stones sell at auction for $6,000-$8,000 per carat up to three carats, rather than the $20,000 or so per carat reported in newspapers and magazines. Furthermore, many auction diamonds come with Gemological Institute of America (GIA) certificates that show the weight, color and clarity of the stone.

Expert advice on how to buy at auction depends in part on what you're interested in. If you're buying contemporary jewelry, where the value of the piece lies almost 100% in the gemstones, it's most important to do a little arithmetic to calculate the value of the stones. Divide the presale estimate by the total weight of the stones.

The size of the stone—separate from their weight—affects prices as well. Example: Two diamond bracelets may have equal total weights, but the bracelet that has fewer and larger stones will be worth more and will sell for more.

For antique jewelry, where condition can count far more than design, workmanship, or the intrinsic value of the gold and gemstones, the rules differ. Reading the description of the piece in the auction catalog and seeing it are far more important. Words such as *repaired, altered, cracked* or *later additions* can lower the value of the piece drastically. Says Joyce Jonas, director of the jewelry department of Phillips, New York, who recommends careful examination of the piece before purchasing: "The most important investment you can make is a 10X jeweler's loupe, which costs less than $25. Carry it with you whenever you're examining jewelry. Look at the front. Look for alterations—the front of a brooch may be pink gold, but the pin in back, added later, may be yellow gold. That reduces the value. Look for marks of soldering repair. Gold solder, if used carefully, will not alter the value of the piece. Lead solder, which leaves gray marks, can reduce the price by 50%. Condition is crucial."

Auction houses are bound legally by their catalog descriptions. Look for listed imperfections (often printed in italics) such as *stone missing, stone cracked, lead solder marks, repaired, enamel worn, later additions,* etc. More pleasantly, catalogs also note the shape and weight of large stones (sometimes with GIA diamond ratings), karat of gold (if not listed, it's 14K), and whether a piece is signed. Descriptions are often so detailed that collectors who become familiar with catalogs can visualize the pieces.

If you're planning to buy frequently, make friends with the auction-house jewelry curators. They will often point out the merits or flaws of a piece and can advise you on the maximum reasonable bid. Subscribe to and keep catalogs and lists of prices paid at auctions. They are excellent reference tools in helping you decide how much to bid at future auctions.

When it comes to bidding itself, there are pros and cons to attending the auction in person versus leaving a written bid. Many people, realizing their susceptibility to auction-fever overbidding, find that it's wiser to have a written bid. Others, including many dealers, prefer to attend in person so that they can better control their bidding. Delaying a bid until just before the hammer comes down can get you a piece for a lower price. Strategy: If you sit in the rear of the room, you'll be able to see who's bidding against you.

Auctions are generally advertised in the "Arts and Leisure" weekend section of major newspapers: *The New York Times, The Boston Globe, The San Francisco Examiner, The Washington Post,* etc. The ads list viewing dates and times (usually three or four days before the auction), as well as the date and time of the auction itself.

Says one collector of antique jewelry, fingering her diamond bracelet, "I could never afford jewelry unless I bought at auction. And I get such a wonderful feeling when I see jewelry in stores that's vastly inferior to mine for thousands of dollars more."

Source: Judith H. McQuown, author of *Inc. Yourself: How to Profit by Setting Up Your Own Corporation,* Warner Books, New York.

RESTORING ANTIQUES

The care and repair of fine treasures from the past is a craft in itself and a satisfying hobby to many collectors. For David Rubin,[*] whose

[*]D is the highest rating.
[*]David Rubin, Springfield, MA.

expertise is shared on the Public Broadcasting Services series *Antiques,* it is a profession that takes him all across the country.

For home-restoration enthusiasts, Rubin recommends the following books as the best guides to repair techniques. Most are out of print but can be found in large public libraries and museum libraries.

• *China Mending and Restoration: A Handbook for Restorers* by Cual & Parsons, London, 1963.

• *The Painter's Methods and Materials* by A.P. Laurie, New York, 1960.

• *Pigments and Mediums of the Old Masters* by A.P. Laurie, London, 1914.

• *Antiques, Their Restoration and Preservation* by A. Lucas, London, 1932.

• *The Artist's Handbook of Materials and Techniques* by Ralph Mayer, New York, 1957.

• *The Care of Antiques* by John Fitzmaurice Mills, Hastings House, New York, 1964.

• *Care and Repair of Antiques* by Thomas H. Ormsbee, Medill McBride Co., New York, 1949.

• *The Preservation of Antiques* by H.J. Plenderleith, New York, 1956.

• *The Art and Antique Restorer's Handbook* by George Savage, Praeger, New York, 1967.

• *Restoring and Preserving Antiques* by Frederick Taubes, Watson-Guptill, New York, 1963.

• *Handbook of American Silver and Pewter Marks* by C. Jordan Thorn, Tudor Publishing Co., 1949.

• *How to Restore China, Bric-a-Brac and Small Antiques* by Raymond F. Yates, Harper, New York, 1953.

COLLECTING CARVED CHINESE JADE

Jade was for centuries the precious gem of the Chinese nobility, and carved jade pieces have long been one of the most important facets of Chinese art and antiques.

Collecting jade is almost as venerable an activity as the art of carving it. Today the center of collecting is the West, where most of the finest antique jade carvings are now found. Both for aesthetic satisfaction and the potential appreciation in value, jade collecting is attracting wider attention in the United States. So far, good antique jade is available.

True jade:

Only two minerals, nephrite and jadeite, can truly be called jade. They are very similar but have slightly different compositions. Jadeite was virtually unknown to the Chinese before the 18th century.

Although jade is tough (difficult to shatter), it is not as hard as gemstones such as rubies and emeralds. It can scratch more easily. (Jadeite is the preferred form of jewelry because it is beautifully colored and harder than nephrite.) It is the toughness of jade that lends itself so well to precision carving and accounts for the survivability of antique jade.

To most people, jade means green. However, a great variety of colors are available. Jade is found in natural shades of blue, lavender, white, red and brown as well as green. One of the most prized types of nephrite is called mutton fat for its lustrous grayish-white color with tinges of pale green.

Small jades that are old, historically important, unusually colored and beautifully carved can command steep prices. However, a collector beginning with an investment of several hundred to a thousand dollars can find a valuable small-jade carving that is 100–300 years old. Besides being a fascinating work of art (owners seem to develop an intimate relationship with their small jades), a fine piece is likely to increase in value (with reservations due to uncertain economics).

A good recommendation often followed by new collectors is to specialize. The collector might narrow a collection to only zodiac animals, or to flowered snuff bottles.

Best; simple and handmade:

A good carver has made use of the different patterns and textures of the raw material. Even imperfections become part of the design. Much of the carving done in Hong Kong today is machine-powered. Experts feel that something is lost in the process and that the result is often too elaborate. However, Hong Kong is still a source of fine, hand-carved contemporary pieces.

Much of modern jade has been dyed to alter or enhance its natural color. And much ''jade'' is not jade at all. The commonest substitute is serpentine. A buyer should beware of both intentional deception and honest mistakes. In addition, jade is very hard to date. Even museum experts can find dating a piece problematical. A trustworthy dealer offers on the bill of sale a description confirming that the item is what it is presented to be.

Attending auctions of Chinese art is one way to learn possibilities and prices. Museum collections also offer a way to survey some of the finest examples of jade workmanship. The Metropolitan Museum of Art in New York City has on permanent display the most impressive pieces from the Bishop Collection, one of the best jade collections in the world. Also notable is the collection in the De Young Museum in San Francisco. A beginner would find *Jade of the East** by Geoffrey Wills worth reading.

*Available from Charles E. Tuttle, Rutland, VT.

Source: Simone Hartman, collector and co-owner of Rare Art galleries, New York, Dallas and Palm Beach.

COLLECTING STAMPS

How much must you invest initially if you want to collect for fun?

Not much for starters, and that's one attraction of the hobby. Unlike coins, which are fairly expensive individual items, you can get started in stamps for $20.

How does one start?

By going through a learning curve. Consult the Yellow Pages for stamp shops in your area. Meet the owners. Find out about the weekend shows, called bourses. Subscribe to philatelic publications.

What are some collecting areas?

Topicals are an excellent way to begin. If you have an interest in aviation, for instance, zero in on stamps depicting airplanes. Space stamps are a hot topical. Tropical fish are also popular.

First day covers are another way to collect. Covers (envelopes) have the stamp canceled at first date of issue, from the town that is issuing for that particular stamp. (Example: The cover for the 75th anniversary of flight was issued at Kitty Hawk on December 17, 1978.) Covers bear a cachet (engraving) related to the subject. They are pretty and inexpensive, but they have no investment value.

Will they appreciate quickly?

Slowly, because modern covers are issued in such quantity. Scarcity and historical importance are the key factors in philatelic value. Of course, if you could find a cover dated September 9, 1850, mailed from California it would bring $100,000. That's the date California became a state, and such a cover is prized.

How high do prices go?

Recently $1 million was paid for *The Blue Boy,* issued at Alexandria, VA, in 1846. This is actually a stampless cover. The postage stamp was invented in England in 1840 but not established in the United States until 1847. Before that, letters were either franked (passed by official signature) or paid for on the receiving end.

What about stamps as an investment?

Stamps seem to be recession-proof. Between January 2, 1978, and December 31, 1980, the Dow rose 2%. A cross-section of 86 classic US stamps rose 85% in value during that same period. Demand for the supply of quality US stamps is great. The number is finite. There are 20 million collectors in the US. (Incidentally, over 95% are males. No one has explained that.)

How do you care for stamps?

Investment stamps should be kept in a vault and not handled. Hobby stamps are slipped into glassine mounts for safety and arranged in albums.

What's the difference between a stamp collector and a philatelist?

Knowledge. A philatelist reads and has an eye toward a specific goal. The choice is limited only by imagination.

Source: Bruce Stone, president of Stamp Portfolios, Inc., Stamford, CT.

COLLECTING COINS

Coin collections fall into two categories: Those done for the fun of it, and those undertaken by collector-investors who mix value with the fun.

Collectors looking only for a pleasant hobby usually restrict themselves to inexpensive coins. Basic procedure: Obtain the standard books and buy albums in which to mount the coin purchases. Join clubs and attend shows to build up expertise at your leisure.

Collector-investors approach their coins with a higher level of commitment. Main difference: They spend significant amounts of money in the hope of reaping financial rewards.

Salient facts:

• The market for US Treasury-minted coins was once fairly steady, since only collectors bought and sold. But starting in the mid-1960s, noncollecting investors began to move cash in and out of the market, buying and selling coins as speculative investments much as they might stocks and bonds. This injection of volatile money transformed a relatively steady market into one of cycles, with booms and busts. Speculation increases demand for investment-grade coins, which makes those that are extant more and more valuable.

• Experienced collector-investors and dealers often use their expertise to take advantage of the novice investor. Result: Thousands of new collectors find they are stuck with inexpensive junk when it is time to sell.

How to avoid being skinned:

• Study well before making major money investments. There are a number of books about each major US coin series. These volumes discuss the historical background of the coins. Examples: How well the coins were struck, and the condition of the dyes when the coins were made. The rare years and common years for the coins and dozens of variations that make each coin distinct from others. The books often give values for the coins, but these are usually out of date. For the latest figures, consult the coin collectors' newsletters. Point: Learn all you can about a coin before investing. This background knowledge helps keep you from being cheated by a fast-talking dealer.

• Learn from dealers. Get acquainted with several to gain a sense of them as people. Be alert to their willingness to protect beginners from their own errors.

• Do not depend on the advice of dealers for long. To wean yourself away, spend lots of time at coin shows and auctions. Learn to identify and grade individual coins and note their sale prices. Subscribe to and study the literature read by professionals.

Crucial advice: Sell part of your collection every year. This shows you whether or not you knew what you were doing when you bought.

What to sell: Duplicates for which you have better samples. Coins from periods that no longer interest you. Samples that have lost their fascination.

Why to start or rebuild a collection now: In the late 1970s and into 1980, a major speculative boom shot prices far beyond sustainable levels. After some panic selling, many paper profits disappeared. Now the market is pretty well cleared of all excess pricing. The boom drove away many novice and casual collectors as prices soared. But recently these people started drifting back into the marketplace as coins became more affordable.

Preservation: The value of a coin does not depend entirely on the market cycle. It can drop rapidly from poor handling or cleaning or even from coughing on the coin. Best: Check with dealers and consult literature on the best methods of preservation. Avoid: Plastic holders made from polyvinylchloride (PVC). This material breaks down with time and releases an oil that oxidizes the copper in coins, turning them green and oily. Note: Although damaged coins can be cleaned, they never look the same to an experienced eye.

Useful literature:

• *Coin Dealer Newsletter,* Hollywood, CA.
• *David Hall's Inside View,* Newport Beach, CA.
• *Rosen Numismatic Advisory,* East Meadow, NY.
• *Fortune Teller,* West Palm Beach, FL.

Source: Dr. Martin G. Groder, consultant to a coin dealership in Durham, NC.

COLLECTING AUTOGRAPHS FOR PROFIT

Autograph collecting is not limited to signatures. Collectors look for letters, manuscripts, documents and checks—anything signed or written by a person of interest. Most popular are presidents, composers, authors, scientists, black and feminist leaders and movie stars.

A doctor who is a music lover, for example, may concentrate on the correspondence of famous composers regarding their health. Many collectors strive to complete a "set," such as Pulitzer Prize winners or Mexican War generals. The classic set of autographs to collect, the signers of the Declaration of Independence (known simply as "Signers"), also contains the most famous of rarities—the signature of Button Gwinnett, a Georgia pig farmer who perished in a duel less than a year after the signing. A genuine letter signed by Gwinnett (he is frequently forged) was found in an outhouse in 1927 and was auctioned for $51,000. A brief receipt signed by Gwinnett brought $100,000 at auction in 1979, the record price paid to date for a single signature.

Inexpensive and easy to find are signatures and signed promotional photographs of many entertainers and athletes and signatures that have been clipped from the letters or documents they were once part of (a common practice in the 19th century). Complete letters or documents are much more desirable. A handwritten letter, manuscript or diary with historical interest is most valued of all.

What affects value:

Content or context. This extremely important factor brings history alive, thus ensuring enduring worth. A letter or journal by an unknown person describing field conditions during the Civil War is of far greater interest than a note from a famous person saying "Sorry, I can't make it on Tuesday," or "Here's the autograph you requested." Many collectors especially youngsters, begin by writing to living noteworthies for their autographs. It is preferable to ask an original, thought-provoking question that will elicit a written reply rather than a form letter or glossy photograph. Even a short response that reveals something of the personality of the writer will be of greater value later on.

Collectors of presidential signatures prefer examples dating from the term of office. Ironically, it can be harder to find a signed, handwritten letter from a modern president (starting with Theodore Roosevelt) than from one of our "fore-fathers." Reason: The advent of the proxy signature, the typewriter and the autopen. A record was recently set for the highest price ever paid for a letter from a living person $12,500 for a signed, handwritten letter from President Reagan. But signed typewritten letters from Ronald Reagan before he became president sell for $50–$500, depending on content.

Rarity. The collector must learn what is scarce or common in his own field. Abraham Lincoln signed thousands of military appointments during the Civil War, but complete letters and signed photographs are rare. Charles Dickens seems to have written letters daily throughout his long life, while Edgar Allan Poe's signature tempts the finest forgers.

Demand. This has more to do with fashion than with fame. Even as revered a figure as Sir Winston Churchill could easily follow his predecessor, David Lloyd George, into relative obscurity as public attention shifts. A rare contract signed by ragtime composer Scott Joplin was sold for $5,000, outpricing a comparable piece by Beethoven.

As a general rule, villains outsell good guys. A John Wilkes Booth signature outprices Lincoln's, while Lee Harvey Oswald's is worth more than JFK's. Murderers and Nazis are likely to remain popular.

Condition. The strength and clarity of a signature, size and length of the material, condition of the paper and postal markings, among other variables, all affect the value of a piece. Important: Do not attempt repairs yourself. Never use cellophane tape on old papers.

Display. The value of any collection can be enhanced by creative, attractive framing. Even inexpensive signatures take on a new life when mounted with a portrait of the subject. Contemporary newspaper clippings, program covers or tickets, reproductions of documents and artwork can make exciting companion pieces of autograph material, as can early daguerreotypes, engravings, posters or other historical ephemera. Striking graphic design adds to the fun, and for this, a skilled professional framer is necessary. Examples: Irving Berlin's autograph, mounted on a background of red, white and blue stripes with his photograph and the original sheet music to *This Is the Army*. A check signed by Orville Wright, mounted next to an early photograph of his airplane. A Bela Lugosi autograph, set against a black cutout of a bat, beneath an early still from *Dracula*.

Investing and the market:

Unlike other collecting areas, there has been no slump in the market for autographs. Record prices continue to be set. This seems to be due to our increasing awareness of the importance of our cultural heritage, along with the desire to preserve as much as possible in this age of the telephone. For investment purposes: Specialize in several areas at once. Perhaps interest in the American West will decline, while the astronauts hold their value—or vice versa. Select your purchases for the interest of their content or their relevance to a historical event. Don't be afraid to pay healthy prices for important material.

Private dealers and auction houses who will vouch for the authenticity of their material are the best sources for important pices. A thorough knowledge of one's field is necessary to be able to recognize chance finds, should they occur. Be careful of inscriptions in the flyleaves of old books, a favorite ground for the forger. Check the drawers in antique furniture, and don't throw out old family papers before consulting an expert.

For further reading: *Collecting Autographs and Manuscripts* by Charles Hamilton, University of Oklahoma Press, Norman, OK.
Collectors' organization: Universal Autograph Collectors' Club (UACC), Box 467, Rockville Centre, NY 11571 (publishes the bimonthly journal, *The Pen and Quill*).
Source: Charles Hamilton, founder of Charles Hamilton Galleries, Inc., New York, the first auction house in the US devoted exclusively to autograph material.

COLLECTING MAPS

Map making goes back to at least 2300 BC, the date of the earliest known clay picture of how to get from here to there—found in Iraq. The ancient Chinese made sophisticated silk maps, Eskimos carved them in ivory, the Incas etched them in stone and prehistoric Europeans drew them on cave walls.

Collectors revere maps for a number of reasons. Many old maps are beautiful (all early world maps are fanciful as well) and very deco-

rative. Historians look for changing political boundaries, documents of military campaigns or journeys of early explorers. Homebodies like to trace changes in their country or city layout over the years.

• Early maps: Maps from the Middle Ages—now seen in museums and libraries—were more symbolic and religious than realistic. World views included imaginary places or vast expanses of *terra incognita,* often with remarkable creatures to match. These delusions and distortions are the delight of collectors, but their rarity makes them irreplaceable treasures.

Maps for practical purposes began to proliferate in the 15th century with the establishment of printing. Explorers needed up-to-date guides to the oceans and lands of the world. They helped to chart new areas and revise old standards. Although it is possible for a collector to find a 16th-century map, it will cost in the thousands. Prices for 17th- and 18th-century maps—most are pages from bound atlases—will vary according to scarcity and demand. Good reproductions of such maps, while handsome and interesting, are of no investment value, so collectors must be careful of their sources.

• Nineteenth-century maps: Fine examples of these more recent world or local maps can be bought for less than $100. Some come from atlases. Others are official maps used to define states or territories. US Geological Survey maps, published since 1879, indicate elevation, roads, swamps, railway stations and churches. Many early city maps show landmark buildings in addition to the streets. Particularly popular at the moment are maps of the American West.

• Twentieth-century maps: Even early 1900s maps are of little value so far. Dealers do not yet carry them so the interested collector must cull flea markets and garage sales.

Determining value:

Rarity, authenticity, beauty, and condition make a map valuable. Even maps that were run off on printing presses in great numbers can become quite scarce over time. The paper they are printed on is fragile, for they were never meant to endure. When a map gets out of date, for whatever reason, it faces what one expert calls "a dangerous interval of vulnerability" when it has no value in contemporary, practical terms and yet arouses little interest in the scholar or historian. Not many maps survive that interval.

Determining the authenticity of old maps is difficult. The best protection is knowledgeable dealers who stand behind what they sell. (A good dealer will also search for specific maps for you.) Although beauty is in the eye of the beholder, condition is an obvious asset to an old map. Creases hurt a map, so potential collectibles should be stored flat.

Learning the ropes:

A beginning collector must start by browsing and reading. Most major libraries have cartography sections with a variety of maps and books on map making that can help you zero in on the types that interest you most. A good general book on the subject is *The Mapmakers* by John Noble Wilford.* Many libraries also have dealers' catalogues which can give you a sense of what is available and the going prices.

Great Britain is the world center for map collecting. In the US, about six major dealers specialize in maps, and interest here is picking up rapidly. An extensive guide** to the world's antique-map dealers is available.

* Knopf, New York.
** *The World Directory of Dealers in Antique Maps,* Chicago Map Society, Chicago.

Source: Ruth Shevin, map specialist at the Argosy Gallery, New York.

COLLECTING FIREARMS

Firearms are among the oldest and most distinguished collectibles. (Henry VIII was a keen collector, as were George Washington and Thomas Jefferson.) And because firearms have been made since the 14th century, the field is vast. No individual can be expert in every aspect.

Most US collectors concentrate on Americana. For the past 40 years, they have tended to specialize—even down to a single gun series. A collector might choose the Colt Single Action Army group, the guns you see in Western movies, for example. They were called "the peacemakers" and "the thumb busters." The US Army adopted this series as a standard sidearm in 1873.

What are the criteria for collecting?

Aesthetics play a great role. The finer guns are exquisite. The engraving can be compared with the work of Fabergé. Historical relevance is important, and so is condition. But quality and maker count more. Even excellent condition cannot make an ugly gun desirable. Add the allure of fine mechanics and also romance. Can you imagine Buffalo Bill without his six-shooters and Winchester Rifles?

Who were the leading makers?

The big four are Colt, founded in 1836; Remington, founded in 1816; Winchester, founded in 1866 but really dating back to 1852, the same year as Smith & Wesson. (The last two companies trace their origin to the same firm.)

What about guns not from those firms?

Many are very desirable. Tiffany was big in the gun business until 1911. And the great Kentucky rifle is a classic collectible. These date from the early 18th century and continued to be made for about 100 years. Kentucky rifles sell for $5,000 and up. One of them sold at Christie's firearms auction for $55,000. They were made in small workshops, often by wonderful craftsmen.

Are pairs more valuable than singles?

Yes, indeed. Also triplets: A rifle, a revolver and a knife made as a set, for example.

Some collectors specialize in miniatures. These tiny weapons were a test of the gunsmith's art, and they were made for fun. (You can fire the little guns, though it's not advisable.) A society of miniature-collectors exists.

Modern engraved guns are also very collectible. In the last 10 years, they've become a $15-million-per-year business. Colt, Remington and Winchester (among others) make them. The craftsmanship is magnificent. Some are the equal of anything done in the past. These are not replicas, and owners do not discharge them. One reason for collecting modern firearms is assurance of authenticity. However, after 1840, most US firearms were given serial numbers. If you own a weapon made after that date, a factory may have it on record.

How do you care for a collection?

Rust is the great enemy. Try a light film of oil. Put on a pair of white cotton gloves, spray oil on the palm of one glove and rub the gun with it. If you use a rag, sweat from your hand will eventually mingle with the oil.

Should fine weapons ever be fired?

Never! Well, hardly ever—only if the antique arm is not of much value. Black powder, outdated in the 1890s, is still available for shooting today. It is corrosive to metal and scars wood. If you do wish to shoot antique-type guns, you should buy replicas. About $100 million is spent on them annually. Even if black powder isn't used, wear and tear on the firearm lowers its value. Excessive refinishing or polishing is also not recommended.

Do you need a license for antique guns?

Generally not, if they were made before 1898, the federal cutoff. But check with local authorities.

Gun collecting is expensive. How much need you spend?

About $500 is the least; you can find very good Derringers for that price. These sidearms were made from 1830 to 1930. However, before you invest any money, spend several hundred hours studying. There are over 12,000 books on the subject, but you should begin with the basic source: *Flayderman's Guide to Antique American Firearms and Their Values* by Norman Flayderman, Digest Books, Northfield, IL.

Source: R.L. Wilson, historical consultant for Colt Firearms Division.

COLLECTING OLD TRAINS

Every child remembers the thrill of receiving that first model train set. Many people like to recapture the excitement as adults, by collecting model trains as either a hobby or an investment or as both. Certain old model railroad cars and sets have become so expensive that counterfeiters are making forgeries. Although most collectors are train buffs who belong to model railroad societies throughout the country and often attend "train swaps," the collectors also include some famous names. Newscaster Tom Snyder is a collector, as are Graham Claytor, former secretary of the Navy, and Mick Jagger, who occasionally buys Lionel.

Finding bargains is difficult. Don't expect to discover valuable old train sets at garage sales or country auctions. Train collecting is a well-explored area. A price guide to all old Lionel cars is available. (*Greenberg's Price Guide to Lionel Trains,* Greenberg Publishing Co., Sykesville, MD.)

Top collectors' items in the United States consist primarily of pre-World War II standard gauge Lionel cars. (Standard gauge refers to the 2⅛-inch width popular before the war.) Lionel stopped making the large-size sets in 1939 because the metals were needed for the war. Afterward, all trains were smaller. Other makes collected include American Flyer and Ives. (Both these firms merged eventually with Lionel, so there is not so large a pool of items.) Marx was the manufacturer of smaller, cheaper trains that were sold through Woolworth's and other variety stores. They were eventually bought by Quaker Oats, and the line was discontinued. Marklin, a German manufacturer which began making trains in 1856, is the most prominent European producer.

The highest price on record for a model train was $23,000, paid for a Marklin "crocodile train" made in the early 1920s. The most expensive train set sold at auction at Parke Bernet was a Lionel "state set" for $12,000. Its boxcars are decorated with the names and maps of states of the union. More expensive purchases may have been made privately, but there is no record of them.

The age of trains does not necessarily determine their price. Scarcity and demand are more important factors. Example: Any Lionel train with a Disney motif is likely to be very valuable. Lionel made an entire Disney circus train. In this case, the market is not limited to train buffs. Circus-memorabilia collectors and Disney collectors also covet these trains.

Another rarity: Lionel made a special train for girls in the 1950s. The locomotive was pink and the caboose was blue. It sold poorly, and Lionel did not produce very many. Some dealers painted the trains black to get rid of them. Those that are still pink and blue are very valuable.

Reproductions. There are counterfeiters who may also call themselves "restorers" because they rebuild damaged trains. Such trains are not very valuable. Some may be as much as 75% restored, in which case they are, for all intents and purposes, counterfeit. The most valuable trains are "in the box" or in mint condition. Since many trains were made of a zinc alloy called Zamac, which frequently became contaminated with other substances and disintegrated, many cars are partially original and partially restored.

How to tell: Lettering on counterfeit and restored pieces is usually stamped instead of using the old decal lettering. Another telltale: Original Lionel trains were dipped in paint. People look for marks and imperfections in the paint job. Today, people spray-paint the cars, so it is easy to tell the difference. Other differences are more subtle, and it takes a great amount of expertise to distinguish a reproduction from an original.

Modern pieces: Manufacturing for the collector has become an important part of Lionel's business now. Example: The GG1 was first put on sale in 1956 for $49.95. When Lionel remade it in the 1970s, the list price was approximately $320. Not too many parents spend that much on children's toys, but an investor might be interested.

Specializing: Many serious train buffs specialize in a single item, such as Number 8 locomotives, or a certain kind of boxcar. There is a broad spectrum.

Displaying trains: While many collectors like setups (tracks on which the trains run), collectors' items should be kept on display shelves.

Source: Alan Spitz, owner of The Red Caboose, New York, and Bruce Manson, editor of *Train Collectors Quarterly.*

COLLECTING DOLLS

Collectors of fine art and antiques have discovered dolls in recent years. Dolls have surpassed coins in popularity and are now the world's second largest collectible. (Stamps are number one.) The attractions are not only the investment potential of dolls but also their aesthetic appeal and cultural and historic significance.

Most collectors concentrate their attention on the "golden age of dollmaking" from 1840 to 1920, on modern dolls from 1920 to 1950, on artists' dolls from 1910 to the present or on contemporary dolls like Shirley Temple and Barbie dolls.

The doll market did not suffer from the recession as did coins and stamps. Reason: Doll collectors are accumulators. Coin collectors don't buy multiples of the same thing, except for examples in better condition or for trading, but doll collectors do. One collector with 50 Brus (valuable French dolls) has 12 of the same size and mold number, yet each one is different because they are hand made and hand decorated.

Dolls have "presence"—recognizable characteristics and human-like personalities. As collectors grow more sophisticated, they become more aware of these distinctive characteristics and can recognize dolls they have seen before.

Good buys in old dolls:
• German character dolls made between 1900 and 1917 by Simon & Halbig or Kammer and Reinhardt.
• All dolls made by American artists. The Georgene Averill baby has doubled in value in recent years.
• Kamkins dolls made by Louise Kampus. Buy any that is reasonably clean.
• Kewpie dolls (not figurines) are all good investments.

New dolls with potential:
• Original creations of members of the National Institute of American Doll Artists.
• German dolls by Kathe Kruse.
• Steiff stuffed animals (keep the tag and pin that come with them).
• Smurfs and Peanuts dolls will probably appreciate, but not in our lifetimes.

Advice to new collectors:
Educate yourself. People who are in a hurry make mistakes. Become familiar with dolls. There are several excellent museums. Leading ones: The new Margaret Woodbury Strong Museum in Rochester, NY, and the doll collections at the Smithsonian Institution in Washington, DC.

A better way to learn about dolls: Visit stores and antique shows where you can touch and handle the dolls.

Guidelines: Many dolls are easy to identify because most manufacturers of bisque dolls numbered them. (Bisque is a form of china introduced in 1870 and used extensively until 1940.) But get a guarantee when you buy. Anyone who purchases a valuable object should be able to sell it back at any time. However, a guarantee is only as good as the dealer.

Dangerous buy: A damaged doll. You can't go wrong paying $500 for a damaged Bru doll worth $8,000—the parts alone are worth that. But don't pay $5,000. A damaged doll will always be a damaged doll.

Many people have dolls stored in attics, basements or closets. One woman heard a description of a rare doll on television. She realized she had just thrown away a similar doll. She retrieved it from the trash can and sold it for $16,500, the American record for a doll sold at auction.

Books on dolls:
- *All Dolls are Collectible* by G. Angione and J. Whorton, Crown, New York.
- *The Doll Registry: A Guide to the Description and Value of Antique and Collectible Dolls* by Florence Theriault, Annapolis, MD.
- *The Spinning Wheel Complete Book of Dolls* edited by A. Christian Revi, Everybody's Press, Hanover, PA.

Source: George and Florence Theriault, Dollmasters, Annapolis, MD.

The 1959 Barbie doll that cost $3 now brings up to $1,000—but only if in mint condition, with original striped bathing suit and gold earrings. And if you've lost the box, you've lost half the value. Rule of thumb: The more common the doll, the better shape it must be in.

COLLECTING COMIC BOOKS

Comic books sell for as little as 15¢ each and for as much as $15,000. It is estimated that there are over 100,000 collectors in the US.

When did comic books begin?

There were comics in the 1920s but they were reprints of newspaper strips. The first "superhero" comic book, *Action Comics No. 1,* was issued in 1938. The early books had 64 pages, with five or six stories featuring different heroes, and sold for 10¢.

What are the criteria for establishing worth?

The first issue of anything is most valuable. The spread in price between the first issue and the second one is always great. A first may be worth $100 and the next only $35.

Condition is extremely important. Ten years or so ago, you'd have paid twice as much for a comic book in mint condition (practically untouched) as for a well-read one. Now, if a mint book is worth $1,000, the same in well-read condition brings only $200. Mint condition is particularly important for books from the 1960s.

Scarcity also determines value. Books from the 1930s and early 1940s are rarest. Fewer were issued, and wartime paper drives prompted patriots to donate their collections.

How do you define scarce?

Scarce is under a hundred known copies. Under 25: Rare.

How is a collection built?

Usually, collectors will try to get every issue of a particular title. It isn't easy, but the chase is part of the fun.

How do you decide on a title?

Often, nostalgia. Older collectors want comics from the Golden Age, from 1938 up to 1956. After that, it becomes the Silver Age, starting with *The Flash,* a new character, in 1956.

How should one buy contemporary comics with an eye to future collectibility?

Look for a good story line, superior artwork and popularity with fans. *X-Men* and *Moon Knight* from Marvel and *New Teen Titans* from DC are good choices.

What about cartoon animals and other categories?

The Walt Disneys, especially those drawn by Carl Barks, appeal to specialists. A few of the scarcest sell for thousands of dollars. *Big Little Books,* small thick and hardbound, range from $3 to $50. *Classic Comics* appeal to some older collectors. There's a trap in the *Classics.* They were used in schools and reprinted every six months from the original plates. The dates were not changed. Many people who think they have originals have only valueless reprints.

How should you store comic books?

Upright, in a box of some sort. Never store them flat—the spines of the bottom books will become crushed. Also, you must handle them all to get at the lower ones. For valuable books, use inert plastic mylar cases.

Source: Michael Feuerstein, owner of M&M Comics, Nyack, NY.

COLLECTING ANTIQUE PLAYING CARDS

Antique playing cards are amusing, interesting, inexpensive and, possibly, undervalued (worthwhile ones may start as low as $50). But collect them only for sheer pleasure; a buyer might be hard to find.

POPULAR SHEET MUSIC

The mass production of sheet music of popular songs is a uniquely American commercial phenomenon that started in the early 19th century and began to wane only with the popularity of the phonograph record at the time of World War I.

Few titles or editions of the two million songs published in the last 150 years are of investment value. An early printing of *The Star Spangled Banner* (1814) is worth $25,000. Civil War songs are valuable because of their scarcity. And original printings of Scott Joplin rags can bring as much as $800 at auction because jazz buffs have recognized the musical importance of 1890s ragtime tunes.

But most sheet music is collected for fun—by era, by subject, by composer or by artwork on the cover. The staple of home entertainment, popular music that could be easily played on the piano and sung in groups reflected the popular culture of its time. Early 19th-century songs told stories of romantic love, tragic death, home and mother. Minstrel-show music was catchy and sentimental (like Stephen Foster's songs).

After the Civil War, songs were topical: *The Price of Meat Is Going Up Again* is one example. Lyrics discussed the stock market, sports fads, inventions and scandals. Sheet music became big business in the 1890s with *After the Ball* by Charles K. Harris, a best-seller that earned up to $25,000 a week. The industry was concentrated on New York City's 28th Street, dubbed Tin Pan Alley. Songs at the turn of the century could sell a million copies or more, and these songs are the ones most collected.

Where to find sheet music: There are few dealers who specialize in it. Flea markets, thrift shops and even garage sales are good places to start. Be prepared to plow through dusty cartons. Ephemera shops usually carry some sheet music. Offers are made in the newsletter of a national collectors' group. The New York chapter holds its meetings at the Songwriters Hall of Fame at 1 Times Square in New York City. This museum has fascinating exhibits of sheet music, and the research staff is very helpful to collectors.

Source: Dave Jasen, vice president of the New York Sheet Music Society and author of *Rags and Ragtime,* Continuum Publishing Co., New York.

COLLECTING STOCK CERTIFICATES

One type of certificates is "live" certificates, representing ownership in a company. These have wonderful engraved designs, called vignettes. (The New York and American Stock Exchanges require that all certificates carry a genuine engraving and a design with tones. This makes counterfeiting more difficult.) There are advantages to owning a single share in a company. You are on the company's mailing list and receive all financial information including the annual report, which can be a collectible.

For someone starting a current collection, the following is recommended: One share each of Playboy Enterprises, Wells Fargo and Co., Lion Country Safari, Dynamics Corp. of America, International Bank Note and Toro. That gives you six beautifully engraved stock certificates. These are beautiful, and they represent the New York and American Stock Exchanges and over-the-counter trading as well. Also, International Bank Note's annual report is quite a work of art.

Another collection you might want to start is of used, canceled stock certificates. Certain certificates are part of American financial history. For example, you might find an American Express certificate that was issued in the 1860s and signed by Mr. Wells and Mr. Fargo, then president and secretary of the company. (Many people's major interest in certificates is the autograph.) Millard Fillmore, John D. Rockefeller and Jay Gould once signed stock certificates.

A very valuable certificate is Standard Oil, signed by John D. Rockefeller. Its current worth is around $1,500.

Old certificates needn't cost a lot of money. You can buy 20–30 for around $50. Some collectors specialize. They'll collect only oil companies, or railroads, or only New York railroads, but you don't have to specialize. You should collect certificates for the fun of it as well as the investment value.

Source: Edward Mendlowitz, CPA, Siegel & Mendlowitz, New York.

COLLECTING ROCK-AND-ROLL MEMORABILIA

These articles are becoming increasingly valuable to collectors. High-priced items: Letters and signed pictures of deceased rock stars, such as John Lennon and Janis Joplin, as well as their costumes and instruments. Problem: Since the field is relatively new, the network of buyers and sellers is unsophisticated. Where to find out what's available: Classified advertisements in *Rolling Stone* and *The Village Voice*.

COLLECTING CELEBRITY MEMORABILIA

Do you remember Rosebud, the sled that meant so much to Orson Wells in the 1941 film *Citizen Kane?* Rosebud means a lot to well-heeled movie buffs, too—the sled fetched $60,500 (including the buyer's fee) at Sotheby's New York.

Collectors have long cherished relics of the famous, but a market in recent celebrities artifacts is just being established. It was sparked by auction houses that found a willing market for rock 'n' roll and movie memorabilia.

Examples:

In December 1981, Sotheby's London sold

a drawing of a seated nude figure for 8,000 pounds ($14,080). Artist: John Lennon. On October 1, 1981, Christie's East, New York, sold a pair of ruby slippers worn by Judy Garland in the 1939 film *The Wizard of Oz* for $12,000. Few movies are strong enough in themselves to draw high prices for props or clothing. What could vie with the ruby slippers: Probably only a recognizable gown (in good condition) worn by Vivien Leigh in *Gone With the Wind.*

At Sotheby, a Beatles wristwatch sold for $375, a pastel drawing of Patty Boyd by Paul McCartney brought $850 and a *Two Virgins* album signed by John Lennon went for $950.

Who collects: A mixed group—friends of the famous as well as fans. Investment is always a consideration, but it takes a back seat to nostalgia.

The future: Both New York auction houses reported that there are queries about selling items (a tie that once belonged to Elvis Presley, for example) but not many requests to buy. Problem for the auctioneers: People tend to exaggerate the value of relics they want to sell. While legendary figures and great films will draw, the field is still too new to make assumptions or venture prognoses.

Source: Pamela Brown Sherer, Sotheby's York Avenue Galleries, New York, and Julie Collier, Christie's East, New York.

COLLECTING BASEBALL MEMORABILIA

When most people think of collecting baseball memorabilia, they think first of cards. Cards with players' pictures have been issued since the early days of the game, first by tobacco companies, more recently by chewing gum companies.

It's too late, from the viewpoint of investment, to collect cards. Recent cards will probably not be a collectible in the future.

Look back to the last era when people identified with baseball as the true national game, the late 1950s. Collect programs, autographs and *Baseball Registers* from that time. For example, if you were a Dodger fan as a kid, you might like to have a number of old Ebbets Field programs.

An item that has gone up in value every year for the last 25 years is a publication called *The Baseball Register*. It's put out by *The Sporting News* and is a record of everything that happens in the major and minor leagues in a single year, including the results of every game played. Like any good investable book, *it's rare*. There's only one first edition. The 1981 *Baseball Register* is bound to be worth something; a game-by-game record of the craziest season that ever was, and a whole history of the seven-week strike.

Autographs from 1930 to 1950 are desirable. Get those of good players who didn't give them out too freely. Jackie Robinson and Babe Ruth were great, but their signatures may not be worth much. They gave too many away. Buy autographs only from authorized dealers, so you'll know they're not fake. But buy programs, *Registers* and old baseball magazines from anyone. They're self-explanatory.

Cards are not the repositories of our memories any more. What is? Television. For earlier fans, radio. It's logical now to start collecting videotapes. And old audiotapes by announcers Red Barber and Mel Allen would be worth a fortune.

Source: Louis Ehrenkrantz, vice president of Rosenkrantz, Ehrenkrantz, Lyon and Ross, New York.

APPRAISING YOUR VALUABLES

Valuable items worth over $100 should have written appraisals every two years. Replacement values change with current-day economics.

More information: American Society of Appraisers, New York.

INSTANT ART APPRAISALS

Available by phone from Telepraisal. The company has computer files on over 50,000 artists and more than 600,000 works of art, including paintings, lithographs and prints. Information includes prices at auctions over the last five years. Cost of service can be charged to your credit card. If the search doesn't turn up the artist in question, a lesser rate is charged.

COLLECTING SEASHELLS

She sells sea shells by the sea shore—and in cities, museum shops and through the mail. You can buy your shells or you can have the pleasure of finding them yourself. You needn't worry about investment, auctions or authenticity. Shell collecting is a just-for-the-fun-of-it hobby.

Begin by collecting as many types of shells as appeal to you. This way you can learn their names and become familiar with the distinctive qualities of each type. Most collectors are eventually drawn to one or two species and narrow their scopes.

Prices within every species range from 25¢ to several thousand dollars. But it is easy to put together a very broad collection of several thousand shells for $1–$10 apiece, with an occasional splurge into the $20–$25 range. Most popular species:

• Cones (Conus): Cone-shaped shells that exhibit an astonishing variety in pattern and color. One, Conus bengalensis, brought the record price ($2,510) for a shell sold at an auction. At the time, it was only the fourth specimen known. However, several more were found shortly thereafter. It now sells for $400–$750, a warning to would-be investors. C. textile: Named for its wonderful repeating pattern, which resembles a Diane von Furstenberg knit. C. marmoreus: the model for a well-known Rembrandt etching.

• Cowries (Cypraea): Very rounded shells, with lips rolled inward to reveal regularly spaced teeth. Naturally so smooth, hard and glossy that they appear to have been lacquered, they are often considered the most pleasurable shells to handle. Cypraea aurantium: Deep orange. A classic rarity. The famous tiger cowrie, C. tigris, speckled brown and white. C. mappa: Striking pattern resembles an antique map.

• Murexes: Swirling shells favored for their pointy spines, though many are delicate and hard to store. Murex pecten (Venus comb): Spectacular curving spires. M. palmarosae: Rose-branched murex, has floreate tips. M. erythrostomus, has ladylike white ruffles and a luscious pink mouth.

• Scallops (Pectens): Shaped like ribbed fans

in surprisingly intense reds, oranges, yellows and purples.

- Volutes (Voluta) and Olives (Oliva): Equally popular species. Best-loved classics are the triton, Charonia tritonis and the chambered Nautilus pompilus.

Choose live-collected specimen shells in perfect or near-perfect condition, without natural flaws or broken spines or tips. Stay away from lacquered shells. Avoid ground lips (an edge that has been filed will feel blunt rather than sharp). A label should accompany each shell, with its scientific name and location information.

Dealers have a worldwide selection of shells, access to professionally collected deep-sea varieties and experience in identifying tricky species. Dealers advertise in a shell-collecting periodical. Most sell through the mail. The thrill of finding that new box of shells in the mailbox never wanes. Clubs provide new friends to trade with, up-to-date information on new species, travel opportunities, and techniques for cleaning and storage. Check with the nearest natural-history museum to find a local club.

The most colorful shells are found near coral reefs in tropical waters. Many areas offer special arrangements for shell collectors, from boat trips to uncombed beaches to guided snorkeling or scuba diving. Much of Southern California and Australia's Great Barrier Reef are closed or limited for environmental reasons.

Sanibel Island, FL, is the best-known shelling spot in the US. It is especially well geared to the collector. Contact the Chamber of Commerce for information. Costa Rica offers both Atlantic and Pacific varieties, with pre-Columbian ruins as an added attraction. The Philippines are known for their many local dealers and good values, as well as for fine beachcombing, snorkeling and diving. Cabo San Lucas, Mexico, on the southern tip of the Baja Peninsula, and the Portuguese Cape Verde Islands off Senegal offer great shelling.

Of course, you need never go near an ocean to start a fine collection of seashells. If camping in the mountains or dining in Paris is more to your taste, just bring along your copy of *Hawaiian Shell News*.

Source: Jerome M. Eisenberg, The Galleries at La Jolla, and William Gera, The Collector's Cabinet, New York.

COLLECTING BUTTERFLIES

Papillon, Schmetterling, farfalla, mariposa—in almost any language, the word for butterfly trips across the tongue like the flitting, colorful creature it describes. Butterflies were held in lofty esteem by the ancient Greeks and by the early Christians, who saw in them symbols of the human soul.

The common names for some favorite butterflies range from painted ladies, jezebels and jungle queens to emperors, rajahs, and Apollos. Ironically, these short-lived symbols of transient beauty, once captured and carefully mounted in a collector's cabinet, retain their shimmering colors for centuries, like frozen rainbows.

The lover of lepidoptera (butterflies and moths) must also be a lover of labels. There are 140,000 species of lepidoptera, about 20,000 of them butterflies. If the prospect of learning 20,000 scientific names is enough to give you butterflies in your stomach, you will understand why most collectors specialize in one family of butterflies (lepidopterists generally agree on 15 basic families) or further limit themselves to one genus or even to one species. Within any family, the price for a single specimen can range from less than $1 to several hundreds. Only extreme rarities sell for $1,000 or above. Females may be more costly than males because they are often left in the field to breed.

Major collecting categories:
- Morphiodae ("Morphos") are the most popular (and flashy) butterflies to collect. The Morpho genus is conveniently small, about 80 species. What attracts collectors is their intense color—a dazzling, metallic blue that reflects light like satin, changing from deepest navy to royal blue to icy turquoise as one moves past them. Other Morphos, patterned like watered silk, appear to be translucent white until, as one moves closer, they show subtle, opalescent colors, like mother-of-pearl. Examples: The large Peruvian Morpho didius, an iridescent blue outlined in black, is extremely popular. A female, in softer pastels, sells for more.
- Papilionidae is a family of about 700 species.

Particularly sought are the various swallow-tails and the Ornithoptera, or "birdwings," including the largest known butterfly, Ornithoptera alexandrae.

• Nymphalidae contains several thousand species. Some of the subgroups most favored by collectors: Vanessidi (vanessas), Charaxes (rajas), Argrias (a rare and expensive genus) and many others equally showy and varied, with colors, patterns and wing shapes resembling laces, leaves, Rorschach tests, stars in a night sky, maps, Dubuffet designs in magic marker, animals' eyes and Florentine bargello. An extreme rarity is the African species Charaxes fournierae, worth about $1,000 per pair.

Butterfly values are determined almost exclusively by their rarity. In this era of ecological abuse and species protection, this can be a tricky business, however, and it doesn't always work the way one might expect. For example, the O. rothschildi, for years worth $150 per pair, now sells for $20. Reason: About five years ago, it was bred in captivity and then released by the government, so it has become fairly common. Of course, the inverse is more often true. Fire or construction can wipe out a habitat in a short time. The top price ever paid for a single butterfly was $1,750 brought by an O. allotei at the 1966 sale of the Rouseau Decelle collection.

Sets of 10 or so different butterflies are available for very little from hobby shops or mail-order dealers. The new collector must learn to mount specimens in open-wing position. Mounting equipment and instructions are available from the same sources.

Butterflies are usually kept in flat cases with glass or Plexiglas dust covers that can be stored away from the light. A small container of mothballs in the storage area prevents other insects from attacking the collection. Some species, including many Morphos, have greasy bodies that can harm the delicate wings. After the butterfly is mounted, the body can then be replaced with a dab of glue.

Buy only perfect specimens. Be sure each comes with its identification and date and location of capture for your labels.

The International Butterfly Book by Paul Smart is a good source of information. It's out of print but is available in libraries. Some copies are available from The Butterfly Company.

Source: Michael Berman, The Butterfly Company, New York.

PORTRAIT PHOTOGRAPHY SECRETS

People are the most popular subject for photography. People pictures are our most treasured keepsakes. There are ways to turn snapshots of family and friends into memorable portraits. Techniques:

• Get close. Too much landscape overwhelms the subject.

• Keep the head high in the frame as you compose the shot. Particularly from a distance, centering the head leaves too much blank background and cuts off the body arbitrarily.

• Avoid straight rows of heads in group shots. It's better to have some subjects stand and others sit in a two-level setting.

• Pose subjects in natural situations, doing what they like to do—petting the cat, playing the piano, etc.

• Simplify backgrounds. Clutter is distracting. Trick: Use a large aperture (small f-stop number) to throw the background out of focus and highlight the subject.

• Beware of harsh shadows. The human eye accommodates greater contrast of light to dark than does a photographic system. Either shadows or highlights will be lost in the picture, usually the shadowed area.

For outdoor portraits:

• Avoid the midday sun. This light produces harsh shadows and makes people squint. Hazy sun, often found in the morning, is good. Cloudy days give a lovely, soft effect.

• Use fill light to cut shadows. A flash can be used outdoors, but it is hard to compute correctly. Best fill-light method: Ask someone to hold a large white card or white cloth near the subject to bounce the natural light into the shadowed area.

• Use backlight. When the sun is behind the subject (but out of the picture), the face receives a soft light. With a simple camera, the cloudy setting is correct. If your camera has a light meter, take a reading close to the subject or, from a distance, increase the exposure one or two stops from what the meter indicates.

• Beware of dappled shade. The effect created in the photograph will be disturbing.

For indoor portraits:

• Use window light. A bright window out of direct sun is a good choice. However, if there is high contrast between the window light and the rest of the room, use filter-light techniques to diminish the shadow.

• Use flashbulbs. A unit with a tilting head lets you light the subject by bouncing the flash off the ceiling, creating a wonderful diffuse top lighting. (This won't work with high, dark or colored ceilings.)

• Mix direct light and bounce flash. An easy way to put twinkle in the eyes and lighten shadows when using bounce light is to add a little direct light. With the flash head pointed up, a small white card attached to the back of the flash will send light straight on to the subject.

• Keep a group an even distance from the flash. Otherwise, the people in the back row will be dim, while those in front may even be overexposed.

HOW TO PROCESS YOUR OWN BLACK AND WHITE FILM WITHOUT A DARKROOM

Although not recommended for a rank beginner, you can process black-and-white film yourself without a darkroom, using a changing bag and a few dollars' worth of equipment.

This will result in—believe it or not—higher quality negatives than you are likely to obtain even from a professional photo lab, due to exposure, light-ratio and development standardization that you will establish for yourself. The end product is consistently superb pictures.

Self-processing of black-and-white film will also enable you to see your results immediately. You don't need to make contact sheets or prints to accomplish this. Simply place your developed and dried negatives under a bright light (like direct sunlight or photoflood bulb)

and view them against a black background. When you angle the emulsion, the negative appears positive. Voila! Your photographs suddenly become visible.

This trick is used by newspaper photographers working against deadlines that leave no time for contact proofs. Later, you can have a lab make contacts and study your pictures in detail.
Source: Ralph Ginsburg, magazine publisher and ardent photographer.

• Store film in the refrigerator or freezer if you don't plan to use it for a while. Refrigerated film can last one year past the expiration date. Film stored in the freezer will last up to two years.

• Color prints and transparencies fade faster than black and white photographs. Even professional color wedding pictures do not last through the decades. And the light of slide projectors hastens the fading process of transparencies. How long they last: Prints on Ektacolor 74RC paper have about four years of prime color and 20 years in all. Dye-transfer prints also fade quickly in light. But in a cool, dark storage area they could last a century. To save transparencies: Wrap valued slides in moisture-proof packing and store them in the freezer. Refrigeration retards the fading process, and the transparencies will last for a lifetime.

• When loading 35 mm film, you can ignore the instructions that tell you to wind off two empty frames. Instead, wind off one. That gives you an extra frame at the beginning and one at the end of the roll. Result: 38 printable frames instead of the normal 36.

TIPOFF THAT BAD SNAPSHOTS ARE PROCESSOR'S FAULT

Check finished snapshots before leaving the photo print store. If you spot any processing mistakes, ask for reprints. Common processing foul-ups: Dirt or dust spots. (The negatives weren't thoroughly cleaned before printing.) Unbalanced color. (Flesh tones are the best reference points.) Uneven exposure. (If

the same sky comes back in three shades of blue, you can probably get a better print.)
Source: *Changing Times.*

HOT WEATHER HAZARDS TO CAMERA GEAR

Humidity is the summer photographer's nemesis. Here are some defensive maneuvers:

• Don't open new film until you are ready to load and shoot. (It is packed in low-humidity conditions in sealed packets.)

• Have exposed film processed as soon as possible. Don't leave it in the camera for long periods —it may stick.

• Use slow advance and rewind to avoid moisture static.

• Keep equipment dry with towels or warm (not hot) air from a hair dryer. Store film and gear with silica gel to absorb excess moisture. (Cans of silica gel have an indicator that turns pink when the gel is damp. They can be reused after drying in the oven until the indicator is blue.)

Source: *Modern Photography.*

LEVEL SUPPORT WITHOUT A TRIPOD

If you don't have a tripod, use a small beanbag to make a level support for cameras or binoculars. Put the beanbag on an irregular surface like a rock, railing or tree limb to form a firmer surface.

Source: Pinwheel Systems, New York.

HOW TO HOLD A CAMERA STEADY

Hold your camera steady by "thinking still". . . simply concentrate on how heavy and inert the camera feels in your hands. Other tricks: Tuck your right thumb under the camera base. Hold the camera upside down, with its base pressed securely against your forehead. For slowest shutter speeds *without a tripod:* Sit down and support the equipment on your drawn-up leg, positioning the lens on your knee.

Source: *Popular Photography,* New York.

13. Credit Cards

Credit Cards

WHEN A CREDIT CARD IS NOT A CREDIT CARD

Not all cards bearing the name Visa or Master-Card are credit cards. Some are debit cards.

• Credit cards. When you charge a purchase to your credit card, the bank extends you credit until the bill is paid. At most banks, no interest is due if you pay in full by the due date. But interest is levied on any amount outstanding after that date.

• Debit cards. A debit card works like a check. An amount charged to your debit card is immediately withdrawn from your account. No credit is advanced.

Advantages of a debit card:

• It is more acceptable than a check at many merchant outlets.

• It is ideal for people who do not want credit. A debit card limits the shopper to the amount available in the account.

WHAT VISA AND MASTERCARD DON'T TELL YOU

One Visa card or MasterCard could be very different from another Visa card or Master-Card. What counts is the bank issuing it.

The MasterCard and Visa organizations do not issue credit cards themselves. They provide a clearing system for charges and payments on the cards and license banks to use the Visa or MasterCard name. It is the issuing bank that determines the interest rates and fees.

A bank's name on a credit card does not necessarily mean that it is the bank actually issuing the card. Issuance of credit cards is a high-risk, low-profit business. Seldom does a small bank issue its own.

Generally, a small bank will act as an agent for an issuing bank. The agent bank puts its name on the card, but it is the issuing bank that actually extends any credit.

Aside from costs, this can be important if the cardholder encounters an error. The correction might have to be agreed upon, not by a friendly local banker, but by an unknown, larger institution, perhaps, in a different state.

Visa, for example, has about 1,400 issuing banks in the US and about 10,500 agent banks.

Choosing which card to take is becoming more difficult, because some of the nation's largest banks have begun active solicitation of customers throughout the US. Individuals must be especially careful about accepting any offer that might come in the mail.

A recently discovered quirk in the federal law allows federally chartered out-of-state banks to ignore state usury laws that limit the amount of interest or fees that the issuing bank may charge on its credit cards. In Arkansas, for example, state usury laws prevent local banks from charging more than 10% interest on credit card balances. But a federally chartered out-of-state bank, in lending to Arkansas residents, may charge whatever its home state allows. Even within individual states, the terms on credit cards can vary widely.

Aside from the actual rates and fees, individuals must carefully check the fine print of their contracts. Most banks, for example, do not charge interest on balances stemming from purchases until the customer is billed for such purchases. If the bill on which the charges first appear is paid in full by the stated due date, there is no interest charge to the holder. But some banks, those in Texas, for example, begin charging interest as soon as they receive the charge slip and make payment to the merchant. Thus, interest begins accumulating even before the cardholder receives the bill. These interest charges continue until the bank receives payment from the customer.

Source: Robert A. Bennette, banking correspondent, *The New York Times.*

USE CREDIT CARDS WITH TRAVEL AGENTS

Credit cards are best when using a travel agent. They minimize difficulties if the agent goes into bankruptcy. Reason: The credit card company immediately becomes the middleman —and the financial solvency of the travel agent is no longer an issue.

CREDIT CARDS: BEATING THE SYSTEM

Credit cards have become a way of life for most Americans. However, very few people realize the unnecessary costs they incur by not utilizing their cards to their advantage or by not choosing the least expensive card to begin with.

Determine which card is best for you. Banks offering VISA or MasterCard services have a wide variety of fees and interest charges. Some levy a $35 charge, while others will nick you for only $5 or $10. Moreover, interest charges for goods purchased range from 18% to 22%. And some banks charge interest from the date of purchase, while others charge no interest if you pay your monthly bill on time.

Watch out, too, for bank cards that bill on a 24-day cycle, which means customers receive 14 bills per year. If you are used to paying all your bills once a month, one of those 14 could easily get delayed in the shuffle. Then you will be charged interest on the missed bill and get a reputation as a slow payer.

Even if the credit terms and service charges are to your liking, find out if there is any time limit on them. Some banks offer attractive deals as part of a special promotion that expires after nine months or a year. Take advantage of such offers—but be ready to switch over to another bank card if it is less expensive once the promotion expires.

Credit cards also can be used as a bargaining chip to receive a discount from a merchant. Merchants typically pay a fee of 2%–7% of your charge when you use your credit card. With an American Express or Diners Club card, they may have to wait a while to get paid. It may be to the advantage of the merchant to go along with your suggestion of a 5% dis-count if you pay cash.

Another way to beat the system: Take a cash advance on your credit card, and pay directly for goods and services, rather than charging them if bank-interest charges are less (up to 6% less, in some cases) for cash advances. If you already are being charged interest for merchandise purchases, take a cash advance and switch the balance due to the lower rate.

If no interest charge has yet been levied, then time the cash advance to a day or two before the bill would be past due, and pay off the merchandise portion of the bill. Reason for the timing maneuver: Cash advances are charged interest from the day that they are taken. Multiple credit cards come in handy if you want to go to the limit of allowable cash advances on each without having to use your card to purchase merchandise at high rates.

If you have gotten in over your head it may be best to take out a consumer loan to pay off a number of credit-card bills. Although the consumer loan rate may not be much cheaper than the credit-card cash advance rate, it can be significantly cheaper than the card's basic interest rate on merchandise purchases. In addition, since bank credit-card payments are based on a 24-month term, one big advantage to consolidating such debt with a 36-month consumer loan is lower monthly payments.

Source: Edward Mendlowitz, a partner with Siegel, Mendlowitz & Rich, CPAs, New York.

BUILDING A GOOD CREDIT HISTORY FOR YOUR CHILD

The sooner your child starts to establish a good credit history, the easier it will be for the maturing child to have access to bank loans when needed in the future, particularly when a family is being started.

State regulations on giving credit to minors vary, but even if your state is one of the more restrictive ones, you may still be able to get your child a credit card. How: Many bank credit-cards firms and department stores skirt the issue by authorizing the use of cards to children of any age when parents are willing to assume responsibility for their debts.

Exception: American Express, which allows card members to take additional cards for dependents only when they reach 18. If a member does, the parent or child—or both—are liable for charges on the child's card.

Credit-card issuers can successfully sue parents of minors for bad debts even if the parent disclaims knowledge of the child's purchases. Few such suits have been brought, however.

The better way is to set guidelines at the time you authorize the credit card for a minor:

• Let the card be used only for purchases agreed upon in advance. Give permission purchase by purchase.

• Set monthly limits to the amount your teenager can charge.

• Insist that teenagers save receipts of purchases.

• Act as a cosigner on any charge card your teenager assumes, even if your signature isn't required for a purchase, so that you can monitor the child's spending.

• Require teens to pay for credit purchases with earned income and to use their allowances for daily expenses. This builds in an incentive for a teenager to supplement income for major purchases.

Source: Meredith Fernstrom, senior vice president, Office of Public Responsibility, American Express Co., New York.

CARBON COPIES OF BILLS CAN BE DANGEROUS

Keep the carbon copies of bills charged to your credit card at stores or restaurants. Alternative. Tear up the carbons on the spot. Why: Thieves often dig these copies from the trash of business establishments. They then use the name and number to charge goods and services to your card by phone.

BEWARE OF LOW CREDIT CARD RATES

In many cases, bank cards with the lowest rates can cost much more than cards with traditional charges. Reason: A growing number of banks begin tacking on interest charges the minute a transaction is posted to their books. This interest charge accrues until the charge amount and the interest are paid in full. Even if you pay your charges off as soon as you receive the bill each month, you'll still have to pay an interest charge. Solution: If you pay in full whenever you use the credit card, choose a bank that charges interest only on balances that are still outstanding following the payment due date on the bill.

Source: *Money.*

YOUR LIABILITY FOR LOST OR STOLEN CREDIT CARDS

Your liability for unauthorized use of your credit card is limited to $50—and then only if the card company has informed you of the rules and provided you with a postage-paid notification form to use if the card is lost.

Once you have reported the card missing, you are not liable for its use—even if someone makes a purchase with the card five minutes later.

Suggestion: When you phone or mail notification of loss, have a witness, and note the exact time.

Although liability is strictly limited, lost cards can be a problem, especially if you have a lot of them. You have to report and replace each one; in addition, your credit standing can be damaged if someone runs up big bills in your name, and your cards could be cancelled if you make a habit of losing them or don't report promptly. One solution: Credit card protection services. Just call the service and report your cards missing; they will take care of notifying all card issuers, getting replacements. In addition, they insure against the $50 potential liability, which might be substantial if you have a lot of cards.

CREDIT CARD CAUTIONS

Debit card risk. If lost or stolen, unauthorized

use of your bank-automation card leaves you liable for the first $50, even if the loss is reported before use. It's up to $500 if you delay reporting it until after someone has tapped your account for a teller-machine withdrawal. Point: That makes the convenience of a debit card potentially ten times costlier than a credit card, which limits your liability to $50 tops and charges you nothing if a loss is reported in time to flag it before use.

Check your credit card statement against your receipts. It's very easy for a dishonest storeowner to run off several slips when you present your card and submit them later for payment.

Be sure that it's your card that the store clerk returns. Accidental switches do happen. The number of switches is increasing. It's not costly, but it can be inconvenient, especially if you're traveling.

You are not automatically responsible for any of the credit card charges of family members, even if they're using a family card. Example: An executive's son continued to use his father's credit card after he was told to return it. Under a Federal Trade Commission ruling, the father had only to inform the credit card issuer that the card was being used without permission. Having done so, the father would be responsible only for the next $50 charged.

YOU CAN WITHHOLD CREDIT CARD PAYMENTS

Disgruntled consumers may be able to withhold payments on a credit card they used to purchase goods or services that proved substandard. This is the result of a provision of the Fair Credit Billing Act, which enables the credit card companies to reclaim disputed amounts from merchants after credit card slips are signed.

Four conditions must be met for a consumer to be entitled to withhold credit card payments:

• The amount of the charge must be more than $50.

• The charge must be made within the customer's home state, or within 100 miles of the customer's home.

• The customer must first attempt to settle the dispute with the merchant directly.

• The customer must give the bank that issued the card written notice that the attempt to settle has failed.

How it works: When the bank receives the customer's notice, it credits the account with the amount of the charge. It then charges this amount back to the bank that serves the merchant. The bank then charges the merchant.

This provision of the law has been little publicized by the banks and credit card companies. Reason: They fear that if too many customers take advantage of this feature of the law merchants will begin to refuse credit cards.

CREDIT CARD BILLING ERRORS

The error may be a charge for goods you never bought, never received, or rejected; a failure to credit a payment; a mistake in amount; or any item on which you want a clarification.

To protect your rights, you must notify the card company of your objection, in writing, within 60 days after your bill was mailed.

• Do not just telephone; this is not considered proper notice. If you do phone, follow up with a letter within the 60-day period.

• Do not just write your objection on the invoice; this isn't proper notice, either. Use a separate sheet of paper and include your name, address, account number, and what you object to on the bill.

The card company must acknowledge your notice within 30 days, and within two billing cycles (but not more than 90 days) it must either:

• Correct the bill and send you notice. If the correction doesn't agree with your figures, the company must explain the difference, and if you request, furnish documentary evidence, or

• Send you a written explanation of why it thinks the bill is correct. On request, it must furnish documentary evidence. If you claim the goods weren't delivered, the company must give you a written determination that they were "delivered, mailed, or otherwise sent" before it can charge you.

During this period, you don't have to pay

the disputed amount and the company cannot:

• Make any attempt to collect it.

• Revoke your card or accelerate payment.

• Report you as delinquent to any credit bureau.

Caution: While you don't have to pay the disputed amount, you must pay at least the minimum due on any undisputed balance. If you don't, the company can accelerate your debt, revoke your card, report you as delinquent, etc., as to the undisputed amount.

Penalties: If the company fails to comply with all requirements, it forfeits the first $50 in dispute, even if it turns out the bill was correct. In addition, you can sue for any actual damages —for example, damage to your credit if the company improperly reports you as delinquent.

Note: The Fair Credit Billing Act applies only to consumer credit—credit for "personal, family, household, or agricultural purposes." It doesn't apply to business credit cards.

CREDIT CARDS AND THE LAW

• A cardholder continued to make purchases and get cash advances after filing for bankruptcy. The bank that issued the card claimed these debts should not be discharged in bankruptcy because they were obtained "by false pretenses or false representations."

A federal court of appeals held in favor of the cardholder. Banks voluntarily assume the risk of non-payment when they issue credit cards. They have the right to cancel at any time, but, until the card is cancelled, the cardholder is not making any false representation when he uses it.

• The wife of an American Express cardholder was issued a "supplementary" card in her own name. When her husband died, the company automatically cancelled it. A federal court of appeals ruled this was illegal discrimination on the basis of marital status and violated the Equal Credit Opportunity Act.

• If you are turned down for a credit card, you can demand to know why. If the reason is a poor credit rating, you have a right to know

the name and address of the credit bureau that reported on you.

You can then go to the credit bureau and demand to know what's in your file. They must tell you the "nature and substance" of all information about you, the sources of the information, and the names of all persons who were sent a credit report on you within the last 6 months (2 years, if sent for employment purposes).

If you dispute the report, the bureau must reinvestigate and correct any error. Even if you can't prove the record wrong, you have the right to insert a brief statement in the record about any disputed item. You can also demand that a corrected report be sent to everyone who received a credit report within 6 months (2 years for employment inquiries).

You must assert your rights. If, for example, you don't request that corrected reports be sent out, the credit bureau doesn't have to— and they're not likely to bother.

• Credit cards and marriage. A husband opens up a credit-card account in his name alone, but asks for two cards, one for himself and one for his wife. Later the couple separate. He has to pay for her credit-card purchases until he (1) tells her to stop using the card and demands its return (words are enough, and he doesn't actually have to get the card back) and (2) notifies the card issuer that he has revoked his wife's authority to use the card. After that, payment of her purchases on the card is not his responsibility. However, he is liable for all purchases made by his wife in the period after he tells her to stop and before he notifies the issuer.

Source: FTC Staff Letter by Justin Dingfelder, deputy assistant director for credit practices.

CREDIT CARD CALLING

When you have more than one pay phone call to make from a hotel or pay phone, don't hang up after each call. Push the # button between calls. This will allow you to stay connected with your chosen long-distance carrier. Added benefit: Most hotel computers will register several calls made this way as a single local call, saving you surcharges.

Source: *Travel & Leisure*, 1120 Ave. of the Americas, New York 10036.

14. Personal Money Management

Personal Money Management

HOW TO KEEP YOUR FRIENDLY BANKER FROM ROBBING YOU BLIND

If you are a person of average means and assets, your bank will rob you of well over $100,000 during your lifetime. You will pay more than you should for your mortgages, credit cards and other loans. You will be cheated out of a fair return on your savings and bank IRA deposits. And along the way, you will be outrageously overcharged in fees and penalties for every service your bank provides.

Bankers are not your friends.

Bankers are, in fact, your worst financial enemies. The community banks—which once weighed a loan applicant's character above his collateral—are being squeezed out by a handful of big banks. These huge institutions cater to major corporate accounts and are scarcely regulated by the government, which depends on their financing to keep it afloat. The banks' attitude toward small customers is simple—our way or the highway.

Basic rules:

• Do business with one of the smaller banks in your market area, where you will have most leverage in negotiating more favorable terms.

• Comparison-shop each banking service among at least three institutions. After you find the best deal, negotiate for even better terms.

Forget about finding a one-stop financial supermarket. You may wind up at Bank A for a checking account, at Bank B for a savings account, and at Bank C for a mortgage. Anyway, banks do not value your loyalty. They value only your money—and the more of it they can take from you, the better they like it.

The mortgage is the largest investment most people ever make—and the one where banks take greatest advantage. Most people decide on a mortgage based on whether they can afford the monthly payments. They rarely consider—

nor do banks openly disclose—that at prevailing interest rates, homeowners repay about four dollars for every dollar they borrow over the standard 29- or 30-year term. In other words, a $100,000 mortgage will cost them about $400,000.

Advice: Accelerate your payments against the mortgage's outstanding principal. A negligible increase in your monthly payment—perhaps 4%—can save you 25% or more of the amount you ultimately repay the bank, and shorten your obligation to 20 years or less. While some experts advise keeping the longer term for its tax advantages, this is a big mistake for the great majority of consumers. Even if you are in the 28% tax bracket, every dollar of unnecessary interest will still cost you 72¢ after taxes—money you could be investing for your own benefit, rather than the bank's.

Other mortgage scams:

• The adjustable-rate mortgage (ARM) represents the banking industry at its worst. It is a blatant marketing gimmick—complete with the deceptive come-on of an initial "discounted" rate—that fleeces the most vulnerable and over-extended. The ARM was created to ensure that banks might skim the absolute maximum from their borrowers, no matter where interest rates head. The risk is virtually all yours. (It is also possible, of course, that interest rates will fall—but since bankers control the rates, rates will always fall more slowly than they rise.)

Unfortunately, the prime interest rate will tend to increase in reverse proportion to our economy's health. In other words, your mortgage payment soars just when it is most likely that you may lose your job or business. Even if you hold steady, there's a fair chance you won't be able to afford the larger payments. Consider: If your ARM is based at 10% interest and then rises to 13%, your interest costs have actually risen by 30%—not the innocuous-sounding "three percentage points" advertised by your bank. On a $100,000 mortgage, that could translate to several hundred dollars more a month—a prescription for foreclosure.

Advice: Stick to a fixed-term mortgage, unless you are certain you will be selling your house before your ARM interest rate can substantially increase.

• Negative amortization mortgages are special ARMs which allow for fixed monthly payments regardless of interest-rate fluctuations. What most customers don't understand (and what most bankers fail to make clear) is that the bank may be siphoning their equity into its profit center. If the mortgage rate rises, the difference between what you pay each month and what you owe is assessed against a balloon payment, usually due in five years. At the end of the balloon, you may actually owe more than when you took out the loan. Aside from pocketing your interest payments, the bank now owns a substantial portion of your down payment.

Worst case: When you need to refinance the loan after paying off the balloon, your increased mortgage needs may exceed the property's appraised value. After the banks turn you down, you may have no option except to sell the house—at a loss.

Advice: Avoid this one at all costs.

• Reverse mortgages, recently in vogue, are supposed to enable people (mainly the elderly) to stay in their homes when they are no longer able to afford upkeep expenses. The borrower receives a monthly check from the lender, either for a set term or until the borrower dies. The loan balance plus interest is repaid by the sale of the house.

This new mortgage vehicle is very popular these days. In most cases, however, it is a gigantic rip-off. After 30 years of monthly mortgage payments, the homeowner trades in all that equity for five or 10 years of moderate income.

An "open-term" reverse mortgage allows for permanent residence until death, but it is available only on premium homes in excellent condition. And if something unexpected happens to the elderly homeowners, the bank has hit a bonanza.

• Home equity credit lines represent new packaging for a dog-eared product—the second mortgage. While they remain tax-deductible, that advantage is quickly wiped out by fees for the application, credit check, appraisal and closing, among others. For every dollar you save in taxes (versus an unsecured personal loan, for example), you may pay the bank two dollars in fees.

Since your home equity is your least liquid asset, you should save it for true emergencies. Any other purpose (to finance a car or home improvement, for example) represents an unacceptable risk . . . if you default on the loan, after all, you could be faced with foreclosure.

Source: Edward F. Mrkvicka is president of Reliance Enterprises, a national financial-consulting firm in Marengo, IL, and publisher of *Inside Financial* newsletter. He is also author of *The Bank Book: How to Revoke Your Bank's "License to Steal"—and Save Up to $100,000,* published by Harper & Row.

FLOAT WORKS BOTH WAYS

The textbook definition of float is "converting a negotiable instrument into cash or the transit period required to turn a contingency into an asset." This means the time lapse between your deposit and the date the bank allows you to use those funds; or, the time lapse between when you make a payment and the date that debit is charged to your account.

Assuming that the money in question is "working," using float is a way of "creating money." If you doubt this, be assured that while the sums involved may seem small, taking advantage of float on deposits is one of the ways commercial banks expect to make a profit. A very small ($10,000,000) bank, for example, can easily make $50,000 a year simply by instituting a policy that gives them free use of your money for as long as possible.

Perhaps the first step in dealing with float is to minimize its use against you. Find a bank with a reasonable "hold" policy (the delay in crediting deposits to customer accounts). The difference between a hold policy of three calendar days and 14 business days on a NOW account with an average balance of $3,000 could be the difference between annual earnings of $165 and $0.

Once you have arranged to make your deposits work as long and hard as possible, you might give some attention to making float work to positive financial advantage. If you have a NOW account or a money-market account, by making payment by mail on the last possible day, you may keep that money earning as much as a week longer than otherwise, given mail delivery time and time for the draft to clear through the system. (A post-marked mailing is the legal equivalent of making payment in person on the same date.)

There are ways to use float in your savings program, too. There are still banks that offer an in-by-the-tenth, earn-from-the-first policy. You can routinely turn this to your advantage by the simple expedient of opening a second account in a day-of-deposit-to-day-of-withdrawal bank (we'll call it Bank 2) and playing one bank against the other. Withdraw funds from Bank 2 on the tenth of the month, depositing them in Bank 1, thus earning an extra 10 days' interest on the sum every month. On the last day of the month, simply transfer funds back to Bank 2 and begin again. (Note: Some in-by-the-tenth banks offer this privilege only on a quarterly basis. Still, that's 40 days' double interest per year.)

Source: Edward F. Mrkvicka Jr., founder and president of Reliance Enterprises, Inc., P.O. Box 413, Marengo, IL 60152, a financial consumer-advocacy corporation.

HOW SAFE IS YOUR BANK?

Banks don't have to fail in order to hurt the customers with whom they do business. Even as financial problems are just begining to develop, the bank's operations may begin to deteriorate, and ultimately the bank may need to rein in its growth.

When banks run into financial problems, they behave like any other troubled company. They sometimes try to hide problems and limp along the best they can. For the customer, services can quickly deteriorate. Growing companies can be especially hurt because most rely on their banks to expand credit lines. On the contrary, too often a troubled bank will call in its loans because the bank needs the money —not because the customer is at any growth risk.

Ironically, thousands of customers are unnecessarily hurt. Many could have avoided problems by watching for early-warning signals of bank weakness. Typically, these distress signals show up as early as two years before an outright failure.

Chances are good, of course, that your bank is among the vast majority of healthy ones in the US. But ignoring the signs of problems now adds to your future risks.

Most recent bank problems stem from decisions to grow aggressively. Some banks that failed funded an ambitious growth strategy with ''purchased'' funds (such as large CDs), as opposed to deposits from their local customer base. That strategy puts them on shaky ground.

Customers that have dealt for some time with banks in this situation usually sense something is wrong:

• There's high turnover among the officers.
• Paperwork and record-keeping become sloppy.
• The bank encourages customers to extend credit when officers know it really isn't necessary.

But even when customers suspect that a bank is going through some sort of change, they rarely take the trouble to find out if it's merely because of routine personnel problems, for instance, or because of more serious financial trouble.

Essential steps: If a friendly bank officer has recently quit, invite him to lunch and ask him tough questions about his former employer.

If you think there's a problem, get a copy of the bank's Call Report. This twice-a-year document has the data that tell the financial conditions of a bank. (In fact, regardless of whether a customer senses trouble, his finance officer should routinely get Call Reports for banks with which the company does business.)

Although Call Reports are public documents, not all banks make copies available (usually obtainable from the bank's shareholder relations department). But if a bank balks, copies are available from the state agency that regulates banks or from the federal agency under whose jurisdiction it falls (Comptroller of the Currency, Federal Reserve Board or the Federal Deposit Insurance Corp.).

What to look for: By comparing figures of Call Reports over time, a customer can read the warning signals. According to Cates Consulting Analysts, Inc., the signals include:

• Rapid expansion as reflected in a big increase in loan yield relative to other similarly sized banks.

• Loan recovery rate of less than 20%. This is the percentage of written-off bad loans that a bank is ultimately able to recover. It should be well over 20% and is an excellent indication of how riskily the bank is willing to operate.

• Low return on assets for a bank its size (can range from 0.6% for large banks like Citibank and Chase Manhattan to over 1.0% for a small bank).

• High overhead ratio. Failed banks had overhead expenses that amounted to nearly 80% of their income base, compared with a nationwide average of 56%.

TRICKS BANKS PLAY WITH INTEREST RATES

Banks teach their loan officers a number of strategies to get an extra ¼% or even ½% from borrowers. Recognize some of their tricks:

• Doing the negotiating at the bank, which is familiar territory to the banker, intimidating to the borrower.

• Not mentioning the rate at all, but simply filling it in on the note.

• "Since you need the money today, let's write it up at X%. Then we can talk later about changing it." The banker hopes you'll never bring it up again. He certainly won't.

• Flat statement: "The rate for this type of loan is X%." (Never true except for small consumer loans. There is always room to negotiate.)

• Postponing the rate discussion as long as possible, hoping borrower will weaken under deadline pressure.

• Ego-building. Bank president stops by during negotiations.

• Talking constantly about how little the interest costs after taxes. And comparing it with finance company rates, secondary mortgage rates, or the cost of equity capital.

The banker looks at the company's account as a package, including loans, average balances maintained, and fees for service. Borrower options: Trade off higher average balances for a lower interest rate on borrowings, or vice versa.

The borrower is at a disadvantage because he probably negotiates a loan only once a year or less, while the banker spends full time at it. So prepare carefully for negotiations.

Good tactics for the borrower:

• Ask interest rate question early—in your office, not his. Don't volunteer suggestions.

• Negotiate everything as a package—rate, repayment schedule, collateral, compensating balances. Banker's strategy will be to try to nail down everything else and then negotiate interest rate when the borrower has no more leverage and no room to maneuver.

Source: Lawrence T. Jilk, Jr., executive vice president, National Bank of Boyertown, PA, in *The Journal of Commercial Bank Lending*.

WHAT BANKS DON'T TELL YOU

• Banks like to publish their effective annual yield, whereas money-market funds are legally permitted to advertise only the simple interest rates. The long-standing rule inadvertently conceals the fact that money-market funds do compound interest on a daily basis. If a bank and a money-market fund pay the same rate, the bank will appear to offer more by advertising the effective rate.

• Some banks say they let you draw on all checks immediately, provided you put up another bank account as collateral. Catch: If a check backed by a six-month certificate bounces, the bank can break into the certificate before maturity. If this happens, you will have to pay an interest penalty.

HOW PRIVATE ARE YOUR BANK RECORDS?

When it comes to providing information to nongovernmental sources, each bank establishes its own rules regarding the information it will make available. Ask your bank to explain its policies. Some can provide a written policy statement.

Many banks refuse to disclose any information about you to a private individual, unless there's a court order. But most banks will be very open in supplying information to credit bureaus and other genuine grantors of credit, such as department stores. They certainly will if you list the bank as a credit reference. Generally, the bank will give such information over the telephone if it is familiar with the calling institution. It might, however, ask for a written request if it does not have a standing relationship with the inquirer.

A bank usually discloses:

• Whether your checking account is good or whether there have been overdrafts.

• Whether it has loaned you money, how much, for how long and whether or not you have made your payments on time.

• The size of your savings accounts. Bank officials will talk of ''high four figures,'' or ''low five figures,'' and so on.

• What kinds of loans you have with the bank: mortgage, personal, auto.

Banks keep credit agencies up to date about your loan payments and the amount of credit available to you. This information pertains to lines of credit on credit cards as well as other credit lines and actual loans.

The Bank of America, the country's largest bank, has a typical policy. ''We will respond to a recognized business or a credit-rating bureau,'' reports one of their vice presidents.

On an installment loan, the Bank of America will disclose the approximate size of the monthly payment and the remaining balance on the loan. On a practical level, it would be impossible for the bank to single out individual accounts on which it would not give out any information.

If a merchant calls a bank to determine whether a check you are presenting is good, or if a credit card is good for a certain amount, the bank usually will tell the merchant. Department stores' computer terminals often provide the same kind of information, disclosing whether the amount involved can be covered by the account. But the computers usually do not give the exact amount in the customer's account.

Can you prevent a bank from giving out this information? At this time, it is impossible to prevent disclosure of this information unless you do business with a small bank that knows you well. Problem: Most banks have this information on computers and the technology, at least technology at a reasonable price, has not been developed to isolate individual accounts to block the dissemination of such information. Many people want their banks to supply information to credit grantors because this enables them, the individuals, to obtain additional credit more easily.

If you choose a small bank, however, especially one that is not automated, it is possible that the bank would agree not to give out information about you to anyone unless ordered to do so by a court.

• Form 1099s supplied by banks that still process them manually are likely to escape the IRS computers because of the sheer volume of forms involved. There is also an increased chance that the forms themselves may get lost. (For just these reasons, some people invest their money only at small ''country'' banks that do not have sophisticated computers.)

SWISS BANK ACCOUNTS

Swiss bank accounts are mysterious and secret. Only multimillionaires and Arab oil sheiks have them. And they're illegal. Right? Wrong—on all counts. Neither US nor Swiss law puts any restrictions on American citizens' opening Swiss bank accounts. Many Swiss banks accept modest accounts (some have no minimum). And they're no more complicated to open than an American account.

You should open a Swiss bank account for the following reasons:

• *Privacy.* Under Swiss law it's a crime for a bank or bank employee to disclose information—even to the Swiss government. Indeed,

French tax inspectors tried to obtain information on French depositors but could not. In America, many government agencies can get information. Even private investigators, such as credit bureaus, can usually find out a great deal about your financial affairs. Swiss law and tradition make leaks nearly impossible. A "numbered account," identified by code number, is the most private. The owner's name is locked in the bank vault.

• *Currency restrictions.* We have none now, but who knows about the future? Many governments have imposed heavy restrictions on the movement of currency in bad times. The worse the economy, the greater the restrictions.

• *Convenience.* If you travel or live in Europe or have business interests there, a Swiss account is useful for European dealings.

• *Services.* Swiss banks are universal banks. A single bank can perform all the services performed in America by a commercial bank, a savings bank, an investment bank, a brokerage house and other financial institutions. Many private, unincorporated banks specialize in portfolio management and handle international investments especially well.

The limits of secrecy: Banks may disclose information needed to investigate or prosecute crime. During the Howard Hughes autobiography hoax, it was disclosed that an endorsement had been forged on a check deposited in a Swiss account. By treaty, the US government can get information in some cases involving organized crime. A recent treaty covers violations of Securities and Exchange Commission insider-trading regulations. The Swiss authorities make the final decision on disclosure in each case.

There can never be disclosure in cases of tax evasion, currency exchange violations or political offenses. These are not crimes under Swiss law. Disclosure may be made to courts (not to the public) in bankruptcy cases and in some inheritance cases.

How to open an account:

The Big Five among Swiss banks are the Swiss Credit Bank (Zurich), the Union Bank of Switzerland (Zurich), Bank Leu (AG) (Zurich), the Swiss Bank Corporation (Basel) and Swiss Volksbank (Berne). All are accustomed to doing business with American depositors.

Books listing the names and addresses and other pertinent information for these banks and others are in your library. Check in the card catalog under Banking—Switzerland.

It's best to open an account, especially a large one, in person.

However, you can easily open an account by mail. Just write to the bank, asking for forms and information. (Type your letter. Swiss bankers complain of illegible mail from America.)

You must have your signature verified at a Swiss consulate or bank or by a notary public. The bank will provide forms.

You should execute a power of attorney over the account (unless it's a joint account). Under Swiss law, the power of attorney remains in force even after the depositor's death. If you have qualms about a power of attorney, you don't have to deliver it to the person. Leave it with your attorney, to be delivered only in case of your death or disability.

If you take or send more than $10,000 in cash or bearer securities out of the US, you must notify the government. However, you can send checks or money orders. Bank money orders are most private.

Swiss banks offer current accounts (checking), deposit accounts (saving) and custodial accounts (the bank will hold your stock certificates, gold or other property for a fee).

As in America, there are demand deposits and time deposits. Some accounts require notice to withdraw more than a specified amount. Interest varies with the type of account. The rates are not high, however, compared with those of American banks. The appeal of Swiss banks lies in safety and the soundness of the currency.

Accounts may be in Swiss francs, American dollars or another stable currency (depending on economic conditions when the account is opened).

Taxes and regulations: Although there are no US restrictions on Swiss bank accounts, your income tax form asks if you have any foreign bank accounts. If you answer yes, you must fill out Form 90-22.1.

Interest on foreign accounts is taxable like any other income. You can take a credit for foreign taxes paid.

If you have an account in Swiss francs, and the franc increases in value relative to the dollar, you may be liable for a capital gains tax when you withdraw money and reconvert it to dollars. Losses arising from decreases in value may not be deductible in regard to personal accounts.

Switzerland imposes a withholding tax on interest, but Americans can get refunded by showing they are not Swiss residents. Your bank will send you the forms. (Note: The bank sends in the tax without disclosing depositors' names. To claim the refund, however, you must, of course, disclose your identity.)

The Swiss formerly imposed severe restrictions on foreign accounts. Only the first 50,000 francs of an account could draw interest, and accounts above 100,000 francs were charged "negative interest" of 40%—nearly a confiscatory rate. All these restrictions have been dropped. They could conceivably be reinstated if economic conditions change.

Even when the restrictions were in force, however, they were not retroactive. They did not apply to existing accounts—only to deposits made after the rules were adopted (another reason you might want to act now).

Source: Stanley C. Ruchelman, tax partner, Touche Ross & Co., New York.

HOW TO SPOT A FORGED CHECK

• See if the check has perforations on one side. (A false check often has four smooth sides, since the forger cuts them with a paper cutter after printing.)
• The code numbers printed on a legitimate check reflect no light. They are printed in magnetic ink, which is dull.
• About 90% of all hot checks are drawn on accounts less than one year old. The numbers in the upper right-hand corner of the check indicate the age of the account. Be suspicious of those that are numbered 101–150 or 1001–1050 (the starting numbers).

Source: Frank W. Abagnale, once a master forger and now a consultant to banks and retailers, writing in *Real Estate Today.*

HOW TO DEPOSIT AN UNSIGNED CHECK

Write or type the word *over* on the line where the signature would normally appear. On the bank, type *lack of signature guaranteed...* and add your company's name, and your name and title. Then sign. This guarantees your bank that you'll take back the check as a charge against your account if it isn't honored. Most banks will then process the check and remit the funds. This saves you the trouble of returning the check to your customer for signature.

Source: *Credit & Financial Management.*

HOW SAFE IS YOUR SAFE DEPOSIT BOX?

Don't assume that when you put your valuables in a safe deposit box there is no further need for worry. Safe deposit vaults in banks get robbed in real life as well as in the movies. Then the questions arise: Who is responsible —and for what? Is the bank insured for the loss? How does the bank or the insurance company know what was actually in your box?

There is no law that a bank must have theft insurance for its boxholders. If the bank does have insurance, it may cover only damage to the bank, not losses sustained by box renters. The bank may choose not to put in a claim on its own insurance, denying responsibility for any losses. In actual practice, banks will usually attempt to reimburse their safe deposit boxholders after a robbery, for public relations purposes, but there are no guarantees. If the bank's insurance won't cover the claims made, the individual boxholder may have trouble collecting, especially if he is unable to prove what was inside his box.

To protect yourself, do the following:
• Purchase your own protection through a rider on your homeowners policy or a separate policy. (Rates may depend on the vault security system at your particular bank.)
• Make a complete list of all the valuable items in your box, documenting each as fully as possible. The documentation should include photographs, appraisals and receipts. Don't keep

the list in your safe deposit box.
• Keep photostats of all the important documents in your box at home or with your lawyer.
• Do not keep cash in a safe deposit box. Many banks prohibit it, and cash is almost impossible to insure.

CASH FOUND IN DECEDENT'S SAFE-DEPOSIT BOX

What was the source of any cash in a safe deposit box or in your home or office? In the absence of proof to the contrary, the Internal Revenue Service will consider any unexplained cash to represent previously untaxed income. This presumption can be refuted if there is credible evidence. For example, there may be a letter to your executor stating that Social Security checks or horse track winnings (reported) will be converted into cash, to be kept in the box as an emergency fund. Correspondence can identify cash as having been found money, which has been turned over to the police department and given back to the finder when no claimant appeared.

Source: *Encyclopedia of Estate Planning* by Robert S. Holzman, Boardroom Classics, Springfield, NJ 07081.

WHEN HOLDER OF SAFE DEPOSIT BOX DIES

A safe deposit box may not be the best place to keep items you want a spouse or child to inherit with the least taxation or red tape. In planning for your family's future, it is important to know the laws concerning safe deposit boxes.

When a keyholder dies: The box may be leased by a single renter or by two renters (called colessees). Upon the death of one, the box is immediately "sealed" by the bank for appraisal of its contents by local tax authorities.
• How do banks know when a keyholder has died? Very often, they don't know. In a small town, a death would be general knowledge. Upon hearing of the death, the bank would seal the box. However, in a large city, it is

unlikely that the bank would know unless someone informed them. Bank officials do not review newspapers and obituary pages for this purpose.
• How do you get into a box once it has been sealed? The executor of the estate must go to court for letters of administration in order to claim the contents of the box. If there might be a will in the box, the court issues a will search order. This directs the bank to witness the opening, along with the local tax authorities. The will is then personally delivered by the bank to the court. It is wise for the executor to get a will search order even if he already has found a will. There might be a later will in the box. The court can also direct the removal of other important papers, such as insurance policies, death certificates and GI papers.

Joint ownership: People tend to assume that the colessee of a safe deposit box automatically inherits the contents when the other lessee dies. This is not true. Joint rental of a safe deposit box is not like a joint bank account. It resembles the rental of an apartment by roommates. When one roommate dies, the other does not automatically inherit all of the property in the apartment, unless this is specifically provided for in his will.
• How does inheritance work when a safe deposit box is involved? The same way as when a box is not involved—according to the will. The colessee on a box has no more right to inherit its contents than anyone else. If there is no will, the courts might or might not interpret co-ownership of a box as reflecting the intention of the deceased to leave the box's contents to the colessee, depending on the relationship between them.
• Is there any way to set the box up so that the colessee inherits? Not with absolute certainty, unless there are no other heirs who might contest it. Clear inheritance depends primarily on the contract both renters sign with the bank when they rent a joint box. Some banks include a clause in their contract when the renters are husband and wife. It reads: The box is the joint property of both and upon the death of either passes to the survivor, subject to estate taxes, if any. However, since even this clause may not hold up in court if there is no will to back it up and other heirs have strong claims,

many banks do not include an inheritance clause in their rental contracts. Others won't rent joint boxes at all, to avoid litigation.

• What happens if the other keyholder cleans out the box before the sealing? It depends on the situation. If there are heirs who feel entitled to some of the box's contents, they are likely to sue, if they can prove that the colessee had access. However, access may be difficult to prove, because many banks throw away nightly the access slips indicating who entered their safe deposit boxes that day. Some states require that these access slips be kept. Others don't.

The state tax commission is unlikely to prosecute after the fact, even if access can be proved. It's very difficult to prove that a keyholder took assets which didn't belong to him, especially if he claims that the box was empty when he opened it. But, if the tax commission does prove illegal removal of assets, penalties can be heavy.

• What is the best way to set up a joint safe deposit box? If there are several heirs to an estate, it is a good idea to rent the box in a single name, with the other keyholders as deputies rather than colessess. "Deputy" is the bank's term for power-of-attorney. He has complete access to the box during the lifetime of the lessee. The deputy has no rights to enter the box after the lessee's death. The will should determine who inherits the contents. In any joint safe deposit box rental, read the contract you sign with the bank to see what it says regarding inheritance.

The bank and executor are responsible for the following:

• The bank is not responsible for the contents of the box after the death of a keyholder unless the bank was put on notice about the death. The bank can be held responsible if the deceased had bank accounts. If after his death the bank accepted papers regarding the bank accounts of the deceased, it can be held liable for not checking to see if he also had a safe deposit box.

• The executor has no automatic access to the safe deposit box and is not responsible for its contents until authorized by the court. He is then responsible for distributing them according to the will.

If your family has a business, renting a safe deposit box in the name of your corporation can assure you continued access after the death of a family member. Corporations never die. They just keep on electing new officers, and the box will not be sealed when an officer dies. To take out a safe deposit box in a corporate name, you must show the bank papers proving that there is an actual corporation in existence.

Source: Jay A. Jones, vice president of Williamsburgh Savings Bank and president of the New York Safe Deposit Association, New York.

WHAT TO PAY FIRST—AND LAST—WHEN SHORT OF CASH

When you're temporarily short of money, you must defer or finance some bills. Do not skip a rent payment. By tradition, landlords act quickly to evict. Utility bills can be delayed for a month, or two at most. Avoid having your phone disconnected. The process of hooking it up again is expensive, and the company usually demands a hefty deposit. Mortgage payments can sometimes be skipped for one month. Best: Notify the bank first. The same applies to a car loan. Notify the lender. See if the loan can be rewritten with smaller monthly payments. Credit-card balances are satisfied as long as you make the minimum monthly payment. The easiest bills to defer: Department store, medical and dental. But don't simply ignore them. Initiate honest, open discussions about the payment schedule.

STRETCHING DUE DATES ON BILLS

Due dates on bills can be stretched—but not far—without risk. Typical grace periods: Telephone companies, eight days. Gas and electric utilities, 10 days. Banks and finance companies, 10 days. Even after a late charge is imposed on an unpaid bill, your credit rating should be safe for 30 days.

Source: Terry Blaney, president of Consumer Credit Counseling Service of Houston and the Gulf Coast Area.

PERSONAL BANKRUPTCY

Even prudent people can find themselves facing a debt problem. A careful businessman may discover that a major customer is going under with six months' worth of bills unpaid. An executive may be told that his unprofitable division of the company will be eliminated, along with his job.

Most people have many more options for handling debt problems than they realize. Bankruptcy is an important factor that influences negotiations with creditors. But there are few situations where bankruptcy can't be avoided if the matter is handled with intelligence and integrity.

There are no fixed guidelines, but there are factors to take into account (such as a certain dollar amount of debts, or a certain percentage of income going to loan payments, or even a ratio of assets to debts) that can be used for deciding when bankruptcy makes sense. All of these factors must be considered, of course. But in every case, there is the balancing of pluses and minuses of a bankruptcy proceeding and the possibility of negotiations that can be undertaken rather than filing a proceeding. Examples:

• *What kind of debts are involved?* Some, such as taxes, back alimony and child support, or student loans that became payable less than five years previously, can't be discharged in bankruptcy.

• *What else would be affected?* Family members or friends who have cosigned loans may be drawn into the situation.

• *Are any inheritances, trusts or life insurance proceeds about to be received?* Anything of this nature received within six months of filing for bankruptcy will be subject to creditors' claims. In some cases, it pays to have a benefactor change his will to leave only a small income for the debtor and the balance held for the children.

• *What are the future consequences?* In one recent case, a banking executive had been involved with a side business that failed. If he had filed for bankruptcy, his career would have been stymied. Point: Even without special situations, out-of-court negotiations with creditors can frequently lead to a settlement that is quicker and less public than a filing for protection under the Bankruptcy Code.

Nevertheless, there are situations in which bankruptcy is the best solution, particularly if one of the creditors is hard to deal with.

For individuals, the bankruptcy law's three important alternatives:

• *Liquidation.* It's possible to simply turn everything over to a bankruptcy trustee (Chapter 7 of the Bankruptcy Code). The debtor is allowed to keep exempt assets. Under federal law, the most important exemption is up to $7,500 worth of equity in a home or, for those who don't own a home, $7,500 worth of any other assets or a combination of equity in a home and personal property. This is sometimes called the wild card exemption. Exemptions exist for equity in an auto and household furnishings, tools used to make a living, etc.

The debtor is allowed to choose either the federal or the state exemptions, whichever is more favorable. Exception: Some states have opted to force their residents to forgo the federal exemptions.

Any property not exempt is turned over to the bankruptcy trustee, along with a list of creditors and the amount each is owed. The trustee converts the assets to cash, establishes the legal priorities among the creditors and distributes what he has collected in accordance with these priorities.

As long as the debtor has been honest in dealing with this creditors and with the bankruptcy court, his debts are then discharged, except for those in the categories (referred to above) that aren't eligible for discharge. The debtor cannot file for relief under Chapter 7 or Chapter 11 for six years after the initial filing.

• *Installment plans.* Under Chapter 13, a debtor who has a regular income may pay off his debts over a period of three to five years. Nondischargeable debts must be paid in full. But other creditors may be forced to accept a percentage of what they're owed. The debtor must make a good-faith effort to meet his obligations, and creditors must receive no less than they would get in a straight liquidation bankruptcy. And even the nondischargeable debts are spread out over a manageable period. Bonus: IRS interest and penalty charges on tax debts stop running once the bankruptcy petition is filed.

• *Reorganization.* Most people think of reorganization under Chapter 11 of the Bankruptcy Code as something that applies only to corporations. But there's nothing to stop an individual from filing under Chapter 11. There may be advantages, particularly if he or she has a business worth continuing.

Once the petition is filed, everything is frozen. Creditors who are suing to collect or trying to seize the debtor's property must back off. Even IRS levies are barred or can be set aside. Interest and penalties stop running upon filing of the petition.

In order to continue essential services such as utilities, the debtor must post a new deposit (usually 50% of the average monthly bill for the last three months). If any mortgaged property is involved, the mortgage does not become due, and foreclosure is barred if the debtor has any equity or if the property is needed in business. The court may set a monthly payment for the use and occupancy of premises or assets covered by a valid lien.

Next, the creditors are organized into categories, usually secured and unsecured. Then a compromise plan is worked out. Generally, it calls for a portion of the debt in each category to be paid off, dependent on the liquidation value of the assets. Once the plan is confirmed, and payment is made, the balance of the debt is forgiven.

To win acceptance, the plan must be accepted by one class of creditors wherein a majority in number and two-thirds in amount of those voting have consented to the plan. If these guidelines are met, all of the creditors are bound by the plan.

Sidestepping bankrupcty: Once the debtor knows the law, it's often possible to achieve the same result, or even a more favorable one, without going to court.

First, the creditor and his attorney must take stock of the entire financial situation, listing assets, liabilities, pending court actions (if any), extra resources and so forth. The next step is to work out a compromise offer that's fair both to the creditors and to the debtor—something the debtor can live up to that will give the creditors more than they would get in bankruptcy. A full disclosure of the assets, liabilities and prospects for the future must be made.

Unless a major creditor is irrationally vindictive, it should be possible to make an offer attractive enough to win over the bulk of the creditors. Reason: Bankruptcy is an expensive process. Trustees' fees, attorneys' fees and other administrative expenses are high. And, in effect, these expenses are borne by the creditors. Administrative expenses are treated as first-priority debts. They must be paid in full before anything is paid toward any other debts. Also: In making a compromise offer, the debtor can often draw on resources, such as borrowing from a relative, that wouldn't be available to the creditors in a bankruptcy.

One or two small creditors may feel an offer in compromise isn't worth accepting. Usually, if 90% or so of the debt can be compromised, the other 10% can be taken care of. To maintain leverage, the offer is generally set up so that it must be accepted by enough of the creditors to make a compromise worthwhile or enforceable in a Chapter 11 proceeding utilizing consents in proper form. Otherwise, it is automatically withdrawn. In that case, the creditors are likely to end up with a bankruptcy that gives them even less. Even the IRS has been known to accept a compromise of back taxes under these circumstances.

For a simple wage earner with relatively few assets and an overwhelming debt load, a simple, straight liquidation bankruptcy may be the best course. Such a debtor is likely to lose little or none of his property because of the exemption rules. And he will be freed of creditors' harassment. But most people should first explore other options with a competent attorney. The public embarrassment and damage to reputation that bankruptcy entails can often be avoided.

Source: David N. Ravin, partner in the law firm Ravin & Kesselhaut, West Orange, NJ.

TAX ADVANTAGES FOR FILING FOR PERSONAL BANKRUPTCY

Tax considerations are hardly ever the main reason an individual files for bankruptcy. But the tax aspects of personal bankruptcy can be very favorable, especially for taxpayers who are heavily in debt to their employers or to their own closely held corporations. Main benefits:

* *Cancellation of indebtedness.* As a general rule, when a debt is forgiven, the debtor must report the amount forgiven as income. But a debt cancelled in bankruptcy is not treated as income.

Example: Among other debts, a financially troubled taxpayer owes his employer $25,000. If the debt is simply forgiven by the employer, the employee must report the $25,000 as income. If, however, the employee files for bankruptcy and the debt is cancelled, he does not have to treat it as income.

Example: An individual had credit card charges of $10,000 last year. This year the credit card debt is discharged in bankruptcy. If any of the credit card charges were previously deducted (e.g., as a business entertainment deduction) they would have to be reported as income. But the other part of the discharged debt wouldn't have to be reported.

Example: Five years ago, an individual borrowed heavily for his closely held corporation. For other reasons business is now so bad that the corporation must file for bankruptcy. If the individual also declares bankruptcy and the loan is discharged, he has a big tax windfall. He will not have to pick up the money he borrowed from the company as income.

* *Cancellation of back taxes.* Unpaid federal income taxes are cancelled in bankruptcy if they become due more than three years before the bankruptcy filing.

* *Deductible expenses.* Fees paid to an accountant to prepare an individual's personal records for Bankruptcy Court are tax deductible. So are legal fees, to the extent they involve the tax aspects of bankruptcy.

* *Carryovers.* Some carryovers are retained by the individual after bankruptcy. Included: Net operating loss carryovers (business losses), capital loss carryovers, tax credit carryovers and charitable contribution carryovers. Limit: Net operating loss carryovers must be adjusted downwards to the extent that the debt giving rise to the carryovers is cancelled in bankruptcy.

The negative tax consequences of personal bankruptcy:

* *Recapture of credits.* Any investment credit taken on an asset that is disposed of in the course of the bankruptcy proceeding must be recaptured (that is, added back to the tax due on the individual's post-bankruptcy tax return).

* *Payroll taxes.* Individuals who are personally responsible for payroll taxes (e.g., officers of a company) cannot cancel their liability for those taxes in bankruptcy.

* *Tax refunds* are payable to the trustee in bankruptcy, not to the individual who files for bankruptcy. Loophole: Taxpayers who expect to file for bankruptcy next year should arrange payroll withholding this year so that no tax refunds will be coming from the government. Alternative: If large refunds are expected, file for bankruptcy prior to December 31, before the refund becomes an asset payable to the bankruptcy trustee.

Source: Edward Mendlowitz, partner, Siegel, Mendlowitz & Rich, CPAs.

SECOND MORTGAGE CHECKLIST

It's difficult for homeowners to sell without giving the buyer help with the financing. Typical dilemma. The buyer can't qualify for a full first mortgage at the bank. He asks the seller to help close the gap by taking back a second mortgage for the balance of the purchase price.

Problems: Many sellers have been hurt by incautious secondary financing arrangements. The buyer can't come up with the payments, so the seller must go through costly foreclosure proceedings. In many cases, the seller ends up with nothing—the bank holding the first mortgage takes all proceeds from the forced sale.

To minimize the risk before agreeing to any secondary financing:

• See a lawyer. Don't sign papers without first getting sound legal advice. No reputable broker will urge a seller to get involved in secondary financing unless the seller has relied on an attorney for advice.

• Get a credit check on the prospective buyer. A strong, creditworthy buyer is the best protection an owner-financer can have. If you're working with a real estate broker, the broker will run the check for you. If not, you can tell a credit company and have the company run the check. Or, the bank holding the first mortgage might help.

• Give a second mortgage only if the purchaser is putting at least 25%–30% of his own money into the property. The more of his own equity the buyer has tied up in the deal, the less chance he'll walk away from it.

• Avoid very short-term balloon mortgages.* The balance of the second mortgage should not be due for at least three to five years. If you give only a one-year balloon and interest rates are worse in a year, you'll have put the buyer—and yourself—in an impossible position. If he can't come up with the money or refinancing, you'll have to force a foreclosure.

• Have someone in the area watch the property to make sure that the buyer is maintaining it properly. Rundown property can hurt you badly.

• Prepare to take steps should the buyer fall behind in his payments. Banks, for a service charge, will collect mortgage payments for you. Alternative: Sell the second mortgage. You'll take a loss, but you might be better off in the long run.

Some advice: Keep it clean. Drop your selling price before you accept secondary financing.

*The buyer makes small monthly payments for a limited time, then makes one large (''balloon'') payment of the full amount due.

Source: Margot Robinson, G.R.I., C.R.S., John Garrison Real Estate, Stamford, CT.

SECOND MORTGAGE SECURITY

Two programs are taking most of the risk out of owner-financed second mortgages:
• Seller-financed mortgage insurance.
• Federal National Mortgage Association (Fannie Mae) seller-financed second-loan program.

Taking back a private second mortgage is often the deciding factor in selling a house today. But these loans were not always good investments. Individuals usually can't make proper credit checks. If the buyer should default, holders of second mortgages are last in line.

Five companies now insure seller-financed loans against default. They work through banks, savings and loan institutions and mortgage companies.

The buyer must put at least 10% of the price of the house down in cash. He must be found creditworthy. He must be buying the house as his primary residence. The mortgage must be drawn on acceptable standard forms. Origination fees run 1–2% of the face value of the mortgage. Insurance costs vary, averaging about 1% for 50% coverage. Banks charge ½–1% for servicing the mortgage.

The Fannie May program buys second mortgages from individuals through local lending institutions. It discounts the difference between the private loan's interest rate and its current 10–12% rate. Restrictions: The buyer must plan to live in the house full time. The combined value of the first and second mortgages cannot exceed 80% of the price of the house. The loan must be written to Fannie Mae specifications. To be sure your second mortgage qualifies, work out the details of the loan with a local bank or savings and loan institution before you close the deal with your buyer.

PROS AND CONS OF HOME-EQUITY LOANS

Second mortgages, often called home-equity loans, are becoming an increasingly flexible and attractive means of raising fairly large amounts of money.

One of the latest and most convenient wrinkles in the second-mortgage business is the ability to write checks against a line of credit secured by the borrower's equity interest in his home. An individual can get a large loan for almost any purpose merely by writing a check.

Moreover, the interest rate on the loan probably will be lower, possibly considerably lower, than it would be if the borrower had obtained an ordinary personal loan. Generally, the interest rate on a second mortgage (because it is secured by residential real estate) is one to two percentage points lower than the interest rate on a personal loan.

A borrower should be aware, however, of some of the dangers inherent in second mortgages. First of all, the borrower is using his home to collateralize the loan. If for some reason the loan cannot be repaid as originally planned, there is the possibility that the house will be lost.

Considering this risk, a potential second-mortgage borrower should think carefully about what he plans to use the loan for. Is it prudent to put a lien on a home to take a vacation paid for by writing a check against a second-mortgage credit line?

Second mortgages have a very legitimate role to play and should be carefully considered, especially when large amounts of money are needed—paying for a child's education or an addition to a home, for example, or dealing with a large medical bill.

Potential second-mortgage borrowers should shop carefully. Different institutions offer substantially different kinds of second mortgages and a wide range of interest rates.

A critical element is the amount of money needed. Some lenders set relatively low limits, such as $50,000 or $60,000, while some will go several times higher.

Of course, the amount an individual can borrow under a second mortgage is limited by the equity he holds in his home. That is the appraised value of the property minus the amount owed under the first mortgage. The second mortgage allows the borrower to obtain cash for the increased value of his property and for the amount of principal he has paid on his first mortgage. He thus can "unlock" the frozen cash equity in his home.

Key consideration: Is the loan fixed-rate or variable-rate? Usually, the initial interest rate on a fixed-rate second mortgage is higher than it is on a variable-rate loan. Reason: On a fixed-rate loan, the lender is assuming the risk of a rise in interest rates. Even if rates were to rise dramatically, the interest paid by a fixed-rate borrower remains unchanged. On a variable-rate mortgage, however, the borrower assumes this risk, or at least a substantial part of it.

Therefore, an individual should consider the purpose of the loan in deciding whether to opt for a rate that is fixed or variable. If the loan is for a long-term purpose, such as adding an extension to a home, it might be wise to take a fixed-rate loan, viewing the initial higher interest rate as a form of insurance against a sharp rise in interest rates in the future. If interest rates were to drop sharply, the fixed-rate loan could be refinanced. Warning: Check for prepayment penalties, and shop to see which lender's offer is least onerous.

Variable rates usually are better suited for loans that the borrower expects to pay off in a relatively short period. Loans used for investments could be expected to generate enough cash flow to at least keep up with sharply rising interest rates.

Borrowers also should be careful about so-called balloons. These are second mortgages that fall due within a few years, usually three to five. But the repayment schedule might have been calculated on a basis of up to 20 years. Thus, at the end of, say, five years, although very little might have been paid on the principal, the lender could demand immediate and full repayment. If that were to happen and the borrower could not raise the needed money, he might lose his home. It is therefore essential that the contract have a clause requiring the borrower to renew the loan. Note: It is critical that you borrow from a reputable lender. The last thing most well-established financial institutions want to do is take over your home. They will always try to work things out if the going gets tough. That is not always the case with unknown lenders.

If your needs are special, many second-mortgage lenders will try to devise a program that fits your requirements. For example, they might agree to postpone payments for a specified period of time.

SHOULD HIGH-INTEREST MORTGAGE BE REFINANCED IF RATES DECLINE?

Much depends on the terms of the mortgage and the state in which you live. In New York, it's reasonable to refinance a mortgage if rates decline by as little as two percentage points. But if you live in California, it requires a decline of four or five percentage points before refinancing becomes profitable.

The most important variable: The penalty charged for paying the mortgage before it matures. Under New York State law, no penalty is applied on fixed-rate mortgages after they have been in effect for one year.

California, however, has no laws regarding prepayment penalties and banks can set whatever standards they please. Result: It is usually far more expensive to refinance a mortgage in California than in New York.

When to refinance: Calculate what time period it should take for the monthly saving in mortgage payments (due to the lower interest rate) to offset the cost of refinancing.

Example on which the following calculations are based: A 30-year mortgage of $60,000 has a fixed rate of interest of 17%. The monthly payments of principal and interest are $855.41.

New York: According to Sigfred L. Solem, senior executive vice president and mortgage officer of the Dime Savings Bank of New York, the costs of prepaying a mortgage in New York (after one year) is $783. This includes cost of title update, recording, attorney and appraisal fees.

The most expensive factor in refinancing is the up-front fee, the points charged for a new mortgage. This comes to about 3%–4% of the mortgage. At 3%, that is $1,800 on a $60,000 mortgage. The total cost of refinancing is $2,583 ($1,800 in points and $783 in fees).

Let's say the mortgage rates drop a percentage point, to 16%. In the switch from a 17% mortgage, monthly payments decline by $48.55, to $808.86 (from $855.41). Dividing the $48.55 saved per month into the $2,583 cost of refinancing shows that it takes about 54 months (4½ years) to make back the cost.

But if the mortgage rate drops to 15% from 17%, it takes 27 months. To 14%, 18 months. To 12%, 11 months.

Such an analysis assumes that you pay for the refinancing costs with cash. It neglects the opportunity cost of not having that money for investment. The analysis changes if the refinancing costs are integrated into the new mortgage. Then, you add the $2,583 to the original $60,000 owed, and the mortgage increases to $62,583.

On this basis, it takes more than 14 years to recoup the $2,583 in refinancing costs if the interest rate dropped only one percentage point, to 16%. To regain the refinancing costs at 15% takes 40 months. At 14%, 23 months. At 13%, 16 months. At 12%, 13 months.

California: Generally, each year a borrower can pay up to 20% of the outstanding balance on a California mortgage with no penalty. Thus, you can pay off the loan in five years and incur no penalties.

But say it is refinanced at another institution. The homeowner then repays the principal to the lender beyond the annual 20% limit during the first three years. Penalty: One-half of the original interest rate applied to the loan's balance.

If a homeowner decided in the second year to fully repay a $60,000 mortgage at 17%, the prepayment penalty would be $4,560—the $60,000 mortgage, minus $12,000, which represents the 20% leeway, times .085 (half the 17% interest rate).

If the homeowner refinances at the institution that gave the original loan: The prepayment penalty is 1¼% of the outstanding balance for each one-quarter-of-a-percentage-point reduction in the original interest rate.

The maximum penalty is 5%, which is reached with only a one-percentage-point decline in the rate.

If the interest rate on a $60,000 mortgage is readjusted downward by one percentage point or more, the penalty is about $3,000. In addition, the borrower has to pay a 3% fee for the new mortgage, plus $200. This comes to $2,000. Other charges and costs: $853. Total cost of refinancing a $60,000 mortgage: $5,853, more than twice the cost in New York.

Even without considering the opportunity cost of this $5,853 expense, it takes 10 years for a homeowner to break even if a 17% mortgage is refinanced at 16%. That means five years if the new rate is 15%, and a bit less than 2½ years if the rate goes to 12½%.

But if the opportunity cost is factored in, the borrower actually pays $18.69 more each month for this loan at 16% than 17%. At 15%, it takes 14 years to break even; at 12½%, almost three years.

tween the loan principal remaining and 100 percent.

	Loan Remaining After					
Interest rate	5 years	10 years	15 years	20 years	25 years	30 years
Life of mortgage – 30 years						
7%	94%	86%	74%	57%	33%	0%
7½	95	87	75	59	34	0
8	95	88	77	60	36	0
9	96	89	79	63	39	0
10	97	91	82	66	41	0
Life of mortgage – 25 years						
7%	91%	79%	61%	36%	0%	
7½	92	80	62	37	0	
8	92	81	64	38	0	
9	93	83	66	40	0	
10	94	85	69	43	0	
Life of mortgage – 20 years						
7%	86%	67%	39%	0%		
7½	87	68	40	0		
8	87	79	41	0		
9	89	71	43	0		
10	90	73	45	0		

Source: *How to Make Money in Real Estate,* Steven James Lee, Boardroom Books, Milburn, NJ.

BEST TIME TO REFINANCE A MORTGAGE

The most common type of mortgage is the conventional credit agreement for a fixed-rate, self-amortizing loan. Since each periodic payment is a fixed amount for each installment, the division between principal and interest will change constantly. In the early years almost all of the payment will cover interest costs. As time goes on, the principal is repaid, the proportion changes. There will eventually come a point where most of the payment will be applied to principal.

Since the interest expense is deductible, the early period of a fixed-rate, self-amortizing loan provides a larger tax deduction. Therefore, most real estate investors prefer to refinance a loan at the point where principal repayments become a major portion of the installment payment. Below is a table setting forth the percentage of loan principal remaining for various interest rates and maturities of loans. The percent equity buildup in a particular mortgage will be the difference be-

WHAT HAPPENS IF MORTGAGE PAYMENTS CAN'T BE MET

The most frequent reasons individuals may find it impossible to meet their mortgage payments are losing a job, getting divorced or separated, or encountering a sudden big expense such as a giant medical bill.

If you get hit—don't panic. Most legitimate financial institutions will do as much as they can to keep you from losing your house, although some will be more accommodating than others.

The worst reaction is to ignore the problem. It is critical that the borrower show the lender that he is a responsible person. Explain the details of the problem. Together, the lender and the borrower will try to determine the extent of the problem and possible resolutions.

• How soon can the borrower start repaying the loan?

• How much, ultimately, will the borrower be able to pay on a monthly basis?

If the problem is temporary, such as a big bill or the loss of a job, the lender generally will agree to accept smaller payments for a time and work out a schedule for future repayment of the delayed payments. Each situation must be worked out in accordance with the specific problems.

• The lender might agree to forgo payments for a few months. It might, for example, also be agreed that in the fourth month payments will begin as usual, with an additional 25% until the missed payments are brought up to date.

• If the loan has ''aged,'' and the borrower has built up equity in the home, the bank could ''recast'' the payments. That is, it could lengthen the maturity of the remaining loan, making each of more payments smaller.

• Refinancing is another alternative. This is possible if equity has been built up in the house, either through past payments or an increase in the house's value, or both. This approach is especially useful if the problem has arisen from an unexpected large bill. The bank gives the homeowners a new loan with which to pay the bill, and the loan is then incorporated into the mortgage. This increases the monthly payments—but only by a relatively small amount, as payments are stretched over many years.

• A second mortgage is a similar device. The homeowner might prefer a second mortgage for a number of reasons. First, it would not affect the first mortgage, which might be at a rate far lower than the bank is willing to charge on a refinanced mortgage. Next, the homeowner might want to pay the extra money needed over a shorter period of time than the life of his mortgage. He also might not be able to get a credit of the required size without putting up collateral, and the house could serve that purpose. And he might not be able to afford paying off a loan of the required size in only three years or so, even if he could get such a loan. Second mortgages can be as long as 15 years.

In some situations, it appears that under no circumstances will the owner be able to keep the house. Then it is as important as ever to work closely with the banker.

BEWARE OF INVESTMENT ADVICE

Odds are that you'll lose money if you invest in the stocks that are recommended by guests who appear on television's *Wall Street Week*. Most stocks rise in the weeks before the show ... peak on the Monday after the show has aired as viewers rush to buy them ... drop an average of 3.2% over the next six weeks ... and then continue to decline over the next three, six, nine and twelve months. Wouldn't it be wonderful if you could get in touch with the show's schedulers two weeks ahead to find out who the guest analysts will be? Then call the analysts' firms to find out what stocks they're recommending ... then buy shares of those stocks, hoping they'll be mentioned on the show ... then sell them on the Monday after the show has aired.

Source: Norman Fosback, president of The Institute for Economic Research.

SELECTING A STOCK-BROKER

Be sure that you do the interviewing. Don't let the prospective broker turn the tables and interview you. Here are some key areas to cover when interviewing a potential stockbroker:

• Where did he study? What?

• How long has he been with the brokerage firm? How long has he been in the securities industry? What was his prior employment? Why did he leave his last place of employment?

• From where does he get his investment recommendations? His firm's research department? Company contacts? Friends in the business? His own research? A combination?

• Can he supply a certified history of his firm's and his own research recommendations?

• Does he have any client references?

• What is his theory on giving sell advice and profit taking?

• How many clients does the account executive service? (You want your telephone calls to be answered promptly.)

- How diversified is the brokerage firm? Does it have, for example, a bond department? How about an economist? An in-house market technician (essential for timing)? Money-market experts? Commodity department? Option department? Tax shelter experts?
- How many industries does his firm's research department follow? How many companies? How many senior analysts does the firm have?
- Will you be getting weekly, monthly or only occasional printed research reports?
- What fees, if any, will be charged for such services as securities safekeeping?
- What is the firm's commission structure? What discounts is it willing to offer?
- Can the investor talk directly to the investment-research analyst to get firsthand clarifications and updates on research reports? Must everything be funneled through the account executive?
- What is the financial condition of the brokerage firm? (You want the latest annual and quarterly financial statements.)
- How many floor brokers does the firm have at the various stock exchanges? (You want prompt order execution.)
- Is the potential broker willing to meet personally on a regular basis (monthly or quarterly, depending on portfolio size and activity) to discuss progress?
- What kind of monthly customer statements are prepared? (More and more firms now offer tabulation of monthly dividend income, portfolio valuation and annual portfolio yield estimate.)

If you are reluctant to ask all the above questions, select at least some of them and have the answers supplemented with a resume. After all, if you entrust your financial future to an individual, you should be fully informed about his background.

HOW TO SELECT A DISCOUNT BROKER

Just because a firm calls itself a discount broker doesn't mean it really is. Rule of thumb:

Commission fees should be at least 50%–75% less than at a full-service firm, or you should continue searching.

In fact, there's an enormous variation in fee structures among brokers and even among discounters. Some brokers offer extremely low rates only for large trades but slim discounts for small transactions. Others do precisely the opposite. . .and some are in-between.

Shrewd investors should consider accounts at different discount brokers in order to benefit from the lowest fees for different-sized transactions within their portfolios.

Smart traders also know that in the discount brokerage business everything is negotiable. To keep a good client, discount brokers regularly offer fees below their published rate sheets, just as the big, full-service brokerage houses do. But you have to ask for those better deals.

While there's no substitute for comparison shopping, discount brokers with a single office generally offer lower fees than the large national brokers with many offices (and a lot of overhead).

In the best Wall Street tradition some discounters offer free investment advice to their best clients—but again, only if the client asks for it. The single-office brokers with an 800 number are likely to do this, although it may be possible for the client who trades at the local office of a national discount broker to develop a similar rapport with a particular trading agent.

Important limitations: Tax shelter syndications are traditionally part of the full-service brokerage function. A smaller number of discount brokers offer these syndications.

If a discount broker doesn't offer these services, an investor should search elsewhere:

- Trading. Nearly all reputable discounters trade stocks and bonds as well as options. Some firms offer lower rates for over-the-counter trades.
- Securities deposit. Discount brokers should either hold the security being purchased or deliver it to the client at no charge. Avoid brokers who insist that the client take delivery or those which charge a delivery fee.
- Insurance. SIPC insurance, which insures a

client up to $500,000, is standard industry practice, just as it is at the full-service brokers. Some have an extra insurance charge of up to $2.5 million per client.

• Cash balances. All cash from sales or dividends should be automatically reinvested in a money-market fund. Sometimes this is done only upon client request. Investors with large cash balances should shop for a broker who reinvests this cash immediately.

• Margin trading. The usual rate for both discount and full-service firms is ½%–2% over the broker call rate (which is based on the prime rate), depending on the amount borrowed. The more borrowed, the lower the rate.

• Keogh and IRA plans. Some plans are free, but most charge $25 to open the account plus a $25 annual service fee. Some firms even charge considerably more.

Most good brokers are willing to take the time to tell a prospective client what services they provide. Bad sign: If the phone isn't answered quickly, the broker may be understaffed or overworked. In the long run, this will waste a considerable amount of your time.

Source: David L. Scott, professor of finance, Valdosta State College, Valdosta, GA, author of *The Investor's Guide to Discount Brokers,* Praeger Publishers, New York.

USING A DISCOUNT BROKER

This can make good financial sense for simple transactions or if you play the market according to your own research. Saving: 25–75%. There is a minimum fee per trade. The size of the discount will depend on the size of the transaction. What is offered: Discount brokerages don't offer research services, advice or an individual broker. All buy and sell stocks. Most deal in stock options and some in government securities, municipal bonds and mutual funds. Find a discount broker in the standard ways: From friends, ads, *Yellow Pages.*

SPOTTING THE TRAPS IN EARNINGS FIGURES

Figures on company earnings are deceptive. They are useful guides only to investors who interpret them correctly.

• Retained earnings for some American companies can be overstated by significant amounts. Example: $1 in after-tax profit shrinks to just 60¢ after 40% is subtracted to adjust for the effect of inflation on depreciation and costs. Another 40% might then be deducted in order to pay out a dividend.

• The real corporate tax rate is elusive. Reason: Inflation boosts costs, resulting in inventory profits and underdepreciation of plant and equipment. Advice: Have more confidence in the earnings reports of companies that use last-in, first-out (LIFO) inventory accounting methods that make adjustments for inflation.

• Return on equity is often one-fourth of the reported percentage. Reason: Profits are nearly halved by inflation. But the book value might be almost doubled when current prices are used to calculate.

In most cases, it is not worth trying to make a quick trade based on a quarterly report. Reason: There is almost always a correction that brings the stock price back to where it was before the report. When to trade: After the price settles back.

What to focus on:

• Deviation in the long-term trend of a company's earnings.

• Changes in net margin. If sales move ahead but income is level, watch for a trend toward lower profits. And vice versa.

• Underlying changes, such as currency fluctuations, tax rate, and number of shares outstanding. They all affect earnings per share.

Translating the earnings figures into the price/earnings ratio is even trickier because the price of a stock is based on anticipated earnings, but the ratio is calculated on earnings in the previous 12 months.

Brokers are quite shameless about recommending one stock to a client as a good value (because the p/e ratio is low) and another as an excellent growth stock (because company prospects are so exciting that the p/e ratio is meaningless).

Rationale for buying low-multiple stocks: There is less downside risk in a declining market. And they have higher upgrade potential in an advancing market.

Rationale for buying high-multiple stocks. If the company really grows by 40% a year for the next 10 years, paying 40 times earnings is acceptable. Current earnings of $1 compounded for 10 years at a 40% rate amounts to nearly $30 of earnings 10 years from now. Even if the p/e ratio falls to 10 by then, the stock will have gone up more than seven times in value (from 40 to 290).

Bottom line: Keep a clear head when earnings, earnings forecasts, and p/e ratios are being loosely presented as reasons to buy now.

Source: Peter De Haas, portfolio strategist, L.F. Rothschild, Unterberg, Towbin, New York.

HOW TO ANALYZE CORPORATE EARNINGS

There are ways that a dedicated investor who's willing to do some serious work can get an edge on the market. That's by looking for significant data in the financial reports that managements issue each quarter. Many professionals overlook the early warning signs that are revealed in corporate shareholder reports.

Start with a company's annual report. Read the *Letter to Shareholders* that's usually the first thing in the report. Compare what management is saying now with what it said last year. Was it right? Is it glossing over bad news? The purpose of this review: To assess the integrity of management. That's an important fact in company performance that most security analysts and money managers ignore.

A double check on management: Ask the company (as a stockholder or potential investor) to be put on the list to receive the company's 10K report that's filed with the Securities & Exchange Commission (the company's annual report to the SEC) and also the 10Q report (quarterly report to the SEC). Compare what the company reports to the SEC with what it reports to the shareholders. What you can learn from focusing on the differences:

• The Rolm Corp. 10Q reported that the company was being impacted severely by price competition, whereas this information was not disclosed in the company's quarterly shareholder report. That was a real red flag. Shortly afterward, Wall Street was "surprised" by bad news from Rolm, but any investor who had looked carefully at the 10Q would have been forewarned to act.

• Baldwin United had tremendous differences between its public and its SEC reports long before the company's problems surfaced. For instance, in its quarterly reports, Baldwin was reporting after-tax earnings to the shareholders. But the more detailed 10Q revealed that the company was running pretax losses that were covered by tax credits.

Significance of these differences: If management cuts corners in its reports to its shareholders, what is it doing in company operations and in the accounting department to dress up earnings?

Secrets in taxes: Look, too, at the item called Deferred Taxes on the company's year-end financial sheet. The more aggressive a company is in its accounting, the greater the difference is likely to be between its shareholder books (its regular profit and loss statement) and the way it reports income to the IRS. Companies can legally report income and expenses differently to the public and to the tax authorities. Example: Capital purchases can be depreciated more slowly in the shareholder's report (enhancing earnings) than in the report to the IRS (where accelerated depreciation decreases earnings and taxes). The difference is captured in Deferred Taxes.

Lesson: You can rely more on the earnings reports and the projections made by managements that are conservative in their accounting. For example, two of the best-run companies, IBM and General Electric, use accelerated depreciation for both their tax and shareholder accounts.

Tax rates are important to look at, too. Here the important thing to observe is a change in the tax rate from year to year. If the company's tax rate (usually noted in the P&L review) goes down suddenly in the fourth quarter—say, from 40% to 29%—earnings for the quarter may look very good. An investor probably can't count on that boost in earnings turning up again. This can mean that future earnings may be disappointing, and Wall Street may be caught with another earnings "surprise" on the downside.

The signs are often not what they seem. A big drop in the cost of goods sold, general and administration expenses, or research and development as a percent of overall revenues may not be all good news either. The decline may be nonrecurring. Then what does the company do for an encore in comparative reporting?

Sharp investors keep a keen eye on inventory figures. If inventories are rising faster than sales—especially for a retailer—there's trouble ahead. Get out of any stock where the inventory turns* are steadily declining. That was an early warning sign for W.T. Grant —long before it filed for bankruptcy. Declining retailer inventory turns in many cases are caused by a buildup of slow-moving goods that should have been pushed out the door rather than kept in inventory.

Another trick that works like a charm for firms—especially high-tech firms—but is very rarely used by the so-called experts on Wall Street: A big increase in finished goods in inventory, but work-in-process inventories that don't go up nearly as much, and raw materials inventories that actually drop. What that means: Management is bearish regarding its near-term prospects and so has slowed down buying raw materials. The reverse, of course, is positive: A bigger increase in raw materials inventories than in finished goods means that management is filling the production pipeline because incoming orders are excellent. (Be

*A few companies report their inventory turns in their financial reports. But if this information isn't there, divide the cost of the goods sold by the company's average inventory for the year.

careful that the increase isn't due to some major price increase in raw materials for the industry.) Probability: This inventory indicator works about 80% of the time.

The fundamentals to check in every earnings report:

• A bulge in accounts payable. The company may be short of cash and stretching out bill payments. Watch out!

• Short-term debt. Look carefully at this because many companies are covering up short-term liabilities (such as commercial paper) and calling it longer-term debt since it's covered by a bank's line of credit. Short-term debt is a burden on a company, making it vulnerable to interest rate increases. Also, the company's bankers may force the company to amend loan covenants, curtailing the operating flexibility of the company in a way that can be detrimental to the long-term interest of all the present shareholders.

• Dividend payout. Too many managements are unwilling to cut dividends during tough strikes or other sharp reverses. When a company's resources are drained to pay a dividend, start worrying about the quality of management. It takes tough managers to cut a dividend. And, in the long run, tough managers are usually very good to shareholders.

One of the most bullish signs in an earnings report is a big bath —a big writeoff, often associated with a long overdue restructuring of operations, including the sale of losing or low-margined businesses. Among the recent classic examples: Beatrice Foods, Gulf & Western and Ralston Purina. Chances are good, with a big bath, for a real turnaround in earnings. Wall Street may be disappointed at first, but it usually reads a big bath positively and increases the price/earnings multiple on the stock.

Source: Ted O'glove, author of *The Quality of Earnings Report,* published by Reporting Research Corp., Englewood Cliffs, NJ.

BUYING NEW ISSUES

Don't expect wire houses and general stockbrokers to service you on new issues as well as they do on conventional stock transactions. Find a source by monitoring the formal announcements of new issues (called tombstone ads) that appear in *The Wall Street Journal*. Identify the lead underwriter (the first name listed among the brokers handling the issue), and keep track of what happens to the issues brought out by that underwriter over time. If the prices in the aftermarket hold a premium above the issue price on a fairly consistent basis, call that underwriter directly.

Ask for the company's biggest producer. Tell him that you want to be on his primary mailing list for prospectuses. Aim: To get them as soon as they are issued. Read the prospectuses carefully. Note people or firms (lawyers, accountants, etc.) where you have contacts. Ask them about the company. While they probably will not say much directly helpful, with experience you can do some very valuable reading between the lines.

When an issue is really hot, you can buy only so much. The superstar has an allotment, just as everyone else in the firm does. The reason to build a relationship with him is that his allotment is bigger.

It's only reasonable to believe that good customers get the lion's share.

Many investors who do get in on a few hot new issues then make a crucial mistake. They buy at the new-issue broker, hold the stock for a short time as the price runs up and then sell it through a wire house. If everyone runs out after the first day or week, the reputations of both the stock and the original underwriter are hurt. The broker at the new-issue house will soon find out what the customer is doing and will not work eagerly with him any more, either.

Suggestion: Tell the broker that you need some liquidity as soon as possible, and ask what you can sell in a short time without hurting the market. A common practice: Sell enough to get back the original investment at the issue price, and hold onto the rest for a free ride.

Danger signals: When the new-issue market gets hot, excesses build up and everyone gets hurt. When the cycle is over, few new issues come to market. The opportunities are in a down market. Companies that do go pub-

lic then are usually stronger and will probably outperform, on average, companies brought out in a frothy market.

Private placements: More and more investment bankers arrange private placements for start-up firms and get them ready to go public eventually, when the market is right. That is another reason for a sophisticated investor to build up a relationship with a firm that is regularly raising capital for new businesses. His broker can put him into a private placement when he is ready. (The minimum investment for an individual is about $50,000.) That can be the very best place for an investor. That was where all the real money was made in Syntex and Xerox some years ago.

When more seasoned companies go public, the public generally pays a premium price for the stock.

During the seasoning period between a start-up and a fully developed company, the privately raised money is used to create a pretty financial and people picture for the prospectus that is to be issued several years down the road. The pretty picture justifies the higher price. There is generally much more publicity with such seasoned issues, too. That can be a danger. The price shoots up on the issue day because a lot of unsophisticated investors read the publicity and place buy orders. But then the price often drops in the aftermarket.

Source: Patrick Rooney, president of Rooney Pace, Inc., New York.

SELLING SHORT IN A BULL MARKET

Short selling opportunities develop even during bull markets. Most such markets are interrupted at least once by a severe decline.

Suggestions for profitable short selling:

• Sell only heavily capitalized issues with a low outstanding short interest. They are less likely to be subject to a short squeeze (sharp rallies caused by many short sellers rushing to cover and too few shares available).

• Cover short sales during moments of market weakness. Take advantage of market declines that are stimulated by bad news to cover into periods of weakness. Warning: Do not wait for a rally to cover shorts. What the pros do: Cover short sales just before weekends in case favorable news triggers sharp Monday rallies.

• As an alternative to selling short, consider the purchase of puts (selling an option contract at a stated price on or before a fixed expiration date).

• A stock that is sold short can decline by only so much, but there's no limit on how much it can rise. Result: Short selling bucks the odds because the ultimate risk is always greater than the potential reward. Place stop loss orders to cover when the short sale goes against you by more than 10%-15%.

• Sell short stocks that show definite signs of overhead resistance (areas of heavy trading in that stock just above your short selling level) on their charts. Such areas tend to impede upside progress.

• Do not sell those short issues that have just made new highs. Wait for definite signs of weakness before selling short.

Source: *Personal Finance,* Kephart Communications, Alexandria, VA.

THE ART OF SELLING SHORT

Short selling is the process of borrowing common stock from an investor who holds it and selling it with the hope of profiting from a decline in price. In that case, the borrower replaces the stock at a lower price. This type of transaction is viewed as highly risky by most individual investors. But although we do not recommend that investors jump into short selling, we believe that with more knowledge, much of the risk is removed.

Insight: A study of security-price movements shows that security prices taken as a whole tend to move down about as far as they move up over long periods of time. But oddly, even during the worst-performing investment environments, prices are going up two-thirds of the time. Implication: Stock prices move downward twice as fast as they go up. If prices fall faster than they rise, money can be made very quickly—hence the appeal to a short seller.

Psychological negatives: Short selling is a concept that has been maligned by many people. Investors are suspicious of advisors who recommend it. Reason: We get most of our investment information from the media. But much of what appears to be business ''news'' is really public relations handouts that present corporations in a glowing light. For this reason, most business communications are too optimistic.

The following are the practical benefits of using a short sale:

• As a speculation. This will benefit an individual if the market or an individual stock declines. Most people who think the market is too high and expect a decline merely refrain from buying stock. Although there is justification, that doesn't help capital grow. It merely protects it. A short sale might enable the investor to make money grow in a weak market. Naturally, you can't select just any stock to short in a bear market, just as you can't buy just any stock in a bull market. Selection of the correct security is crucial. Logical choice: A company whose raw-materials costs are soaring in price but is unable to raise prices because of customer resistance. Although most investors would just eliminate such a company from their holdings, a venturesome person might not only sell his shares but also short some of them.

• As a portfolio hedge. An investor who is uncertain about the intermediate-term outlook for the stock market might arrange a portfolio that is 80% long and 20% short. Those proportions could be adjusted, depending on the investor's uncertainty or pessimism. Since stocks decline faster than they rise, some shorting might afford some protection during uncertain times.

• As a ''transactional hedge.'' Within a single industry, better-managed companies tend to rise faster than their peers during a good cycle for the industry, and poorer companies tend to fall faster during weak periods. Possibility: Being long on the shares of the strongest company in the group and going short on the weakest company.

• To defer taxes. This is also called ''shorting against the box.'' If an investor has made a big gain in a single year and wishes to defer it, he might short the equivalent number of shares he already owns. Such shorting is not treated as profit-taking. The investor may close out the short sale by delivering his own shares in the year he wishes to take the gain without paying any commission. The original short sale serves to guarantee the profit at the price the shares were sold short, whereas the gain need not be declared until the year in which the entire transaction is terminated.

• Short sale combined with an option eliminates risk. Most people fear short selling because the stock might run away on the upside. Few stocks, though, go straight up. Still, with the advent of listed call options, a short position can now be protected through purchase of a call option. It establishes a limited liability on the short sale.

Example:

An investor decides he wants to short XYZ at $50 but is worried that the stock might advance sharply. If XYZ has a call option with an exercise price of $50, he may then purchase that option to protect his short. If he buys a six-month call for $600 and his worst fears are realized (say, the stock goes up to $70 per share), he may at any time until the option's expiration date exercise the call option at $50 and deliver the stock against his short position. The only loss: The amount he paid for the option, plus commissions on the transaction—substantially less than the potential loss if he hadn't purchased the option.

• Variations. There are dozens of other possibilities for combining short sales and options. They range from aggressive trading to low-risk portfolio hedging with a maximum risk of $50 plus commissions. It is the conservative way to short.

THE BEST DAY TO SELL STOCKS!

Friday is the best day to sell stocks. Reason: Historical data show that stocks generally rise more on Fridays than on any other day of the week. The rule holds especially for stocks with the lowest market capitalization (price times total number of shares outstanding). Moreover, those shares consistently outperform most higher-valued shares throughout the month of January. To take advantage of these trends: (1) Add to your portfolio in late December. (2) Sell large capitalization stocks at the very end of a week.

Source: Norman Fosback's *Market Logic*, 3471 N. Federal Highway, Fort Lauderdale, FL 33306.

TIMING A STOCK SPLIT

Stock splits are not necessarily a bullish sign. General rule: Stocks that split usually outperform the market only before the announcement. After the announcement the stock performs no better than average.

HOW TO AVOID SELLING TOO SOON

Investors who are nervous about the direction of stock market movement can adopt the following method to avoid selling securities just as the market may be gathering upside momentum:

• Each week, record the number of issues making new highs for that week on the New York Stock Exchange. (These and other key data are recorded in *Barron's* among other sources.)

• Maintain a moving four-week total of the number of issues making new highs on the NYSE.

• Presume that the intermediate uptrend is intact for as long as the four-week total of issues making new highs continues to expand. Investors can hold long positions in most issues without fear until the four-week total turns down. This method is not foolproof, but in a 53-year period there has never been a market decline not foreshadowed by at least one week's notice in this indicator.

Source: *Timing and Tactics,* Ventura, CA.

WHEN NOT TO LISTEN TO YOUR BROKER

The few words the average investor finds hardest to say to his broker are, ''Thanks for calling, but no thanks.'' There are times when it is in your own best interest to be able to reject the broker's blandishments.

• When the broker's *hot tip* (or your barber's or tennis partner's) is that a certain stock is supposed to go up because of impending good news. Ask yourself: If the ''news'' is so super-special, how come you (and/or your broker) have been able to learn about it in the nick of time? Chances are by the time you hear the story, plenty of other people have, too. Often you can spot this because the stock has already been moving. That means that insiders have been buying long before you got the hot tip. After you buy, when the news does become ''public,'' who'll be left to buy?

• When the market is sliding. When your broker asks, ''How much lower can they go?'' the temptation can be very great to try to snag a bargain. But before you do, consider: If the stock, at that price, is such a bargain, wouldn't some big mutual funds or pension funds be trying to buy up all they could? If that's the case, how come the stock has been going down? It's wildly speculative to buy a stock because it looks as if it has fallen ''far enough.'' Don't try to guess the bottom. After all, the market is actually saying that the stock is weak. That is the fact, the knowable item.

• Don't fall for the notion that a stock is ''averaging down.'' It's a mistake for the broker (or investor) to calculate that if he buys more ''way down there,'' he can get out even. The flaws are obvious. The person who averages down is busy thinking of buying more just when he should be selling. And if a little rally does come along, he waits for his target price ''to get out even''—so if the rally fades, he's stuck with his mathematical target.

Stock market professionals average up, not down. They buy stocks that are proving themselves strong, not ones that are clearly weak.

HOW TO SELECT A MUTUAL FUND

Investors willing to assume risk sometimes seek aggressive mutual funds for rapid capital appreciation during a rising market. Other investors, to maximize safety, opt for mutual funds that show the greatest resistance to decline. And still others, who prefer to remain invested at all times, try to find mutual funds that perform better than the market averages during both up and down swings.

Techniques useful to investors for evaluating performances:

For aggressive investors: Each week that the market rises, divide the closing price of the mutual fund at the end of the week by the closing level of either the Standard & Poor's 500 Stock Index or the N.Y.S.E. Index. Plot the results on a graph for comparison. If the fund is indeed stronger than the average during a rising market, it will show up clearly, indicating that it is suitable for an aggressive investor.

Since such funds also frequently decline more sharply than the averages during falling market periods, these mutuals may be suitable vehicles only for investors with an accurate sense of market timing.

For safety-oriented investors: Each week that the market declines, divide the closing price of the mutual fund at the end of the week by the closing level of one of the averages. If your fund resists the downtrend more than the average stock during a falling market, the plotted results will show the fund's line declining less than that of the average.

Such funds may advance less than more aggressive funds during rising market periods.

For investors who want to try to beat the averages: At the end of each week divide the price of the mutual fund (rising or falling) by the price of one of the broad market averages, and plot the results. The result will demonstrate the relative strength curve of the fund, indicating whether it is outperforming the broad market, regardless of the price trend. Caution: As soon as your fund's relative strength curve begins to show weakness, consider switching your holdings into a better-performing vehicle.

MUTUAL FUNDS HIDDEN INVESTMENT FEES

Mutual funds have a responsibility to disclose their fees fully. That is required by the securities laws. But not all mutual funds structure their fees the same way.

Front-end load fees are easy to spot. The front-end commission to a broker runs up 8½%. In a few cases, the performance of a particular fund may justify that fee, but generally fees should be avoided. That can easily be done by buying a no-load mutual fund.

Back-end loads are less obvious. Although details are in the prospectus, the stockbroker may tell you it is a no-load fund. However, the investor winds up paying a back-end load if he takes his money out of the fund before a specified period of time, usually five years. If you are buying a fund from either a broker or an insurance agent, you can be sure there is a commission somewhere.

Low loads: You probably won't encounter this structure if you buy directly from a "family" of funds. However, in some of them there may be a "charismatic" fund—well advertised and high-profile—that charges a low load.

Example: At the Fidelity Group, the Magellan Fund charges a low load. However, a similar fund, Discoverer, with similar investment precepts and performance, is a no-load fund. Fidelity's Select Portfolio charges a 3% front-end fee and a 1% back-end fee. But once you are in the family of funds, with any of the funds, you can switch as much as you want from financial services to high-tech to leisure without paying a penny extra.

Management fees: Look for a fund's 12B1 plan. That is the section of the securities law that permits the use of the fund's assets to pay for distribution. Some funds pay and some don't. Paying for distribution is not necessarily an evil. You have to decide for yourself.

Example: Kemper Group has two money-market-type funds that are quite similar... the Kemper Cash Equivalent Fund and the Kemper Money Market Fund. The Cash Equivalent Fund is distributed by stockbrokers, while the Money Market Fund is a direct-sale operation. The Cash Equivalent Fund is a no-load money-market fund with a management fee that is ¼% higher than that of the Money Market Fund. The extra ¼% is paid to reimburse the brokers.

Why are investors willing to pay the extra ¼%?

They may want to have the money-market fund at their broker's instead of with the Kemper Group. They may be parking their funds there between other investment instruments. Kemper Cash Equivalent Fund and Kemper Money Market Fund are consistently two of the top-performing money funds in the country. They are large funds, and research indicates that the net yields on larger money-market funds outperform smaller funds by as much as half to three-quarters of a percentage point. So if one pays one-quarter of a percentage point extra for the 12B1 plan and that money is used for extra advertising, giving the fund more investment and more clout in the money markets, then there can be a reward to the investors for the greater size of the fund.

Bottom line: Despite the extra management fee, you're better off than if you bought a small fund through your broker's office.

Evaluating fees: The reporting of yields on mutual funds is formulated net of all management fees. If you had a choice of a fund paying 11% after a 1% management fee or one that paid 9½% after a ½% management fee, you would obviously want the one that yields 11%, despite its higher management fee. You always want the one that nets more.

Some fund shareholders have instituted suits against funds, insisting that their management fees are too high. That is silly. If the return is very high, they should be satisfied. If it is not, they should take their money out—a vote with cash. A management that is doing a good job deserves a good profit.

Perspective: Management fees can be warranted by good performance, but brokerage commissions are easy to avoid if you don't need hand-holding.

IRAs: Most mutual funds charge an annual fee for custodial duties—and a fee for setting up the account. The custodial fee is a pass-along because of charges by the bank's trust department, which provides the accounting services required by the IRS.

Frequently the largest expense for IRA investors is the transfer fee incurred if they wish to change their IRA from one brokerage or fund to another, from a broker to a mutual fund, etc. The problem: This entails a change in trusteeship (the bank providing the custodial service). And that can be costly as well as time consuming. Believe it or not, it often takes three to six months. Reason: Those trusteeships were set up with the belief that the accounts would be held there until retirement. The trustees never expected to give up these accounts quickly. To discourage transfers they require all kinds of information and material from the investor...and they charge heavily for making the transfer.

Better transfer method: Roll over your IRA account instead of transferring it directly. In a rollover, you close your account and take personal possession of your IRA money for up to 60 days. You are allowed one rollover per year. All funds, brokers and trustees are set up to do this easily. Rollovers are faster than transfers, and at most firms they are less expensive.

Another way to avoid transfer fees: Use a no-load family of mutual funds. Then, when you are unhappy with the stock market, you can switch into another type of investment fund free of charge...and switch, and switch...

Banking alternative: Banks don't charge fees for setting up IRAs, since they are trustees for themselves. There is, however, a hidden fee. Banks give a lower rate of return on your money. The differential between what an investor can expect to earn in bank certificates of deposit and a growth stock mutual fund over a 10-20 year period is very large. Our estimate:

Banks will average 10%, while growth stock mutual funds can average 20%.

Source: William E. Donoghue, chairman of The Donoghue Organization and publisher of *Donoghue's Moneyletter* and *Donoghue's Mutual Fund Almanac*.

HOW TO READ A MUTUAL-FUND PROSPECTUS

A mutual-fund prospectus is not easy reading. The way to pry out the information needed to make a good investment decision is to focus on the following:

• Does the fund's portfolio mesh with the buyer's investment goals? Some funds have highly volatile portfolios and employ leverage or margin selling to enhance return, but at greater risk. Investors can evaluate these practices in light of their own willingness to assume risk. Those who in the past have found themselves adept in market timing can more safely opt for volatile funds.

• What's the fund's performance record? It's prudent to select a fund that has matched or surpassed *Standard & Poor's 500* during periods of both rising and falling markets. Most prospectuses include several years' performance data. Best performers are usually funds with less than $50 million in assets.

• What are the minimum initial and subsequent investments? The lower the better.

• Is there a switch privilege? It is highly desirable to pick a fund that allows investors to switch back and forth between a firm's equity and money-market funds by phone.

• Are there fees for opening and closing an account? There is no reason to pay such fees. As a group, no-load funds, those without a salesperson's commission to pay, perform pretty much as well as those with fees. (Some funds charge for switching, but the charges usually don't amount to much, except for the frequent trader.)

• What are the limitations on how the fund can invest money? Some funds must diversify their portfolios, while others allow management to concentrate highly on one or more industry groups. As a general rule, diversification reduces risk. Investors may also want to find out (by asking management, if necessary) whether the fund has a policy of moving into cash during bear markets. While a fund can cut losses this way, it may also delay reinvestment in equities when the market starts to rise. Long-term holders often adopt the strategy of investing in funds that have a record of increasing cash positions by selling equities before bear markets or at least at their earliest stages.

Source: *Switch Fund Advisory,* MD.

WATCH YOUR ARITHMETIC WHEN MUNICIPALS ARE CASHED IN

Many owners of municipal bonds pay more tax on appreciated value than they should.

Trap: The increase in the value of the bond is not all capital gain. The IRS has held that any increase in value which is attributable to the discount given when the bond was originally issued is really interest income. Benefit to taxpayers: Interest on a municipal bond is tax-free.

Reality: A municipal bond is rarely held by the same person from the day it is issued until the day it matures, which may be many years later. It is much more likely that the bond will be traded several times during that period. And the price of a bond issued at discount will tend to rise as its maturity date approaches. Tax treatment: The amount of the discount is attributed to the owners of the bond evenly over the bond's life. Example: A bond issued at a $300 discount has a 30-year term. The discount is attributed (or amortized) at the rate of $10 a year. So a person who holds the bond for two years may sell it for a $20 profit and have no taxable gain.

Complications: The price of the bond may be affected by many other factors. And a price change resulting from another factor, such as a change in interest rates, will result in a gain or loss that is capital in nature. But a taxpayer who properly amortizes the original issue dis-count will benefit regardless of whether the bond is sold for a gain or a loss. Reason: The taxpayer adds the amortized discount to the price he paid for the bond when he computes his profit or loss on the subsequent sale. Result: If the bond is sold for a profit, the taxable gain is reduced. But if it is sold for a loss, the available loss deduction is increased.

BUYING BONDS ANONYMOUSLY

Bearer bonds, although a perfectly legitimate form of debt security, have become a favorite investment for the underground economy. Why: They are a convenient way to stash cash, earn interest on it, and (illegally) hide that income from the IRS. This is possible because bearer bonds are not registered in the purchaser's name. They belong to anyone who possesses (bears) them.

Types of bonds that are bought in bearer form:

• Corporate issues predating the late 1960s. (After that, the Department of the Treasury required corporate bonds to be registered when sold.)

• Treasury notes and bonds (but not Treasury bills).

• Most federal government agency securities (such as GNMAs).

• Virtually all state and municipal issues.

Dangers: If lost or stolen, bearer-bond certificates are, for all practical purposes, impossible to trace and recover. Because there is no name on them, investors risk having someone else (perhaps a family member) cash them in without permission. And if the interest is not declared as income, and the IRS discovers the concealment, the bondholder faces criminal as well as civil penalties.

ZERO-COUPON BONDS

Zero-coupon bonds are touted as one of the safest investments around, but if you don't watch your step, you could wind up losing big.

Zeros are bonds that are "stripped" of their dividend coupons (thus the name zero coupon). They are sold at deep discounts from their face value. When they mature decades hence, they can return seven or eight times your original investment. For example, a zero-coupon Treasury bond that will be worth $1,000 when it matures in the year 2004 was recently selling for $121. That's a yield to maturity of 11.25%.

Nearly all zeros are backed by US Treasury securities and go by catchy feline nicknames such as CATS* and TIGRs.** Even though holders of these bonds do not receive any interest payments while the bonds are outstanding, for tax purposes, holders are treated as though they received interest payments year in and year out. Since no one in his right mind wants to pay taxes on income he has not received, those taxable Treasury-backed zeros are considered suitable only for tax-favored retirement accounts such as IRAs and Keogh plans.

Zeros have proved immensely popular since they were introduced in 1982. But it's starting to look as though some of the brokerage firms that sell these securities to individuals are taking advantage of a good thing. Trap: The markup that brokers tack onto the wholesale price of the bonds.

A group of Michigan doctors has filed a class-action suit against Merrill Lynch, alleging, among other things, that the giant brokerage firm charged an excessive markup on $680,000 worth of zeros purchased by their pension plan. (Merrill Lynch denies the charges.) The Securities and Exchange Commission and the National Association of Securities Dealers are also conducting investigations of retail pricing practices on zeros. NASD guidelines say the markup on corporate bonds should not exceed 5%. However, the markup on zeros, which are virtually unregulated either by the federal government or by industry watchdog groups, sometimes exceeds 15%, according to some industry observers.

*Certificate of Accrual on Treasury Securities.
**Treasury Investment Growth Receipts.

But it's difficult for the individual investor to determine the markup on zeros because the bonds are sold "net," after figuring in the markup. About the only way to find out whether your broker is charging you a fair price is to phone around to see what the competition is charging. The larger the broker's markup, the higher the price of the bond —and the lower the yield to the investor.

Comparison shopping isn't easy. The firms often package their zeros differently, so their zeros may be similar but not identical. Furthermore, it's unlikely that the firms you question will have on any given day the same inventory of products with identical maturity dates.

Nevertheless, shopping around can pay off. A recent unscientific sample found variations as large as one-third of a point on the yield of several identical long-term Treasury zeros. If you had purchased $100,000 face value in bonds from the firms offering the highest yields (and lowest prices), you would have saved almost $750 on a transaction of about $11,350.

You also have to watch your step if you purchase zeros backed by tax-free municipal bonds, which account for a small but growing segment of the market. Although the yield on these zeros is lower than the yield on the Treasury-backed variety, the imputed interest is not taxable to the holder each year. This feature makes them ideal investments for high-bracket taxpayers who would like to purchase zero municipals for their regular investment portfolios.

But even here, you must be wary. The biggest danger: The bonds may be called before maturity at a price that is only a slight percentage above their "accredited value" (their value if interest had been accruing on them up to that moment). The problem is that many people have purchased their zeros at a price above accredited value. Rapid compounding of interest on zeros doesn't begin until the last third of the holding period. Consequently, you may be forced to accept a price that is less than what you paid for the bonds if they are called during the first two thirds of the holding period.

Your best defense: Purchase zero municipals that are not callable. Alternative: Buy bonds that are the last callable ones of the particular series. If you can't, be sure to at least ask your broker the accredited value of the bonds you're considering. If the asking price is above accredited value, keep on looking.

Source: Deborah Rankin writes the Personal Finance column for *The New York Times.*

A HYBRID VERSION: THE ZERO-JUNK BOND FOR SOPHISTICATED INVESTORS

Corporate bonds that pay no interest for an initial five years or so, and then transform into high-yield bonds (13%–16%) thereafter, are increasingly popular with sophisticated investors.

Two major advantages of these zero-junk hybrids are: Like zero-coupon bonds, price appreciation is magnified if interest rates drop—and the exceptionally high interest rates should more than compensate investors for the extra risk of the underlying company.

The major disadvantage of these hybrids is: Early redemption by the company may prohibit investors from collecting the high interest rates paid after the zero-coupon bond phase is over.

Source: *Fortune,* 1271 Ave. of Americas, New York 10020.

JUNK BONDS: DON'T LET THE NAME FOOL YOU

"Junk" bonds are riskier than Treasury bonds or investment-grade corporate bonds (rated A or above) like AT&T's. The reward: they produce better returns for investors. Many institutions (pension funds and insurance companies) aren't allowed to buy bonds rated lower than A, so the market prices them inefficiently.

The typical high-yield "junk" bond can yield 350–450 basis points (3.5%–4.5%) more than long-term US Treasury bonds—up to 18½%.

If you're afraid of high-yield bonds, consider this: The scariest thing in the world is buying an AAA bond at par (face value). You have paid for everything good that can ever happen to your investment. If the bond goes up much in price, the company will call it (buy it back from you), and if it goes down, you may have to take a loss, or wait out the bond's maturity. But if you buy a B bond, any number of things can happen. Many high-yield bonds are issued at 85% or so of face value, so there's room for the price to go up. Another possibility: Instant upgrade through merger.

If the issuing company goes bankrupt, all is not lost, by any means. You may lose some interest and some sleep, but if you are willing to wait a while and don't panic, you can still do well. The people who held Penn Central's debt now control the company. There was more money lost on the downgrading of Ford's bonds from AA to A than on all the bankruptcies of B bonds in 10 years put together.

The volatility of interest rates makes the prices of high-grade bonds gyrate, and that makes junk bonds even more attractive. Low-grade bonds tend to trade like stocks, so they have always fluctuated in price. (Many are even convertible to stock.) That is part of what gave junk bonds their image problem. People think bonds shouldn't be volatile. When even the high-grade bonds are fluctuating in price the risk/reward ratio shifts still more in favor of lower-grade credits.

How to invest in junk bonds: As always, the key to success is to do homework and to spread risks. Most individuals should not buy one or two issues of B-rated bonds. Although the risk on a broadly based portfolio is minimal relative to the yield differential, the risk on any one issue could be catastrophic. By diversifying, you reduce the risk of a thermonuclear event in your portfolio.

If you can afford to buy an assortment of high-yield bonds issued by different companies in different industries, that's great. For smaller investors, there are a dozen or so high-yield bond mutual funds that have diversified portfolios and will do your homework for you. Typical minimum investment: $1,000.

Source: G. Chris Andersen, managing director, corporate finance department, Drexel Burnham Lambert, New York.

HOURS WHEN EXPERTS DO THEIR TRADING

Popularly traded issues show distinct tendencies during the course of the day. Reason: Traders tend to buy and sell at certain hours. Astute investors can take advantage of these patterns:

• Day traders often buy early in the morning or on evidence of overall stock market strength that day. If the market is weak, traders will sell short at the earliest opportunity. Positions on the New York exchange are normally equalized between 3:30 and 3:45 p.m. there.

• On stronger days, expect temporary weaknesses in the issue at about 3:30 when most traders close out their long positions. Buyers should try to place orders during this period. Sellers should wait until just near the close when prices often recover. (Another point of market weakness is between noon and 1 p.m.)

• On weaker days, short sellers should expect some price recovery at about 3:30 p.m. when some traders are covering their shorts.

GUIDE TO STOCK MARKET INDICATORS

• Speculation index: Divide the weekly trading volume on the American Stock Exchange (in thousands) by the number of issues traded. Calculate the same ratio for New York Stock Exchange trading. Divide the AMEX ratio by the NYSE ratio to calculate the speculation index.

To read the index: Strategists believe the market is bearish when the index is more than .38 (and especially so if it rises to .38 and then falls back). Less than .20 is bullish.

• Member short selling: Divide the number of shares NYSE members sell short each week by total NYSE short selling.

To read the index: It is bearish when read-

ings of .87 are reached. A reading below .75 is very bullish, particularly if it lasts several weeks.

• New highs-new lows: The market is usually approaching an intermediate bottom when the number of new lows reaches 600. The probable sign of an intermediate top is 600 new highs in one week, followed by a decline in number the next week.

• NYSE short interest ratio: The total number of outstanding shares sold short each month divided by the average daily trading volume for that month. A strong rally generally comes after the ratio reaches 1.75.

• Ten-week moving NYSE average: Compute the average NYSE index for the previous 10 weeks. Then measure the difference between last week's close and the average.

How to read it: When the gap between the last weekly close and the 10-week average remains at 4.00 or below for two to three weeks, investors can expect an intermediate advance. Market tops are usually near when the last week's index is 4.00 or more above the previous 10-week average.

• Reading the indicators together: Only once or twice a year will as many as four of the five indicators signal an intermediate bottom, but when four do, it is highly reliable. The same is true for intermediate tops.

Source: All indicators available weekly in *Barron's*. The Speculation Index was developed by *Indicator Digest*.

HOW PROFESSIONALS SPOT LOW-PRICED STOCK THAT IS READY TO BOUNCE BACK

Value has little to do with telling a good company from a bad company. A top-quality large company which is selling at a high price/earnings multiple is less attractive than a lesser-quality company which is selling at a depressed price in terms of its past and future earning power, working capital, book value, and historical prices.

What to look for:

• Stocks that have just made a new low for the last 12 months.

- Companies that are likely to be liquidated. In the liquidation process, shareholders may get paid considerably more than the stock is selling for now.
- Unsuccessful merger candidates. If one buyer thinks a company's stock is a good value, it's possible that others may also come to the same conclusion.
- Companies that have just reduced or eliminated their dividends. The stock is usually hit with a selling wave, which often creates a good buying opportunity.
- Financially troubled companies in which another major company has a sizable ownership position. If the financial stake is large enough, you can be sure that the major company will do everything it can to turn the earnings around and get the stock price up so that its investment will work out.

Opportunities, also, in stocks that are totally washed out—that is, situations where all the bad news is out. The stock usually has nowhere to go but up.

How to be sure a stock is truly washed out:

- Trading volume slows to practically nothing. If over-the-counter, few if any dealers are making a market.
- No Wall Street research analysts are following the company any more.
- No financial journalists, stock market newsletters, or advisory services discuss the company.
- Selling of the stock by company's management and directors has stopped.

Signs of a turnaround:

- The company plans to get rid of a losing division or business. If so, be sure to learn whether the company will be able to report a big jump in earnings once the losing operation is sold.
- The company is selling off assets to improve its financial situation and/or reduce debt.
- A new management comes on board with an established track record of success with turnaround situations.
- Management begins buying the company's stock in the open market.
- Also, be sure to follow the Form 13d statements filed with the SEC. (A company or individual owning 5% or more of a public company must report such holdings to the Securities and Exchange Commission.) If any substantial company is acquiring a major position in a company, it's possible a tender offer at a much higher price is in the wind.

Source: Robert Ravitz, director of research, David J. Greene & Co., New York.

THE SCANDALOUS WALL STREET "SPECIALS"

One of the more insidious stockbroker-dealer practices is the use of "specials" to dispose of inventory. When a brokerage firm wants to dump an over-the-counter (unlisted) security which it has in its own inventory, it substantially increases the commission it pays to its account executives if they sell it promptly.

Since the security comes out of the firm's inventory, the transaction is called a principal transaction. These are generally done on a net basis. On the confirmation slip that the customer receives, there is no breakdown between the actual price of the security and the commission charged. Result: The customer doesn't really know the exact commission or the stock's precise price. This obfuscation allows the broker to charge a higher price for the security than may be dictated by supply and demand. As a result of this ploy, the firm can afford to give its account executives the higher commissions.

Why is the account executive so eager to sell you a particular security? Does it really fit into your investment program? Does he have a research report recommending it?

There are two main reasons why brokers want to unload stocks in their inventory. They have become disenchanted with the stock's prospects, or the carrying (interest) charges have become excessive. Some firms announce "specials" to the account executives on an almost daily basis.

Safeguard: One of the most important safeguards any investor should employ is to ask his account executive for a research report on any recommendation that is made, even if it is only a brief one.

Confirmation slips should indicate when a brokerage firm is selling stock out of its own inventory by stating that it is a principal transaction. Some brokers, however merely indicate that the transaction was done on a net basis and that the firm is a "market maker." An investor who sees these terms may have been an unwitting purchaser of a "special" which was sold to him only because his account executive was eager to get a higher commission. In order to mislead clients, some brokerage firms merely put a small code number on the front of the confirmation slip. On the back of that slip, in tiny print, one can find that the code number means that, in fact, a principal transaction was done.

Bottom line: Instruct your broker to always inform you beforehand whether the transaction is likely to be a principal or an agency transaction, which means that the broker is acting as a middleman or on behalf of another investor. Confirmation slips for agency transactions should state separate price and commission charges.

SIGNAL THAT A LARGE BLOCK OF STOCK IS ABOUT TO BE DUMPED ON THE MARKET

Very frequently, knowledge that a large block of shares of a particular stock is up for sale can influence the decision on whether to buy or to sell those securities. For example, you might postpone or permanently avoid purchasing shares about to come under institutional liquidation. Or you might choose to sell before a competing large sell order becomes operative.

While mutual funds and other institutions don't "advertise" that they plan a liquidation prior to actual sale, such information, not infrequently, manages to "leak out," and this often puts a sizable dent in the stock's price. There usually are hints available to the alert investor that a liquidation of the block is imminent.

The major indication that a block is coming up for sale lies in a sudden shrinkage of the trading range of the issue in question. For example, a stock might usually demonstrate an average trading range of perhaps a full point or point and one-half between its daily high and low in a typical trading day. If, for two or three days, this trading range shrinks to, say, one-tenth to three-eighths of a point, you might anticipate a block is coming up for sale at near current market levels or below.

The shrinkage probably represents awareness on the part of knowledgeable floor and other traders that a large sell order exists and an unwillingness to bid up for the stock until the overhead supply, which is immediately forthcoming, is fully liquidated.

HOW TO BUY A STOCK AT LESS THAN ITS MARKET PRICE

• Select issues of interest that have listed puts available.

• Sell listed puts in the amount of shares that you might wish to purchase. Emphasize puts that are slightly out of the money (exercise price below the current market price of shares).

If the stock falls to the exercise price of the put, you will have purchased your shares at lower than the current price. If not, you will have pocketed the put premium free and clear.

Example: Stock X was selling at 28½, at which time a July-25 put was selling at ⅝. If you owned Stock X at the time, you might have sold one July-25 put for each 100 shares you had planned to purchase. If Stock X was to decline to 25 or below, the put might be exercised, and you would be obligated to purchase the shares at 25—an effective cost of 24⅛ since you had previously received ⅝ of a point from the put. If the stock were to remain about 25 through the period before the option's expiration, you would receive the premium free and clear as a profit.

Alternate strategy: If put premiums are low, you might, as an alternative, purchase the shares immediately, and also purchase a put to protect against loss. If the market declines in the near future, you could sell your put at a profit.

PROTECTING PAPER PROFITS WHEN THE MARKET DIPS

There's a way to safeguard paper profits against the stock market dropping without selling out entirely. It's called covered-option writing. How covered-option writing works:

Sell short one 100-share call option* for every 100 shares of stock owned. If the stock goes down, the option will go down, too. Then there'll be a profit when the investor buys it back at a loss, or when it expires worthless. If the stock goes up (providing more paper profits), the option will go up, too. The investor must then buy it back (that's a cash loss, not a paper loss). Otherwise, the option will be exercised, which means he's forced to sell the stock at the option exercise price.

The technique is a bit complicated, but many brokers are familiar with it and will guide the investor. Be aware that this is a strategy for uncertainty. If an investor feels sure the market will drop, he probably should sell his stocks outright.

• Points to remember: Covered-option writing gives only limited downside protection. If the market drops faster than 10% in six months (which could happen), this program loses money. And the cost of getting this protection is that the investor gives up most of the additional profits he'd make if the market goes higher.

Also, commissions are high, especially on one or two options. (Example: One option at 3 ($300); the commission is $25 to sell and another $25 to buy back.)

*An option to buy 100 shares of stock at a fixed price within a specified time limit; nine months is the maximum.

HOW TO TELL WHEN A FAST-RISING INDUSTRY IS TOPPING OUT

Typical pattern: Initial price gains attract wide public speculative interest which finally gives way to sharp price declines. The declines often trap unwary investors.

How to recognize when such groups may be topping out prior to a sharp price drop:

• The industry group already has had a very sharp runup.

• Very heavy trading volume. Stocks in this group dominate the list of most actively traded stocks.

• Near the top of the rise, the stocks gain and lose in violent price swings. But little ground is gained in the process.

• Price/earnings multiples for the group soar far above historical norms.

• Heavy short selling appears. Early short sellers of the stocks are driven to cover by sharp rallies. Their covering of shorts adds fuel to late rallies within the group. (Short sellers who enter the picture later, however, are likely to be amply rewarded.)

Trading options that work for professionals: Extreme caution first and foremost. Close stop-orders are placed on any long and/or short positions taken. Short sales are entered into only after these issues have shown signs of fatigue and of topping out, and then only after recent support levels have been broken. Wait for a clear sign that the uptrend has ended before selling out.

HOW BEAR MARKET RALLIES CAN FOOL YOU

Bear market rallies are often sharp. They're fueled, in part, by short sellers rushing to cover shares. However, advances in issues sold short often lack durability once short covering is completed. Details:

• Bear market rallies tend to last for no more than five or six weeks.

• Bear market advances often end rapidly— with relatively little advance warning. If you are trading during a bear market, you must be ready to sell at the first sign of weakness.

• The first strong advance during a bear market frequently lulls many analysts into a false sense of security, leading them to conclude that a new bull market is underway. The majority of the bear markets don't end until pessimism is widespread and until the vast majority is convinced that prices are going to continue to decline indefinitely.

• Although the stock market can remain "overbought" for considerable periods of time during bull markets, bear market rallies generally end fairly rapidly, as the market enters into "overbought" conditions. An "overbought" condition occurs when prices advance for a short time at a rate that can't be sustained.

One way to predict a decline—using the advance-decline line as a guide: Each day, compute the net difference between the number of issues that rise on the Big Board and the number that decline. A ten-day total of the daily nets is then maintained. During bear markets, be careful when the ten-day net differential rises to +2,500 or more, and be ready to sell immediately once this figure is reached and starts to decline. The decline will usually indicate that the advance is beginning to weaken.

SPOTTING THE BOTTOM OF A BEAR MARKET

Here's how sophisticated investors recognize that a bear market is near its last phase:

• Downside breadth increases. That is, market declines become broader, including even stocks that had been strong before. More issues are making new lows.

• "Oversold" conditions (periods in which the market seems to decline precipitously) extend for longer periods of time. Technical recoveries are relatively minor.

• Pessimism spreads, but analysts and bullish advisories still discuss "bargains" and "undervalued issues."

• Stocks continue to be very sensitive to bad news. The market becomes very unforgiving of poor earnings reports and monetary difficulties.

• Trading volume remains relatively dull. Prices seem to fall under their own weight, the result of a lack of bids rather than urgent selling.

Important: The bear market isn't likely to end until pessimism broadens into outright panic, and until public and institutional selling becomes urgent.

Some of the most reliable nontechnical signals that the bear market is over:

• When the mass media begin to headline the fact that the stock market is hitting its bottom.

That's when *Time* and *Newsweek,* and the TV networks, warn of even lower Dow levels. When those reports appear regularly, wise investors know the bottom has already passed.

THREE WAYS TO SPOT MARKET DECLINE BEFORE IT STARTS

Strong market moves frequently end in one- or two-day reversal spikes. Those spikes often provide advance warning of significant market turning points. Here are signs that show when a market decline may be coming:

• The market will rise sharply in the morning on very high volume running at close to 15 million shares during the first hour of trading.

• From 10:30 a.m. (Eastern time) on, the market will make little or no progress despite heavy trading throughout the day.

• By the end of the first day, almost all the morning's gains will have been lost, with the market closing clearly toward the downside. Occasionally, this process will be spread over a two-day period.

Steps to take: When you see the pattern, either sell immediately or await the retest of the highs that were reached during that first morning. Such a retest often takes place within a week or two, on much lower trading volume. This may prove to be the last opportunity to sell into strength.

The patterns seen during one-day reversals occasionally take place early in intermediate advances, with the backoff representing a test of previous lows. If such action appears prior to significant market gains, do not sell. Rather, buy during any near-term weakness. The market will probably resume its rise.

However, if such a trading pattern occurs following a period of several weeks or months of rising prices, the odds increase that a genuine one-day reversal is occurring. Then you must take protective action.

MAKING PROFITS ON A STOCK SPLIT

When a stock splits, the average profit to an investor is 20%. But the greatest profits are generally made in three to six months before the split is announced. The general pattern is that the price stays high for two days after the split announcement and then declines. To spot a candidate for a split, look for:

• A company that needs to attract more stockholders, diversify, or attract additional financing.

• A takeover candidate (heavy in cash and liquid assets) whose management holds only a small percentage of the outstanding shares. (Companies with concentrated ownership rearely split stock unless there are problems with taxes, acquisitions, or diversification.)

• A stock price above $75. A split moves it into the more attractive $35–$50 range.

• A stock that was split previously and price has climbed steadily since then.

• Earnings prospects so strong that the company will be able to increase dividends after the split.

Likely prospects are over-the-counter companies with current earnings of $2.5 million, at least $2 million annually in preceding years, and less than 1 million shares outstanding (or under 2,000 shareholers). A stock split is necessary if management wants to list on a major exchange.

Source: C. Colburn Hardy, *Dun & Bradstreet's Guide to Investments,* Thomas Y. Crowell Co., New York.

TECHNIQUES FOR EVALUATING OVER-THE-COUNTER STOCKS

Growth potential is the single most important consideration. Earnings increases should average 10% over the past six years when acquisitions and divestitures are factored out. Cash, investments, accounts receivable, materials, and inventories should be twice the size of financial claims due within the next year.

In addition, working capital per share should be greater than the market value of the stock (an $8 stock should be backed by $10 per share in working capital). Long-term debt should be covered by working capital, cash, or one year's income. And the balance sheet should show no deferred operating expenses and no unreceived income.

The criteria for final selections include ownership by at least 10 institutions reported in *Standard & Poor's Stock Guide,* and public ownership of between 500,000 and one million shares, with no more than 10% controlled by a single institution. There should also be continued price increases after a dividend or split, and a strong likelihood of moving up to a major exchange. (A good sign is strong broker and institutional support).

OTC stocks to avoid are those of companies expanding into unrelated fields, where they lack the required management experience and depth, and stock selling at prices far below recent highs. This sign of loss of investor support can take months to overcome.

Source: C. Colburn Hardy, *Physician's Management.*

BEST TIME TO INVEST IN NEWLY LISTED STOCKS

Most investors believe that a stock will rise in price as soon as it moves from an over-the-counter listing to the New York Stock Exchange. That's rarely true. What happens:

• The prices of such shares tend to run up sharply on the smaller exchange in the year preceding the NYSE listing. Foreknowledge of listings may or may not be available to shareholders, however, and you can't necessarily presume that you'll benefit from this information.

• During the average nine-week period required for the NYSE to consider applications for listing, stocks that move from the over-the-counter markets usually outperform other stocks. If you hold such an issue, keep it until the listing procedure is completed.

• Once listing has been achieved, expect the price performance of such issues to fall to below average. Weakness is usually particularly acute during the first six weeks following listing, and this weakness can linger for as long as a year.

Hold or buy as soon as applications for an NYSE listing are made, but plan to sell when the application is approved. Be careful: A few issues will rise in price even after listing is complete, and some will fall during the periods just prior to listing.

Source: *Market Logic.*

HEDGING YOUR INVESTMENTS WITH STOCK MARKET INDEX FUTURES

For the first time in the financial markets, there is an opportunity for people to call a turn in the stock market without having to pick and choose individual stocks. At times, it is easier to call a turn in the market than to determine the individual stocks to "bet" on. Since it's just as easy to be short on a commodity as to be long, an investor can just short one of the indexes if he thinks the stock market is going to move downward. He doesn't have to choose specific stocks to short.

Right from the beginning, it was obvious to everyone that these were going to be viable contracts. They have attracted both speculators—the traditional commodities traders—and more conservative equities investors who can use the futures contracts to hedge their investments.

Attraction for speculators: Enormous leverage can be obtained on the initial outlay of cash. Each contract is valued at the index multiplied by 500. For instance, with the S&P 500 index at 155, the value of the S&P futures contract would be $77,500. Margin requirements: 10%, or, in this example, $7,750. But for each dollar the index moves up or down, the speculator makes or loses $500, according to how he was positioned.

Obviously, this leverage factor can work either for or against the investor. That potential for volatility and the possibility of a margin call frighten some people. It is the same as the margin calls for gold and silver futures contracts. An investor will be called to add to his margin requirement if the market gets out of his trading range and moves against him. Ac-

tually, stock market index futures are even more risky than gold and silver futures contracts, since there are no limits on the contract's movements as there are in gold and silver.

For that reason, brokerage houses insist that potential buyers of any futures be high-net-worth individuals.

Hedging opportunities: Besides speculating on which way the market is blowing, there are some savvy uses of stock market index futures for the moderately large equities investor.

For the investor with a sizable portfolio—say, in the $1 million range—who is worried that the stock market is moving down and is in for a serious correction, there is great opportunity in selling the index short. If the investor is correct, and the market falls, he will profit from the position in the futures contract while he loses money on some of his stocks. This is especially true if the investor wishes to take a capital gain at the end of a year and has not been holding many of his stocks long enough. The maximum income tax on a commodities profit is 32% for those in the highest bracket. This way, there is profit at a lower tax . . . and the investor is able to qualify for the holding period on his stocks.

For many individuals, accumulating a good, balanced portfolio takes a long time and a lot of thinking. Selling the index short against an equities portfolio ensures investors of not having to upset that balance. And they aren't later forced into selling those stocks into a weak market where they must take panic prices if the market is falling fast.

If an investor shorts the index instead of selling his stocks and there is a false start—the market appears to be plunging and then turns back upward—it is a lot easier to "cut bait and run" with a stock market index contract than it is to buy back stocks once you have sold them. And you save a great deal in commissions if you substitute shorting the future for selling the stocks.

Buy hedge: On the opposite side of the fence, people can go long the index futures contract as a hedge. By definition, a hedge in the futures market is taking a position opposite to what your inventories are. Thus, if you buy a futures contract, you are holding no stocks, but you are anticipating a future purchase.

For example, you have a strong feeling that the market will make a major bullish move, but your cash-flow situation is poor. Although you have the money, it is tied up in various money-market instruments. You wish you had the money in hand to put into the stock market. At that point it is a hedge to buy the futures contract. If you are correct, you will have to pay more for any stocks you want to buy when your instruments come due a few months later. On the other hand, you will have made at least a comparable amount of profit on the futures to make up for the higher prices. Point: You have fixed the cost of your purchase when the market is just beginning to take off.

For foreign investors: Going long the stock market indexes can be a good substitute when you can't get your money out of your country quickly enough to participate in a stock market rally.

An unusual use of the sell hedge: When there is a possible merger of two corporations, and one of the participants asks you to tender stock. In many cases, the merger doesn't materialize, and the stock value has gone down by the time it is finally released. You could have sold a stock market futures contract short against the stock you tendered. Condition: If the merger is so dramatic that it affects the whole stock market in one way or another (which has happened in a few cases). This could cause the contract to move in an unusual way.

To learn more about index futures: An assortment of pamphlets and books details the specifics about the new index futures.

• *The Future Is Here* (The Value Line Composite Average, the Index Behind the Futures). Published by the Kansas City Board of Trade, the free pamphlet runs 36 pages. Contact the Marketing Department at 4800 Main St., Suite 274, Kansas City, MO 64112.

• *Inside S&P 500 Stock Index Futures.* A free 24-page report published by the Index and Option Market of the Chicago Mercantile Exchange, 444 W. Jackson Blvd., Chicago 60606.

• *The Market Will Fluctuate.* A free 20-page pamphlet on the New York Stock Exchange index published by the New York Futures Exchange, 20 Wall St., New York 10005.

Source: Malcolm "Mac" Fellman, first vice president, Prudential Bache Securities, New York.

HOW TO KEEP AHEAD OF THE WALL STREET CROWD

Good rule of thumb in any investment planning: Don't trust the conventional wisdom. In fact, in some situations the prudent investor should do just the opposite of what the conventional wisdom indicates.

Example: When a significantly large majority of investors, financial publications, and advisers, turn bullish, it's probably time to sell. Reason: By that time, prices have been bid up to about their top. Conversely, when most people turn bearish, it's time to buy because prices have probably ebbed.

Clue: When *Time* or *Newsweek* publishes a story on the bullish market, that is clearly a signal to turn bearish (and vice versa).

The real trick in investing is knowing when to get out and when to get back in. If you do the "right" things—remain diversified, etc.— you'd still do no better than about 90% a year over the long term, and that is because doing the right thing according to the conventional wisdom is essentially staying in the market. Some mutual funds think they're out of the market when only 10% of their funds are in cash.

Investment vehicles. I'd rate bank trust accounts at the bottom. Their two drawbacks: They almost always stay in stocks, and they move too slowly, missing good buys and holding bad ones.

Better: No-load mutual funds. They, too, fall into the fully invested trap, but many are flexible and follow the swings. They tend to do better than bank trust.

Better yet: Use mutuals as your investment base, but don't be afraid to sell out when you feel a turn coming and move into cash. By selling out, all you've lost is opportunity—no real dollars. That is important.

Dealing with a broker. Don't believe it when people tell you that you can't bargain with a broker over his commission. You may not be able to bargain with the giant firms, but medium and small firms are going to be flexible. If you're talking about a trade in the $5,000 range and don't seek special research or any "hand holding," the discount on the commission could be 30%.

Source: Dr. Martin Zweig, editor, *The Zweig Forecast*.

WHAT MAKES "THE DOW" TICK AND HOW IT CAN FOOL YOU

The Dow Industrials Average is computed by adding the prices of the 30 stocks that comprise the average and dividing the total by a divisor, published every Monday in *The Wall St. Journal*, that changes periodically to reflect stock splits.

As a result of this method of computation, the higher-priced issues in the Dow contribute more to the average than do lower-priced ones.

Were each of the 30 components of the Dow to gain 8 points on average, or 240 points in total, the Dow would rise by approximately 165 points (240 divided by 1.443). If each component lost 8 points, the Dow would go down by 150 points. Of course, this is unlikely, since the higher-priced issues are more likely to show wider fluctuation than the lower-priced issues, on a point-change basis.

A deceptively rising Dow. Very frequently, bull markets end with the Dow rising to new heights, but investors don't make that profit. Such situations come about when one or two influential issues (like DuPont and Kodak) rise to new highs, pulling up the averages significantly because of their weight. However, the rest of the list is faltering, but their troubles are buried in the computation of the Dow Industrials Average. Result: A deceptive rise in the Dow, luring in investors, although the bulk of the market is either standing still or falling.

Remedy: Track either the Advance-Decline Line, which shows how many issues on the New York Stock Exchange are actually rising and falling, or check on how many components of the Dow Industrials Average are actually contributing to its rise. The Advance-Decline Line figures are published daily in *The Wall Street Journal*. (A convenient place to review a majority of the Dow components in one place is the American, PBW, or CBOE options listing in the *Journal*.)

HOW TO BUY STOCK IN AN UP MARKET

Some thoughts on how to approach the timing of stock purchases during an up market:

Basic rule (expressed in exaggerated form here): There is never a second chance to buy a good stock. However, if the stock is genuinely strong, any downward correction is usually minor, so the longer you wait the more you'll pay. Don't be too concerned about getting in at the lowest price. If it's a good stock (and a steady rise in price confirms that), it will probably be good even if you have to pay a bit more by not jumping in.

How to handle that dilemma of either waiting for a correction or chasing it up:

Consider that a stock has gotten "too far away" if it has already advanced three days in a row or gained 15% in price or both. You should have acted before the rise. But if you missed that point, wait.

How long to wait: Since the normal retracement is about 50% of the rally (if the stock has gone from 25 to 30, a 50% retracement of that 5-point gain would mean back to about 27⅔). Then "shade" that upward, not only to the next higher round number (in this case 28) but also tack on a small fraction to be first in line ahead of those who more typically use the round number as a convenient place to enter numbers. In this example, putting in a limited price order to buy at 28¼ and then waiting to see if the order is executed during the next correction is a sensible approach.

Finally, though, not to miss a stock that is really wanted (one that didn't dip back to the buy-order level), it makes sense to jump on it the moment the stock shoots up past 30 (its prior high point) because that usually means the stock you're interested in is on its way again.

QUESTIONS AND ANSWERS ABOUT CONVERTIBLE BONDS

When are convertibles a good investment?

When convertibles are undervalued, they can be much more attractive than either a straight bond or the underlying common stock. Best choice: From time to time, you can find a convertible bond that has as high a yield as a straight bond. You get the equity kicker for nothing. Why this happens: Since many people don't understand convertibles, the market is thin and there are often valuation discrepancies.

When should a convertible be converted into a common stock?

Only when the stock sells well above its redemption price. Further, take into account the interest-rate payment date of the bond. Convertibles generally pay interest semiannually. In the interim, the interest is accrued. However, if you convert a bond before interest is payable, you could lose up to six months' interest, especially since the bond interest is usually greater than the stock's dividend. If you want to liquidate a convertible-bond position, you can do it by selling the bond or by converting into the resulting stock. Check both ways to see which is more profitable. Be wary of lost interest upon conversion.

How do you measure the value of a convertible?

First: Compare the yield of the bond with the yield of the stock. Next: Compare the current price of the bond with the redemption price. There is a high likelihood of redemption of the bond by the issuing company when the stock is selling for much more than the redemption price. At such time, the convertible will not sell at a premium to its stock value. Find out if there are any special provisions that could affect the value of the bond, such as the expiration of the conversion privilege, which sometimes is set before the bond matures.

What happens to convertible bonds if interest rates increase or decrease dramatically?

Convertible bonds are interest sensitive, but not as much as straight bonds. Other things being equal, they would rally if interest rates decline and drop if interest rates rise.

How can you reduce the risk of owning convertible bonds?

Look for undervalued convertibles and hedge them by shorting stock against it. There are other hedging techniques which make use of options.

Where do I find more information?

Subscribe to leading convertible bond publications:

Value Line Convertible Survey, 711 Third Ave., New York 10017.

RHM Convertible Survey, 417 Northern Blvd., Great Neck, NY 11021.

Standard & Poor's Bond Guide, 25 Broadway, New York 10004.

Source: Paul Singer, president, Braxton Management Services, New York.

A convertible bond is convertible into the common stock of a company. It generally carries a lower interest rate than a straight bond because of this kicker. Evaluate:

• Its attractiveness as straight, subordinated debt.

• Its long-term warrant (which allows you to buy the underlying stock at a specific price for an indefinite time period).

• The right of the company to redeem the bond and when.

SECRETS OF A COMMODITIES TRADER

Perspective: Go in on the assumption that the money is already lost. Those who worry about profit don't make the right moves or get the rhythm of the market.

Goal: To justify the risk entailed, a player should aim to double his money within a year or less. Otherwise, the game is not worthwhile. But doing so takes discipline. To improve your chances of winning:

Work with a reliable broker. Find out what

is being recommended by the firm's technicians (those who base the odds on historical data) and by the fundamentalists (those who look at environmental factors). When the two coincide, and you agree with their perspective, take a position. If you think the price on a commodity will rise, buy with the intention of selling later (long). Conversely, if you think the price will drop, sell with the intention of buying later (short). Rule: Look for opportunities where the reward/risk ratio is at least 3:1 (2:1 is only for speculative traders who always have access to a phone).

Play the ranges. Determine how much money to risk and buy and sell within that range. What it takes: To be a real player, you need to risk at least $10,000. That way, if you win only 40% of the time, you come out ahead. (The math: If a trader loses $5 five times, he's out $25. But if he wins three times, he makes $45.) Beginners shouldn't risk their shirts just to take a position.

Note: Diversify by taking a position in multiple commodities rather than a few in one commodity. Or, if you prefer a single vehicle, be ready to drop out of the market at intervals. Nothing is ever good all the time.

Source: Henry Hanau, account executive, Bache Halsey Stuart Shields, Inc., New York.

BEFORE JUMPING INTO A COMMODITY POOL

Commodity pools have many attractions to the speculatively inclined investor who wants the leverage of commodity trading but also wants to cut some of the risk. Before investing:

• Look for performance consistency over at least five years. Pools with outstanding records are often successful for only a relatively brief period. Monthly or even annually computed returns can vary from excellent to terrible.

• Be wary of a pool that pays the manager more than 5% in commission.

• Make sure the pool is getting a favorable commission rate if it's organized by a brokerage house. Although the typical brokerage house does provide a commission discount to its pool, these discounts are often minimal compared with what can be achieved elsewhere. So compare the commission expenses of the various pools.

HOW TO WIN WITH LARGE-LOSS REAL ESTATE TAX SHELTERS

The major impact of Tax Reform on real estate investing is the restriction placed on the use of passiveactivity losses and passive-activity income.* Before Tax Reform, one of the great advantages of real estate investing was that investors could receive the cash flow from a property while at the same time reporting large tax losses for depreciation.

Under Tax Reform, however, losses from passive activities such as most rental-property investments and limited partnerships are allowed as deductions only if they are taken against income from other passive activities. (Unused losses can be carried forward, however, to offset future income in the activity or partnership.) Losses can no longer be used as deduction against ordinary income—wages or portfolio income (interest and dividends).

Losses not taken in one year as a result of restrictions on passive-activity income can be carried forward indefinitely. Benefit: Losses can be used to offset passive-activity income in future years, or even taken against gains made on the sale of the properties from which the losses originated.

You could find investments now that would generate passive-activity income to be sheltered by your passive-activity losses. Best bet: Real estate purchased for all cash or with very little debt that has large annual cash flow. Look for properties (or partnerships buying properties) with established occupancy levels and attractive locations to guarantee adequate rental income after operating expenses. A reasonable rate of return: 7%–8%.

Some investors in rental real estate will be able to deduct up to $25,000 in losses each year. Such an investor must have an income of below $100,000 (there's a phaseout between $100,000 and $150,000); must "actively participate" in the property's management; and must have more than a 10% direct interest in the investment.

*Passive activity is any business or trade in which the investor does not participate directly. The investment could take the form of a sole proprietorship, a limited or general partnership, or an S corporation.

Source: Robert A. Stanger, chairman, Robert A. Stanger & Co., publisher of *The Stanger Report: A Guide to Partnership Investing*, 1129 Broad St., Shrewsbury, NJ 07701.

REAL ESTATE: BARGAINS FROM BANKS

Individuals or companies that want to buy real estate at distressed prices should search for banks with portfolios of foreclosures and repossessions. They're difficult to find, but the search can really pay off.

When commercial or savings banks foreclose on commercial property, they're often in a hurry to sell the property to remove non-income-producing assets from their books. If the real estate market is weak or the property is not prime, you have substantial leverage in negotiating with the bank.

Insiders, however, know that: Banks don't generally advertise real estate they want to sell. They usually find buyers through private contacts.

Three excellent ways to overcome this problem are:

• Ask loan officers at your bank to put you in touch with colleagues in their real estate department. A real estate workout officer is usually in charge of selling foreclosed property.

• Use business contacts to get introductions to real estate officers in other banks.

• Make cold calls to bank real estate departments. Lenders who are anxious to sell property sometimes will provide information about available real estate to total strangers. Once

you've located a property for sale there are certain things to bargain for:

Price and favorable financing.

One bargain hunter I know of has been able to buy high-quality property for up to 50% of the original cost. Of course, the discount is biggest when the property is in a distressed area.

Banks are often willing to offer enticing mortgages to the purchasers of foreclosed property. But it's usually possible to go even further.

For example: A New York bank foreclosed on an apartment building whose owner couldn't meet the debt sevice on an $8 million property. Because of the soft market, the bank could sell it for only $6 million. But instead of selling, the bank found a buyer who agreed to take over the building for $8 million, paying 10% down with a $7,200,000 mortgage at a low interest rate and extended repayment schedule.

Because the rental market was weak, the bank agreed to accept all cash flow from the property for eight years if scheduled debt service couldn't be met, and also waived its right to foreclose for eight years. Any shortfall in debt service was to be added to the mortgage balance and come due as a balloon payment at maturity. After eight years the mortgage reverted to normal terms.

The advantage to the buyer: The market rebounded after five years, and rental income was then more than enough to cover mortgage payments. Meanwhile, the bank couldn't foreclose while the property became healthy. From the bank's point of view, it was worth postponing part of the mortgage payments in order to find a buyer willing to pay the price quickly in a soft market.

Source: Malcolm P. Moses, president, Malcolm Moses Associates, 3428 S. Hewlett Ave., Merrick, NY 11566.

HOW REAL ESTATE INVESTORS GET TRICKED

The urge to invest in real estate exposes buyers to sharp practices by sellers. Most common distortion: Claims of high-paying tenants. Example: The rent roll of a commercial building shows that nine tenants pay $6–$8 per square foot and three pay $12. Essential: Find out who the high-paying tenants are. One may be the building owner, and the others may be affiliated with the seller.

Any fudging of current and future income can cost an investor tens of thousands of dollars. Example: In a small building, the seller reports that 10 tenants each pay $400 a month ($48,000 a year). If buildings in the area sell for six times gross, the market price would be $288,000. But suppose the owner had prepared to sell the building by raising the rents from $350 to $400 a month. Impact: That increase in the rent roll cost the buyer $36,000 (the difference between six times $48,000 in annual rents and six times $42,000).

Even worse: The impact on future rent increases. If the rents in the building were close to market before the increase, the owner may very well have offered the tenants a free month's rent or a delayed increase. A delayed increase means that the buyer will not realize as much income as forecast. A free month's rent means that the actual increase in rents was only $17 an apartment, not $50. If the new owner tries to jump rents well above that, tenants may move.

Other claims that buyers must investigate:

• Low operating expenses. Sellers may be operating the building themselves to avoid a management fee. If buyers cannot take care of the building personally, this fee must be added to real operating expenses. And if sellers do not factor it in, the bank will when it calculates the maximum supportable mortgage.

• Reasonable property tax. If the building has not been assessed for several years, the buyer may have a substantial tax bite on the next reassessment. Another trap: The seller has made an addition to the building that has not yet been recorded with the tax assessor. Ask the local assessment office for tax card or listing sheet. It will show the building's assessment and when it was assessed. If it was assessed a year and a half ago and there has been no significant addition to the building, reassessment may not hurt the buyer. But if it has

not been assessed for eight years, there could be a significant tax boost.

While checking the tax card or listing sheet, check the owner's property description against the one listed. If the owner says that 20,000 square feet are being sold, but the tax card says 15,000 square feet, there has been some addition to the structure that has not been recorded and, therefore, has not been assessed. Or there may be an assessment error that, when corrected, will raise costs.

• Low insurance premiums. Is coverage in line with the structure's current value? What does the policy cover? Ask to see the policy. Ask an insurance advisor: If coverage is insufficient, how much more will proper coverage cost?

• Energy efficient. Verify the owner's claim with the local utility to determine actual energy costs. Also: Check with regulatory commissions to see whether utility companies are scheduled to increase their tariffs.

• A real buy: Check the income statement with those of comparable buildings in the area. Helpful: The annual income and expense analysis by geographical area and building type of the Institute of Real Estate Management, 4390 N. Michigan Ave., Chicago 60611.

Source: Thomas L. O'Dea, O'Dea & Co., Inc., investment real estate consultants, Winston-Salem, NC, and senior editor, *Rental House and Condo Investor.*

YOUR REAL ESTATE TAXES CAN BE MUCH LOWER

Many people pay too much in property taxes year after year without ever realizing it or questioning the system. Yet it is fairly easy to get property taxes reduced.

Statistics show that more than 60% of home owners who challenge assessments succeed. Our own firm's success rate on behalf of clients varies from 70% up to 100% in some counties.

No lawyer is needed to challenge an assessment, and there's no fee. All you have to do is put in the effort.

The savings you reap can become huge over time. Not only do you cut your tax bill every year, but your savings grow each year as property taxes go up on a percentage basis in line with inflation. And, by lowering your tax rate, you increase your home's resale value.

The key to cutting your tax bill is understanding how the system works. The big trap is that many people believe their homes are assessed at bargain rates. That's because assessed value is typically only a percentage of market value. Thus, a house with a $200,000 market value may be assessed at only $100,000, and the owner may think he's getting a bargain tax rate.

What most people don't know is that property tax is computed by multiplying assessed value by an "equalization ratio" which is determined by the state. If the ratio on a $200,000 housed assessed at $100,000 is 2.5, the owner is being taxed on a house value of $250,000 without even knowing it.

Equalization ratios are determined by the state and are applied countywide or throughout a tax district. The ratios are increased periodically to keep track with inflation and market transactions. But the fixed ratio often can easily be shown to be inappropriate for a particular property. If you can change your equalization ratio, you can cut your tax bill.

• Analyze your current assessment. Call your local tax assessment office and ask what equalization ratio is used to make the adjustment. Your tax bill may show an assessment at $100,000 but if the multiplier used is 2, then your assessment is really for $200,000. A challenge should be made if your home is actually worth less than $200,000.

• Justify your opinion of market value. Your opinion that the tax assessment is too high is probably right. Tax assessors usually base their assessment on the cost of replacing your home plus the land.

More accurate: A comparison of actual sales of similar homes in your area. This will produce a more realistic (and lower) valuation of your home. Sales prices and information about houses sold are a matter of public record at your local deed recording office.

Write all the information down in an organized format to be presented to the tax assessor. Don't forget to include adjustments for differences between your home's value and a recent local sale due to conditions, location, date of sale, amount of living space, etc.

• Research other assessments. Your property should be assessed at about the same rate as comparable homes in your neighborhood. If yours is higher, you are entitled to a reduction. Get information about other assessments at the assessor's office. (Your neighbors will never know.) All you need to find is three or four homes that are very similar to yours that are assessed at a lower value.

• Challenge the opinion of the tax assessor. Tax assessments are based on the market value of your land and the buildings on that land, in the opinion of the tax assessor. Yet tax assessors rarely have any kind of professional training in this area. Even professionals in the real estate business reach different opinions when valuing property.

Compare any recent professional appraisals of your home with the assessor's. If you recently purchased your home, you paid your bank to perform an appraisal before it lent you the money. Call your lending officer and ask for a copy of that appraisal. If it's lower than the tax assessor's opinion, use it to show that you are overassessed.

• Hire your own appraiser. Tell the appraiser that you need it for a real estate reduction appeal. Shop around and get quotes from several appraisers. The cost is usually small compared to the amount of tax you will save, especially since a reduced assessment will stay in effect for several years.

• Look for the lowest value. Use anything you can to explain why your property's value is lower than what the tax assessor determined it to be. Put yourself in the place of a buyer who is trying to justify why you should lower the selling price of your home.

Examples: Water in the basement, radon or general deterioration in the condition of your home since the last assessment was made.

• Look at the assessor's worksheet. Go to the tax assessment office and ask to see the worksheet that the assessor used for valuing your property. You have the right to see this document. Check to see if the assessor properly describes your home, land, zoning and public services. Check that the numbers of bathrooms and garages are correctly listed.

• Review property descriptions for mechanical errors. Check that the dimensions of the house were measured correctly and that the correct mathematics was used in calculating the number of square feet.

• Look for clerical errors. The amount of the assessment on the worksheet should be the same as the amount on your tax bill.

• Check that personal property wasn't included. Personal property is anything that is easily movable and is not fixed to land. Example: A shed that is not permanently affixed to your real estate. Items that can be removed relatively easily are considered personal property and are not subject to real estate taxation.

• Calmly present your facts. Go to the assessor's office and tell the assessor what reduction you want and why. The assessor will probably make an adjustment if you have a good case. If the tax assessor doesn't agree to reduce your assessment, ask for a hearing with the local board of review. These boards have been established to give an impartial opinion. If the board decides against you, you can take your case to a court of law.

Source: Howard J. Udell is president of Property Tax Reduction Services, Inc., 2647 Russell St., Allentown, PA 18104.

HAMBRECHT & QUIST'S HIGH-TECH INVESTING SECRETS

We don't think that high-tech stocks are inherently more dangerous than other kinds. It is merely that they get more attention. Their progress up and down is watched more closely.

High technology is not an industry group. It is an economic sector, like financial services or extractive industries. Technology is really just a way of describing leading edge companies in many different areas. The 600 companies that we follow may be making software for banks or medical devices or biotechnology ingredients. A wide variety of economic activities is involved. Some are influenced by consumer spending, some by capital spending, and some by defense spending or even interest rates. We don't expect all these different types to move at the same time and react in the same ways as a group.

Our current investment posture: We are looking for cyclical growth industries. Example: Companies that supply semiconductor production equipment, since the semiconductor industry will be expanding. Obviously that area rises and falls with the semiconductor industry. There are two parts of semiconductor fabrication . . . front end and back end. The front end is wafer fabrication, which we prefer. The back end is assembly and testing, where the Japanese competition is more severe. We prefer smaller companies in semiconductor production to the larger ones. The large companies have too many extraneous businesses.

Considerations in stock selection:

• Check out relative price. Just as in any investment, don't pay too much for these companies.

• Try to get a company that has a new product line coming out. It is in a lot better position than one with an aging product line.

• Look for a company whose management has experience and a track record that is underwritten by a respected investment firm. There is a continuing flow of new companies.

Red flags in technology investing:

• Companies going public that have neither profit nor significant revenues. It is one thing to say a company is about to become profitable. It is entirely different when it hasn't begun to sell the product or service yet. Many companies that are really only a gleam in someone's eye are being brought public.

• Fly-by-night underwriters who bring the deal to the public. When the market is frothy, a lot of these firms try to push new issues out. However, the opposite may not be true. Just because a firm is being brought out by a solid, reputable underwriter, doesn't mean it is automatically going to be wonderful.

• A venture capital group that may not be solid. Even the best venture people get into sour deals. But the point is, check out the group. You want to examine carefully who is already in the deal.

• Industries where new, small companies rarely have a chance. For example, one industry where small companies historically have problems is consumer electronics. The market is so huge that a company has to sell millions of units. So it must be able to produce at very low cost. Since the distribution chain takes bites out of every item as it goes by, a manufacturer needs to be fairly large to get economies of scale. It does happen every now and then. But only an exceptional company can do it. We regard small companies in consumer electronics with a more jaundiced eye than we do a small industrial equipment manufacturer. There a company can operate in an area where none of the big guys are paying attention.

Areas we like: We choose big, fast-growing markets where the activity is already a reality, like computers. We are obviously in the Computer Age. Small companies that can enhance computer capability have an advantage. Why: No one knows how large these markets will become, and the big, mean kind of competition tends to wait until a significant market is clearly developing. That, in effect, gives the "mice" a chance to run through the elephant's feet. So products like peripheral equipment for personal computers and applications software for microcomputers are areas where small companies can grow fast.

Areas to avoid: Technological changes are so rapid that investors shouldn't look too far into the future for a company's development and profit. One to three years is about the maximum. Companies can have a fairly concrete idea of what they expect during that time frame, so one can make calculations and investment decisions on that horizon. But you can't expect a specific development to come along in five or seven years—you are just extrapolating a trend line if you do that.

You'll be wise to avoid solar energy stocks. There are really no favorable technological factors. Biotechnology prices have been bid up to the stratosphere on developmental contracts. Those developments take time, and all

the usual glitches and problems are in store. The current prices are discounting at least four years' growth.

Investors are better off with technologies that are already successful. For instance, computers offer an opportunity in and of themselves. They are also used in financial services, energy, medicine and other fields, and one can find interesting plays throughout. In reality, high-tech industries are everywhere. However, they do elude easy definition.

Source: Albert Toney, Jr., general partner and portfolio manager, Hambrecht & Quist Equity Management, San Francisco.

HOW TO REALLY READ FINANCIAL REPORTS

The growing complexity of corporate finance and recent changes in accounting standards can make it difficult for even the most sophisticated investor to accurately judge a company's health from its financial reports.

However, we have come up with simple ways to translate the increasingly garbled language of financial reports. What we watch:

• Annual reports. Compare the latest report with the two previous ones. Though the chairman's letter usually portrays the company in a positive way, the best way to measure management integrity is to watch what was promised in years past and see how those promises turned out.

If the chairman's letter is so optimistic that he would be better suited to work as a Florida sunny-weather forecaster, beware. Coleco was like this. Management projected nonstop optimism all the way to bankruptcy. Now the company is in Chapter 11. Tipoff: Any glossing-over of obvious negatives.

• Income statements. Helpful: Pay close attention to income statements in the company's financial reports. Aim: To see how clear the earnings statement is of nonoperating items such as deferred income tax credits, sale of assets and interest income. Such earnings are real, but they're not the same as operating earnings. They may not occur again.

• Balance sheets. A key element: Debt. How much debt is short-term (due within a year) and how much is long-term? Too much short-term debt can squeeze the company's operating flexibility by hurting cash flow.

For most industrial companies, a balance of 40% debt and 60% shareholders' equity is about right. Above 40% of total capital debt can become worrisome.

• Footnotes to financial statements. These tie in with, and further explain, the income statement and the balance sheet. Sometimes there can be as many as 30 footnotes. And they can be very complex. Always read them, however, because they often contain information you can't get anywhere else. Example: Details about lawsuits against the company which could represent big future liabilities.

Source: Ted O'glove, whose *The Quality of Earnings Report*, is published by Reporting Research Corp., 560 Sylvan Ave., Englewood Cliffs, NJ 07632.

ABOUT INVESTING IN BROADWAY SHOWS

Broadway investors seldom earn their money back, let alone make a profit—even with shows that are hits. Investors are the last people to be paid. Royalties go to stars, producers, directors, authors, composers, lyricists and choreographers. These royalties, percentages of the box-office gross receipts, are paid whether the show is making money or not. Of course, operating costs are met. Then, if anything is left over, investors get theirs.

Why invest: A few shows reward investors handsomely. After they pay back the original investment, the investors split further profits from the box office with the producers.

INVESTING IN DIAMONDS

Diamonds are a bad investment, unless you're in the business. Why: Most of us buy at retail (at a markup of 100%) and have to sell at wholesale. What your diamond is worth: About 20% of the appraised value. Also: Diamonds are not really rare. De Beers has artificially maintained the rarity of diamonds by withholding them from the market, but its monopoly is currently breaking down. Possible result: A total collapse of world diamond prices. Good investment stones: Rubies, emeralds, sapphires and colored diamonds. These are naturally rare.

WHAT A GREENBACK IS WORTH IF PART OF IT IS MISSING

Worn and torn paper money will be replaced by the Department of the Treasury if three-fifths or more of the bill remains intact. If less than three-fifths but more than two-fifths exists, the bill is worth one-half its face value. For redemption of a smaller fragment, proof must be offered that the missing portion is destroyed. Such bills will be replaced at face value by your local bank.

15. Insurance and You

Insurance and You

BEST INSURANCE BUYS

We spend a lot of money for insurance. The industry, directly or indirectly, takes in about $3,600 a year from every four-person household in America. Each family could save hundreds of dollars a year by simply learning some rules of the game.

A savvy consumer must personally cut through the sales pitches (there are currently 250,000 agents selling just life insurance in the United States) and find the best protection for the least cost. Practical guides through the maze:

Life insurance:

Almost all adults—if they need life insurance—should buy renewable term insurance and do their saving and investing elsewhere. It stretches your dollars farther. You can comparison shop and find the best price. There is no practical way that a bright consumer can make an intelligent choice among other types of life insurance.

In certain situations—a business partnership, for example—there may be some tax advantages to other types of insurance. But don't deal with an insurance agent until after your tax expert has helped you define exactly the policy that you need.

If you are still hanging on to an old whole life policy, you should:

• Borrow against it up to the limit you are allowed at the advantageous guaranteed rate (some are as low as 5%). Invest the money in safe, long-term Treasury bonds or some such investment and get the higher return the policy will never pay. Or:

• Consider dropping the policy, taking out the cash value and starting over again with term insurance and a separate investment fund. (Make sure the new policy is in effect before you cancel the old one.)

Health Insurance:

If you qualify for a group plan, that is the best deal. Just be sure the maximum benefit keeps up with inflation ($25,000 is not really enough any more). In buying supplementary insurance, avoid duplication of coverage.

If you are not part of a group, Blue Cross/Blue Shield generally offers the best coverage. Major medical plans sold by life insurance companies do allow you to save by taking higher deductibles, and many offer low rates to the young and healthy. Shop around.

If you leave a group plan with an option to convert to an individual policy, you can get the new policy without a physical, a good option if you have medical problems.

Auto insurance:

Compare prices. For example, one company in California (20th Century Insurance) limits its coverage to good risks. If you qualify, you can save up to 50%. Rather than going through an independent agent, you should at least consider saving money by dealing with the direct writers like State Farm, Wausau Insurance and GEICO.

Choose the highest deductible you can afford. Bonus: Unreimbursed casualty losses over $100 are income-tax deductions.

For old cars with little book value, don't buy collision or comprehensive coverage.

Homeowners insurance:

Shop around and take high deductibles. Put the difference in premium costs for high deductibles in a savings account for covering small losses. Chances are you will be well ahead very soon. However, there is no saving in underinsuring your home. In the case of a partial loss, your insurer will not pay you fully unless your house is covered for at least 80% of its replacement cost. Don't skimp on liability coverage.

Disability insurance:

Unless you are covered by an employer, you should have enough coverage to supplement

Social Security payments. The only way to save on costs is to take a six-month or full-year waiting period before the benefits begin to pay out.

Source: Andrew Tobias, author of *The Invisible Bankers: Everything the Insurance Industry Never Wanted You to Know,* The Linden Press, New York.

INSURANCE POLICIES YOU ONLY THINK YOU NEED

Avoid special policies for cancer or other diseases and mail-order hospitalization plans. The payout on such plans is typically just 50¢ of each premium dollar—or less.

Credit life insurance: This is a very poor bet unless you are quite old or in poor health.

Auto rental insurance: Only on an icy night in a strange town when you have had a few drinks might this coverage be worth the price. (Best: Don't drive at all.) Otherwise, about $4 of each $5-a-day you pay goes not to insurance but to the rental company's expenses and profit.

Source: Andrew Tobias, author of *The Invisible Bankers: Everything the Insurance Industry Never Wanted You to Know,* The Linden Press, New York, as well as *The Only Investment Guide You'll Ever Need, Fire and Ice* and *Getting By on $100,000 a Year.*

LOW-PRIORITY INSURANCE POLICIES

"Slice-of-life" insurance policies such as mortgage life insurance, credit life insurance (to pay off installment loans on a car, furniture, etc.) and flight insurance should be low-priority items in the family budget. More important— and more economical—are comprehensive life insurance policies that cover a family's total financial needs no matter how the major breadwinner dies. A renewable term life insurance policy large enough to pay off the mortgage, the car loan and business debts and to cover college costs for the children is far better than a series of special policies to cover individual situations.

Source: J. Robert Hunter, president, National Insurance Consumers' Organization, and Joseph M. Belth, professor of insurance, Indiana University, quoted in *The New York Times.*

HOW TO COLLECT CLAIMS FROM INSURANCE COMPANIES

In many situations, you can negotiate successfully with an insurance company without retaining a lawyer. It is important to know when to negotiate yourself and how to negotiate effectively.

Where to start:

Your insurance agent, if he is not an employee of the insurer, should be your first line of inquiry. An independent agent is better able to assist in obtaining the full amount to which you are entitled. A good relationship with clients is what keeps him in business.

He will often present your claim, negotiate it and obtain a satisfactory settlement for you without charge. He's especially valuable on smaller claims. Also, if you negotiate yourself, he can be a major source of information and advice.

Should you hire a lawyer:

The major deciding factor is economic. On small claims, a lawyer's fee might be prohibitive, but on larger claims you could lose money by negotiating with an insurance company yourself.

In some cases, you might simply pay a flat fee for the attorney's review of your claim. Initial consultation will usually provide you with helpful information and assist the attorney in deciding whether or not it will pay for him to take your case.

Other considerations:

• Subjective factors. If you don't feel comfortable retaining a lawyer, go it alone.

• No-fault versus at-fault states. Negotiating your own claim makes a lot more sense in a no-fault state, where the insurance company is bound by law to reimburse you for your losses. But even in a no-fault state, or if you don't apply in time for all of the benefits to which you were entitled, your claim may not be honored if the forms are presented incorrectly.

• Language. Understanding the convoluted terminology used in insurance policies and law is a major stumbling block for the layman. To negotiate successfully, you must be comfortable with the language.

• Reputation. Some insurance companies deal fairly and quickly. Others are notoriously difficult and slow. Ask your insurance agent or a negligence attorney about the company you are dealing with. You may need legal help to negotiate a favorable settlement with a difficult company.

• Pain and suffering. When multiples of out-of-pocket expenses are involved due to pain and suffering, it is best to hire a lawyer. Lawyers can point out losses you have not even thought of. Also, the insurance company will take into account what you are saying by not hiring a lawyer and offer you less.

If you go it alone:

• Read the policy very carefully. Pay special attention to exclusions and coverages. Before presenting your claim, take a close look at the policy. Make sure you're presenting it in a way that makes it evident that your claim is covered. (If you can't find your policy, the insurer is obligated to give you a copy.)

• Document everything completely. It is the most important part of an insurance claim. Support every aspect of your claim, including doctor bills, receipts for medicines, transportation for medical reasons and a letter from your employer stating lost wages. Think of everything. Witnessing an injury to a loved one may cause compensable emotional trauma. A husband (wife) may recover for the lost services and companionship of his (her) injured spouse.

• Find out what your claim is worth. Ask your insurance agent or a negligence lawyer what a reasonable offer would be in your situation.

• Be prepared to take a discount. There has to be a motivation for the insurer to settle a claim. One advantage of negotiating without a lawyer is that a quick settlement may be offered to avoid legal expenses. So decide what amount you are willing to settle for. The settlement offer will depend on various factors, including clarity, proof of coverage, damages, documentation, how likely you are to prevail at trial and the caseload of the court you would have to sue in. (Some insurers offer nothing until the trial date.)

Bodily injury:

Claims for bodily injury can be the most complicated and negotiable, especially when based upon pain and suffering.

• In a no-fault state, you are limited to out-of-pocket expenses in a nonserious injury. This includes lost wages. In a fault-governed state, you can negotiate for more.

• Don't miss damages. Start at the top of your head and go down to your toes, to include every part that's been hurt.

• Photograph your injury. In addition to medical reports, photos are the best documentation of suffering.

• Consider every aspect of your life affected by your injury. Include your career, sports, hobbies, future interests and family relationships.

• Ask what a lawyer would ask—at least twice the actual expenses when there has been no permanent disability. Where liability is clear, the insurance company will be likely to give you what you ask, if they believe that you really had difficulties and were out of work for a few weeks. However, where there has been permanent disability, multiples of expenses do not apply. Example: Your medical bills for a lost eye might have been only $3,000, but a jury might award you 50 times that amount.

If you cannot reach a settlement:

An insurance company has a fiduciary duty (a relationship based on trust, like that with your lawyer or stockbroker) to deal fairly and in good faith with its insured. What to do if you are not treated well:

• If you feel that the company is either unreasonably delaying your claim or acting in bad faith, make a complaint to your state insurance regulatory agency. In most cases, the agency will write a letter to the company.

• If your time is being wasted by the insurance company's bureaucracy, the small claims court may be appropriate. Such action will pressure the company to settle with you more quickly on your terms.

• Many states have laws penalizing an insurer for bad faith. If you feel the company has been acting in bad faith, you can initiate a lawsuit and possibly collect a multiple of your claim in punitive damages.

Source: Dan Brecher, a New York attorney.

INSURANCE COMPANY HARASSMENT

During a dispute over $146.71, an insurance company deceived, harassed and generally made life miserable for a policyholder. When he sued, he was awarded the $146.71, plus $5,000 for intentional infliction of mental distress and $200,000 in punitive damages. On appeal, the court brushed aside the company's complaint that its wealth had been continually emphasized during the trial. Punitive damages, the court said, were intended to deter wrongdoers from repeating their actions. The richer the defendant, the higher the penalty had to be.

Chodos v. Insurance Co. of North America, 178 Cal. Rep. 831.

SHREWD LIFE INSURANCE PLANNING

Many people go about getting life insurance in the wrong way. They don't buy life insurance— they are sold it by an aggressive salesperson. This happens because few people understand life insurance or have the time to spend to understand it. And the salesperson pushes those policies that produce the highest commission.

The real way to look at life insurance: Don't think of it as an investment, but merely as temporary protection against your untimely and early demise. If you buy other things besides protection (such as investments), you will pay a lot more. Also consider whether you really need life insurance. For instance, after you have reached a certain age (the kids are grown up, the mortgage is paid off, your pension is vested, your spouse is entitled to Social Security and you have accumulated some capital), you may not need life insurance at all.

Of the two basic types of life insurance— whole life and term—the temporary (term) insurance wins hands down, in my opinion.

The first and most important factor is the cost. You can currently get no-load (no commission), nonsmoker's term insurance for as low as 60–70¢ annually for each $1,000 of coverage. A $500,000 policy might cost you only $300 a year. By contrast, if you paid $350 annually for a whole life policy, you might get only $20,000 worth of protection.

The second factor: Term insurance is so cheap that people can usually afford to keep it up. But with a whole life policy that may cost, say, $1,750 annually for a $100,000 policy, people find themselves in a temporary cash bind and let the policy lapse.

Third: Looking at whole life insurance as an investment is a big mistake. The part of your premium that is invested returns at best 3–5% annually. This compares very unfavorably with the rate paid on a Treasury bill, and on a tax-free bond, and considerably higher than that in the stock market recently. To those who argue that whole life is a necessary forced savings plan, I say buy term—and invest the difference at a substantially higher rate than you could get under a whole life policy.

Perhaps the worst aspect of whole life is the commission schedule that heavily favors its sales, giving salespeople a hefty incentive to push it over other types of policies. On the $500,000 term insurance policy mentioned above, the commission for the first year might be as low as $200. But the first-year commission on a $100,000 whole life policy, including overrides and incentives, can equal 200% of the first year's premium. In the case above, that's $3,500 for a $100,000 whole life policy. Given this disparity in commissions, it's small wonder that salespeople are so enthusiastic about the benefits of whole life.

Unfortunately, some consumers get caught on a real treadmill with life insurance salespeople. They agree to buy a whole life policy and make the payments for two years or so, at which time the bulk of the heavily front-end-loaded commissions is paid out. Then the salesperson comes back, offering the customer a new whole life policy with another insurance company at a lower price than the first one. Not understanding the details, the customer agrees to cancel the first policy and buy the new one, thinking that he's getting a great deal. The problem: Little, if any, cash value (or saving) is accumulated in those two years because most of the extra premium beyond insurance coverage went to pay commissions.

Some customers get duped like this for as long as 10 years, never really building up any cash value.

Another common mistake is buying too much insurance. A general rule: If the mortgage is paid off and there are no outstanding debts of note, you will need only $300,000 of coverage to take care of your spouse, assuming interest rates remain at today's levels. Add in another $100,000 per child to cover education, clothing, etc. If interest rates go higher or lower, you would have to decrease or increase the amount needed. Of course, if your spouse earns $30,000-40,000 a year now, you wouldn't need as much coverage.

When you do buy term insurance, shop very carefully. The cost of term insurance varies widely. A couple of companies offer nonsmoker's term insurance for 60¢ per thousand, but others charge as much as $4 a thousand. Also, zero in on the first five years' cost of the policy. A typical ploy: Charging, say, 60¢ a thousand for the first year and then raising the cost to $1.50 in the second year. By getting a five-year-cost calculation, you can better evaluate the overall cost of the policy.

Source: Terrance M. Gill, La Jolla, CA.

MOST COMMON MISTAKES IN BUYING LIFE INSURANCE

In addition to offering protection for your family, life insurance can also be a good investment. But life-insurance policies are complicated, and without facts and comparisons it's easy to spend a lot of money for the wrong coverage.

The most common mistakes to avoid and recommendations on what you should buy:

• Mistake: To buy life insurance when you have no dependents. Agents tend to create needs where none really exists in order to sell policies. If you are single, you don't need life insurance.

• Mistake: To buy mail-order insurance. It's most often a bad bargain for most people.

• Mistake: To buy life insurance for your children. Unless there's some extraordinary reason, there are better ways to save money.

• Mistake: To put money into a cash-value life insurance policy...unless you have an IRA for yourself and your spouse. (Cash-value policies are whole life, universal life, variable life or any form of life insurance that contains a saving element.) Stay away from variable life. It has very high built-in expenses. If you want a cash-value policy, buy universal or whole life—provided you know how to choose the right policy and company and intend to keep the policy at least 10 years. Otherwise you'd be a lot better off with term insurance.

• Mistake: To buy a cash-value policy from a high-pressure salesperson. Keep in mind that agents make five to 10 times as much commission selling you a $100,000 cash-value policy as a term policy for the same amount. So you should always be alert to the hard sell for such policies.

• Mistake: To buy life insurance and not disability insurance. People may automatically buy life insurance without realizing that a long-term disability can be an even worse financial event for their family than dying. If you're disabled, you not only lose your income, but you are still around incurring expenses. You don't have to buy disability insurance if you're covered at work. However, only 30% of workers have such coverage. Everyone is covered by Social Security disability, but it's very restrictive, especially for white-collar workers.

• Mistake: To buy riders on your policy —such as the accidental-death benefit or the additional-purchase option. These should be treated like options on a car—high-profit items that are best avoided.

Example: Double indemnity. Contrary to popular belief, you're not worth more dead in an accident than dead otherwise.

Controversial rider: The waiver of premiums in case of disability. You don't need it if you're covered for disability. If you become disabled, you'll have enough money to keep up your life-insurance premium.

The safest and best insurance protection is

the purchase of annual, renewable term insurance. A non-smoking male can buy $250,000 coverage for about $250 a year at age 30 and $300 at age 40. Women pay 10% less, smokers 30%-75% more, depending on their age. For a family with one wage earner, five times annual income is the rule of thumb.

Compare any cash-value or term policy you're thinking of buying with the policies sold by USAA Life of San Antonio, Texas.* Salaried representatives at its home office sell by phone. It has the best values on whole life, universal life and term insurance. Also: Check with the rate-of-return service run by the non-profit National Insurance Consumer Organization (NICO).** Some policies are so complicated that it's impossible to figure out exactly what you're getting without a special computer program.

Example: If a universal life policy says it pays 11%, that may be figured on whatever is left after a lot of expenses. You have to compare it with what you would have earned if you'd bought term and invested the difference. Assuming you hold the policy 20 years, 11% may turn out to be more like 9½%.

Reevaluate your older policies. If your old policy is a term policy, you should assume you can replace it with a lower-priced policy, at least if you're a nonsmoker. If your old cash-value policy doesn't pay dividends, it probably should be replaced. If it does pay dividends, you'll be better off keeping it, especially if it has a low policy-loan interest rate that allows you to borrow on it and reinvest elsewhere.

*Phone (800) 531-8000
**344 Commerce St., Alexandria, VA 22314, (202) 549-8050. Cost: $25 for the first proposal and $20 for each additional one.

Source: James H. Hunt, director of National Insurance Consumer Organization, a life insurance actuary and former commissioner of banking and insurance for the state of Vermont.

LIFE INSURANCE TEST

Add up your assets—IRAs, savings, investment, etc. Subtract the amount that will be needed for estate taxes, mortgages, children's education, etc. If the balance won't generate enough income to support survivors, you need more life insurance. Best buy: Annual term insurance. Don't forget disability insurance. At age 50, you're more likely to be disabled than die suddenly.

Source: P. Kemp Fain Jr., Asset Planning Corp., Knoxville, TN, quoted in *Dun's*.

WHAT LIFE INSURANCE COMPANIES DON'T TELL YOU

Buying the wrong kind of life insurance is one of the major reasons people fail to become financially independent. The other major reasons: Investment procrastination. Lack of financial goals. Ignorance of what to do with money to accomplish those goals. Failure to apply tax laws to advantage.

Life insurance traps to avoid:
• A policy that does not use a current mortality table. Many premiums are still being paid and policies are still in force based on the American Experience Table. That's the death rate from the days of Abraham Lincoln. Another table, the 1941 Commissioner's Standard Ordinary (CSO) table, was devised before penicillin. The current 1958 table is out of date. If you have a policy based on an old table, you may be paying as much as 300% more than you need to because you are on the wrong table. (Most policies are based on the 1941 table.)
• Cash surrender policies. Many consider them one of the greatest frauds in our country today. People are convinced by insurance companies that these are worthwhile because the company gives you a level premium on a whole-life policy and you can borrow your cash value. That may sound attractive. Reality: Insurance is based on a mortality table, and all the funny banking in the world won't change that. The companies are willing to give you a level premium on whole life because you are overpaying until you reach age 72. Then you can underpay when you don't need the insurance anyway. Parallel: Would you go to the telephone company and say, ''Could I over-

pay my bill for each of the next 30 years for the privilege of underpaying after age 72?''

On the cash-value side, you would never go to a bank that takes away everything you deposit the first year and then charges you to deposit money in the account. Then, if you want to borrow, it charges 5½% for your own money. And if you die, the insurance company can keep the money. No one would open that kind of bank account. Neither should you accept such terms from an insurance company. Principle: People are willing to believe they can combine a living estate and dying estate. In reality, these are incompatible. Insurance should be bought as an umbrella in case you die before building up a life estate. Don't ever consider it a method of building up your net worth (or ''living'' estate).

• Dividend participating policies. These are not really dividends. They are partial returns of an overcharge. Again, people are victims of the belief that they can combine nest eggs for life and for death. A controversial Federal Trade Commission report says that if you keep a policy for an average period, you would receive 1.3% on your money. That means it takes 55.4 years for $1 to become $2. Worse: If you hold the policy under five years, you could have as high as a negative 18% interest. Holding for 10 years could produce a negative 4%.

• Insurance that is in your pension plan. The incidental costs are much higher than most people are led to believe. After all, your pension plan is for living, not for dying.

Better methods of insuring:

If you can pass a physical, you get a lower price per thousand on insurance if you switch to annual renewable term or 10-year deposit-level term.

Which to choose: If you know you are going to need insurance for the next 10 years, there is merit in the 10-year deposit-level term, since your premiums will be level for 10 years. However, realize that you are being overcharged in the beginning and undercharged at the end. But by making a deposit, you do get a discount on the rates you pay.

Best: If you believe you will soon start making enough to take care of your family out of your living estate (the money you build up out of investments over a lifetime), you will want to drop your insurance incrementally as your estate grows.

How to manage it: If you have a dependent who requires $1,000 a month if you die, then you need an estate of $200,000 (at a 6% return a year—half of that at 12%). If you have only $20,000 in your living estate, you need a $180,000 death estate (or insurance policy). As you build up your living estate, you can annually decrease your death estate. When your living estate rises to $50,000, then your death estate should go down to $150,000. Naturally, you may want to adjust this in accordance with inflation. However, your goal is to be self-insured, so that benefits don't hinge on death.

Insurance should be viewed as a way to buy time before you build up your own future.

Source: Venita Van Caspel, financial planner and author of *Money Dynamics for the 1980s,* Reston Publishing Co., Reston, VA.

HOW TO PICK AN INSURANCE COMPANY

Your number one consideration as you're selecting an insurance company should be its financial strength. Buying insurance (especially life and health insurance) is—we all hope—a long-term proposition. You want to be sure that the company you are buying it from will be healthy for many years.

Nevertheless, most people fail to verify the strength and stability of the company they are choosing. It has taken the failure of several firms to drive home the point that not all insurance companies are created equal. But analyzing a company on your own is virtually impossible. Their statements are inscrutable, even to accountants without special training. Leave the analysis up to the professionals.

The main source of financial information about insurance companies is *Best's Insurance Reports,* published since 1905 by A. M. Best Co., Oldwick, NJ. The Life/Health volume rates many of the companies it lists. Companies are given a rating of A+, A, B+, B, C+ or C. The report costs more than $200 but is available in many libraries.

It's wise to deal only with companies rated

A+. To be even safer, check back further. Reason: Before 1976, Best Co. used a more rigorous system ("recommending" companies instead of assigning a letter rating).

The most conservative customers should choose a company that, in addition to having rated A+ for the past 10 years, also received the strongest recommendation in 1975. (For a list of companies, send $2 to *The Insurance Forum*, Box 245E, Ellettsville, IN 47429. Ask for the November 1985 issue.)

In order to read Best's 1975 recommendations, however, you have to know its code—the qualifying adjectives and adverbs. The strongest companies are described as having "most substantial margins for contingencies" and "most favorable operating results." The word very substituted for most indicates a weaker company. And if the qualifier is omitted, the company is even weaker.

The best way to gauge the service of an insurance company is to find out how satisfied its current customers are. Unfortunately, there is no comprehensive nationwide ranking.

The best alternative: A few state insurance commissions publish "complaint ratios" for companies licensed to operate within their borders. This gives consumers some indication of the kind of service a company will provide.

If you do not live in a state that publishes complaint ratios, you can use another state's listing as a guide. A company that offers poor service in one state is unlikely to do much better in another.

Source: Joseph M. Belth, publisher of *The Insurance Forum*, a monthly newsletter for the insurance industry.

WHAT YOUR INSURANCE AGENT DOESN'T WANT YOU TO KNOW

Most people don't want to think about the possibilities of fire, illness or the head-of-household's premature demise. Result: Insurance companies spend a bundle trying to get people to buy the insurance they need. Who pays for that sales effort? The consumer, of course.

Opportunity: If you're willing to take the initiative and cope with your insurance needs without using an agent, you can save a lot of money.

Recognizing that a growing number of consumers are willing to buy insurance independently, several insurers now offer so-called low-load insurance. Because this insurance is purchased directly from the company, it can carry a lower sales commission than traditional agent-sold policies. Advantages:

• Separation of advice from the product. When agents advise you to buy insurance, there is an inherent conflict of interest. Their livelihood depends on making sales, regardless of whether the insurance is right for you.

With low-load insurance, you're free to get advice anywhere you like—from your own research in books and periodicals, from fee-based financial planners or from insurance consultants who charge a flat hourly fee.

• Reduced cost of making a bad choice. With most agent-sold policies, if you cancel in the first year or two, you get back virtually none of your premiums—all the money goes toward the commission. With a low-load policy, in contrast, you usually get back almost everything you've paid, and you might get some interest as well. Bottom line: The cost of changing your mind is much lower with low-load insurance.

How likely is it that you will change your mind? Inside information: In setting prices, some insurers assume that 15% of insurance-buyers will cancel their policies within one year ... and more than two out of five will cancel within five years—an indication of how often people are sold insurance they don't need or can't really afford.

Source: Glenn Daily, author of *The Individual Investor's Guide to Low-Load Insurance Products*, International Publishing Corp., 625 N. Michigan Ave., Chicago 60611.

A NEW POLICY MAY BE BETTER THAN AN OLD ONE

Buying a new policy may be cheaper than re-instating a lapsed one, if you're considerably older now. Age is only one factor in setting premiums. Of equal or greater importance are fluctuations in the interest rate. The higher the rate, the lower the premium. Generally higher interest rates over the past decade may have lowered premiums more than your increasing age may have raised them.

Source: Christopher Collins, CLU Solomon, Collins & Associates, Lincoln, NE.

YOU CAN AVOID A PHYSICAL EXAM

Insurance medical exams are quietly being abandoned by insurance companies, even for $100,000-200,000 term-insurance sales, according to a major insurance broker. The reasons are the high cost of the exams and the poor reliability of the information given by those seeking insurance. Even the best exams, say the insurers, protect them only for about six months, anyway. Now they often rely on a medical history taken by the insurance broker. They may also request an electrocardiogram and a chest X-ray.

INSURING THE VERY HIGH RISKS

People who face life-threatening operations may be insurable under a special 30-day, single-premium policy offered by Lloyd's of London. The policies have face values of $50,000-500,000. Premium: 1-5% of the face value. Payoff: If the patient dies within 30 days as a result of the operation, Lloyd's pays the proceeds to the beneficiary or patient's estate. Hitch: A patient with only a slim chance of recovery will probably be ineligible.

TEMPORARY INSURANCE AT A PREMIUM

Temporary health insurance, already expensive and likely to become more so, remains the best hedge against the financial devastation of an accident or sudden illness while you are between corporate-benefit packages. It's the only way by which you can get guaranteed first-rate medical care if disaster should strike while you are not covered by a group plan.

You should probably get temporary insurance if:

• You're moving to a new job but will be between jobs for a few weeks or months.

• You quit your job for a limited period to try your hand at independent consulting. (Consultants may be eligible for cheaper ''one-person group'' insurance for the long term. These policies usually require the additional purchase of at least $100,000 in group life insurance.)

• You've been covered under your spouse's health plan but are now getting a divorce.

Although several companies have dropped out of the market, temporary insurance can still be obtained from Prudential, Aetna and Kemper. They offer both hospital coverage and major medical, which applies to visits to doctor's offices. In most cases, the policies run for 90 or 180 days. However, the policies can be canceled quite arbitrarily at the end of the period, so you should be working on more permanent coverage after the gap.

Most temporary policies do not cover any ongoing conditions that required a doctor's consultation within the preceding year. If you have a chronic medical problem, you may need to convert your old company's group insurance to an individual contract. Anyone can maintain Blue Cross coverage, regardless of job status, but with major-medical conversions, the new contract will be both expensive and limited in coverage.

There are some alternatives to temporary insurance. If you leave a job on good terms, your old employer may agree to keep you on the company's health policy for one to six months. Your new employer may agree to cover the transition period. Or you may be eligible under your spouse's company plan. If so, the spouse's coverage can be revised at any time to include you. Don't accept any delay by the company's benefits department.

But suppose none of these work out, and you simply can't afford a full temporary policy. One solution: Opt for a partial policy that covers only hospitalization, where potential costs are most dramatic. Such basic coverage will run about half as much as a comprehensive policy.

Source: Leonard B. Stern, insurance broker, New York.

AGED PARENTS NEEDING VERY EXPENSIVE CARE

There's nothing underhanded about making an effort to conserve aging parents' assets to pass along to children, while using Medicaid (or, under the Medicare Catastrophe Act) Medicare to pick up much of the cost of home care or nursing home care. In fact, Congress has made clear that it doesn't want middle-class families to deplete all their assets for such care.

The key legal device to conserve an elderly parent's assets is the Medicaid Qualifying Trust. The parents divest their assets into the trust and receive annual interest payments. Those interest payments are then used to meet the bills of home and nursing home care, with Medicaid picking up qualifying expenses over that amount. The principal in the Trust would remain intact, to be inherited by designated beneficiaries.

Until the beginning of this year, when the Medicare Catastrophe Act became law, this divestiture had to be made at least two years before a family applied for help from Medicaid. Under the Act, 2½ years is the requisite period.

It is essential, however, to get expert legal advice on how this law works now in your particular state. Ask your local bar association to recommend lawyers who specialize in legal counseling on problems of the aged.

Source: Lewis Kamin, partner, Cappa, Kamin and Goldberg, 244-14 Jericho Turnpike, Floral Park, NY 11001, a law firm that works with Corporate Consultations in Aging, Inc.

MEDICARE: WHAT IT DOESN'T COVER

Don't fool yourself that all your old-age medical needs will be taken care by Medicare. This program is riddled with coverage gaps. Be aware of what not to expect from Medicare.

What is Medicare:

Medicare must be distinguished from Medicaid, which is the federal program providing medical coverage for the indigent of all ages. Most elderly people wind up on Medicaid when their assets are exhausted paying for what Medicare doesn't cover. This can be a tragedy for people who had hoped to leave something to their children.

Medicare is an insurance program for people over 65. It is subsidized by the federal government through the Social Security Administration. Each month, elderly people pay premiums to private insurance companies (Blue Cross/Blue Shield or companies like them), which act as fiscal intermediaries for Medicare. The program is overseen by a watchdog agency, Professional Standards Review Organization (PSRO), which makes sure hospitals are not used improperly. Drawbacks: Private insurance companies, acting in their own best interests, tend to deny benefits whenever possible. PSROs interpret Medicare regulations restrictively, since they must save government money.

Major problems with Medicare:

• Congress passed much of the Medicare legislation with the intention of helping the elderly by keeping them out of institutions. However, the local agencies administer Medicare restrictively in a misguided attempt to save money. Actually, money is being wasted by forcing the elderly into nursing homes unnecessarily. Result: Benefits we thought would go to the elderly simply don't materialize.

• Medicare does not deal with the problem of custodial care. It is geared toward rehabilitation, which is hardly realistic for the population it serves.

• Medicare is part of an overall supply-and-demand problem. There are simply more and more old people every year, as modern medicine enables us to live longer. While the over-65 population expands, nursing homes are filled to capacity and have long waiting lists, and Social Security benefits and services to the elderly are being cut back. Fear for the future: Some see the frightening possibility that euthanasia may be discussed.

Hospital cutoffs:

Hospital cutoffs are the biggest problem with Medicare today. Example: An elderly woman goes into the hospital with a broken hip. After surgery, she cannot go home because she can't take care of herself. She needs nursing home rehabilitation or an around-the-clock companion at home. Because of the shortage of these long-term-care alternatives, she has to remain in the hospital, though everyone agrees she is ready to leave. But Medicare cuts off hospitalization benefits, claiming that she no longer needs hospitalization. The family gets a threatening letter from the hospital—if she isn't out in 24 hours, the family will have to pay privately. At approximately $300 per day for a hospital bed, the family's assets will be wiped out very quickly.

The appeal process:

The only way to deal with such unfair (and inhumane) bureaucratic decisions is to appeal them aggressively. Appeal is a long and costly process, but a $300 per day hospital bill is even more costly. Also, as good citizens we must make our government accountable for benefits promised but not delivered.

Chances on appeal: Very good. At the highest level, Federal Court, the reversal rate on Medicare cases is extremely high.

There are four levels of appeal:

• Reconsideration is a paper review by a bureaucrat. You can request this when Medicare is first denied. Some 95% of reconsiderations confirm the original denial of benefits.

• An administrative law judge will review the case after the reconsideration is denied. You present evidence at this hearing, and a lawyer is recommended. Some of these judges are competent and sympathetic. However, many judges fail to understand the issue.

• The Appeals Council in Washington is the next step. They will usually rubber-stamp the decision of the administrative law judge.

• Federal Court is your final crack. You do stand a good chance of winning here, because judges at the federal level are not employees of the Social Security Administration. They tend to be less sympathetic to the agency's viewpoint.

At this level a lawyer is necessary. Important: No new evidence can be presented in Federal Court, so be sure all your facts are presented to the administrative law judge.

Medicare and nursing homes:

Under the law, up to 100 days of skilled nursing care in a nursing home are to be paid for by Medicare. In fact, Medicare pays for an average of only five days, claiming that nursing homes do not provide skilled care. This is another patently unfair decision that must be appealed on an individual basis.

Beyond 100 days, you're on your own as far as nursing-home care is concerned. Medicaid will take over only after your assets are totally exhausted. At an average cost of $30,000 per year, few families can afford long-term nursing-home care. Important: Plan ahead for this possibility well before a nursing home becomes necessary. Transfer your assets to your children, or set up a trust fund that the government can't invade. Be aware: You may be liable for payment if your assets have been transferred within less than an average of two years before entering a home, depending on the state.

Recommended: Consultation with a specialist in geriatric law. Ask your lawyer or a social worker in a local hospital or nursing home to recommend one.

Home care:

The home care situation under Medicare is also dismal. Medicare will pay for a skilled person to come into the home occasionally on a doctor's orders to perform tasks such as giving injections or physical therapy. There is virtually no coverage for the kind of help most elderly people need—a housekeeper/companion to help with personal and household tasks. Many senior citizens groups are currently lobbying for this type of home custodial care to be provided by Medicare.

Assignment rate:

As far as general health care is concerned, Medicare supposedly pays 80% of the "reasonable rate" for medical care as determined by a board of doctors in the community. In reality, the "reasonable rate" is usually set so low that most doctors will not accept it. So instead of paying 20% of their doctor bills, the elderly frequently wind up paying 50% or even more.

Suggestions:

• Don't drop your major medical insurance when you retire. If you keep it up, it will cover the gaps in your Medicare insurance. It is extremely difficult to buy such coverage after you reach 65.

• Be wary of insurance-company policies that supplement Medicare. You must be extremely careful when you buy one. Be sure it complements rather than duplicates Medicare coverage.

• Get together with other senior citizens to create consumer leverage. If a group of 50 seniors goes to a doctor and all promise to patronize him providing he accepts the Medicare assigned rate, it might be worth his while.

Source: Charles Robert, an attorney specializing in geriatric law, Hempstead, NY.

DISABILITY INSURANCE CONFIDENTIAL

When disability strikes, you have to replace your income with something or face losing your house, your lifestyle, savings and investments. Ironically, most people routinely buy life insurance to protect their families in case they die, but they neglect to buy disability insurance. Fact: Chances of being disabled during your working years are four to five times greater than chances of dying during the same period.

Figuring out how much is enough: First, assess what resources you already have that would enable you and your family to manage. Compare these resources with your expenditures. Then, make up any gap with disability insurance. Key questions:

• Would you get partial pay from your employer? How much? For how long?

• Do you have a benevolent family member you could count on to keep you going or at least to help?

• What assets do you have that could be converted quickly?

• Are you already covered by disability insurance policies? (Don't forget to check what's provided by credit cards and association memberships.)

• What could you expect from Social Security?

Comparing policies:

Concern #1: How the policy defines disability. You want the broadest definition you can find and/or afford. Some policies, for example, define disability as inability to perform any of the duties required by your occupation. Be careful: under many definitions, including that of Social Security, disability is the inability to perform any occupation. Under that definition, you get no payment as long as you can work at something, even if the job you can perform after being disabled is low paying.

A split definition of disability that's often used: Strict for a specific period of time and broad for the duration of the benefit period.

Concern #2: The length of the benefit period. Will the policy continue to pay you after age 65? Many policies stop paying then and you may still need funds. Unless another retirement fund kicks in, you'd have an income gap.

Also, check the waiting period, the time between the start of the disability and the actual beginning of payment of benefits. If you can wait 90 days before you need income, the premiums will be significantly lower than if you wait only 30 days.

Example: A person who is 45 years old wants a disability policy that will protect his income of $55,000 a year. Yearly premiums with a 30-day waiting period will cost $1,900—with a 60-day wait, $1,700—and for a 90-day waiting period, $1,550.

Reassess your disability coverage when:

Income changes. Almost everyone increases lifestyle and financial needs when income increases.

Financial responsibilities increase. Examples: You have a new child, a new mortgage, build a new house.

Investigate both individual and group coverage offered through your company, professional or other organization. Get quotes from several different companies. Also check to see what occupations they primarily insure. Some companies specialize in insurance for white-collar executives, while others insure blue-collar workers or high-risk occupations and charge much higher premiums.

Choosing an insurer: When you talk with

insurance salespeople, avoid their jargon. Insist on concrete examples by using "what if" stories to obtain the real facts from them.

Example: What if I were hit by a car and after six months could go back to work only part-time. How much would I be paid? Only policies with a residual benefit would pay in such a case.

Be wary of some group policies advertised on TV or sold by mail. Their definitions and coverage are usually so restrictive that you may never be paid.

There's a Social Security trap to watch out for in planning your insurance needs. To get disability payments from Social Security, you must have paid into the system for 40 quarters. But there are errors in the Social Security records, and you may find out too late that records are wrong and you're not covered.

As a safeguard, write to the Social Security Administration (6401 Security Blvd., Baltimore 21235) every three years for a copy of your account. If there's a mistake, correct it immediately (you have a three-year time limit to make changes).

Source: Karen P. Schaeffer, Schaeffer Financial, Greenbelt, MD.

• Waiting period. One- to six-month periods are common. Choose as long a period as you can. Why? You'll get higher coverage for the same premium. With a short waiting period, you may be paid for some illnesses you could probably ride out without help; but you'll get proportionately less in time of real need, if you're hit by catastrophic long-term disability.

• Definition of disability. You want a policy that defines disability as inability to work at your regular occupation. Also, the policy should pay for illness that first manifests itself while the policy is in force. This protects you if you have a condition (such as heart disease or cancer) that you don't know about when you buy the policy.

• Residual-disability benefits. A residual-benefit clause pays partial benefits if you can work part-time or at a lower-paying job. Example: A violinist who lost the use of his fingers from arthritis took a teaching job at a lower income. He could collect a percentage of his disability benefit equal to the percentage of his lost income.

Source: Leonard B. Stern, president of Leonard B. Stern & Co., insurance and consulting firm, New York.

HOW TO BUY DISABILITY INSURANCE

You can generally get coverage up to 50% of your income. Policies cover all illnesses not specifically excluded. This includes psychiatric disabilities. Pregnancy is usually excluded, but not complications from pregnancy. What to look for in a policy.

• Noncancelability. As you get older, you're more susceptible to disabilities, and they last longer. You can get a policy that's noncancelable to age 65, with option to renew if you keep working.

• Cost-of-living clause. This pays additional benefits when the cost-of-living index goes up. The annual adjustment is usually limited to 6% although some policies pay more than this. There's also usually an upper limit, such as twice the original benefit.

DISABILITY INSURANCE FOR HOMEMAKERS

Full-time homemakers can now get insurance that lets them hire replacement help if they become disabled. About one-third of the country's largest disability insurance firms now offer such policies. Rates are based on age and coverage.

Source: American Council of Life Insurance, Washington, DC.

PROPERTY INSURANCE TRAP

Traditional policies pay only the "actual cash value" of an item that's lost, stolen or destroyed. Example: A sofa purchased five years ago for $600 is destroyed in a fire. At today's prices, a comparable replacement costs $900. But the cash value of that five-year-old sofa—if you tried to sell it secondhand—is only, say, $150. So all you could collect under a traditional policy would be $150.

Replacement-cost insurance seems like an attractive alternative. But in practice, most of these policies pay off only the smallest of either replacement cost, repair cost or four times the actual cash value.

In the example just given, the payout would be $600, four times the actual cash value. And the policyholder would be $300 short of the price of a new sofa. Cost of coverage: About 15% higher premiums on a typical homeowner's policy, 25% higher for condominium and co-op owners and 40% extra on a tenant's policy.

COVERING COMPUTER EQUIPMENT

Computer equipment, like any other household possession, is covered by home insurance policies. Exception: Expensive equipment may necessitate upgrading of your present policy.

INSURING PAINTINGS

• If you have art holdings valued at over $5,000, you should insure them separately. Reason: The standard homeowners policy does not list artworks individually, and valuation isn't made until after the object has been lost, making it difficult to settle a claim. Also: Standard policies do not take into account the tendency of art to appreciate rather than depreciate in value. Recommended: A fine-art floater as an extension of your regular policy. This will list each object at its appraised value, providing all-risk coverage that includes all loss and damage. Important: Have your art collection reappraised every two or three years. Then change the policy accordingly.
• Buy all-risk insurance, including loss and damage. If you plan to lend a work, get "wall-

to-wall" coverage, which insures the work from the moment it leaves your custody until its return. Standard exclusions in art policies: Damages from wear and tear or stemming from restoration, moths, normal deterioration, war and nuclear disaster.

Source: *Investor's Guide to the Art Market, ART newsletter.* New York.

LOW-COST LIABILITY PREMIUMS

Take at least $100,000 of liability coverage when buying homeowners insurance. The premium difference between $25,000 and $100,000 is often less than $10.

Source: *The Invisible Bankers: Everything the Insurance Industry Never Wanted You to Know* by Andrew Tobias, The Linden Press, New York.

UMBRELLA POLICIES: HOW TO PROTECT AGAINST CATASTROPHES

In a litigious society, if you have substantial assets, you are fair game for lawsuits and heavy damage judgments simply because you do have those substantial assets.

Homeowners insurance and automobile insurance policies offer basic liability coverage for injuries and damage caused by you or your family (even your pet) and by your car or small boat. (Larger boats and many recreational vehicles require separate policies.) These policies cover accidents that happen on your property as well. You pay higher and higher premiums as you raise the limits of your liability coverage.

However, the amount you owe when you are sued for damages is determined by the courts, not by the limits of your insurance coverage. Judgments in the last decade have skyrocketed. If you are not prepared, a judgment can be financially ruinous. The more you own—houses, jewelry, boats, cars, investments—the more you can be expected to pay.

Minimum liability recommendations:

• Automobile bodily injury: $100,000 per person, $200,000 per accident.

• Automobile property damage: $25,000 per accident.

• Boatowners liability: $100,000 per occurrence.

• Homeowners liability: $100,000 per occurrence.

Enter the umbrella:

If your net worth is a great deal more than these minimums, you need more protection. This is where umbrella liability insurance becomes useful. An umbrella policy provides excess coverage for all your primary liability insurance. Example:

A guest is injured at a party around your swimming pool. The courts award him $300,000 for medical costs and lost pay. Your homeowners policy has only a $100,000 liability limit. The umbrella policy covers the $200,000 gap. And then, your car goes out of control and plows into a new addition on a neighbor's house. The courts assess the damage at $40,000. Your car insurance pays a maximum of $25,000. Again, the umbrella policy picks up the $15,000 shortfall.

Cost of umbrella policies:

Personal umbrella liability insurance is sold in increments of $1 million of coverage. Premiums start at $50–$60 a year. More than 75 companies now offer this blanket coverage for personal (rather than business) liability. Biggest difference in policies: Requirements for minimum liability coverage in primary homeowners, car, boat and recreational vehicle contracts. Each personal umbrella liability policy has its own conditions, definitions and exclusions, too. In shopping around, look for a policy that includes all your family's potentially hazardous activities.

Interesting bonus: Personal umbrella policies give primary coverage for one area of liability not touched on by other general types of liability insurance—slander and libel.

Bottom line: Personal umbrella liability insurance is designed to protect individuals with substantial property, who are vulnerable to lawsuits and costly judgments. For them, it is an inexpensive insurance against catastrophic losses in court.

Source: Leonard B. Stern, an insurance consultant and broker, New York.

CANCELLED CHECK IS PROOF THAT FIRE INSURANCE IS PAID FOR, RIGHT? WRONG

Fire and casualty policies should be in hand (on file) before the full premium is paid. One firm, after finding its plant burned to the ground, didn't have the policy it had paid for. Though it produced the canceled check to the broker, its claim was disallowed. The wise course is to buy insurance as you would an automobile: Give the broker a small deposit, but don't pay up until the policy is delivered.

HOW TO CUT CAR INSURANCE COSTS

Chances are you're now overpaying due to changes in your life since you applied for coverage. Update now, save money and get refunds for past overpayments:

• If you have two or more passenger cars, be sure they're all covered by the same insurance company. A multi-car discount can save you 20% off your annual premium.

• If your car is worth $1,500 or more, carry collision, but save with a higher deductible. As a rule of thumb, you can increase the collision deductible to equal a week's take-home pay, thus lowering your collision premium by as much as $100.

• Comprehensive coverage (for vandalism and "acts of God") is normally worth carrying no matter what the value of the car. Save $30–$40 by choosing a higher deductible.

• Rates can also be cut by paying attention to auto use. Highest premiums: Business or commercial use. Lower: Commuters driving 100 miles a week round trip. Lower still: Those driving 30–100 miles a week round trip to and from work. If your commuting distance has changed, get your premium rate changed, too.

• Males under 30 years old and females under

25 should consider having their car registered in the name of someone older for a considerable saving. Example: Your 25-year-old son marries a woman, also 25. They have a car. If they register it in her name, with your son as nonprincipal driver, they save 25% on the total premium. If the car is registered under your name, they save an additional 20% for a multi-car discount (if you have another car). If they drive it less than 7,500 miles per year, they save an additional 15%. If you have drivers under 21 living at home, driver training and good-student discounts (B grade average) are available for a saving of 5–10%.

Source: *You Can Save a Bundle on Your Car Insurance* by Paul Majka, St. Martin's Press, New York.

• Avoid high-performance, high-priced and sports-type cars. They are more expensive to insure. Labor and replacement parts cost more, too.

• Drop collision coverage entirely. Such clauses make little sense for older cars that are worth only a few hundred dollars.

• Ask about eliminating duplicate coverage. Car insurance and health-accident insurance may pay for some of the same things.

• Stay with one company. Most firms consider your longtime record when rates are reappraised after a claim. This can be more important than constantly changing companies to achieve the lowest premiums.

Drivers with good safety records and graduates of defensive driving courses are often eligible for insurance discounts. Certain types of cars and safety equipment can put you in a position to bargain for lower premiums. Examples:

• Makes and models with a good insurance history. These may vary among insurers.

• Vehicles equipped with air bags, passive seat belts (which automatically belt the passenger in) and antitheft devices.

Source: *Journal of American Insurance.*

Insurance savings for minors: Auto insurance saving for drivers under 21 years old: Having them rated on your least valuable vehicle. It'll save you at least 10% off your premiums.

AUTO INSURANCE WISDOM

Collision: Increase the deductible on a new car from $100 to $500 and pay for minor dents yourself. You save 45% on the premiums and are still protected in a major accident. Also: Don't necessarily drop collision on an old car. As new-car prices have risen, so have used-car prices. Comprehensive coverage: Take a $100 deductible and reduce your premium by 30%. Liability: Don't stint. $1 million is a safe floor for professional families. Extra liability is relatively inexpensive if it is bought through an umbrella policy.

WHEN YOU ARE HIT BY THE UNINSURED (OR UNDERINSURED) MOTORIST

An accident with an uninsured or underinsured motorist can be financially ruinous. As part of your own policy, underinsured (in some states) and uninsured motorists coverage is obtainable to deal with such accidents.

Uninsured coverage:

Most states have statutory requirements that automobile liability insurance policies include uninsured motorists coverage.

• Financial responsibility limits. The law requires that uninsured motorists coverage be provided in an amount mandated by the state. These financial responsibility limits vary.

• Getting more coverage. Usually you can buy coverage up to your liability limits. Example: If you carry $300,000 in liability, you can get the same amount in uninsured coverage.

• Proof of fault. Under uninsured coverage, your company has to pay you only what the other party is legally liable for. So, the other party must be proved at fault.

• Comparative negligence provisions. In some states, if the other driver is proved somewhat at fault, you can recover proportional damages from your own insurance company.

• Making a claim. You are placed in an adversarial position with your own insurance company. You must prove the extent of the injury, establish its value and negotiate with your own carrier to settle. If you can't reach a settlement, most claims will go to arbitration, not to court.

• Limits. Most mandatory uninsured motorists protection covers only bodily injury. Property damage is covered under your collision insurance, after the deductible. (As with any collision claim, your rates may go up after filing.)

Underinsured coverage:

This type of coverage is becoming more and more popular. Some states require that underinsured coverage be offered. In others, it is optional.

With underinsured coverage:

• You must first recover the maximum amount from the other party's liability policy before you can collect on your own policy.

• As with uninsured coverage, you are in an adversary position with your carrier and must prove that the value of your injury has exceeded the liability limits of the other party's policy.

Important: Uninsured motorists coverage will not pay you if the other driver has any insurance at all, no matter how inadequate.

Pedestrian accidents:

You will be covered by your uninsured motorists coverage just as if you were in a car at the time. If you don't own a car, you might be able to get coverage under the policy of a family member in your immediate household who does own one. If neither you nor anyone in your family has coverage, you can apply to a fund that some states maintain to cover such accidents, or pursue a court action directly against the responsible party.

Source: Richard P. Oatman, assistant claim counsel for Aetna Life & Casualty, Hartford, CT.

SUPER CAR INSURANCE

You can now buy insurance coverage that pays for repairing a damaged auto even if the cost of repairs exceeds the car's book value. (Regular policies usually pay only book value.) The new coverage also pays whatever it would cost to replace the car with one of comparable value, if it is beyond repair. Available:

In most states, from either Kemper Group or Royal Insurance. Cost: 10–30% more than the usual combined collision and comprehensive.

NO-HIT PROTECTION

Auto-insurance policies are required by state law to cover hit-and-run accidents. One driver wrecked her car when another vehicle veered at her, forcing her off the road. The other car then sped off. But the insurance company refused to pay for the accident because the damaged car had not actually been hit by the other one. So the car's owner sued. Court's decision: A hit-and-run accident is any accident caused by a person who runs away. There doesn't actually have to be a hit involved. The insurance company had to pay.

Su v. Kemper/American Motorist Insurance Cos., R.I. Sup. Ct.

CHILDREN CAN SUE INSURED PARENTS

A child could sue its parents for damages from an auto accident caused by the parents' negligence. (The doctrine of parental immunity from lawsuits is waived in negligence cases to the extent to which the parent is covered by insurance.) The court noted that the insurance company could have protected itself by putting an appropriate clause in the policy.

Ard v. Ard, S. Ct., Fla., 414 So. 2d 1066.

BUYING INCOME TAX INSURANCE

Income tax insurance now can be purchased by families that earn $125,000 per year or more. Central National of Omaha protects the policy owner against inadvertent mistakes on a tax return. Cost: $100–600. You get reimbursed for up to $1,000 in additional tax preparation charges and up to $100,000 in additional tax liability. Coverage is now available in: California, Illinois, Colorado. Nationwide coverage is planned.

ALL ABOUT UNEMPLOYMENT INSURANCE

Benefits are not paid automatically. A claim must be filed in person at the local unemployment-insurance office as soon as possible after termination of employment. Reason: Benefits begin when the claim is filed, not from the time the job is ended. Also, benefits could be lost in some cases.

Who can collect: Anyone who has lost his job through no fault of his own and has worked a minimum number of weeks and/or earned a minimum salary. In New York, a claimant must have worked at least 20 weeks out of the previous 52 and earned at least $800. New Jersey offers an alternative—either 20 weeks of work or earnings of $2,200. In California, it's either eight weeks of work in a 12-month base period with earnings of at least $900 or earnings of $1,100 during the period.

How much will you be paid?

Benefits are based on the previous earnings. They generally amount to 50% of salary up to a maximum. Alabama, Georgia and Mississippi pay a maximum of $90 per week. District of Columbia, $196. In Connecticut, the maximum is $140. Pennsylvania, $175. New York, $180.

A claimant may be paid partial benefits if his regular hours of employment are reduced because of lack of work. If a claimant obtains part-time work while he is collecting unemployment insurance, he may continue to collect partial benefits. In Pennsylvania, a claimant can earn up to 40% of his weekly benefit rate without reducing benefits. Any amount over the 40% will be deducted from his weekly benefit rate. In California, any amount over $21.99 will be deducted.

Some states (including Connecticut and Pennsylvania) have dependency allowances in addition to weekly benefits. Connecticut allows $10 per week for each child and for a spouse who has been unemployed for three months. Maximum: $50 per week. The maximum for dependency allowances in Pennsylvania is $8 per week with two or more dependents; with one dependent, $5 per week.

How long will benefits last?

With few exceptions, the maximum number of weekly benefits is 26. New York pays all eligible claimants 26 weekly checks whether for $25 or $125. New Jersey pays three weeks of benefits for every four weeks worked during the previous year.

During periods of high unemployment, benefits may be extended beyond the maximum 26 weeks. Extended benefits are triggered on a state-by-state basis by increases in state insured-unemployment rates.

When applying for unemployment benefits, the claimant must have with him his Social Security number and a record of his unemployment for the previous year. Important: Fill out forms completely. Incomplete information will delay benefits.

There is never any preferential treatment. Mechanics' and office managers' claims are processed in the same manner.

After the application has been filed, the claimant will have to wait three to five weeks before receiving his first check. The first week of unemployment is a waiting week. Some states will not pay for this week. Others will pay for this week only after the claimant has collected benefits for three or four consecutive weeks.

For the duration of a claim, the claimant must report in to affirm that he is still unemployed and is still actively seeking work. In New York, he must appear at his local office at an appointed time, once a week. In New Jersey, claimants report once every two weeks.

The claimant cannot refuse a job offer for which he is fitted by training and experience. This also means that a key punch operator will not be required to take work as a waitress.

Free handbook:

Each state provides a free handbook of its unemployment-insurance rules and regulations. The handbook is must reading for anyone facing unemployment in the near future.

Tax liability:

Benefits are subject to federal income tax.

GROUP INSURANCE OVERCHARGES

Some insurance companies may be overcharging their group insurance customers. Slight amounts can add up over the years. Because buying group insurance is so automatic, and complicated, the insurers usually can get away with it. But by knowing what the group contract is and how to negotiate with their carrier, most customers can cut costs by as much as 10% or more. Remember, the rate is not the annual cost of the insurance, it is only the advance premium. Most important: Get a breakdown of the premium charges. A common area where overcharge could occur is carrier retention. Only one out of a hundred insurance brokers really understands what goes into these surcharges, which are intended to cover a broad range of miscellaneous carrier costs. Insurers aren't eager to teach brokers either. Some of the costs included in retentions are:

- Carrier processing.
- Insurance company's profit.
- Contract and booklet printing.
- Carrier administrative service.
- Late payment.
- Pooling and conversion.
- State premium taxes.
- Commissions.
- Claim determination and processing.

Many of these items should rightfully be picked up by the insurer.

Often as much as one-third of a year's premiums are held in reserve by the carrier to protect itself against the time when the customer terminates his or her policy.

Very often, the carrier pays little interest on this money. How to earn higher interest, or get the entire reserve refunded:

- Negotiate a lag time for premium payments equal to the amount held in reserve.

- Offer the carrier a letter of credit that guarantees payment for claims filed after the company switched insurers.

Signs that your company may be overcharged include:

- A retention percentage above 10% of annual premiums. Retention rates commonly vary between 8% and 12% of the annual premiums. In some cases, the higher retention is offset by a lower premium rate. Frequently, however, it is a gross overcharge.

- A reserve that exceeds 30% of annual premiums, or one on which little or no interest is being paid.

- A large number of small claims. It may indicate that a plan is misdesigned.

- A consistent retrospective charge levied by the carrier to compensate for an excess amount of claims. Negotiating the retrospective trigger level from 75% of premiums to 80% can save $5,000 on a $100,000 annual premium bill.

- A customer is dealing with a captive insurance agent of a specific company. No matter how smart the agent may be, the likelihood is that the agent is partial to his own carrier. Alternative: Have an independent broker examine the policy to see if there's a better deal elsewhere.

Source: Arthur Schechner, president of Schechner Corp., insurance brokers and group consultants, Millburn, NJ.

HOW TO NEGOTIATE FOR BUSINESS INSURANCE

The same medical and life insurance coverage can cost your company less if the buyer negotiates for one or more of these advantages:

- 90-day (instead of 30-day) grace period, with payment made toward the end of the grace period.

- Insurance company discounts premium rates in advance (say 10%). Employer pays the discounted premium each month, but agrees to make up any deficit at the end of the policy year if premiums don't cover claims, reserve adjustment, other charges. (The deficit payment is limited to amount of discount.)

- Insurance company provides service at real cost plus a set charge for profit and overhead. (Obviously, for very large accounts only.)

- Employer self-insures major portion (90% to 95%) of anticipated medical claims. The insurance company covers claims over that amount.

16. Points of Law

Points of Law

ABOUT COMPANY LAWYERS

If you're asked to discuss something about your job with the company attorney, you can't assume that all statements you make will be kept confidential. As a matter of fact, in most cases, the lawyer would be violating his duty to his client (the company) if he even reminds you that your statements may be reported to company officials. Exception: If the lawyer has represented you on some personal matter, such as drafting your will or handling some traffic tickets, he might have a duty to explain the situation to you and point out that he is not representing you in this instance.

Source: *American Bar Association Journal.*

LAWYER-CLIENT CAUTION

Lawyer-client privilege may be lost if a third party sits in on the conversation. Trap: When a complicated financial matter is to be discussed, the lawyer may want an accountant or banker, for example, to sit in. But since the third party cannot claim the lawyer-client privilege, confidentiality is lost. Better way: Have the lawyer hire a financial expert to sit in as an employee, or have the lawyer talk to the expert separately.

NONCLIENTS CAN SUE LAWYERS

Case: The owner of some shares of restricted stock needed a letter from a law firm in order to sell his shares. It took 10 months for the firm to issue the letter. Meanwhile, the price of the shares dropped significantly. But when the shareholder sued for damages caused by the delay, the lawyers thought they had a solid defense.

Their argument: We were the lawyers for the company whose shares were being traded, not for the shareholder. Since the shareholder was not our client, we did not owe him any duty. He has no basis for suing us.

Court: The shareholder is entitled to sue. He need not be a client to recover if he can show that the firm deliberately favored some shareholders by promptly issuing the letters that let them sell their stock while delaying the issuance of letters to others.

Singer v. *Whitman & Ranson,* 186 N.Y.L.J., No. 35, p. 12.

WHEN TO SUE A LAWYER FOR MALPRACTICE

The legal profession is entering its own malpractice crisis. The number of suits against attorneys being brought by clients is increasing and the availability of malpractice insurance is decreasing.

Ground rules for considering a suit against your lawyer:

• Where malpractice is charged in connection with litigation, the client must show that the litigation would have ended with a result more favorable to the client if it were not for the attorney's neglect.

• Where the attorney fell below the standards of skill and knowledge ordinarily possessed by attorneys under similar circumstances, expert testimony is needed to support this charge. And the standard may be affected by specialization (which raises the standard of care required), custom and locality. Locality and custom can't lower the standard, but they may be used as a defense to show that the procedure or law involved is unsettled.

The best ways to avoid malpractice charges:

• See that there is good communication between lawyer and client.

• Avoid a situation where a lawyer is handling serious matters for personal friends. The tendency is to deal with them more casually.

• The attorney should give an honest opinion of each case, good or bad. The client shouldn't press him for a guarantee as to the result.

• All fee arrangements should be in writing.

• The attorney should spell out the scope of his responsibilities, including appeals, and a limit should be placed on costs.

• The agreement should provide for periodic payments, unless the matter is one involving a contingency fee, and for withdrawal, if there is a default in payment.

COST OF BANKRUPTCY

Lawyer's fees start at $500. An average charge for a Chapter 7 action—a straight discharge of debt—is $600. The more complicated Chapter 13 bankruptcy is about $750, plus a $60 filing fee.

Source: Robert H. Bressler of the law firm Bressler and Lida, New York.

EXEMPTIONS IN BANKRUPTCY

A debtor who had a tax refund coming argued in Bankruptcy Court that the refund should be considered as unpaid wages; after all, the money had been withheld from his salary. (Under his state's law, 75% of unpaid wages was exempt from creditors' claims.) The court rejected his argument. Reason: Once money is sent to the government as taxes, it loses its character as "wages" and also loses any exempt status.

In re Kalelin. W.D. KY., 19 B.R. 39.

LOVE AND LIABILITY

"Don't worry. My doctor says I'm sterile, so you can't get pregnant." He wasn't, and she did. After an abortion, Alice sued Bill for fraudulent misrepresentation. The court found Bill believed what he said. Nevertheless, he was responsible for the false statement, and Alice could recover the cost of the abortion, her lost wages, and damages for the pain and suffering of the operation. But no damages for the break-up of the romance, said the judge.

In re Alice D. (William M.), NY Civil Ct., Small Claims Part, reported in *NY Law Journal.*

YOUR NAME AND THE LAW

The American legal system, with its emphasis on freedom and avoiding "big brother," has surprisingly few rules on what people call themselves. Mostly it's a matter of custom. The price we pay for this freedom is confusion and sometimes thorny legal problems for innocent people.

Your legal name:

Most people acquire legal names when their birth certificates are filed. (If the parents haven't named their child when the certificate is filed and never get around to it, the child may not have a legal name other than boy Jones or girl Smith.) The only way to change a legal name is by court order.

Getting married does not obligate a woman to use her husband's surname. However, a woman who has been using her husband's name may find that a divorce court is hesitant to grant her permission to go back to using her birth name if she has children in her custody who will continue using their father's name.

Aside from that, people are not generally required to use their legal names in the course of day-to-day activities. You can use any name you choose, as long as you're not engaging in unfair competition (for example, setting up a dance studio and calling yourself Fred Astaire) or committing some kind of fraud.

Most people, of course, do use their own legal names and expect others to do the same. But in important business transactions with people you don't know well, it's a good idea to make sure they are who they say they are.

Example: John Johnson is being sued by his creditors. So he withdraws all his money from the bank and buys an apartment building, taking title in the name Henry Stevens. A year later, you want to buy the building. Checking property records, you find no liens outstanding and no judgments against Henry Stevens. Six months after that, one of John Johnson's creditors sues to enforce a judgment lien against the building.

Cases like this have turned up all over the country. In some jurisdictions the creditors have won. In others, the innocent purchaser is protected. But even if you win, you suffer the cost and aggravation of a lawsuit. The only real protection: Verify the identity of anyone with whom you have a major business dealing.

Most people are never asked to prove their identity. John Johnson had no trouble buying property under an assumed name.

Even getting false identity papers is fairly easy. Common ploy: A 30-year-old con man checks old newspapers for the obituary of a three-year-old who died 27 years earlier. He writes to the dead child's home town for a copy of the child's birth certificate. (In most places, anyone can request another person's birth certificate.) Using the birth certificate, the con man obtains a new driver's license and Social Security card. He's off and running.

Best defense: A full-scale credit check to make sure the person you're dealing with has a substantial credit history.

A woman who chooses to continue using her birth name after marriage may later have problems establishing her right to spouse's benefits under Social Security or her right to serve as executrix of her husband's estate. Suggestion: Request extra certified copies of the marriage license at the time of marriage and store them with other important papers. (Courthouses sometimes burn down. Computers can fail. Proving that a marriage took place 30 or 40 years ago could turn out to be difficult.)

A woman who does adopt her husband's surname should make sure all important records are updated. The same is true when a woman is divorced and goes back to her birth name. To square the records with Social Security after a marriage, divorce or remarriage, women need only fill out and file the same form requested when applying for the original card. This form must be accompanied by documen-

tary proof of identity, such as a marriage license. Otherwise, when later applying for benefits, the applicant will then have to document a marriage or divorce to establish her rights under her name. Credit cards and charge accounts require particular care.

Whatever name you use, be consistent. One married couple was audited by the IRS four years in a row, even though the couple never owed any additional tax. Reason: The wife had kept an old bank account in her birth name. Since the IRS had no tax return in that name, bureaucracy went into action. Once the name on the account was changed, the audits ceased.

Source: David Schechner of the law firm of Schechner & Targan, West Orange, NJ.

PROVING YOUR AGE AND CITIZENSHIP

The US Census Bureau will perform a search for anyone who needs help to prove age or citizenship. How: The applicant fills out a form, listing the names of both parents and where they lived at the time of past censuses. Then the bureau checks past censuses to certify whether the person was listed with those parents at that address and whether a place and date of birth were given.

For information: Write US Census Bureau, Pittsburg, KS 66762.

PARKING LOT LIABILITY

A customer who was assaulted in a store's parking lot, where there had been five muggings in recent months, could sue the store for negligence. The court didn't spell out exactly what the store was supposed to do. But it held that customers should have been informed of the danger.

Butler v. Acme Markets, Inc., S. Ct., NJ. 445 A2d 1141.

COLLECTING ON A JUDGMENT

After getting a judgment, many people find that they have spent much time and money and gone to a lot of trouble to get a worthless piece of paper. Estimated projections of the percentage of judgments that are collected in full are very low—according to one lawyer, less than 25%. Few people are willing to go to the trouble and expense of pursuing a reluctant debtor. To make winning a judgment worthwhile, it is important to know what to do and what to avoid.

Before you sue:

The biggest problem with judgment collection is suing the wrong entity. For instance, Joe at Joe's Garage puts a defective part in your car. You sue Joe but later find out that the XYZ Corporation owns his shop. Even though Joe owns every piece of stock in XYZ, your judgment is not collectible out of the corporation's assets.

Some guidelines for a successful suit:

• Don't sue a firm just because its name is on a sign outside a place of business, or the person you assume owns the business. Always check further. Example: A large national fast-food chain has a number of restaurants in New York City which are not owned by the chain but by another large food corporation.

• Check with the local county clerk's office, business-licensing bureau, department of consumer affairs or police department to find out the real name in which the business is registered.

• Sue where the assets are. The service person who did the damage, the franchise owner, the corporate owner or the parent corporation may all be liable if you can prove wrongful involvement. Sue whichever entity or entities have enough assets to pay your judgments. You can sue more than one.

Finding assets:

Unless your judgment is against a well-established corporation, you may have to deal with a debtor who will not pay voluntarily. Hiding assets is the most popular method of avoiding payment. These assets must be uncovered in order to collect.

• If you have ever received a check from or given a check to the debtor, you may have a clue to the whereabouts of the debtor's bank account.

• If you have a judgment against someone who owns a home, check the county's home-ownership records in that area of residence.

• If you have won a judgment against a business, go personally to the business location to see what equipment and machinery are on the site.

• If the judgment is large enough, hire an agency to do an asset search. Before paying for a professional search, find out what the agency is actually going to do to uncover assets and what results you can realistically expect.

Watch out for fraud. To avoid creditors, an unscrupulous company will often go out of business in one name and start up the same business the next day with a different name— on the same location and with the same equipment. To collect on your judgement you will need a lawyer to prove that the transfer of assets took place for the purposes of fraud.

How judgments are collected:

Judgments can be forcibly collected only by an enforcement officer (a local marshall, sheriff or constable) or sometimes the court clerk. You are responsible for informing the officer where to find the debtor's assets.

Collection procedures:

• Property execution: The officer seizes any property that is not exempt and sells it at auction to pay the debt.

• Income execution: The officer granishees a debtor's salary. You may collect 10%–25% of take-home pay, depending on state law. For an income execution, you must tell the officer where the debtor works.

Collectible Property:*

• Exempt from collection: Household and personal items, including furniture, stove, refrigerator, stereo, TV, sewing machine, clothing, cooking utensils, tools of a person's trade.

• Collectible items: Motor vehicles, valuable jewelry, antiques, real estate, bank accounts, business equipment, stocks, bonds and the like.

• A home lived in by the debtor is exempt up to a certain amount (which varies from state to state). The major problem in collecting on a home: Many are jointly owned by a married couple. If a judgment is obtained against only the wife, for instance, the house can't be touched if it's also in her husband's name. But if only

*These are general guidelines. Details vary from state to state. Check with the local marshall or other enforcement officer for more information.

the debtor owns it, you can have it seized, sell it and return the exempt amount.

Out-of-state collections:

Under the US Constitution, judgments are reciprocal from one state to another. If you have a judgment against an individual or business in one state that has assets in another, you or your lawyer can have the judgment docketed (registered) in the state or state where you wish to collect. The judgment is then viable in both places at the same time and can be collected in either. A judgment can be good for as along as 10 years, depending on the jurisdiction, and can be renewed by the court for an equal amount of time.

Getting help:

• Legal help is recommended if you are suing for an amount over the small-claims-court limit. After you win the judgment, your lawyer may arrange an asset search for you or recommend an agency to do one.

Collection agencies are not recommended. They deal mostly with large accounts and not with one-shot cases. Also: A collection agency can only dun a debtor in a formal, legalistic way to convince him to pay voluntarily. After assets have been uncovered, only an enforcement officer can actually collect.

Source: Kenneth D. Litwach, director, Bureau of City Marshalls, New York City Department of Investigation.

UNCHARITABLE CHARITIES

Generous people who donate to charities like to think they're helping a philanthropic cause and people in need. Very often this is not the case! Many times the only cause being helped is the charity itself—or its officers.

Problem: There are no federal guidelines specifying the amount of funds charities must channel toward their cause. As long as some of the money raised goes to the charities' cause the organization can still call itself a charity. Because of "creative" accounting practices used by charities and professional fund-raisers, it is often difficult for donors to assess how well a particular charity is performing.

Background: According to the standards developed by the Council of Better Business Bureaus, each charity must apply at least half of all income to its particular activities. Fund-raising activities are not to absorb more than 35 percent of the contributions received by the charity.

Because of incompetence or outright fraud, many charities flout these guidelines.

To protect yourself: Before donating to a charity, contact the local Better Business Bureau or the state charities registration office in your area. In addition, it is important to obtain the following information:

• The percentage of funds raised that are donated which actually go to the cause. (For example, The American Heart Association collected more than $9 million in charitable donation in 1988, and spent $8 million on fund raising.)

• Examples of how the charity has benefited the cause over the past years. If they tell you what they plan on doing . . . Remember, big plans for the future do not count!

Source: *The Washington Spectator.*

17. Crime Prevention

Crime Prevention

PERSONAL PROTECTION FOR EXECUTIVES

A bodyguard may be advisable if your company is becoming very controversial or getting involved in an area receiving a great deal of attention. Otherwise, unless an executive has gotten a personal threat, violence against executives is so rare that personal protection isn't necessary.

Source: Oliver B. Revell, manager of the FBI's criminal investigation operations, quoted in *Personnel Administrator.*

HOW TO OUTSMART MUGGERS

Getting mugged these days is a real and personal threat, not something that happens just to other people. Not only must you prepare yourself, but your entire family should be taught how to act to survive an attack. If only one member of a group that is held up responds badly, all of you might be hurt.

Fortunately, most muggings are simple robberies in which neither the criminal nor the victim is hurt. However, the possibility of violence is always there.

First rule: Cooperate. Assume the mugger is armed. No matter how strong or fit you are, you are no match for a gun or knife. Remember: Your personal safety is far more important than your valuables or your pride.

Specific recommendations:

• Follow the mugger's instructions to the letter. Try not to move too quickly or too slowly—either could upset him.

• Stay as calm as possible, and encourage companions to do the same.

• Give the mugger whatever he asks for. Don't argue. But if something is of great sentimental value to you, give it to him, and then say, "This watch was given to me by my grandfather. It means a lot to me. But if you insist, I will give it to you."

• When he has all he wants of your valuables, ask him what he wants you to do while he gets away—stay where you are, lie face down, whatever. If he dismisses you, leave the scene immediately, and don't look back. Don't call the police until you are in a safe place.

Most criminals are not anxious to hurt you. If there is no violence, the police are not likely to pursue the offender. Mugging is like a job to many practitioners. If you respond in a businesslike way with a minimum of words and gestures, it will likely be over quickly and without injury.

Some important dont's:

• Don't reach for your wallet in a back pocket without explaining first what you plan to do. The mugger might think you are reaching for a gun.

• Don't give him dirty looks or make judgmental remarks.

• Don't threaten him with hostile comments.

• Don't be a wiseguy or a joker. Even smiling is a dangerous idea. He may think you are laughing at him.

• Don't try any tricks like carrying a second empty wallet to give to a mugger. This common ruse could make the mugger angry. Some experts even recommend that you carry at least $25 with you at all times to keep from upsetting a mugger. Muggers are often as frightened and inexperienced as you are, which is why it is important not to upset them.

Source: Ken Glickman, co-director of the Self-Defense Training Center, New York.

If you're assaulted, scream *fire!* People are more likely to come to your aid than if you shout *help!*

FINANCIAL AID FOR THE MUGGING VICTIM

Financial compensation programs for mugging victims exist in 34 states. Compensation can cover both medical expenses and lost earnings. However, most of these programs utilize a means test that eliminates all but lower-income victims from compensation. Additionally, the victim's own medical unemployment insurance must be fully depleted before state compensation is granted.

• Workers compensation may cover you if you were mugged on the job or on your way to or from company business during your workday. It will not cover you while traveling from home to work and back.

• Homeowner's policies may cover financial losses suffered during a mugging.

• Federal crime insurance insures up to $10,000 against financial losses from a mugging. This program is for people who have had difficulty purchasing insurance privately. Policies can be bought from any licensed insurance agent.

• Mugging insurance is an idea whose time has come. It is available in New York. It covers property loss, medical care and mental anguish. If successful, it may spread rapidly to other states.

• A lawsuit may be successful if it can be proved that the mugging was the result of negligence. Example: Celebrity Connie Francis was attacked in her room at a major motel chain. She won $2 million in damages by proving that the motel's security system was inadequate.

Source: Lucy N. Friedman, executive director, Victim Services Agency, New York.

LIMITING LARCENY LOSSES

Safest places for a wallet: Jacket breast pocket and front pants pocket. Insert the wallet sideways so it's harder for a pickpocket to remove. Leave unnecessary credit cards at home. Don't put all your money in the same pocket. Always have some cash to give to a mugger.

Don't keep your keys with your wallet or with any other form of identification.

Source: *Crime Prevention Manual for Business Owners and Managers* by Margaret Kenda, AMACOM, New York.

PICKPOCKET DETERRENTS

Pickpockets work in pairs. One is the stall and the other the pick. The stall distracts the targets by bumping into them or otherwise detaining them. The pick takes advantage of the moment of confusion to lift a wallet or a purse. Pickpockets carry newspapers in their hands to conceal the stolen goods. They stand too close to you. And they wear caps to keep people from seeing their eyes, which makes future identification more difficult.

Precautions: Men should not carry their wallets in their back pockets. Women should keep their bags zippered shut. Hold the bag under your arm. When you're walking with someone else, keep the bag between the two of you.

Source: Andrea Forrest, president, Preventive Security Services, New York.

HOW TO CATCH A THIEF

Report a crime in progress immediately. Waiting even a minute or two makes it nearly impossible to catch the perpetrators in the act. Most crimes last only a few minutes, at most.

INSTANT REVENGE AGAINST OBSCENE PHONE CALLER

Keep a referee's whistle handy to respond with a shrill, earsplitting blast right into the speaker of your telephone.

BREAKING IN ON A BURGLARY

If you walk in on a burglar by accident, just asking an innocent question may defuse potential violence. Example: Oh, you're the guy who's supposed to pick up the package, aren't you? If, at this point, the burglar tries to run away, it's smart to step aside.

Source: *Crime Prevention Manual for Business Owners and Managers* by Margaret Kenda, AMACOM, New York.

If an intruder is in your house when you arrive home, resist the temptation to yell or otherwise bring on a confrontation. You then become an obstacle to the burglar's escape, escalating the chances that you may be hurt. Better: Go as quickly and quietly as possible to a neighbor's and call the police from there.

Source: *How to Protect Yourself From Crime,* Avon Books, New York.

How to avoid walking into your home while a thief is there: Leave a $20 bill conspicuously placed, near the door. If the bill is gone when you return home, someone else may be there. Leave at once and call the police.

Source: *Venture.*

18. Computers and Office Equipment

Computers & Office Equipment

WHO NEEDS A HOME COMPUTER AND WHO DOESN'T

If you haven't already bought a personal computer, it pays to carefully evaluate whether it's worth the price.

• About 50% of personal-computer owners don't use their machines at all. The other 50% are just playing the games on them after the first few days. Or they can't get to it at all because the kids have taken it over. The computer hobbyists and those using computers for business at home are still rather few in number.

• After the initial entertainment phase, a few owners use prepackaged programs for one chore like household budgeting, but never run the machine anywhere near its capacity.

• Many people are buying computers for status. The computer becomes an expensive, high-tech objet d'art.

The value of personal computers is depreciating. Today's technology becomes outmoded almost as soon as it hits the stores. Cheaper and better equivalents are coming out constantly.

Should you buy one for the kids? If you can afford it, and you believe your child will use it, the answer is a resounding yes. Kids love personal computers, and up to the age of 15 they are much more likely than adults to really use them to advantage.

• Buy your child an inexpensive computer with a keyboard rather than a simple video game device. The child may start out playing games that teach hand/eye coordination, but you can encourage him to switch to more sophisticated games like Wilderness, chess or Dungeons and Dragons. These games will teach your youngster to interact with the keyboard by using high-level logic and reason. Bonus: He'll learn how to type.

• The youngster who actually learns how to use a computer will have a great advantage in the future, no matter what career he eventually chooses. There is a stong trend toward the infusion of computers into all areas of endeavor.

• A personal computer makes a great babysitter. If your youngster gets involved with the home computer, he won't be in the neighborhood arcade.

If you are a professional accustomed to dealing with some form of computing device, such as a desk calculator, you might be able to use a computer profitably. But don't assume you can pole-vault from no-tech to high-tech just by spending money.

If you have been moving toward data processing, even if it just involves keeping highly organized manual files, you are a good computer bet. If you never kept good records but always yearned to get organized, a computer won't do it. Without motivation, an expensive, unused machine will simply make you feel more guilty.

If your whole family participates in learning to use the computer, the likelihood of a successful investment is improved substantially. Recommended: Get together with your spouse and one or two of your kids and designate at least one hour a week together to learn how to use it.

Source: Charles P. Lecht, president of Lecht Sciences, Inc., New York.

• Best time to buy computers: Discounts are most likely at the end of the month, since retailers receive a break from suppliers only if they make their preset monthly quota.
Source: *Dun's Business Month.*

• Buying computer software. If you can't understand the instruction book don't buy the software. Chances are good the programs will be incomprehensible as well.

WHAT TO COMPUTERIZE AND WHAT TO LEAVE ALONE

Before a particular function or operation in the business is computerized, answer the following questions:

• How often will the program be run? It takes four to six times as long to create a program as it takes to do the job once, without a computer. If the job isn't done fairly often, it may not pay to computerize it.

• Can data be entered into the computer easily? The more work that's involved in collecting, keying, and proofreading the data, the fewer the advantages of computerization.

• How complicated is the job? The more complex the work, the greater the potential savings from automating.

• How many different ways will the information be used? The more outputs required, the greater the advantages of using a computer.

Source: *Computer Programming for the Complete Idiot,* Design Enterprises, San Francisco.

COMPUTER PLANNING TIPS

• Trap when planning for a new computer system: Putting 80% of the effort on the hardware and software acquisitions and only 20% on preparing the staff. Reality: Most of the benefit of a new system comes from people working smarter and faster. To accomplish this, employees need to understand the concept behind the new system. They may need new skills, and they must have the right attitude toward the change.

Source: Charles B. Andrews, management consultant, W. Hartford, CT.

• Measure peak work load, not average work load, when planning a computer purchase. And be sure the system can be expanded as the company grows. Common problem: Machine turns out to be too slow and to have too little memory for rush jobs. Expansion features to look for: Multiprocessing, multiterminals, networking, communications capability, modular expansion.

Source: *Interactive Computing.*

STAY WITH THE TOP COMPUTER VENDORS

Buy only from a vendor that will still be in business in the years ahead (to provide service as the technology gets more complex). Most of today's vendors won't survive even five years.

Source: Survey of 22 computer experts by *Computer Decisions.*

PURCHASE AGREEMENT POINTER

Purchase agreements should indicate what charges, if any, are to be made for upgrades and future enhancements. The user should try for something like a Most Favored Nation clause, which guarantees charges that are at least as low as the charges given to any other customer of the vendor.

Source: *Computer Negotiations Report.*

MAINTENANCE CONTRACT CAUTION

Computer maintenance contracts that can be canceled after a year by either side (the general practice) may seem to provide desirable flexibility but actually benefit the vendors. They often threaten to cancel in order to raise prices above the agreed level. Solution: Amend the standard contract so it calls for a minimum period of guaranteed renewable maintenance of at least several years.

HOW TO READ A COMPUTER VENDOR'S CONTRACT

Never accept the standard purchase contract the vendor offers. Scrap the vendor's forms and write new ones that are not weighted overwhelmingly in favor of the vendor.

The standard computer contract's inadequacies:

• Disclaims two traditional key warranties that are a buyer's best protection under the Uniform Commercial Code. The buyer wants the warranties that state that the product meets minimum standards of serviceability and that the buyer relies on the seller's expertise in deciding what to buy.

• Expressly negates all the claims, promises and technical descriptions the seller may have made in discussions about a purchase.

• Describes software in general, nonfunctional terms that ignore the marketing claims made about it.

• Refuses to include quality or performance standards against which the system can be measured.

• Limits to a maximum of three months warranties that the system will be free from defects.

A fair contract's basics:

• Spells out the performance characteristics, capacity and other capabilities of the system. Example: The software package can compute and print 5,000 payroll checks per hour on a single printer. Also spells out expertise and experience of the vendor that made the company select it as a seller.

• Describes the timetable of delivery, installation, training, maintenance, etc.

• Sets a method to determine whether standards have been met.

• Clearly and precisely defines technical jargon. Example: What is downtime?

Problem: Vendors resist giving up the huge advantages of the standard contract. To get the best deal:

• Negotiate only in a competitive bidding environment.

• Persuade the vendor to make a substantial marketing investment in the deal. Examples: Get the seller's representatives to arrange demonstrations of the unit by other users. Write a sample program. Produce sample displays or reports.

• Until the last minute, avoid steps or comments that suggest even a tentative commitment to any one computer vendor.

Source: Dick H. Brandon and Sidney Segelstein, computer experts.

When buying or leasing a computer system:

• Insist that the vendor handle the service for all components even if the system includes components from several manufacturers.

• Request that the last payment not be due until after the system is operational. Goal: To motivate the vendor to perform well.

• Itemize the purchase price and payment schedule. Also specify a firm delivery date and a penalty if that date is not met.

• Have the software and hardware listed on separate bills if the company does not intend to take an investment tax credit for the software (opting, instead, to deduct it as an expense).

• Specify maintenance and repairs. Key questions: Service contract or by the call? Who will do work, when, where? Press for service beyond the initial contract period.

• Do not surrender rights to legal recourse in the event that an unresolvable dispute arises.

Source: Hillel Segal, president of Association of Computer Users, Boulder, CO.

COMPUTER CARE

• Negative-ion generators, the new devices that supposedly make the air healthier, should never be placed near delicate electronic equipment. Especially vulnerable: Computer storage units. Reason: The generators create static electricity, which can erase stored data and damage other equipment.

Source: *Popular Computing.*

• Covering computers when the equipment's not in use appears to make them less susceptible to static-electricity damage. Covers also reduce dust contamination, a major hazard to electronic equipment.

Source: *Update.*

• Buy a voltage regulator that filters the electricity going into your home-computer system. It protects against power surges that can damage the machinery. Adding accessories, such as additional memory capacity, means drawing more electricity, which creates more heat. Remedy: Buy an add-on fan that cools the mechanism by pulling fresh air through it. Note: The information on disks and tapes is stored magnetically. Keep them away from sources of magnetism.

SAFER COMPUTER SCREENS

It's easy to redesign a workplace in which video display terminals can be used safely. One organization, The Fund for the City of New York, changed its office layout so that employees sit an arm's length—28 to 30 inches—from their VDTs. They found that the electromagnetic radiation drops off sharply at that distance.

But radiation from VDTs doesn't just come from the screen—it comes out the back and sides as well. So the organization does not allow anyone to sit within 40 inches of another employee's VDT.

Even safer: Lap-top computers use safe liquid crystal displays (LCDs) that do not give off hazardous magnetic fields.

WHAT COMPUTER SALESMEN DON'T TELL YOU

• "Burn in" your computer by leaving it on for the first two weeks you own it. If there are any electrical problems, most will surface during this period (when the machine is under warranty). The good news: 80% of electrical circuits that survive a burn-in will last an estimated 500 years.

Source: *The Personal Computer in Business Book* by Peter A. McWilliams, Prelude Press, Allen Park, MI.

• Frequent cleaning of floppy-disk-drive heads is unnecessary if you buy quality disks, handle and store them carefully and discard them when worn. Cheap, dirty or defective disks will give off oxide particles. Then the disk-drive head will need regular cleaning.

Source: *Business Computer Systems.*

• Executives at the very top may not need computers. Their job involves policy direction, historical performance and examining prospects and choices for the future—not up-to-the-minute figures, numbers and details. That's the business of their staff.

Source: Frank Gatewood, Bank of America, quoted in *Popular Computing.*

• Computer services can be leased from many universities for as much as 50% less than the usual commercial rates. The schools get government aid to buy giant supercomputers. Often they buy bigger computers than they need and sell the excess capacity to outsiders.

• Stand-alone word processors aren't much more powerful and capable than microcomputers equipped with word processing software, contrary to claims. A word-processing program can give a microcomputer as much WP power as a specialized WP system. Big bonus: The micro can be used for other duties.

Source: *Word Processing Buyer's Guide* by Arthur Naiman, McGraw-Hill, New York.

• Team up with other local companies for word-processor or computer training. Pool together enough students (usually 10–15) to fill a course, and contract with the vendor for an instructor. Typical cost: Half that of a course open to the public, plus saving on travel expenses for the trainees.

Source: *Computerworld.*

• Water does not damage computer hardware provided the equipment is cleaned and dried within 12–24 hours after wetting. Most important: The wet components should be washed down with demineralized water to remove any contaminants and then dried with a fan or ordinary hair dryer.

Source: Ron Reeves, Factory Mutual Engineering and Research, quoted in *Computer Decisions.*

• Sending computer data over the cut-rate long distance telephone services like MCI and sprint doesn't always work too well. Reason: The independent companies cram so many "conversations" through their systems that some information is inevitably lost along the way. That's OK if you're *talking* to someone on the phone—you can always ask the person to repeat a word or two. But it won't do for most computer applications. *Even a small loss of data can invalidate an entire transmission.*

BEST COMPUTER REPAIR SERVICE

Local dealers are usually not best for repair and other services. It's better to go with a third-party maintenance outfit such as Bell & Howell, GE, RCA, Serbus and TRW. They have nationwide locations, generally charge less than other service groups and provide service quality that is standard from location to location. They may also provide a "loaner" personal computer for the duration of the repairs.

CHOOSING A COMPUTER SERVICE BUREAU

Here are some basic risks to be aware of if computer chores are handled by a service bureau—and some suggested remedies, which should be included in the contract signed with the bureau.

• Financial responsibility. A number of service bureaus have gone bankrupt, and in some cases such failures have resulted in government or creditor impoundment of equipment and media. User data on the medium is irretrievably lost. But even if the data is returned, it may be temporarily unusable if the bureau's programs aren't available.

Remedy: Deal with financially strong service bureaus. Contractually require quarterly copies of their financial statements. Cover ownership of data, programs, tapes and disks in the contract to protect them from impoundment.

• Ability to correct errors. A service bureau prepares your paychecks and mails them directly to your employees. If there's an error, who's liable? Probably the bureau is, if you can collect.

Remedy: Same as above—pick a bureau with financial strength. Also, don't abdicate output. Check it. Sign the checks at your office. Institute your own controls.

• Lowballing. A service bureau in desperate need of business prices your job on an "incremental cost" basis, giving you an unrealistically low price. If their business improves, the squeeze is on, and your data or programs are held for ransom for service price increases. The bureau may argue that the programs are its property and may demand a "transfer fee" to release the data.

Remedy: Get multiple bids before signing. Be sure that the question of program ownership is resolved in the contract.

• Confidentiality and security. You ask the bureau to print a confidential list of your most important customers. By coincidence, a programmer for your principal competitor, testing a program at the bureau, uses a work-file containing the list, and realizes what he has found. Or he finds the carbon sheets "deleaved" from your multipart paper and notes that by holding it up to the light he can read the entire list. Or someone sells or uses your data or mailing list. Or he determines through your data that your earnings are up (or down) and then buys (or sells) your stock accordingly.

Remedy: For all confidential data, obtain all work-files, carbons, and the like. Establish security procedures and inspections contractually. Execute confidentiality clauses with all employees of the bureau. Also be sure to provide backup storage on your site for all key files in case of accidental loss or destruction.

CHOOSING THE RIGHT WORD-PROCESSING SUPPLIES

• Paper. Many offices use a higher quality than necessary for the job at hand. Always buy in quantity.
• Floppy disks and tape cartridges. Unless special features are desired, ignore brand names and buy on the basis of price. Most so-called magnetic media on the market are made by a few reputable manufacturers and sold under a variety of brand names. Note: Tapes and disks should come packaged in a plastic box rather than the traditional paper box. More damage is done by poor handling than by actual wear.

Source: *Word Processing Systems.*

PERSONAL COMPUTERS AS WORD PROCESSORS

Microcomputer: This is the core unit that features the keyboard. It also contains the internal circuits (chips) that provide processing functions, the power supply and the so-called ports where such peripherals as display screens, disk drives and printers can be plugged in.

Power: Judge the power of the personal computer by its main memory size, i.e., the thousands of bytes (eight-bit or -digit codes roughly corresponding to words) it can temporarily store and work with. Note: Computer memory disappears forever when the power is switched off. For storage, the working memory must be transferred to (recorded on) tape or magnetic disks.

Keyboard: This is all-important for word processing and it should closely resemble a conventional electric typewriter. Watch out for small computers that have flat or too compact keys that are hard to operate. Consider only models that have 10 or more general-purpose function keys that can be used for such common word-processing functions as centering or searching through the text for specific lines or words.

Video display: While it may be adequate just to hook up to an old TV set for some purposes, the CRT, or screen, is usually all-important in word processing. Three primary areas of concern:

Format: Screen space is at a premium, since most personal computers offer only 24 lines and some of that must be used for special commands or file information. Look for a model that either has the capacity to display 80 columns of characters.

Color. A green screen is easier to look at for extended periods than a black screen. Next best: Amber.

Formation of characters. Images formed on CRTs are actually composed of a tiny matrix of dots. The finer this dot matrix, the higher the resolution and the easier to read over long periods.

Source: *How to Evaluate a Personal Computer for Word Processing Applications,* Datapro Research, Delran, NJ.

JUDGING WORD-PROCESSING OPERATIONS

Productivity standards for word-processing operations can be hard to establish by conventional time and motion techniques.

• Set a standard unit of productivity for an average mix of original, revisions and repetitive materials. In ordinary commercial business use: 125 six-inch lines, with 12 characters to the inch (12-pitch printer element).

• Pick a standard time-frame: Four hours to turn around 50% of the work, eight hours to turn around 95%.

• Quality standard: Two format errors per draft page, but none in grammar or spelling. (Permissible errors: Names, technical jargon.) Final copy: No errors of any kind, including formatting.

• Using these standard units, a satisfactory one-day performance (six working hours) would be:

	Lines per hour	Lines per day
Original copy	100	600
Revisions	150	900
Repetitive copy	200	1,200
Repetitive copy with automated paper feed	300	1,800

Source: J.R. Little, Reg Little & Associates, Fairfax Station, VA.

OFFICE COPIER: WHEN TO RENT AND WHEN TO BUY

• Low-volume copiers: Generally, these should be purchased. Caution: The dealer should have an established reputation for properly servicing the machines.

• Medium-volume copiers: If purchased, amortization should be no longer than four years, and preferably only three years. Constant usage wears out even the most durable copiers during that period of time.

• High-volume copiers: If they cost more than $10,000, buy them outright only when usage exceeds 30,000–40,000 copies per month. With lower use, outright ownership of an expensive copier isn't justified, especially in view of the industry's track record of constantly coming out with improved, more efficient machines.

Source: Datapro Research Corp., Delran, NJ.

• Things to look for in a copier: A short, straight paper track. A simple method for clearing paper jams. Electronic rather than mechanical components. Important: Pick a manufacturer or dealer with ample service capability.

Source: Clapp & Poliak, industrial-show management firm, New York.

• When buying a small copier, do not buy a service contract from the manufacturer or distributor. Calling a service technician as needed is more economical provided the machine is properly maintained in-house. But when buying a large-volume, plain-paper machine, do buy the service contract from the manufacturer.

• Copy speed: First-copy speed is as important as copies per minute when the machine is being used for short runs.

Source: *Purchasing World.*

• Do not select a slower machine when the estimated volume of copies a day is high, even if the machine can theoretically handle it. A machine pushed to or beyond its limits will not hold up. Guidelines:

Volume (copies/mo.)	Machine speed (copies/min.)
Under 5,000	10
5,000–10,000	15
10,000–20,000	20
20,000–30,000	30
30,000–50,000	45
Over 50,000	60

Source: Datapro Research Corp., Delran, NJ.

• Use carbon paper whenever possible if documents will be circulated in-house only and their appearance doesn't matter. Make more expensive photocopies only when material is to be sent out.

HOW TO BEAT COMPUTERPHOBIA

Though most employees are no longer afraid to touch a computer keyboard—as many were a few years ago—businesses now face a new kind of computerphobia . . . fear of trying something new. Examples:

• In the 1980s, workers in many companies switched from typewriters to word processors. Now they're being asked to switch to powerful computers that can handle word processing—and many other previously non-computerized functions. Problem: Many of these employees feel so comfortable with word processors that they resist the change.

• Over the last few years, many managers took time to learn computer basics, but they haven't kept up with new developments. Result: They're afraid to look into new hardware and software products.

That fear has recently been exacerbated by virus programs that destroy vital parts of a computer and its accumulated data.

The cost of computerphobia can be high. Businesses miss out on opportunities to increase profits and productivity and to accomplish many tasks, such as desktop publishing and spreadsheet analysis, for which computers are uniquely suited.

For most companies, the greatest missed opportunity is in marketing. Here, the potential is dramatic because of a computer's ability to quickly spot buying patterns and relationships between them that can help develop more effective marketing plans and even new products.

Example: By developing a customer database, a business can constantly monitor what products customers buy, where they live, where else they shop, the size of their income and other valuable demographic data. The data can then be used to market certain products selectively to the group of customers, most likely to buy them. Or data can be used to design new products for a select group of customers known to buy them.

• Involve employees in an early stage of planning for the company's next step in computerization. Those involved should include key employees who will be in charge of the system, employees who use the computers and those who use the end product.

The type and degree of involvement will vary among companies. But the first step for all businesses should include a meeting at which each worker describes what he expects from a new program or computer system.

That kind of exchange gets employees thinking that they're part of the change process, and when that occurs, resistance is greatly reduced. Just as important, employees are likely to offer computer solutions management hasn't even thought about.

Employee feedback can often steer the company away from the first choice of a new system and toward a more effective or cheaper product.

Caution: When an employee becomes irrationally reluctant to change computer systems, consider the possibility that he/she may be using the computer to cover a trail of embezzlement or other crimes. When that red flag is raised, bring in outside accountants to check through the data the employee is using. However, don't make accusations before an impropriety is discovered. Reason: Some honest employees are almost irrationally afraid of changing computer systems, too.

• Encourage managers to keep up a high level of computer literacy. Consider paying for managers' computer training courses at community colleges or computer-training institutes. It can also help to buy or lend them home computers so they can familiarize themselves with basic operations. Helpful: Software that coincides with a personal interest, such as programs that help with investments, word processing, playing chess, etc. Most of today's programs have excellent tutorial exercises that help newcomers.

Computer-knowledgeable managers can help lower-level workers make transitions to new software or hardware and answer questions as they arise, without the anxiety and resistance that often results in the absence of such hands-on guidance.

Supervisors who keep up their computer skills are also more likely to spot new software programs that are useful to the company.

Example: Managers who visit other companies or read trade journals often hear about new computer applications. But the knowledge is of little use unless they know enough about computers to understand how their own company could benefit.

Buy an effective anti-virus program and keep it updated. Nothing makes a company more reluctant to try new software than having experienced the destructive consequences of a virus. Until recently, viruses were transmitted mainly by free software available through computer bulletin boards. Now, malicious computer hackers have found other ways to transmit them, including hardware.

Self-defense: An anti-virus program that scans new software and eliminates viruses—when it finds them. The problem with anti-virus programs is that it's difficult for them to keep pace with new ploys from the malicious hackers.

Source: Brooks Hilliard, president, Business Automation Associates, a computer consulting firm, 2720 E. Thomas Rd., Phoenix 85016.

19. Tax Cutting Tactics

Tax Cutting Tactics

WHAT'S THE BEST TAX YEAR

Calendar-year companies with seasonal businesses should consider adopting a fiscal year for tax and financial reporting purposes. The year can end on the last day of any month and be timed so that:

• The financial statement looks best: High cash and low receivables.

• The company has more time to take inventories and utilize internal controls.

• The company gets more attention from its tax advisers (since it does not have to prepare its return during the advisers' busy season).

IRS permission is required and can usually be obtained by filing Form 1128. The IRS seldom objects to a switch when there's a good business reason behind it.

Common fiscal year-ends:

Manufacturing
Building supplies . . . . June
Electrical equipment . . . . September
Meat packing . . . . October
Office equipment . . . . June

Wholesaling
Auto accessories . . . . January
Groceries . . . . June
Plumbing supplies . . . . February
Paper . . . . June

Retailing
Books . . . . June
Department stores . . . . January
Furniture & appliances . . . . June
Hardware . . . . January

Services
Building contractors . . . . February
Real estate agencies . . . . September
Garages . . . . September
Warehouses . . . . March

TAXWISE TIMING FOR START-UP OF SUB S CORPORATION

New S corporations must adopt a calendar year. An exception is made only where there is a strong business purpose for the use of a fiscal year. Furthermore, if there is a more than 50 percent change in ownership, then a calendar year must be adopted or the S status ceases.

If the stockholders are confident that the period of losses will be brief, they should time the start-up so that the first taxable year will be very short. For example, start the business in September and the first fiscal year will only be three or four months. The stockholders get the benefit of the losses during the brief start-up period. Then they can terminate the Sub S status for the second fiscal year beginning January 1.

This can be most applicable to a service business that started as an unincorporated organization, keeping its books on the accrual basis. In that case, the accounts payable are negligible as most of the expenses are labor.

In a service business on the accrual basis, taxes are paid on profits represented by accounts receivable. As an example, let's say that such profits in the first year's accounts receivable amounted to $50,000; the profit equals that amount, and taxes are paid on it.

At this point, the business is restructured as an S corporation on the cash basis. But the old organization keeps collecting the cash on its existing accounts receivable, while the new Sub S company pays all expenses. Assume that three months' expenses come to approximately $50,000, and that billed but uncollected accounts receivable also come to $50,000. Cash to pay the bills of the Sub S company can be generated by transferring the $50,000 in accounts receivable collections from the old organization as an investment in the new business. Meanwhile, however—at least for the roughly 90-day period during which no cash collections are coming into the Sub S from its own new accounts receivable—the new company reports a loss.

Source: *Successful Tax Planning* by Edward Mendlowitz, Boardroom Books.

S CORPORATION MAGIC

New tax law has greatly expanded the number of ways in which Subchapter S corporations can be used to cut business and personal taxes. The new rules make it possible to use S corporations:

• In syndications and other money-raising ventures.

• In tax-shelter arrangements, subject to passive loss rules.

• As a tax-cutting tool for personal investments.

An S Corporation combines the tax benefits of personally owning a business with the legal protection of the corporate form. The income and deductions of the firm flow directly to the shareholders, in proportion to their stockholdings, to be claimed on their personal tax returns.

For example, business losses can be used to cut the tax on shareholder salaries. But, at the same time, shareholders have personal protection from corporate liabilities (such as lawsuits and unsecured debts).

The new law, for the first time, makes it possible for an S corporation to receive most of its income from investments in the form of rents, dividends and interest. It also allows different shares of an S corporation's stock to bear different voting rights. These changes create many new tax-saving opportunities.

Tax shelters: Until now, the typical tax shelter has been arranged as a limited partnership. The shelter business (such as oil drilling or equipment leasing) incurs losses in its early years, which flow through to the partners and offset other passive income.

Drawback: Each limited partnership must have at least one general partner who has unlimited liability for the shelter's debts. The remaining partners are limited partners who are liable only up to the amount they invest. But, since limited partners can't have any regular input into the management of the business, they have little say as to how their money is being spent. Furthermore, it's difficult to get out of a partnership because partnership interests aren't freely transferable.

S corporation advantages: Tax benefits flow through to investors in much the same way as in a partnership, and the same shelter advantages (subject to passive loss rules) result. But in addition:

• The corporation protects all the investors from personal liability.

• Since shareholders can be executives and managers of the firm, they can control how their money is spent.

• Shares of stock may be much easier to sell or give away if the investor wants to get out.

Business opportunities: Because most businesses incur tax losses during their start-up phase, syndicators and entrepreneurs can attract investors by starting up a new business in the S corporation form. The flow-through of losses will offset income from other shelters.

Similarly, a large, established business that wishes to expand (by purchasing new equipment or real estate, for example) can have some of its executives and shareholders form an independent S corporation to acquire the new property. The company can then lease the property on terms that are arranged to be advantageous to it and the new firm's shareholders.

Personal tax planning: Because an S corporation may now have passive income, it's possible for a top bracket investor to incorporate his personal portfolio. Shares of stock without voting rights may then be given to (or placed in trust for) other family members. At the same time, by keeping all the voting shares of the S corporation's stock, the taxpayer retains complete control over the investments. Of course, the same tactic is available to the top-tax-bracket owner of a family business.

Restrictions: There's no limit to the size of a company that elects S corporation status. But the company can have no more than 35 shareholders (with husband and wife counting as one). Another corporation can't be a shareholder.

While an S corporation's losses flow through to its shareholders, the amount of losses a shareholder can claim is generally limited to the amount he paid for his stock plus the amount of any loans he has made to the company. Excess losses can be carried forward and deducted from the company's future income.

The loss limitation rule means that S corporation status may not be best when company losses result from heavy interest payments on borrowings for which the shareholders aren't personally liable. Example: Real estate tax shelters, when a mortgage is secured by the property alone. Tactic: Shareholders can increase their deduction limit by substituting themselves for the company as the party primarily liable on the loan. (They're then assumed to have reloaned the borrowed amount to the company.) If the business is successful, they will never have to pay off the loan out-of-pocket. And since the owners of a closely held company are usually required to guarantee its major debts personally anyway, the substitution doesn't really increase their liability, even in the worst case.

There are other technical rules that apply to S corporations, making it necessary to consult with a tax professional to see if an S corporation election is a good idea in your case. But don't overlook the flexible planning opportunities that result from the liberalized new law.

Even an established company that's highly profitable may gain by electing S status:

• The election eliminates corporate income tax at the federal level, and sometimes at the state level as well.

• Income can be collected by shareholders at favorable rates if they have tax benefits or offsetting losses from other investment (such as tax shelters).

• The election eliminates the risk of two common IRS challenges, namely, that the company pays unreasonably large salaries or has accumulated too much in earnings in the business.

A firm that expects to lose money can elect S corporation status to pass its losses through to its owners. It can then return to regular corporate status when it returns to profitability.

Normally, S corporation status can't be elected more than once every five years. But the new law allows the company to reelect S corporation status now if it ended its previous election under prior law.

Source: Barry D. Sussman and Martin Galuskin, partners of Milgrom, Sussman, Galuskin & Co., CPAs, New York.

BUYING OUT A SHAREHOLDER AND DEDUCTING THE COST

One of the worst things that can happen to a closely held company is trouble among the shareholders. Buying out the dissenting shareholders can be very costly.

Some companies have tried to minimize the cost of a buyout by deducting it as a business expense. Problem: Company stock is a capital asset. And the cost of a capital asset is generally not deductible. Opportunity: Show that there is a compelling business reason for the buyout. The elimination of friction between shareholders is not enough. The company must show that without the buyout its business will be in jeopardy.

How the rule works:

• Winner. A company produced a patented product under license. But the conduct of one of the shareholders upset the patent owner, who threatened to cancel the license agreement if the shareholder was not removed from the company. So the company bought the shareholder out and deducted the cost. Court of Appeals decision: Without the license, the company would have been out of business. So there was an overriding business motive for the deal, and the deduction was ruled okay.

• Loser. A company wanted to close an unprofitable subsidiary. But it was contractually committed to buy out interest of the subsidiary's manager first. IRS objection: The company business was healthy on the whole. The fact that the company had made a bad investment in the subsidiary did not entitle it to specially favored tax treatment. The Court's decision: The fact that there was some business motive for the deal did not outweigh the fact that it was a purchase of capital stock. The deduction was disallowed.

Winner: *Five Star Mfg.*, USCA–5, 355 F.2d 724. Loser: *Harder Services*, 67 TC 585.

INTEREST DEDUCTIBLE; PRINCIPAL TOO

Employee stock ownership plans are a tax-saving means of corporate financing. The essence: A firm sets up a plan, which borrows money from a bank on a note guaranteed by the corporation. The plan uses this to buy stock from the corporation. The corporation makes contributions annually in cash or stock to the plan, for which it gets tax deductions. The contributions are used to pay off the bank loan. In effect, the corporation raises capital with tax-deductible dollars.

The ESOP can be used as a personal financial planning tool for the shareholder-owners of a close corporation who are otherwise locked into the corporation.

If the corporation redeems part of their shares in an ordinary way, they're almost certain to be taxed at ordinary income rates. And that transaction will be treated as a dividend distribution (which the shareholder pays taxes on) rather than a sale or exchange taxable at capital gains rates.

The corporation itself faces a major problem on redemptions. It must accumulate the necessary funds. They can be accumulated only out of after-tax dollars.

By interposing an ESOP, the picture changes dramatically. The shareholders have a market for their shares—the ESOP. The plan buys their shares with deductible contributions made with pre-tax dollars.

If there isn't enough money in the ESOP at the time to effect the purchase, then the plan borrows money from a bank in the procedure outlined above.

The same approach may be used by the shareholder's estate as a means of realizing cash on stock held by the estate, without getting dividend treatment.

Insurance angle: The ESOP, as an alternative to borrowing to raise cash to purchase stock from the estate, may, according to current thinking among practitioners, carry life insurance on a key shareholder. If the corporation itself were to carry such insurance to facilitate redemption, the premiums paid wouldn't be tax deductible. By interposing an ESOP, the premiums effectively become tax deductible, since they're paid by the Plan out of tax-deductible dollars contributed to it by the company.

Other benefits: The shareholder-executive will be able to participate in the plan himself and enjoy its benefits.

• His company will make tax-deductible contributions to the plan.

• He won't be taxed until the benefits are made available to him.

• He'll get favorable tax treatment on lump-sum distributions through a special averaging formula.

• The payout is required to be made in company stock and he won't be taxed on the unrealized appreciation in the stock over the cost to the plan until he sells the stock.

Chief problem. Valuation of shares on a sale to the ESOP. Another is the necessary distribution of corporate information to the employee-shareholders. If corporate progress isn't to the liking of employees, expect worker dissatisfaction.

The concepts are new. But the idea is one well worth exploring.

LOOPHOLES EVERYWHERE

Some federal tax loopholes are created intentionally to attract private investors into fields the government can't cope with. Example: Tax credits for investors in low-income housing. Other loopholes are accidental, created by flaws in the writing of legislation. The best of the new loopholes:

• Tax-favored long-term capital gains loophole. Capital gains are taxed at a top rate of 28%, while ordinary income is taxed at a top rate of 31%.

• Education savings bonds. Interest on US savings bonds issued after December 31, 1989 that are cashed in to pay for education expenses will be tax-free income for certain taxpayers. Main restrictions:

• Applies only to people who buy the bonds after reaching age 24.

• Interest is fully tax-free only for joint filers whose Adjusted Gross Income (AGI) is less than $60,000 ($40,000 for single filers). It is partially tax-free for joint filers with AGI under $90,000, and single filers with AGI under $55,000. These figures are adjusted annually for inflation.

• Early withdrawals from IRA accounts loophole. The 10% penalty tax on pre-age-59½ withdrawals from IRAs does not apply if the money is taken out in the form of an annuity, that is, in a series of payments over one's life expectancy or the joint life expectancies of a couple. This loophole can be put to good use if there is a fair amount of money in your IRA, say $100,000, from the rollover of a company pension plan.

Source: Edward Mendlowitz, partner, Mendlowitz Weitsen, CPAs, Two Pennsylvania Plaza, New York 10121. Mr. Mendlowitz is the author of several books, including *New Tax Traps/New Opportunities,* Boardroom Books, Springfield, New Jersey 07081.

BEST TAX LOOPHOLES

Taxes have become much more complicated in recent years. We've had the biggest tax cut in history followed by the biggest tax increase in history. And the stomping ground for tax professionals remains—loopholes. There are always loopholes. Here are the best:

Pension and profit-sharing plans: Probably the very best tax shelters. Amounts put into a pension plan are deductible by the business. Neither the original amount contributed, nor any of the earnings, are taxed until actually paid to the individual (presumably after his retirement, when he will be in a lower tax

bracket). For a business owner/officer, this amounts to a bonanza. He can put a share of the business profits aside for his retirement and see the government contribute a sizable additional amount (equal to the taxes saved by deducting the contribution).

For the self-employed: The limits for Keogh plan deductions are the the same as those that apply to regular qualified plans. This is a tremendous benefit for people who have unincorporated businesses, but new rules applicable to all plans require much more coverage for employees.

Charity loopholes: Instead of giving cash to charity, give securities that have increased in value. You get a charitable deduction for the present market value of the securities and you avoid paying tax on the gain. (Watch out for potential alternative minimum tax (AMT) liability.) Deferred giving: Get an immediate income tax deduction for a gift that won't be completed until sometime in the future by setting up a charitable remainder trust. In the meantime, you or your beneficiaries can enjoy the income from the assets you put into the trust.

Q-TIP trusts: You don't have to leave property outright to your spouse to take advantage of the estate tax marital deduction. By setting up a Qualified Terminable Interest Property Trust (Q-TIP trust), you can provide an income for your spouse for her lifetime, get an estate tax deduction for the amount put into the trust, and control who gets the trust assets when your spouse dies.

Source: Edward Mendlowitz, partner, Mendlowitz Weitsen, CPAs, New York.

HANDLE BIG GAINS

Stock market gains. Gains on real estate sales. Gifts and inheritances. Bonuses. Pension-plan distributions. There are many ways you can get windfalls, and all are taxed differently. Here are some ways to soften the tax bite on big gains.

Capital gains:

Any time you sell a capital asset (stocks,

bonds, real estate) for a profit, you have a capital gain.

Look for built-in losses in your portfolio: Did you buy oil stocks a year ago, when they were at their peak? If you sell, those losses can help shelter your other gains.

Real estate angles:

If you sell your house and reinvest the proceeds in another, more expensive one, within two years, you can defer paying tax on the gain. You can also defer tax on commercial property—if you swap with someone else rather than selling.

Gifts and inheritances:

Gifts are easy—the recipient pays no tax. For example, if your uncle gives you a $2,000 wedding present, you don't have to pay taxes on it. Exception: Capital gains on property you receive as a gift. Say I bought XYZ stock for $10 and gave it to you when it was worth $30. When you sell the stock, you pay tax on that $20 gain, as well as on any gain that has arisen since you received it.

Protect your beneficiaries: Rather than give away highly appreciated assets, keep them in your estate. When you die, the cost basis of everything in your estate is revalued to market value. When your beneficiaries sell the property, they will be taxed only on any gain that has arisen since they inherited it.

Although inheritances are tax free to the recipient for federal estate tax purposes, many states impose a 10% to 12% inheritance tax. The only way around this is to have the will probated in a state that doesn't have the tax. (Nevada, California, Florida are favorites.) But the person making the will must be a resident of that state. You may not have to spend more than six months of the year in the state to be considered a resident. The authorities will look at the broad picture to decide where you belong. Examples: Where are you registered to vote? What state is your driver's license from?

Bonuses:

If you can see a bonus coming ahead of time, you may be able to elect deferred compensation if your company allows it. That avoids paying tax until you actually get the money. (Your company may even pay you interest while you wait.) Caution: You must make the election before you have a right to the money.

If your employer has "cafeteria-plan" benefits, take tax-free fringes. Examples: Medical benefits, pension contributions, group-term life insurance. The plan must not discriminate among employees. Also: See if your company's stock-option plan qualifies for "incentive stock option" (ISO) treatment. If so, you pay tax only when you sell the stock, not when you exercise the option—and even then at capital gains rates. Be aware of any potential impact of the alternative minimum tax when exercising ISOs.

Lump-sum distributions:

You have a clear-cut choice with lump-sum payments from a retirement plan. Either take the money now and pay tax on it now, or roll it over (transfer it) within 60 days into an IRA or annuity and pay tax as you receive the income.

Source: Matthew Levitan, vice president and director of financial services, Dean Witter Reynolds, New York.

LOOPHOLES FOR BUSINESS OWNERS

The Tax Reform Act of 1986 closed many corporate-tax loopholes—however it created a few new ones. The best of them:

• Timing loophole I: Partnerships, S corporations and personal service corporations are required to use a taxable year that generally conforms to the taxable year of their owners—in most cases a calendar year. For these entities, it's no longer possible to get certain officer salary deferrals by having the company on a fiscal year while the owners are on a calendar tax year. Loophole: The deferral ability continues to be available to regular C corporations that are not personal service corporations.

• Timing loophole II: Arrange your own leverage buyout after you have become a legal resident in a low-tax state such as Florida. Reason for a leveraged buyout: You need personal funds, but all your money is tied up in the business. The company borrows the money then distributes it to you. Reason for moving to Florida: To avoid paying state income tax on the money you get in the buyout.

• Size loophole: Regular corporations can't use the cash method* of accounting if the business has average annual gross receipts of over $5 million. Loophole: Split the business into a number of corporations, each with annual sales of under $5 million.

*Cash method: You report as income only the money actually received, not the accounts receivable.

• Profit loophole: Corporations are required to pay tax on a certain amount of book profit. Loophole: Consider changing the method of reporting so that the company's financial statement will more closely agree with its tax return on book profit items.

• Incorporation loophole: Elect Subchapter S status for your business. S corporations pay no corporate taxes. Instead, income, deductions and credits are passed through to the shareholders and reported on their individual income tax returns. Starting in 1988, for the first time in many years, the top individual tax rate (31%) became lower than the top corporate tax rate (34%). Use S corporation status to take advantage of the tax rate spread. This could be the biggest new loophole for owners for closely held corporations.

• Pension loophole: Invest more of your pension-plan funds in equity investments. Loophole: Under tax reform, capital gains are taxed at the same rate as other income. There is no longer a tax disadvantage to holding capital gains property in your pension plan. You'll have nothing to lose, from a tax point of view, by investing pension funds in the stock market.

Source: Edward Mendlowitz, partner, Mendlowitz Weitsen, CPAs, Two Pennsylvania Plaza, New York 10121.

AVOIDING A GAIN ON INSURANCE PROCEEDS

When property is destroyed by fire or accident, the insurance proceeds may give you a taxable gain. But you can avoid being taxed on the gain by reinvesting the proceeds in similar property within two years (three years if the property is real estate used in business). Make sure that the first replacement property you pick is the right one. Recently, a taxpayer avoided tax by designating a replacement property, then filed an amended return to designate a different property that was more attractive. IRS ruling: Even though the replacement period had not expired, it was too late. The first pick was final.

DEDUCTIBLE GAMBLING LOSSES

A vacation trip may include time spent at a race track or casino. With luck, you might win big. Trap: Winnings are taxable, and winnings over $600 are reported to the IRS.

The tax can be cut by netting the gain against gambling losses, but few people document their losings. Result: A person who scores a big win may wind up paying tax on the gain without getting any benefit from his losses. He may wind up paying extra tax even if he lost more than he won over the entire year.

Better way: Keep tabs on your gains and losses. The IRS recommends wagering tickets, cancelled checks, credit records, bank withdrawal statements and credit receipts as proof. An accurate diary is also recommended.

Bottom line: The result of all kinds of gambling is netted at year-end to determine the size of any gain. So if you are planning to be lucky at all this year, keep records for the entire year.

Source: Dr. Robert S. Holzman, professor emeritus of taxation at New York University.

THE FINE DISTINCTION BETWEEN COLLECTOR, INVESTOR, AND DEALER CAN MAKE YOU OR BREAK YOU

For tax purposes, it makes a big difference whether you collect as a hobbyist, an investor or a dealer. And for most collectors, the best tax category to be in is investor.

Gains and losses:

Hobbyist: If you sell items from your collection at a profit, your gains are taxable and qualify for capital gains treatment. Losses: Not deductible.

Investor: Your profits qualify as capital gains and your losses as capital losses. Impact: Losses are deductible dollar for dollar against capital gains. If the losses exceed capital gains, losses are deductible from your other income, subject to a $3,000 per-year limit until the loss is used up.

In addition, your investment expenses are deductible subject to a 2% of AGI floor. These include insurance, safe deposit-box rent, subscriptions to collectors' journals, appraisal fees and depreciation on safes and other security systems.

Dealer: You don't get capital gains treatment, but you do get ordinary loss deductions (business losses).

A fine line between hobby and investment:

The distinction between hobbyist and investor is a very fine one. To maintain investor status:

• Make occasional sales. Collectors almost never make sales. Sell when items in your collection don't meet your investment needs or goals. Sell when you can get a good price. Sell to a dealer or to an auction house. Trap: Don't make sales at the retail level, and don't advertise in trade magazines. If you do that, you might be considered a dealer and lose capital gains treatment. Note: Your sales do not have to be at a profit.

• Keep detailed records. Make a major effort to keep really good records. If you do this, you're obviously not just a hobbyist. The extent of the detail may be the deciding factor whether an item is bought for hobby or investment purposes.

Bottom line: The IRS follows a simple rule: If you spent it, you should be able to prove it. Without proof, you cannot fight. And without good records, you won't be able to convince the IRS that you're collecting as an investor.

Source: Edward Mendlowitz, partner, Mendlowitz Weitsen, CPAs, New York.

INCOME-SHIFTING OPPORTUNITIES AFTER TAX REFORM

Traditional family income shifting techniques have been radically changed, for the worse, by tax reform. It's now harder than ever for taxpayers to spread income among the family as a tax-saving device. The options have been cut back for shifting income from higher-tax-bracketed family members to those with lower tax brackets (so the income is taxed at the lower rate).

Wiped out by tax reform: Clifford trusts allowed a high-income taxpayer to put an asset in a short-term trust set up for the benefit of a child. The child was taxed on the income at his low tax rate. The parent got the asset back at the end of the trust term. New law: Income earned in the trust is taxed to the person who set up the trust.

Gifts of income-producing assets allowed high-income taxpayers to give their child cash or investments. The child was taxed on the income from these investments at his/her lower tax bracket. New law: Unearned income (income other than wages or salary) of a child who is not age 14 by the end of the year will be taxed at the parent's tax rate.

Loopholes in the new law:

• Give generously to children age 14 or older because they have escaped the new rules. Income from gifts to children at this age is taxed in the child's lower tax bracket. Strategy: In the year your child is going to turn 14, start giving him gifts so he can accumulate money for college. As long as your child is 14 by the close of the tax year, he is exempt from the new rules. Smart gift: Appreciated securities that you were thinking about selling. Give them to your child and let the child sell the securities. The gain will be taxed at his/her lower tax bracket rather than your higher one.

• Take advantage of the $1,200 allowance. The first $600 earned on an income-producing gift may be offset by the child's standard deduction. The next $600 earned on income-producing property given to your child is taxed at his lower tax rate.

• Hire your children in your business.

Salary earned by children of any age is safe from the new rules (except for the loss of the personal exemption). The children must really work for you, and you must pay them a reasonable wage. Double advantage: Your business gets a deduction for the wages. Your child, depending on how much he earns, will pay little or no tax in his low income bracket. And, sole proprietorships don't have to pay Social Security for a child under age 18.

• Refinance your home to pay for your child's education. Interest on student loans has been phased out as a tax deduction for you and your child. Loophole: Convert this nondeductible interest into a deduction. How: Take out an equity loan on your home and use this money instead of a student loan to pay for college. You can deduct interest on a home equity loan up to $100,000, provided that sum doesn't exceed fair market value less acquisition debt.

• Give "deferred income" gifts to children under age 14. These are gifts for which taxable income won't have to be reported for many years, preferably until the child reaches age 14. Examples:

Low-income securities. These usually don't pay large dividends over the years, but will appreciate in value and sell at a large profit by the time the child reaches age 14.

US Savings Bonds. Your child won't have to pay tax until the bond is cashed in (unless the child elects to report each year's income as it is earned).

And don't forget the old folks:

• Buy a home for your parents. Elderly parents are likely to be in a lower tax bracket and wouldn't get much of a tax benefit from the purchase of a small home or condo. Consider buying the home or condo and renting it to them. This will create tax deductions for you while you are providing them with a place to live. You can only deduct up to $25,000 of losses from the home. However, this $25,000 loss allowance is phased out on adjusted gross income from $100,000 to $150,000.

• Give appreciated securities to your parents instead of cash if you are supporting them. They can cash in the securities and pay tax on the appreciation in their low tax bracket. You'll avoid paying tax in your high tax bracket. Caution: A large gain could push your parents into a higher bracket.

Source: Edward Mendlowitz, partner, Mendlowitz Weitsen, CPAs, New York.

TAX BREAKS IN RENTING A HOME YOU CAN'T SELL

Taxpayers who relocate often have trouble selling their old home before they move into a new one. To avoid paying for two places, they rent out the old home. Here are the tax consequences of these living arrangements...

• The taxpayer has two years from the time he moves out of his home to sell the old home and buy another and still preserve the tax break on replacement residences.

The break: Your gain on the sale of the house is deferred for tax purposes if, within two years after you move, you buy and live in another home that costs at least as much as the old one.

• If you rent the old house out to a tenant, you can claim deductions for expenses involved, thus shielding the rental income from tax. Key: You must sell this house and buy a new one within two years to get tax deferral*

There are almost no exceptions to the two-year rule. It's a rigid rule. You must replace your old home within two years or you lose the right to defer tax both on that home and any others on which tax has been deferred. Taxpayers who waited longer than two years lost the right to defer in the following cases...

• The real estate market took a downturn and the replacement period ended.

• The new house was destroyed by fire before the new owners could move in and the replacement period expired.

• The taxpayer was hospitalized and the replacement period expired.

• Two deals fell through and the replacement period expired.

• FHA's authority to insure mortgages had

*One way around the two-year rule: Form a personal corporation and sell the house to the corporation. Because a personal corporation is a separate taxable entity, tax deferral will be allowed on the sale (if it's a *bona fide* sale).

temporarily expired so the lender refused to close and the period expired.

In all these cases, taxes were due on the sale of the old residence. The courts will allow no excuses. The Tax Court has said that "the Courts are without authority to weigh the merits of the events precipitating delay to determine whether the time limits may be waived or extended."**

You can claim deductions up to the amount of the rental income. These deductions include mortgage interest, property taxes, maintenance, and even depreciation.

Limit: Your total expenses must not exceed the rental income you receive on the place. You can depreciate to shelter positive cash flow, but you cannot show a loss on Schedule E or C. If you do, you've turned the place into an income property—a business—and you will lose the right to defer tax on the profit when you sell. Note: Mortgage interest and property taxes are always fully tax-deductible, even if they exceed rental income.

**James A. Henry, TC Memo 1982–469.

Source: Jack Killough, tax analyst, relocation and real estate, The Hessel Group/Runzheimer International, Wilton, Connecticut 06897. Mr. Killough is the author of *The Tax Saver: A Tax Guide for Homesellers and Relocated Employees*, published by Runzheimer International, Chicago.

MINOR INCOME SHIFTING

For a child under age 14, the first $600 of income from property given by his/her parents may be offset by the child's standard deduction. The next $600 is taxed at the child's tax rate. Investment income over $1,200 is taxed at the parents' top rate.

HOW HIRING YOUR KIDS CAN SHELTER INCOME

If you have children old enough to work and responsible enough to earn their pay, you can cut thousands of dollars off the family tax bill by putting the kids on your payroll. The wages you pay will be shifted from your tax return to the children's returns, where as much as $5,600 a year for each child can escape tax entirely.

A child can earn $5,600 each year without

paying any federal income tax by utilizing:

• The standard deduction ($3,700 in 1993, annually indexed for inflation), plus

• The $2,000 that can be invested in an Individual Retirement Account (IRA).

If the child earns more than this amount during the year, the excess will be taxed at the lowest tax rates.

The benefits are almost as great, even if the child has substantial income of his own—for instance, a trust fund from grandparents. In that case, he already pays taxes (at your rates, if he is under 14) and has used up $600 of his standard deduction. But the balance of the standard deduction and the $2,000 IRA deduction are not available for "passive" income (interest, dividend, etc.). If, however, you put the child on the payroll, he can earn up to the standard deduction amount, apply it to these two items, and pay no tax on the money. The wages are "earned" income and qualify for the standard deduction and IRA. Bonus: The income earned on the IRA funds is sheltered from current tax.

The wages you pay can be generous, but must not be unreasonably high for the kind of work the child does. And the child must have genuine duties. Recommended: Have the child keep a log showing the hours he's worked and what he's done.

Meet the obligations of an employer. You won't have to withhold and pay Social Security taxes if the child is under age 18, but any state or local payroll taxes may apply. You needn't withhold income tax, as long as the child files Form W-4, certifying he had no tax liability the previous year and expects none for the current year.

"CHILD LABOR" AND THE IRS

• A business owner paid his three children (ages 7, 11, and 12) for the part-time work they did for The Business. He deducted their salaries, a total of $8,400, including $2,100 for the 7-year-old. The IRS ruled that 90% of the children's pay was unreasonable and not deductible, including the entire amount paid to the

7-year-old. Tax Court: For the father. Deduction allowed with only a slight reduction of the youngest child's salary. Key: The children actually performed a number of duties, including clean-up and office services. Value of the 7-year-old's services: $1,900.

Source: *Walt E. Eller,* 77 TC 934.

• A professor paid salaries to his children for helping out with his correspondence, filing, answering telephones and cleaning. They did all the work at his home. Tax Court: Deduction allowed for the filing and correspondence, but since his home wasn't a "home office" the cleaning wasn't deductible. And, the telephone answering salary wasn't deductible because there were no records separating personal calls from business calls.

Source: *L.J. Moriarity,* TC Memo 1984-249.

NEPOTISM PAYS

A favorite tax-planning tactic is to have a minor child work for the faily-owned business. The first $3,700 (indexed for inflation) earned by the child is tax-free, and further income is taxed at low rates. In addition, the company gets a deduction for the child's salary. Now, a dramatic taxpayer victory shows just how effective this tactic can be.

The facts: The taxpayers owned a mobile-home park and hired their three children, aged 7, 11 and 12, to work there. The children cleaned the grounds, did landscaping work, maintained the swimming pool, answered phones and did minor repair work. The taxpayers deducted over $17,000 that they paid to the children during a three-year period. But the IRS objected, and the case went to trial. Court's decision: Over $15,000 of deductions were approved. Most of the deductions that were disallowed were attributable to the 7-year-old. But even $4,000 of his earnings were approved by the court.

Key: The children actually performed the work for which they were paid. And the work was necessary for the business. The taxpayers demonstrated that if their children had not done the work, they would have had to hire someone else to do it.

Source: Irving Blackman, Blackman Kallick Bartelstein, CPAs, Chicago.

DIVORCE PLANNING

Robert and Ethel Burkle were married for 36 years. Robert built quite a business in that time. When they divorced, Ethel received annual payments equal to a percentage of Robert's income from the business and a $50,000 note payable on Robert's death. When Robert died, Ethel claimed the $50,000 was tax-free property distribution recognizing her contribution to the business.

Tax Court: The $50,000 was alimony that was taxable to Ethel and deductible by Robert's estate.

Key facts: The note was payable only if Ethel survived Robert and didn't remarry. If it really had represented an interest in the business, it wouldn't have been subject to such restrictions.

Source: *Ethel H. Burkle,* TC Memo 1986-394.

TAX SHIFTING IN THE FAMILY

A husband and wife owned property that the husband used in his business. The husband paid his wife rent for using her half of the property and treated the rent as a business expense. The couple then filed separate returns. The rent was deducted on the husband's return as a business expense and treated as income on the wife's return. But since the wife was in a much lower tax bracket, the result was a net tax saving. IRS ruling: The arrangement is OK.

IRS Revenue Ruling 74209.

DANGEROUS FAMILY LOANS

Parents who don't press their children to re-pay money they've lent them can fall into a trap. Recent example: A father lent his child $500,000. In return, he got an interest-bearing note payable on demand. Three years later, the father still hadn't demanded repayment. Problem: At the end of those three years, the father was legally barred (by the statute of limitations) from enforcing the debt. Result: The loan plus interest automatically turned into a taxable gift to the child.

INTRA-FAMILY LOANS

The IRS disallowed the deduction a taxpayer claimed for interest paid on a loan from his brother. IRS: The loan was not genuine because there was no repayment schedule or security. Tax Court: The taxpayer had signed a document acknowledging the debt and promising to pay interest at a set rate. This was enough to establish a genuine loan, even though there was no specific repayment schedule. The interest was deductible. Catch: The taxpayer could not deduct the interest paid on similar loans from his sister and mother, because there was no written document evidencing the debt.

Source: *Badi Zohoury,* TC Memo 1983-597.

MULTIPLE FAMILY SUPPORT

Suppose you're chipping in with other family members to support a dependent relative. It may seem that no one is entitled to a dependency exemption because no one provided more than half of the dependent's support. Election: If all of you sign a multiple support declaration (Form 2120) you can take turns claiming the dependency exemption for the relative you're supporting. Requirements: The people signing, as a group, must provide more than 50% of the dependent's support. And, the person claiming the exemption must furnish more than 10% of the support.

Source: Edward Mendlowitz, partner, Mendlowitz Weitsen, CPAs, New York 10017.

DON'T MARRY: SAVE TAX ON $125,000

Two adults, each owning a home, get married. Their plan is to sell one house and live in the other. Problem: Loss of tax-free capital gain on one residence.

Homeowners over 55 are allowed to sell a house without paying any tax on the capital gain up to $125,000. But this tax break can be used only once in a lifetime. And if it is used once by a married couple, it cannot be used again by either spouse.

The only way to have two tax-free sales is for them to sell both houses before getting married (if they are both over 55). If they get married first and then sell one house, they forfeit the chance for a tax-free sale of the other.

ALL IN THE FAMILY

A taxpayer who owned a duplex lived in one unit with his wife and rented the other to his daughter. He deducted a $2,000 business loss on the rental unit, which the IRS disallowed.

IRS reasoning: A father renting to his daughter isn't renting for profit. Thus, his deductions couldn't exceed his income from the unit.

Tax Court: The full loss was deductible. The taxpayer had a genuine intention to make a profit from owning and renting the unit. The daughter was paying a reasonable rent. Even if the taxpayer had rented to a stranger, he couldn't have rented the place for more.

Source: *J.V. Keenon.* TC Memo 1982-144.

BEWARE THE DOUBLE TRAP

The Tax Reform Act of 1986 made sure that dependents can no longer take the personal exemption for themselves if they are claimed as a dependent on their parents' income tax return. Double trap: Both the child and the parent are deprived of all or part of the personal exemption on joint returns showing over $150,000 of income for married couples ($100,000 for singles). Personal exemption are phased out above this income.

BUYING RELATIVES' TAX LOSSES

If you are a high-bracket taxpayer and have a relative with little or no taxable income, consider taking advantage of a tax law provision that allows you, in effect, to acquire your immediate relatives' deductible losses.

How it works: If a member of your immediate family sells property to you at a loss, that loss can't be deducted. But, when you turn around and sell that property, you don't have to pay tax on any gain unless the gain is more than your family member's loss. Even then, only the portion of the gain that exceeds the previous loss is taxable.

Example: John White's mother is very ill. She has some income from dividends and a modest pension. But her deductible medical expenses are so high that her taxable income is zero. Her portfolio includes 100 shares of Consolidated Conglomerate that she bought at $35 a share. The current price is $11. If Mrs. White sells on the open market, she'll have a $2,400 loss that won't save a penny in taxes. If John buys the stock, he can hold on to it until the price recovers. And although he bought the shares at $11, he won't have a taxable gain until the stock hits $35 again.

Added twist: John can give his mother a note for the purchase price of the stock with a reasonable interest rate, say 10%. The money can help defray Mrs. White's medical costs, while John gets an interest deduction.

Who can do it: This special rule applies on any transaction between you and your parents, grandparents, children, grandchildren, brother, sister, or any corporation in which you own more than 50% (by value) of the shares.

WHEN A WIDOW CAN FILE A JOINT RETURN

A widow or widower with dependent children living at home can qualify as a *surviving spouse* and file using advantageous joint return tax rates for each of the two taxable years after the year in which the spouse died. Check filing status box 5 on your Form 1040.

HOW MARRIAGE MAY SAVE TAXES

The privilege of filing a joint federal income tax return is available only to people who are legally married. In some years, filing a joint return is advantageous. In others, it isn't.

Usually a joint return works out better. But there are a couple of situations in which separate returns can save taxes. Consider filing separately in these situations:

• The spouse with the lower income has very large medical expenses. The expenses may be deductible on a separate return. On a joint return they would have to exceed 7.5% of the couple's combined adjusted gross income (AGI) to be deductible.

• One spouse has large casualty losses. If separate returns are filed, the loss is reduced by only 10% of the income of the spouse claiming the loss. On a joint return, casualty losses must be reduced by 10% of combined AGI.

Warning: Don't file separate returns unless you've figured the tax both ways and are certain you'll benefit by filing separately. Remember, the rates paid by married people filing separately are the highest rates that anyone pays.

Estate tax savings:

A major tax advantage of being married is the ''unlimited'' marital deduction for gift and estate taxes. An unlimited amount of cash or other assets can be left by one spouse to the other completely free of federal estate tax, so long as the property goes to the survivor without strings attached.

Source: Dr. Robert S. Holzman, professor emeritus of taxation at New York University.

TROUBLE WITH THE IRS

If you've been having trouble with the IRS—say you owe back taxes from a business that failed—it may be a good idea for you to file this year's return listing your spouse's name first. The IRS computers are programmed to pick up the Social Security number of the spouse whose name appears first on the return. By filing under your spouse's name, there's a good chance that your refund won't be held up.

Source: Edward Mendlowitz, partner, Mendlowitz Weitsen, CPAs, New York 10017.

NEGLECTED LOOPHOLES FOR DIVORCED COUPLES

Divorce settlements reached in anger, or by picking numbers out of the air, can have disastrous tax consequences. All too often the IRS ends up with too big a piece of the pie. But this won't happen to a couple who carefully work out in advance the tax implications of their settlement.

Alimony loopholes:

Alimony paid under a divorce decree or written separation agreement is deductible by the husband and taxable to the wife. But child support, lump-sum property settlement payments, and the wife's legal fees (if paid by the husband) are not deductible, and they don't have to be reported as income by the wife. The loophole: In a properly worded agreement the legal fees can be made deductible by including them as alimony.

Lawyer's fees: If the husband agrees to pay the wife's divorce lawyer, estimate the fee and add that amount to the alimony to be paid to the wife. The husband can then deduct the amount—as alimony. The wife includes it in her taxable income and uses the funds to pay her lawyer.

Income after taxes:

Where the husband has a large taxable income and the nonworking wife has little or none, it makes sense to have all payments treated as alimony. Reason: Income is shifted from the husband's high-tax bracket to the wife's lower bracket.

In negotiating a settlement, the parties must calculate the income that each will have after taxes. Factors that affect after-tax income:

• The parent having custody is entitled to claim the children as dependents for tax purposes. He or she may waive this right by filing a consent to allow the exemption to the other parent. A copy of the consent to waive the exemption must be attached to the father's return.

• A parent who has a child living with him or her can file tax returns at lower head-of-household rates.

• Both parents might have head-of-household filing status. This could happen if the younger children live with the mother, but an older child, who is away at college, lists his father's home as his regular residence and stays with him when home on vacation.

• Child support normally stops when the kids become independent. Alimony often goes on until the wife remarries.

• Professional fees for advice about the tax aspects of a settlement are deductible. Fees for nontax services cannot be deducted. Make sure your advisers submit two bills, one for tax services and the other for nontax matters.

Alimony traps:

Alimony must be paid as a result of a written agreement or a court order, otherwise it won't be deductible.

Informal payments that a husband gives his wife after he moves out of the house, but before there is any written agreement or court order, are not deductible. Solution: Get a formal written agreement from the wife that amounts paid to her as alimony during negotiations are taxable to her. To protect her position, state in the agreement that she is not giving up the right to demand bigger payments later.

Vague wording: Too often judges don't consider tax consequences when wording an order. Vaguely worded orders that don't specify the exact nature of the payments simply invite the IRS to interpret the language in their favor. Always carefully check the wording of the order.

Reporting requirements: The spouse who claims an alimony deduction must show the social security number of the spouse receiving the alimony on his or her return, or face penalties. The payee spouse must provide the number. Penalty for failure on either spouse: $50.

The last joint return:

Even though they're separated, a couple who are still legally married on the last day of the year have the right to file either a joint return or as married filing separately.

Pitfall: Failing to provide in the separation agreement that a joint return will be filed and that both spouses will sign it. Without such an agreement, the husband's income will be taxed at the highest rates. If a couple agrees to file a joint return, they should also agree in advance how they will apportion the tax owed or share the tax savings.

IRA benefit. The spouse receiving the alimony can treat it as earned income for IRA purposes. Maximum benefit for a non-working divorcee: $2,000.

Source: Edward Mendlowitz, partner, Mendlowitz Weitsen, CPAs, New York.

DIVORCE AFTER TAX REFORM

The 1986 tax reform law has profound implications for divorcing couples. It is more important than ever for couples involved in a matrimonial dispute to seek the advice of a knowledgeable tax professional. Special tax considerations:

• Changing tax rates. While alimony is still fully deductible by the spouse who pays it, lower income tax rates diminish the value of the deduction. Husbands, who traditionally pay alimony, may balk at making alimony a big part of the divorce settlement. And because of the increased tax on capital gains, they may be more disposed to give low-basis, appreciated property, such as the family home, stock, and interest in a business, etc., to the other spouse as part of the settlement. Reason: The spouse who gives the property would avoid paying increased tax on the gain, which could be as high as 28%. The spouse who receives the property could sell it and have the gain taxed in her lower bracket. The tax saving would then be factored into the amount of the settlement.

• Reduced value of home-mortgage interest deductions, caused by lower income tax rates, may be an additional incentive for one spouse to give up his or her interest in the family home.

• Increased exemptions for dependents makes the right to claim children as dependents after a divorce a more valuable bargaining ship. Tax reform almost doubled the amount of the dependency exemption, raising it from $1,080 per dependent to $2,350 for 1993 (indexed for inflation). (Under 1984 tax law, the spouse awarded custody of the children is automatically entitled to claim the dependency exemptions. But these can be signed over to the non-custodial spouse.) Spouses may consider trading dependency exemptions for increased child support. Flip side: High-income spouses may not want dependency exemptions, since the exemptions could cause the spouse to pay more income tax. Starting in 1991, the benefit of the exemptions is phased out for taxable income above the following breakpoints... $162,700 for joint returns, $135,600 for head-of household, and $108,450 for single taxpayers.

• Medical expenses. The 1984 tax act allows either divorced parent to treat a child as a dependent for purposes of claiming medical expense deductions. The 1986 act increased the floor on medical expense deductions to 7.5% of adjusted gross income (from 5%). Planning point: Have the low-bracket spouse pay the medical expenses. That way, more of the expenses are likely to be deductible.

• Legal fees. The portion of a divorce lawyer's fee that is for tax advice is deductible (if separately stated on the bill) as a miscellaneous deduction. But you may claim miscellaneous deductions only to the extent they exceed 2% of your adjusted gross income. Planning point: Bunch your miscellaneous deductions into the year you pay the divorce lawyer, so that as much as possible of the bill will be deductible.

• Alimony complication. The 1984 tax act imposed recapture rules to prevent nondeductible property settlement payments from being deducted as alimony. Excess up-front alimony payments (those that exceed the limits set by the law) must be added back into income by the spouse who paid them. These complicated recapture rules were completely revised by the 1986 Tax Act. Bottom line: This change in the law is reason in itself to get expert tax advice on your divorce settlement.

Source: Sidney Kess, retired, KPMG Peat Marwick, 55 E. 52 St., New York 10055.

TAX EVICTION

A husband who was ordered by the court to vacate the marital home and who was then slapped with a temporary order to pay alimony and child support still could not use the lower tax rates available to single persons. Reason: A person who has lived under the same roof with his separated spouse during the taxable year and is still married can file as single only if legally separated under a decree of divorce or separate maintenance. A temporary order covering alimony, child support and occupation of the residence is not a legal separation.

SWAPPING PROPERTY

Garcia had real estate that, for tax purposes, he wanted to exchange rather than sell. But the person who wanted the property had nothing that Garcia wanted. Other parties were contacted, and after a series of deals involving three properties, four parties, and several escrow arrangements, the taxpayer managed to exchange his property for another rental property. The IRS held that the transaction was a sale because cash had been involved in the escrow arrangements. But the Tax Court disagreed with the IRS. Reason: The final result was that the taxpayer had in fact exchanged one property for another.

TAX FREE EXCHANGE OF REAL ESTATE

By far the most common tax-free method of disposing of real estate is the like-kind exchange. "Like-kind" does not mean that the properties must be identical. Improved real estate, like an apartment house, can be exchanged for raw land, provided both properties were held for investment purposes or trade or business purposes. The exchange may include cash or other additional payment, called "boot," to equalize the value of the exchange. By continuing to exchange, the seller can defer paying taxes and reinvest the full amount of capital in new properties. In effect, the IRS is giving the taxpayer an interest-free loan. Be aware, however, that a tax-free exchange applies to profits and losses alike, so if you have a loss and make an exchange, the loss will not be recognized.

It is not uncommon to find a three- or four-party like-kind exchange. For example, A has a property that B wants to buy. A will not sell outright but will swap it with B if he will buy the properties owned by C and D and include them in the exchange. B must first buy the two properties and then swap them with A for the property he wishes to own. One caveat: never try to short-circuit the whole mess by having C and D transfer their properties directly to A. For the best possible savings of an extra transfer tax you may lose the tax-free status of the transfer.

You may swap real estate for a lease interest and still have a like-kind tax-free transaction. As long as the lease is for more than 30 years it is treated as an interest in real property.

Let's look at the case of Mr. A who owns an apartment building worth $2,500,000 in which he has an equity of $1,600,000. There is an assignable mortgage on the building of $900,000. Mr. B has a shopping center worth $3,000,000 in which he has a $2,000,000 equity and a $1,000,000 mortgage. Mr. A and Mr. B want to exchange properties. There is an equity difference of $400,000 between Mr. A's apartment building and Mr. B's shopping center. Mr. A will have to pay "boot" of $400,000, which can consist of cash, notes, property, or anything that Mr. A and Mr. B can agree upon. For simplicity we shall say that lower and higher rate mortgages have been taken into account and the mortgage figures above are net after premiums or discounts.

First, net out the mortgages. Mr. A was

relieved of a $900,000 mortgage and Mr. B of a $1,000,000 mortgage. Mr. B was relieved of a net $100,000 of mortgage and this gets added onto his $400,000 "boot" for tax purposes to make it total $500,000. (Note that if B had a $2,000,000 mortgage he would not make the swap because he would have a $1,500,000 "boot"!)

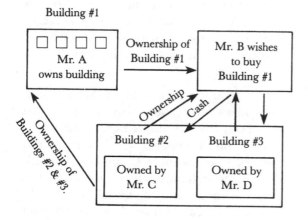

Building #1

1. Mr. B wishes to buy Building #1 owned by Mr. A.

2. Mr. A will not sell outright because of tax on his appreciated value but will swap Building #1 for Buildings #2 and #3.

3. Mr. B buys Building #2 and Building #3 from their owners and pays the transfer tax. He now owns Buildings #2 and #3.

4. Mr. B swaps Buildings #2 and #3 with Mr. A for Building #1.

If the value of the qualified property transferred plus the boot received is greater than the calculated basis in the property transferred, a gain is recognized but not in excess of the boot.

We apply the following formula:

Old Basis in the Property Swapped
1. Increased by basis in the boot
2. Decreased by any money received; and
3. Increased by any gain; and
4. Decreased by loss on boot; and
5. Increased by additional mortgage liabilities; equals Basis in new property.

Don't panic, as this is not really very dif-

ficult; it is purely mechanical. In our example, let us say that Mr. A will pay the $400,000 difference in the "boot" by giving Mr. B stock he bought for $500,000, which is now worth $400,000. Here is the result of our formula:

	For Mr. A	For Mr. B
Old basis in property swapped	$600,000	$1,500,000
1. Plus basis in "boot"	500,000	– 0 –
2. Minus money received	– 0 –	(400,000)
3. Plus gain on transaction	– 0 –	500,000
4. Minus loss on "boot"	(100,000)	– 0 –
5. Plus additional mortgage liabilities	100,000	– 0 –
Basis in new property	$1,100,000	$1,600,000

Mr. A will recognize his $100,000 loss on the stock part of his "boot." He will take over the shopping center with a $1,100,000 basis. Mr. B will take over the apartment house with a $1,600,000 basis. Mr. B will have to pay a tax on the amount of his gain realized up to the fair market value of the "boot" Mr. B paid $1,500,000 for the shopping center and swapped it for $3,000,000 so he has a gain of $1,500,000. This gain will be recognized up to the value of the "boot" (or $500,000). Don't worry if you can't immediately repeat all of this formula. Your accountant will do the actual work. Just be aware that in these swaps there are changes in basis and potential taxes in the "boot."

Source: *How to Make Money in Real Estate,* Steven James Lee, Boardroom Books, Millburn, NJ.

ESTIMATED-TAX PLANNING

As year-end approaches, individuals often find themselves facing an estimated-tax penalty for underwithholding. To avoid this: Have your employer withhold the necessary additional tax before the end of the year. The total amount withheld will be prorated by the IRS over the entire year.

Example: You had originally calculated your estimated-tax liability to be $4,000. You paid $1,000 for each of the first three quarters and plan to pay the final $1,000 on January 15. But it now becomes clear that you should have figured on an estimated tax of $6,000 and paid $1,500 each quarter. Solution: Have the extra

$2,000 withheld from your salary before the year ends. Then $500 (one-fourth of the amount withheld) will be credited against your estimated tax liability for each quarter. Result: The penalties will have been avoided. Important: If you simply add that $2,000 to your last quarter's estimated tax payment, you'll still face penalties for the first three quarters.

Suggestion: If the additional liability is the result of some end-of-the-year income you didn't anticipate, you may be able to take advantage of an exception to the underestimation penalty provisions. There is one other exception that you may be able to qualify for, particularly if last year's tax bill was lower than this year's. Review these with your adviser.

Warning: You can't use this exception to the penalty provisions if your Adjusted Gross Income is more than $75,000, increased by more than $40,000 over the previous year, and you paid estimated taxes in any one of the three previous years.

GETTING MAXIMUM PROTECTION FROM YOUR ACCOUNTANT

Something's wrong if all you've been getting from your accountant is a tax return every April and a bill. An accountant who isn't coming up with new suggestions each year for you to mull over and discuss with him is not doing anything for you.

More than the basics:

Beyond taxes: The advice you get from a first-rate accountant will not be limited to your needs this year. He will be planning for the long term, for your retirement and after. Nor will his advice be limited to tax preparation and tax savings. Expect from your accountant: An evaluation of your insurance coverage, the pros and cons of various types of life insurance, guidance in retirement and estate planning, personal financial statements for bank loans or divorce settlements, evaluations of investment advice from other professional services, help with record keeping for your business and help in getting credit.

Look to your accountant for objectivity: For example, expect him to explain to you the advantages and disadvantages of various kinds of life insurance without recommending any specific company or policy. Expect him to explain the risk in any investment or aggressive tax strategy and to avoid recommending particular investments (such as a specific tax shelter program).

Is he doing his job?

A crackerjack accountant knows his clients. He's looking for ways to transfer knowledge and experience. When he puts a tax-saving plan into action for Smith, he remembers that Jones is in a similar situation and might benefit from the plan.

Your accountant is doing his job when:

• You are kept informed of changes in the tax law.

• Periodically you are asked if there has been any change in the information originally given to him, especially personal data.

• It is clear that your file has been reviewed before your session with him.

• He regularly presents tax-planning suggestions even if they were rejected in the past. For example: Isn't it time you reconsidered getting into a tax shelter? Have you done any more thinking about a gift program for your children?

• His advice is objective and within his range of competence. Beware of an accountant, or any financial adviser, who is dogmatic about a specific investment.

A two-way street:

There are a number of things you can do to get the most from your accountant:

• Keep him informed about changes in essential personal and financial data. For example, if you don't tell him that you've started to support an aged parent, he isn't likely to recommend setting up a way to use gifts to support him.

• Organize information as efficiently as possible. This saves his time and your money. If he sends you an income tax questionnaire, use that to organize the necessary information.

• Be sure the information is complete. The bane of an accountant's existence is to be told after he's prepared a tax return about deductions the client forgot to mention earlier.

Changing firms:

The best way to find a new accountant is through recommendations from satisfied clients. When you switch accountants, the greater knowledge and capability of the new one should be obvious.

You can judge a new accountant by the number of questions he asks you. How probing is he? How creative? Avoid an accountant who gives off-the-cuff advice without knowing anything about your personal financial situation.

Source: Leon M. Nad, national director, technical tax services, Price Waterhouse, New York.

YOUR FAULT OR ACCOUNTANT'S FAULT?

Most individuals get professional advice when preparing their personal tax returns. But when a return contains a mistake, a taxpayer cannot avoid a negligence penalty by simply showing that the return was reviewed by a professional. The taxpayer must also show that the adviser was competent and given all the information needed to fill out an accurate return.

Suggestion: Keep a careful record of all the information given to the adviser. This is protection against the unfortunate fate suffered by a taxpayer in a recent case. He had used an adviser to prepare his return. But years later, when the return was challenged, he couldn't prove what information he had given his adviser to work with. The Tax Court doubted that the adviser had been provided with adequate records. Therefore, it held the taxpayer liable for negligence penalties.

NEGLECTED TAX LOOPHOLES FOR HOMEOWNERS

It's common knowledge that the Tax Code is more generous to homeowners than to tenants. Deductions for mortgage interest, real estate taxes and casualty losses amount to hidden tax subsidies for home ownership. Two other well-known tax benefits:

• Anyone who sells a principal residence can postpone the tax on the profits. Requirement: Buy a new residence that costs more than the selling price of the old one within 24 months before or after the old residence is sold.

• Anyone age 55 or older who sells a home that has been the principal residence for at least three of the previous five years can elect never to pay tax on the first $125,000 of profit from the sale. If a married couple sell their home, only one of the spouses need be 55 or over to qualify for this tax break. But this election can be made only once in a lifetime. And if either member of a married couple has previously made the election, both are barred from making it again, even if the previous election was made before they got married.

Uncommon tax angles:

Tax-free cash when you sell: The key to postponing taxes when you sell a residence is the purchase price of your new residence. As long as you trade up to a more expensive home, and do it within the specified period, there's no current tax on the transaction, no matter how much cash you draw out of the deal. In order to make this work, you simply have to minimize the down payment on the new house. Of course, that means a higher mortgage and larger interest payments on your new home. But the interest is deductible. And you'll have tax-free use of the cash in the meantime. How it works:

Mr. and Mrs. Brown bought their home for $35,000 in 1967. By 1984, they've reduced the mortgage balance to $15,000 and are able to sell the home for $85,000. After paying off the mortgage, they have $70,000. They can buy a new home for, say, $90,000. If they put one-third down ($30,000), the Browns can keep $40,000 cash without paying any tax.

Deferring tax when you buy a co-op: In the last few years, many urban neighborhoods have been revitalized or "gentrified," often by converting older buildings to co-ops. With a co-op, each resident owns a certain number of shares in a corporation that owns the building. Those shares entitle the shareholder to live in one of the apartments or units. A monthly maintenance fee covers the day-to-day expenses of running the building plus real estate taxes and mortgage payments on the building. The portion of each monthly fee that covers taxes and mortgage interest is deductible, like the interest and taxes on a private residence.

Problem: For many people, the cost of the co-op shares is less than the selling price of their old home. And that would seem to make some or all of the profit on the old home taxable.

Solution: Add on to the cost of the shares that percentage of the building's mortgage that the shareholder is responsible for.

Example: Mr. and Mrs. Jones sell their suburban home for $100,000 and buy a co-op apartment in the city. The cost of their shares is only $80,000. They seem to have traded down by $20,000. That would make the first $20,000 of their profit taxable. But suppose there are 35 apartments of approximately equal size in the co-op and a $900,000 mortgage on the building. The Joneses can add 1/35 of the mortgage (just over $25,000) to the cost of their shares. Result: None of the profit from selling their old residence is currently taxable.

Deducting a loss on your residence: In the last few years, home prices have actually fallen in some parts of the country. Ordinarily, a home is considered a personal asset. That means if you sell it and lose money, the loss is nondeductible. Solution: Convert the home to an income-producing asset before you sell.

The best way to do this: Rent the house out before you sell it. If you can't rent it, at least make genuine efforts to do so. And prepare to document your efforts. Keep copies of listing agreements with rental agents and of ads in local papers. If there's a school nearby, write to the student housing office, and keep copies of your correspondence.

But if the house is not put up for rent before it's sold at a loss, do not give up. Look at the surrounding circumstances for evidence you can use to show that your intentions in owning the house had changed. In one case, a widower sold his old home at a loss shortly after he remarried. But he presented evidence that his married children had moved into the house rent-free just after his first wife died. And he moved out four months later. He convinced the court that he didn't intend to use the house as his personal residence following his first wife's death and that thereafter he had held it as an investment. That made his loss deductible.[*]

[*]*H.V. Watkins,* TC Memo 1973-167.

Source: Gerald J. Robinson, partner in the law firm Carb, Luria, Glassner, Cook & Kufeld, New York.

REHABILITATE A BUILDING

There are tax advantages for qualified realty rehabilitation expenditures—expenditures that are bound to increase in popularity under the latest incarnation of the tax code. There are two tiers of tax credit: 20 percent for rehabilitations of certified historic structures and 10 percent for rehabilitation of nonresidential buildings that were first placed in service before 1936. The expenditures during a two-year period must be more than the greater of $5,000 or the adjusted basis of the property. (The credits are phased out for taxpayers with adjusted gross income above $200,000 and disappear altogether when adjusted gross income reaches $250,000.)

Credits are even available for expenditures incurred by lessees, provided that at the time the rehabilitation is finished, the remaining lease term is at least 27½ years for residential property or, for nonresidential property, at least 31½ years.

There are tests, naturally, regarding just what qualifies as rehabilitation. For example, for structures other than those certified as historic, the test is whether at least three quarters of both the outside walls and the internal framework remain in place. If your building was standing even before Jesse Owens took all the gold at the '36 Olympics, you may want to redo it for an extra 10 percent credit.

STRICT RULES ON HOUSE SALE GAIN POSTPONEMENT

Gain on a house sale will not be taxed if the sale proceeds are reinvested in another home within 24 months. This time limit is strictly enforced. Recent case: A couple sold their home and contracted to buy another within the permitted period. But at the last minute, the seller refused to close the deal. By the time the deal was closed, the deadline had passed. The couple protested that they should not be penalized because of the seller's delay. Tax Court: There is no exception in the law to cover this situation. The couple had to pay tax on the gain.

James A. Henry, TC Memo 1982-469.

• A couple bought a new home, but stayed in their old one while the new home was being re-modeled. The IRS ruled they will lose the right to defer tax unless they sell the old home within two years of purchasing the new one. But they don't have to move immediately if the remodeling isn't complete.

IRS Letter Ruling 8316087.

REAL ESTATE CONFIDENTIAL

Through a sale and leaseback of the house, children in high tax brackets can help support their parents and at the same time improve their own tax picture. How it works: The children buy the house from the parents, using an installment sale, and then rent the house back to the parents. (The installment payments can be set larger than the rental payments, increasing the parents' cash flow.) Since the place is now the children's rental property, they can deduct depreciation, mortgage interest and operating expenses. The parents' gain on the sale may be entirely tax free because of the $125,000 lifetime exclusion that is available to taxpayers age 55 and older. Any gain in excess of $125,000 would be a capital gain. (Note: Installment sale treatment will be denied if the children resell to a third party within two years.) Alternate tax saver: Buy a condominium for your parents and rent it to them at fair market rent. You can deduct depreciation, operating expenses, interest, etc. Planning point: Go over the numbers very carefully. It doesn't always make tax sense to charge rent and take depre-

ciation and operating expenses. You may be better off simply deducting real estate tax and mortgage interest, especially if your income is too high to allow you to deduct the operating losses.

Source: Randy Bruce Blaustein, Esq., Blaustein, Greenberg & Co., New York. Mr. Blaustein is author of *How to Do Business With the IRS*, Prentic-Hall, Inc., Englewood Cliffs, NJ.

RENTING OUT YOUR VACATION HOME

If you have a vacation home and want to pick up some extra cash by renting it out when you aren't using it, you need to know the tax rules. They severely restrict the deductions you can claim as expenses. You can't ignore the rules. Your tax return (Schedule E) specifically asks if you deduct expenses on a vacation home. Except for "qualified rental periods," the rules apply to any dwelling (including trailers, houseboats, co-ops, etc.) used for part of the year and rented for part. (The rules also apply if you rent out rooms in your home.)

The primary rules:

If the vacation home rules apply, you can't deduct more than the amount of rent you receive. Losses are not allowable. In addition, you must deduct expenses in the following prescribed order:

1. Taxes and mortgage interest that are attributable to the rental period. (You can deduct the balance on Schedule A.)

The IRS says you must prorate on the basis of actual use. If you use the home for one month and rent it for two (and close it down for the rest of the year), you allocate two-thirds of interest and taxes to the rental period.

The Tax Court, however, has ruled that you can prorate over the year. If you rent for two months, you allocate $2/12$ of taxes and interest to the rental period. This helps the taxpayer. You get these deductions whether you rent or not. So the less interest and taxes you deduct from rental income, the more you can deduct for other costs and depreciation.

2. Operating expenses, such as repairs, electricity, water, etc. are prorated on the basis of use. If you use the home for one month and rent it for two, deduct two-thirds of operating costs.

3. Depreciation is prorated on the basis of use, like operating costs. This is your best deduction. You couldn't claim it if you didn't rent the home. (This also applies to operating expenses.) In addition, it costs you nothing out of pocket. Remember, though, that you can't show a loss. If you received $2,000 in rent and deducted $1,900 for interest, taxes and other costs, you can take off only $100 for depreciation, no matter what the actual figure may be. Example:

You use the house for one month and rent it for three. Total rent is $2,000. Interest and taxes for the year are $1,000. Under the IRS rule, you allocate ¾ ($750) to the rental period; under the Tax Court rule, you allocate $\frac{3}{12}$ ($250). If operating costs are $800 and depreciation is $2,000, you can deduct ¾. Here's how your figures would look for your tax return:

	IRS rule	Court rule
Income	$2,000	$2,000
Expenses:		
Interest & taxes	$ 750	$ 250
Operating expenses	600	600
Depreciation, limited to	650	1,150
Total expenses	$2,000	$2,000
Schedule A deductions (interest and taxes)	$ 250	$ 750

When you can avoid the rules:

If you rent for 14 days or fewer, you don't have to report the income. Usually only trivial sums are involved. However, if your home is in an area where some annual event shoots up rents for a week or two (Mardi Gras, the Kentucky Derby, a big tennis or golf tournament), you can pick up meaningful tax-free dollars.

If personal use of the vacation home is fewer than 15 days or less than 10% of the number of days rented during the year, whichever is greater, the vacation home rules don't apply. You can deduct all expenses, even when this gives you a tax loss. Any such loss would be a "passive loss," deductible only against passive income, except that $25,000 might be deduct-

ible under the rental loss exception. Check with your tax advisor.

Another problem, if you show a tax loss: The so-called "hobby loss" rules will apply. This means, in general, that the losses could be challenged by the IRS under the presumption that activities generating losses in three out of five consecutive years may not be engaged in for profit.) So if you use the place for a month (30 days) and rent it for nine months (about 275 days), consider leaving a few days early to come within the 10% limit.

You must always prorate expenses, no matter how short the period of personal use. Example: You use the house for only five days and rent it for 50. You deduct $\frac{50}{55}$ (or $\frac{10}{11}$) of total depreciation and operating costs.

Figuring personal use: You count every day the house is used by you, your family or anyone else you allow to use it, unless that person rents for fair value. Lending the place to friends counts as personal use. You can't evade the rule by charging nominal rent.

You do not count days you visit the house to open or close it or to attend to maintenance, repairs and the like.

Renting to relatives: At one time, all rental to relatives, whether of a vacation home or of regular rental property, was considered subject to vacation-home rules.

Now, however, the rules for relatives are exactly the same as for anyone else provided that you charge normal fair-market rents. But you must be prepared to prove it. The IRS is always suspicious of transactions between relatives.

Profit motive: Even if you meet the days-of-use test, the IRS may still disallow any tax losses on the grounds that you were not renting the property with the purpose of making a profit or gain.

The Tax Court upheld the IRS ruling that the entire transaction (purchase, rental, etc.) was entered into for personal reasons, not for profit or gain. All losses were disallowed.

Note: Despite the decision described above, buying a retirement home before actually retiring may be a smart move. First, it's possible the IRS won't disallow your losses. Second, you can deduct at least the amount of income received, so you won't owe any taxes. Third, if the property is likely to increase in value, you'd have a strong argument that the property was held for purposes of gain, despite the initial losses. Finally, if you do show a profit for at least three of any five consecutive years, it will be presumed that you are renting for profit.

Source: Sam Starr, tax manager, Coopers & Lybrand, Washington, DC.

TAX RULES ON EDUCATION SCHOLARSHIP

Educational scholarships are generally not taxable, except to the extent they include room and board. Exception: If the person is required to perform services (such as teaching) as a condition of getting the money. Some or all of it may be considered taxable compensation for services rendered.

Scholarships are not counted in determining child support. If you provide half the support or more for your child's education, you can claim his or her dependency exemption.

CO-OP ALIMONY

When a married couple separated, he got title to their co-op. She got the right to live in the apartment rent free. He agreed to pay all maintenance charges and assessments to the cooperative. Alimony? The IRS said the payments were taxable alimony to the ex-wife (and were deductible by her ex-husband). She said the payments benefited her husband because they enabled him to hold on to his investment. Tax Court: The IRS was 99% right. Except for a small part of the payments that resulted in a tax benefit to the husband (the portion that went for real estate taxes and interest on the co-op mortgage), the payments were taxable alimony to the wife and deductible by her former husband.

Doriane Grutman, 80 TC No. 18.

BACK ALIMONY

A divorced husband fell $45,000 behind in his alimony payments. His ex-wife agreed to accept a lump-sum payment of $36,000 worth of property in satisfaction of all alimony obligations. The wife argued that she shouldn't have to pay tax on the payment because it wasn't ''periodic'' (the tax law formerly defined alimony as periodic payments). Tax Court: The lump-sum was taxable. The nub of the payments was back alimony. And a payment to satisfy unpaid back alimony retains its taxable character.

Dorothy Olster, 79 TC No. 29.

WHEN A STATE REFUND IS TAX-FREE ON FEDERAL RETURN

A state income tax refund is taxable only if the state tax was deducted on your previous federal return and the deduction reduced your federal taxes. If you didn't itemize your federal return last year, you don't have to pay tax on the state refund when you file your federal return this year. Even if you did itemize last year, a portion of your state refund may have been nontaxable.

Shortcut for figuring the nontaxable portion:

• Find out your standard deduction for last year.

• Find your total itemized deductions and subtract your state income tax deduction.

• Compare the result of the subtraction with your standard deduction. If the subtraction result is lower than your standard deduction, the difference between the two figures is the nontaxable portion of your state tax refund. If higher, your state refund is fully taxable.

IRS Revenue Ruling 79-15, 1979-1 CB 80.

SALES TAX CAN ADD UP— TO SAVINGS

Sales taxes no longer qualify as itemized deductions. They are absolutely out—but not always (because we are talking about taxes, after all).

If you buy a big-ticket item, you will not be able to claim an itemized deduction for the state or local levy on the new purchase. But don't throw away the receipt—add the sales tax to your cost basis.

For property used in your trade or business, you will be able to increase your depreciation deductions. For other assets, adding the sales tax to your cost will reduce any eventual gain you might have to report on a subsequent sale.

For example, suppose you buy a delivery truck to be used exclusively in your business. The purchase price is $25,000 plus an additional $1,500 in state sales taxes. The whole $26,500 is depreciable. Suppose, further, that you buy a painting for $25,000 plus $1,500 for the sales levy. When, after the artist has passed on, you sell the work for $30,000, your taxable gain will not be $5,000 but only $3,500. Keep records. They'll save you money.

Source: Special reports, *New Tax Loopholes for Investors*, written for Boardroom Reports by Robert A. Garber, a tax attorney and vice president of a major investment-banking house. He writes frequently on tax matters and is the author of several books.

LIFE INSURANCE DIVIDENDS

No income tax is due on dividends paid on life insurance policies. This is true whether you receive a check or have the dividends applied against next year's premium. Dividends are viewed as a refund that reduces the cost of your policy, not as part of your income.

EMBEZZLER'S SPOUSE INNOCENT

A man escaped paying any penalty even though he filed a joint return with his wife who was an embezzler. Reason: He didn't significantly benefit from the embezzled funds. And, she had complete control over the family finances.

RULES FOR DEPENDENCY EXEMPTIONS

Your 18-year-old son lives with you and you support him. Last year, though, he worked and earned $4,500. Can you claim him as a dependent on your joint tax return?

Yes, you can, if you furnished over half of his support. The income limitation on dependents does not apply to children under 19 (or children of any age who are students) who are part of the taxpayers' household.

A parent who provides over half of a child's support can claim a dependency exemption if the child is under 19 or a full-time student. Beginning in 1990, the full-time student provisions applies only to those under age 24.) The cost of a child's wedding is considered support. If the child lives with a spouse after marriage, the wedding may push the parent's support over the 50% mark and entitle the parent to the exemption. Drawback: The child cannot file a joint return for the year. Nor can the child claim his own exemption on his tax return.

A US citizen who lived overseas since he was nine couldn't claim his child as a dependent on his tax return, because the child was not a US citizen or resident.
IRS Letter Ruling 8318016.

DEPENDENCY LOOPHOLES

• You can claim a dependency exemption for unrelated individuals. But these dependents must live with you for the entire year, and your relationship can't violate local morality laws.
• In many cases, greater overall tax savings result if parents claim a newly married daughter as a dependent than if she files a joint return with her husband in the first year of their marriage.

THE ALTERNATIVE MINIMUM TAX

Perhaps fewer taxpayers will now be infected with the notorious alternative minimum tax, or

AMT, because large long-term capital gains no longer carry the AMT germ. Yet, paradoxically, it may be possible occasionally to use the latest version of the alternative minimum tax to gain a tax advantage and recognize capital gains at a preferential rate.

The AMT is really a flat tax, at the rate of 24 percent, on a broader base of income (after an exempt amount) than the regular tax. That broad base has been expanded. It includes various items of "tax preference" and excludes certain preferential deductions from the minimum taxable income. Now added to the list of preferences are, for example, deferred gains from certain installment obligations and the untaxed appreciation on charitable gifts of property.

The exemption amounts, $40,000 for joint returns and $30,000 for single taxpayers, are phased out at the rate of 25 cents on the dollar to the extent that the base on which the tax is figured, the "alternative minimum taxable income," exceeds $150,000 on a joint return or $112,500 for single taxpayers.

A taxpayer must first calculate his or her income tax liability the regular way and then figure out the alternative minimum tax on the broader base—the regular taxable income plus the tax preference items, without the frowned upon deductions. Whichever calculation produces the higher tax is the one that must be used.

After all the other disallowances, don't forget passive activity (alias tax shelter) losses. The five-year phase-in of disallowance of such losses applies only to the normal tax computation. But such losses are, starting in 1987, completely disallowed when it comes to calculating the AMT; total shelter losses have to be added back to arrive at alternative minimum taxable income.

Once it appears that the alternative tax may be applicable, it's time to do some tax planning. Since every dollar subject to the AMT is taxed at a flat 24 percent, the strategy is to increase income as much as possible until the amount of regular tax reaches the indicated alternative minimum tax bill. The flat 24 percent rate, payable anyway, is probably a better bargain than the usual tax rate.

The technique in such cases has always been to increase ordinary income. Certificates of deposit, E bonds or T-bills could be redeemed, bonuses could be advanced, or other methods of taking in ordinary income could be recommended, but, in most cases, there was not enough control over significant amounts of such income to really make a difference. Now that capital gains are to be subject to the same regular tax rates as other kinds of income and no longer give rise to tax preferences, planning may be easier. The sale of capital assets, after all, can be planned. A taxpayer's control over the recognition of capital gains is often much more exact than it is over ordinary income. If the alternative minimum tax looms, therefore, consider selling capital assets for a tax bargian. With the correct planning, the applicable rate may be just 24 percent.

Another method of dealing with the AMT is the deferral of certain deductions that lessen the regular tax, but don't reduce the broad-based alternative minimum taxable income. For example, estimated state and local income tax payments may be made in January, rather than before the end of the prior year. The deduction, good against regular taxes but not the AMT, is deferred that way. Similarly, if the alternative minimum tax is going to apply, deductions such as charitable contributions may be put off until the next year since, during the AMT year, they are worth no more than 24 cents on the dollar.

20. Tax Deductions

Tax Deductions

STATE TAXES CAN LOWER FEDERAL TAXES

State and local taxes can reduce your federal taxable income in a variety of ways.

Real estate taxes are deductible, of course. Many people own vacation homes or land held for investment. Real estate taxes on these properties are deductible along with taxes on your personal residence.

If you bought or sold a home during the year, the real estate tax deduction is shared between buyer and seller. It's based on the length of time each held title. You can usually find out how the taxes were prorated by looking at the closing papers for your house.

State and local income taxes. You're allowed to deduct all the state or local income tax withheld from your pay even if you expect part of it to be refunded when you file your state or local return. Beyond that, if you filed a return last year with a balance due, that balance is deductible on this year's federal return provided you paid it this year.

Did the IRS audit you this year? If it did, and if you ended up with a balance due, you probably got a bill for additional state income tax as well. (The IRS exchanges audit information with state taxing authorities.) If you paid any back state income tax this year, don't forget to deduct it on your federal return.

Other taxes. If you live in a state with a disability tax, or one where employees have part of the unemployment tax withheld from their pay, you can add that to your state income tax deduction.

Auto registration fees are deductible in some states. If the amount of the fee is based on the value of the vehicle, you can deduct it. In some states, a portion of the fee is based on value. That portion is deductible. States with vehicle fees partly or fully deductible: AZ, CA, CO, IA, IN, MA, ME, NH, NV, OK, WA, WY. Any other personal property tax or fee based on the property's value is also deductible. Examples: Fees for boats and motorcycles.

DEDUCT A BOAT AS A "SECOND HOME"

Question: Can I qualify my boat as a "second home" in order to get an interest deduction under tax reform rules for the loan used to finance its purchase? If so, how?

Our experts say yes. The IRS has ruled many times that a boat can qualify as a residence. And under standard IRS rules, a property qualifies as a residence if it is used by the owner as such for the greater of either 14 days during the year or 10% of the total days during which it is leased to outsiders. Thus, if you're not in the practice of leasing out your boat, it seems that a simple two-week vacation trip taken in it will qualify it as a second home.

CAPITAL LOSSES LOOPHOLE

Under the Tax Reform Act of 1986 capital losses are fully deductible. As under the old law, however, only $3,000 of ordinary income (e.g., salary) can be offset by capital losses in any one year. Also, as before, unused losses can be carried over into future years. Old law: Only 50% of net long-term capital losses were deductible. So it took $6,000 of long-term losses to offset the limit of $3,000 of ordinary income.

ALIMONY LOOPHOLE

Under the old law, alimony payments (exceeding $10,000 a year) had to be spread out over at least six years in order to be fully deductible. New Law: Payments only have to be made for three years. This means bigger deductions for alimony.

TIMING YOUR DEDUCTIONS

Medical costs are deductible to the extent they exceed 7.5% of adjusted gross income. The figure is 10% for casualty and theft losses.

Strategy: Maximize tax benefits by piling two or more years of deductions into a single year (thus topping the limits). It may seem as though you have little choice as to when to take these deductions. But often there is a choice. That's because these items are not deductible until it is clear they will not be compensated for, by insurance or otherwise. Even if the chance of an insurance recovery seems remote, you should file a claim. Otherwise, the IRS can deny the deduction on the grounds the insurer might have paid off.

When you want a deduction immediately, process your insurance claim as quickly as possible. Pressure the insurer for a quick response, so you get either the money or the deduction right away. It may even be worthwhile offering the insurer a compromise, to get a quick determination.

If you feel you will be in a higher tax bracket in a future year, you can delay the deduction by processing your insurance claim in a very deliberate manner. Take your time collecting relevant information, ask for clarifications. The insurance company is not likely to hurry you. Also: Seek reimbursement for your loss from other related parties. Put your requests in writing. Even if there is little chance of their coming through, the possibility they might will help justify your delaying the deduction until a later year.

Source: Dr. Robert S. Holzman, professor emeritus of taxation, New York University.

WHEN TAX STATUS DEPENDS ON WHICH CREDIT CARD YOU USE

The general rule is that you only get a tax deduction in the year you actually pay for a deductible expense. But there's an important exception when you pay with a credit card. For tax purposes, payment is considered made on the date of the transaction, not on the date you pay the credit card company. You can sign now and deduct this year but pay next year.

Many charities accept credit card donations. The IRS gives you a choice. You can claim a charitable contribution deduction either in the year the contribution is charged or in the year payment is made to the issuer of the credit card. The same rule applies to payment of medical or dental expenses with a credit card.

Caution: If you charge a deductible expense on a credit card issued by the company supplying the deductible goods (or services), you can't take a deduction until the credit card bill is paid. Example: If you have a prescription filled at a department store pharmacy and charge it on a credit card issued by the store, you can't deduct the cost of that medication until you get the bill and pay it. But if you charge the same prescription on a credit card issued by a third party, such as MasterCard or Visa, you can deduct it right away.

WONDERFUL DEDUCTIBLE MOVING EXPENSES

The expenses of a job-related move are deductible without regard to the 2%-of-Adjusted-Gross-Income limitation that applies to miscellaneous itemized deductions. Requirements:

• The distance between your new place of work and your old principal residence must be at least 35 miles farther than the distance from your old residence to your old place of work.

• You must work at least 39 weeks during the 12-month period immediately after your arrival in the new work location. This work need not be for a single employer, nor do the 39 weeks have to be consecutive.

Deductible moving expenses include...

1. Travel expenses, including meals and lodg-

ing, for the taxpayer and his family while en route to the new location.

2. The cost of moving household goods, personal effects, and automobiles owned by yourself and members of your household.

3. The cost of house-hunting trips prior to the move (provided you've already secured a job).

4. The cost of temporary quarters at the new work location for 30 consecutive days after obtaining work.

5. The cost of selling an old residence, or acquiring a new one.

6. The cost of settling a lease on your old residence and acquiring a new one.

The total deduction for items 3, 4, 5, and 6 is $3,000, of which no more than $1,500 can be for items 3 and 4.

Source: Robert S. Holzman, PhD, professor emeritus of taxation, New York University.

NEGLECTED MEDICAL DEDUCTIONS

• You can deduct medical bills paid for a person who qualifies as a dependent, even though you can't claim a dependency exemption for that person, provided that you paid more than half that person's support in either the year the bills were run up or the year they were paid. A similar rule applies to married couples. You can deduct bills paid now for a former spouse, so long as you were married when the bills were incurred. You can deduct medical costs paid for your child if you are divorced and the child lives with and is a dependent of your divorced spouse.

• No-smoking and weight-reduction programs to improve your general health are not deductible, even when recommended by a doctor. But a weight-reduction program prescribed as treatment of hypertension, obesity, and hearing loss was ruled deductible. Key: The program was prescribed to treat specific ailments. The IRS would probably rule the same way on a no-smoking program prescribed by a doctor for a specific ailment, such as emphysema.
IRS Revenue Ruling 79-162; IRS Letter Ruling 8004111.

• A transplant donor can deduct surgical, hospital and laboratory costs and transportation expenses. So can a prospective donor, even if found to be unacceptable. If the recipient pays the expenses, the recipient gets the deduction.
IRS Revenue Ruling 68-452, IRS Revenue Ruling 73-189.

• Removing lead-based paint and covering areas within a child's reach with wallboard, to help prevent and cure further lead poisoning, are deductible expenses. But paint removal and wallboard for areas beyond the reach of the child are not—nor is the cost of repainting.
IRS Revenue Ruling 79-66.

• A clarinet and lessons are deductible medical expenses when prescribed to cure teeth defects.
IRS Revenue Ruling 62-210, 1962-2 CB 89.

• Both the installation and the operating cost of a home-computerized visual alert system to offset a taxpayer's deafness are deductible as medical expenses.

IRS Letter Ruling 8250040.

• Also deductible: Whiskey prescribed for heart disease.

HOW TO BEAT THE 7.5% LIMIT ON YOUR MEDICAL DEDUCTIONS

Everyone has medical expenses and everyone now faces a tough limit on deducting them—you can only deduct those expenses in excess of 7.5% of your adjusted gross income. But there are ways to beat the limit.

• Double up. Maximize your medical deductions by bunching payments in alternate years. If you're not going to meet the 7.5%

threshold this year, defer paying medical bills until next year, when your combined expenses may put you over the limt.

On the other hand, if you're clearly going to meet the limit this year, stock up on medicine and drugs, pay outstanding medical and dental bills before year-end, and consider having planned dental work and voluntary surgery done (and paid for) this year, rather than next.

• Hold off. If you plan not to itemize your deductions this year, hold off paying medical bills until January. You'll get no deduction for them this year, while next year you might.

• Charge it. Medical and dental expenses paid by credit card are deductible in the year you *sign* for the charge, rather than in the year you pay the credit card company. You can boost your deductions this year by putting year-end medical expenses on your credit card.

• Drugs. Only prescription drugs and insulin can be deducted now as medical expenses. Tip: Many over-the-counter drugs can also be bought on prescription. Ask your doctor for prescriptions for patent drugs you use. Trap: The price, as a prescription, may be higher.

• Dependents. You are entitled to include in your deductions medical expenses you pay on behalf of a dependent. Bonus: You can deduct medical expenses for a family member who meets all the requirements for being claimed as your dependent except that he or she has too much income. Suggestion: Make your support dollars do double duty by paying the medical bills of a person you're helping support. Those payments could get you both a dependency deduction and a medical expense deduction.

• Life care. The medical expense portion of a lump-sum life-care fee paid to a retirement home for a parent is fully deductible as a medical expense in the year the fee is paid. You may be better off taking a deduction now for future medical care rather than making annual payments.

• Separate returns. It is sometimes advantageous for a married couple to file separate returns when one spouse, but not the other, has heavy medical expenses. On a joint return,

medical expenses must exceed 7.5% of a couple's combined adjusted gross income. But if separate returns are filed, only the income of the spouse with the big medical bills is considered for the deduction limit. (The only way to tell for sure whether it's better to file jointly or separately is to work out the figures both ways.)

• For bosses. Owners of closely held corporations, especially those with a few other employees, may avoid the 7.5% limit by setting up a company medical reimbursement plan. As long as the plan covers all employees and does not favor those who are highly compensated, the company can reimburse its employees (including officer-stockholders) for their actual medical bills. The reimbursed amounts are tax deductible by the corporation and are not taxable income to the employees. The 7.5% limit does not apply. Caution: The IRS can rule that the plan is discriminatory if it favors highly paid employees. If this happens, the value of the benefits will be taxed to the recipient.

Doctor's orders: Obvious medical expenses include prescription drugs, doctor, dentist and psychiatrist bills, hospital costs and laboratory fees. Less obvious expenses include:

• Transportation costs back and forth to the doctor's office or the dentist's, cab, train or bus. If you drive, you can deduct as a medical expense either your actual car expenses or the IRS allowance of 9¢ per mile (plus tolls and parking, whichever method you use).

• Lodging. A patient and an individual accompanying him can each deduct up to $50 per night of lodging expenses—but not meals —on a trip to an out-of-town hospital facility to get necessary medical care.

• Marriage counseling is deductible if performed by a licensed psychologist or psychiatrist. So is sex therapy.

• Home improvements that are medically required are deductible to the extent they do not increase the value of your property. (If a pool for an arthritis sufferer costs $10,000 to install, and increases the value of the house by $6,000, the deduction is limited to $4,000.)

• Travel simply for a change of scenery is not deductible. But trips recommended by a doctor to treat a specific ailment are deductible. Example: A trip to Arizona by an asthma victim, or by a person whose post-operative throat condition is aggravated by cold weather.

• Weight-loss programs prescribed by a doctor as treatment for a specific medical condition such as hypertension are deductible. Not deductible: Weight loss to improve general health and well-being. Get a letter from your doctor recommending a specific program as treatment for a specific disorder.

Also deductible if prescribed by a doctor as treatment for a specific medical condition are:

• Stop-smoking programs.

• Speech therapy.

• Health-club visits.

• Special filters for air conditioners. Ionizers to purify the air. Filters to purify drinking water.

• Special foods taken in addition to your normal diet.

Other deductible medical expenses include:

• Birth-control pills, abortions that are legal under local law, vasectomies.

• Acupuncture, hearing aids, eyeglasses, contact lenses, dentures and braces.

• Orthopedic shoes, medically required shoe lifts, support hose and surgical belts.

Source: Edward Mendlowitz, partner, Mendlowitz Weitsen, CPAs, New York.

SPLITTING HEADACHE

Suppose your mother lives with you and you support her. She becomes severely ill for several months, and you hire a private nurse to take care of her while you're working. Should you claim a medical deduction, or take the dependent care credit, or both?

You can take your choice—figure out which gives you the biggest tax saving. Or you can split the expense between the two. For example, if you spent $5,000, you might allocate $2,400 to the dependent care credit (the maxi-

mum allowable), and claim the $2,600 balance as a medical expense deduction. But you can't get a credit and a deduction for the same money.

MOTHERAID

A son paid his mother's medical expenses with money he withdrew from her bank account under a power of attorney. The IRS disallowed the son's deduction for these expenses, saying the money was really the mother's. But the Court of Appeals allowed the deduction. The money was legally his—a gift from his mother to him.

Source: *John M. Ruch*, CA-5, 82-4463.

DEDUCTION FOR SPECIAL SCHOOLS

Two children suffering from language learning disabilities were sent to a special school. Costs were $1,800 above regular tuition. The school had no staff psychiatrists or psychologists, and no doctor had prescribed that the children be sent there. The IRS refused the $1,800 as a medical deduction. The Tax Court reversed. Although the children didn't need medical treatment, their disorders were severe enough to make normal education impossible. The teachers, though not medical personnel, were trained.

Lawrence F. Fay, 76 T.C. 408.

HOW TO AVOID THE 2% FLOOR FOR MISCELLANEOUS DEDUCTIONS

Miscellaneous itemized deductions include expenses directly connected with the production of investment income, such as...

1. Fees for managing investment property.

2. Legal and professional fees.

3. Fees for tax preparation and advice, investment advice and financial planning.

Problem: Most taxpayers are unable to deduct any investment expenses on Schedule A because their total miscellaneous expenses don't exceed 2% of their Adjusted Gross Income.

Solution: Put as many expenses as possible out of reach of the 2% floor by accounting for them elsewhere on your return. Possibilities:

• Schedule C. Report non-wage miscellaneous income, such as that earned from consulting, lecturing, or speaking engagements, on Schedule C as business income, rather than as "other income" on Schedule A. The expenses you incur in producing that income are deductible on your 1040, where they are not subject to the 2% floor.

• Schedule E. Expenses of earning rent, royalties, or other income that is reportable on Schedule E are deductible on Schedule E, where they are not subject to the 2% floor.

• Adjust the cost of assets. Add the expenses of acquiring a capital asset to the asset's cost. This will reduce the amount of capital gain you must report when you eventually sell. While this approach doesn't give you a current deduction for the expenses, it does reduce the tax you pay on the gain.

• Bunch payment of expenses so that you get two years' worth into one year and exceed the 2% floor in at least one year.

Source: Richard Lager, national director of tax practice, Grant Thornton, CPAs, 1850 M St. NW, Washington, DC 20036.

HOME IMPROVEMENTS

If you make a capital improvement to your home for medical reasons, you get a medical deduction, but not for full cost. It must be reduced by any increase in the resale value of the property. Example: Your wife has a respiratory illness. On her doctor's orders, you install a central air conditioning system at a cost of $12,000. The new system increases the value of your home by $8,000. You can claim a deduction of $4,000. You can also deduct, in full, the costs of operating, maintaining and repairing the system.

Medically required home improvements, such as elevators, air conditioners and swimming pools, qualify in part as deductible medical expenses. In order to get the deduction, the taxpayer making the improvement must have a property interest in the home. Recent ruling: A polio victim who had a specially designed swimming pool installed at his parents' home could not deduct part of the cost. Although he lived in the house, he had no ownership interest in it.
IRS Letter Ruling 8249025.

HOTEL STAY NOT DEDUCTIBLE

An asthmatic was told by her doctor to stay in air-conditioned rooms. When her home air conitioner broke down, she spent the night in a motel. IRS ruling: While the cost of operating the home air-conditioning system might be a deductible medical expense, the motel bill was not deductible. Reason: No medical care was furnished at the motel.
IRS Letter Ruling 8317035.

CHARITY LOOPHOLES

The easiest way to make a charitable donation is by a check. But other kinds of gifts to public charities can also produce large tax savings and may accomplish the same charitable objectives at less cost.

Donate appreciated assets (stocks, bonds, real estate) rather than cash. If you've held the property for more than a year, you're entitled to a double tax benefit. You can deduct the full market value of the property as a charitable contribution, and you avoid paying capital gains tax on the appreciation. Deduction limit: 30% of your adjusted gross income. Any excess is deductible in the five succeeding tax years. Warning: Charitable gifts of appreciated property may trigger the alternative minimum tax. Check with your tax adviser.

Set up a charitable remainder trust, preferably with securities that have gone up in value. Most commonly, this kind of trust pays you a fixed amount of income each year until your death and then distributes the remaining assets to charity. Loophole: You get a tax deduction now for a gift the charity won't receive until some time in the future. In the meantime, you continue to have the use of the money.

Example: A man of 55 sets up a charitable remainder trust with securities that cost him $25,000 but which are now worth $50,000. He reserves an income of $3,000 a year for life. Tax benefits: An immediate charitable deduction of nearly $20,000 (the present value of the charity's remainder interest). And even though this deduction is based on the stock's current value, no tax has to be paid on the appreciation.

Fund the trust with municipal bonds and you will also avoid paying tax on the income you receive from the trust. If you set up the trust with very long-term municipal bonds, your yield might well exceed current money-market rates. And it's completely tax free.

Contribute to a pooled income fund. Many charities maintain investment funds called pooled income funds. The fund "pools" the contributions of individual donors, each of whom has retained the right to receive an income for life from their contributions. Tax loopholes: Similar to those of a charitable remainder trust. Investment benefits: Funds are diversified. You get the benefit of professional management without having to pay for establishing and administering a trust. Drawback: Pooled income funds are not permitted to invest in municipal bonds or other tax-exempt securities.

Charitable lead trusts are the reverse of charitable remainder trusts. Instead of providing you with an income, the charity gets the income from the trust assets for a number of years, usually eight to ten. When the trust's term is over, the assets are returned to you. Loophole: You get a big up-front tax deduction for the value of the charity's income interest.

Lead trusts make a lot of sense for high-earning taxpayers who intend to retire in a few years. The trust gives them a big tax deduction in an earning year, lets them continue to provide for their favorite charity, and gives them the security of knowing that the trust assets will be available for their own use in retirement.

Community trusts. Another way to get maximum tax benefits from your charitable donations is to set up a fund in your own name through a recognized public charity that will serve as a conduit to other charities that you

recommend. Loophole: You get a deduction when you set up the fund without the pressure of having to name specific charities at that time. Set up the fund and get big tax deductions in high-income years—for example, the years just before retirement. In the years after your retirement, the fund will make donations in your name to the various charities that you suggest. Problem: You can't order the charity that is administering the fund to make donations. You can only suggest the beneficiaries. But the administering charities usually do follow a donor's suggestions.

Gifts of life insurance. The mere naming of a charity as the beneficiary of a policy on your life will not provide you with an income tax deduction. To guarantee a deduction you must give up all ownership rights in the policy. Loophole: Have the charity own the policy. Make annual contributions to the charity. The charity will use its own money to pay the premiums. You will get a current income tax deduction for your annual gifts and you will have given the charity a very large gift—the proceeds payable on your death.

Source: Edward Mendlowitz, partner, Mendlowitz Weitsen, CPAs.

FAIR MARKET VALUE DEFINED

The fair market value of property donated to charity means the price paid in a market transaction by the ultimate user. If, for example, you donate used furniture to charity, its value is not the price a used furniture dealer pays you, but the price at which he sells it to a customer.

Goldman, CA6, 388 F. 2d aff g. 46 TC 126.

PERSONAL DEDUCTION FOR CORPORATE DONATION

A way for owners of closely held companies to use company funds to get a charitable deduction on their personal income tax returns: The owner gives the charity stock in his company.

Subsequently the company redeems the stock from the charity. Advantage: A 100% owner would not give up any ownership interest in the company, since his interest in the company after the charity is redeemed would still be 100%. How a bailout works: The owner makes an informal agreement with the charity to offer the stock for redemption shortly after the charity receives it. The owner gives the stock to the charity. He takes a deduction on his personal return for the fair market value of the stock. A week or so later, the company redeems the stock from the charity. If the transaction is properly handled, the stock's redemption will not be taxed as a dividend to the owner. Caution: The agreement with the charity must be informal. The charity must not be under a binding obligation to let the company redeem the stock. It must have the legal right to retain the stock or to sell it to an outsider. Tax rule: Normally, if a 100% shareholder in a closely held company has some of his stock redeemed, income from the redemption will be taxed to him as a dividend. But the IRS has agreed that a redemption will not be considered a dividend if it is handled by an informal prearranged plan with a charity. Such a transaction must be structured properly to ensure the desired tax results. Check with your accountant or attorney.
Source: Tom C. Klein, CPA.

BARGAIN SALE TO CHARITY

A business owner sold some of his company's stock to a charity for less than its market value. The charity, to obtain usable cash, intends to have the company redeem the stock at market value. IRS: The owners can claim a charitable deduction for the discount he gave on the price of the shares. Benefit: The owner gets to deduct a cash payment that will be made by the company.
IRS Letter Ruling 8307134.

FAMILY GIFT TRAP

If you help a family member to make payments on his home mortgage, neither of you may be able to deduct the interest.

Trap: To deduct the interest, you must actually pay and be legally obligated to pay it. If you're not named on the mortgage, you are not legally obligated to pay and can't deduct the payments you do make. The family member you're helping can't deduct the payments either, because he/she is not making them.

Solutions: Make cash gifts to the family member, who can then use them to make payments and claim the deduction, or...if you want to claim the deduction yourself, acquire a partial interest in the home to become jointly liable on the mortgage.

MARKET VALUE OF DONATED LAND

Three persons donated adjacent tracts of land to a university. They valued the tracts as one when determining the property's market value. This increased the value and their charitable deductions. But the IRS said the tracts should be valued separately. Tax Court: The university intended to use the three tracts as a single property, on which it planned to build a research facility. So it would have to pay the higher price to buy similar land in the market. The higher deduction was justified.
Charles Ivey, TC Memo 1983–273.

MAXIMUM DEDUCTION ON DONATED LAND

When you donate property to charity, your maximum deduction may be less than the property's market value. Recent case: A partnership owned valuable real estate. One of the partners gave his interest in the partnership to a charity and claimed a $180,000 deduction. The IRS challenged it. Court of Claims: The property was subject to a mortgage. Moreover, the other partners had to be paid off before the charity could liquidate its holdings. So the net value of the charitable contribution was only $1,000.
Dan L. Beaird, Ct. Cl., No. 491–80T.

ART DONATIONS

The IRS challenges and eventually alters

more than half of the art appraisals it receives to justify deductions for gifts to museums and other nonprofit institutions. And yet, according to the IRS, properly prepared appraisals are accepted readily.

What makes the difference: A good appraiser who documents the figures with research. Such experts charge by the hour, not a percentage of the appraisal figure, and provide the essentials for substantiating the deduction.

They include:

• A careful description of the piece of art, including the size, medium and artist and the date and place of origin.

• A statement of the work's condition, including the relative importance of flaws and imperfections.

• Research establishing the authenticity of the work and the historical significance of the artist.

• Documentation of recent sale prices of similar pieces of art and/or works by the same artist.

Important: Record the date, place and price of purchase.

Source: *The Collector-Investor.*

The gift of a painting to a nonprofit retirement center entitled its donor to a charitable deduction for the painting's full fair market value. IRS ruling: The charity's use of the painting was related to its charitable function. The center displayed works of art in its public areas to keep the residents alert and to encourage their arts and crafts activities.

IRS Letter Ruling 8247062.

TAX DEDUCTION FOR ART DONATED TO MUSEUM BUT STILL HANGING ON YOUR WALL

A taxpayer intends to make a bargain sale of artwork to a museum, and to take a corresponding charity deduction. The museum doesn't have room enough to display the artwork, so the taxpayer will continue to keep it in his own home. But the museum will have the right to remove the artwork at any time. IRS ruling: The taxpayer can claim the deduction despite the fact that he will keep possession of the artwork.

IRS Letter Ruling 8333019.

CHARITY TRAPS

Anselmo donated 461 colored gems to a museum and claimed a charitable contribution for their retail value. But the IRS objected. Tax Court: If Anselmo were to sell the gems, he would have to do so to a wholesale dealer. So he was entitled to a deduction only for their lower wholesale value.

Ronald Anselmo, 80 TC No. 46.

The cost of tickets to a benefit performance for a charitable organization may not be deductible. The cost of tickets to a concert or show is deductible to the extent it exceeds the going rate for tickets to similar events. That's because you can't deduct a contribution when you get something of equal value in return. So if there's no premium built into the price of the tickets, there's no deduction.

GIVE MONEY TO CHARITY AND KEEP EARNING INTEREST ON IT

It's possible to give money to charity, take a deduction, and still receive interest for life.

It's called a charitable remainder trust. The trustees can agree to pay the donor a percentage of the principal every year. Or a fixed number of dollars. Or the trustees may pool the gift with others and pay a pro rata share of the earnings of the combined fund. The payments continue as long as the donor lives.

The full contribution is not deductible. The deduction will be the actuarially determined value today of the money at some time in the future, when the charity gets full use of it. It depends on the giver's age. For a man of 55, it would be 42%. For a woman of 55, 34%.

If the property has appreciated, the calculation is based on current value, and there's no capital gains tax. But in the case of a gift of appreciated property, the deduction can't be more than 30% of adjusted gross income. The usual limit is 50%. (Any excess can be carried forward.)

Most charities have already set up the procedures and paid the lawyers; there shouldn't be any fees. But you can't change your mind. It must be a permanent transfer of ownership.

GIVE A HOUSE TO CHARITY AND KEEP LIVING IN IT

It's possible to give a home to charity but continue to live in it for as long as either spouse lives. Then the charitable organization takes title and possession. It works for vacation houses or any other real estate, but not for personal property (paintings, jewelry, etc.).

The catch: The tax deduction for the charitable contribution is less than the full value of the property. It's some fraction of the value, determined by an actuarial calculation according to life expectancy. Since the charity won't get the property until sometime in the future, the present value of the gift is less than the full value of the property.

Example: Home is donated by 70-year-old man and 68-year-old-wife, with provision that they keep the house as long as either one lives, then it goes to the charity. In the year of the gift, they would get a charitable deduction for 41.5% of the value of the house.

LEFTOVER OIL FOR CHARITY

Homeowners who convert from oil to gas heat may be able to get a charitable deduction for the oil left in their tanks. IRS ruling: Homeowners who had the unused oil removed from their tanks by a utility company, which then delivered it to a local charity, were allowed a deduction for the retail price of the oil at the time the gift was made.
IRS Letter Ruling 8134209.

DEDUCTIBLE ANTIDRUG CAMPAIGN

After two of his children had fallen victim to drug addiction, a taxpayer dedicated himself to stamping out drugs in the community. He worked with law enforcement agents, providing money for informants and for purchases from pushers. The Tax Court ruled he was entitled to a charitable deduction for his expenses, as they were directly related to state law-enforcement services, even though his motivation was strictly personal.
Sherman H. Sampson, TC Memo 1982–276.

RELIGIOUS ACTIVITIES CAN BE DEDUCTED

All out-of-pocket expenses of volunteer work for your church are deductible (but not the value of your time). Say you provide auto transportation for a church group. You can deduct either your actual out-of-pocket car expenses or the IRS standard mileage allowance of 12¢ a mile. Whichever you choose, parking and tolls are deductible.

DEDUCTION RULES FOR VOLUNTEER WORK

How can a couple get a deduction for all the time one spouse puts into volunteer work for charity?

Unfortunately, they can't deduct the value of the spouse's services. But they can deduct all out-of-pocket expenses, such as luncheons and dinners, transportation, parking fees and tolls, telephone calls and uniforms, such as those worn by Red Cross volunteers: Meals and lodging are also deductible, where the work required the volunteer to be out-of-town overnight.

THRIFT SHOPS AND CHARITIES

A charitable organization allowed the operator of a "thrift shop" to use the charity's name in return for a total of 20% of gross sales. The IRS ruled donations to the thrift shop were not deductible; they were neither "to" nor "for the use of" the charity.

NONDEDUCTIBLE PROMISE

A taxpayer claimed a charitable deduction for a promissory note she had given to a charity. The IRS disallowed the deduction and the courts agreed. Decision: A promise to make a gift is not deductible. The taxpayer must wait until she actually sends the charity money, before she can take a charitable deduction.

Nancy J. O'Neil, CA-9, No. 82–4128.

VOLUNTARY ALIMONY PAYMENT NOT DEDUCTIBLE

Before the divorce, a husband paid his wife $2,100 in ''temporary'' alimony. The IRS disallowed this deduction because it wasn't paid pursuant to a separation agreement or divorce decree. Tax Court: For the IRS. For the husband to deduct alimony payments, the wife must be required to include them in income. But wives don't have to include predivorce payments that aren't made under a written separation agreement or a support order.

James J. Klobuchar, TC Memo 1981–482.

COHABITATION PENALTY

A husband who continued to live in the same house with his estranged wife pending their divorce was ordered by the court to pay all mortgage and utility costs. The husband deducted these payments as alimony. Tax Court ruling: No deduction. Alimony payments are deductible only when a couple is living separated and apart. Living estranged in separate parts of the same house does not constitute separation within the meaning of the tax law.

Alexander Washington, 77 TC NO. 44.

FIXED-AMOUNT ALIMONY

Support payments a husband made under an agreement to pay his separated wife whatever it took to maintain her former standard of living may be deductible by the husband even though the agreement did not set a specific dollar amount. Tax Court: The IRS was wrong to automatically deny the husband a deduction simply because the agreement didn't fix a sum. The tax law on separation agreements says nothing about fixing a sum.

Patience C. Jacklin, 79 TC No. 21.

ORAL ALIMONY

Additional payments a separated husband made to his wife under a verbal modification of their written separation agreement were not deductible as alimony. Reason: To be deductible, payments to a separated spouse must be required under the terms of a written separation agreement. Verbal agreements won't do.

Eugene H. Bishop, TC Memo 1983–240.

FINE POINTS OF ALIMONY

• A separated couple hasn't gone through any court proceedings and isn't planning to. Does he get any deductions for the money he sends to help support her and the kids? Is it considered alimony?

If there is a written separation agreement between the husband and wife, he can deduct amounts specified as alimony. If there are children, the custodial spouse has the right to claim dependency exemptions for them, unless he or she formally waives the right to the exemptions.

• A husband agreed to give his wife property valued at more than half of their combined net worth. But the divorce papers did not describe any part of the settlement as alimony. When the husband claimed an alimony deduction for his monthly payments, the IRS said they were a nondeductible part of the property settlement. The husband appealed and the Tax Court issued a split decision. The payments were alimony to the extent that the wife received more than half of the marital estate.

Robert H. Hall, TC Memo 1982–605.

• A divorced wife was injured in an accident and confined to a convalescent home. Her ex-husband agreed to pay the costs, even though they came to more than the alimony specified in the divorce agreement. The wife's conservator wrote a letter spelling out the agreement and sent it to the home, with a copy to the husband. He paid the money and deducted it as alimony. The Tax Court held that the conservator's letter satisfied the requirement that alimony payments be made under a written agreement. The husband hadn't signed it, but his actions proved he accepted and ratified it.

ALIMONY SUIT EXPENSES

The cost of suing to protect your right to receive taxable alimony is deductible as an expense for the production of income. Also deductible: Litigation costs of suing for an increase in taxable alimony.

Source: *Elsie B. Gale,* 191 F2d 79.

PERSONAL INTEREST AND MORTGAGE INTEREST

To get the greatest tax benefit for your interest costs, you'll have to know how to handle each interest charge.

Personal interest, which includes charges incurred on credit cards, car loans, personal loans and the like is not deductible.

Interest paid on a mortgage on your primary residence or a second home (as defined in the new law) is deductible. Limit on deduction: $1 million of mortgage debt on original purchase plus capital improvements.

There is also a way to get around the deduction limit on personal interest. A person who has partially paid off the mortgage on his home may obtain a home equity loan and use the cash obtained to make personal purchases

(items such as a car, boat, new furniture, etc.). Since the interest paid on the refinancing is deductible, the home owner in effect gets an interest deduction for a personal loan.

Limit: The interest deduction on a home equity loan is limited. The amount of a new loan incurred after October 13, 1987, must not exceed the fair market value of the home up to a limit of $100,000.

Example:

A taxpayer bought a house 20 years ago for $80,000. He later spent another $25,000 adding an extra room and other improvements to the house. The house has also appreciated in value by $40,000 so that it's now worth $145,000 on the market. Remaining mortgage debt is $40,000.

Based on these facts, the taxpayer will be able to deduct all the interest on a home equity loan of up to $100,000. The new loan doesn't exceed fair market value ($145,000) less acquisition debt ($40,000).

Planning point:

• Many homeowners are careless about keeping records concerning the cost of home improvements. But now these records are important. If your records aren't complete and up to date, pull them together now.

• If you own more than one second home, you can deduct only interest that's paid on one of them. But you get to choose which home you'll claim a deduction for, and you can change your designation each year (for example, if you increase the interest paid on one home by refinancing it).

Source: Jerry Williford, partner, Grant Thornton, 2800 Citicorp Center, Houston, TX 77002.

INTEREST DEDUCTION LOOPHOLE

If you borrow money from your margin account and use the money for personal purposes (for instance, to take a vacation), the interest is personal interest, and not deductible. But if you use the money to buy stock, the interest is investment interest (fully deductible up to the amount of your investment income for the year).

To get full deductions for interest on money borrowed for personal use, sell some of the stock you currently own, use the proceeds to take your vacation, and buy the stock back on margin. Your margin interest charges will be fully deductible investment interest (assuming you have enough investment income to cover it).

Caution: Keep records that clearly show where borrowed money came from, what it was spent on, and all interest payments you make.

Source: Edward Mendlowitz, partner, Mendlowitz Weitsen, CPAs, 310 Madison Ave, New York 10017.

ALL ABOUT INTEREST DEDUCTIONS

• Prepaid interest is not deductible in full in the year you pay. Recent case: A taxpayer bought a building in October. His mortgage called for a first-year interest-only payment, due when the deal was closed. He deducted the total payment on his tax return. The IRS disallowed 9/12 of his deduction. The Tax Court agreed. Prepaid interest must be pro-rated.

Joseph A. Zidanic, 79 TC No. 40.

• Zero interest equals 10%. A taxpayer bought a house for one-third down with the balance to be paid over seven years in equal monthly payments of principal only. No interest was charged. IRS ruling: The home buyer can claim an interest expense deduction of 10% of his annual payments. Rationale: When no interest is payable in an installment sale, the IRS assumes for tax purposes that interest at 10% is incorporated into the deal. (Note: The seller must include 10% interest as taxable interest income each year.)

IRS Letter Ruling 8228113.

• Mortgage interest deductions were lost to a separated husband who no longer lived in the house, even though he paid support to his wife and she paid the mortgage. Reason: He could not prove that she made the mortgage pay-

ments with funds that he gave her. Better way: The husband could have made the payments himself and kept the deduction.

IRS Letter Ruling 8246073.

HOBBY VS. BUSINESS

Housewife-painter was able to claim a home office deduction for a room in her house that she used as a studio. The IRS said her painting was only a hobby, but she showed that she made a serious effort to sell her paintings (even though she wasn't successful). So she qualified as being in business.

Source: *Gloria Churchman,* 68 TC 696.

PROPER APPRAISAL OF CASUALTY COST

A casualty loss (fire, theft, accident, etc.) is usually easy to prove from police and fire department records, insurance reports or witnesses' statements. But proving the amount of the loss can be tricky. And there are rules restricting the amount of the deduction you can take.

Stolen or destroyed property. If the property has risen in value (e.g., jewelry, works of art, some buildings), you can normally deduct its original cost. The best proof of the cost is a sales slip. Second best: Insurance records or appraisals made at the time of purchase. Next: Statements of the purchaser or other knowledgeable person. Often none of these are available, especially if the property was received as a gift. The only solution is to describe the property as fully as possible and get expert testimony on what the price would have been at the time of purchase. For inherited property, you can deduct the value at the time of the inheritance. Best proof: The valuation used for estate tax purposes.

If the stolen or destroyed property has depreciated in value (e.g., automobiles, household furnishings), you can deduct the lower of the original cost less depreciation or its actual market value—not the cost of buying a new or used car or new or used furniture. For automobiles, *Blue Book* value is a common measure. If you claim more, you'll need proof, such as a mechanic's testimony that your car was in unusually good condition or had low mileage. For household items such as furniture, clothing, TV sets, you can deduct the original cost less depreciation, based on the estimated life of the property and its actual age or its value, whichever is less.

If you had a large-scale loss, such as the loss of a home by fire, try to list every item you can possibly think of. Even if individual items have small value, the aggregate may be extremely large. If some of your household goods were far above average in value (e.g., a large wardrobe of expensive clothing), get records or statements from the stores you deal with. If you don't have invoices for everything, you can show a pattern of expensive purchases.

Damaged property. You can deduct the difference in market value before and after the damage (but not more than the original cost). One method of proof is to get an appraisal. Cost of repairs may also be a measure of damage —provided the repair just restores the property to its previous condition. Remember to reduce the amount of the loss by any insurance or other reimbursements.

Source: Allan I. Weiss, national director of tax services, and Thomas P. Donnelly, partner, Pannell Kerr Forster, CPAs, New York.

ALL ABOUT CASUALTY LOSS DEDUCTIONS

• A tornado blew down 12 trees on a taxpayer's 10-acre wooded property. The IRS disallowed the taxpayer's casualty-loss deduction of $28,000 for the loss of the trees. Its reasoning: There are so many trees that the loss of 12 couldn't make a difference to the value of the property. The taxpayer, however, had a tree expert value each lost tree according to its size, species, condition and location in relation to the house. Tax Court decision: The taxpayer was entitled to a $20,000 casualty-loss deduction for the reduction in the property's value because of the loss of the trees.
Thomas R. Bowers, TC Memo 1981-658.

• All the trees on a homeowner's new property

died from a lethal yellowing disease shortly after he moved in. The disease started by insect infestation and took about six months to kill the trees. The Tax Court disallowed the homeowner's casualty loss deduction, because the loss wasn't sudden enough. Homeowner's appeal: The event precipitating the disease— insect infestation—was a sudden event. Court: No deduction. A loss attributable to disease does not constitute a casualty loss.
John A. Maher, CA-11, No. 81-5561.

• A casualty deduction for earthquake damage to a building could include the cost of repairs, even though the repairs were not made. The Tax Court agreed with testimony on lowered market value given by an appraiser, who said prospective purchasers would either demand that repairs be made, or insist that the price be lowered by the amount the repairs would cost.
Paul Abrams, TC Memo 1981-231.

• Unusually heavy winter rains altered the soil density under a taxpayer's new house. The house settled and was extensively damaged in the process. But the IRS and the courts disallowed a casualty loss deduction for the damage. Reason: While the rain was heavy, it was not unforeseen. The ordinary action of the elements on a poorly constructed house does not qualify for a casualty loss the court said.
Portman v. U.S., CA No. 81-4433.

• A middle-Atlantic-state taxpayer whose car engine froze during a period of extreme cold could not claim a casualty-loss deduction for the damage. IRS reasoning: Very cold winter weather was not extraordinary and nonrecurring in the taxpayer's state. And to qualify as a casualty, an event must be unexpected or unusual.
IRS Letter Ruling 8247060.

DEDUCTING POINTS ON A HOME MORTGAGE

In 1983, a person bought a home using a 29-year mortgage. He paid three points to finance the purchase, and another four points to obtain a lower interest rate over the life of the loan. The homeowner deducted the three points in 1983. He also deducted 1/29 of the four points in 1983 and in each year since. In 1986, he took out a new mortgage and paid off the old one. IRS ruling: The homeowner can deduct the remainder of the four points immediately. The old loan has been completely paid off, so all interest on it is deductible as paid.

Source: Letter Ruling, 8637058.

DEDUCT FEES FOR ADVICE ON TAXES AND INVESTMENTS

Legal fees for advice about the taxation and management of investments are deductible, subject to the 2% of AGI floor on miscellaneous deductions. However, fees for legal advice that results in the sale of an investment currently cannot be deducted as an investment expense. The legal fees must be capitalized (that is, added to the cost to determine your profit in resale). What to do: Make sure your lawyer gives you an itemized bill showing how much he charged for general investment and tax advice and how much for handling the sale of an investment.

Paul W. Learner, TC Memo 1983–122.

The beneficiary of a trust could deduct fees he paid an attorney to keep him informed of the handling of trust property, even though the beneficiary received no income in the year he paid the fees. The Tax Court said the fees were ordinary and necessary expenses in connection with the production of income.

Source: *Hobart J. Hendrick,* 35 TC 1223.

NONTAXABLE INCOME EXPENSES ARE NOT DEDUCTIBLE

If a taxpayer incurs expenses for investment advice, accountants' fees, safe deposit box rentals, etc. that apply to both taxable and nontaxable income, he can deduct only the expenses (or percentage of expenses) allocable to taxable income. Failure to establish the allocation can jeopardize the entire deduction.

DEDUCTIBLE IRA FEES

An IRS official has confirmed that the startup costs and custodial fees that brokerage firms and mutual funds charge IRA account holders are tax deductible as a cost of producing income. The fees do not reduce the amount an individual can contribute to an IRA. No penalty will be charged if the fees put the annual contribution over the $2,000 limit.

DEDUCTING COST OF HOME SAFE

The cost of a home safe bought to store securities and other financial investments as well as jewelry and personal effects is partially deductible through depreciation deductions. The part of the safe's cost relating to the production of taxable income—storing securities and income-producing financial instruments—can be deducted as it is depreciated. Not depreciable: That part of the cost allocated to personal use, that is, storing jewelry and personal effects.

IRS Letter Ruling 8218037.

PROTECT YOURSELF FROM THE IRS WHEN YOU MAKE A LOAN

Whatever risks you take on when you make a loan, you need not risk trouble with the IRS when it comes to deducting bad debts.

Look before you lend:

A careful review of the options often shows that other, more tax-wise methods of employing capital can be used instead of loans. Reason: Taxpayers who have money to lend are likely to benefit most from tax deductions or credits. Loans, however, offer no direct tax benefits to lenders.

Strategy: Consult a tax professional about ways to get more advantageous tax treatment by becoming a partner, a shareholder, an equipment lessor, or a landlord, instead of assuming the role of lender. These and other options can serve the same purpose as loans, while providing you with considerable tax benefits.

Protective measures:

Businesslike lending practices offer you the best means of supporting bad debt deductions, should the IRS question them. Guidelines:

• Document all aspects of the loan. Included: A formal note, your reasons for lending, what steps you took to collect both interest and principal, how you arrived at the conclusion that the debt was worthless. Goal: To prove that you intended the transaction to be a loan—that you expected repayment in full.

• Determine the borrower's creditworthiness. For individuals, use credit reports. For businesses, use both credit ratings and debt/equity ratios. Alternative: A copy of a commercial lender's loan approval.

• Lend at a "reasonable" rate of interest. What's reasonable: Using the AFR rate is both expedient and safe. IRS releases AFR rates on a monthly basis.

• Use fixed-term loans, rather than demand loans. Why: By definition, term loans clearly indicate when payment is due. They emphasize your intention to be repaid. This fine point can work to your advantage if the IRS questions your bad debt deduction.

Proof of worthlessness:

Be prepared to prove that a bad debt is worthless. How: Retain all relevant documents and receipts (copies of return-receipted letters, lawyer's letters, loan payment checks returned for insufficient funds by the borrower's bank, etc.). Also retain any evidence of the debtor's insolvency, bankruptcy or disappearance. Save envelopes marked "Refused" or "Unable to Deliver." These can be used as proof of a debtor's disappearance.

Strategy: Since worthlessness is generally a subjective determination, your actions should demonstrate reasonableness. Although it may be perfectly reasonable to rely solely on telephone calls and letters to collect, say, a $100 debt, limiting yourself to the same steps for a $10,000 debt just doesn't make sense. Whatever seems "unreasonable" is more likely to be disallowed by the IRS.

Family loans:

Loans to relatives invariably prompt IRS questions. The closer the relation, the closer the IRS will scrutinize the transaction. Trap: If the IRS denies your bad debt deduction and rules that your "family loan" was really a gift, there may be gift-tax consequences. Note: If you guarantee a loan made to a family member by a bank or third party, and are forced to pay it back, this may also be treated as a gift. Check with your tax adviser about how to handle family loans.

Not deductible:

Nondeductible losses result in each of the following situations:

• Monies owed but never paid (such as salaries owed to employees or rents owed to landlords) can't be deducted as bad debts. Rule-of-thumb: You can't get a bad debt deduction for amounts not previously reported as income.

• Loans that were worthless when made are not deductible.

• Unrepaid loans to political parties or to candidates for elective office cannot generally be deducted as bad debts by individuals and non-bank corporations. Caution: Check with your tax adviser about the very limited exceptions allowed by law.

Source: Marvin J. Dickman, tax partner, small business division, Arthur Andersen & Co., Rolling Meadows, IL.

CAPITAL LOSS TRAP

If you have stock or other property that has gone down in value, do not sell it to your spouse, child (or other descendant), parent (or other ancestor), brother, sister, or any corporation, trust or organization that you control. If you do, you will probably not be allowed to deduct the capital loss.

DEPRECIATION TRAP

Make sure you take all you're entitled to. If you sell the property, the IRS will compute your profit, based on the depreciation that was allowable, even if you didn't claim it. As to the amounts you could have deducted but didn't, you're just out of luck—except for the last three years, for which you can file amended returns.

DEDUCTING THE COSTS OF A SECONDARY BUSINESS

The Tax Court allowed a working couple to deduct losses from a boat-charter business they ran for two years. The couple had gotten professional advice before buying the boat, had listed it for charter for two years, and managed it in a businesslike manner in a genuine attempt to make a profit. And they used the boat for personal pleasure no more than seven days a year.

Patrick Edward McLarney, TC Memo 1982–461.

WEEKEND FARMER'S COSTS ARE DEDUCTIBLE

Reversing the Tax Court, the US Court of Appeals ruled that a weekend farmer's hope that his farming activities would produce a profit when he began full-time operations entitled him to deduct his current losses. The fact that he could not make a profit from his weekend activities did not mean that he lacked a profit motive for operating the farm. His expectation of making a profit in the future and his lack of a recreational motive justified his deduction.

Melvin Nickerson, CA-7, 82–1323.

EXPENSE FOR FUTURE INCOME IS DEDUCTIBLE

A taxpayer took a 50-year lease on undeveloped land on which he intended to build and operate an office building. He deducted the first-year lease payments as a business expense. But the IRS denied his deduction, arguing that since the building hadn't yet been constructed, the taxpayer wasn't in business. Tax Court: The lease payment was deductible as an expense incurred for the production of future income—though not deductible as a business expense. The fact that the taxpayer wasn't actively engaged in business didn't cost him his deduction.

Herschel Hoopengarner, 80 TC No. 26.

COMPANY GIVES TO CHARITY—OWNER TAKES PERSONAL DEDUCTION

The controlling shareholder of a private company plans to give some of his shares to a charitable foundation that he has established. The charity will then redeem the shares for cash, and the owner will claim a charitable deduction on his personal return, even though it will be the company that pays out the cash to the charity. IRS ruling: The deal will be legitimate so long as there is no legally binding agreement that requires the foundation to submit the shares for redemption.

Source: Letter Ruling 8639046.

HOW TO TAKE OFF 100% OF A BUSINESS MEAL

The Tax Reform Act of 1986 slapped a tough new limit on deductions for business meals and entertainment. For tax years beginning on or after January 1, 1987, only 80% of these expenses are deductible. The limit applies to food, beverages, taxes, tips, tickets, cover charges, and whatever else you spend, for business purposes, on eating out and entertainment. All are just 80% deductible.

Even though the value of deducting an extra $1 of business-meal expenses is reduced because of the drop in tax rates, the incentive to get the biggest deduction legally possible still exists. Many taxpayers will discover that tax reform actually means higher taxes. For them, the ability to squeeze out a few hundred or even a few thousand dollars more of deductible business-meal expenses will make all the difference.

The angles:

• Reimbursement angle. Employees are not subject to the 80% rule if their company reimburses them for business-meal and entertainment expenses. It's the company that's subject to the rule—the company must limit the amount of the deduction it claims on its tax return to 80% of the amount given to reimburse the employee. Bottom line: The tax reform law has no adverse effect to an employee on an expense account who is reimbursed in full for business meal and entertainment costs. It may be more desirable to have your employer reimburse you than for you to receive an expense allowance and deduct meal and entertainment expenses on your own tax return where the deduction will be limited to only 80%.

• Company party loophole. The 80% rule does not apply to certain traditional employer-paid social or recreational activities that are primarily for the benefit of the employees. Holiday parties and annual summer outings will continue to be fully deductible.

• Company dining rooms, employee cafeterias, and other "eating facilities" operated by an employer for employees are not subject to the 80% rule if: the facility is located on the business premises of the employer; and brings in revenue that normally equals or exceeds its direct operating costs; and does not discriminate in favor of highly compensated employees.

(New IRC Section 274 (n) (2); Amended IRC Section 132(e) (2).)

Source: Randy Bruce Blaustein, former IRS agent now a partner, Blaustein, Greenberg & Co., New York. Mr. Blaustein is the author of *How to Beat The IRS*, Boardroom Books, Springfield, NJ 07081.

MEDICAL EXAM LOOPHOLE

Medical examinations are usually in included with the rest of your medical expenses—they are only deductible to the extent that the total of all your medical expenses exceeds 7½% of your Adjusted Gross Income (AGI).

Loophole: When the medical exam is taken because it's required by your current job or potential employer, it's counted as a *miscellaneous* expense. These expenses are deductible to the extent that the total miscellaneous deductions exceeds only 2% of your AGI.

BUSINESS LUNCH TRAPS

• A lawyer often took business guests to lunch at a club located in the same building as his office. He kept invoices from the club, showing the date and amount spent. However, the invoices didn't indicate the name or business relationship of the taxpayer's guests. Result: He lost over $6,000 in deductions. The Tax Court said that "only those expenditures for which (the taxpayer) has identified the guests are deductible."
Lennon, TC Memo 1978–176.

• Every business day, 52 weeks a year, the partners of a Chicago firm lunched together and discussed the firm's business. The firm deducted the cost of the lunches. But the IRS disallowed the partner's share of the lunch deductions as personal living expenses. The Tax Court agreed with the IRS. The fact that the meetings were necessary to the firm's business did not convert the personal cost of daily meals into a business expense to be shared by the government, the court said. The partners met at lunch because it was convenient.
John D. Moss, Jr., 80 TC No. 57.

BEST TAX SHELTER IN AMERICA IS A BUSINESS OF YOUR OWN

• Deductible executive dining room and living quarters. Meals furnished by a corporation to a shareholder-employee are tax-free to the employee if furnished for the business convenience of the corporation. This includes meals furnished on the corporation's premises so that the employee will have more working time or so that there will be a responsible person on hand at all times to provide supervision or handle business communications.

If the business is large enough to warrant it, a separate executive dining room may be set up. The cost of the meals will be deductible by the corporation and not taxable to the executives, including shareholder-executives, if business decisions take place during the meal either among the executives themselves or with customers, suppliers, or consultants invited to dine.

Living quarters may be provided on a tax-deductible basis for the corporation and tax-free to the shareholder-employee if the corporation requires him to live on the premises for a good business reason. This might apply for a shareholder serving as a hotel, motel, farm, or ranch manager. It might also apply to the manager of a nursing home, hospital, or funeral home, and other occupations requiring close and more or less continuous availability in connection with the business.

• Personal use of deductible company car. The use of a company car, especially a luxury car, can be a valuable fringe benefit. The expenses of the car, including depreciation, are deductible by the corporation and not taxable to the shareholder-employee if it is used on company business. The IRS has informally taken the position that if the car is used primarily for business, income will not be imputed to the user because he takes the car home on weekends and makes incidental use of it for nonbusiness purposes.

If a shareholder-executive is given the use of two cars, and it is clear that one of them is being used by *his wife* for nonbusiness purposes, he will be taxed on the value of the use of the car. But his tax liability will be less than the cost of renting a car, and most likely less than it would cost him to buy, finance, and maintain the car on his own. If the extra car is treated as extra compensation, the attending expenses are deductible by the corporation as compensation, subject to the overall limitation of reasonableness. If treated as dividend income to the shareholder, it would not be deductible by the corporation.

• Deductible chauffeur. The cost of a chauffeur may be deductible by the corporation and not taxable to the shareholder-employee if deemed an "ordinary and necessary expense," sometimes translated as "appropriate and helpful."

• Capital loss transformed into ordinary loss. A special form of stock (Section 1244 stock), within limits, permits an ordinary loss rather than a capital loss if the business turns sour.

If the stock qualifies, an ordinary loss of up to $50,000 per year ($100,000 on a joint return) may be taken. This may be spread over several years. Whether or not a loss is anticipated, stock should be issued under the aegis of §1244 to qualify for such treatment. Briefly, the requirements are that it be common stock of a domestic small-business corporation and the total it has received for stock (including §1244 stock) doesn't exceed $1 million. For the five years prior to the loss, the corporation must have derived more than 50% of its gross receipts from sources other than rents, royalties, interest, etc.

• Bail-out loophole for family members. Income and estate tax considerations generally make it desirable for family members to hold stock in a close corporation. The family head may wish to give them money to buy stock from the corporation, or they may already have their own money to buy in.

There are two good reasons why it may be desirable for family members to acquire their stock directly from the corporation as soon as the corporation is set up:

1. The stock will be cheaper at that time than later, assuming that the corporation succeeds; and

2. The rules governing corporate redemptions are less restrictive when the stock is acquired directly from the corporation rather than by a transfer from the family head or other family member.

If the stock is acquired from a family member, it must be held for at least ten years before it can be redeemed to yield capital gains. This ten-year requirement does not apply if the stock is acquired from the corporation. Thus, it will be possible for the holder to bail out corporate earnings and profits as capital gains whenever the need arises or when it is desirable to do so.

• Leasing assets to your own corporation. The fact that the corporate form is selected as the basic means of conducting a business enterprise does not mean that all of the physical components of the enterprise need be owned by the corporation. Indeed, there may be legal, tax, and personal financial planning reasons for not having the corporation own all the assets to be used in the business.

Whether the corporation is to be the continuation of a sole proprietorship or partnership or a wholly new enterprise, decisions can be made about which assets owned by the predecessor or acquired for use in the corporation are to be owned by the corporation and which assets are to be made available to the corporation through a leasing or other contractual arrangement. For the assets that go to the corporation, decisions must be made about how they are to be held and on what terms they are to be made available to the corporation.

There are several possible choices. The assets may be owned by:

1. An individual shareholder or some member of his family;

2. A partnership, limited or general, in which family members participate; or

3. A trust for the benefit of family members.

A separate corporation is still another possibility, but the risk of being considered a personal holding company and incurring penalties due to passive income (including rent and royalties) may make this impractical.

Normally, a leasing arrangement is used for the assets to be made available for corporate use. Assuming that the rental is fair, it would be deductible by the corporation and taxable to the lessor. Against the rental income the lessor would have possible deductions for interest paid on loans financing the acquisition of the asset, depreciation, maintenance and repairs, insurance, and administrative costs.

These deductions and the credit might produce a tax-free cash flow for the lessor. When depreciation and interest deductions begin to run out, a high tax-bracket lessor might find that he is being taxed at too high a rate on the rental income. At this point, he may transfer the leased property to a lower tax-bracket family member. He might also consider a sale of the property to his corporation, possibly on installment terms to reduce the impact of tax liability. This sale would serve to extract earnings and profits from the corporation at favorable tax rates. At the same time, it would give the corporation a higher tax basis for the asset than it had in the hands of the lessor, thus increasing the corporation's depreciation deductions. This, of course, would reduce the corporation's tax liabilities and benefit the shareholders—the lessor included, if he is a shareholder.

Source: *New Financial Planning Opportunities for Owners of Closely Held Corporations* by Bertil Westlin, Boardroom Books.

HOW TO DOCUMENT ENTERTAINMENT EXPENSES

• If you take customers to dinner and pay by credit card, the credit-card record is not enough to prove your deductions for entertainment.

Don't be misled by ads saying a credit card will "give you proof of travel, entertainment and hotel bills for the IRS." The credit-card record will prove how much you spent and where you spent it. But you still have to prove the business nature of the expense, and this means keeping a record of who you were with, the person's business relationship to you, and the business purpose of the meeting. Tip: Make a record on the back of your credit-card receipt, enter it in your business diary as soon as possible; and keep the receipt.

• Cancelled checks are sufficient to document a travel expense deduction (provided the taxpayer shows the travel had a business purpose), but they are not enough to document entertainment expenses. Reason: The cancelled checks alone do not indicate who was entertained, or the business purpose of the entertainment.

Donald Sap, TC Memo 1981–167.

MUST ESTABLISH A TAX HOME

A salesman spent most of his time on the road, but rented a room in his sister's home in the same city as his company's main office. The Tax Court ruled this was his "tax home," and he could deduct expenses while away. But where another salesman, in almost the same situation, did not pay his sister any rent for the room, IRS ruled he had no "tax home" to be away from. Hence, no deduction.

Sapson, 49 TC 636; Rev. Rul. 73–529.

HOW TO DEDUCT YOUR VACATION

There are several ways to get tax deductions for vacation travel. One is to plan a trip with business as its primary purpose. Even if a trip is essentially personal, it's desirable to tack on business activities and get a partial write-off. And sometimes you can combine good works with leisure and get a charity deduction for the cost of your travel.

Business vs. pleasure:

Basic rule: When business and personal activities are mixed, traveling expense are deductible if the primary purpose of the trip is business. Included: All fares; room and meals; and incidental expenses such as phone calls, laundry and local transportation.

Whether a trip is primarily business or personal depends on various factors. Key question: Is this a trip that would not have been made but for the business activities that were planned? The amount of time you spend on each activity is an important indicator of the primary purpose. But you can spend a reasonable amount of time on recreation without changing the primary focus of the trip.

Overseas travel:

If you spend more than one week outside the US and more than 25% of the days you're away are not business days, your write-offs are reduced. Amount of the reduction: A percentage of the write-offs equal to the percentage of nonbusiness days.

When traveling overseas, a business day is a day in which:

• Your principal activity during normal business hours is business. Note: Even if you spend more time on nonbusiness activity than on business, the day can still be a business day. Important: Don't cram all your business appointments into a single day. Spread them out over the course of your trip.

And even a day on which you don't do any business at all can be counted as a business day, provided:

• You're traveling to or from a business destination.

• You would have done business, but circumstances beyond your control, such as a blizzard or a strike, kept you from doing so.

• It's a weekend or holiday that's preceded and followed by days on which you actually do business.

Business travel essentials:

Keep a simple diary showing what your principal business activities were each day. Include:

• Who you saw.

• When and for how long you met.

• The business purpose of the meeting.

For business entertainment, include the place you met and the amount of the bill; a receipt if the bill is over $25.

Alternate strategy:

If you can't make business the primary purpose of your trip, see if you can arrange to travel on behalf of a recognized charity. It may take some imagination. This tactic has worked in a variety of situations. Examples:

• Lay delegates to a church convention, attending in an official capacity.

• American Legion convention delegates.

• A safari to bring back specimens for a museum.

• Members of the National Ski Patrol.

• Not useful: Conventions that are open to all members of the sponsoring organization unless you are designated to fulfill some special role in the proceeding.

To qualify for this type of write-off, the benefit to the sponsoring charity must be primary. Suggestions:

• Arrange in advance to represent the organization in some official capacity.

• Document the relationship between your trip and the organization's goals.

• Show what tangible benefit the organization is getting from your trip.

• If possible, have the charity reimburse a small part of your costs.

Discuss travel plans with your tax adviser as

early as possible. Innovative tax planning is your adviser's business. Focus on how to make the trip deductible and how to maintain the kind of records you'll need. And have a good trip.

- Ship travel can be an asset on a combined business-vacation trip. Reason: Days spent in transit count as business days in the allocation formula. Example: A two-day business meeting in Paris is followed by a two-week European vacation. If you fly (one day each way), only 22% is deductible (two business days plus two days of travel out of a total of 18 days away). But if you sail (five days each way), 46% is deductible (two business days plus 10 days of travel out of a total 26 days away).

Source: Edward Mendlowitz, partner in Mendlowitz Weitsen, CPAs, New York.

DEDUCTIBLE COMMUTING

Most commuting expenses aren't deductible, but if a person works at two jobs in the same day, the cost of traveling from first job to second job is deductible as an itemized miscellaneous deduction (subject to a 2% of AGI floor). (He still can't deduct travel from home to the first job or from the second job back home.)

DEDUCT YOUR JOB-SEARCH COSTS

Job-hunting expenses are deductible, even if you don't find a new job, as long as you're looking for work in the same trade or business as your current position. Deductible: Amounts spent for typing, printing and mailing resumes. Also deductible: Long-distance telephone calls, job-counseling and employment agency fees, travel, transportation, meals and lodging (if the travel is undertaken primarily for job-hunting purposes). These items are only deductible as miscellaneous itemized deductions.

DRUMMING UP BUSINESS IS DEDUCTIBLE

A CPA deducted the expenses he incurred visiting clients to see if they would retain him if he went into business for himself. The IRS disallowed the deduction, holding his travel costs were really capital expenses in connection with setting up a new business. Tax Court: The expenses were deductible costs of seeking employment in the same trade or business. The taxpayer, the court said, was trying "to improve his employment opportunities in his profession as a CPA." Since the nature of the employment was the same, it was immaterial that he would be self-employed rather than employed by another.

Howard L. Cornutt, TC Memo 1983–24.

EDUCATION-EXPENSE TRAP

Your kids have reached school age and your wife wants to resume her career. She plans to take some brush-up courses first. Are they deductible?

Educational expenses are deductible only if related to a taxpayer's trade or business. What your wife should do is get a job first—then take the courses. A part-time job will do—just as long as she can show she is currently engaged in an occupation to which the courses are related.

DEDUCT EDUCATION-RELATED LIVING EXPENSES

An official temporarily moved to another state to take a nine-month course in his specialty. Afterwards, he intended to go back to his old job. IRS: He may deduct all expenses related to the course, including his personal moving and living expenses, but he may not deduct expenses incurred by other members of his family.

IRS Letter Ruling 8307067.

LOSS OF APARTMENT SECURITY DEPOSIT IS DEDUCTIBLE

A taxpayer who was transferred to another city lost the security deposit on his old apartment. Can he get a tax deduction?

Yes. Deductible moving expenses include the cost of getting out of any leases on his previous residence—as well as the cost of finding a new one, such as real estate brokers' fees. (But not the security deposit on the new apartment; presumably, he'll get that back someday.)

WITHDRAWAL PENALTIES ARE DEDUCTIBLE

A couple cashed in a certificate of deposit before maturity and the bank charged a penalty. Is it deductible on their tax return?

Yes, early withdrawal penalties are deductible and are subtracted from gross income to arrive at adjusted gross income.

YEAR-END HOLIDAY DEDUCTIONS

Holidays bring many once-a-year deductions and tax-saving opportunities for individuals. Don't overlook them.

• Christmas and holiday cards sent to clients and customers are deductible as a miscellaneous item on Schedule A or a business expense on Schedule C. Include the cost of the cards and postage.

• Charitable contributions are most often solicited at this time of year. Keep records of every charity you donate to. The safest way to contribute is by check. Contributions of property over $5,000 must be accompanied by an appraisal.

• Charitable driving. If you use your own car, deduct 12 cents per mile or your actual driving expenses (excluding depreciation and insurance). Add parking fees and tolls.

• Holiday payments. Don't put your holiday purchases on your charge card if you can help it. Instead, pay with cash. Reason: The interest paid on these accounts is only partially deductible after 1986 and is gradually phased out over the next five years by tax reform. By 1991, the interest deduction for consumer items won't be available.

• Holiday turkeys and hams that you get from your employer don't have to be included in your income. But the employer can deduct their value as a business expense.

• Holiday business parties and entertaining: only 80% of the cost of business entertaining is deductible, and then only the cost that is in excess of 2% of your adjusted gross income.

Source: Cary R. Mikles, tax partner, BDO Seidman, 700 Union Bank Plaza, Grand Rapids, MI 49503.

HOW TO SET UP A HOBBY AS A BUSINESS

You can set up a hobby as a business and deduct your losses. However, you must be able to prove that the hobby is a for-profit business. If you realize some profit in at least three out of the most recent five consecutive years, it is presumed that the business is for profit. But even if you don't show a profit, you may be able to prove that the business is intended to make a profit.

To prove you have a profit motive in conducting your business, keep detailed records. Present evidence of your advertising campaigns, attempts to generate new business, and sales analyses. It's not necessary to show that you run a big business, reaping huge profits, but only that you have genuine intentions of running the business in a businesslike way.

Source: *New Tax Traps/New Opportunities*, by Edward Mendlowitz, Boardroom Special Report, Springfield, NJ 07081.

21. Tax Strategies for Investors

Tax Strategies for Investors

DEDUCT! DEFER!

The year-end rallying cry for most investors should be: Deduct! Defer! Deduct losses this year to offset income to be taxed next year.

Your investment decisions should be governed by the current market outlook for your holdings, not by tax savings. Get professional tax advice: Individual situations create vastly different tax consequences. Also, many year-end strategies involve complicated tax rules. Consult your tax adviser before undertaking such transactions.

Defer current income through the purchase of utilities whose dividends are expected to be partially or wholly recognized as return of capital.

Defer gains by selling short against the box. You sell stock your broker has arranged to borrow this year. Your own shares are delivered next year to replace the borrowed shares. Since the sale isn't consummated until delivery is made, you nail down your profit now, while not paying tax on the gain until next year.

Defer capital gains through installment sales. Under an installment sale, a pro rata portion of the gain is taxed each year. Warning: Installment sales should not be attempted without the help of a tax expert.

Defer income to next year by purchasing short-term unit trusts or one-year government securities. Suggestion: Liquidate money market assets and reinvest in a pooled fund composed of six-month vehicles (CDs, bankers acceptances, Treasury bills). There will be no tax liability this year because interest isn't paid until maturity.

Deduct losses this year. Losses are deductible from ordinary income on a dollar-for-dollar basis up to $3,000. Losses beyond $3,000 can be carried forward to future years.

Deduct losses in bonds or securities through tax swaps, or doubling up. These techniques will turn a current paper loss into a deductible loss.

Doubling up involves buying an equal number of shares at today's prices of stock on which you have paper losses. After 30 days, you sell your first purchase. This gives you a deductible loss which does not violate the wash-sale rules.

Deduct margin interest. Caution: The tax code disallows interest expense deductions on money borrowed to finance tax-free investments; it also denies interest deductions until income is realized. Seek advice from your expert.

Source: Alfred F. Palladino, corporate vice president and resident manager, Bache Halsey Stuart Shields, New York.

TAX-SWAPPING STRATEGIES

Tax swapping is a traditional year-end tactic for generating losses in an investor's portfolio. These can protect gains that have already been taken, allow additional gains to be realized or shelter up to $3,000 of income from other sources.

Typical tax swaps:

In an ordinary tax swap, the investor inspects his portfolio as the year is drawing to a close. He looks for fixed-income securities that are trading in the market for less than their original cost. The investor sells these securities. Then he can use the proceeds to purchase comparable ones (similar coupon value, maturity date and credit rating).

As a result, the investment position is maintained, and a tax loss is established. Because of the wash-sales rule, the investor cannot repurchase identical securities unless he waits at least 31 days. These tax losses are fully deductible to the extent the investor has capital gains to offset them against. Beyond that, up to $3,000 worth of noncapital income can be offset with capital losses in any one year.

Watch this: Rules for taxable bonds issued after July 18, 1984, make the market discount on those bonds taxable as ordinary income. So there may be a tax advantage to retaining the old bonds already in your portfolio. This rule does not affect your stock swaps.

A better way of swapping:

More sophisticated investors don't wait until the end of the year to do their tax swapping. And they seek to improve their investment position rather than just maintain it.

The end of the year is not the best time to do a tax swap. Too many people do it then. With many investors looking for swappable securities during the last calendar quarter, supply/demand imbalances develop. These cause prices to rise. The later in the year it is, the more pronounced this effect will be. So if you haven't acted already, do so as soon as possible (without rushing into anything until all angles have been considered).

Watch the market all year long. Market conditions, rather than an artificial date for the closing of a tax year, should dictate the best time to buy or sell.

Upgrading investment quality:

Spreading swap activities throughout the year reduces the pressure to reinvest sales proceeds right away. Instead, the investor can pick and choose, ending up with a better investment position as well as a tax loss. Possible aims: More current income, a better maturity, reduced credit risk.

Source: Peter J. Schmitt, director, fixed income research, Prescott, Ball & Turben, New York.

INVESTOR TIPS AND TRAPS

Stock investors should keep records sufficient to identify specific shares of stock. That way, they can pick shares to sell that will produce the greatest tax benefit.

Example: Say you own two lots of shares of Gem Corp., one bought at $7 per share and the other at $12. Today, the stock is worth $20.

If you sell a share, you'll get $20 cash, but the tax will vary depending on which share you sell, being based on either a $13 or $8 profit. You can minimize your reported profit and the resulting tax by electing to sell one of the more expensive $12 shares.

Conversely, if you have other capital losses, you could elect to sell a cheap $7 share and use the offsetting loss to shelter the larger profit from tax.

Trap: If you don't have records identifying specific shares, the IRS can rule that shares are disposed of on a first-bought, first-sold basis. In a rising market, this will generally mean that the cheapest shares are sold first, increasing both your profit and the taxes due.

Source: *Personal Financial Planning*, by G. Victor Hallman and Jerry S. Rosenbloom, McGraw–Hill, 1221 Ave. of the Americas, New York 10036.

DEDUCT STOCK LOSSES WITHOUT SELLING YOUR SHARES

Examine your portfolio for stocks and securities that have gone down in value. Their sale will produce losses that can be used to offset capital gains and other taxable income. Problem: You may not want to sell the securities. What should you do? Use one of the following strategies that allow you to lock in losses while substantially retaining your current investment position.

1. Double up by purchasing a matching amount of the same securities you already own. Hold the new lot for 31 days, then sell the old lot. You get your tax losses on the sale of the old lot, yet emerge with the same investment you started with. Your tax losses may far outweigh the cost of carrying a double position for 31 days.

2. Sell and buy back the same securities, but be sure to wait 31 days before making the repurchase. Again, you get your losses while retaining your position. Caution: If you don't wait the full 31 days before making the repurchase, the loss won't be recognized.

3. Repurchase similar securities immediately after you sell the old ones. You don't have to wait 31 days to secure your losses. What is considered similar? (1) Stock of a different company in the same business. (2) Bonds of the same company with a slightly different maturity date and coupon rate.

SMART INVESTORS

When you make a new investment, be sure that you break down the cost between what's deductible and what's not.

Deductible subject to the 2% limit: The cost of an investment counselor's advice, management fees, amounts paid for investment-related publications, fees charged by a lawyer or accountant for advice and insurance that protects your investment.

Not deductible: Any costs that are directly related to buying or selling the investment. These must be capitalized—added to the price of the investment to reduce your capital gain (or increase your capital loss) when you sell it or otherwise dispose of it.

Trap: A broker, lawyer or accountant may provide both deductible and nondeductible services on the same deal. For example, when a broker recommends an investment, a lawyer provides a legal opinion of it, and an accountant estimates its tax impact, the fees involoved are deductible. But when a broker charges a commission on a purchase, a lawyer handles the closing papers, and an accountant adjusts your books to reflect the purchase, the fees involved are nondeductible capital costs.

Advice: Always have your professional advisers provide itemized bills that spell out what's deductible.

TAX-FREE INTEREST

Savings bonds are popular baby gifts. Plan to file a tax return for the baby's first year, if your child is given them. On that return you can elect to report the bond's interest annually, rather than let it accumulate. Loophole: The election to pick up the interest annually will result in a very small tax (as long as it's not over $1,200 a year). If you let the interest accumulate, when the child is 15 or 20 and wants to take the money out, he'll have to pay tax on 15 or 20 years of interest.

BIGGER WRITE-OFFS FOR MONEY LOST IN NEW BUSINESS

Tax law provides a very favorable opportunity for those who invest in starting up a small business. If both investors and new companies follow a few simple rules, they can be certain that, if the business fails, investors can be protected through an ability to deduct their loss against ordinary income rather than taking it as a capital loss. The provision is not new, but it has been streamlined and liberalized in recent years.

An ordinary income deduction is better than a capital loss:

Capital losses of any size can be used to offset capital gains. But if the net result of all capital transactions is a loss, it can be deducted from ordinary income only at the rate of $3,000 per year. The remainder can be carried forward and used in later years. But even so it would take over eight years to write off a $25,000 loss.

Any unused capital losses expire at the taxpayer's death. Thus, if an older investor realizes a large loss, he may find it impossible to take advantage of all of it. Accordingly, a provision for turning all kinds of capital losses into ordinary income losses is very valuable. And that's what is offered by Section 1244 of the Internal Revenue Code.

How the investor deducts the losses:

The basic feature of Section 1244 is that the annual $3,000 limit on capital losses that may be used to offset ordinary income does not apply. Section 1244 capital losses can be deducted from ordinary income up to $50,000 a year ($100,000 for a married couple filing jointly). Losses in excess of these amounts are then treated the same as other capital losses.

There is no lifetime limit on Section 1244 losses. Accordingly, if a corporation is failing, a better strategy than immediate liquidation might be to keep it (barely) alive for several years and sell part of the stock every year in order to take deductions far in excess of the one-year limit.

It is important to realize that the investor cannot deduct the corporation's operating losses against his taxable income, as he would with a Subchapter S corporation. He can deduct his capital loss on the sale of the stock, but not until he sells it or until he can show that it is worthless.

How a corporation can qualify under Section 1244:

To safeguard its investors, a company must meet the following requirements:

1. The total capital contributed (that is, the amounts paid to the company by its stockholders when they buy newly issued stock) may not at any time exceed $1,000,000. (Retained earnings are not counted toward this limit.) The stock may be sold in a single transaction or in several transactions spread over a period of time. And it may be sold in a private sale or a public offering.

2. The corporation must operate a business. It cannot be a passive investment vehicle owning real estate or securities or a tax shelter.

3. It is no longer required that the corporation have a written plan covering the offering.

4. Stock issued in exchange for personal services does not qualify under Section 1244. To meet the test, the stock must be issued for money or property.

Gratuitous benefit:

Section 1244 is one of the very few provisions of the tax law that has no disadvantages and doesn't cost anything to use. Obviously, if the business prospers, Section 1244 will never be used, but that is hardly something to complain about.

Source: *Successful Tax Planning*, by Edward Mendlowitz, Boardroom Books.

DEFERRED ANNUITIES THE DARLINGS OF TAX REFORM

With tax reform now in place, the insurance industry's deferred annuities are one of the most attractive investment products around...

• Deferred annuities serve as an alternative for individuals whose incentive to continue to make IRA contributions is greatly weakened by tax reform. Although contributions to a deferred annuity are not tax deductible, earnings do accumulate tax deferred. Advantage over an IRA: There is no limit to the amount of money you can invest in an annuity.

• The new variable annuity could serve as the ideal replacement for investments that used to receive the benefit of favorable long-term capital-gains treatment. Reason: Long-term gains from investments in stock, which are now going to be taxed as ordinary income, can be sheltered in a variable annuity. That income is not taxed until you withdraw your money.

How annuities work:

An individual buys an annuity from an insurance company, paying a lump sum or a series of payments over time. In return, the insurance company guarantees that the funds will grow at a certain tax-free rate. Then, beginning on a specified date, the individual receives regular income payments for the rest of his life.

Payments depend on the amount of money contributed to the account, the length of time the funds are left in it, and the rate of return earned on the funds. Also a factor in determining the size of the payments is whether you include your spouse and other heirs as beneficiaries. Different options enable you to have payments continue to your wife, or to your children, or for a minimum of, say, 20 years, regardless of who is there to receive them after you die.

Deferred annuities therefore can be considered part insurance and part investment. If you are willing to part with at least $5,000 (the minimum amount can differ from company to company) for five years or longer, you can be guaranteed a competitive, tax-free return on your funds. Because the earned income is not taxed until you begin withdrawing the money (presumable at a much lower tax rate), your funds accumulate much faster than they would if they were taxed. The insurance component, of course, is guaranteed regular monthly income payments for the rest of your life—taking the worry and risk out of budgeting for your retirement income. Also, should you die before you begin receiving payments, your heirs are guaranteed to receive the full amount of your original principal.

Fixed rate vs. Variable:

There are two basic types of deferred annuity, fixed and variable.

Fixed annuity: The insurance company guarantees that your funds will grow at a specified rate (the current range is 7.5%-9%) for a specified period of time. Most companies guarantee a specific rate of return for at least the first year. Thereafter the rate usually fluctuates at least once a year, according to the then prevailing interest rates. Advantage: Although the rates of return for fixed annuities may vary, your principal always remains intact.

Variable annuity: The rate of return is determined by the performance of investments you select from a broad range of mutual funds offered by the insurance company. Investing in a variable annuity is almost identical to investing in a family of mutual funds. You have the same exchange privileges and the choice of putting all your money into one fund or a blend of different funds, or even of dividing your money between a fixed annuity and variable annuity. Advantage: You can earn a much larger return than you might with a fixed annuity. Risk: If your investments perform poorly, your original principal may diminish. The minimum investment for a deferred annuity is generally $5,000. However, some single-premium annuities can require a one-time lump-sum investment of as little as $2,500. A flexible-premium annuity, paid over time, may have an initial minimum as low as $1,000 and require small monthly payments.

Most companies levy an annual management change of .5%–1.5% of total assets. If you invest in a variable annuity, you will also pay a percentage of your total assets to cover management costs for the mutual fund.

Insurance companies typically charge a declining surrender fee of 5%-6% (which usually falls to zero after five or six years) if you liquidate the principal of your annuity. And if you withdraw your money before age 59½, the IRS will charge you a penalty.

Source: Alexandra Armstrong, Alexandra Armstong Advisors, Inc., 1140 Connecticut Ave. NW, Washington, DC 20036.

HOW TO SPOT A FRAUDULENT TAX SHELTER

By their very nature, tax shelters are risky investments. But an investor who prepares for the worst, while hoping for the best, stands a good chance of cutting any losses and reducing the basic risks to an acceptable level. Steps to take:

When you invest: Of course, it's essential to check out the people you're dealing with. You should also make sure the offering documents include a comprehensive tax opinion written by a reputable attorney or accounting firm—such an opinion is extremely helpful in evaluating the program. In addition, if the deal goes sour, you'll probably have at least one potential defendant with "deep pockets" (the ability to pay a judgment if you sue, and win.) Tax shelter promoters and general partners often turn out to be shell corporations, with virtually no assets you can recover against, even if you sue successfully.

Another simple protection, but one a lot of people surprisingly overlook, is getting a full set of investment documents.

Any representation the promoter makes should be confirmed in writing before you invest. You can do this in a low key way by writing a letter after each meeting: "Dear Mr. Jones, thanks for coming by and explaining the Super-shelter-85 program to me. I understand that XYZ Corporation has already agreed to rent 40% of the office space in the proposed office plaza..."

Important. Insist that the promoter provide you with a list of all the other investors. Most tax shelters are set up as limited partnerships, and you're entitled to know who your partners are. If the offering hasn't been fully subscribed when you put your money in, your cash should be held in escrow until the deal is set to go. You should get a list of all the partner's names and addresses at that time. Contact your fellow investors at the outset and lay the groundwork for any future cooperation that may be appropriate. Be on the alert for partners who have received their share without putting up hard cash, people who have contributed services or are taking a partnership share in lieu of some preexisting debt. Such investors, sometimes referred to as "shills," may be an indication that the deal is already in trouble, or at least having difficulty raising cash.

The first year: Review your position approximately eight to ten months after the venture begins. Look for danger signs, such as too many shill partners, failure or refusal to supply interim financial data, failure of third parties to enter into anticipated contracts, difficulties in obtaining outside financing, vague, evasive or nonexistent communications from the promoters.

This review should be completed before the first year is up. It may be your last chance to withdraw from the deal with relative ease. Reason: Most shelter promoters don't go through the lengthy and expensive process of registering their offerings with the Securities and Exchange Commission (SEC). They rely instead on exemptions from the registration requirement. But these exemptions are very complex. It is common for shelter promoters to be technically in violation of the SEC rules. Such a violation may give you the right to rescind your investment at any time during the first year. Threatening to raise this issue is often enough to get the promoters to refund your investment.

After the first year: Frequently the problems don't surface until sometime in the second or third year, when cash flow is supposed to begin or some other commitment isn't met. The statute of limitations under the federal securities law, which usually provides an investor's strongest basis for suing, is three years. If there is going to be a lawsuit, it normally should be started within three years after the investment is made. There may be a way around this problem, if the investors had no way of knowing about the misrepresentations at the outset. In that case, the three-year limitation period starts from the date the investors know, or should have known, about the problem. But pinpointing this date can be difficult, and the burden is on the investors.

Before filing suit: Use an attorney who has experience with this type of lawsuit. There are three things to determine.

• Are there grounds for suit? Remember, shelter investments are supposed to be risky. Presumably, legitimate tax benefits make the risk less onerous, but they don't eliminate it.

There have to be some grounds for arguing that a material fact was knowingly misrepresented, that you, as an investor, used due diligence in checking out the investment . . . and that the misrepresented fact was one of the items you relied on when you made your investment. If these conditions are met, a lawsuit can often be maintained under the federal securities law. Sometimes state securities laws can also be used. They may place less of a burden on the investor to show due diligence or reliance on the misrepresented facts.

• Is there a defendant worth suing? It's usually hard to collect a judgment from the promoter/general partner. But it may be possible to sue the professionals who prepared the tax opinion or financial projections, the bank that provided financing, brokers and sales organizations, or individual officers, directors and backers of the promoter or general partner. You must show that some or all of these people knew or should have known about the misrepresentation and aided or abetted the making of it.

• Can the investors work together? Given the risks involved, usually no single investor should put in more than 15%-20% of his original cash contribution to finance a lawsuit. Costs can easily run $200,000 or more if a full-fledged trial is required. That calls for coordinated action among 10-20 investors. If the group is larger than that, it can become unwieldy. Very large groups may designate representatives to act on their behalf. Each plaintiff must be prepared to put up the cash and to commit the energy and effort necessary to follow through. A case like this can easily run two to four years. A plaintiff who won't cooperate by answering interrogatories and preparing for depositions can torpedo the whole project.

Settling: Once the lawsuit is filed, the various defendants often will file motions seeking to be dismissed from the suit. As soon as these motions have been dealt with and the lineup of defendants is set, efforts should be made to settle. If some of the defendants are represented by insurance companies experienced in suits like this, they will know that even a successful defense can cost them $100,000 or more if the case goes to trial. Assuming the case has some merit, they may be willing and wise to settle for 40%-60% of this amount to avoid litigation expense. If a reasonable settlement offer is made, consider it seriously. Pressing the lawsuit will be time consuming and expensive.

If the suit is not settled early, be prepared for a long battle. Getting to trial may take over four years and post-judgment motions, appeals and new trials could possibly double that time. Realistically, the battle usually isn't worth fighting unless there is solid evidence of securities law violation and at least a few hundred thousand dollars at stake.

Source: J.H. Mitchell, Jr., partner, Mihaly, Schuyler & Mitchell, lawyers.

REAL ESTATE TRAPS AND NEW OPPORTUNITIES

Tax reform contains dangers for many real estate investors, but it also presents opportunities for those who act cleverly.

Tax shelters;

The toughest provision of tax reform took dead aim at tax shelters. The trap: Real estate investment produced large tax losses as a result of depreciation and interest deductions. Many people made long-term real estate investments to obtain such losses, which they used to cut tax they owed on income from other sources. But since tax reform prohibited the deduction of real estate losses against salary or investment income, the main purpose behind these investments is defeated.

What you can do:

• Under tax reform, losses from real estate can be used to offset income earned from real estate. Thus, a real estate tax shelter can remain a tax shelter under tax reform, as long as you're earning income from other real estate investments. Look for real estate deals that promise taxable income and cash flow.

• You may be able to cut tax losses or increase reported gains from current real estate investments by restructuring terms. Consider refinancing loans to cut interest costs, raising rents to increase income (even if

this means bargaining with tenants by extending leases, etc.) and attracting extra capital to retire debt.

Under tax reform there are still many ways for individuals to use real estate to cut their tax bills. Ideas:

• While tax reform doesn't let you currently deduct real estate losses from salary or investment income, it does let you carry such losses forward to future years to offset future gains from real estate. Thus, if you own property that's appreciating in value, it may pay to hold it for a few years, then sell it and use your accumulated losses to shelter your gain from tax.

• If you own your own business, you can retain personal ownership of real estate used by the business, then have the business lease the property from you. Advantages: You can set the terms of the lease (though it must provide for a rent that's reasonable in relation to the market). Thus, you can fix the lease to provide you with income that will be sheltered from tax by losses you're receiving from other investments. Or the lease can provide losses that you can use to shelter your other passive income.

• Under a special provision of tax reform, those with income of under $100,000 can still make direct investments in real estate and deduct up to $25,000 in losses each year. Thus, a person can buy an apartment or house, rent it out and use the tax losses that result to cut the taxes owed on salary or investment income. Requirements: You must own the property directly, not as an investor in a limited partnership. And you must actively manage the investment property yourself. The market for real estate investments remains as active as ever after tax reform, but there are dramatic changes in the way these deals are packaged and sold.

• Income deals. Most attractive under the new law are real estate deals that are structured to produce annual cash flow for the investor. Because depreciation deductions remain under the new law, this income can be sheltered from tax, with excess depreciation being accumulated to shelter ultimate gain when the property is sold. Result: The investor receives tax-free income similar to that which might be obtained from an investment in tax-exempt bonds—with a chance for additional large profits through the property's appreciation.

The day of the real estate deal made purely for tax reasons is over. Today prospective real estate purchases must be evaluated on the basis of economic fundamentals. Before buying now, it's important to evaluate property carefully. Will it appreciate in value? Provide sufficient cash flow? Meet your personal or business needs?

Tax savings through real estate are still possible—but it's more important than ever that the tax aspects of any deal be crafted to match your specific circumstances. Be sure to consult an expert before acting.

Source: Glenn Davis, partner, BDO Seidman, 15 Columbus Circle, New York 10023.

HOW TO PICK THE RIGHT FRANCHISE

Corporate executives and "semi-executives," disillusioned about corporate life, see the virtue of making a large investment of money, time and effort in a promising franchise.

Many see it as the best of both worlds: Entrepreneurial independence coupled with a successful business record and a serious organization that will do some hand-holding if necessary.

Besides the career motive, there is also the attraction of a fairly large return. For example, a McDonald's franchisee can put down $250,000-$400,000 and expect a gross of $800,000-$1,400,000—and make a profit of $100,000-$150,000. That is a very attractive return. Guideline: A franchisee should recover his investment within three years.

There are two major elements to assess when buying a franchise:

• Assessing the market. Is the franchisor promoting an enduring product or service, such as food or auto repair? Or is it a transient fad like trampolines or miniature golf courses? One organization that develops franchising programs for corporations rejects over 80% of the companies that seek their advice because the ideas just don't have endurance. If it is a novelty that has not been proven, the investor is taking a real gamble.

Among the tried and proven, there are different styles. One must choose carefully. In restaurants, for instance, choose a franchise that conforms to the ethnic taste and general socioeconomic environment where you want to locate. Example: Today, the type of franchise that is surging forward is the Mexican food restaurant, because of the growth of the Hispanic population and its influence on the rest of our culture.

Also take into account the marketing position of the franchisor—its image and reputation. Look for one that has positioned itself distinctively in the market. For example, Wendy's Hamburgers' "fresh and juicy" image is in direct competition with the precooked image of Burger King and McDonald's. Wendy's uses that competitive edge as a benefit and sets up its stores right next to the big chains' outlets.

• Assessing the organization. If the franchise already is operating and there are other franchises, interview as many of them as possible — at least 10. Twenty is better. They have put their money into it and are experiencing the day-to-day problems.

If the franchise is new, you are really buying just a concept, and you will be the prototype. The figures you are receiving from the franchisor are theoretical. So first check out the market for the product by interviewing people in other organizations or independent entrepreneurs who are selling similar or related products. Then examine the previous business record of the franchisor with whom you are interested in working. He may be inexperienced or unprepared to work closely with you, and that could spell disaster. Franchising should be a proven operating business that can be duplicated elsewhere.

Expenditures. Once you have chosen a franchise, expect three types of fees:

• The one-time franchise fee that enables you "to become a member of the club." It reimburses the franchisor for recruitment screening and training costs.

• The costs of the structure and equipment necessary to run the franchise. With a fast-food franchise of the McDonald's type, this could run to $600,000.

- Residuals—a percentage of gross sales.

Some franchisors want an additional percentage of gross sales to pay for advertising. Advertising is absolutely essential to bring good traffic to the operation. However, when a franchise system is just beginning, advertising is so limited that it would be an injustice to pay that percentage. A better choice would be to negotiate for limited local advertising and a lower price tag until the franchise rolls out heavy nationwide campaigns. When buying into an existing franchise, be sure that it has sufficient units in your area to allow the share of the cost for expensive prime-time advertising to be affordable for each franchisee.

Expensive vs. inexpensive. It is accepted in franchising circles that it is easier to sell the expensive franchises —the $5 million and $10 million Holiday Inns and Quality Inns and Burger Kings —than the $10,000 bottom-of-the-line outfits. The reason is simple: Small-scale franchisees fall apart if there are a bad few weeks. They don't have sufficient experience to promote themselves and spend their own money to get customers. They shy away from taking risks. For the investor, it is best to be involved with more sophisticated, management-oriented franchisees.

The work load. McDonald's won't permit a franchisee to be an absentee owner. Franchisees must get involved in management. Yet it need not be a full-time occupation. It is possible to find a good motivated manager and give him some equity —some shares of stock that can be increased with good performance. Participation breeds better performance — and in franchising, entrepreneurial enthusiasm is absolutely essential.

Source: David D. Seltz, Seltz Franchising Development, Inc., New Rochelle, NY.

PERSONAL TAX SHELTERS

If you're afraid of owning any of the high-return but tricky tax shelters you hear about, or if you'd like to keep more control over your investments, there are many personal tax shelters. These are ways of investing your money to get maximum tax advantages.

Real estate opportunities.

All real estate purchases have tax advantages. Even if you just buy a better home for your family, you get deductions for mortgage interest and real estate taxes—so Uncle Sam is picking up part of the tab.

Renting out a house: If you decide to rent out your old house (or if you buy a house to rent), you can deduct all your expenses from the rent you receive. You can also deduct the depreciation on the house (based on cost or on the market value at the date of conversion to rental property, whichever is lower). During this period, you're likely to have a tax loss, even if the property is producing cash income. A loss up to $25,000 may be recognized, provided your income is not too high.

Caution: You can depreciate the cost of the house only. Land is not depreciable.

Renting to relatives. If you rent to relatives at a fair market value rental, you may realize substantial tax savings. Example:

Your parents want to retire in Florida. If you buy a house or condominium there and rent it to them, you can deduct expenses and depreciation. If your parents buy the home, they can deduct only interest and taxes. Should your parents die, you can rent the property to someone else or sell it and pay only capital gains tax. Or you might decide to keep the home for your own retirement.

Caution: You must charge the normal market rent on the property. Otherwise, the IRS will be able to claim that there was no bona fide business transaction.

Equipment leasing. This common tax shelter device can be combined with a trust for family purposes. The owner of a business sets up a trust for a family member. Business property or equipment is transferred to the trust and then leased back to the business. The trust gets the income, and the business gets a deduction for the rental it pays. Or the trust could purchase equipment for lease to the business, thereby obtaining deductions for interest and other expenses. Some deals have been challenged by the IRS, so get advice.

Other shelters:

Municipal bonds: Income from these is tax free. But bonds pay less. To see whether they're good for you, figure what your money would earn in other investments and how much tax you would pay. Compare the after-tax income with the yield you could get from municipals. Municipals pay a fixed interest rate. You lose on them if other interest rates go up and win if the rates go down. So your decision may depend on what you expect the economy to do in the future.

Deferring income: By now everyone knows about IRAs and Keogh plans for the self-employed. You put money in a retirement trust and pay no tax until you actually withdraw it—withdrawals must start at age 70½. Meanwhile, the trust income accumulates tax free. Some executives also have arrangements with their employer to defer part of their compensation until after retirement. But simply deferring income is no longer a very attractive option. Now that the top tax rate is down to 28%, most executives won't be in a substantially lower tax bracket after they have retired. They're better off taking the money now and investing it.

Source: Norman J. Ginstling, partner, Deloitte & Touche, New York.

INVESTORS CAN PROFIT MORE UNDER TAX REFORM

First: Long-term capital gains are taxed at a preferential rate—28%.

Second: "Passive losses" (e.g. from limited partnerships) will no longer be deductible, except as an offset against "passive income" (the anti-tax shelter provision).

These changes dictate an entirely new strategy for many investors. Here are investments that look good under the new rules.

• Buying your own home may be the best investment you ever make. First of all, you'll have a place to live. And you get tax deduc-tions, not available to people who rent, for real estate taxes and mortgage interest. You can sell the home and defer tax on the gain by purchasing another within two years. At age 55, you can exclude from tax $125,000 of gain whether you buy another home or not.

New advantage: The tax reform law killed the deduction for consumer interest (on car loans, credit cards, student loans, etc.). Home owners, however, can obtain cash—not exceeding $100,000 for such purposes through home equity loans—for which interest is deductible.

• Real estate investment trusts (REITs) and the new real estate mortgage investment companies (REMICs) receive favorable treatment under the new tax reform law and may become the hottest investments in the field.

• Real estate limited partnerships are still good but only if they produce positive cash flow and income. If you already have investments that are producing passive losses, it's important to find investments that produce offsetting passive income.

• Municipal bonds, at first glance, seem less valuable under the new law. Their tax-exempt status is worth less because of the lowered tax rates. On the other hand, many municipals with high yields are available. And the exemption from state and local taxes is important to investors in high-tax states.

• US Series EE Savings Bonds are attractive, especially to conservative investors. You're guaranteed 6% even if the interest rate drops. If it rises above 6%, you get 85% of the difference (adjusted every six months). Series EE bonds come in denominations as small as $50. Like all Treasury securities, they're exempt from state and local taxes. And you have the option of deferring federal taxes until the bonds are cashed. Moreover, interest on bonds purchased in 1990 or later may be tax-free if used to pay education costs.

Investing for retirement:
• Keogh plans for the self-employed are still great investments. The new law changed the rules only slightly.

• 401 (k) plans. Contributions are limited (about $9,000 for 1993, indexed for inflation annually), and the rules on withdrawals have been tightened. But contributions are still effectively "tax deductible" and accumulate tax free until withdrawn. If your employer has a 401(k) plan, take advantage of it

• IRAs. Many taxpayers will no longer be able to make deductible contributions because they are covered by their company's retirement plan. They can, however make nondeductible contributions to take advantage of tax-free accumulation.

Example: $2,000 invested in an IRA at 8% will grow to more than $9,500 in 20 years. If annual taxes had to be paid on the income, the investment would grow to only slightly over $6,000.

Source: Robert A. Garber, vice president, executive financial services. Salomon Brother, Inc., One New York Plaza, New York 10004.

SUBSTITUTE FOR MUNICIPAL BONDS LOOPHOLE

To get muni-like tax-free income from rental real estate, buy the property with a low enough mortgage so that your deduction for depreciation equals the income the property earns. The lower mortgage interest payments make the cash flow, up to the depreciation amount, tax-free.

Opportunity: An arrangement of this kind is valuable for taxpayers with Adjusted Gross Income in excess of $150,000 who do not qualify for the $25,000 exception to the passive activity rules.

Source: Edward Mendlowitz, partner, Mendlowitz Weitsen, CPAs, Two Pennsylvania Plaza, New York 10121.

22. Fighting the IRS

Fighting the IRS

SOLVE YOUR TAX PROBLEMS IN ADVANCE

Many financial decisions turn on tax considerations. But what if you're not sure of the tax consequences of your decision? For example:

• You're considering an exchange of property, but only if the exchange is ruled tax free.

• A modification of a divorce settlement is proposed. How will it affect the status of payments?

• You're working out an arrangement to defer compensation. But if it doesn't meet all the tax requirements, you could find yourself being taxed on income you won't receive for years.

• You want to know if a scholarship is tax free.

• A family member needs extensive physical therapy. Can you build a swimming pool and deduct the cost as a medical expense?

You can't make a sound decision until you know how the IRS will view the transaction.

The solution: Get a private letter ruling. Any taxpayer (or authorized representative) can get an IRS ruling on the tax effect of most proposed transactions. The IRS charges a fee for these rulings. Corporations have used this procedure most often. A ruling is equally available to an individual. And it applies to tax questions involving estates, trusts and gifts, as well as to personal income taxes.

Tax protection:

If you get a favorable ruling in advance, your tax position is fully protected. Even if other taxpayers are treated differently, or if the IRS changes its mind, the ruling in your case will not be changed retroactively except in unusual circumstances. (Note: A private letter ruling is binding on the particular transaction it covers. Similar situations involving other taxpayers will probably be treated the same way, but not necessarily.)

The IRS gives you a chance to talk the situation over before a ruling is issued. If it ap-

pears that some aspects of the transaction may lead to adverse tax results, you can modify or amend your proposal to come up with a plan that will qualify for the ruling you want. Caution: There's no point in asking for a ruling if you're sure it will go against you. Study the rulings issued to other taxpayers with similar problems. These rulings are all published, and you can find them through several tax services. Also, your accountant or attorney probably can talk with IRS people and sound them out informally.

Letter rulings generally can't be appealed. You can appeal to the courts only after a return has been filed and tax assessed.

How to get a ruling:

There is no prescribed form. Send a letter to the Internal Revenue Service. The IRS will generally get in touch with you within 21 working days. Include in your letter:

• A complete statement of all the facts.

• A carefully detailed description of the transaction.

• Names, addresses and taxpayer identification numbers of all persons involved.

• Copies of all relevant documents.

• An explanation of the transaction's business purpose. ("Business" includes personal and commercial financial dealings.)

• A statement of what ruling you are asking for.

• Citation of authorities (regulations, decisions, etc.).

• Arguments supporting your position.

• Whether the issue, or an identical issue, is being examined, litigated, etc.

• A request for a conference to discuss the matter.

• The location of the district office having jurisdiction.

• A penalty of perjury statement.

• Some of the confidential information (names, addresses, etc.) is deleted before publication of IRS rulings. You should state which information you want deleted and why.

Other requirements:

You must put everything in writing. If you supply any information verbally, it must be confirmed in writing within 21 days or the IRS will not consider it. If the IRS requests additional information, it must be submitted in writing. Information must be complete. If you leave out or misstate material facts, the ruling could be invalidated.

Conference:

You're entitled to a conference with the IRS. Ask for it when you submit your original letter. The conference is more informal than a hearing. You'll get a chance to argue your position with the IRS representatives and see what their opinion is likely to be.

This is the time to find out what objections, if any, the IRS has to your proposal and what changes are necessary to make it acceptable. You or your representative may well be able to come up with modifications to the proposed transaction that will lead to a favorable ruling.

Safe strategy:

If the IRS reaction is negative, and you can't come up with an acceptable modification, withdraw your request. Having no ruling at all is better than having an unfavorable one. Reason: You must attach any unfavorable ruling to your tax return.

When the IRS will not rule:

There are some issues the IRS will not rule on, either by law or as a matter of policy. Examples: Purely hypothetical questions: Issues involving determinations of fact. Other major "no-ruling" issues:

• The prospective effect of estate taxes on the property of a living person.

• Issues on which there are court decisions the IRS may be planning to appeal.

• Issues on which no regulations have yet been issued (unless the application of the law itself is obvious).

• The effect of pending legislation.

• Whether a proposed action would subject a taxpayer to criminal liability.

Source: Arthur S. Gordon, a partner with Arthur Andersen & Co., New York.

LAST-MINUTE FILING TIPS

Don't forget to sign. Both husband and wife must sign a joint return.

Be sure to put your name and Social Security number on every form and every piece of paper attached to the return—if they get separated they may never find their way back.

Check your arithmetic. Make sure you used the right tax table. Mistakes will delay your refund. If you owe money, you may be charged interest.

Tip: Round figures to the nearest dollar. You'll make fewer errors.

Put forms in order: The return on top (Form 1040), then Schedules A, B, C, etc. followed by numerical forms in order.

Don't forget the following forms, if they apply:

• Form 2210, if you owe more than 10% of the total tax. Use the form to figure whether you owe a penalty or come within one of the exceptions (e.g., your current year tax payments at least equal last year's tax.)

• Form 6251 (Alternative Minimum Tax). If you are liable for the alternative minimum tax, you must file Form 6251. It applies if you have tax preference items, such as accelerated depreciation, or intangible drilling costs.

• Form 4684, casualty and theft losses.

• Form 8283, if you gave more than $500 in property to charity. This is a statement showing nature of the property, valuation, etc.

Answer all questions or check the correct boxes.

• Your occupation: You can use general terms like executive or administrator.

• On Schedule B (Interest and Dividends): Questions on foreign bank accounts or trusts.

• On Schedule C (Self-Employed): Questions on accounting methods and home office use.

• On Form 2441 (Child Care Credit): Questions on employees hired to work in your home.

Attach all W-2 forms from employers. But you can file without a W-2 if you have to. Attach an explanation of why the form is missing, along with any evidence of wages paid and taxes withheld, such as a final pay stub.

Put on enough postage when you mail the return. If it comes back you could be hit with a penalty for late filing. Don't use a postage meter. The date may be unacceptable as proof. If you're worried about proving you filed on time, use certified mail. Better yet, deliver the return to IRS personally and get your copy receipted.

Extensions: If you aren't able to file on time, you can get an automatic four month extension by filing Form 4868. Further extensions are available only by showing good cause.

Caution: You get an extension of the time to file, not the time to pay. Estimate the tax due and send it in with Form 4868. If you estimate too low, you'll be charged interest. If you're too low by more than 10%, you may be subject to a penalty.

Source: Tom C. Klein, CPA.

UNANSWERED QUESTIONS CAUSE PROBLEMS

Income tax returns with unanswered questions are considered no returns. That means the statute of limitations never expires and you can be audited no matter how many years have passed. Unanswered questions can also delay refunds, result in interest charges, and call attention to your return by IRS agents (since the computer automatically spits out the return). If a question doesn't seem to apply to you—Do you have any foreign bank accounts? Do you claim a deduction for an office in your home—just answer no—but answer.

DEALING WITH THE IRS

There are ways to make the IRS bureaucracy work for you and work efficiently. But you

must know how the system operates, and where to call or write to get results.

Collection notices:

Problem: Even though you've written the IRS an answer to its collection notice, the notices keep coming. You get a second notice, and a third one, and then one that says, "Past Due Final Notice (Notice of Intention to Levy)." This final notice (sometimes it's the third in a series) is the one to watch out for. Trap: The IRS can seize your bank account without first having an IRS employee meet with you. They can notify you by mail and then automatically take money from your account.

Self-defense: If you get such a final notice, immediately call the phone number given on the notice and explain that you've already written to them and you don't owe tax. The Collection Division employee who answers the phone at that number has the authority to put a hold on collection action if given a good reason to. Unfortunately, not all of them will take that step.

Loophole I: If the person who answers your call isn't receptive, excuse yourself and call back. You won't get the same person. There's a decent chance that your second call will be answered by someone who is willing to put a hold on the levy.

Loophole II: You can delay collection action on a tax deficiency you're protesting by filing a claim for a refund. The refund claim will cause the IRS to automatically put a hold on collection action. This is a smart move if you've missed the deadline for filing a Tax Court petition.

Source: Peter A. Weitsen, partner, Mendlowitz Weitsen, CPAs, Two Pennsylvania Plaza, New York 10121.

LATE FILING EXCUSES THAT WORK

Any person who fails to file a federal income tax return without obtaining a filing extension faces the prospect of stiff tax penalties. But penalties can be avoided if the taxpayer acts quickly to present the IRS with an adequate late filing excuse. Here are some excuses that usually work:

- The death or serious illness of an immediate family member.
- Incapacitating illness of the taxpayer himself.
- Unavoidable absence of the taxpayer from home due to circumstances beyond his control.
- Destruction of the taxpayer's records due to circumstances beyond his control, such as fire or flood.
- A competent and informed tax adviser told the taxpayer that a tax return was not necessary.
- The IRS failed to provide the taxpayer with necessary forms, after he requested them to do so in timely fashion.

To present the excuse, the taxpayer should file the overdue return as quickly as possible, with an explanation of the delay attached. If the IRS is satisfied the taxpayer acted reasonably under the circumstances, it will abate any penalty. But the IRS is not required to accept any excuse, so expedient action by the taxpayer is a must.

Taxpayers who face penalties for misfiling returns or misreporting income will do the best they can to come up with a good explanation. Some excuses work—others don't.

Excuses that work:
- Reliance on bad IRS advice from an IRS employee or an IRS publication. If the advice came from an employee, you must show that it was his job to advise taxpayers and that you gave him all the facts.
- Bad advice from a tax professional can excuse a mistake if you fully disclosed the facts to the adviser. You must also show that he was a competent professional, experienced in federal tax matters.
- Lost or unavailable records will excuse a mistake if the loss wasn't the taxpayer's fault and he makes a genuine attempt to recover or reconstruct the records.
- Incapacity of a key person can be a legitimate excuse. Examples: Serious illness of the taxpayer or a death in his immediate family.

Excuses that don't work:
- Pleading ignorance or misunderstanding of the law generally does not excuse a mistake. Exception: Where a tax expert might have made the same mistake.
- Someone else slipped up. You are personally responsible for filing your tax return correctly. You can't delegate that responsibility to anyone else. If your accountant or lawyer files late, for example, you pay the penalty.
- Personal problems don't carry much weight with the IRS. For example, don't expect to avoid a penalty by pleading severe emotional strain brought on by a divorce.

EASY WAYS TO FILE FOR EXTENSIONS

Better late than never is not a good idea when filing your tax return. Each year, more and more Americans face April 15 without the complete information they need to file a proper return. Frequent problem: Partnership data from tax shelters is missing. Some promoters are months late in sending out the K-1 schedules that contain individual partners' tax information. What should you do?

Fortunately, there is an easy answer—file extension Form 4868 on or before April 15. The extension automatically gives you until August 15 to file. But it does not give you extra time to pay. The form requires that you estimate the tax you still owe and send it in with your extension request.

Not filing your tax return when due is an expensive disaster. You must pay interest from the due date of the return to the date the tax is finally paid.

There are two additional penalties. The first is a penalty for failure to pay on time. It is .5% per month on the net amount of tax due, up to 25%. This penalty can be avoided if, when you file your return (having gotten a proper extension), the balance of tax still due doesn't exceed 10% of your total tax liability, and you pay the balance with your return. There is an even stiffer penalty for failure to file your return on time. This penalty is 5% per month (for each month or fraction of a month), up to 25% maximum. The failure to pay penalty goes up to 1% a month after you receive an IRS notice to pay tax.

Example: Joe Lately mails his return on June 4, along with a $10,000 check for the tax he owes. Since Joe had not filed an extension request, the IRS bills him for the interest plus a $1,100 penalty (5% for one full month plus 5% for a fraction of a month, or 10% plus .5% for two months for failure to pay). If Joe had filed Form 4868, the most he would pay would be interest plus the .5% penalty for two months (1% × 10,000 or $100).

Sometimes even a four month extension is not enough. An additional extension is possible. Use Form 2688 or send a letter to the IRS Service Center where your return is filed. This time the extension is not automatic. In your letter (or on Form 2688), report: (1) Type of return you're supposed to file and the tax year involved. (2) Reason for the delay. (3) Whether you filed your returns for the last three years on time (and, if not, why you were late). (4) Whether you were supposed to have been paying estimated tax and, if so, whether you made each payment on time.

If you can't pay:

Some people put off filing their returns because they owe a sizable balance that they can't pay right away. This is not a good idea. For one thing, the penalties will be much higher ultimately. And putting off filing because you can't pay is probably the most common way that people fall into the trap of not filing at all. That can be disastrous. It may even lead to criminal charges.

How to handle it: File the return but omit the payment. Over the next couple of months, you'll receive a series of three notices requesting payment. The last will be a 10-day warning. Before those 10 days are up, contact the IRS collection division. If you don't have a pattern of tax delinquencies and you're genuinely unable to pay at once, the IRS will work with you to set up a schedule of installment payments.

Source: Irving Blackman, Blackman Kallick Bartelstein, CPAs, Chicago.

TAXPAYER PENALIZES IRS FOR LATENESS

You file your tax return in February, and get a refund check in May—but no interest. Does

the government owe you interest on the money?

No. The government doesn't have to pay interest if it sends your refund within 45 days of the date the return was due—April 15—not 45 days from the date you filed it. But if it doesn't get the refund out within the 45 days, it has to pay interest all the way back to April 15, even if it's only one day late.

NO PENALTY FOR LATE-FILERS

Late tax filers may escape penalties because the IRS has *no way of checking* whether or not a person filed an extension request on time. The General Accounting Office (GAO) reports that the IRS has no procedures for tracking Form 4868 extensions and that "as a matter of policy," it generally does not assess failure-to-file penalties because of this lack. The GAO also reports that, in many cases, taxpayers avoid penalties by producing copies of extensions that were "purportedly" filed on time, even though the IRS has no record of them.

HIDDEN TREASURES IN YOUR OLD TAX RETURNS

It's surprising how often people pay more income tax than they have to. Overlooked deductions, alternative (money-saving) ways of computing tax liability, little-known exemptions and credits—there could be big dollars in missed tax-saving opportunities on your old returns, up to three years old, in most cases.

You can still get refunds you overlooked the first time around by filing an amended return (Form 1040X). The procedure is simpler and safer than most people think.

All the form requires is some basic identifying data, an explanation of the change that's being made and a recomputation of the tax. You don't have to re-do the entire return. And the IRS will figure out how much interest it owes you.

The IRS does not automatically audit you just because you've filed for an additional refund. But it is useful to thoroughly document the basis for amending your return. The clearer it is, the less the likelihood that it will be looked at twice.

What if there's a problem area on your return that's unrelated to the item you're amending? For example, you've just found out that you could have claimed a dependency exemption and a large medical deduction for your mother-in-law, whose nursing home bills you were paying two years ago. However, you deducted a lot of travel and entertainment business expenses that year, and you'd have a hard time pulling those records together if the IRS decided to check them.

In practice, the possibility that the IRS will even look at such an unrelated area of your return is low. But you can make things even safer by working with the statute of limitations. How: You wait to file until a week or so before the deadline for requesting a refund. The same deadline applies to the IRS. It can't assess additional tax unless you failed to report more than 25% of your income or committed tax fraud.

The worst that could happen, in the unlikely event that the IRS does examine other areas of your return and find a deficiency, is to apply that deficiency against the refund you've requested. It can't bill you for additional tax due.

The deadline is three years from the original or extended due date of the original return.

Here are items to look for:
• Medical expenses for medical dependents. You can sometimes deduct, for tax purposes, medical expenses you've paid on behalf of someone for whom you can't claim a dependency deduction because he or she has too much gross income. That person must have met all the criteria for being claimed as a dependent, except that his or her own income was too high. You must have provided more than one-half of the total support for a medical dependent.
• Tax computations: If you received a lump-sum pension or profit-sharing distribution, you may qualify for special 10-year averaging. This right is generally repealed from 1987 on, for those under 50 on December 31, 1985; five-year averaging is substituted.

Another one of the alternative tax computations: If you received a lump-sum pension or profit-sharing distribution, you may qualify for special 10-year averaging. This right is generally repealed from 1987 on, for those under 50 on December 31, 1985; five-year averaging is substituted.
• Exemptions: Occasionally, someone who's not a member of your household could have been claimed as a dependent if he or she is related to you, received more than half his support from you and didn't have too much nonexempt income of his own.
• Shared support: Several people may have been contributing to support someone, with no one person contributing more than half that person's support. With the consent of the others, one member of the group can claim a dependency exemption, if the group as a whole provides more than half the support.
• Dividends on public utility stocks: Sometimes part or all these dividends are tax free, but information on how much of the dividend is tax free may have been announced after you filed your return. Check with your broker.
• Miscellaneous possibilities: Job-hunting expenses, non-cash charity contributions or subscriptions to business, investment and tax publications.

Once you've filed your return, it takes three to six months to get your refund. You are entitled to interest from the due date of the return. The IRS will figure out the various interest rates that applied back to when your original tax return was due.

Don't get impatient. One taxpayer hadn't gotten his refund from an amended return when he filed the next year's regular return. So he just subtracted the money he figured the IRS owed him. That maneuver cost him some heavy underpayment penalties. The two transactions were treated separately.

Source: Steven L. Severin, a tax partner with Deloitte & Touche, New York.

ATTORNEYS' FEES COLLECTIBLE

Attorneys' fees will continue to be collectible from the government after tax reform if the government takes an unreasonable position and the taxpayer eventually wins the case. The old allowance of up to $25,000 has been replaced with a $75-per-hour cap on attorneys' fees.

IRS ENVELOPE LABELS— WHAT THE NUMBERS REALLY MEAN

Here's the scoop on the numbers and symbols on the peel-off label the IRS sends with your tax package.

A. Two-letter "alpha code" that is computer shorthand for your name.

B. Your Social Security number. By entering the two-letter code and your Social Security number, the IRS can identify the correct account. The data-entry clerk doesn't have to type your full name and address into the computer.

C. Postal Service home delivery route.

D. Type of package mailed to the taxpayer—1040, 1040A, etc.

E. IRS service center where you filed your return last year—in this case, Fresno, CA. (S29 is the Ogden service center, Kansas City is S09, and so on.)

F. Your postal ZIP code.

G. The IRS's presort mail for the US Postal Service.

H. Certain labels, to help with mail distribution, have either PP, SS, or PL directly under the "S" in IRS. These letters indicate:

- PP—Package (first label in a package).
- SS—Sack (first label in a sack).
- PL—Pallet (first label in a pallet).

Source: George S. Alberts, former director of the Albany and Brooklyn IRS district offices.

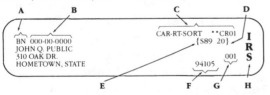

NO STATUTE OF LIMITATIONS FOR FRAUDULENT RETURNS

The Supreme Court of the US has ruled that the IRS has unlimited time to assess tax when a fraudulent return has been filed—even if the taxpayer later files a nonfraudulent amended return correcting his mistake. Filing an amended correct return does not start the running of the usual three-year limitation period, the court held.

Badaracco v. Comm., 104 S.Ct. 756, 1-17-84.

KEEPING A LOW AUDIT PROFILE

Can you take full advantage of all allowable deductions but keep the chance of being audited to a minimum?

What are your chances of being audited? Is there anything you can do to lower your profile? The exact formula for choosing the returns to be audited is an IRS secret, but history shows the high-risk areas.

Before we look at the audit process, here are two important points to keep in mind:

- There is no guarantee you won't be audited: Some returns are chosen entirely at random, just to keep taxpayers guessing. Others are picked at random for the Taxpayer Compliance Measurement Program, an extensive audit for statistical purposes.

- Don't be intimidated by the very thought of an audit: You should never forego a legitimate deduction just because of the possibility of being audited. But you should take the precaution of preparing your documentation and proof. Don't wait until you get actual notice of an audit. By then, papers could be lost and details might be forgotten.

The odds on being audited:

The IRS can audit only a small percentage of the returns filed each year. It's now running at about 1% (about 5% of those making over $100,000). IRS purpose: To recover as much money as possible for the government and to discourage incorrect returns in the future. Its focus: On "problem area" items where it has found the highest percentage of "errors."

Most audits are of one or two items only. The simpler ones are conducted by mail. Relatively few are field audits (covering extensive areas of the return). The IRS considers your total income—not just your adjusted gross income. (A taxpayer with total income of $70,000 and a tax shelter loss of $30,000 has the same adjusted gross income as one with $40,000 of income and no losses. But the first taxpayer is much more likely to be audited.)

Items likely to trigger audits:

• High tax-shelter losses. Shelters considered "abusive" are high-priority audit items. Moral: Be careful when you invest. Be especially wary of shelters offered near the end of the year, when taxpayers are hungry for deductions.

• High Schedule C or Schedule F losses, especially on secondary businesses or farms.

• Casualty losses. (The IRS often challenges the valuation.)

• High charitable contributions, especially contributions of property rather than of cash.

• High miscellaneous expenses, particularly those for travel and entertainment.

• Any deduction significantly higher than the average for your income level.

Strategy to follow:

If your deductions are below average: You probably won't be audited, but perhaps you're being overly conservative. Of course, if you gave $500 to charity, you can't deduct $1,000 just because that's the average. But are you declining to claim deductions you actually incurred, simply because you aren't certain you may have absolute proof? You may even have overlooked or forgotten some deductible items. Go over the possibilities again.

If your deductions are above average: You may want to be less aggressive on borderline items, particularly if you lack documentation. But take what you're entitled to. Use the averages as guidelines. If you have higher deductions, claim them, but be prepared to support the figures on your return.

When to file: Some tax advisors think there's less chance of being audited if you file near the April 15 deadline, when the IRS is swamped with returns. The IRS insists it makes no difference, and there's no real evidence that it does. However, if you want to wait until then, it probably won't do any harm, either.

Tax protests: Unless you want to be audited, don't refuse to pay because you think the tax is unconstitutional, you don't like the way the government spends the money, etc. The IRS always audits such returns, and you will be subject to a $5,000 penalty for filing a "frivolous" law suit if you go to the Tax Court.

Choosing a preparer. Pick a reputable firm, one you can work well with. Find out something about the firm. You might, for example, check with other clients you know personally. A bad preparer can get you audited. In fact, the IRS maintains a "problem preparer" list.

Plan ahead: Keep tax considerations in mind in your financial dealings during the coming year, especially if you're thinking of buying into a tax shelter. If you do have any transactions, losses, deductions, etc. that increase your audit risk, be careful to get together all records, documents or other evidence that may prove necessary.

Source: Lawrence S. Lioz, Deloitte & Touche, New York.

TAX BREAK ON RETIREMENT FUND WITHDRAWALS

The IRS has simplified the withdrawal rules for taxpayers who have more than one retirement account, including all IRAs, company pensions, Keoghs, 401(k)s, or other qualified plans.

You can calculate the minimum required withdrawals, but you can also add them all up and withdraw the total amount from *any* account or accounts that you choose. You might withdraw the entire total from one account and leave all the others untouched.

Actually, your choice isn't entirely unlimited, as company pension plans are *required* to make certain minimum distributions to participants who have reached age 70½. However, you do control your IRAs and can decide which ones to make withdrawals from, and how much.

OUTWITTING THE IRS COMPUTERS

The IRS computers are quite sophisticated and it is virtually impossible to do anything legally to divert their eagle eye from your tax return. By and large this is true, but there are at least two things that may help minimize the effect of the IRS's high-tech capabilities.

First, how income is reported on the return may make a difference. Suppose you have freelance income. If it is merely reported as "Other Income" with an appropriate description as to its source, chances of having the return selected for audit may be smaller than if the same income is reported as business income on Schedule C (Income from a Sole Proprietorship).

Second, you can minimize your chances of being audited by filing as late as legally permissible. A tax return filed around April 15 generally has a greater chance of being audited than one filed on October 15 (the latest possible date). This is because the IRS schedules audits more than a year in advance. As returns are filed and scored by the computer, local IRS districts submit their forecasted requirements for returns with audit potential. The fulfillment is made from returns already on hand. If your return is filed on October 15, there is a smaller chance that it will be among the returns shipped out to the District Office in the first batch. As a result of scheduling and budget problems that are likely to develop in the two years after your return has been filed, it may never find its way into the second batch slated for examination.

Although the IRS is wise to this ploy and has taken steps to make sure that the selection process is as fair as possible, inequities invariably result. Why not try to be part of the group that has the smallest chance of being audited?

Source: *How to Beat the IRS* by Ms. X, Esq., a former IRS agent, Boardroom Books, Millburn, NJ 07041.

IRS HIT LIST

Doctors and dentists are high priority targets. Items IRS agents look for: Dubious promotional expenses. If the same four people take turns having lunch together once a week and take turns picking up the tab, a close examination of diaries and logbooks will show this. Agents also take a close look at limited partnership investments, seeking signs of abusive tax shelters. And they take a dim view of fellowship exclusions claimed by medical residents. Other target occupations:

- Salespeople: Outside and auto salespeople are particular favorites. Agents look for, and often find, poorly documented travel expenses and padded promotional figures.
- Airline pilots: High incomes, a propensity to invest in questionable tax shelters, and commuting expenses claimed as business travel make them inviting prospects.
- Flight attendants: Travel expenses are usually a high percentage of their total income and often aren't well documented. Some persist in trying to deduct pantyhose, permanents, cosmetics and similar items that the courts have repeatedly ruled are personal rather than business expenses.
- Executives: As a group they are not usually singled out. But if the return includes a Form 2106, showing a sizable sum for unreimbursed employee business expenses, an audit is more likely. Of course, anyone whose income is over $50,000 a year is a high-priority target just because of the sums involved.
- Teachers and college professors: Agents pounce on returns claiming office at home deductions. They are also wary of educational expense deductions because they may turn out to be vacations in disguise.
- Clergymen: Bonafide priests, ministers, and rabbis aren't considered a problem group. But if W-2s show income from non-church employers, IRS will be on the alert for mail-order ministry scams.
- Waitresses, cabdrivers, etc.: Anyone in an occupation where tips are a significant factor is likely to get a closer look from IRS nowadays.

Many people, aware their profession subjects them to IRS scrutiny, use nebulous terms to describe what they do. Professionals in private practice may list themselves as simply "self-employed." Waitresses become "culinary employees," pilots list themselves as "transportation executives." But there's a fine line here. Truly deceptive descriptions could trigger penalties. And if the return is chosen for audit, an unorthodox job title for a mundane profession could convince the agent you have something to hide. Then he'll dig all the deeper.

Source: Ralph J. Pribble, former IRS field agent, president of Tax Corporation of California, San Francisco.

SURVIVING AN AUDIT

Knowing how the system at the IRS works gives an experienced practitioner an advantage when it comes to representing a client at an audit. Here are some of the truly "inside" things that go on.

• Postponing Appointments: It is possible, though not likely, that the IRS will actually change its mind about auditing you if you have postponed the appointment enough times. The IRS is constantly under pressure to start and finish tax examinations. If the return selected for an audit becomes "old" (i.e., more than two years have passed since the return was filed), the IRS may not want to start the audit. This situation may develop if you are notified of an audit about 15 to 16 months after filing. By the time you have canceled one or two appointments, the 24-month cut-off period may have been reached.

When is the best time to cancel? The day before the appointment. By that time, the next available appointment will probably not be for six to eight weeks.

Source: *How to Beat the IRS* by Ms. X Esq., a former IRS agent, Boardroom Classics, Springfield, NJ 07081.

HOW TO REDUCE YOUR CHANCES OF BEING AUDITED

Once a year, you face the same dilemma. . . . You want to keep your tax bill as low as possible, but you don't want the IRS to audit you.

While there is no way to eliminate the danger of an audit completely—since some returns are selected totally at random—you can significantly reduce the overall risk. Here are some suggestions:

• Follow instructions precisely—those on the return and in the accompanying instruction kit. Avoid mistakes that might draw attention to your return. Attach all required schedules and forms. Answer all questions, including those that don't apply to you, such as, "Do you have bank accounts in a foreign country?" The computers at the IRS automati-

cally flag questions that go unanswered. While you won't necessarily be audited just because you forgot to answer a question, the oversight may lead the IRS to look more closely at your return and may well trigger an audit if the return indicates a complexity of investments.

• Verify all calculations on the return. The math is fully checked by IRS computers and correction notices are sent to taxpayers who make mistakes. Beyond that, a return with a math error is more likely to be audited than one that is error-free. Common mistakes: Putting figures on the wrong lines. Bringing the wrong totals forward from schedules.

Source: P. Thomas Austin, consultant, Ernst & Young, CPAs, 1300 Huntington Building, Cleveland 44115.

TAX FRAUD: WHO GETS CAUGHT

Executives, lawyers, doctors, and other high income professionals are accused of tax fraud more often than the general population. Charges stem from IRS challenges that there was willful or intentional failure to file, understatement of income, or claiming of fraudulent deductions. About one out of every five charges brought by the IRS in a recent year involved a professional or business executive. The average claim for back taxes is nearly $70,000.

	Investigations	Convictions
Total	8,901	1,476
Of which:		
Business Owners	2,059	328
Other Executives	485	94
Company Officers	485	94
Attorneys	299	46
Managers	232	37
Dentists & Doctors	199	33
Non-CPA Accountants	164	40
CPAs	89	13

Less than 20% of IRS fraud investigations end in convictions. Other cases are dropped, Justice Department refuses to prosecute, or they end with acquittal or dismissal.

ALL ABOUT IRS NOTICES

The first thing to do when you get an IRS notice is to understand what it means. The notice may not be anything to get excited about. For example, the automatic notice IRS sends when you file an amended return.

Never ignore an IRS notice for payment, no matter how wrong the notice is. Respond quickly, within the time limit given on the notice. Once the IRS computer has you targeted, you'll continue to get threatening notices until you do something to take the problem out of the system.

• Don't panic and pay without first checking the figures on a payment notice. The IRS may have made a mistake.

• Avoid trying to straighten out mistakes in person at your local IRS office. The clerk you deal with won't be a person who can resolve the problem—you'll be wasting your time. Telephone or write to your local Service Center.

• Keep copies of your letters to the IRS. You may need a copy if the Service Center loses your letter and says you didn't respond in time.

• Put your Social Security number on every letter you send the IRS.

• See your tax adviser if sizable amounts are involved or if you have the slightest question about the notice. Send your adviser a copy of the notice and copies of all your correspondence to the IRS, to keep his files up to date.

HOW TO DEAL WITH IRS MISTAKES

Common IRS mistakes and what to do about them:

If you receive an incorrect payment notice:

One of the most troubling warnings a taxpayer can get from the IRS is a ''matching'' notice. This is a long computer printout summarizing income you've failed to report and recalculating your tax. The notice is generated by an IRS computer program that matches information forms (1099s) that report income from various sources, such as banks and financial institutions, with what taxpayers report on their returns. The program is good, but it isn't sophisticated enough to deal with some fairly common situations. One problem: The computer matching is done by Social Security number.

Example of mismatching: You have a joint bank account with your brother. But only *your* Social Security number is on the account. If you reported only half of the interest on your tax return, you'll get a matching notice saying that you omitted the other half and owe more tax.

What to do: Call your local IRS Service Center and explain the situation—that the other half of the interest was reported on your brother's return. (There's usually a toll-free number printed on the top of the computer notice.)

Most matching notice mistakes can be resolved over the telephone with Service Center personnel. If you get nowhere with the Service Center clerk, ask to speak to his supervisor, or, call the local District Office of the IRS and ask for a Problems Resolution Officer. It's his job to cut through IRS red tape and help taxpayers resolve problems quickly.

If you receive a penalty notice:

Check penalty notices carefully to see whether you are actually liable for the penalty. Common IRS error: Sending automatic penalty notices for underpayment of estimated tax to individuals who haven't paid 90% of their estimated tax, but who come within one of the exceptions to the underpayment penalty. Defense: Send back a copy of Form 2210 (Underpayment of Estimated Tax by Individuals) along with a copy of the computer notice.

If you didn't file form 2210 and you get a penalty notice for underpayment of estimated tax, go back to the professional who prepared your return. You may be able to use one of the exceptions to avoid the penalty.

Two exceptions to the underpayment penalty for taxpayers who haven't paid in 90% of their estimated tax:

• You paid an amount equal to last year's tax. (This exception may not be available if you make over $75,000 a year.)

• Current year's payments equal 90% of the tax on your ''annualized'' income for the first three, five and eight months of the year.

If an auditor makes mistakes:

When you're called in for an audit, it's very important that you check the revenue agent's figures before you agree to any adjustment of your tax bill. Auditors do make mistakes. Make sure that the agent picked up the correct amount when he recalculated a deduction, and check to see that he's recalculating your tax correctly. Common error: When the agent redoes your tax, he could forget that you used income averaging that year.

More mistakes to watch out for:

Misplaced estimated tax payments: Sometimes checks get credited to the wrong year. You get a notice saying your payment doesn't show up on the IRS computer. What to do: Send a copy of your estimated payment voucher, together with your cancelled check showing when the payment was made.

Interest errors: Always check the interest the IRS charges you on tax underpayments. The rate changes every quarter, so it's easy for the IRS to make a mistake.

Source: Jerry P. Leamon, tax partner, Deloitte & Touche, Cincinnati.

• The IRS mistakenly informed a taxpayer that he had overpaid his taxes, although he had actually underpaid. In an exchange of letters, the IRS took inconsistent positions. In one letter, it said that the return would be accepted as filed—case closed. Then it sent a letter assessing more tax. The taxpayer argued that the IRS should be bound by its "case closed" letter. Court's decision: Taxes must be paid. IRS confusion did not give the taxpayer the right to duck out of taxes he legally owed.

Arthur I. Kaufmann, TC Memo 1982–205.

AUDIT DANGER SIGN

If an IRS agent examining your return asks you to fill out Form 4822 (statement of annual estimated personal and living expenses), be sure to get professional help before you do anything else. Reason: This usually means the agent is looking for signs that you've been spending more money than the income you've reported.

Source: *The Taxpayer's Survival Guide: All You Want To Know About IRS Tax Audits,* TC Publications, El Segundo, CA.

TWO KINDS OF TAX AUDIT

An office audit usually concerns only a few items on your return. These items are checked off in the notification letter, which also sets an appointment for you to appear at an IRS office. A field audit is a more general examination. The letter asks you to make an appointment for an agent to come to your home or business.

Preparing for an office audit:

The notification letter usually gives you two or three weeks to prepare for the audit. The items the IRS is interested in are checked off or written in on the back of the letter.

• If the items checked off can be readily documented by canceled checks and receipts, you may be able to resolve the issue by mail. Make a copy of the documentation and send it in. But first, call the agent and tell him you're mailing in your proof. He'll tell you how to address the envelope so it won't go astray. Hopefully, you'll eventually get a letter back from the agent advising you that your return has been accepted as filed—examination closed.

• The letter may take months to come. If you send the information in and hear nothing for a couple of months, chances are it has been accepted.

• If the questioned item is something that really cannot be answered by mail, you or your representative must assemble your documentation and keep your appointment.

• Ask for a postponement if the date in the notification letter does not give you time to prepare thoroughly. Auditors are very cooperative when you call up and ask for a short delay.

• Important: You have to present substantiation only for items that are checked off in the letter. Take only this documentation to the audit. Don't answer questions about items not checked off. Another notification letter is required for items you were not told to prepare for.

Preparing for a field audit:

In a field audit, your whole return is open for examination. When you telephone the agent to set up an appointment, ask him what he's looking for. You may be able to narrow down the issues. Have documentation ready. While the agent can ask for proof of all items on your return, he has only a limited amount of time.

If the documentation you give him in the first meeting doesn't satisfy him, ask him to list the questions he still has and set a second appointment.

FOUR KINDS OF IRS AUDIT

Correspondence Audit:

Some IRS audits are more thorough than others. The least thorough is a correspondence audit. Here, the IRS seeks to test compliance with perhaps one item on either a regional or national basis. For example, the IRS may send out hundreds of letters asking for verification of energy credit expenditures. On receipt of this notice, all you have to do is mail in the appropriate documentation to support your deduction.

Technically, this inquiry constitutes an audit. Once it takes place, there is very little chance that the rest of your return for that particular tax year will ever be audited. If the IRS should decide it wants to audit your return at a later date, it must go through a formal "reopening procedure"—which is rarely done. The obvious advantage of the correspondence audit is that if the IRS does not select an area in which you may be vulnerable, it will never know that it could have made other adjustments to your return that might have resulted in more tax.

Office audit:

The next level of audit is the Office Audit. This examination is handled at a local IRS office. Typically, one or two deductions on your return will be questioned. Absent special circumstances, such as suspicion of fraud or gross errors in other areas of the return, the audit will not be extended to other issues. The primary advantage of the Office Audit is that it is generally conducted by individuals who lack the sophistication in tax matters needed to rec-

ognize more significant issues. The training and method of operation at the Office Audit level consists of telling the examiner (called a Tax Auditor) exactly what to look for in a given issue. The audit will be conducted mechanically and "by the book."

Field audits:

These are conducted by the best educated employees at the IRS, known as Revenue Agents. They are usually assigned the tax returns of businesses and wealthy individuals. An audit conducted by a Revenue Agent is usually quite complete, and although it will not examine every item in depth, it will attempt to cover many areas. One of the jobs of the Revenue Agent is to identify promptly areas with the potential for extra tax dollars and then to spend time developing the tax issues.

The chances of having the IRS uncover unreported income or disallowing deductions that are either personal or otherwise not deductible are more likely at the Field Audit than at any other type of IRS examination. It is unwise to try to handle a Field Audit yourself because the potential adverse ramifications can be severe—even if you think you did everything right! A sharp Revenue Agent can be quite creative when it comes to interpreting the Internal Revenue Code in the government's favor. Your ability to survive such creativity is enhanced by having an experienced practitioner representing your interests.

TCMP audit:

The most encompassing type of IRS audit is the TCMP Audit. TCMP stands for Taxpayer Compliance Meaurement Program. TCMP audits are conducted to gain a statistical sample of the kinds of adjustments that are being uncovered. (For example, are adjustments of medical deductions on returns with an adjusted gross income of $25,000 or less more likely than on returns with an adjusted gross income of $100,000 or more?) The results of these audits are used to reprogram the IRS computers so that in the future they can select those returns most likely to result in additional tax dollars.

TCMP audits are usually conducted by Revenue Agents. The biggest problem with these examinations is that the Agent is required to comment on every item appearing on the tax return, starting with the spelling of your name. This does not mean that every line is audited, but the audit is lengthy and there is greater risk that adjustments will be found that will cost you a lot of money. One of the required audit techniques is the analysis of all a taxpayer's bank accounts for possible monies that were deposited but not reported.

HOW TO HANDLE AN IRS AUDIT

Don't try to handle an IRS audit yourself. Find an experienced professional to battle the IRS for you. A professional knows how to field an auditor's trick questions.

Finding the right representative:

Not every accountant or lawyer knows how to deal effectively with the IRS. Many are just as unsure and just as afraid of the IRS as the clients they represent. Look for a professional who has handled many IRS audits. Best: An accountant or lawyer who has worked for the IRS as a revenue agent.

Why you should be buying time:

The more time you put between initial contact by the IRS and your first appointment with the auditor, the better off you'll be. Reason: Revenue agents are under considerable pressure to close their quota of cases within a set period of time. The longer your case has been in the agent's inventory, the more likely he is to rush through the audit—to your advantage.

How to buy time: Telephone to ask for an extension. Do this the day before your appointment, not the day you get the appointment letter. By then, the agent will be booked up with other cases for six weeks or so.

If you're persistent, and you have legitimate reasons for extensions, you can generally postpone the audit for up to six months. Caution: Don't ask for a postponement without a good excuse. Stalling can backfire by antagonizing the agent.

Presenting your case:

Prepare meticulously for the audit. Gather all your receipts for the deductions the IRS has questioned. List each, in detail, on a sheet of paper. Also, meticulously reconstruct cash expenditures for which you don't have receipts. Explain exactly how and when you made those expenditures.

By presenting your case in factual detail, you establish your credibility. And credibility is everything at an audit. It will be easier for the auditor to allow nondocumented items if you can show him that you kept some receipts, that you made an effort to comply with IRS rules and regulations, and that you've reconstructed, as best you could, your cash outlays.

Travel and Entertainment audits:

Travel and entertainment is the most commonly audited deduction. Your goal: To limit the items the agent examines by persuading him to do a test check of your expenses. Let the auditor choose a three-month period for detailed examination. Or talk him into limiting the audit to items over, say, $100. Make sure you can document all items in the test-check period or in the amount. Double benefit: A test check cuts down on your work in assembling backup data, and it prevents the agent from rummaging through all your travel and entertainment expenses.

How to bargain during the audit:

Don't expect to walk out of an audit not owing a dime. Your objective is to strike the best possible deal. To get an auditor to see things your way: Keep harping on the items he says must be adjusted. Keep talking. Don't give up until he reduces the adjustment. Even the most hardnosed agent will ultimately concede some proposed adjustments if you're stubborn enough. But you must be prepared to give a little, too—to concede items you're weak on, to bargain. Keep in mind that the agent's goal is to close the case and move on to his next audit.

How to deal with special problems:

Business audits: If your business is being audited, have it done at your accountant's office, not at your home or your place of business. You don't want the auditor to see your standard of living nor run the risk that an employee will say something to the auditor that could hurt you.

Unreported income: Generally required to be asked at IRS audits is: Have you reported all your income? Never answer this or other potentially embarrassing questions with a lie. Deliberately failing to report all your income is a crime. So is lying to an IRS employee. To avoid incriminating yourself, deflect the question with: Why do you want to know that? or: I'll get back to you on that later. The question may not come up again. Another way to avoid answering this question is to not show up for the audit. Then the deductions you've been asked to prove will be automatically disallowed. But you can appeal the agent's disallowance at the appeals level of the IRS. At the appeals level, you're generally not asked whether you've reported all your income.

Special agents: Their job is to develop evidence for criminal tax cases. If they show up at your door, don't answer any of their questions, even seemingly innocuous ones. Tell them to talk with your lawyer. Then retain a lawyer who is knowledgeable in criminal tax matters. Best: A former assistant US attorney.

Source: Randy Bruce Blaustein, former IRS agent, partner, Blaustein, Greenberg & Co., New York.

AUDIT PLOY TO AVOID

Readers of popular tax services are frequently advised to confront IRS auditors with such a stack of bills and receipts that the overwhelmed agent will assume, in frustration, that the proof he wants is somewhere in the pile. This is bad advice. An experienced auditor will recognize this ploy at once. And as one court said recently, "Merely presenting an 'avalanche' of receipts falls woefully short of meeting the [substantiation] requirements. . ."

Lynch, TC Memo 1983–173.

CHOOSING TAX AUDIT SITES

You can meet an IRS agent at your attorney's or accountant's office for an audit even though your report was filed from a home address. It's wise to do so if your home surroundings are luxurious. The IRS instruction book tells the examiner to use his eyes as well as his calculator to assess your tax liability.

"Taxpayer's standard of living is subject to observation. The agent should observe the neighborhood, furnishings, automobiles, etc. The quality of clothing worn by taxpayer and family, as well as their shopping places and methods, should be noted. Their travel, entertainment and recreation styles are good barometers. The schools attended by the children afford another good guide. The observant agent can draw a very good picture of taxpayer's income by evaluating these signs of taxpayer's standard of living."

Source: *Technique Handbook for In-Depth Audit Investigations,* IR Manual MT 4235–1 (12–13–7), Section 642.4

IF IRS AGENT COMES TO YOUR DOOR

The IRS has issued new instructions to be followed by auditors making field visits to a taxpayer's home or place of business. New rule: Agents may enter private premises "only when invited in by the rightful occupant." The IRS is concerned about the growing number of taxpayer lawsuits for violation of privacy rights.

Manual Transmittal 4200–471.

WHEN IT'S SMART TO ASK FOR A TAX AUDIT

• When a business is closed down, the records and key personnel who can provide tax explanations may disappear. A subsequent IRS examination could prove very costly to the business' former owners.

• When someone dies, the heirs can count only on sharing in the after-tax size of the estate. So the sooner the IRS examines matters to settle things, the better.

When a taxpayer requests a prompt assessment of taxes due, the IRS must act within 18 months. Otherwise, the IRS has three years to conduct an examination. Use Form 4810 to ask for the prompt assessment. You don't have to use this form, but if you don't use it, eliminate any uncertainty on the part of the IRS by having your letter mention that the request is being made under Code Section 6501(d).

AUDITS THE IRS FORGETS TO DO

Asking the IRS to transfer your case to another district may be the key to avoiding an audit. Don't expect the IRS to admit it, but transferred cases often fall between the cracks and never get worked on even though the taxpayer has been notified of the examination. Delays caused in processing the case file between districts, combined with the fact that the case is likely to go to the bottom of the pile when it is assigned to a new Agent, may bring help from the statute of limitations. Rather than asking the taxpayer to extend the statute of limitations, as is the usual practice, many agents are inclined to take the easy way out and close transferred cases without auditing them.

Source: Ms. X, a former IRS agent, still well-connected.

WHAT TO DO IF YOU HAVEN'T KEPT GOOD RECORDS

Under the law, a taxpayer has the burden of proving his deductions. If you haven't kept good records, get duplicate receipts from the people you paid money to. Alternatives: Sworn affidavits, copies of canceled checks from your bank (usually available for a fee).

Under IRS guidelines, agents generally will give you adequate time to come up with proof if they believe you're making a good faith effort to cooperate.

Most agents will allow only what you can substantiate under the circumstances. The balance is negotiable. Always present a plausible story to explain your lack of records. Example:

"I realize I didn't follow the law 100% but I couldn't because I had to do so much traveling and there was so much illness at home that I had to take care of. I'm willing to take a reasonable disallowance and prove the illnesses."

What records you should have:

Itemized deductions are a common IRS target. Here's the information you'll need to support your numbers:

Medical expenses:
- Doctor and dentist bills
- Copies of prescriptions
- Doctor's letter describing the illness and treatment to justify travel costs
- Copies of premium invoices and policies to prove medical insurance coverage

Taxes:
- Copies of state and local returns
- Tax bills and receipts (property tax)

Interest:
- Copies of promissory notes
- Mortgage amortization tables

Contributions:
- Letters from the organization that prove the donation
- Appraisals or other proof of value

Casualty losses:
- Police or fire department reports
- Description of property and proof of ownership
- Appraisals to establish value
- Itemized list of stolen/destroyed items
- Documented insurance recovery

Professional fees:
- Invoices or letters itemizing services and detailing percentage of tax-deductible work

Source: Stuart R. Josephs, tax partner, BDO, Seidman, San Deigo, CA.

Inadequate records notice:

That's what you'll get from the IRS after an audit if you haven't properly kept records to substantiate your income and deductions. Despite poor record keeping, you can often work out a satisfactory settlement; the IRS may take your word on a lot of things, if it's reasonable. But don't try it twice. One taxpayer was charged with fraud when he made the same "mistakes" two years later. The government said he had received an Inadequate Records Notice, so he must have known exactly what was wrong.

WHEN YOU DON'T HAVE RECEIPTS

Contrary to wide publicity by the IRS, it is possible to have many deductions allowed at a tax audit even if you don't have receipts. The trick is to reconstruct your expenditures and back them up with corroborating evidence.

Home entertainment:

Suppose you claimed a business expense deduction of $1,000 for home entertainment expenses, but you can't prove, with receipts, that the money was actually spent. First step: Establish the dates that you entertained people in your home. Check your diary. If it's lost, speak to a few people you remember entertaining and ask them to look at their calendars. Next: Make a list of all the people you entertained at each party and record the company they were affiliated with. Jot down your business relationship with each person. This will help you establish, for the IRS, that people were entertained. At the same time, it will refresh your memory. If you mailed invitations or received thank-you notes, it will help you prove your case to show them.

Reconstruction:

Now, reconstruct the amount of money you spent each time you entertained at home. What did you serve? Did you keep a menu? Figure out the approximate cost of the food you purchased. Make a list of the quantity of food and beverages bought, the approximate prices and the name and address of each store that you shopped at. Include items purchased at the supermarket, butcher shop, bakery, fruit store, liquor store and party shop. Don't forget to include the approximate value of food and beverage items served which were on hand and that did not have to be specially purchased.

Other helpful evidence. Photographs taken at each gathering and sworn statements from people attending each party attesting to its date, the approximate number of people present and the types of food and beverages served.

Out of town travel:

Say you drove to Boston from New York for a three-day business trip, but you can't find your hotel bill or most of your receipts from the trip. Start off by reconstructing the fact that you really were in Boston on the days you claim. Do you have toll receipts or gasoline charge-card expenses in the Boston area? Did you make any phone calls and charge them to your home or office during the days you claim to have been away?

If no expense records exist, then try to get affidavits from the people you met with, attesting to the dates you were there and the business that was discussed.

Lodging: Technically, you must have the actual hotel bill to be entitled to a tax deduction for lodging away from home. But it may be possible to convince a revenue agent of the validity of your deduction if you can show him a canceled check paid to the hotel or a charge-card receipt. If neither a check nor a receipt exists, the next best documentation is a hotel rate brochure showing what you were charged.

Other expenses: As part of the reconstruction of your business trip expenses, include the approximate costs of all tips, meals, telephone calls and laundry service.

Minor expenses:

The IRS recognizes that it is virtually impossible (or impractical) for taxpayers to obtain receipts for certain types of business expenses. If a daily diary entry is made to record money routinely spent on taxis, newspapers, magazines and pay-telephone calls, then the chances are quite good that these items will be accepted by an auditor even though no receipts can be produced to prove that the money was actually spent.

After 1984: The rules above will help you prove travel and entertainment costs for prior years. But from 1985 on, the tax law itself requires written records to prove such costs.

Home entertaining. Monthly at-home dinner parties that a publishing executive hosted for prominent guests were a deductible business expense, even though the executive wasn't able to prove that business was actually discussed at the dinners. It was enough, the Tax Court ruled, to show that the dinners were generally conducive to a business discussion.

Key Fact: The taxpayer also did a lot of purely social home entertaining for which he did not claim a deduction.
Jack R. Howard, TC Memo 1981-250

PROOF OF CHARITY

The IRS has imposed tough new substantiation rules for charitable contributions. For cash gifts: Taxpayers must have a canceled check, receipt, or other written evidence showing the amount, date of the gift and the charity's name. For gifts of property: A receipt and a reliable written record about the property will be required. The receipt must include the taxpayer's name, the date and location of the gift, and a detailed description of the property. For property over $500, you must use Form 8283. Written appraisals are necessary for property gifts worth $5000 or more.

Prop. Reg. Sec. 1.170A-13.

IRS POWER TO GET AT FINANCIAL RECORDS

The IRS can compel production of any records of a taxpayer's financial dealings—not only from banks and brokers, but also from department stores, etc. Objective: To find out if the taxpayer is spending more than the income he reported on his return. If he is, he may be asked to explain where he's getting the money—and to pay taxes on it.

HOW TO PROTECT YOURSELF FROM EXCESS IRS INTEREST CHARGES

When the IRS comes up with a deficiency as the result of an audit, the taxpayer is given a waiver to sign and mail back to the Service. According to the tax law, if the IRS doesn't demand payment of the tax bill within 30 days after the waiver was executed, interest on the deficiency stops running.

Problem: The IRS has been charging some taxpayers interest right up to the date of billing, which is often several months after the waiver was signed and returned. This extra interest can be several hundred dollars more than you should pay.

What to do: Carefully check interest charges before paying the deficiency bill. Interest should be charged for the period beginning with the due date of the return and ending 30 days after you sign the waiver and mail it back to the IRS. Pay the tax you owe and the interest that you determine to be correct. Clearly explain in an accompanying letter how you arrived at your figures, including a detailed computation of the correct interest. Note: Pay the deficiency bill within 10 days after you get it. If you don't, interest will start running again.

Source: Peter A. Weitsen, former IRS agent, now with Mendlowitz Weitsen, CPAs, East Brunswick, NJ.

STOPPING IRS INTEREST

Audited taxpayers can stop interest from building up on proposed tax liabilities (while preserving their right to contest the auditor's findings in Tax Court) by depositing the contested amount with the IRS. Conditions: The deposit must be made before the IRS sends a statutory notice of deficiency—a 90-day letter. The taxpayer must say in writing that the payment is "a deposit in the nature of a cash bond." Drawback: If the taxpayer wins in court, the IRS doesn't have to pay interest on the refunded deposit.

IRS Revenue Procedure 82-51.

HOW TO APPEAL A TAX AUDITOR'S DECISION— AND WIN

The best place to settle a tax dispute with the IRS is at the audit or examiner level. However, if you don't reach a satisfactory settlement there, you can request an IRS Appeals Division hearing. If you document your appeal with sound facts or a good legal argument, you have an excellent chance of winning at least some reduction in your tax bill without having to go to court.

In dollars, the Appeals Division settles about

50–60¢ for the taxpayer, per tax dollar dispute.

Why appeals pay off:

Experienced hearing officers: Appeals are handled by highly trained and experienced IRS personnel called appeals officers. Most are CPAs and/or attorneys who have experience as revenue agents. They can generally tell when an auditor has been unreasonable.

Settlement authority: Appeals officers have broad settlement authority—their mission is to resolve tax disputes, without litigation, in a way that is fair and impartial to both the government and the taxpayer. Unlike auditors, who are bound by IRS rulings and record-keeping requirements, appeals officers can settle disputes on the basis of hazards of litigation. This concerns the government's chance of winning or losing if the case goes to court.

If, for example, the appeals officer feels that the government has only a 20% chance of winning in court, he'll settle for an 80% reduction in the tax increase proposed by the auditor. If the officer feels that the government has a 70% chance of winning, he'll offer you 30¢ on the dollar to settle the case.

Best chance of settling: Legal issues where the IRS position has been rejected by the courts. Auditors will follow the Service's position despite taxpayer victories in the courts. But an appeals officer will look at both sides and will settle depending on how well he thinks the IRS would make out in court. Issues the IRS has a bad record on in the courts:

• Is rent paid under a gift-leaseback arrangement a deductible business expense?

Tax shelters:

If you're looking for settlement of a tax shelter case beyond your out-of-pocket expenses, you can only get it at the appeals level. Auditors can't offer you more than your out-of-pocket costs even though the IRS has labeled the shelter a "settlement vehicle." But you may be able to convince an appeals officer that the economic reality of the investment exceeds the tax benefits you received.

Winning strategies:

To win a good settlement in the Appeals Di-

vision you must have a strong factual case or a good technical (i.e., legal) argument. The game is to convince the appeals officer that you will beat the IRS in court—if the case goes to court. Pointers:

• Present new facts at the start of your session with the appeals officer—facts that were not available to the auditor or which the auditor wouldn't accept. Aim: Convince the appeals officer that the agent sped through the audit or rigidly applied the tax law.

• Be prepared to horse trade with the appeals officer, to concede issues you're weak on in return for concessions on other issues.

• The Appeals Division can partially settle a case. For instance, it can agree to settle two out of five issues in dispute. The other three you'll have to take to Tax Court.

• Nuisance settlements are not allowed. If your chances of winning in court are greater than 80%, the appeals officer must give you the full amount in dispute. He can't extract 20% from you just to save you the cost of going to court.

PROLONGING THE AGONY: RULES FOR A SECOND LOOK AT YOUR RECORDS

A second examination of a taxpayer's records can be made only after written notification by the Secretary of the Treasury. (The taxpayer must request it before producing any records, or he waives any objection.) If an IRS agent is just trying to harass the taxpayer or to fix up an error he made the first time around, he's likely to drop the matter at this point. But, if you never produced the records you were asked for originally, the first examination isn't over yet. It is deemed complete when the taxpayer is notified in writing that an adjustment has been made or that the return has been accepted as filed.

WHEN YOU CAN DECLINE AN AUDIT

Under their own rules, the IRS will not audit you if the same item was examined in the past two years and no change was made by the auditor. Problem: Audit invitations are computer-generated. If you get an audit notice but you fall within the two-year rule, call the IRS and request cancellation of the audit.

Source: Louis Lieberman, former IRS agent, Great Neck, NY.

KNOW YOUR RIGHTS IF YOU OWE THE IRS

Several little-known provisions of the tax law expand the rights of taxpayers who are being pursued by the IRS. Highlights:

• Increased exemptions: The amount of wages, salary and other income exempt from IRS levy increased to an amount of weekly wages equal to the sum of your standard deduction plus personal exemptions for the tax year in which the levy occurs, divided by 52 (up from $75 a week for the taxpayer and $25 per week for each dependent). Also raised: The exemption for fuel, provisions, furniture and household effects (to $1,650). The exemption for books and tools of a trade went up to $1,100.

• Written notice: The IRS must give at least ten days written notice of its intention to levy on a taxpayer's salary, wages or property. The notice must be given in person, left at the taxpayer's home or business or sent by registered or certified mail. Formerly, notice was not required before a levy on property. Notification by registered or certified mail was not required.

• Seized real estate: The law now extends from 120 to 180 days the time a taxpayer is allowed to redeem real estate that was seized and sold by the IRS. Wrongful seizure: If the IRS wrongfully seizes and sells property that doesn't belong to the taxpayer, it must refund the greater of the property's fair market value at the time of the seizure or the proceeds from the sale.

• Quick release: Lien notices must be lifted within 30 days after the taxpayer has paid up. IR-82-133.

UNDERCOVER IMPOSTERS

The hottest news from the IRS Criminal Division is the new requirement that National Office approval must be obtained before Agents can pose as lawyers, doctors, reporters and clergymen during criminal investigations. Each of these occupations carries with it a recognized privilege of communication, which will likely be breached when the target confides his illegal activities to the undercover Agent. Promoters of phony tax shelters are likely targets of make-believe doctors and lawyers. The Agent tells the promoter that he wants to save tax, at any cost . . . and he doesn't care if documents have to be backdated or papers signed reflecting nonexistent assets.

Source: Ms. X, a former IRS agent, still well connected.

IMPACT OF BANKRUPTCY ON DEBTS TO IRS

Income tax debts can be discharged in bankruptcy if they're at least three years old when the bankruptcy petition is filed. This three-year period is measured from the due date of the tax return if it was filed on time. If the return was filed late, the three-year period starts from the filing date. But a bankruptcy discharge won't release the taxpayer from fraud penalties or from liability for income and Social Security taxes withheld from ex-employees' salaries that wasn't paid over to the IRS.

Source: Kenneth Zuckerbrot, partner in the law firm Wiener, Zuckerbrot, Weiss & Brecher, New York.

Property attached by the IRS, but not yet sold at tax sale, is still legally the taxpayer's property. If he goes bankrupt, it can be taken by the trustee, under the turnover rules of the Bankruptcy Law.

US v. Whiting Pools, S. Ct., No 82–215.

SHIELDING JOINT PROPERTY FROM IRS SEIZURE

If a married man is about to file a return and knows he can't pay the taxes due, he should consider filing separately. This may increase the tax liability, but it may also shelter his wife from the debt. That means jointly owned property (even the family house in some circumstances) will be exempt from seizure, unless there's evidence of fraud or collusion.

Source: Kenneth Zuckerbrot, partner in the law firm Wiener, Zuckerbrot, Weiss & Brecher, New York.

PROTECT YOURSELF FROM THE IRS

Tax professionals make their living relying on IRS policies they know about and you don't. There's no secret about these policies, which have the force of internal law for IRS employees, but they're not well-publicized. In fact, the IRS may not even tell you about them unless you ask.

• *Policy Statement P-9-35*, approved in 1987:

Legal rights of persons being investigated to be observed.

But there's a catch here. The use of eavesdropping devices, such as tape-recording telephone calls, is quite legal if the IRS is participating in the conversation. The only requirement to legally record a conversation is the consent of one of the parties to the conversation—it's usually the IRS that does the consenting—and the approval of IRS higher-ups. A court order is only required in cases where none of the parties to the conversation consent to the eavesdropping.

What this means to you: Listening in to conversations is not uncommon in criminal investigations. If you're a target, assume your telephone calls with the IRS are being recorded by the IRS.

Source: George S. Alberts, former director of the Albany and Brooklyn, IRS districts.

PAY THE IRS SIX MONTHS LATE...

The form no one at the IRS talks about is Form 1127. That's the form you file when you can't pay your taxes on time. It's called "Application for Extension of Time for Payment of Tax" and it gives you up to six months from the due date to pay the tax you owe. Problem: You must be able to show that you can't borrow money to pay your tax bill except under terms that would cause severe loss and hardship. Note: Though late-payment penalties are excused when you're granted an extension, you still owe the IRS interest on late-paid tax.

NONPAYMENT SURPRISE

Can't pay your taxes? Don't worry, you won't go to jail. Nonpayment isn't a crime unless you intentionally squirrel away assets to evade taxes. The worst that will happen to a person who legitimately can't pay is that the IRS will constantly inquire about his financial status and will try to seize, whenever possible, his salary and bank accounts. Because of the volume of cases it has, the IRS often stops actively pursuing collection after a few years.

NOT-SO-PRIVATE RETURNS

New rules enable the IRS to hire outside contractors to process tax return information for it. The new rules state that providing tax returns information to the outside companies will not violate taxpayer confidentiality.

Source: *Regulation 301.6103(n)-1*, amended.

23. Retirement Planning

Retirement Planning

HOW TO PAY LOWEST TAX ON IRA/KEOGH DISTRIBUTIONS

The primary rule: Any money taken out of the account is taxable income. For that reason, it's best to take out only as much as you have to. Any large distribution can put you in a high tax bracket, and you lose the benefit of tax-free earnings whenever money is taken out of the fund.

Keogh Plan distributions get a better tax break. They may qualify for the five-year-averaging method applicable to lump-sum pension distributions. If you were 50 years old or older on December 31, 1985, you may even qualify for 10-year averaging. This method does result in large savings. Distributions of up to $20,000 are taxed at an effective rate of only 11%. Even for a $100,000 distribution, the rate is less than 16%.

Distributions after a taxpayer's death are also taxable, and there may be an estate tax.

When is distribution required?

You must begin to distribute your account by April 1 of the year after the year you reach age 70½. (Contributions to an IRA must stop—except for rollovers—even if you're still working, but you can still contribute to a spousal account for a nonworking spouse who is under age 70½. Contributions to a Keogh may be made at any age.)

You can withdraw the whole account in a lump sum, but you don't have to. You must, however, withdraw enough each year to distribute the entire account during your life expectancy at that time (or the combined life expectancies of you and your spouse) as shown on IRS life expectancy tables. How to figure the minimum withdrawal:

Look up your life expectancy (or yours and your spouse's). Let's suppose it's 15 years. You must withdraw at least 1/15 of the account during the year. Then repeat the process each succeeding year, using the life expectancy shown for that year.

If you withdraw less than you should, there's a 50% penalty on the difference. Example: You withdraw only $2,000 in a year when the minimum required is $8,000. You can be penalized $3,000 (50% of the $6,000 difference).

You do, however, get a tax break. The minimum requirement is figured as of the first of the year, but you don't have to take it out until December 31. The account's earnings for the year are tax-free and remain in the account. Example: The account is $100,000, invested at 8%. In a particular year, you're required to withdraw 1/10. By December 31, the account will have grown to $108,000, but you have to take out only $10,000.

Source: Louis Wald, vice president, tax advisory department, Merrill Lynch, Pierce, Fenner & Smith, New York.

THE SUPER KEOGH LOOPHOLE

Under tax law, anyone who has some self-employment income can set up a Keogh retirement plan and make bigger deductible contributions than ever before. But there is more than one kind of Keogh. And if you set up the "Super Keogh" you can contribute—and deduct—more than twice as much as with the run-of-the-mill Keogh. Here's how.

Types of Keogh plans:

• *Defined-contribution plan.* Your tax-deductible contribution is a set amount each year, usually a percentage of your self-employment income. Maximum deductible contribution: 25% of "salary" or $30,000, whichever is less.

Note: Because of a technicality in the law, "salary" and "total self-employment income" are not equal amounts for a self-employed person. "Salary" is your total self-employment income minus your Keogh contribution. But how can you figure out what 25% of your salary is when you haven't even made your Keogh contribution yet? A special formula provides the answer—take 20% of your total self-employment income to find out what 25% of your "salary" is. That amount is your maximum contribution.

- *Defined benefit plan,* or "Super Keogh." This provides for a specific or defined retirement benefit. You can contribute an amount which is actually necessary to fund your specified benefits.

Maximum: A retirement benefit of $90,000 a year (indexed for inflation). . . or 100% of your self-employment earnings averaged over the past three years, whichever is less. The contribution needed to produce this benefit can be enormous, depending on your age. It may be far larger than the normal $30,000 or 25%-of-income limit.

To determine how much larger, you should consult an actuary. But in general, the older you are, the larger your contributions can be.

How to choose: There are many factors that you must consider when weighing the two types of Keogh Plans before deciding which one is the right one for you.

- If you are under age 45, a defined contribution plan is probably better than a "Super Keogh." Reason: The younger you are, the more years you will have to contribute until retirement. The acutal cost per year that will allow you to end up with a retirement benefit of $90,000 per year is a lot less for a young person than for someone near retirement.

- If you are over age 45, a defined benefit "Super Keogh" is probably best. In some cases, you will be able to contribute more than twice as much as you could to a defined contribution plan. Reason: You must contribute a lot more to fund a $90,000 benefit in fewer years.

Other considerations:
- What will you need at retirement? If your Keogh Plan is going to be your only source of income at retirement, you should set up the type of plan that will give you the most retire-

ment income, regardless of the tax benefits.

With a defined benefit plan, you will know the exact figure that your benefit will be. With a defined contribution plan, you won't know the exact figure because it depends on the success of the plan's investments over the years.

- What are the tax benefits of the Keogh Plan? Although Keoghs are an excellent way of sheltering your income from tax, be sure that you need and can use the tax deduction you get.

- Other employees. How many people work for you? If you set up a retirement plan for yourself, you also must set one up for all employees in your business. You may not want to spend that much.

Source: Edward Mendlowitz, partner, Mendlowitz Weitsen, CPAs.

YOUR IRA—AFTER TAX REFORM

- Taxpayers who are not "active participants" (see below) in a qualified pension plan can continue to make deductible contributions of up to $2,000, as before.

- Taxpayers who are "active participants" in qualified pension plans can continue to make deductible contributions of up to $2,000, provided their adjusted gross income (AGI) is no more than $40,000 (joint filers) or $25,000 (individual filers).

- Joint filers with income between $40,000 and $50,000 and individual filers between $25,000 and $35,000 can make deductible contributions. But, the deductible amount is reduced by 20% of AGI in excess of $40,000 (joint) or $25,000 (individual).

Example: Brown, a joint filer, has AGI of $44,000. He can make deductible contributions of $1,200—$2,000, less $800 (20% × $4,000, the excess over $40,000). Brown can contribute up to $2,000, but only $1,200 will be tax deductible.

- Joint filers with incomes over $50,000 and individual filers over $35,000 can make no deductible contributions. They can, however, make nondeductible contributions up to $2,000, and the earnings from their contributions will accumulate tax free.

Note: For taxpayers who qualify for spousal IRAs, the maximum is $2,250, rather than $2,000.

Nondeductible contributions can be withdrawn at any time without tax or penalty; but earnings on the contributions are taxable and are subject to early withdrawal penalties. And if you do withdraw nondeductible contributions, a pro rata part of the withdrawal will be allocated to earnings.

"Active participants" in qualified plans. Anyone covered by a qualified pension plan is a participant, even if he/she has no vested rights. However, employees who have not met the eligibility requirements (e.g., they haven't worked long enough) are not active participants.

A self-employed person who has a Keogh plan for himself is considered a participant in a qualified plan.

Trap: If your spouse is a participant in a qualified plan, the "participant" rules apply to you, even if you yourself are not covered by any plan.

Early withdrawal penalties. Starting as of 1987, taxpayers under age 59½ will not be penalized if the withdrawal is to be paid out in equal installments over a lifetime (e.g., an annuity). Other rules on early withdrawals remain unchanged, with one exception. If the amount withdrawn is more than $150,000, the excess is penalized 15%, rather than 10% (does not apply to withdrawals of contributions made before August 1986).

Source: Deborah Walker, partner, KPMG Peat Marwick, 1990 K St. N.W., Washington, DC 20006.

MAKING THE MOST OUT OF SPOUSE'S IRA

A married couple with only one spouse working can make deductible Individual Retirement Account (IRA) contributions of up to $2,250 in a single year. Special considerations:

• There must be two accounts to make the maximum contribution, since a single IRA can't receive more than $2,000 in one year. However, subject to that limit, the $2,250 can be divided between the two accounts in any manner.

• When most of the contribution is placed in the younger spouse's account, it may accrue tax-free earnings longer, until that spouse begins mandatory withdrawals at age 70½.

• A working person aged 70½ can't make IRA contributions for himself or herself. But that person can make a full $2,000 deductible contribution into the IRA of a nonworking spouse who's under 70½ years old, provided neither spouse is covered by a company plan, and the couple's income doesn't exceed $50,000.

IRA INVESTMENT TRAPS

The April 15 tax deadline for personal income taxes is also the deadline for making IRA contributions. Everyone who can afford to should make the maximum contribution the law allows. But before you invest . . .

• Read the fine print in the plan. Watch for set-up charges, management fees, and early withdrawal penalties that institutions charge (over and above the tax-law penalties). The penalties can be steep and fees vary widely. Shop around.

• Make IRA contributions in cash or check only. That's the law. You won't get a deduction for a transfer of stock from your investment account into an IRA.

• Stay within the contribution limits. Contribution limits:

If you exceed the limit, you're liable for a nondeductible excise tax (6% of the excess amount) for each year the excess remains in your account. To avoid the penalty, you must withdraw the excess along with the earnings attributable to such excess, before your return is due (including extensions).

Investments to avoid:

• Don't put your IRA in an investment that already provides tax-exempt income, such as municipal bonds or a municipal investment trust. Reason: Tax-exempt bonds typically yield less than taxable bonds because the tax exemption is of value to investors. By law, the income earned in an IRA builds up tax free until withdrawn. Thus, tax-free interest on municipal bonds is of no value to an IRA.

• Remember this: You can't deduct your IRA contribution if you or your spouse are covered by a company plan, and your income exceeds $50,000.

Source: Brett D. Yacker, tax partner, and Leonard J. Senzon, tax manager, Price Waterhouse, New York.

IRA administrative fees are tax deductible. The start-up costs and annual custodial fees that financial institutions charge IRA holders are deductible as an investment expense—a cost of producing income. The fees don't reduce the amount you can contribute to an IRA. Nor will you be penalized if the trustee's charges put your annual contribution over the $2,000 limit.

LOOPHOLE IN USE OF IRA LIFE-EXPECTANCY TABLES

Most people want to keep their IRA accounts intact for as long as possible, accumulating tax-deferred interest. They want their beneficiary to get maximum benefits from the account. But the tax law requires quick distribution of an IRA account after the death of the owner.

General rule: The entire account must be paid out within five years of the owner's death or the death of the surviving spouse, whichever comes later. Exception: If the owner or beneficiary started to receive payments from the account before death, the account balance can be paid out over the life expectancy of the surviving spouse on a joint life expectancy.

The loophole: Begin to take token distributions from your IRA after you reach age 59½ — say, $10 or $20 a month. Leave the bulk of the account intact. Your required distribution is calculated, based on your joint life expectancy

when distributions begin. Starting nominal distributions early enables you to use a longer life expectancy. However, payments don't have to be the minimum required under that life expectancy.

Source: Deborah Walker, senior manager, and Peter I. Elinsky, partner of KPMG Peat Marwick, CPAs, Washington, DC.

PARTIAL IRA ROLLOVERS

Partial rollovers of IRA distributions are permitted. The amount rolled over will not be taxed if it is reinvested within 60 days. But any amount you retain is subject to tax in the year that you receive it.

Tax Equity Act, Section 335.

ROLLOVERS—YOU CAN CHANGE YOUR MIND

A taxpayer who rolls over a lump-sum pension distribution into an IRA can change his mind, withdraw the IRA and use five-year averaging to compute a tax on the distribution—provided he acts before his tax return is due (normally the following April 15, plus any extensions).

IRS Letter Ruling 8311127.

TWO-MONTH INTEREST-FREE LOAN FROM YOUR OWN IRA

Generally, IRA borrowings are prohibited. But it is possible to move funds from one IRA to another, so long as the transfer is completed in a 60-day period. Benefit: You have use of the funds for 59 days. Warning: The exact amount you take out of the first IRA must be placed in the second one within the 60 days. And you can use this device only once a year.

IRA PROCRASTINATION DOESN'T PAY

Make your full contribution on the first business day in January of the tax year rather than the deadline of April 15 of the following year. (A working couple contributing $4,000 in January of the tax year will have $50,000 more after 30 years—at an 8% return—than if they wait the extra 15 months.)

GOLD COINS AND IRAs

Uncle Sam's newly minted gold coins are the only collectibles that can be included in an Individual Retirement Account. Cost: The spot price of gold plus about a 5.5% premium (less-than-one-ounce coins carry a higher charge).

CREDITORS CAN GRAB YOUR IRA

Individual Retirement Accounts can be tapped by creditors when a debtor declares bankruptcy. Pension plans are exempt from the bankruptcy estate. But because the debtor controls an IRA and needn't wait until a particular age to withdraw funds, an IRA is treated like any other liquid asset.
Source: *In re Innis*, US Bankruptcy C, So. Calif., 7/14/86.

IRA PITFALL

Broker's fees and commissions are not deductible when incurred on an IRA investment. Neither may the account owner reimburse the IRA for these expenses. Helpful: Get an itemized breakdown of all charges made against your IRA, so that brokers' fees and commissions can be clearly distinguished from management fees, which are deductible.
Source: *Revenue Rulings* 86–142 and 84–1.

SWITCHING IRAs AFTER DEATH

A woman was the beneficiary of her parent's Individual Retirement Account. Her parent died before any distributions were made. IRS letter ruling: The daughter is allowed to transfer the IRA to a new trustee, as long as the new trustee maintains the IRA in her parent's name. She is also allowed to receive annual distributions from that account for 16.9 years, the life expectancy of her parent.
Source: IRS Letter Ruling 8716058.

NEW RETIREMENT STRATEGIES

You can no longer make deductible IRA contributions if your adjusted gross income is more than $50,000 ($35,000 if you're single)—and either you or your spouse is covered by a company pension plan or a Keogh plan.

If your adjusted gross income is between $40,000 and $50,000 (between $25,000 and $35,000 for single taxpayers), you may make partially deductible contributions. If your income is less or if you and your spouse aren't covered by any retirement plan, you may make fully deductible contributions as before.

Even if you are no longer permitted to make deductible contributions, you still may make nondeductible contributions, which grow tax-deferred until withdrawal. The contributions themselves may be withdrawn tax-free, but all earnings taken out are taxed.

Caution: You can't just designate a withdrawal as being made from nondeductible contributions. The new law provides a formula for determining which portion of a withdrawal is taxable and which part is nontaxable:

$$\text{Nontaxable percentage of a withdrawal} = \frac{\text{Total nondeductible contributions}}{\text{Total value of all your IRAs}}$$

Example. Your present IRA or IRAs are worth $48,000. You make a nondeductible contribution of $2,000. Suppose you then decide to withdraw $1,000. The nontaxable percentage of the withdrawal will be $2,000/$50,000...or only 4%. The remaining 96% will be taxable. Bottom line: The higher the value of your current IRAs, the higher the taxable percentage of withdrawals.

If you're still eligible to make mostly or fully deductible contributions, they're as good an investment as ever. But if you may make only nondeductible contributions, the only advantage of an IRA is tax-deferred growth. In deciding whether to contribute, take into account the following:

• For younger taxpayers: Nondeductible IRA contributions can be a good investment, because the money will have many years to grow free from taxation. Be cautious, though, if you expect to need cash in the near future—to buy a home, pay for children's education, etc. Taxable IRA withdrawals made before age 59½ are penalized 10%. Because early withdrawals are taxed according to the same formula as regular withdrawals, if accumulated earnings and deductible contributions are substantial, an early withdrawal can be expensive.

• For middle-aged taxpayers: You're closer to retirement, and tax-deferred accumulation is less valuable. If you already have a sizable IRA, the taxable percentage of any withdrawals will be high. Other investments may be more suitable for retirement funds than nondeductible IRAs

Attractive alternatives to IRA's include:

• Municipal bonds. Interest is tax free except for certain bonds that are subject to state taxes and the alternative minimum tax.

New twist: Zero-coupon municipal bonds, which are sold at a deep discount and paid off at face value at maturity tax-free. Advantage: You lock in not only an interest rate on your principal but also the same rate on reinvested interest. Risk: If interest rates rise, the market value of zero-coupon bonds falls further than that of ordinary bonds—a problem if you sell the bonds before maturity.

• Savings Bonds (Series EE) guarantee a 6% minimum return if the bonds are held at least five years. If the equivalent of 85% of the interest rate on five-year Treasury notes rises above 6%, the bonds pay that proportion of the five-year Treasury rate. Income is exempt from state and local taxes.

Certain investments that previously were unappealing or illegal for IRAs are now worth considering thanks to the 1986 tax reform law.

• Growth stocks. Long-term capital gains used to qualify for favorable tax treatment not available to IRAs, so most taxpayers would buy growth stocks outside their IRAs and put income-producing securities into their IRAs.

Now, however, tax advantages for long-term capital gains have been repealed, so IRAs have become one of the best ways to shelter long-term gains from growth stocks. If a stock is sold at a profit within an IRA, no tax is incurred on the gain, all of which can be reinvested. (Of course, all gains are eventually taxed at withdrawal.)

• Gold and silver. IRAs used to be prohibited from investing in precious metals or collectibles. But the new law permits investment in certain US-issued gold and silver coins. Taxpayers interested in hedging against inflation may want to consider this new option.

*The decision will depend on your complete financial picture and retirement plan . . . so you should consult your financial adviser before making any contribution.

Source: Deborah Walker, partner, KPMG Peat Marwick, 1990 K St. NW, Washington, DC 20006.

BETTER THAN AN IRA AND NO $2,000 LIMIT

Cash or deferred profit-sharing plans, technically called 401(k) plans, offer retirement-minded employees much bigger tax benefits than Individual Retirement Accounts (IRAs). Key to the potential tax windfall: A cut in pay. These plans also provide tax savings for the employer.

How they work: The company sets up a qualified profit-sharing plan, or conforms its present plan to the tax law's 401(k) requirements. The plan permits employees to defer taking a portion of their salary—let's say 5%. The deferred salary is contributed directly into the plan by the company.

As with an IRA, the employee pays no tax on the contribution. And the income earned builds up tax-free in the plan. Bonus: No Social Security tax has to be paid on the amount deferred, which will result in a saving, even though the employee's salary is less than the Social Security wage base. The employer would also save by paying less Social Security tax if employee salaries do not exceed the wage base. (But contributions cannot be integrated with Social Security; that is, Social Security taxes cannot be counted as part of contributions.)

Compared to an IRA, a deferred-salary program offers significant tax advantages to the employee:

• There is no $2,000 annual limit on contributions, as there is with an IRA. The 401(k) limit is about $9,000 for 1993, and is indexed annually for inflation.

Source: William Grinde and Jay Dengrove, tax consultants, New York.

THE DEFERRED COMMERCIAL ANNUITY TRICK

Few people have heard of the deferred commercial annuity (DCA), a completely legal personal tax shelter that can contribute greatly to an individual's retirement wealth.

How it works: An individual pays one or more premiums to an insurance company in exchange for the right to receive annuity payments beginning at some future date. The insurance company invests the premium proceeds and credits the earnings to the investor's account.

Tax benefits:

• Earnings accumulate in the account tax free until they are distributed. They can thus be reinvested to produce more tax-free earnings.

• When the annuity is paid, a portion of each payment is tax free. That's because a portion of each payment represents a return of the original premiums. Tax is due only on the earnings of the premiums that are paid out.

• If the annuity is paid after the recipient retires, the portion of the annual payment that is taxable will probably be taxed at lower rates.

A DCA can be set up in addition to an IRA, and there is no limit to the amount of money you can put into it. DCA contributions are not deductible the way IRA contributions are, but a DCA is still such a good deal tax-wise that the government does not want you to begin collecting payments from one too soon. So withdrawals from a DCA taken before age 59½ are subject to a 10% penalty.

Source: Irving Blackman, Blackman Kallick Bartelstein, CPAs, Chicago.

EARLY WITHDRAWALS FROM IRA ACCOUNTS LOOPHOLE

The 10% penalty tax on pre-age-59½ withdrawals from IRAs does not apply if the money is taken out in the form of an annuity, that is, in a series of payments over one's life expectancy or the joint life expectancies of a couple. This loophole can be put to good use if there is a fair amount of money in your IRA, say $100,000, from the rollover of a company pension plan.

Source: Edward Mendlowitz, partner, Mendlowitz Weitsen, CPAs, Two Pennsylvania Plaza, New York 10121.

BORROWING FROM YOUR IRA

Borrow from an IRA legally by making a short-term loan. Generally, IRA borrowings are prohibited. But it is possible to move funds from one IRA to another, as long as the transfer is completed in a 60-day period. Benefit: You have use of the funds for 59 days. Warning: The exact amount you take out of the first IRA must be placed in the second one within 60 days. And you can use this device only once in a 12-month period.

SOCIAL SECURITY CARD SECRET

Few people know it, but the first three digits of a Social Security number are a code for the state in which the card was issued. This code, which can be used to confirm a place of birth or an employment history, is not public knowledge. However, many private detectives have the key to the code and will crack the Social Security number for a fee.

Source: Milo Speriglio, director and chief of Nick Harris Detectives, Inc.

FOUR KINDS OF PAY THAT ARE EXEMPT FROM SOCIAL SECURITY TAXES

• Wages paid to family members, including a child under 18, when the business is a proprietorship. Wages paid by a corporation are subject to tax.

• Loans taken out from the company by an employee or shareholder. But be sure the loan is fully documented so that there is no doubt about its legitimacy. If th IRS concludes that the loan will not be paid back, tax will be imposed. The loan must carry an interest rate equal to 110% of the applicable federal rate at the time of the loan. IRS will announce this rate monthly.

• Health-insurance payments made into an employee accident, health or medical reimbursement plan.

• Educational benefits which add to employee's on-the-job skills.

• Moving-expense reimbursements when a move is job-related, covers more than 35 miles, and the worker stays at the new job site at least 39 weeks during the next year.

DEFERRED-PAY RETIREMENT PLAN CUTS YOUR SOCIAL SECURITY TAXES

The new Social Security tax rules generally toughen up the way the tax is imposed. But there is one break for well-paid executives who participate in deferred-salary programs. These popular arrangements allow a person to delay taking part of his salary until after retirement, when he will probably be in a lower income tax bracket.

Under old rules, these deferred salary payments were subject to Social Security taxes when made.

Under the new law, they are taxed at an earlier date, when earned. But they are not subject to Social Security tax when paid.

Trick: Social Security and Medicare taxes apply to only the first $130,200 of earnings. A person who is paid more than that does not have to pay any tax on the excess. So when salary payments in excess of the maximum amount are deferred, Social Security tax need not be paid at all. The deferred amount is exempt from tax when both earned and paid.

Planning point: The rules apply to amounts earned after 1983, and there are many technical rules that apply. So you should consult with an expert now to form your compensation strategy for coming years.

CONSULTANTS DON'T ALWAYS HAVE TO PAY SOCIAL SECURITY TAXES

A retired executive continued to work for his company as a consultant and a member of the board of directors. The IRS said he had to pay Social Security taxes on the fees the company paid him. Tax Court decision: For the executive. He was not self-employed in the trade or business of being a consultant and board member. Key facts: The executive had agreed not to work for any other company after retirement. He did no work for any other company. His duties as a director took up about six hours of his time each year.

Fred W. Steffens, TC Memo 1981–637.

BIGGER SOCIAL SECURITY INCOME FOR WIFE WHO NEVER WORKED

Making your wife a partner in your business could boost her ultimate Social Security retirement benefits. As a partner, the wife now has self-employment income. When she reaches retirement, her benefits will be based on that income. This could far exceed the 50% of her husband's retirement benefits that she would get if she had no earnings of her own on which to compute her Social Security entitlement.

Source: Dr. Robert S. Holzman, professor emeritus of taxation at New York University and author of *The Encyclopedia of Estate Planning,* Boardroom Books.

PROTECT YOUR SOCIAL SECURITY RIGHTS

Are you getting credit for all the Social Security taxes you've paid? If your earnings aren't credited properly by the Social Security Administration (SSA), you may be stuck. Mistakes must be corrected within 39½ months after the year the earnings were supposed to be credited. And it makes no difference whether you, your company's payroll department or the government caused the error. Even younger workers should be keeping track of this. An error by the SSA could mean lower benefits for disability as well as retirement.

Anyone who ever worked under Social Security has a lifetime earnings record at the Social Security Administration headquarters in Baltimore. It's your responsibility to make sure that your record is accurate. If it isn't, you could lose out on benefits.

To check to see whether your earnings have been properly credited to your Social Security account, fill out Form 7004 and mail it to:

Social Security Administration, Box 57, Baltimore, MD 21203.

You will receive (in about three months) a statement of your earnings together with the number of quarters of coverage credited to your account. Don't expect an up-to-date record —the SSA is 1½ to 2 years behind in posting their records.

SOCIAL SECURITY SECRET

Collecting Social Security early can pay off. Even though benefits are reduced, you won't lose out—at least not for a long time. Example: If full benefits are $750 per month for retiring at age 65, you can get reduced benefits of $600 a month by retiring at age 62. You'd have to collect full benefits for 12 years to make up the $21,600 you'd receive during the three years of early payments.

Source: *Changing Times..*

SOCIAL SECURITY SECRETS FOR THOSE UNDER 65

It's your right as a working person to apply for disability insurance from the Social Security Administration if at any point you're unable to work because of a mental or physical disability. Before applying, you should know how the system works, who is eligible and what kind of medical criteria a decision is based on. When dealing with any government agency, the more you know before you walk in, the better your chances are of walking out with what you want.

There are two disability programs under Social Security. One is the needs-based program, Supplemental Security Income Program. SSI is basically a nationalization of welfare benefits for the unemployable. The other, which applies to working people, is the basic insurance program that you pay into as the FICA tax: Old Age and Survivors Disability Insurance (OASDI).

Although the disability criteria for acceptance are the same under both programs, you don't have to prove financial need for OASDI. You're eligible if you've worked and paid into the system for 20 quarters out of the last 40 (five years out of the last 10) and have the necessary years of work credit, depending upon your age. If your last day in the system was 10 years ago or more, you're not eligible for disability benefits now, though you may be eligible eventually for retirement benefits.

Benefits are based on what you've paid into the system.

The system works as follows:

• The first step. File an application with your local Social Security office. You'll be interviewed by a claims representative, who will ask you basic questions about your disability: What is the nature of it? When did you stop working? How does it interfere with your daily activities and ability to work? Which doctors and hospitals have treated you? You'll be asked to sign medical releases so Social Security can obtain information from your medical sources. The interviewer will also note any evidence of your disability that he observed.

• This material is sent to a trained disability examiner at a state agency, who will contact your medical sources.

• If the medical information you have submitted isn't sufficient, the agency will send you to a consulting specialist, at the government's expense, and this information will become part of your file.

• If you've met the medical disability requirements (which are extremely stringent), you'll be granted benefits. But you can still be found disabled even if you don't meet the medical requirements. Age, past work experience and education are also taken into account. Anyone over 50 is put in a special category because his vocational outlook is less favorable. A 55-year-old construction worker with minimal education who suffers from mild heart disease might be eligible—he can't do his past work and probably wouldn't be able to find another job. Another construction worker of the same age and disability, but with more education and skill, might be expected to find light or sedentary work. The approach is individualized throughout the process.

• The final eligibility decision is made and signed by the disability examiner, together with a physician who works for the state (not the consulting physician).

• If benefits are denied, you can appeal the decision or reapply.

Social Security's definition of medical disability: The inability to do any substantial, gainful activity by reason of any medically determinable physical or mental impairment which can be expected to result in death, or which has lasted or can be expected to last, for a continuous period of not less than 12 months. To meet the definition you must have a severe impairment that makes you unable to do your previous work or any other gainful work that exists in the national economy. How to prove it:

• It's crucial that your doctor submit very precise medical information, including all test results—the same kind of information a doctor would use in coming up with a diagnosis and treatment plan. Social Security won't accept your doctor's conclusions. It wants the medical evidence that led to the conclusion.

• Social Security has a long list of impairments under which your disability should fall. The listing, broken down into 13 body systems, covers about 99% of the disabilities that people apply for. This listing outlines exactly what tests must be met for eligibility. Examples: An amputee is eligible only if he has lost both feet, both hands, or one hand and one foot. Angina pectoris victims must show certain results on a treadmill test and/or a number of other listed tests. Recommended: You and your doctor should take a look at the listings before you apply. If your doctor answers in enough detail, you might avoid a visit to the agency's consulting physician.

Filing an appeal:

When benefits are denied, a notice is sent. A brief paragraph explains the reason in general terms. At that point you can go back to the Social Security office and file for a reconsideration, which is simply a review of your case.

If the reconsideration is denied, you can take your case to an administrative law judge within Social Security's Office of Hearings and Appeals. You don't need a lawyer for this hearing, but many people do have one. At the hearing you present your case, review the evidence in your file, add other relevant evidence and personally impress the judge. The reversal rate at this level is fairly high (40%–60%.)

If denied at this hearing, you can go to the Appeals Council and then up through the courts. The chances of reversal improve at each level. Most people just go up to the administrative law judge level. If they're turned down there, they file a new claim and start all over. Often delay works in a claimant's favor, since disabilities may worsen over time.

• Look into state disability programs. If your disability is temporary, you might be covered by your state. State programs bridge the gap for people who are disabled for less than a year. Be aware: Many state disability programs and private insurance companies require that you apply for Social Security first, before you can collect from them.

• File soon. Don't wait until you've been disabled for a year. There's some retroactivity (up to 12 months), but the sooner you file, the better.

• Call the Social Security office before going in. You can save yourself a lot of trouble. Find out first what you should bring with you and which are the best days and times to come in.

• Ask at your local Social Security office for the Listing of Impairments, or look them up in the library. Request the Code of Federal Regulations—see 20CFR404 and 20CFR416.

Source: Dan Wilcox, disability program specialist, Social Security Administration, Disability Programs Branch, New York.

WHEN YOU RETIRE AS A "CONSULTANT"

A long-time executive of a company plans to retire but also plans to continue working for the company as a consultant. As a consultant, he'll be paid an hourly rate. The amount of consulting work to be done isn't fixed. IRS ruling: The retired executive will be considered to have separated from service with the company, in spite of the fact that he'll continue to do consulting work. Thus, the payout from his company's retirement plan will qualify as a lump-sum distribution and get favorable tax treatment.

Source: *IRS Letter Ruling* 8635067.

GET BACK THE TAX PAID ON EXCESS SOCIAL SECURITY BENEFITS

Question: I paid tax on Social Security benefits that I received, then was told I had to repay some of the benefits because I had too much income during the year. Is there any way I can get back the tax I paid?

Answer: Yes. File an amended tax return, Form 1040X, for the year in which you paid the tax. On it, report your accurate income total for the year—excluding the benefits you had to repay. You'll get your refund.

SEP's OR IRA's

Question: Are Simplified Employee Pension plans (SEPs) considered to be qualified plans under tax reform's new rules concerning IRA contributions?

Answer: Yes. Thus, individuals who are covered by a SEP will not be able to make deductible contributions to an individual retirement account unless they report adjusted gross income of under $50,000 on a joint return or $35,000 on a single return.

WHEN RETIREMENT HOME CHARGES ARE DEDUCTIBLE

A retirement home charges both an entrance fee and a one-time service fee. IRS ruling: These fees qualify as deductible medical expenses to the extent that they are used to cover the cost of providing medical services to residents.

Source: *IRS Letter Ruling* 8641037.

ALL ABOUT "TOP-HEAVY" RETIREMENT PLANS

A "top-heavy" retirement plan, whether maintained by a corporation, partnership or sole proprietorship, does not qualify for beneficial tax treatment unless certain conditions are met.

Meaning of "top-heavy": More than 60%

of the plan's benefits go to "key employees." These are: Officers of the company, over-5% owners, over-1% owners earning more than $150,000, and employees with the 10 largest ownership interests in the company.

To qualify a top-heavy plan for tax purposes, the employer must:

- Vest* benefits faster. Either 100% vesting after three years of service or six-year graded vesting.

- Provide minimum benefits for non-key employees. In determining these minimum benefits, Social Security can't be taken into account. For a pension plan: The benefit must be at least 2% of pay for each year of service (but not more than 20% of average annual compensation). For a profit-sharing plan: 3% of the pay.

*A benefit is "vested" when the employee's right to that benefit can't be forfeited.

HOW SAFE IS YOUR PENSION?

How to check on the safety of your retirement income:

For employees of public companies: Basic information is included in the firm's annual report. Usually the size of a firm's unfunded pension liability and the size of its past service liability are disclosed in footnotes. More detailed information is available in the financial section of the firm's 10K report, filed with the Securities and Exchange Commission.

For employees of private companies: Everyone who is in a qualified plan (one approved by the IRS under the Code) has the right to obtain information about his pension from the trustees of the plan. They may be either internal or external trustees. The average person may not be able to decipher the information. If you can't, then take it to a pension expert, actuary, lawyer or accountant for an analysis. Whether you are examining pension information of public or of private firms, you are seeking the same sort of basic information.

Principle: The size of a company's liability for retirement payouts is not as important as the assumptions about funding these liabilities. Like a mortgage, these obligations don't exist 100% in the present. Concern yourself with how the company expects to fund its liabilities.

Types of liabilities:
- Unfunded pension liabilities. The amount a firm expects to need over the next 20–30 years to supply vested workers with promised pension benefits. These figures are derived from various actuarial assumptions.
- Past service liabilities. Created when a company raises its pension compensation. For instance, a company may have been planning to provide 40% of compensation as a pension. One year, they may raise that to 45% and treat it retroactively.

Trouble signs:
- A poor record on investing. Compare the market value of the assets in the pension with their book value. If book value is more than market value, the trustees have not been investing wisely. Point: If the fund had to sell those assets today, there would be a loss. I would also get a bit nervous if the fund is still holding some obscure bonds or other fixed-income obligations issued at low rates years ago.
- Funding assumptions are overstated. Actuaries have a myriad of estimates on how long it takes to fund pension plans and what rate of return a company will get.

What to look at:
- Time frame: This should not be too long. If the firm is funding over 40 years, I would want to know why and how, since 10–20 years is more customary. Reason: We don't have a crystal ball, and the investment world will be different in as little as 10 years from now. Assumptions made on 40 years may not hold up at all.
- Rate of return: If a company assumes a conservative 6%–7% or less right now, you can be comfortable. If the assumed rate is 10% or more, I would want to know how they are going to meet that expectation for the entire fund over the long run.
- Salary and wage scales: The company should be assuming an increase in compensation over years. Most plans have such provisions. They

must start funding now for future salary increases.

• Assumptions about the employee turnover rate: These should be consistent with the historically documented turnover of the company. If a firm has a very low turnover rate and assumes a 4% turnover, the company will be underfunded at some time. Estimates should be conservative.

To assess your own status in a corporate pension plan, see how many years you have been vested. Many people have the illusion that they are fully vested for maximum pensions after only five years or so. In truth, companies couldn't afford to fully vest people with such short service. They may offer some token pension for such service. But most people are not fully vested until they have worked for the firm for 10 or even 20 years, and then they might be vested only to the extent of their accrued pension to date, not the full pension expected at normal retirement. With so much job-hopping in the past two decades, an individual's pension-fund status may be much less than imagined.

Employees of troubled or even bankrupt companies need not panic. Trustees of the plan have an obligation to the vested employees. The assets of the plan are segregated, and no creditor can reach them. In fact, as a creditor, the corporate pension plan can grab some corporate assets under certain circumstances. And if there has been gross mismanagement of pension funds, stockholders of a closely held company can be held personally liable.

Source: James E. Conway, president of The Ayco Corporation, Albany, NY.

Index